THE LAWBOOK EXCHANGE, LTD.

Foundations of
Spanish, Mexican and Civil Law
Series

Series Editor WARREN M. BILLINGS

Distinguished Professor of History, Emeritus,
University of New Orleans and Visiting Professor of Law,
William and Mary School of Law

This series addresses the history of the civil law in the Americas,
with an emphasis on Spanish and Mexican law

A Compilation of Spanish and Mexican Law,
in Relation to Mines and Titles to Real Estate,
in Force in California, Texas
and New Mexico

And in the Territories Acquired under the Louisiana and
Florida Treaties,
When Annexed to the United States
Volume I [ALL PUBLISHED]

BOOKS IN THE SERIES

J. P. KIMBALL, translator
Laws and Decrees of the State of Coahuila and Texas
In Spanish and English

With a New Introduction by JOSEPH W. McKNIGHT

Larry and Jane Harlan Faculty Fellow and Professor of Law,

SMU Dedman School of Law

JOSEPH M. WHITE
A New Collection of Laws, Charters and Local Ordinances of the
Governments of Great Britain, France and Spain
Relating to the Concessions of Land in their Respective Colonies
Together with the Laws of Mexico and Texas on the Same Subject, to Which is Prefixed
Judge Johnson's Translation of Azo and Manuel's Institutes of the Civil Law of Spain

With a New Introduction by AGUSTÍN PARISE

Research Associate, Center of Civil Law Studies,

LSU Law Center

JOHN A. ROCKWELL
A Compilation of Spanish and Mexican Law, in Relation to Mines and
Titles to Real Estate, in Force in California, Texas and New Mexico
And in the Territories Acquired under the Louisiana and Florida Treaties, When An-
nexed to the United States. Volume I [All Published]

With a New Introduction BY PETER L. REICH

Professor of Law and Sumner Scholar;

Director, Whittier Mexico City Program, Whittier Law School

A COMPILATION

OF

SPANISH AND MEXICAN LAW,

IN RELATION TO

MINES, AND TITLES TO REAL ESTATE,

IN FORCE IN

CALIFORNIA, TEXAS AND NEW MEXICO;

AND IN THE TERRITORIES ACQUIRED UNDER THE LOUISIANA AND FLORIDA
TREATIES, WHEN ANNEXED TO THE UNITED STATES.

VOLUME I.

CONTAINING A TRANSLATION OF THE MINING ORDINANCES OF NEW SPAIN—GAMBOA'S MIN-
ING ORDINANCES—THE LAWS IN RELATION TO MINES OF GOLD, SILVER AND
QUICKSILVER, CONTAINED IN THE

"NOVISIMA RECOPILACION," AND THE "RECOPILACION DE LAS INDIAS;"

AND IN THE DECREES OF THE CORTES OF SPAIN AND OF FERDINAND VII.,
ALSO OF THE LAWS AND DECREES OF MEXICO, ON THE SUBJECT
OF MINES, COLONIZATION, AND THE RIGHT OF FOREIGN-
ERS TO HOLD REAL ESTATE.

ALSO, EXTRACTS FROM PUBLIC DOCUMENTS, AND FROM THE LAWS OF CALIFOR-
NIA, IN RELATION TO MINES AND MINERAL LANDS:

TOGETHER WITH
A DIGEST OF THE COMMON LAW, ON THE SUBJECT OF
MINES AND MINING.

With a New Introduction by Peter L. Reich
Professor of Law and Sumner Scholar,
Director, Whittier Mexico City Program, Whittier Law School

THE LAWBOOK EXCHANGE, LTD.
Clark, New Jersey

ISBN 9781584779803 (hardcover)
ISBN 9781616190798 (paperback)

Lawbook Exchange edition 2011

The quality of this reprint is equivalent to the quality of the original work.

THE LAWBOOK EXCHANGE, LTD.
33 Terminal Avenue
Clark, New Jersey 07066-1321

*Please see our website for a selection of our other publications
and fine facsimile reprints of classic works of legal history:*
www.lawbookexchange.com

Library of Congress Cataloging-in-Publication Data

Rockwell, John A. (John Arnold), 1803-1861.
 A compilation of Spanish and Mexican law, in relation to mines, and titles
to real estate, in force in California, Texas and New Mexico : and in the
territories acquired under the Louisiana and Florida treaties, when annexed to
the United States. Vol. I, [all published] Containing a translation of the
mining ordinances of New Spain, Gamboa's mining ordinances, the laws in
relation to mines of gold, silver and quicksilver, contained in the "Novisima
recopilacion," and the "Recopilacion de las Indias," and in the decrees of the
cortes of Spain and of Ferdinand VII, also of the laws and decrees of
Mexico, on the subject of mines, colonization, and the right of foreigners to
hold real estate : also, extracts from public documents, and from the laws of
California, in relation to mines and mineral lands, together with a digest of
the common law, on the subject of mines and mining / by John A. Rockwell ;
with a new introduction by Peter L. Reich.
      p. cm.
 "Foundations of Spanish, Mexican and Civil Law series."
 Includes bibliographical references.
 ISBN-13: 978-1-58477-980-3 (hardcover : alk. paper)
 ISBN-10: 1-58477-980-2 (hardcover : alk. paper)
 ISBN-13: 978-1-61619-079-8 (pbk. : alk. paper)
 ISBN-10: 1-61619-079-5 (pbk. : alk. paper)
 1. Mining law--California. 2. Land titles--Registration and transfer--
California. 3. Mining law--Texas. 4. Mining law--New Mexico. 5. Mining
law--Mexico. 6. Land titles--Registration and transfer--Mexico. I. Title.
 KFC400.A4 2011
 343.73'077--dc23
                    2011021089

Printed in the United States of America on acid-free paper

Introduction[1]

The minister officiating at the 1861 burial of John Arnold Rockwell noted his numerous legal and political accomplishments, most significantly the treatise, *A Compilation of Spanish and Mexican Law, in Relation to Mines, and Titles to Real Estate*.[2] The eulogy described the deceased as having "engaged in the study of Spanish law, and by translations furnished a work that has been adopted as a valuable and reliable digest . . . ."[3] Rockwell's lifetime of litigation and public office gave his book credibility among lawyers active in America's mid-nineteenth- century commercial and territorial expansion into Mexico and the Southwest. What we know of his background, Whig party affiliation, expertise in Hispanic law, production of an influential treatise, and attempts to forestall the country's sectional tragedy elucidates his important role in antebellum law and politics. Ultimately, Rockwell succeeded at mediating foreign and American jurisprudence, but failed at navigating the winds that would tear the nation apart.

Rockwell's family came from England to Massachusetts in 1630 as part of the Puritan migration, and finally settled in Connecticut.[4] Born in Norwich in 1803, he graduated from Yale College in 1822 and returned to his hometown to read and practice law.[5] Elected a state senator as a Whig in 1838, Rockwell became a judge of the New London County Court in 1840 and served two terms in Congress, beginning in 1845. Leaving his seat in 1849, he stayed in the capital to litigate claims involving Mexico before special arbitration commissions and ultimately in the U.S. Court of Claims, which he helped establish in 1855.[6] An attorney in a variety of international and domestic cases, Rockwell compiled his extensive treatise while simultaneously becoming caught up in the divisiveness of those years and the consequent disintegration of the Whig party.

---

1. Most of the primary source material used for this essay is contained in the John Arnold Rockwell Collection at the Huntington Library, San Marino, California. The author is grateful for the valuable assistance of Dr. Peter J. Blodgett, the Huntington's Curator of Western Historical Manuscripts. Thanks are also due to Whittier Law School for supporting this project with a Faculty Summer Research Stipend.

2. ALVAN BOND, A DISCOURSE OCCASIONED BY THE DEATH OF HON. JOHN A. ROCKWELL 17 (1861) (original in Rockwell Collection, Huntington Library). *See* JOHN A. ROCKWELL, A COMPILATION OF SPANISH AND MEXICAN LAW IN RELATION TO MINES, AND TITLES TO REAL ESTATE IN FORCE IN CALIFORNIA, TEXAS AND NEW MEXICO (1851).

3. *Id.*

4. *Id.* at 33.

5. JAMES GRANT WILSON & JOHN FISKE, 5 APPLETON'S CYCLOPEDIA OF AMERICAN BIOGRAPHY 295 (1888).

6. *Id.*

The Whigs had emerged in 1834 as an alternative to the Jacksonian populism of the Democratic party, enjoyed particular sway in New England, and dissolved by 1856 in the national debate over slavery and other issues.[7] Their platform derived from Henry Clay's "American System," which proposed to achieve national economic integration through internal improvements, a national bank, and protectionist tariffs.[8] Whig political rhetoric drew upon legal texts and portrayed the party as the voice of reason in contrast to Jacksonian mob rule.[9] Indeed, recent scholarship emphasizes a unique "Whig lawyering" style focusing on neutral dispute resolution and an appeal to law and order, epitomized by Abraham Lincoln's practice and oratory.[10] (This view has been contested with the rejoinder that resolving disputes and maintaining order were interests shared by all attorneys in the period, Whigs or not.)[11]

Another dimension of Whig policy was the encouragement of peaceful commercial expansion and border negotiation with foreign countries, as opposed to the Democrats' advocacy of territorial seizure through war. The Whigs promoted Western Hemisphere trade, sought accords with Britain over the Maine and Oregon boundaries, and opposed the dispossession of the Indians, the annexation of Texas, and the Mexican War of 1846–48.[12] In 1849, Whig president Zachary Taylor sent diplomatic missions to Central America to obtain transit rights across Honduras and Nicaragua.[13] Though exclusive U.S. control over an isthmian passage was waived in the 1850 Clayton-Bulwer Treaty with the British, historians have described how Yankee entrepreneurs then began to spread into Southern Mexico and beyond.[14] In fact, as much as a decade earlier, an American merchant had already penetrated this area, sparking a case that would involve the Mexican and U.S. governments and would launch John A. Rockwell's career as a specialist in Hispanic law.

The remote and swampy state of Tabasco was racked with political instability following Mexico's winning independence from Spain in 1821. During the 1830s

---

7. *See generally* MICHAEL F. HOLT, THE RISE AND FALL OF THE AMERICAN WHIG PARTY (1999). *See also* DANIEL WALKER HOWE, THE POLITICAL CULTURE OF THE AMERICAN WHIGS 5 (1979) (discussing the Whigs' New England origins and power base).

8. HOWE, *supra* note 7, at 16, 137.

9. *Id.* at 23–25.

10. MARK E. STEINER, AN HONEST CALLING: THE LAW PRACTICE OF ABRAHAM LINCOLN 56–61 (2006).

11. Polly J. Price, Book Review, 26 LAW & HIST. REV. 753 (2008).

12. HOWE, *supra* note 7, at 40–42, 93, 14–45, 212.

13. WILLIAM H. GOETZMANN, WHEN THE EAGLE SCREAMED: THE ROMANTIC HORIZON IN AMERICAN DIPLOMACY, 1800–1860 81 (1966).

14. *Id.* at 81–83.

there were repeated military incursions from neighboring Campeche and Yucatán, along with internal uprisings linked to the conflict between "centralists" and "federalists" over state autonomy.[15] To encourage investment, the Tabasco government promoted logging in the state's extensive forests, as well as cacao and sugar plantations.[16] In 1831 William Brown, a commercial agent for New York merchant Aaron Leggett, obtained an exclusive concession to operate steamboats on Tabasco's rivers, and began cutting and shipping lumber for export.[17] But in October of the next year Leggett's ship *Hidalgo* sunk under questionable circumstances, and in 1833 Brown filed a claim for the loss in Tabasco's capital, San Juan Bautista.[18] At a certain point in the litigation Leggett engaged Rockwell to represent him, and the attorney's personal papers contain a complete file of memoranda relating to the case, as well as correspondence from the U.S.-Mexico Claims Commission "umpire" (arbitrator), the Prussian aristocrat Baron Friedrich Ludwig von Roenne.[19]

Following the model for international claims tribunals established by Jay's Treaty of 1794, the 1839 convention between Mexico and the United States set up a commission of two representatives from each country, with final decisions and awards to be made by an umpire appointed by the King of Prussia.[20] Before this board the U.S. commissioners found that the steamboat *Hidalgo* had been illegally seized by the Tabasco authorities during a rebellion, and that Leggett's logging business was destroyed.[21] On the other hand, Mexico's representatives considered that the ship had been justifiably requisitioned to transport troops, for which Leggett had been indemnified, and had sunk afterwards due to his overloading it with logs.[22] The umpire, Baron von Roenne, regretted "that there is an entire disagreement between [the parties] not only on the merits of the claim, but in regard to the essential facts of the case."[23] Based on these dramatically inconsis-

---

15. CARLOS MARTINEZ ASSAD, BREVE HISTORIA DE TABASCO 68–69 (1996).

16. *Id.* at 63.

17. Gobierno Supremo del Estado Libre de Tabasco, … establecimiento de los buques de Bapor en las aguas navegables de su territorio …, Noviembre 24 de 1831 (original in Rockwell Collection).

18. Guillermo H. Brown, …petición …, Marzo 13 de 1833 (original in Rockwell Collection).

19. William H. Brown, Papers relating to claim against the State of Tabasco, 1831–49 (originals of 20 letters in Rockwell Collection); Letters from Friedrich Ludwig von Roenne to John Arnold Rockwell, 1849–60 (originals of 9 letters in Rockwell Collection).

20. *See* SAMUEL FLAGG BEMIS, JAY'S TREATY: A STUDY IN COMMERCE AND DIPLOMACY 438–88 (2d ed. 1962) (describing the Jay's Treaty template for resolution of debts and other disputes between Britain and the U.S.); H.R. DOC. NO. 190 (1840) (Convention – United States and Mexico).

21. H.R. DOC. NO. 269, at 6–9 (1842) (Memorial of Aaron Leggett, of the State of New York).

22. *Id.* at 9.

23. *Id.* at 10.

tent accounts, the Americans awarded $407, 079.41 for the loss, the Mexicans refused to concede any remuneration, and the umpire compromised by allowing the claimant $99, 487.94.[24]

Despite repeated requests for reconsideration, Baron von Roenne declined to reevaluate the award, and Leggett wrote various U.S. officials throughout the 1840s in a fruitless attempt to pressure the Mexican government.[25] In one of these communications, Leggett proposed to Secretary of War William Marcy that the American government seize California from Mexico in order to satisfy his claim.[26] Shortly thereafter the Mexican War resulted in the annexation of that province, but Leggett remained unpaid and U.S. steamboats returned to Tabasco as part of a military campaign rather than for commerce.[27]

While the war was bitterly condemned by the Whigs as an unconstitutional act of aggression, it did boost the international legal practice Rockwell pursued in Washington, D.C., after leaving Congress in 1849.[28] In 1850 he argued that Mexico should compensate the family of an American officer killed while serving in one of the revolutionary armies during the independence struggle against Spain.[29] By 1855 Rockwell was handling the cases of French citizens arising out of the Mexican War.[30] That year he also began advertising a practice before the new U.S. Court of Claims, a tribunal he had helped establish while in Congress.[31]

Perhaps Rockwell's most complicated litigation came with his work for the claimant in *United States v. Castillero*, the attempt by the beneficiary of an 1845 Mexican land grant to obtain federal confirmation of his title to a quicksilver (mer-

---

24. H.R. Doc. No. 291, at 52 (1842) (Claims of Citizens of U.S. on Mexico).
25. H.R. Ex. Doc. No. 83 (1848) (Aaron Leggett).
26. *An Important Letter, Aaron Leggett to William L. Marcy, October 16, 1845*, 11 Cal. Hist. Soc'y Q. 33 (1932).
27. *See generally* K. Jack Bauer, Surfboats and Horse Marines: U.S. Naval Operations in the Mexican War 108–122 (1969) (discussing the 1847 occupation of Tabasco's river ports by Commodore Matthew C. Perry).
28. Bond, *supra* note 2, at 17. *See* Form Letter from John A. Rockwell, June 12, 1849 (announcing practice before the U.S. Supreme Court and the Board of Commissioners on Mexican Claims) (Original in John D. Gordan, III Collection). *See also* Howe, *supra* note 7, at 93–95 (detailing Whig criticisms of the Democrats' war policy as unnecessary, imperialist, and a violation of the separation of powers).
29. J.A. Rockwell, Argument in the Case of the Heirs of Guildford D. Young Before the Commissioners on Claims Against Mexico ... (1850) (original in Rockwell Collection).
30. Lists of French Claims in the War with Mexico, April 18, 1855 (original in Rockwell Collection).
31. John A. Rockwell, Will Practice Before the Supreme Court of the United States and the Court of Claims (1855) (original in Rockwell Collection); Bond, *supra* note 2, at 16 (discussing Rockwell's sponsorship of the legislation creating the Court of Claims).

cury) mine at New Almaden, California, near San Jose.[32] The California Land Commission upheld the title, and on appeal to the U.S. District Court Rockwell drafted numerous memoranda along with his co-counsel Judah P. Benjamin (later Confederate Secretary of State), John J. Crittenden, and Reverdy Johnson.[33] Federal judge Ogden Hoffman also confirmed the grant, although the requested area surrounding the mine was reduced.[34] But despite voluminous documentation and eyewitness testimony (some obtained in Mexico) that the customary registration procedures in pre-annexation California had been followed, in 1862 the U.S. Supreme Court rejected the claim, four to three, on the grounds that compliance with Mexican legal procedures had not been exact.[35] Since Rockwell died in 1861 he did not live to see the final result of his extensive work on the case.[36]

Rockwell's research on these matters had necessitated his studying Spanish and Mexican law, which in turn led him to produce the volume reprinted here.[37]

_____

32. *See generally* KENNETH M. JOHNSON, THE NEW ALMADEN QUICKSILVER MINE (1963) (surveying the history, operations, and legal proceedings concerning the mine).

33. REVERDY JOHNSON, JOHN A. ROCKWELL, ET AL., CORRESPONDENCE IN RELATION TO THE NEW ALMADEN QUICKSILVER MINE OF CALIFORNIA (1859); REVERDY JOHNSON, JOHN A. ROCKWELL, ET AL., FURTHER CORRESPONDENCE IN RELATION TO THE NEW ALMADEN QUICKSILVER MINE OF CALIFORNIA (1859) (originals in Rockwell Collection). *See generally* W.W. ROBINSON, LAND IN CALIFORNIA 91–109 (1948) (detailing the federal California Land Commission's role in evaluating the validity of titles originating in the Mexican period); Edgar M. Kahn, *Judah Philip Benjamin in California,* 47 CAL. HIST. SOC'Y Q. 157 (1968) (discussing Benjamin's participation in the New Almaden case); ROBIN W. WINKS, FREDERICK BILLINGS: A LIFE 98–116 (1991) (chronicling the role of San Francisco law firm Halleck, Peachy, and Billings as the California-based counsel for Castillero).

34. *See* Transcript of Record, United States v. Andres Castillero, No. 420 (N.D. Cal. 1859) (proceedings before Judge Hoffman). *See also* WINKS, *supra* note 33, at 110–11 (discussing the arguments and decision in the District Court, technically functioning as a Circuit Court). *See generally* CHRISTIAN G. FRITZ, FEDERAL JUSTICE IN CALIFORNIA: THE COURT OF OGDEN HOFFMAN, 1851–1891 134–79 (1991) (discussing Hoffman's influence on land title jurisprudence).

35. United States v. Andres Castillero, 67 U.S. (2 Black) 17 (1863). The Court's decision, including documents, testimony, the majority's opinion, and the dissent, occupied 354 pages in the U.S. Reports. *Id.* at 17-371. *See* Letters from Frederick Billings to John Arnold Rockwell, 1859–60 (originals of 11 letters in Rockwell Collection) (reporting on legal research in Mexico and other aspects of the New Almaden litigation). *See also* FREDERICK BILLINGS, LETTERS FROM MEXICO, 1859 (Mary M. Billings French ed., 1936) (recounting Billings's observations of conditions in Mexico).

36. Prior scholarship has stated that Rockwell participated in *Castillero* only at the U.S. Supreme Court level. *See* Leonard Ascher, *Lincoln's Administration and the New Almaden Scandal,* 5 PAC. HIST. REV. 38, 41 (1936); JOHNSON, *supra* note 32, at 68. But the Huntington Library material cited *supra* note 33 clearly shows him to have been an attorney of record as early as 1858, during the appeal from the Land Commission.

37. BOND, *supra* note 2, at 17.

FIGURE I.

1850 letter from Harvard law professor Theophilus Parsons to John A. Rockwell, referring to Spanish colonial codes Parsons sent him. (Original in Rockwell Collection, Huntington Library.)

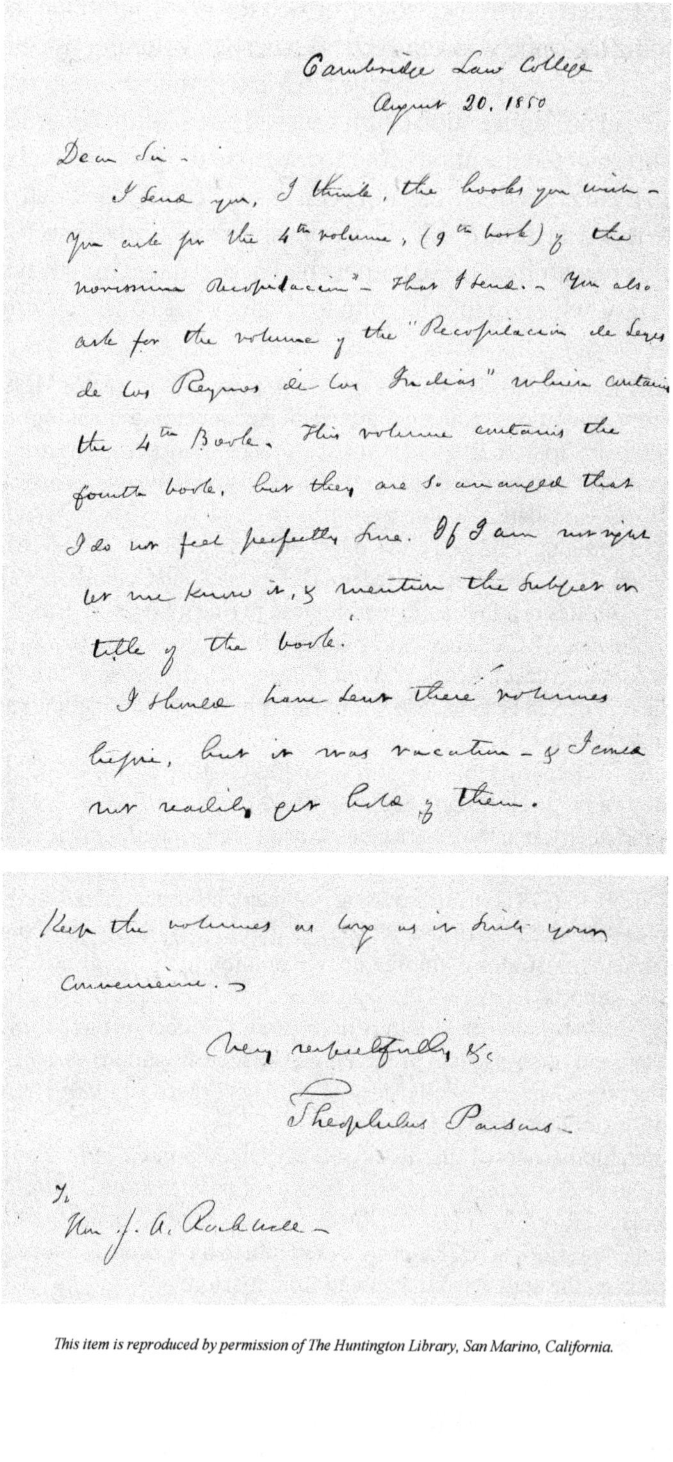

He considered that while his treatise would not be an original analysis, of "far more value, than any commentary on the law, would be a faithful translation and compilation" of the law in force in the Southwest at the time of the 1848 U.S. annexation.[38] In August, 1850, Rockwell enlisted the aid of Harvard law professor Theophilus Parsons, who sent him copies of the Spanish colonial code collections, the *Recopilación de Leyes de los Reynos de las Indias* (1774), and the *Novísima Recopilación* (1805).[39] Taking advantage of his location in the capital, Rockwell also consulted "gentlemen connected with the legations of the Spanish American States" for assistance in translating sources.[40]

The book's comprehensive coverage was noted during the production process. After delivering the manuscript to the publisher, John S. Voorhies of New York, Rockwell received word from his editors that the "large amount of Latin, French, and Spanish notes" would require an "increase of compositors, not to let that circumstance delay the work."[41] A certain amount of pre-publication interest was being generated among other specialists, such as New Orleans attorney Gustavus Schmidt, author of a recent treatise summarizing Hispanic family, property, contract, and inheritance law.[42] Schmidt had been accumulating materials for a further book on Mexican land and mining law, but wrote Rockwell to ask about "the scope and tendency of your work … since if it occupies the same ground as my contemplated publication I shall abandon the undertaking."[43] As it turned out, Schmidt did not proceed.

Indeed, Rockwell's *Compilation of Spanish and Mexican Law* was far more complete than anything else to date on its topic, for it presented new translations, corrected earlier translations, and reprinted relevant English-language materials. The book's new translations included portions of the *Recopilación de los Reynos de las Indias* (1774) and of the *Novísima Recopilación*, including sections on quicksilver mining, which would shortly be at issue in the New Almaden

---

38. ROCKWELL, *supra* note 2, at 8.

39. Letter from Theophilus Parsons to J.A. Rockwell, August 20, 1850 (original in Rockwell Collection). Parsons taught at Harvard Law School from 1848 to 1870 and authored an influential contracts treatise, among other works. Charles Fairman, *Parsons, Theophilus, in* 14 DICTIONARY OF AMERICAN BIOGRAPHY 273–74 (Dumas Malone ed., 1934).

40. ROCKWELL, *supra* note 2, at 8.

41. Letter from O.S. & G.W. Cooke to J.A. Rockwell, September 23, 1851 (original in Rockwell Collection).

42. *See* GUSTAVUS SCHMIDT, THE CIVIL LAW OF SPAIN AND MEXICO (1851). *See generally* Michael H. Hoeflich & Louis V. de la Vergne, *Introduction: Gustavus Schmidt, His Life and Library,* in THE 1877 SALE CATALOGUE OF GUSTAVUS SCHMIDT'S LIBRARY 5 (Michael H. Hoeflich, Louis V. de la Vergne & Kjell Å. Modéer eds., 2005) (discussing Swedish immigrant Schmidt's career as an attorney, civil law scholar, and book collector).

43. Letter from G. Schmidt to John A. Rockwell, September 19, 1851 (original in Rockwell Collection).

case.[44] Rockwell also translated decrees of the Spanish Cortes (representative assembly) from 1811 to 1821, and the U.S. State Department's files of official Mexico City publications regarding silver and quicksilver regulation, mining dispute resolution, and frontier colonization.[45] Some English-language versions of sources already existed, so he corrected previously translated extracts from Francisco Gamboa's *Comentarios a las Ordenanzas de Minas* (1761) and from the *Reales Ordenanzas ... de la Minería de Nueva España* (1783).[46] Rockwell also reprinted certain government pronouncements regarding land and mining in California (including both translated pre-annexation and U.S. post-annexation sources), and sections of a standard British treatise on common law mineral rights.[47] A glossary of mining terms and a table of Mexican land measures concluded the book and ensured its reference value for practitioners.[48] Notwithstanding its 677 pages, Rockwell considered this volume only the first of a series in which he would ultimately summarize federal court decisions relating to Spanish titles in Louisiana, Florida, and Texas, as well as all related public documents.[49]

When the book was released in December, 1851, a flood of congratulations poured in from diplomats, judges, and politicians; some of these plaudits were reprinted by the publisher in promotional flyers.[50] The Spanish ambassador in Washington, D.C., Angel Calderón de la Barca, complimented Rockwell on his use of Hispanic sources — "authorities which we hold as the best" — and on the quality of the translations.[51] U.S. Supreme Court justice John McLean predicted

---

44. ROCKWELL, *supra* note 2, at 14–17. *See also* GUILLERMO FLORIS MARGADANT S., INTRODUCCION AL DERECHO INDIANO Y NOVOHISPANO, PRIMERA PARTE: EL DERECHO INDIANO LEGISLATIVO 11-24 (2000) (reviewing the various editions of the Spanish colonial codes). Quicksilver was crucial to silver mining due to its use in extracting the precious metal from ore. *See generally* Peter Bakewell, *Mining in colonial Spanish America, in* 2 THE CAMBRIDGE HISTORY OF LATIN AMERICA 105, 115–22 (Leslie Bethell ed. 1984) (discussing the mercury amalgamation technique for extracting silver, and the late-eighteenth-century surge in silver output caused by mercury price reduction).

45. ROCKWELL, *supra* note 2, at 18–19.

46. ROCKWELL, *supra* note 2, at 16–17. For the translations he used, *see* FRANCISCO XAVIER DE GAMBOA, COMMENTARIES ON THE MINING ORDINANCES OF SPAIN (Richard Heathfield trans., 1830); THE ORDINANCES OF THE MINES OF NEW SPAIN (Charles Thomson trans., 1825).

47. ROCKWELL, *supra* note 2, at xvii –xviii. The common law work was WILLIAM BAINBRIDGE, A PRACTICAL TREATISE ON THE LAW OF MINES AND MINERALS (1841).

48. ROCKWELL, *supra* note 2, at 653–69.

49. *Id.* at 19.

50. John H. Voorhies, the publisher, included the work in two promotional flyers. NEW LAW BOOKS, LATELY PUBLISHED BY JOHN H. VOORHIES, LAW BOOKSELLER AND PUBLISHER (1852) included other works issued by the publisher. See Figure II for ROCKWELL'S SPANISH AND MEXICAN LAW (1852) which solely promoted the work.

51. Letter from A. Calderón de la Barca to John A. Rockwell, February 10, 1852 (original in Rockwell Collection).

FIGURE II.

1852 flyer issued by law book publisher John S. Voorhies advertising Rockwell's volume, with testimonials from prominent contemporaries. (Original courtesy of The Lawbook Exchange).

ROCKWELL'S SPANISH AND MEXICAN LAW.

A compilation of Spanish and Mexican Law in Relation to Mines and Titles to Real Estate, in force in California and New Mexico, and in the Territories acquired under the Louisiana and Florida treaties when annexed to the United States. By John A. Rockwell. Vol. 1. New York: Published by John S. Voorhies, Law Bookseller and Publisher, No. 20, Nassau street, New York.

This volume contains a translation of the mining ordinances of New Spain—Gamboa's mining ordinances—the laws in relation to mines of gold, silver, and quicksilver, contained in the "Novisima Recopilacion" and the "Recopilacion de las Indias," and in the Decrees of the Cortes of Spain and of Ferdinand VII; also of the laws and decrees of Mexico on the subject of mines, colonization, and the right of foreigners to hold real estate. It also contains extracts from public documents and from the laws of California, in relation to mines and mineral lands, together with a digest of the Common Law, on the subjects of mines and mining.

Judge Rockwell, to whom the profession owes this valuable work, was formerly a somewhat prominent member of Congress from the State of Connecticut. He was Chairman of the Committee on Claims, and author of an admirable scheme, which nearly passed Congress, for the establishment of a Board of Claims Commissioners. He is a sound and accurate lawyer, and has given, in the work before us, all the important laws which affect the titles to mining lands and the process for working them.—*Evening Post, Dec. 24.*

From the President of the United States.

Washington City, Feb. 26th, 1852.

Hon. JOHN A. ROCKWELL:

SIR: Permit me to return my thanks for a copy of your work on Spanish and Mexican Law.

I have not found time to peruse it, but a glance at the table of contents leaves no doubt that the work is at this time a *desideratum.* Nothing could be more timely than a translation of the Mexican laws relating to mines and real estate. Our large acquisition of Mexican territory, and the rich mines found in it, will render this book indispensable, not only to every intelligent man migrating to that country, but to every lawyer who desires to be well informed on so interesting a subject.

I hope that the publication may prove as profitable to yourself as I doubt not it will be beneficial to the community.

I write in much haste, but I am, truly, your obliged friend and obedient servant,

MILLARD FILLMORE.

From Chief Justice Taney, of the Supreme Court, U. S.

December 31st, 1851.

DEAR SIR: Accept my thanks for the first volume of your work on Spanish and Mexican Law. It is a work of much public interest, and much needed at the present time. I have been unable as yet to bestow on it more than a hasty glance, but shall take pleasure in looking into it more carefully during the Term, and giving you a more deliberate opinion of its value. So far as I have examined it, however, the impression has been so favorable that I have ordered twelve copies to be purchased for the Law Library, which is as large a number as we ever purchase of the most approved works.

With great respect, I am, dear sir, your obedient servant,

R. B. TANEY.

Hon. J. A. ROCKWELL.

From Mr. Justice McLean, of Supreme Court, U. S.

Washington, Dec. 31st, 1851.

DEAR SIR: Yesterday I received the first volume of "Rockwell's Spanish and Mexican Law," relating to "mines" and "real estate," for which I thank you. Such a publication I have long thought was indispensable to a thorough and satisfactory investigation of Spanish and Mexican titles to lands, which, for some years past, has constituted no inconsiderable part of the labor of the Supreme Court. The late extension of our jurisdiction over New Mexico and California, which, with Texas, Louisiana, Missouri, Florida, and a part of Mississippi, make an extent of territory equal to one-half of the Union, over which Spain exercised sovereign power, and made grants of land.

I have had but little time to look into the above volume, but, so far as I have examined it, I am struck with the judicious arrangement of the subjects, and I have no doubt, from the known ability of the compiler, that the work will be of very great importance to

the profession. I trust that an ample compensation will be realized from the sale of the work, for the learning and labor required to complete it, on the plan proposed.

With the greatest respect, your obedient servant,

JOHN McLEAN.

Hon. J. A. ROCKWELL.

From Mr. Justice Wayne, of Supreme Court, U. S.

Washington, April 6, 1852.

MY DEAR SIR: I had not time until the recess of the Court to look over your compilation of the Spanish and Mexican laws in relation to mines and titles to real estate in force in California, Texas, and New Mexico, and in the Territories acquired under the Louisiana and Florida treaties, when annexed to the United States. I have now examined it, and some of its chapters minutely. I thank you for the volume. I hope nothing will interfere to prevent the execution of your purpose in respect to the other volumes mentioned in your preface. That already published will be of use to the American legislator and jurist, whether judge or practising lawyer, and to the immigrant in California and New Mexico. The educated emigrant will find it serviceable to his intentions and hopes in the way of fortune. I cannot foresee what will be the legislation of Congress concerning the mines and lands in our recently acquired territory, but your compilation will have an influence upon it, and it will very much lessen the labors of the Supreme Court in cases which that legislation may submit to its adjudication.

Some of your citations I should like to talk with you about, when it shall suit your convenience to give me a call.

Very respectfully and truly, your obedient servant,

JAMES M. WAYNE.

Hon. J. A. ROCKWELL,
Counsellor at Law, Washington.

From Mr. Justice Grier, of Supreme Court, U. S.

DEAR SIR: Accept my thanks for the first volume of your "Spanish and Mexican Law." It is a work much needed, and becoming of greater importance every year, not only to the legal profession, but to all who feel an interest in our lately acquired territory. The matter promised in the future volumes is of equal importance with that of the present. I hope, therefore, you will be encouraged to proceed and complete the design as stated in your preface.

Very respectfully and truly, yours,

R. C. GRIER.

J. A. ROCKWELL

His Excellency Don A. Calderon de la Barca, Envoy Extraordinary and Minister Plenipotentiary of Spain to the United States.

MY DEAR SIR: I thank you for the valuable present you have been so good as to send me, of your work entitled "a compilation of Spanish and Mexican Law in relation to mining and real estate."

that the treatise would be "indispensable to a thorough and satisfactory investigation of Spanish and Mexican land titles" by the Court, especially because of "[t]he late extension of our jurisdiction."[52] Other dignitaries such as Chief Justice Roger B. Taney and sitting president Millard Fillmore also praised the book.[53]

Rockwell's *Compilation* became the principal English-language authority on Hispanic land and mining law in the new territories; nothing else was published on the subject until 1859.[54] The work could be obtained by practitioners in various California and southwestern law libraries.[55] It was referenced multiple times by the California Land Commission in its opinion as well as by the dissent in *Castillero,* the New Almaden litigation.[56] Similarly, Rockwell was cited by both sides in the 1859 case involving explorer John C. Frémont's Mariposa grant, *Biddle Boggs v. Merced Mining Co,* in which the California Supreme Court held that public prospecting was not allowed on private land.[57] In an 1862 Texas decision the book was used to support the state's reserved rights to salt deposits.[58] And in 1888,

---

52. Letter from John McLean to J.A. Rockwell, December 31, 1851 (original in Rockwell Collection).
53. *See* Figure II.
54. *See* sources cited *infra* note 60. Legal historian Joseph McKnight asserts that "Gustavus Schmidt was the last of the compilers of Spanish law for frontier use." Joseph W. McKnight, *Law Books on the Hispanic Frontier,* 27 J.W. 74, 81 (1988). But Schmidt was cited for his references to marital property, contract assignment, leases, and mortgages, and did not include the numerous land and mineral regulations later supplied by Rockwell. *See id* at 84 n.76. *See also* Peter L. Reich, *Siete Partidas in My Saddlebags: The Transmission of Hispanic Law From Antebellum Louisiana to Texas and California,* 22 TUL. EUR. & CIV. L.F. 79 (2007) (assessing the influence of Schmidt and other Louisiana sources and decisions).
55. *See* Gregory Yale, List of Law Books, July 1856 3 (original in UCLA Library Dept. of Special Collections) (listing "Rockwell's Spanish and Mexican law"); W.C. STRATTON, CATALOGUE OF THE CALIFORNIA STATE LIBRARY 67 (1866) (listing ROCKWELL, *supra* note 2); James P.T. Carter, *Report of the Territorial Librarian, in* JOURNALS OF THE FOURTH LEGISLATIVE ASSEMBLY OF THE TERRITORY OF ARIZONA 255, 257 (1868) (listing ROCKWELL, *supra* note 2, as included in the Territorial Library's law book collection).
56. Transcript of Record, Castillero, *supra* note 34, at 81-128.
57. *See* Argument on Rehearing of the Case, Brief for Appellant at 2-3, *Biddle Boggs* (1859) (appellant referencing ROCKWELL, *supra* note 2, at 50–51, 72, 76, 135, 170); Biddle Boggs v. Merced Mining Co., 14 Cal. 279, 337 (1859) (respondent citing ROCKWELL, *supra* note 2, at 53, 112); 14 Cal. at 374–76 (court holding that no federal or state authorization existed for entry on private property to extract minerals). *See generally* Peter L. Reich, *Western Courts and the Privatization of Hispanic Mineral Rights Since 1850: An Alchemy of Title,* 23 COLUM. J. ENVTL. L. 57, 73–74 (1998) (evaluating the *Biddle Boggs* arguments in relation to the decision and concluding that the court deliberately misinterpreted Spanish and Mexican law).
58. Cowan v. Hardeman, 26 Tex. 217, 222 (Moore, J., concurring) (citing ROCKWELL, *supra* note 2, at 49, 53, 83).

New Mexico's territorial supreme court ruled that Mexican land grants did not include subsurface minerals, basing its opinion in part upon the *Compilation*.[59]

Inevitably, later collections and summaries of Hispanic law materials super-seded Rockwell's, but their authors acknowledged his contribution.[60] As recently as 2002, briefing before the Colorado Supreme Court in a grazing and water rights case relied on Rockwell's translation of an 1837 Mexican colonization stat-ute.[61] The court adopted the claimants' argument that Mexican communal land use law was relevant to the dispute's resolution, and ruled in their favor.[62]

While advancing his career in land and mining litigation during the 1840s and 1850s, Rockwell was also deeply involved in Whig politics and the growing sec-tional divide. As a congressman he supported bills to improve rivers and harbors, prevent tariff reduction, and abolish the disbursement of grog in the U.S. Navy.[63] Along with many Whigs, after the Mexican War he feared that increasing antago-nism over slavery would split the party geographically, and so argued for the ex-clusion of slaveholding from the new territories.[64] By the eve of the Civil War the Whig party had disintegrated, and Rockwell sought to escape confrontation by advocating that only states, as opposed to territories, be created.[65] Unlike many of his fellow party members who had joined the antislavery Republicans, during

---

59. U.S. v. San Pedro & Canon del Agua Company, 17 P. 337, 404, 406 (N.M. 1888), *aff'd on other grounds* 146 U.S. 120 (1892) (citing ROCKWELL, *supra* note 2, at 124–27, 130–31, 411).

60. *See* H.W. HALLECK, A COLLECTION OF MINING LAWS OF SPAIN AND MEXICO v (1859) (citing ROCKWELL, *supra* note 2, as a prior work); GREGORY YALE, LEGAL TITLES TO MINING CLAIMS AND WATER RIGHTS IN CALIFORNIA iii (1866) (citing ROCKWELL, *supra* note 2); FREDERICK HALL, THE LAWS OF MEXICO: A COMPILATION AND TREATISE RELATING TO REAL PROPERTY, MINES, WATER RIGHTS, PERSONAL RIGHTS, CONTRACTS, AND INHERITANCES iv (1885) (citing ROCKWELL, *supra* note 2, although criticizing the accuracy of one of his reprinted translations).

61. Brief of Amici Curiae Bi-National Human Rights Commission, et al., at 8, Lobato v. Taylor, 71 P. 3d 938 (Colo. 2002) (citing ROCKWELL, *supra* note 2, at 627).

62 .71 P. 3d at 946.

63. *See* J.A. ROCKWELL, COMPARISON BETWEEN THE INTERNAL & FOREIGN COMMERCE OF THE UNITED STATES, IN A SPEECH ON THE RIVER AND HARBOR BILL, DELIVERED BEFORE THE HOUSE OF REPRESENTATIVES (March 17, 1846) (original in Rockwell Collection); JOHN A. ROCKWELL, SPEECH ... ON THE BILL TO REDUCE THE DUTIES ON IMPORTS ... (June 26, 1846) (original in Rockwell Collection); JNO. A. ROCKWELL, SPEECH ... IN FAVOR OF ABOLISHING THE SPIRIT RA-TIONS IN THE NAVY ... (January 27, 1847) (original in Rockwell Collection).

64. *See* JOHN A. ROCKWELL, SPEECH ... IN RELATION TO SLAVERY IN THE TERRITORIES ... (Febru-ary 17, 1849). *See also* HOWE, *supra* note 7, at 146-47 (discussing Whig president Zachary Taylor's leadership in advocating admission of California and New Mexico as free states, while the Democrats called for a slave code there).

65. JOHN A. ROCKWELL, STATES VS. TERRITORIES, A TRUE SOLUTION OF THE TERRITORIAL QUES-TION, BY AN OLD LINE WHIG (August 15, 1860). *See also* HOLT, *supra* note 7, at 952-53 (viewing the Whigs' demise as due to infighting over slavery, nativism, and prohibitionism).

the presidential campaign of 1860 he condemned the new organization in classic Whig fashion as "subversive of all constitution and government," and supported compromise candidate John Bell on the "Constitutional Union" ticket.

Rockwell's faith in the traditional Whig ideology of reason and neutrality that served him so well in analyzing Mexican law issues could only frustrate him as war approached. According to his eulogy, "[h]e had long forseen the rising cloud of discontent and disturbance, which has at last gathered dark and threatening over the land, and his mind had been anxiously exercised as to the final issue."[66] At work on the New Almaden case in Washington, D.C., on February 10, 1861, he complained of slight illness during the day, returned to his lodgings, and died in the evening before a physician could arrive.[67] In the words of the eulogist, "[s]uddenly was he summoned from the scenes of a busy and responsible activity."[68]

A successful litigator, John Arnold Rockwell was one of the first American attorneys to bridge the international legal gap both in his practice and in his scholarship. Yet when he applied his considerable talents to address antebellum sectionalism, the country's crisis overwhelmed him as it did the Whigs and so many other lawyers who trusted in the power of rules over violence.[69] The reliance on law that helped him incorporate Mexican territories and traditions into the Union proved helpless in the face of stronger centrifugal forces. What does remain, however, are Rockwell's steps to develop a language of international legal communication, and their culmination in his book. His legacy survives today in the growing movement towards North American cooperation and in the cross-cultural nature of current legal practice.[70]

Peter L. Reich
May, 2011

---

66. BOND, *supra* note 2, at 25.

67. *Id.* at 34.

68. *Id.* at 28.

69. *See generally* PERRY MILLER, THE LIFE OF THE MIND IN AMERICA FROM THE REVOLUTION TO THE CIVIL WAR 214 (1965) (discussing the limits of the nineteenth-century legal mentality in restraining political passions).

70. *See* ROBERT A. PASTOR, TOWARD A NORTH AMERICAN COMMUNITY (2001) (evaluating the prospects for commercial, infrastructural, and political integration of Canada, Mexico, and the United States); BAKER & BOTTS, L.L.P., CROSS-BORDER TRANSACTIONS, http://wwwbakerbotts.com/cross-bordertransactions-practice-areas/ (last visited April 5, 2011) (advertising international law firm's expertise in dealing with divergent legal systems and other multi-jurisdictional issues).

A COMPILATION

OF

SPANISH AND MEXICAN LAW,

IN RELATION TO

MINES, AND TITLES TO REAL ESTATE,

IN FORCE IN

CALIFORNIA, TEXAS AND NEW MEXICO;

AND IN THE TERRITORIES ACQUIRED UNDER THE LOUISIANA AND FLORIDA
TREATIES, WHEN ANNEXED TO THE UNITED STATES.

VOLUME I.

CONTAINING A TRANSLATION OF THE MINING ORDINANCES OF NEW SPAIN—GAMBOA'S MIN-
ING ORDINANCES—THE LAWS IN RELATION TO MINES OF GOLD, SILVER AND
QUICKSILVER, CONTAINED IN THE

"NOVISIMA RECOPILACION," AND THE "RECOPILACION DE LAS INDIAS;"

AND IN THE DECREES OF THE CORTES OF SPAIN AND OF FERDINAND VII.,
ALSO OF THE LAWS AND DECREES OF MEXICO, ON THE SUBJECT
OF MINES, COLONIZATION, AND THE RIGHT OF FOREIGN-
ERS TO HOLD REAL ESTATE.

ALSO, EXTRACTS FROM PUBLIC DOCUMENTS, AND FROM THE LAWS OF CALIFOR-
NIA, IN RELATION TO MINES AND MINERAL LANDS:

TOGETHER WITH

A DIGEST OF THE COMMON LAW, ON THE SUBJECT OF
MINES AND MINING.

BY JOHN A. ROCKWELL,

COUNSELLOR AT LAW.

NEW-YORK:
JOHN S. VOORHIES, LAW BOOKSELLER AND PUBLISHER.
1851.

CONTENTS.

I.

CHAPTER I.

Of the Tribunal General of the Miners of New Spain.

CHAPTER II.

Of the Judges and Deputies of the Mining Districts.

CHAPTER III.

Of Jurisdiction in Mining Causes.

CHAPTER VII.

Of Persons who may or may not discover, denounce, and work the Mines.

CHAPTER VIII.

Of Properties and Intermediate Spaces between Properties,—and of the measures in Mines.

CHAPTER IX.

Of working, supporting, and protecting the Mines.

CHAPTER X.

Of Drains in Mines.

CHAPTER XI

Of Mines worked by Companies.

CHAPTER XII.

Of the Laborers in Mines, and in the works and establishments for the reduction of the Metals.

CHAPTER XIII.

Of the supply of Water and Provisions to the Mines.

CHAPTER XIV.

Of the persons who reduce Ores by agreement, and purchasers of the Metals.

CHAPTER XV.

Of the Contractors for supplying Mines, and of the Dealers in the Metals.

B

CHAPTER XVIII.

Of the education and instruction of young persons intended for the mining business.

CHAPTER XIX.

Of the privileges of the Miners.

II.

Laws of Spain concerning Mines of gold, silver, and other metals, contained in the 18th title of the Novisima Recopilacion, with Gamboa's Commentaries on Law 4.

CHAPTER I.

CHAPTER II.

CHAPTER III.

CHAPTER IV.

CHAPTER V.

CHAPTER XIX.

CHAPTER XX.

CHAPTER XXI.

CHAPTER XXII.

CHAPTER XXIII.

CHAPTER XXIV.

CHAPTER XXV.

CHAPTER XXVI.

III.

Extracts from the Recopilacion de leyes de los Reynos de las Indias.

TITLE XX.

Concerning miners and workers in quicksilver, and their privileges.

TITLE XXI.

Concerning the Alcaldes Mayores, and Notaries of the Mines.

1

VI.

VII.

Common Law in relation to Mines and Minerals.

VIII.

Decrees of the Supreme Government of Mexico.

IX.

Extracts from Official Publications of the Laws in the Newspapers of the City of Mexico.

X.

National Colonization Law of Mexican Republic of January 4, 1823.

ERRATA.

Page 25, in caption, before "Miners of New Spain" insert "OF THE IM-
     PORTANT BODY OF THE"

"   45, SEC. 27, 2d line, for *contests* read *consent*.

"   50, 8th line for *making* read *marking*.

"   61, 2d line, after *should*, read *not*

"   " SEC. 2, for *facuttativo*, read *facultativo*

" 107, 6th line, for *adopted* read *adapted*

" 131, 1st line, for *maner* read *manner*

" " 5th " for *obsolute* read *absolute*

" 599, 9th line, for *ten* read *two*.

PREFACE.

THE object of the present work is, to furnish a compilation of the Spanish and Mexican laws in relation to the mines of the precious metals, and the laws governing the titles to land in the states and territories of the United States which were, originally, a portion of the Spanish or Mexican territories. It is intended to aid in the investigation and decision of questions affecting the titles to land, and in relation to mines, arising under Spanish grants within the territory ceded to the United States under the Louisiana and Florida treaties, and especially, titles delivered under Spanish or Mexican law in Texas, California and New Mexico.

The design is to give a translation of all laws and decrees of Spain particularly applicable to those territories, when provinces—the laws entire as contained in the several titles of the " *Recopilacion de Leyes de los Reynos de las Indias* " and in the " *Novisima Recopilacion de las Leyes de España*" also of the Decrees of the Cortes of Spain and of Ferdinand VII. prior to 1822, and the laws and decrees of Mexico, from that time to the time of the cession of California and New Mexico to the United States, so far as those several laws and decrees are applicable to the territories, and relate to the subjects, above mentioned.

The present volume contains a collection of the laws and decrees in relation to mines of gold, silver and quicksilver, and, in addition to the Spanish and Mexican law, in force, the compiler has added a digest of some branches of the common law on the subject of mines and minerals, which, it is supposed, will be of general use: and as the common law of England has been adopted as the law in California, will be of peculiar value, in that state, in relation to questions which may, hereafter arise. In addition to this there is included, in this volume, a considerable quantity of additional matter, most of which is particularly applicable to California,—viz. The messages of the President of the United States,—reports of the Secretary of the Interior, acts of Congress and other public documents of the United States, in relation to California:—the treaties between Spain and Mexico, and the United States and Mexico: the statutes of California in relation to mines :—Also the laws and decrees of Mexico in relation to colonization, and in relation to the holding of land and mines, by foreigners.

The compiler has not the vanity to suppose that he could furnish any original treatise, on these branches of Spanish or Mexican law which would be at all valuable. His professional engagements rendered necessary an examination of these laws, in reference to the titles to land and mines, in territories acquired from Spain and Mexico ; and, although, the study for a year or two would of course, not enable him to compose an original work, which could only be furnished from the accumulated stores of many years of study and practice in the laws of the country, he has thought that a work of much humbler pretension, but far more value, than any commentary on the law, would be a faithful translation and compilation of the Spanish and Mexican law, in force in California and New Mexico, and other territory, originally, Spanish or Mexican, at the time of their cession. Some of these laws have never been translated into English, and, of those which have been translated, the volumes containing the translations are very rare, and can with difficulty be obtained, at very high prices. The compiler has availed himself of these translations taking however the liberty, after a careful comparison with the original by himself and by others more competent, to make some, although very few, corrections.

In this labor, and in the translations made by himself, he has had most valuable aid from gentlemen connected with the legations of some of the Spanish American States, and others, well acquainted with the Spanish law and language.

A brief history of the Spanish codes, and their relative authority, seems appropriate, and almost necessary, in a work of this character ; and this is rendered the more important, as some of those of very ancient date, are still referred to and cited, not only in the courts of Mexico, and other Spanish American States, but in those states which were formed out of territory acquired under the Louisiana and Florida treaties.

Spain, occupied by Phœnicians, Carthagenians, Romans, Goths, and Arabs, adopted, as is claimed by some writers on this subject, the customs, usages and laws of the people who governed it from time to time. Before being invaded by any nation, she undoubtedly had, as they insist, her own regulations and ordinances, customs and laws, appropriate and accommodated to her national character. But history, if any notice at all is taken of the legislation anterior to the Gothic invasion, is so meagre, confused, and unsatisfactory, as to give no valuable information on the subject.

The first code published by the Goths, was of the Roman law, in the time of Alaric. The decree issued in Latin, by king Alaric, commanding the observance of this new code, and the character of the code itself, not only show that the laws of the Goths in Spain were founded on the Roman law, but that that law was, alone, in force in that kingdom at the time, and that it was not until a subsequent period that the Roman law was at all modified by local usages and customs.

The "Fuero Juzgo," also called "Fuero de los Jueces," book of the Judges, originally published in Latin under the title of "Forum Judicum," and, subsequently under the title of "Liber Judicum," is considered by the sages of the Spanish law as the origin of their jurisprudence. It was published at the close of the seventh century.

The distinguished writer Marina, in his historical and critical essay upon the legislation of the kingdoms of Castile and Leon, gives the following definition of the word "Fuero."

"Antiquity furnishes us with many instruments bearing the title of "*fueros*," which are nothing more than writings of donation, issued by some lord or proprietor, in favor of individuals, churches or monasteries, granting lands, estates, &c. Leaving innumerable instruments of this nature—common in Spain and in all Europe, during the eighth and ninth centuries, and as useful in illustrating the history and geography of the middle ages as they are barren respecting an ancient jurisprudence, to which they have scarcely any relation—we will speak solely of those which properly deserve the name of "fueros;" those documents issued by the kings, or by the lords in virtue of the privileges pertaining to their sovereignty, in which were contained constitutions, ordinances and laws, civil and criminal, designed to establish on a firm footing, the common rights of towns and cities, to raise them into municipalities, and to secure for them a moderate and just administration, conformed to the public constitution of the kingdom, and the circumstances of the people : documents exceedingly valuable on account of the merit of some of the laws, as for their antiquity :—many of them being anterior, by more than a century, to those municipal corporations, and chartered companies, so celebrated in Italy and France, and considered as the first rudiments of politics and legislation in relation to cities. Before the 12th and 13th centuries, the epoch of these charters in those foreign kingdoms, we had in the kingdoms of Leon and Castile, those more wise and equitable, and which combined the advantages of true civil liberty, with due subordination to the sovereign and his laws."

The author of this code is in doubt, it being attributed by different writers to

2

three of the kings of that period, and by some regarded as the joint work of all.

This code has doubtless many and notable defects, if viewed with the light of the present age, but in spite of its faults, no one can deny that, considering the period in which it was promulgated, it was a most remarkable production.

It consists of an introduction, containing 18 laws, and 12 books, divided into 54 titles, and containing 559 laws.

Escriche cites the celebrated Marina as saying, in relation to it, that "it is admirable for method and clearness; its style grave and correct, its Latin sufficiently pure; most of the laws are marked by prudence and wisdom; in fine, as a body of law infinitely superior to all those which to that time had been published in the new political associations of Europe; a body of law which forms a complete vindication of the Gothic kings of Spain, and of the philosophical spirit of the Spanish clergy, who had so important a part in its formation; a body of law which will always be a monument of glory to our country, and an undeniable proof that our fathers were farthest advanced in the career of civilization."

Foreign authors of the highest distinction have regarded this code in a similar light. Among these is Gibbon, in his famous historical work, and Guizot, in his general history of the civilization of Europe, from the fall of the Roman Empire to the French Revolution; and other German, French, and Italian writers, of equal note.

In relation to the authority of this venerable code, it is important to observe that it has never, as a whole been repealed. As recently as the 15th July, 1788 a question arose before the Court of Chancery of Grenada, in relation to the succession to property of a deceased person. According to Law 12. tit. 2., lib. 4. of the Fuero Juzgo the relatives of the deceased person are entitled to the property; and according to the Partidas a convert was entitled to the estate. The matter was referred by the Court to the king, Charles III. who, after consultation with his council decided that the said law of the Fuero Juzgo did not appear to have been repealed by any other, and ought to constitute the rule of decision in this and other similar matters without such adherence as had been shown to the Partida, founded only on the provisions of the civil law of the Romans and on the common canon law. (Escriche Dic. de Leg. Fuero Juzgo.)

Another important code, is the "Fuero Viejo de Castilla."—This code received that title in the year 1356, but it is generally stated by Spanish writers that it had its origin between the years 995 and 1000, and that Don Sancho the Sovereign of Castile was its author—that it was also called "Fu-

ero Viejo de Búrgos," " Fuero de los Fijosdalgos," &c. The learned father
Burriel gave this as the results of his investigations, and was followed by subsequent writers, especially by Doctors Asso and Manuel in more than one of
their works; but it is now considered by the best authority that the celebrated
Marina in his Historico-Critical Essay has demonstrated that Sancho was the
author of no code of general and fundamental laws for Castile.

It is not important as to the precise origin of this code. It is agreed that
from time to time it received various additions under various names, and
when in 1356 it received the title of " Fuero Viejo de Castilla," it had been
enriched by contributions from the " Fuero de Búrgos," that of Najera,
Logroño and others less celebrated.

Doctors Asso and Manuel in their preliminary discourse to the edition of
this code, published at Madrid, 1761, (pp. 43. 44.,) say: " The laws of
the *Fuero Castellano* have been observed constantly from the time of Don
Sancho the author of them, to the present time; not only because it was
commanded by many decrees and royal edicts, but because no one could
mention a period when they were not in force."

Although this is not denied, it appears that aside from those which have
become incorporated in other laws and are embraced in the *Novisima Recopilacion* and those which are obsolete, the number of laws having any application to the existing state of things, is very small.

The " Fuero Real" was not published until the years 1254 or 1255.—
The author of this celebrated code was Alphonso the Wise. To remedy the
evils arising from various uncertain and conflicting laws, decrees and grants
proceeding from various sources of real or pretended authority, and in order
as he says in the preface, to abolish a multitude of unjust laws, this code
was adopted. It has been said also, that this Fuero was considered only as
a preliminary step towards the great legislative reform which this wise Monarch meditated by the publication of the famous *Partidas*, thus preparing
the way by a gradual removal of the existing *fueros*, local grants and conflicting decrees for a more complete change.

This code is remarkable for its clearness, method, and conciseness. It
comprehended the most important of the municipal *fueros* and conformed to
the Customs of Castile and the *Fuero Juzgo*, a large portion of which is copied word for word.

In relation to the authority of this code, Don Alphonso XI. in the " Ordenamiento" made by the Cortes of Alcalá of 1348, ordered by Law 1 Tit.
28, that the laws of the *Fuero Real* and the municipal fueros of each pueblo

should be preferred to the Siete Partidas in the decision of civil and criminal cases so far as they were not obsolete nor contrary to said *ordenamiento*. This provision is inserted and continued in the laws of Toro and the collection of laws subsequently made, and finally in the Novisima Recopilacion, where it forms Law 3. tit. 2. of Book 3.

Escriche in his dictionary adds the following : " Don Juan Sala in the brief history of the law contained in his Institute says, that since the royal cédula of the 15th July, 1788 above referred to, it is not necessary to prove the laws of the Fuero Real to be in force in order to claim the application of them in any case ; but it is sufficient that they have not been repealed by other subsequent acts or by a contrary usage."—Reference is not here had to the many laws which are included in the *Novisima Recopilacion*, since they would possess the same authority with the Novisima of which they form a part.

The Fuero Real was speedily followed by " Las leyes del Estilo" in order to render clear some points in the text of the *Fuero* which were of doubtful meaning. At Madrid, and in some other parts of the kingdom, this code went into immediate force ; but it was not until after the death of the king that it become universally adopted throughout the kingdom.

It is scarcely necessary to refer to the numerous Fueros of a less general and public character.—The *Fuero de Leon*, of the year 1020—De Najerá, of 1076—of Logroño, 1093—That of Sepulveda of 1076, shews most distinctly the peculiar civilization which arose out of the war of the re-conquest. It also diminished the theocratic spirit of the Gothic monarchy by showing to the Castilians in the municipal power, a new germ of government, a social element until then unknown, a power which produced in the course of time, the reform of the codes, which corrected the abuse of the royal authority by converting it into that of protector and guardian, and which created afterwards a representative in the Cortes of the popular class.

We next come to that most remarkable body of law the *Siete Partidas*, so called because the work is divided into seven parts. This code is similar to the Roman Pandects and appears to have been formed from the usages and ancient customs of Spain—the Roman laws—various decisions of the canon law—the writings of the fathers and quotations from various sages and philosophers. It was commenced in the year 1256 and finished in 1263, but not published until the year 1348, in the reign of Alphonso XI.

Considering the period in which it was written, this work is regarded not only by Spanish writers, but by those of other nations as one of the most remarkable legal productions that has ever been written.

The illustrious Morina speaks in the following terms of the second of the Partidas which contains the political and military constitution of the kingdom:

" A most precious monument of history, legislation, morality and politics, and beyond dispute, the part of the whole seven which compose the code of Alphonso the Wise, the most complete, whether we consider the gravity and eloquence with which it is written, or the excellent maxims of philosophy which are sown in every part of it, or its intimate connexion with the ancient customs, laws and *fueros*, municipal and general, of Castile : from which it is principally derived.—A work eminently respectable even in these times of philosophy, and worthy of being read, meditated upon and studied, not only by jurists and statesmen, but also by literary men and the curious, especially by our rulers, the nobility and royalty itself."

This work has been translated under the patronage of the legislature of Louisiana and at the expense of that State, by Messrs. Moreau and Carleton, counsellors at law. They speak of the Partidas, in the preface to the translation as " the most perfect system of Spanish laws," and which " may be advantageously compared with any code published in the most enlightened ages of the world," and that these laws are " the unceasing subject of the praise and admiration of every jurist acquainted with them."

They also quote a learned French writer who, speaking of the Partidas, observes :

" We find in every page of that work, the highest wisdom and the most stern justice. It gave to the monarch under whose auspices it was executed, titles more just to the epithet of wise, bestowed upon him by his contemporaries, than his astronomical researches and physical knowledge, however surprising the one and the other may have been considered, in an age when all studies were so much disregarded. It is in that precious code that we must seek the early treasures of the Spanish language," &c.

But although such is the character of the Partidas, as a profound philosophical and literary work it is deserving of most, if not all the praise bestowed upon this famous body of law, its authority in the decision of causes in the courts of Spain is far less high. Instead of the first, it has a much lower place.

The laws of the Recopilacion and those subsequently passed, are of highest authority, and in the absence of these, those of the Fuero Real and of the Municipal Fueros, so far as they are not obsolete, and lastly those of the Siete Partidas.

The *Ordenamiento de Alcalá,* published in the year 1348, contains 32 chapters, and in all 124 laws. It may be called a supplement to the Partidas, and supplies some omissions and defects in the Partidas.—Almost all the laws of the Ordenamiento have been embodied in the Recopilacion, either entire or with some slight alteration. In 1774, an edition of this work was published at Madrid by Asso and Manuel, illustrated by notes.

The " Ordenamiento Real" was published during the reign of Ferdinand and Isabella, and is an alphabetical compilation of the various laws, whether scattered or contained in the *Fuero Real*—the laws of *Estilo* and Ordenamiento de Alcalá divided into eight books, compiled by Alonzo Montalvo, who has added a commentary and index.

This is confessedly a work of great merit and philosophical value ; but some of the most learned of the Spanish jurists are directly at issue on the question of the public authority of the work. Doctors Asso and Manuel, and learned father Burriel, insist tenaciously that the Ordenamiento Real was never sanctioned by the king and never had any authority beyond that of the private work by a learned author, and critics and authors equally learned and distinguished, maintain that it was written by the express orders of Ferdinand and Isabella, and consequently has all the authority of the other codes.

The better opinion seems to be, that as the work does not bear on its face any mark or evidence of the royal sanction, it is to be considered as of private authority, and that the laws included in it have no additional force by being embraced in the collection.

The *Leyes de Toro* consist of 83 laws which were prepared and arranged under the auspices of Ferdinand and Isabella, in the Cortes of Toledo in the year 1502, but were not proclaimed until during the reign of Joana, at a session of the Cortes in the city of Toro, in the year 1505. These laws do not form a complete code, arranged and methodised, like the codes to which we have referred. Their object was to supply the omissions and correct the errors of the previous codes. They are, without dispute, one of the best and most important collections of Spanish Jurisprudence.

These laws, so far as they are in force, are embodied in the *Novisima Recopilacion*, where they are arranged under the appropriate titles.

To these various codes and collections of laws in the year 1537 followed the *Nueva Recopilacion*, or new compilation. This consisted of two volumes, including nine books, and containing the existing laws. In the subsequent editions, issued in the years 1581, 1592, 1598, 1640, 1723 and 1745, were added the numerous laws which were enacted in the periods between the several editions; and in that of 1745 there is added a third volume, in which, under the title of *Autos Acordados del Consejo*, are included more than five hundred *pragmaticas*, *cédulas*, decrees, orders, declarations and resolutions of the Crown, issued prior to that year, which are distributed in the same order into titles and books, as in the two volumes of the collection of the laws.

Three editions were issued in the years 1772, 1775, and 1777, with the addition of the laws passed prior to the latter period. Although this *Recopilacion* contained the laws which were promulgated subsequent to the issuing of the Partidas and the Fuero Real, and many that were in previous codes ; for example, some from the *Fuero Juzgo*, and of the laws of Estilo, and almost the whole in the *Ordenamiento de Alcalá*, and the famous 83 laws of Toro ; those not inserted were not necessarily thereby repealed, as we have seen above.

Finally there was published another edition of the same *Recopilacion*, but with an entirely new order and arrangement, in the year 1805, selecting the laws in force contained in the former edition, and adding more than two thousand distinct provisions, not contained in the edition of 1745. This was entitled *Novisima Recopilacion de las leges de Espana*, and under this title was approved and ordered to be obeyed by Charles IV., by a royal *cédula*, of the 15th July, 1805.

This work constitutes now the great body of the Spanish law, and is of the highest authority in all departments of the government, and in the adjudication of the Courts, except in those cases where any part has been repealed by subsequent laws, or where there exists a special code of laws, appropriate to a particular subject, or to a particular province, that has not been repealed by it.

But although this is so admirably arranged, and so full a body of law, it does not repeal all previous laws, and although the highest, and in all cases where its provisions are clear, and unrepealed by subsequent laws, an absolute authority, yet in those cases where the Recopilacion and subsequent laws furnish no rule of decision, reference may be had as authority to the *Fuero Real*, or *Fuero de las Leyes*, and, so far as they are not obsolete, to the *Fueros Municipales*, and when these furnish no rule, to the *Partidas*.

The 18th title of the ninth book of the *Novisima Recopilacion*, includes the laws "in relation to mines of gold, silver, and other metals." These are six in number, and although some parts of them do not relate directly to the subject of the present volume, it has been deemed important to give all these entire, as they are not very voluminous, and it being more satisfactory to the reader than any abridgement could possibly be. For the translation of the 4th law, he has mainly adopted that furnished by Mr. Heathfield, in his excellent translation of Gamboa's mining ordinances, that law being almost precisely the same as the 9th law, Tit. 13, Book 6, of the *Nueva Recopilacion*, which forms the text of Gamboa's work.

The compiler has thus given a brief, but he hopes a correct account of the different codes and collections of Spanish law, which are of general application, and the degree of authority belonging to them respectively in the Spanish tribunals. It now remains that he should give some account of the systems of laws peculiarly applicable to the Spanish American provinces, and especially to Mexico, and of the Spanish and Mexican law, in force in California and New Mexico, at the time of the cession to the United States.

The " Recopilacion de leyes de los reynos de las Indias," was first published in the year 1661. Spain, possessing immense dominions in North and South America, felt the necessity of regulating the government of those provinces, and of securing by general and permanent laws, the obedience and welfare of the nations who inhabited them. The scattered laws therefore which had been promulgated for that purpose at different periods, were collected and digested by order of Philip IV. in the same form as the Recopilacion of Castile.(a)

Murillo, an able Spanish law writer, in his treatise entitled *Cursus Juris Canonici Hispani et Indici*, speaks of the manner in which the Spanish laws ought to be received in both Indies. On that subject he says, that in the Spanish dominion in the Indies, courts of justice should first have recourse to the royal and special edicts which may have been directed to the chancery of the city or place where the cause is pending; and if there are none, they should then decide according to the common law, which is to be found in the laws of the Recopilacion of the Indies; and when these last are silent, recourse must be had to the Recopilacion of Castile, (Nuva Recopilacion) and the Partidas. This author also observes, that the rescripts or royal ordinances are of no authority in the Indies, unless they have been directed to the supreme council of those countries.(b)

The same course has been pursued in the translation of all the laws relating to the subject in the several titles in the Recopilacion of the laws of the Indies, as in the case of the Novisima Recopilacion, and for the same reason.

(a) 1st Moreau & Carleton, Partidas p. xv.   (b) Idem, p. xxii.

These laws are included in lib. 4, title 19, on the discovery and working of mines, tit. 20, concerning miners, workers in quicksilver, and their privileges, and tit. 21, in relation to the *Alcaldes Mayores* and notaries of mines. The translations are made from the third edition, published at Madrid in the year 1774.

In the year 1783, however, a new and very important code of laws was framed for the purpose of simplifying and rendering more uniform the legislation of the mines under the title of " *Reales Ordinanzes para la direccion régimen y gobierno del importante cuerpo de la Mineria de Nueva-Espana y de su Real Tribunal General.*"

This code was framed in the reign of Charles III., and during the ministry of Joseph de Galvez.

This work was translated by Charles Thompson, Esq., of Lincoln's Inn, Barrister at Law, and published at London in 1825. The compiler has availed himself of this translation of this most valuable work, with the few corrections which were deemed proper, after a careful comparison of it with the original.

In a recent work of great value and authority, in six volumes, published at Madrid in 1844, entitled " Biblioteca de Legislacion Ultramarina en forma de Diccionario Alfabético," by don José Maria Zamora y Coronado, the learned author, under the head of Mines, copies this work almost entire, and introduces it with the following statement :—" This work was so perfect, and prepared with so much wisdom, that its regulations continue without substantial alteration. Since there is nothing impairing its authority, at least in the judicial portion of it, although there has been published the royal instructions concerning mines, issued for the Peninsula, on the 18th December, 1825 ; it is thought that a service will be rendered to the public by the insertion of the essential chapters, and subsequently of the instructions of 1825."

The decrees of the Cortes of Spain, and of the Ferdinand VII., during the short time in which he may be considered as having the authority of a sovereign, have also been carefully examined, from the year 1810 to 1822, and a translation has been made of the few laws that were applicable alike to Mexico and California, and so far as they relate to the subject of the present volume, they have been inserted in it.

In the year 1829, there was published in Mexico a collection of the decrees and orders of the Cortes of Spain, which were considered to be in force in tha Republic. The following is an extract from the preface of that book. It should also be added, that by official acts the Mexican government have recognised as valid the decrees of the Cortes, not inconsistent with the constitution and laws of the Mexican Republic.

" The independence of Mexico having been happily realized by the occupation of its Capital on the 27th of September, 1821 and the destruction of the vice-royal government, although the obligation of dependence on Spain is forever broken, these laws which regulate the obligations and rights of those who compose the new community, cannot and ought not to lose their force. Since it is only in the course of time and by competent authority, that their place can be supplied, the sudden abolition of all former laws would have been equivalent to the introduction of absolute anarchy at a season when the preservation of order was most necessary. Therefore it is that with the exception of such laws as conflicted directly with the memorable plan of Iguala and the new order of things to which it gave rise, all other laws which had emanated from the kings of Spain and the sovereign authority which, until that day had been recognized, are acknowledged and respected : suits at law have been decided under them, justice was administered in conformity to them, and the social life of the Mexican people had become adapted to them. Hence it resulted that the Spanish codes so far as others entirely national, have not been substituted, are constantly consulted by the judges, professors of law and even ordinary citizens, as furnishing the standard of action, the guaranty of their reciprocal rights and the rules of their proceeding.

One of the most celebrated of these codes is the collection of the orders and decrees issued by the Spanish Cortes, in the years 1812, 13, 14, 20 and 21, in which last year our independence was established. This collection, extending to ten volumes, has become amongst us rare as it is costly : and when obtained, the inconvenience exists of finding scattered in the first seven volumes (being those which contain the decrees passed when Mexico was dependent on the legislators of Madrid) those laws which are regarded as in force in the republic from having been so held, or because they related to this country, or from not having been repealed."

The compiler has also, carefully, examined, page by page, the laws and decrees of Mexico, as contained in the printed volumes, from the year 1821 to 1839, and in the same manner, the files of the official newspapers of the City of Mexico, in the Department of State, to the year 1847, inclusive with the view of obtaining a complete collection of the Mexican law applicable to California. A translation of those which relate to the subject of this volume, will be found in their appropriate place.

It will thus be seen that if the design of this work is carried out by the publication of the subsequent volumes, there will be presented, unabridged and entire, in relation to those branches of the law affecting the title to land, the entire chapters and titles in the Recopilacion of the Indies and the Novisima Recopilacion ; also all the laws and decrees of the Cortes of Spain, and of Mexico that were in force in California, at the time of the cession to the United States ;—presenting thus the entire Spanish and Mex-'ican legislation without any interruption. To this will be added a summary of the decisions of the federal courts, in relation to Spanish titles, under the treaties of Louisana and Florida, and arising out of the annexation of Texas ; and all public documents proceeding from Congress or the departments of the government.

In the present volume, confined principally to the laws in relation to mines of precious metals, in addition to the materials furnished from the sources above mentioned, and the translation of the entire work on the Mining Ordinances of New Spain, there will be added the valuable commentary of Gamboa, so far as it is a commentary on the law, and omitting only the lengthened examination into the machinery to be used and other matters, interesting to the engineer and the workers of the mines, but having no relation to the law on the subject.

With regard to the character of this work, as it will deservedly occupy a large part of the volume, we give very nearly entire the preface of Mr. Heathfield, to his translation of it ; also an extract form the decree of the king authorising its publication.

This is a treatise on the laws by which Spain and her several colonies were governed, in their mining affairs, at the period of its publication, and up to the year 1783. These laws were principally contained in certain regulations applying immediately and exclusively to the subject of mining, and consisting :

First,—Of a code of mining laws promulgated in the year 1584, commonly called the New Code, in contradistinction to other ordinances of anterior date, usually referred to as the Old ordinances. When the ordinances of the New Code were promulgated, the mines of America had not acquired much celebrity, and it was for the government of those of Spain alone, that these ordinances were framed. But it was afterwards directed, by a law of the Indies, that the ordinances of the New Code should be observed in those countries, when not at variance with the municipal laws of each province. These ordinances form the text of the work of Gamboa.

Second,—Of Old ordinances, promulgated at different times previous to the year 1584, and remaining partially in force after that period; being repealed by the New Code, so far only as at variance with the regulations thereby introduced.

Third,—Of royal orders, of different denominations, either general or issued for particular kingdoms or provinces only.

Fourth,—Of colonial or provincial regulations, of force in the particular kingdoms or provinces only by the respective governments of which they had been issued.

Besides these, the general law of Spain the laws of the collection of the Indies, applying generally to all those countries, and the local laws of each kingdom or province of the Indies, occasionally required to be referred to, to supply deficiencies in, or assist the construction of, the laws more immediately regulating mining.

Such was the state of the law of mining in Spain and her colonies, in the year 1761, when Señor GAMBOA published his Commentary. The plan of this work may be thus explained. The ordinances of the New Code, which form the text, are classed according to their subject, in distinct chapters; those contained in each chapter being separately considered. In the commentary, the author commonly gives a succinct historical account of the law, upon the points which form the subject of the chapter, from the earliest times to the year 1584; and after shewing how it stood previous to that date, proceeds to investigate how far the old regulations had been annulled by the new code, and how far they still remained in force, not being at variance with the provisions of that code. He next shows what alterations, if any, had been made by royal orders or provisional regulations since the year 1584 touching upon those of Peru, and other kingdoms or provinces, but referring more minutely and particularly, to those of the kingdoms and provinces now constituting the republic of Mexico. Having thus brought into view the regulations more particularly relating to the points under consideration, the author proceeds to illustrate them by comparison with the general rules of the civil law, the law of Spain, and the laws of the Collection of the Indies, and by referring to important cases decided in the courts, within his own experience, clearing up many doubtful points, pointing out deficiencies or redundancies, suggesting important improvements, and, in fine, completely exhausting the subject in a legal point of view. He also gives, besides his exposition of the law, an account of the various methods of assaying and reducing the ores of gold and silver, and of the rules and practice of mine surveying; a variety of particulars relating to the consumption of quicksilver in New Spain; a detailed plan of a mine-supplying company, and many valuable reflections on the working and supplying of mines by companies; a minute account of the regulations of the royal mint of Mexico; a glossary of mining terms, and a list of the principal mining districts of New Spain, with their distances from the capital, and other particulars: interspersing, throughout the work, a variety of incidental information, and many judicious remarks, drawn from his own experience.

The object and plan of the work, which are detailed more at length by the author, in his preface, being thus explained, it is necessary to show what authority it possesses, at the present time, as a legal treatise.

From the year 1761 to 1783, no material alteration took place in the mining laws of Spain and her colonies. In the latter year however, a code of laws was issued, under the title of Mining Ordinances of New Spain. It was framed, as the title imports, for New Spain alone, but was subsequently adopted in all or most of the other Spanish colonies. In the regulations which concern the *working* of the mines, this code very closely follows the former ordinances; and where alterations are made, they are, not unfrequently, adopted from the suggestions offered in the work of Gamboa. As to other points, the most important changes introduced by the ordinances of 1783, were, the erection of the *Tribunal general de Mineria*, and the *Diputaciones de Mineria*, or general and local tribunals, to which the exclusive jurisdiction in mining affairs was confided;—the establishment of a bank of supplies;—and the organization of a school of mines. But this code left the former ordinances and other mining laws in force, so far as they should not be at variance with the regulations it established, and hence the work of Señor GAMBOA, which was, previous to the year 1783, the paramount authority in all doubtful cases in mining affairs, continued, after that date, to be regarded with the highest respect, and was and is still, constantly referred to in the courts of Mexico, and as is presumed, of the other new republic of America also, as a great authority on such subjects.

Upon the establishment of the independence of the Spanish colonies, they all or most of them adopted, in reference to mining, the laws existing previous to their separation from the mother country, with such modifications only, as were rendered necessary by the alteration from a monarchical to a republican and federal form of government. In Mexico, the principal of these alterations, consisted as follows :—

First, in the abolition of the general tribunal of mining, the functions of which were devolved to the mining deputations or local mining tribunals of each state; and,—

Second, in a decree of the sovereign congress of Mexico, promulgated in the year 1823, empowering foreigners to hold shares in the mines furnished by them with supplies of money or stores; a translation of which will be found in the subsequent pages.

The following changes have also been introduced, in several of the states of the federation :—

By a decree of the congress of the state of Durango, dated the 23d of November, 1824, it was resolved, that a *Tribunal de Mineria,* or mining court for appeals in the second instance, should be established, to consist of a lawyer and two miners. And by another decree of the same congress, dated the 18th January, 1825, it was ordered, that the tribunal of mining appeals should exercise the same functions, in that state, as had been previously granted to the tribunal established at Guadalaxara.

By an order of the congress of the state of Chihuahua, dated the 16th of March, 1826, the *contentious* jurisdiction of the mining deputations was transferred to the ordinary courts. And by a decree of the same congress, of the 7th of October, 1826, the mining deputations were made subject to the supreme government of the state, in all matters as to which they had previously depended on the general tribunal of Mexico, not being inconsistent with the present republican system.

Finally, by a decree of the congress of the state of Guanaxuato, of the 24th of April, 1827, the *contentious* jurisdiction of the mining deputations was transferred to the ordinary tribunals of justice, their ministerial and economical authorities as well as the ministerial and economical authorities of the extinct general tribunal, remaining vested in them. These are the only regulations by which any changes of importance are understood to have been introduced into the mining laws of the republic of Mexico, since the establishment of its independence.

No work of authority has been published on the subject of the mining laws of Spain or her colonies, since that of Señor GAMBOA. There exists in manuscript, a series of notes on the code of 1783, committed to writing by VELASQUEZ, a lawyer of great eminence, under whose opinion and advice that code was principally framed; but the work, although considered highly valuable, has never been published.

Don FRANCISCO XAVIER de GAMBOA, was born of a distinguished family in Guadalaxara in New Spain. After a highly honorable career as an advocate in the courts of that country, in the course of which, although he devoted his attention more particularly to the laws of mining, he acquired the reputation of being, generally, one of the most accomplished jurists of his time, he was appointed deputy, at the court of Madrid, of the consulate of commerce of New Spain, and whilst residing at Madrid in that character, he produced his celebrated Commentary. After several years passed in this manner at Madrid, he was appointed regent or president of the audiency or supreme court of St. Domingo, which he accepted, as it is believed, with some reluctance, having entertained the hope that Mexico, which had been the scene of his labours, would also be that of his reward. It is supposed, however, that Galvez, the minister of Charles III. objected, from some concealed motive, to his being placed in Mexico ; and this opinion is strengthened by the fact, that upon the death of Galvez, he was appointed to the high office of regent of Mexico, which he occupied with much credit and distinction, till his death, having lived to see his sons established in high situations in the church and the government, and long enough to acquire the general respect and esteem of all who came within the range of his authority.

The following is an extract from the royal decree :

" BY THE KING.—Forasmuch as Don Francisco Xavier de Gamboa, advocate of my royal audiency of Mexico, and deputy at this court, of the consulate of commerce of the kingdom of New Spain, has presented to me a book, entitled " Commentaries on the Mining Ordinances," which he has written solely with the view of giving publicity, by means of his application and industry, to the acquisitions he has made on the important subject to which the work relates ; and has requested that I would be pleased to grant to him, my royal licence to print the same, in consideration, not only that the new and copious information he has collected, and the exposition he has given of each separate ordinance, embrace matters which concern the private rights of my subjects, as being interesed in the direction, economy and government of the mines, in the determination of controversies concerning them, in the rules of registering, denouncement, taking possession, and all that constitutes mining jurisprudence,—but also that the aforesaid commentaries treat of questions of importance to my own public rights as sovereign, and investigate the means of giving greater extent and facility to the operations of mining, of improving my revenue, and of promoting commerce and the prosperity of the state in general. Having therefore considered the above in my council of the Indies, and heard what my fiscal has thought it fit to submit, and taking notice also, that the object of the work above mentioned is not to propose

new rules, laws or ordinances, but to illustrate and comment upon such as
are now in force in reference to the government and working of the mines,
and that the labour that has been bestowed upon it, is both profitable and
commendable, and by no means adverse to my royal prerogative, or to my
royal laws and orders: I have resolved, under the opinion of my council
aforesaid, dated the 3d of August last, to grant, and I do, by this my royal
order, grant to the aforesaid Don Francisco Xavier de Gamboa, my royal
permission to print and publish the aforesaid work."

As by the act of the Legislature of California, in relation to the future,
the common law of England is adopted, as the law of the land, and of
course, in relation to mines, as in reference to every other subject, except so
far as it is controlled by statutory enactments, the common law will be the
rule of decision; it has seemed proper to add a summary of the principles
of the common law, on certain branches of this subject, and the compiler
has availed himself, principally, of the work of Bainbridge on Mines and
Minerals for this purpose.

The compiler would have gladly enriched his pages by the insertion of
the reports, in relation to California, by the Hon. Thomas Butler King
and William Carey Jones Esq., were it not that each of these valuable
and able reports have been published in pamphlet form, and generally circulated.

A full table of contents is given, in this volume and a similar one will be
prefixed to each of the subsequent volumes, and in addition a copious alphabetical index will be inserted, at the close of the last volume.

The task of a compiler and translator is not one of a high intellectual
order, but in the present instance, as it has proved one of considearble labor
and in the collection of the materials no small expense, the compiler hopes
it may prove useful to the profession. It has certainly been so to himself,
as it has led him to a more thorough examimation of the subjects embraced
in it, and aided him in the professional investigations which first suggested
the undertaking.

ROYAL ORDINANCES

FOR THE

DIRECTION, REGULATION, AND GOVERNMENT

OF THE

MINERS OF NEW SPAIN,

AND OF ITS

Royal Tribunal General.

BY ORDER OF HIS MAJESTY.

MADRID, 1783.

BY THE KING.

By a Letter of the twenty-fourth of December, 1771, my Viceroy of New Spain represented to me, among other things, that in order to ameliorate the condition of the Miners of that kingdom, to correct effectually and suitably the mischievous abuses which have been introduced among the Mine-Proprietors,* and persons working in the Mines, and to obviate the mutual complaints resulting therefrom, he considered it a matter of extreme importance that a new Code of General Ordinances should be framed for the said establishment (*of Miners*), in such manner as to render the government thereof more uniform and complete : proposing, at the same time the means which he judged most likely to secure a right method in the execution of so important a work. From his information, and from what my Supreme Council of the Indies laid before me upon this subject in a Consult of the 13th of June, 1773, I thought fit to enjoin and command my said Viceroy by Royal Letter, (*Cedula*) of the 20th of July next following, among other things, that there should be formed the new Ordinances as above proposed, with explanations and additions of all that might seem necessary with a view to the actual state of affairs ; and after consultation with the Mine-Owners, and a cer-

---

* The Spanish word here is *Mineros ;* it has been found necessary to translate this word occasionally by " Mine-owners, or Mine proprietors," and occasionally by " Miners," i. e. all persons working in or having any connection with mines.

4

tain number of Surveyors (*Peritos**) keeping in view all the documents referred to in his said Letter, and also the collection of Laws and Statutes of
my said dominions, and especially those which are referred to by my said
Royal Letter.   Afterwards, conformably to a Report which was laid before
me on the 7th of August of the said year, 1773, by a Junta of Four Ministers, formed under my Orders, and with my entire approbation, it was commanded to my said Viceroy, by a Royal Order of the 12th of November
then instant, that in the Ordinances which, in consequence of the said Royal Letter, were about to be formed for the Government of the Miners, they
should be regulated and established in an United Body, upon the model of
the Consulates,† in such manner as to secure to its members the necessary
encouragement, permanency, and support: afterwards, by a Letter of the
26th of September, 1774, my said Viceroy represented to me that the Miners of those my dominions had petitioned, in a printed representation, dated
the 25th of February of the same year (and accompanying his Letter,) not
only to be established in a body, similar to the Consulates, as already ordained, but that a Bank of Supplies (*Banco de avios*) should be instituted
for the encouragement of the Mines ; that a College of Metallurgy should be
erected for improving the construction of machinery ; and for other scientific
purposes;   and that a new Code of Ordinances should be framed for the
Mines, proposing to derive the funds necessary for the support of these establishments from the amount of the double seniorage duties payable on the
metals, from which they hoped to be relieved, by reason of what they had
stated in their said representation ;   and upon all these points my said Viceroy suggested what he considered most expedient.   Wherefore, and after
considering the Report laid before me thereupon by my Supreme Council of
the Indies, on the 23d of April, 1776, I was pleased to determine, amongst
other things, and to command by my Royal Letter of the 1st of July of the
some year, that the important Society of the Miners of New Spain should
be erected into a Corporate Establishment, similar to the Consulates of Commerce in my dominions, giving them, for that purpose, my Royal Consent and
necessary Permission ;   and granting them the power of levying upon their
silver one half, or two third parts, of the double duties, payable before that
time to my Royal revenue in the way of seniorage ; but from which I relieved them by the said Royal Letter : in consequence of all which, by a Public
Act or Sitting (*Acta*) of the represesentative Deputies of the said said Society, held on the 4th of May, 1777, they proceeded to incorporate themselves, accordingly, to determine the offices of which their Tribunal should
consist, and to appoint the proper persons to fill those offices.   Their proceedings were laid before the Viceroy, who approved of them in my Royal

---

* *Peritos*, literally " skilful persons ;" but in order to make it consist with the duties which
are afterwards appointed to such persons, I have translated it surveyors.

† Consulates of Commerce.   These are courts consisting of a judge and assistants, for the
hearing and determining, in a summary manner, causes arising out of commercial transactions.

Name, by his Decree of the 21st of June of the same year ; permitting to the said Tribunal until my Sovereign Pleasure should be known concerning it, the exercise of all the powers of administration, direction, and management, as enjoyed according to law by the Consulates of the Monarchy in all respects in which the exercise of all the powers of administration, direction, and management, as enjoyed according to law by the Consulates of the Monarchy in all respects in which the exercise of such powers should be conformable to my Will, restraining them only from the exercise of judicial authority, which is permitted to the tribunals of the said Consulates of Commerce, and that restriction only to operate till the said new Ordinances should be framed and approved of by me. And the Viceroy having informed me of all this by letter of the 27th of the said year 1777, I thereupon thought fit to confirm the same by my Royal Order of the 29th of December then following, addressed to the said Viceroy, commanding him thereby, and again by another Royal Order of the 20th of January, 1778, that if the New Tribunal of Miners had not as yet formed their Ordinances, and laid them before him, he should cause the same to be done with the utmost despatch : this having been completed on the 21st of May of the said year, they were transmitted to me by the Viceroy, with a letter of the 26th of August, 1799; in order that, after considering them, and the representations made concerning them by the Fiscal of the Royal Audiency* (*Real Audiencia*), and by the Assessor-General of the Vice-Royalty, I might express my Royal Approbation thereof. Lastly, having consulted with Ministers of approved zeal and probity, and considered the best means of reconciling most justly the true interests of the State with the particular welfare of the said important body of Miners, I have, for the direction, regulation, and government of that body, and of their Tribunal, commanded the publication of the following ordinances.

ORDINANCES.

CHAPTER I.

OF THE TRIBUNAL GENERAL OF THE MINERS OF NEW SPAIN.

SECTION I.

THE New Tribunal of Miners shall be styled " The Royal Tribunal General of the Important Body of the Miners of New Spain," and shall be esteemed

---

* Royal Audiency. These were courts of justice, eleven in number, established by the Spaniards, and extending respectively over the eleven districts, into which their American dominions were divided.—*See Robertson's America, Vol. IV. p.* 16. *and seq.*

and considered by all other Tribunals with that respect which is conducive to the important purposes for which my Royal Pleasure has credited it.

SECTION II.

The Tribuual shall be perpetual, conformably to the act of its creation approved by me, and shall at all times be composed of an Administrator-General, who is to be its President; a Director-General; and three Deputies-General; which latter persons may, in case of necessity, be reduced to two, but never be increased.

SECTION III.

The said offices are to be filled only by practical and intelligent Mine-Pro-prietors (*Mineros*), qualified for the office by an experience of more than ten years in the operations of mines; this qualification is to be strictly observed; and these persons must be real American or European Spaniards, of unmixed descent, sons and descendants of ancient Christians, and born in lawful matrimony, with preference always, under these circumstances, to such persons as may have been Judges and Territorial Deputies of the mines, or may have been much experienced in them.

SECTION IV.

The Administrator and Director General of this New and First Creation, in consideration of their extraordinary merit in having suggested and promoted the reform of the mines, and the establishment of the body of Miners, by having directed their attention for many years past to the means most conducive to that end; and in consideration also of their especial knowledge and experience in such concerns, of the length of time during which they have followed the mining profession, their families having pursued no other since their first settlement in New Spain; and lastly, in consideration of the time which is necessary to accomplish such a project, and that no persons can be more likely to succeed in its accomplishment than those with whom it has originated, shall hold their said offices for their lives; but the Deputies-General, now first appointed shall only hold their offices for the time regularly allotted to them, according to the rule that shall be laid down for their alternative succession, over and above the time already elapsed since their appointment.

SECTION V.

For the elections of Administrator and Director General, after the death or failure of the present, and for those of Deputies-General at all times henceforward, there shall be held in Mexico, in the beginning of the month of December, once in every three years, commencing from the present time, a Meeting, consisting of one Deputy from each mining district, provided with sufficient powers from the Miners of such district; and if any such Proprietors shall not send a Deputy on account of their being too remote, or too poor to pay the expences of his journey to Mexico, and his residence therein, it shall be sufficient if they send full power and instruction to any person residing in that capital to act for them, provided the same be not a Deputy or Agent for any other mining district; but he must be a Mine-Owner or Mine-Supplier.* (*Person who lends money to carry on mining operations.*)

SECTION VI.

To enable a Mine Town to have a vote at the Election, it must be proved to contain an inhabiting population, and a church and a Curate, or Deputy, a Judge and Deputies of the Miners, six mines in actual working, and four reducing Establishments (*Works for the reduction of metal from ore*).

SECTION VII.

The city of Guanajuato shall have six votes in the said Election; that of Zacatecas four; that of San Luis Potosi three; that of Pachuca and Real del Monte three; and, generally speaking, the mining districts which bear the title of city shall have three votes each; and those which bear the title of town, or in which there are Provincial Treasuries (*Caxas Reales*), two votes each.

SECTION VIII.

Before proceeding to the Election, there shall be held three scrutinies on three several days, for the qualification of persons eligible to these offices, with this proviso, that the person to be elected Administrator-General must have been one of the Deputies-General during one of the preceding triennial periods, except in the case of re-election, when it will be necessary to observe what is laid down in the 10th Section of this present Chapter; observing also, that, at the expiration of each triennial period, only one new Deputy-General shall be appointed to supply the place of the one about to resign, which person so resigning at the end of the first three years, is to be the one who, at the time of the original appointment, had the smallest number of votes. The same rule is to be observed at the end of the second triennial period, and again at the end of the third, with regard to the last of the three original deputies: Afterwards, at the end of each succeeding triennial period, the Senior-Deputy shall always resign in favor of the one newly elected. Conformably to these regulations, each Deputy will, in future hold his said office for nine years, excepting in the case of the death of any of them before the expiration of that time: in which case, at the next Triennial Meeting, besides

* The Spanish word is *Aviador*, a word well worthy of attention, for it describes the class of persons to which the mining associations belong. Its largest sense seems to be, " to advance money for the working of mines, and to carry on the operations therein, either entirely or in part, on condition of sharing the profits with the proprietor."

the Deputy that is to supply the place of him who resigns, from having completed his nine years, there shall be another appointed to fill the vacancy occasioned by such death, which latter, in point of seniority, shall stand in the place of his predecessor, in order to depart as little as possible from the established rule of succession.

SECTION IX.

The Administrator, the Director, and Deputies-General, shall preside over the said meeting of electors, and shall have votes therein : and the election shall take place on the 31st day of December, by secret lots (*Cedulas Secretas*), and those shall be considered duly elected who have the greatest number of votes ; and in case of any dispute arising, the election shall fall upon that person for whom the Administrator-General shall give his vote.

SECTION X.

To enable any person to be re-elected to any of the said offices of the Royal Tribunal, an interval of three years must have elapsed since his last service, and he must have more than one half of the whole number of votes.

SECTION XI.

No person elected to any of the said offices can excuse himself from serving it ; but every such person must accept the same on the day of his election before sun-set, under the penalty of 2000 dollars, and of being obliged to serve such office even after the payment of the penalty.

SECTION XII.

In case of the death of the Administrator, the Director, or any one of the Deputies-general, or of their resignation (which can only be allowed upon just and indispensable cause), the other members of the Tribunal shall elect a temporary substitute, who shall hold the office till the expiration of the triennial period then subsisting, and till the next general meeting, when a proper person shall be elected, conformably to the 8th Section of this present Chapter.

SECTION XIII.

Those who shall be elected Administrator-General and Director-General, in succession to the persons now filling those offices, and others hereafter, shall hold the said offices, the first for six years, and the second for nine ; with a view to this consideration, that from the circumstances already explained, and which are applicable to all persons who compose the Tribunal, the Director ought to be a person well acquainted with the interests, concerns, and resources of the establishment, with the management and working of the mines, and with the theory and practice of the sciences relating thereto, all which is not to be acquired in a short time.

SECTION XIV.

THE Factor, the Assessor, and the Notary may be appointed and removed with or without cause at the free will and pleasure of the Royal Tribunal General.

SECTION XV.

IN the first General Meeting to be held in Mexico, for the purpose of carrying the present ordinances into effect, there shall be chosen 12 Advisers (*Consultores*), experienced Mine-Proprietors, or Mine Suppliers of distinguished reputation, four of whom shall be persons resident in Mexico, and the Royal Tribunal may consult all or any of them in difficult cases, whenever it shall be necessary; and in order that their employments may be temporary, and to avoid the inconvenience which might arise from their being all changed at the end of each triennial period, six others shall be appointed at the next General Meeting, to supply, for the second triennial period, the places of those six of the first elected twelve who shall have been chosen by the smallest number of votes; and afterwards, at the end of each triennial period, the six newly elected shall replace the six who shall have then been the longest in office; so that the number of twelve will always remain complete; and I hereby declare, that the re-election of such Advisers, in the aforesaid General Meetings, shall be permitted, without regard to those intervals of time and other formalities established in the tenth Section of this present Chapter for the regulation of the offices therein mentioned; observing only, that their seniority is to be reckoned from the period of their re-election; and I grant to the said Advisers a seat in the Public Sittings of the Royal Tribunals, next after the Deputies-General; and when any *Mine Proprietor*, from any of the mine districts shall be in Mexico, I grant to him the honour, dignity, and office of Adviser of the Royal Tribunal as long as he shall remain there.

SECTION XVI.

On the days of scrutiny, and before proceeding to the election, there shall be laid before the General Meeting a clear and correct statement of the funds with which the body of Miners have been endowed, what they have produced, and how they have been applied during the preceding triennial period, as well as of the Bank of Supplies, its gains and losses, shewing, at one view, the condition of the body of Miners at that time, their concerns and possessions in money and effects, their claims, debts, dues, and affairs of all kinds.

SECTION XVII.

Before proceeding to the scrutinies, the permission of the Viceroy must be obtained; and after they are concluded, an account thereof must be rendered to him similar to the practice of the Tribunal of Commerce of that capital (*Mexico*).

SECTION XVIII.

To the Director-General shall also belong the offices of Fiscal and Promoter of the important body of Miners, and he shall, in consequence, represent, suggest, and propose to the Royal Tribunal, whatever he may judge conducive to the advancement and success of that establishment; giving them also, in proper time, such advice and caution as might tend to obviate whatever he may consider as prejudicial to their interest.

SECTION XIX.

The Royal Tribunal shall transmit to me annually, through the Viceroy, an account of the working of the mines and of the concerns of the body of Miners; and, moreover, they may communicate with me, extraordinarily, through the same channel, upon great occasions, when it may seem necessary.

SECTION XX.

The Royal Tribunal may have a representative at the city and court of Madrid, for the protection of its interests; and, in case it should seem necessary, upon any weighty occasion, to send a confidential person to communicate with the same Court, they must, in the first instance, satisfy the Viceroy of the importance of the matter which obliges them to incur such expense, and must procure his certificate of the same, which will precede my *Royal Licence*.

SECTION XXI.

The Clerk of the Royal Tribunal shall keep a minute book of resolutions, in which shall be entered, all the determinations relative to the administration and economy of the mines, whether the same be intended only to last for a time, or to be permanent and perpetual.

SECTION XXII.

There shall be preserved in the Royal Tribunal, the originals of the Royal Letters Patent, Orders, and Declarations, which have proceeded, or may proceed, from me; as also the official letters from the Viceroys, and copies of the Orders that have been, or shall be, received through their hands; and lastly, all Acts and fundamental Decrees relating to the creation or administration of the Royal Tribunal; all which shall be carefully preserved in the archives; and there shall be a book kept, in which there shall be an accurate account of the same, which may be referred to as occasion may require; and I prohibit the originals from being ever taken out to be exhibited, but permit accurate copies or extracts to be taken, compared, and corrected in due form, according to law.

SECTION XXIII.

Before proceeding to the Triennial Elections, an inventory shall be drawn up, and the papers, both of the archives, and of the office of the Tribunal, shall be inspected by two of the Deputies, in order that it may be ascertained whether they correspond with the inventory of the preceding triennial period, and the papers received within the last three years shall be then added to the former.

SECTION XXIV.

The Secretary of the Royal Tribunal shall be one of the Royal Notaries (*Escribanos Reales*), duly instructed and admitted to his office, and possessing all those qualifications required by the law in persons filling that office, and must be moreover a person of good birth, character, and education, and of good conduct and respectable habits, in order that by these means the office may be held in honour, and that he who holds it may be respected and esteemed both in the Tribunal and elsewhere, and he is to be addressed by the title of Don.

SECTION XXV.

The Secretary shall propose to the Royal Tribunal three persons, one of whom is to be appointed chief Official (*Oficial Mayor*) to the court, and another second Official, if necessary; but he shall have free permission and authority to appoint and remove at his pleasure the writer or writers whom he shall employ for the Tribunal.

SECTION XXVI.

The Royal Tribunal shall appoint two Messengers or Porters, who are to execute its orders, provided that they be persons of good character, and Spaniards.

SECTION XXVII.

The Royal Tribunal shall draw up a Table of Fees or Wages to be received by persons employed in Mexico, and in the mining districts, but the same is not to be reduced into practice until it shall have been laid before the Royal Audiency of each district, qualified or regulated by them, and transmitted to me for my Royal Approbation.

SECTION XXVIII.

The Administrator, the Director, and Deputies-General of Mexico, and all other persons employed, shall, at the time of entering upon their respective offices, make oath that they will truly and faithfully discharge the duties thereof, that they will observe these Ordinances, and cause them to be observed, and that they will observe secrecy in the causes and affairs submitted to them; and also that they will maintain the mystery of the Immaculate Conception of Our Lady.

5

CHAPTER II.

OF THE JUDGES AND DEPUTIES OF THE MINING DISTRICTS.

SECTION I.

THE respective *Royal Courts* (*Justicias Reales*) shall be Judges of the Mines, conformably to the laws established for the Government of the Indies, in all cases which are not expressly referred by these Ordinances to the Deputations of the body of Miners.

SECTION II.

All those who for more than one year, shall have worked one or more mines, applying, as owners thereof, in whole or in part, their capital, labour, or personal attention and care, shall be enrolled amongst the Miners of the district, and their names shall be noted in the book of enrolment to be kept by the Judge and Clerk of that mining district.

SECTION III.

The Miners so enrolled, and the Mine-Suppliers (being Miners), the person who reduce by contract (*Maquileros*),* and the Proprietors of Works for stamping and smelting ores in each district, shall assemble in the beginning of January in each year, according to custom, at the house of the Judge, for the purpose of electing the persons who are to exercise the office of Depputy for such district, for the ensuing year ; which persons either must be, or must have been, Mine-Proprietors of superior practice and intelligence, men of good conduct, trust-worthy and possessed of all the qualifications requisite for such office.

SECTION IV.

Every one of the Miners thus enrolled shall have one vote at such elections ; moreover, of the Mine-Suppliers, being Miners as aforesaid, the Reducers by Contract, and the Owners of such works as are mentioned in the preceding Section, each two persons shall have one vote between them, and they shall not themselves be eligible as Deputies, unless they be also Mine-Owners, and possess the necessary qualifications.

SECTION V.

Where there is a very great number of voters, as in Gaunajuato, the same practice which has hitherto prevailed, shall be continued in such district, namely, of choosing beforehand the Electors who are to proceed to the election of the Deputies.

---

* Literally Millers—the persons who reduce the ores into metal; they are so called from the mills used in their operations.

SECTION VI.

The Administrators of Mines may vote instead of their principals, provided the latter do not reside in that neighbourhood (*Territorio*), and provided such Administrators be fully authorized by their principals for that purpose, and such Administrators shall be eligible as Deputies, if their occupations permit it, and they have the necessary qualifications.

SECTION VII.

The Judge of Mines of each Mine-Town, or establishment, together with the Deputies of the preceding year, shall preside at and regulate the election, and shall have votes at the same, and in case of dispute, the vote of the Judge shall be decisive, and those persons who have the greater number of votes, qualified and computed as before determined, shall be considered as duly elected.

SECTION VIII.

In each Mine-Town, or establishment, there shall be a deputation, consisting of two Deputies; and to the end that those employments may be for the duration of two years, and that one of such Deputies may be a person well qualified for the office, in the first year alone of carrying this Ordinance into effect, two Deputies shall be appointed, but in every succeeding year only one, who is to replace the Deputy then oldest in office, and as this provision cannot be complied with at the second Election (*i. e.* at the and of the first year), that Deputy of the two first elected shall remain in office during the second year, who at the first appointment was elected by the greatest number of votes, so that the other of the two first elected Deputies will be in office only for one year.

SECTION IX.

There shall also be elected in the same manner, in each Mine Town, or establishment, four Substitutes (*Substitutos*), who are to supply the place of the Deputies, in the case of their refusal to serve, their death, illness, necessary absence, or other just impediment, and to assist at the several Courts of Appeal in such cases and circumstances as may occur, and which will be treated of in their proper place: but in districts where the electors themselves are to be nominated, according to the Fifth Section of this present Chapter, those four who shall have the greater number of votes are to be the Substitutes for the first year, and it is to be understood that these offices are to be also for the duration of two years, and in each successive year only two new Substitutes are to be chosen, observing, with regard to them, the same rule which has been laid down for the election of Deputies in the preceding Section; and for the sake of greater perspicuity, and to prevent all arbitrary acts in the succession, either to the said offices of Substitutes or to those of Advisers, as directed by several Sections of these Ordinances, those persons shall always be preferred, who shall have had the

greater number of votes at their respective elections, when the elections have
been on one and the same day; but in other cases those who have been longest
in office shall be preferred.

SECTION X.

The said Substitutes shall also be Recorders (*Procuradores Sindicos*) of
their respective districts; and shall observe and procure whatever may
appear necessary for the common interests of the Miners in their neighbourhood, and by virtue of this office shall have a superior claim to be elected as
Deputies, or to other offices connected with the Mines.

SECTION XI.

The persons elected as Deputies must accept the cffice within three days
of the time of their election, under a penalty of $1000, which penalty is to
go to the fund of that district, and the person refusing to accept shall be
obliged to serve the office, notwithstanding the payment of such penalty;
and even though there may appear a just cause for his refusal, he must
accept the office notwithstanding, and serve it until such cause shall have
been admitted by the Royal Tribunal General of the Miners, to which body
it must be submitted.

SECTION XII.

It is forbidden to re-elect any person to any one of the before-mentioned
offices until the expiration of two years from his last serving in such office,
and the person re-elected, after such interval, must accept the same office
under a penalty of 500 dollars, which penalty is to be paid to the general
fund of the district, and he shall be obliged to serve the office, notwithstanding
the payment of such penalty; without prejudice, however, to any sufficient
cause of exemption which he may have; but this must be submitted to the
Royal Tribunal General of Mexico, and he must serve the office in the mean
time as directed by the preceding Section.

SECTION XIII.

All the Mine-Proprietors, Mine-Suppliers, persons reducing by contract,
and Owners of reducing establishments of the respective districts, shall confer on the new Deputies power to promote their interests and pretensions,
and for all the usual purposes, and shall swear to obey them in all that relates to the exercise of their offices; and the Deputies themselves shall take
upon them their office according to law, and swear to observe these Ordinances (which are to be read at every election at the time of their entering into
office), and to maintain secrecy in the causes which come under their cognizance.

SECTION XIV.

As soon as the election is over, an account of it, and proper notice, shall be immediately transmitted to the Royal Tribunal General of the Miners, in order that if there shall appear to be no defect or irregularity in the conduct of it, it may be approved of by the Supreme Government of New Spain : and be it understood, that no charges whatever shall be made for the procuring of such approval, nor for any of the formalities which must precede it.

SECTION XV.

The Territorial Deputies (*Disputados Territoriales*), the Inspectors, and Surveyors of Mines, shall receive no pay from my Royal Treasury, but shall be supported from the profits of the respective mines, agreeably to the laws upon that subject ; for which purpose, the Royal Tribunal General of Mexico shall impose certain moderate duties, according to the conditions and circumstances of each mine district, in the manner and under the rules laid down by Section xxxvi. of Chapter III. of these Ordinances.

SECTION XVI.

In the month of February in every year, the Territorial Deputations (*Diputaciones territoriales*) shall submit to the Royal Tribunal General of Mexico, a report upon the condition of the mines and Miners in their respective districts, and their dependencies, suggesting such measures as may appear to them conducive to the preservation and better advancement of the same, and also upon the quantity of silver produced, and of quicksilver consumed in the preceding year: upon the number of mines which are in course of actual working, as well as such as have been abandoned, and why they have been so abandoned ; and upon those which have been newly discovered, or re-established ; requiring for this purpose, from the Provincial Courts and Treasuries, and other offices, all certificates, attestations and other documents which may be necessary: And it is hereby ordered, that the said reports and documents be laid before the Viceroy, in order that, after acquainting himself with their contents, he may submit them to me, with a suggestion of such measures as he may deem advisable, and likely to meet with my Royal Approbation.

CHAPTER III.

OF THE JURISDICTION IN MINING CAUSES, AND THE MODE OF TAKING COGNIZANCE, OF PROCEEDING, AND PASSING JUDGMENT AND SENTENCE IN THE SAME IN THE 1ST, 2ND, AND 3RD INSTANCES.

SECTION I.

I GRANT to the Royal Tribunal General of the Miners the power of hearing and deciding all concerns relating to the administration, direction, and management of the body of Miners, and I therefore declare that the territorial deputations of all the mining districts shall be fully and entirely subordinate to it in all such matters of administration.

SECTION II.

The Royal Tribunal General shall, moreover, take cognizance of all causes, arising out of the discovery, denunciation,* right of property, extent, draining, desertion, and (*despilaramientos*) destruction of the supports or pillars of the mines, and of all that may occur in the same to the prejudice of the operations therein, and in contravention of these Ordinances, and also of whatever relates to the supply of mines, the sale or exchange of ores, or silver and gold, of copper, lead, and other mineral substances, instruments for reducing, (*Maquilas*), and of other things of the same nature ; but I declare, that such power of deciding causes shall only be exercised by the said Royal Tribunal General within twenty-five leagues of the capital of Mexico.

SECTION III.

Without detracting from the peculiar jurisdiction of administration granted to the Royal Tribunal by the First Article of this Section, the same power shall be exercised by the territorial deputations in their respective territories, in causes which may occur, but only by the two Deputies jointly, for the support and encouragement of the mining operations in their particular district, the interest and advantage of the Proprietors of mines, the preservation and increase of the population, the due administration of justice, the welfare of the inhabitants, and the relief of the poor : be it, however, understood, that the same shall be done in immediate subordination to the Royal Tribunal General, as directed in the said first article ; with this proviso, that they are not to exercise any formal acts of jurisdiction, except in such causes as are expressly referred to them by these Ordinances.

SECTION IV.

The territorial deputations shall, in their respective districts, have the peculiar power, or jurisdiction, of deciding causes, which I have in the Second Article of this Section granted to the Royal Tribunal General in all such

---

* *Denunciacion, Denunciar, Denunciante.* These words deserve particular attention, as they denote the mode of acquiring mines, and are constantly occurring throughout the ordinances. *Denunciar* relates as well to original mines, *i. e.* mines which have never before been worked, as to mines which have once been worked, but have fallen into a ruinous state ; in the former case it means, " to give notice that a certain mine exists, and that the person so giving notice, intends to work it." Whereupon, after complying with certain conditions required by the Ordinances the mine is allotted to such person. In the latter it means, " to give notice that some mine owner has either neglected the working of his mine, so that it is reduced to a state of decay, or that he has acted in contravention of these Ordinances, which points being proved, the person so giving notice himself acquires the mine." The word has generally been rendered "to inform of," or " to acquire by informing of, " but as it implies a great deal more than this, and as it has a peculiar technical signification in the Spanish, I have preferred translating it by the word " *denounce.*"

matters as are there expressed, proceeding in, and deciding the same in a manner wholly independent of the said Royal Tribunal General; since, in the exercise of such jurisdiction, they are not to act subordinately to the said Tribunal, which is hereby prohibited from taking cognizance of, or interfering with any such causes and proceedings out of their own jurisdiction.

SECTION V.

Since all the foregoing causes and disputes are to be determined between the parties in the shortest and most summary manner, according to justice, and the customary good faith of commercial transactions, without any of the usual delays and written declarations, or petitions of lawyers, it is my Will, that whenever any person shall appear before the Royal Tribunal, or before the Territorial Deputation of any of the mining districts to commence an action or suit, they shall not allow any complaint or proceedings to be presented in writing, until after they shall have cited before them both parties, where it is practicable to do so, and heard orally their several causes of actions, and replies or objections, and endeavoured to compromise and settle the matter in dispute between them, with the utmost possible dispatch : but if they should not succeed in bringing about the arrangement between the parties, and if the subject in question shall exceed the sum or value of $200 (for all causes relating to sums not exceeding that amount are to be decided orally, whether the parties consent to it or not), then the petitions or claims in writing, may be received, provided the same have neither been drawn up, arranged, or signed by lawyers; and whenever it shall be necessary to proceed in any cause, in consequence of not having been able to arrange and settle the same orally between the parties, then the demands or requests of the complainant shall all be received and attended to, previously to the hearing of any on the part of the defendant.

SECTION VI.

In consideration of the object above expressed, of procuring a decision in all causes and disputes in the shortest and most summary manner, according to justice and good faith, I thereby ordain and command, for the better attainment of that end, that in actions before the said Royal Tribunal and Territorial Deputations in the first instance, as also in causes of appeal and in the judgments to be pronounced therein, they shall pay no regard to any defect in the proceedings, or want of attention to the minute formalities of the law, or any irregularity of diction, but shall, in all causes, decide and judge with a strict regard to the merits of the case, and for that purpose, they shall officially examine the necessary witnesses, provided they do not exceed the number of ten, and take the depositions of parties where it may be thought requisite, and shall thereupon give and pronounce their determination, and judgment or sentence.

SECTION VII.

In order to avoid all useless and malicious appeals, which are made for the sole purpose of preventing the course and execution of justice, I ordain that no one shall be allowed to appeal from the Judges of the said Royal Tribunal, or from the said Territorial Deputations, unless it be in consequence of definitive judgments or interlocutory decrees, containing irreparable aggrievement (*gravamen irreparable*), and any appeal which may be made in contravention of this article shall not be valid, and neither the Judges of the said Tribunal, nor the Territorial Deputations are to admit the same, but shall proceed in the cause, and pronounce their judgment or sentence definitively.

SECTION VIII.

All interlocutory decrees, and judgments or sentences, are to be signed by the Administrator-General, and by both the Deputies-General of the Royal Tribunal, even if any one of them should dissent from the other two: for the opinion of the Administrator-General, and of one Deputy-General, or that of the two Deputies-General, is to decide the sentence or judgment, and the one who dissents is to sign the same notwithstanding.

SECTION IX.

The Territorial Deputies may each separately proceed in causes, for the sake of their brevity and dispatch which are so desirable for the interests of the body of Miners; but in passing and pronouncing definitive judgments or sentences, and interlocutory decrees, which might cause irreparable aggrievement, they shall act in conjunction; and if they should not agree concerning the same, they shall call in the respective Substitute, according to the rules already laid down, in order that the majority of opinions, and such determination shall be signed by all three, as provided in the preceding Section.

SECTION X.

In all points of law, which are not clearly laid down in these Ordinances, the Royal Tribunal General shall avail themselves of the assistance of any able and conscientious lawyer whom they may select for the purpose, and the Territorial Deputations may confer with any such person who may be in the town or place where they reside; and in case he should be objected to, or if there should be no lawyer in the place, then they shall act with the assistance of the respective Provincial Judge appointed by me, which latter is not to be objected to, unless there be another person who can supply his place; and I further declare, both with regard to this, and the preceding Section, that any person who may have given his opinion in causes in the first instance, shall not give it in the second.

SECTION XI.

When the proceedings in any cause are concluded, and final decision is about to take place, or at any time, whenever the Judges of the Royal Tribunal, or the Territorial Deputations may think it necessary, such proceedings shall be submitted to them by the Clerks of the Court, before whom they were taken down, who are to sum up the contents in the usual manner, and with that brevity which is so desirable for the interests of the Miners.

SECTION XII.

The decrees and judgments, or sentences, of the Tribunal General, and of the Territorial Deputations, if not appealed against, and when they have acquired the authority of a final decision, are to be carried into effect, in a short and summary manner; those of the Tribunal by their two messengers, or porters, who are to exercise the functions of executive Bailiffs (*Alguaciles Executores*), and those of the Territorial Deputations by the ordinary Bailiffs (*Alguaciles*) of the places where they reside, and the former, as well as the latter, shall command and desire all other Judges and *Courts** (*Justicias*), whom it may concern, to afford them any aid or assistance which they may require.

SECTION XIII.

In causes of appeal against any such definitive sentences or decrees, by either of the parties, where the matter in dispute shall exceed the value of 400 dollars (for in all causes regarding a less amount no appeal shall be admissible, and the decisions of the Judges of the Royal Tribunal, or of the Territorial Deputations, shall be finally carried into effect), those from the Royal Tribunal General shall be received by the Court of Appeales (*Jusgade de Alzadas*) about to be established in Mexico, and which is to be composed of a Judge of the Real Audiencia of that place, to be appointed by the Viceroy, in the same manner, and for the same term, as the one intended for the Royal Tribunal of the Consulate or Chamber of Commerce; of the Director-General of mines, and of a Proprietor of mines, who is to be elected for that purpose every third year, in the General Assembly of Miners, from amongst such as have been Administrators, Directors, Deputies-General, or one of those Four Advisers (*Consultores*), who are to reside constantly in Mexico, as directed in a former Section; and the appeals from the Territorial Deputations, within the distance of twenty leagues, in every direction from the city of Guadalaxara, shall be in the same manner received by the Court of Appeal, which I have ordered to be created there, and which is to be composed of one of the Judges of the Real Audiencia of that place, to be appointed by the Acting President thereof for the time, and in the same manner as the one for the Consulate, or Chamber of Commerce, in Mexico, and of two Proprietors of mines, of known character, and possessing all the requisite qualifications, who shall be appointed Co-Judges of Appeal in the city of Guadalaxara, from amongst those residing there in the said General Assembly of Miners, to be held every three years in Mexico, as before directed; but if there should not be any resident Proprietors of mines

---

* Tribunals over which the Magistrates of the country preside, as distinguished from any tribunal composed of Miners.

in the aforesaid city, possessing the necessary qualifications for such office, then others, who reside elsewhere, may be chosen at the said triennial election ; provided, that under the same circumstances of eligibility, preference shall be given to such as live at the shortest distance, even if they be substitutes for any mining district ; and the appeals from all the other Territorial Deputations shall be received, in the manner prescribed, by the respective Courts of Appeal to be erected in each province, and which are to be composed of the principal Provincial Judge appointed by me, and of such two of the four Substitutes of Miners for the mining district as may be nearest to the residence of such Judge respectively, according to the rules already laid down ; and if in the same place, or at an equal distance, there shall reside any one or more of the twelve Advisers before mentioned, they shall, by preference, be appointed Co-Judges of Appeal ; and wherever the said Judge shall not be of the profession of the law (*detrado*), the court in which he presides, shall, in all points and matters, where it may be requisite, avail themselves of the assistance of an able and conscientious lawyer.

SECTION XIV.

All such causes of appeal shall be conducted in a short and summary manner, according to the practice in commercial causes, without introducing any new terms or expressions which may give rise to unnecessary delays or proofs, or admitting proceedings and writings of lawyers, or any others, except a statement of the cause of the appellant, and the replies of the other party or parties, with a strict regard to truth, and the customary good faith of commercial transactions ; and in like manner the cause shall be decided.

SECTION XV.

All such appeals are to be entered on or before the third day, after the notification of the decree or sentence, and in no other manner, and they may be commenced by a letter from the Appellant, stating, either that he will transmit full power for carrying on the proceedings, or that he will appear in person.

SECTION XVI.

Whenever the Courts of appeal shall confirm the sentence of the Royal Tribunal General of Miners or of the Territorial Deputations in the several causes, no further appeal shall be admitted, and such sentence shall be immediately carried into effect, and for that purpose shall be forthwith sent back to the respective judges.

SECTION XVII.

But in case they, (the Courts of Appeal), should reverse the same, either altogether or in part, and either of the litigant parties should appeal or apply for a new trial, the Judges of Appeal shall appoint in the respective cases, two other Co-Judges, who, in Mexico, are to be chosen from the four Advisers (*Consultores*) residing in that capital, in Guadalaxara from the Proprietors of mines residing there, with preference to such as are Advisers, if there be any in that city, and in default of either, they may be chosen from the Proprietors of mines, residing elsewhere, regard being shewn to the considerations expressed in the thirteenth Section of this Chapter ; and in all the other Courts of Appeal, the judge may appoint any of the four respective Substitutes, provided, however, that there be no legal objection to any such individuals, and if there should be such objections in respect to all of them, the nomination may fall on any other Proprietors of mines, having the necessary qualifications ; observing, however, that where any one or more of the twelve Advisers of the Royal Tribunal General shall reside, they shall be preferred to the Substitutes.

SECTION XVIII.

From the judgment or sentence, to be given in this third instance (whether confirming, reversing, or amending, the former sentence, either altogether or in part), there shall be no further appeal ; and the cause shall then be returned to the court to which it belongs, for the fulfilment and final execution, which are also to be proceeded with, in a short and summary manner, as before directed ; but I hereby declare, that there shall still remain open to the parties, the legal remedy of a further application to my Royal Person, in my Supreme Council of the Indies, provided it shall appear that the sum in dispute amount to 20,000 dollars or upwards, on finding the security required by law, and without prejudice to the execution of the sentence already pronounced, and after providing further security, that they will submit, to the final decison, whatsoever it may be.

SECTION XIX.

In the decision of the before-mentioned causes of appeal, the sentence shall be determined by two opinions out of the three, whether they be those of the Judge and one of the Co-Judges of the respective Courts of Appeal, or those of the two Co-Judges, without that of the presiding Judge, and in either case the same shall be signed by all three.

SECTION XX.

Causes relating to possession and property, shall be determined jointly (by all the Judges) ; and in the first place, restitution shall be made to persons who may have been forcibly dispossessed of any property ; but this shall not apply to persons who may have been deprived of possession by the decree or sentence of any Judge, even if the same shall be represented to be unjust.

SECTION XXI.

No mine in dispute, shall, for any reasons, or on any account, be shut up, nor shall its working be suspended, even at the request of the parties; but an Inspector (*Interventor*)* shall be appointed, with the approbation of the party requiring the same, without, however, removing from the mine any thing belonging to it, yet such Interventor shall be dispensed with on full and sufficient security being given to the satisfaction of the opposite party, and I declare that the working a mine is then only to be suspended when the same shall be represented to be in a ruinous condition, without the necessary support of timber work, and such shall appear to be the fact in the opinion of Surveyors (*Peritos*), who shall immediately, without loss of time, inspect and proceed to re-establish the said works, and restore them to a good condition, in order that, whenever the working shall be resumed, it may be carried on without danger.

SECTION XXII.

All executive demands shall be proceeded in according to law, as far as respects the order of process, but with a strict regard to truth and good faith, and without letting in any of those delays or subtilties which retard and interrupt the dispatch.

SECTION XXIII.

Whenever it shall be necessary to carry into effect an execution in any mine or reducing establishment (*Hacieuda de Beneficio*), the same shall not be sequestered, nor put up for sale, nor yet the machines, iron-work, or tools, implements, slaves, cattle, buildings, materials, or any of the necessary stores or provisions; but such execution shall only be put in force with regard to the gold and silver ores, and other produce of the mine, after deducting what may be necessary to meet the expence of carrying on the reducing of such ores, which is by no means to be interrupted; for which purpose an Interventor shall be appointed, to be approved of by the plaintiff, if the latter does not choose to undertake the management of the mine himself; or by the defendant, in case the plaintiff shall take the same on his own account; and such Interventor is to be immediately withdrawn on the liquidation of the debts; and in either case he shall render weekly accounts of the produce and expences of the mine, to be in due time laid before the Judges in the cause, together with the several receipts, or vouchers, and proper affidavits on such items, which cannot otherwise be verified, for the benefit of whichever party may be entitled thereto, according to the definitive judgment or sentence pronounced in the cause.

SECTION XXIV.

If the defendant shall give up his property, and the same shall comprise

---

* Inspector is perhaps the nearest English word; but as interventor expresses most correctly the duty of a person who is occasionally to interpose his services, and as we have, in English, the words intervent and intervention, henceforward the word interventor will be used in the translation.

any mine or mines, notice shall be given to his creditor or creditors, to undertake the working thereof on their own account, and not to suffer them to be suspended ; and in default of their compliance before the expiration of the time to be fixed by these Ordinances, such mines shall be considered as deserted and abandoned, and shall belong to the first person who may denounce the same, to the exclusion of all former claims.

SECTION XXV.

The wages of the labourers of any mine or reducing establishment taken in execution, and the salary of the Interventor, shall by no means be placed on the same footing with the other debts, but shall be paid immediately out of the first proceeds, although the whole of such proceeds should not amount to more.

SECTION XXVI.

In case of the suspension of the working, any one of the creditors shall offer to undertake the same with his own capital, the others having refused to contribute their proportions, such creditor shall have preference, not only in the satisfaction of his new demand, but also with respect to his former claims, even where the same may not have arisen from the supply of such mine or establishment.

SECTION XXVII.

Whenever in causes before other courts, whether relating to judgments concerning inventories, hereditary succession, general partnerships, contests of creditors, or cession of property, any mines and the establishments, or other dependencies belonging to the same, are comprised amongst the other property depending in the cause, I ordain that the Judge of such court shall transmit an official letter, with notice thereof to the respective Court of Miners, whose duty it shall be to take care that the working of such mine or establishment be kept without prejudice to the rights or claims of the party or parties concerned ; and the said Court of Miners shall reserve the proceeds thereof for the disposal of the principal Judge in such cause, and shall also, in case of any widows, minors, or absent persons being interested therein, effectually protect and support their claims, and thus maintain that firm and reciprocal union, which contribute to the preservation, welfare, and prosperity of the whole body.

SECTION XXVIII.

In causes and suits relating to mines, an extension of the whole term, may be granted, but be it understood, that this utmost term allowed by the law, shall not take place in behalf of certain privileged persons in which cases half of the original term may be granted.

SECTION XXIX.

In all criminal causes, such as the purloining of ore, gold or silver, lead, tools, and implements, or any other articles belonging to the mines or the reducing establishments, offences committed in the same, whether by one workman against another, or in consequence of any breach of subordination on their part towards the officers or captains set over them; or by the misconduct of either of these classes towards their masters, the Proprietors of the mines; and finally, in cases of insult, contumelious language, or want of respect towards any of the Courts of Miners, the Royal Tribunal General in Mexico, or the Territorial Deputations, shall take cognizance, each in their respective districts, proceeding in and deciding such causes as are of minor importance, in the most summary manner according to law, and the nature of such offences, with a strict regard to good faith, and in the order already established for civil causes; but in those, which on account of their magnitude and aggravation, require by law the infliction of severe penalties, mutilation, other corporal punishments, the said Courts of Miners shall only exercise the limited jurisdiction of apprehending the criminals, drawing up the processes, and transmitting the same to the Royal Judge of the respective provinces, in order that the latter may, in due time lay them before the criminal chamber of the Real Audiencia of the district for their final decision.

SECTION XXX.

If, in such criminal causes of minor importance as are treated of in the preceding Section, and the jurisdiction of which has been granted to the Courts of Miners, for their cognizance and determination, provided they proceed in and decide the same in the manner directed, any parties shall appeal, they are to be entitled to all the legal remedies to be determined by the Courts of Appeal, in the Manner and form already prescribed with regard to civilc auses, observing the order required in cases of this nature.

SECTION XXXI.

Whenever any contentions shall arise between the Tribunal General of Miners, the territorial jurisdictions, and any other courts or tribunals, concerning the extent of their several jurisdictions, I ordain and command, that the Viceroy of New Spain shall decide the same, and that his determination shall be observed and complied with, without any other appeal; and that the Viceroy shall, in such cases, take the opinion of learned and able lawyers not connected with either of the courts between whom such question may have arisen.

SECTION XXXII.

I expressly prohibit the arbitrary application of the pecuniary fines to be imposed by any of the Courts of Miners, in the exercise either of the criminal or civil jurisdiction, granted to them; and I ordain that they shall be applied in equal third parts to my Royal Exchequer, the expences of justice, and to such further objects, as by law directed.

SECTION XXXIII.

THE Administrator and the Deputies General, shall assemble in court every day (except on holy days, and those on which it is necessary to hear Mass,) from the hour of eight to that of eleven; and also on extraordinary occasions in the evening, and on any day whatever when the urgency and importance of any affair may require it.

SECTION XXXIV.

The Director General shall have a vote in all matters relating to the direction, administration, and management, the jurisdiction of which has been granted to the Royal Tribunal General in Mexico, and due and special notice shall be sent to him on all such occasions to attend; but I declare that he shall have no vote in the substantiation and determination of any pleadings or suits, except only in causes before the Court of Appeal in Mexico, of which he has been appointed a member.

SECTION XXXV.

All matters relating to public works or supplies (*Abastos*), to those of the roads or highways, and other objects of the same nature, are to be under the peculiar cognizance and jurisdiction of the Royal Judges and Magistrates of each District, but the Royal Tribunal General in Mexico, and the Territorial Deputations shall give such instructions as they may deem expedient, to the said Judges and Magistrates, in order that all such works and supplies may be regulated and proportioned in the most fair and equitable manner, proceeding therein with a mutual understanding, and acting in concert together.

SECTION XXXVI.

All taxes, and duties, or imposts, as well public as private, between individuals of the mining body, which immediately affect the advancement and working of the mines and reducing establishments, the remuneration or salaries of those who compose the territorial jurisdictions of Miners, and of persons appointed to any of the new offices or situations treated of in these Ordinances, are to be proposed and regulated by the Royal Tribunal General in Mexico, and by the Territorial Deputations, each in their respective districts, but the latter shall be obliged to lay them, together with the requisite proofs or attestations, before the Royal Court (*Justicia Real*) of the district, for their sanction, but such taxes, duties, and imposts, shall not be established or carried into effect, without having been previously submitted to the Viceroy of New Spain, in order that, after the necessary enquiries respecting them by his superior power, they may be laid before me for my sovereign determination, for which purpose a report thereof shall be transmitted to me by the Viceroy.

SECTION XXXVII.

The Royal Tribunal General in Mexico shall also immediately lay before the Viceroy, an exact estimate of the salaries to be allowed to the principal individuals filling offices in the Tribunal, and of the inferior officers appointed, or to be appointed, in pursuance of these Ordinances; in order that the same may be referred to me by the Viceroy, with his remarks thereon, for my Royal Approbation, which is necessary to the secure establishment of the said Tribunal.

CHAPTER IV.

OF THE ORDER OF PROCEEDING IN THE SUBSTANTIATION AND DETERMINATION OF LAW-SUITS, IN CASES OF A VACANCY OR NECESSARY ABSENCE OF ANY OF THE JUDGES OF THE MINERS, OR OF THEIR REFUSALS (*RECUSACIO-NES*) IN THE 1ST, 2ND, AND 3RD INSTANCES.

SECTION I.

THE Royal Tribunal General of the mines shall not enter upon any business which is in litigation, without the assembling of three of its Members; and if at any time on account of illness, necessary absence, or any other just and lawful impediment whatsoever, as by the judge being interested in the question, or by his being related to any of the litigating parties, that number of Judges cannot be assembled, such of the Advisers residing in the capital of Mexico as are properly eligible to the same office, by the rules already laid down; and the proper number shall be thus completed; and the same thing shall be done with regard to the number of the Judges of Appeal, which is never to be less than three, according to what has already been laid down in these Ordinances; and whenever in consequence of any of the before-mentioned impediments, any one of the Territorial Deputies cannot, or ought not, to be Judge in any such litigated cause, his place shall be supplied by the proper substitute accordingly.

SECTION II.

I prohibit the absolute refusal (*recusacion*), of all the Judges of the Royal Tribunal General, and of those of Appeals; but one or two particular members may refuse, assigning reasons, and giving security; it being understood that those refusing shall not be heard, or any refusal admitted, after a determination has been made concerning them.

SECTION III.

In the same manner the two Territorial Deputies, acting as Judges of the mines, shall not refuse, though either of them may.

SECTION IV.

In cases where the refusal shall be lawful and admitted, whether in causes in the first instance, or in those before the courts of appeal, the vacancy shall be filled up in the first instance according to the first Section of this present Chapter, and in the latter, by the appointment of the respective Judges of Appeal, according to Section xvii. of Chapter III. of these Ordinances.

CHAPTER V.

OF THE ORIGINAL OWNERSHIP OF MINES; OF THE GRANTS TO INDIVIDU-ALS, AND THE DUTIES TO BE PAID BY THEM FOR THE SAME.

SECTION I.

THE mines are the property of my Royal Crown, as well by their nature and origin, as by their re-union, declared by the fourth law of the thirteenth Title of the sixth Book of the new compilation (of Laws and Statutes.)

SECTION II.

Without separating them from my Royal patrimony, I grant them to my subjects in property and possession, in such manner that they may sell, exchange, (pass by will, either in the way of inheritance or legacy), or in any other manner, dispose of all their property in them, upon the terms on which they themselves possess it, and to persons legally capable of acquiring it.

SECTION III.

Be it understood that this grant is made upon two conditions: First, that they (my subjects) shall pay to my Royal Treasury the proportion of metal reserved thereto; and secondly, that they shall carry on their operations in the mines subject to the provisions of these Ordinances, on failure of which, at any time, the mines of persons so making default shall be considered as forfeited, and may be granted to any person who shall denounce them accordingly.

CHAPTER VI.

OF THE MANNER OF ACQUIRING MINES; OF NEW DISCOVERIES; REGIS-TERS OF VEINS, AND DENOUNCEMENTS OF MINES ABANDONED AND LOST.

SECTION I.

As it is most just and proper to reward with particularity and distinction those persons who devote themselves to the discovery of new mineral places, and metallic veins found therein, in proportion to the importance and utility of such discovery, I order and command that the discoverers of one or more mineral mountains (*Cerros Minerales*), wherein no mine or shaft has been opened before, acquire in the principal vein as much as three portions (*pertenencias*), together or separate, where it best pleases them, according to the measures hereafter signified; and that on having discovered more veins, they shall acquire a portion in each vein, fixing on and making the said portions within the term of ten days.

SECTION II.

The discoverer of a new vein in a mountain known and worked in other parts, may hold in it two portions together, or separated by other mines, on condition that he specifies them within ten days, as mentioned in the preceding Section.

SECTION III.

He who proposes for a new mine in a vein already known and worked in part, is not to be considered a discoverer.

SECTION IV.

The persons referred to in the preceding Sections must present a written statement to the Deputation of Miners in that district, or in case there should not be one in that district, to the nearest thereunto, specifying in it his name, those of his associates (if he has any), the place of his birth, his place of habitation, profession, and employment, together with the most particular and distinguishing features of the tract, mountain, or vein of which he claims the discovery: all which circumstances, as well as the hour in which the discoverer shall present himself, must be noted down in a register, kept by the deputation and clerk (if they have one); and after this, the said written statement, shall, for his due security, be restored to the discoverer, and notices of its object and contents shall be affixed to the doors of the church, the government-houses, and other public buildings of the town, for the sake of general notoriety. And I ordain, that within the term of ninety days, the discoverer shall cause to be made in the vein or veins so registered, a pit of a yard and a half in diameter or breadth, and ten yards (*varas*) in depth, and that immediately on the existence of the vein being ascertained, one of the deputies in person shall visit it, accompanied by the clerk (if there is one), or, if there be no clerk, by two assisting witnesses, and by the Mining Professor (*Perito Facultatioo*) of that territory, in order to inspect the course and direction of the vein, its size, its inclination on the horizon, called its falling or declivity, its hardness or softness, the greater or less firmness of its bed, and the principal marks and species of the mineral; taking exact account of all this, in order to add the same to the entry in the register, together with the act of possession, which must immediately be given to the discoverer in my Royal name, measuring him his portion, and making him enclose it by poles at the limits as hereafter declared; after which an authentic copy of the proceedings shall be delivered to him for the security of his title.

SECTION V.

If during the above named ninety days any one should appear asserting a right to the said discovery, a brief judicial hearing shall be granted, and judgment given in favour of him who best proves his claim; however, if this should happen after the stated time, he (the new claimant) shall not be heard.

SECTION VI.

The restorers of ancient mines which have been abandoned and left to decay, shall enjoy the same privileges as discoverers, of choosing and possessing three portions in the principal vein, and one in each of the others, and both revivers and discoverers shall, as an especial reward, be on all occasions preferred to other persons, under parity of circumstances.

SECTION VII.

If there arises any question as to who has been the first discoverer of a vein, he shall be considered as such who first found metal therein, even though others may have made an opening previously; and in case of further doubt, he who first gets it registered, shall be considered as the discoverer.

SECTION VIII.

Whoever shall denounce in the terms hereafter expressed, any mine that has been deserted and abandoned, shall have his denouncement received, if he therein sets forth the circumstances already declared in Section IV. of this Chapter, the actual existence of the mine in question, the name of its last possessor, if he is acquainted with the same, and those of the neighbouring miners, all of whom shall be lawfully summoned, and if within ten days they do not appear, the denouncement shall be publicly declared on the three following Sundays; this meeting with no opposition, it shall be signified to the denouncer that within sixty days he must have cleared and reinstated some work of considerable depth, or at least of ten yards perpendicular, and within the bed of the vein, in order that the Mining Professor may inspect its course and inclination, and all its peculiar circumstances, as is declared in the above-named Section IV. The said Professor should, if it be possible, examine the pits and works of the mine, and see if they are decayed, destroyed, or inundated; whether they contain a draft-pit or adit, or are capable of such; whether they have an outer court, (*galera*), a whim, (*malacate*), machines, rooms for habitation, and stables; and an account and register of all these circumstances must be entered in the corresponding book of denouncements, which should be kept separately. And the said examination being made, the portions being measured, and bounded by stakes in the ground, as shall hereafter be explained, possession of them shall be given to the denouncer, without regard to any opposition, which cannot be attended to, unless made within the term before described; however, if during that time any opposition is brought forward, the parties shall have a brief judicial hearing, and the cause be determined accordingly.

SECTION IX.

If the former Mine-owner should appear, in order to oppose the denouncement, when the three public proclamations are over, and when the denouncer has commenced the sixty days allowed for reinstating the pit of ten yards, he shall not be heard as to the possession, but only as to his right in the property; and if he succeeds in establishing this, he must make good the expences incurred by the denouncer, unless the latter is proved to have acted fraudulently, in which case he must lose such expences.

SECTION X.

If the denouncer does not make, or complete, the shaft as prescribed, nor take possession within the sixty days, he loses his right, and any other person has the power of denouncing the mine. If, however, from the ground being entirely broken up, or otherwise difficult and impracticable, or for any other real and serious obstable, he has been unable to complete the same within the said sixty days, he must have recourse to the respective Territorial Deputation, when his difficulties being examined and proved, the period may be prolonged for as long a time as the Deputation may think necessary for the purpose, and no more; no opposition to his claim being admitted after the ordinary term of sixty days.

SECTION XI.

If any one denounce a mine as forfeited, on account of the non-observance of any of these Ordinances, which bear that penalty, such claim shall be allowed to him, provided he can lawfully establish any such cause of forfeiture.

SECTION XII.

If the former possessor of the Mine, or any person claiming in right of him, shall declare the having left therein, any exterior or moveable works made at his expense, such as coverings of outer courts (*galeras*), machines, or other things of this class, and of which the denouncer may usefully avail himself, he shall be paid for them according to the valuation of surveyors.

SECTION XIII.

If any one shall denounce any intermediate space (*demasia*), in the vicinity of mines already occupied, it can only be granted him in case the owners of the adjoining mines, or any one of them, should not desire it for themselves; however, if these persons have not occupied it, or shall not do so within the time which the Deputations of that territory, after considering the circumstances of the case, shall prescribe, it shall be adjudged to the denouncer.

SECTION XIV.

Any one may discover and denounce a vein, not only on common land, but also on the property of any individual, provided he pays for the extent of surface above the same, and the damage which immediately ensues therefrom, according to the valuation of surveyors on both sides, and arbitration in case of disagreement; the same is to be understood with regard to denouncing convenient places for erecting establishments, and also waters for moving the machines employed for the reduction of ores, commonly called reducing establishments, (*haciendas*), provided in each case, that no more of the water be used, than is necessary for such purposes.

SECTION XV.

If, however, any one denounces a mine or establishment within a town or village, whereby its principal edifices might be injured, or other similar inconvenience might arise, the denouncement shall not be admitted without previous application to the Royal Tribunal General of Mexico, in order that they, after consulting with the Supreme Government, may determine the case with all due prudence and circumspection.

SECTION XVI.

Any one may denounce the ancient site of an establishment, without paying any thing for the same, although there may be found thereon, walls, drains, yard, washing-places, furnaces, chimneys, dwelling house, &c. provided they are totally deficient in roofs, machines, tools, and timber-work; if these latter exist, the former proprietor must have notice sent him to re-establish, sell, or let them, within the space of four months, and on his failing to do so, they shall be granted to the denouncer, on condition of his paying the said proprietor for useful moveables, according to the appraisement and judgment of surveyors.

SECTION XVII.

I prohibit any one (not being the discoverer), from denouncing two contiguous mines upon one and the same vein; but I permit any person to acquire and possess one by denouncement, and another or more, by purchase, gift, inheritance, or other just title. And I further declare, that if any one desires to attempt the re-establishment of several inundated or decayed mines, or other considerable enterprise of this kind, and for this purpose claims the grant of several portions, although they be contiguous and upon the same vein, such claim must be laid before the Royal Tribunal General of Mexico, in order that the circumstances and importance of the undertaking being ascertained, they may acquaint the Viceroy therewith, who on finding therein nothing prejudicial to the body of the Miners, the Public, or my Royal Treasury, shall grant him this and other privileges, exemptions, and aids, on condition that my Royal approbation is previously obtained to all such favours, which cannot be granted by the ordinary authority of the Viceroy.

SECTION XVIII.

Beds of ore (*placeres*) and all other depositories (*criaderos*) of gold and silver, on being discovered, shall be registered and denounced in the same manner as mines or veins, the same being understood of all species of metal.

SECTION XIX.

Inasmuch as the waste ground (*desechaderos*), and earth heaps (*terreros*), of abandoned mines, are generally the support of the widows and orphans of the working miners, the old men and invalids, and all other distressed persons of that employment, and even of all the inhabitants of the district, when the mines are not in a course of working, I prohibit any individual from denouncing them, in order to appropriate them to himself, unless he at the same time denounces the mines to which they belong.

SECTION XX.

The same prohibition is to be understood with regard to the dross, (*escoriales*) rubbish, and refuse, (*lameros*), of those smelting houses and establishments of which nothing is left but the walls ; but I order that if they have an owner, notice shall be given to him, and a certain time allowed, in which if he does not avail himself of the vessels (*resocas*) and other remains, nor the community derive any benefit therefrom, they shall be granted to any person denouncing them.

SECTION XXI.

Though in the regular veins, or in the banks, beds, or other mineral depositories, (*rebosaderos*) great natural masses of virgin gold and silver may be found, I declare that the owners of the mines are to acquire and possess them, on paying the just duties ; and I also declare that only ancient deposits of money or jewels, of ingots, or grains, and any other fragments, smelted by man, and buried by thieves, or in any other manner from time immemorial, so that the owner thereof is unknown, shall be retained as treasure.

SECTION XXII.

I likewise grant, that in the prescribed form, may be discovered, claimed, registered and denounced, not only mines of gold and silver but also those of precious stones, copper, lead, tin, quicksilver, antimony, zinc, bismuth, rock salt, or other fossils, whether perfect or mixed metals, bitumen or other production of the earth, the denouncers thereof receiving grants of the same, according to the circumstances : but I declare that although the free discovery and denouncement of the quicksilver mines is permitted, it must be on the express condition of giving an account of them to the Viceroy, and to the sub-delegate of the quicksilver mines of Mexico, in order that it may be considered and determined whether the said mine or mines shall be worked at the expence, and for the advantage, of that individual who discovered and denounced them, on his punctually delivering all the quicksilver extracted from them into the Royal storehouses, under the terms and prices stipulated ; or whether it shall be done on the account of my Royal Treasury, indemnifying the party by some equitable award, having regard to the circumstances of the said discovery and denouncement, the whole of this important subject being regulated according to my sovereign intentions recently declared upon this subject.

CHAPTER VII.

OF THE PERSONS WHO MAY OR NOT DISCOVER, DENOUNCE, AND WORK THE MINES.

SECTION I.

To all the subjects of my dominions, both in Spain and the Indies, of whatever rank or condition they may be, I grant the mines of every species of metal under the conditions already stated, or that shall be expressed hereafter but I prohibit foreigners from acquiring or working mines, as their own property, in these, my dominions, unless they be naturalized or tolerated therein by my express Royal license.

SECTION II.

I also prohibit regulars of religious orders, of both sexes, from denouncing, or in any manner acquiring, for themselves, their convents, or communities, any mines whatever ; it being understood that the working of the mines shall not devolve upon the secular ecclesiastics, as being contrary to the laws, to the orders of the Mexican Council, and to the sanctity and exercise of their profession ; and therefore, in consequence of this prohibition, all such secular ecclesiastics shall be expressly obliged to sell or place in the hands of lay subjects, the mines or establishments for smelting ore, and reducing establishments, which have devolved on them by inheritance or other cause, the same being completed within the term of six months, or within such time as may be considered necessary to ensure a useful result, which is to be fixed by the Viceroy, with a previous intimation to the Royal Tribunal General of the mines, provided that if it is ascertained that, by artifice or fraud, the effects of this article are attempted to be eluded, to the prejudice of the working of such mines and establishments, in which the state is so much interested, they shall be denounced, and disposed of in the same manner as mines in general.

SECTION III.

Neither shall mines be held by Governors, Intendants Mayors, Chief Judges, nor any other public officers whatever, of the Mine-towns and districts, nor their clerks; but I permit such persons to hold mines, in any territory out of their own jurisdiction.

SECTION IV.

Neither shall Administrators, Stewards, Overseers, Keepers of Tallies,* Workers or Watchers of mines, nor in general any person in the service of Mine-owners, whether of superior or subordinate class, be permitted to register, denounce, or in any other manner, acquire mines within a space of a thousand yards round those of their masters, but I allow them to denounce any mine for their said master, even though not authorised by them to do so, provided the aforesaid masters make good the denouncement in the terms prescribed by Section VIII. of Chapter VI. of these Ordinances.

SECTION V.

No one shall denounce a mine under any circumstances of concealment or fraud for another, nor even publicly, unless he has his power or letter of attorney for that purpose, according to established usage.

SECTION VI.

Neither shall any one denounce a mine for himself alone, if he has previously had partners in the transaction; and I ordain that the denouncer shall declare his partners in his written statement, under penalty, if he fail so to do, of losing his share thereof.

CHAPTER VIII.

OF PROPERTIES, AND INTERMEDIATE SPACES BETWEEN PROPERTIES BELONGING TO EITHER; AND OF THE MEASURES, HENCEFORWARD TO BE USED IN THE MINES.

SECTION I.

EXPERIENCE having shown that the equality of the mine-measures established on the surface cannot be maintained under ground, where in fact the mines are chiefly valuable, it being certain that the greater or less inclination of the vein upon the plain of the horizon, must render the respective properties in the mines greater or smaller, so that the true and effective impar-

---

* See this word explained in Chapter XII. Sect. VII. *post.*

tiality, which it has been desired to show towards all subjects, of equal merit, has not been preserved ; but on the contrary, it has often happened that when a Miner after much expence and labour, begins at last to reach an abundant and rich ore, he is obliged to turn back, as having entered on the property of another, which latter may have denounced the neighbouring mine, and thus stationed himself with more art than industry. This being one of the greatest and most frequent causes of litigation and dissension among the Miners, and considering that the limits establishsd in the mines of these kingdoms, and by which those of New Spain have been hitherto regulated, are very confined in proportion to the abundance, multitude and richness of the metallic veins which it has pleased the Creator of his great bounty to bestow on those regions, I order and command that in the mines where new veins, or veins unconnected with each other, shall be discovered, the following measures shall in future be observed.

SECTION II.

On the course and direction of the vein whether of gold, silver, or other metal, I grant to every Miner, without any distinction in favour of the discoverer, whose reward has been already specified, two nundred yards (*varas,*) called measuring yards (*varas de medir*) taken on a level, as hitherto understood.

SECTION III.

To make it what they call a square, that is, making a right angle with the preceding measure, supposing the descent or inclination of the vein to be sufficiently shewn by the opening or shaft of ten yards, the portion shall be measured by the following rule.

SECTION IV.

Where the vein is perpendicular to the horizon (a case which seldom occurs,) a hundred level yards shall be measured on either side of the vein or divided on both sides, as the Miner may prefer.

SECTION V.

But where the vein is in an inclined direction, which is the most usual case, its greater or less degree of inclination shall be attended to in the following manner.

SECTION VI.

If to one yard perpendicular the inclination be from three fingers (*dedos*) to two palms, (*palmos*), the same hundred yards shall be allowed for the square (as in the case of the vein being perpendicular.)

8

SECTION VII.

If to the said perpendicular yard there be an inclination of

2 palms and 3 fingers, the square shall be of 112½ yards								
2	.	6	.	.	.	.	.	125
2	.	9	.	.	.	.	.	137½
3	.	.	.	.	.	.	.	150
3	.	3	.	.	.	.	.	162½
3	.	6	.	.	.	.	.	175
3	.	9	.	.	.	.	.	187½
4	.	.	.	.	.	.	.	200

So that if to one perpendicular yard there correspond an inclination of four palms, which are equal to a yard, the miner shall be allowed two hundred yards on the square on the declivity of the vein, and so on with the rest.

SECTION VIII.

And supposing that in the prescribed manner any Miner should reach the perpendicular depth of two hundred yards, without exceeding the limits of his portion, by which he may commonly have much exhausted the vein, and that those veins which have greater inclination than yard for yard, that is to say, of 45 degrees, are either barren or of little extent, it is my sovereign will that although the declivity may be greater than the above mentioned measures, no one shall exceed the square of two hundred level yards; so that the same shall be always the breadth of the said veins extended over the length of the other two hundreds, as declared above.

SECTION IX.

However, if any Mine-owner suspecting a vein to run in a contrary direction to his own, (which rarely happens), should choose to have some part of his square in a direction opposite to that of his principal vein, it may be granted to him, provided there shall be no injury or prejudice to a third person thereby.

SECTION X.

With regard to the banks (*placeres*) beds, (*rebosaderos*), or any other accidental depositories of silver or gold, I ordain that the portions and measures shall be regulated by the respective Territorial Deputations of Miners, attention being paid to the extent and richness of the place, and to the number of applicants for the same, with distinction and preference only to the discoverers; but the said Deputations must render an exact account thereof to the Royal Tribunal General of Mexico, who will resolve on the measures which they, in their judgment, may consider the most efficacious, in order to avoid all unfair dealing in these matters.

SECTION XI.

*The portions being regulated in the manner described above, the Denouncer shall have his share measured at the time of taking possession of the mine, and he shall erect round his boundaries, stakes or landmarks, such as shall be secure, and easy to be distinguished, and enter into an obligation to keep and observe them forever without being able to change them; though he may allege that his vein varied in course or direction, (which is an unlikely circumstance); but he must content himself with the lot which Providence has decreed him, and enjoy it without disturbing his neighbours: if, however, he should have no neighbours, or if he can, without injury to his neighbours, make an improvement, by altering the stakes and boundaries, it may be permitted him in such case, with the previous intervention, cognizance, and authority, of the Deputation of the District, who shall cite and hear the parties, and determine whether the causes for such encroachment are legitimate.

SECTION XII.

In the mines already opened and worked, the old measures of the portion shall be retained; but they may be extended to the limits prescribed in these Ordinances, whenever such change can take place without prejudice to third persons.

SECTION XIII.

The immutability of the stakes or boundaries already defined in Section XI. of this Chapter, shall also be observed henceforward, in those mines which are in a course of working, or which shall be denounced as deserted or lost, the limits being ascertained in those cases where there are none at present, and each being attended to in their order, beginning with the oldest; and as to any intermediate spaces, (*demasias*), they shall be regulated according to the provisions of Section XIII. of Chapter VI.

SECTION XIV.

As it has been found that the licence or permission of following a vein by working lower down and within the vein, and having enjoyment thereof, until the owner himself has bored it, has been, and is the most fruitful cause of bitter dissensions, litigations, and disturbances among the mine-owners, and further considering that such intrusion is more generally the result of fraud or chance than of the merit and industry of the person so intruding, and that the consequences thereof occasion, for the most part, nothing but serious detriment to, or the total ruin of, the two mines and the two neighbouring Miners, to the great prejudice of the public, and of my Royal treasury, I order and command that no Mine-owner shall enter the property of another, even though merely by continuing his own vein at a greater depth, but that every one shall keep and observe his own boundaries, unless he makes an agreement and stipulation with his neighbour, to be permitted to work in his property.

SECTION XV.

But if a Mine-owner, pursuing his operations fairly, comes to the property of another while in pursuit of a vein which he is working, or discovers it at that time without the master of the property being aware of its existence, he shall be obliged to give such proprietor immediate notice thereof; and the two neighbours shall thenceforward divide the cost and profits equally between them : one for the merit of the discovery, and the other as owner of the property ; all which, until there shall be a communication effected between the mines, either by the principal vein, or a cross lode, or in any manner that may be most convenient ; whereupon after erecting a mutual boundary (*guarda-raya*,) each proprietor shall remain within his own boundaries. But if any one so discovering and following a lode, into the property of his neighbour, fails to give immediate notice thereof to such neighbour, he shall not only lose his right to the half of all the metal, that may be extracted, but also shall pay double the value of what he has already extracted, it being understood, that before exacting this penalty, fraud and misconduct of persons so encroaching must be proved in the plainest and most satisfactory manner, according to the form prescribed in Chapter III.

SECTION XVI.

And in case a Mine-owner shall have advanced so much in his subterranean operations as to have passed beyond the limits of his own property, whether in length or square measure, I declare that he shall not on this account be obliged to turn back or suspend his work, provided the ground he has entered be unclaimed (*terreno virgen*) or within the limits of a deserted mine ; he must however denounce this new property, which shall be granted him, observing always that such new portion must not exceed its former size, and that he must move his boundary marks to his new limits, in order that they may be generally known.

SECTION XVII.

The Mine-owner shall not only possess a portion of the principal vein which he denounced, but likewise of all those, which, in any form or manner whatever, are to be found in his property ; so that if a vein takes its rise in one property, and, passing on, terminates in another, each proprietor shall enjoy that part of it which passes through his particular limits, and no one shall be entitled to claim entire possession of a vein from having its source in his portion, or on any other pretence whatever.

CHAPTER IX.

OF WORKING, SUPPORTING, AND PROTECTING THE MINES.

SECTION I.

It being of the greatest importance that the lives of workmen, and other persons obliged continually to enter and go out of the mines should be endangered, and that the mines should be kept in the state of security and convenience necessary to their being successfully worked, even although they may have been judged useless and impracticable by their first possessors, and abandoned accordingly ; and it not being possible to establish any general and absolute rule on the subject on account of the variety of circumstances of each mine, the greater or less hardness, tenacity, and adherence of the sides, (*respaldos*,) and of the substance of the vein itself ; its greater or less inclination, width, and depth, inducing much diversity in the size and number, of the pillars, arches, beams, (*testeras*), cross-beams (*intermedios*), and other props, which may be left or constructed to support the sides, and also in the distribution of the works necessary to proper ventilation, and the convenient removal of the substances extracted from the mine ; all which cannot be effected without true practical skill and science in the working of mines ; I ordain and command as follows.

SECTION II.

It shall not be permitted to any one to work the mines without the assistance and direction of one of those able and intelligent surveyors, who are called in New Spain, Miners, (*mineros*) or mine-watchers, (*gaurdaminas*) who must have been examined, qualified, and approved by the Mining Professor (*perito facuttativo*) appointed to be in every Mine-town or district, of whom mention will be made hereafter, Chap. XVII. Sect. I. However, in the very poor and remote Mine-towns, where there may be neither Mining Professor, nor qualified and approved surveyor, they may be allowed to proceed under the direction of the most accredited and intelligent surveyors who can be found there, until these, or others, shall be examined and licensed : the same being understood in all cases which require the direction or intervention of a surveyor, in order that, in judicial proceedings, they may meet with the confidence and credit they deserve.

SECTION III.

For the design and execution of shafts (*tiros*) levels, (*contra-minas*) or adits, (*socabones*) and other great and difficult works, which, if they do not turn out successfully, render useless the great expences which have been bestowed upon them, the direction of one or more of the Gaurdaminas, shall not be sufficient, but the inspection or intervention of one of the aforesaid Professors of Mining shall be necessary, with the obligation on his part of visiting the work once every month, or once in two months, as the progress of it may require, in order that, if he perceives any error in the execution, he may amend it in time, and before it occasions further expences.

SECTION IV.

In mines opened on a vein, of which the sides and interior substance are soft, and have so little tenacity, or adhesive property, that on being exposed to the air they moulder away, and open into cracks and crevices, or which, from any other causes, are perceived to be insufficient by themselves to maintain the security and firmness of the mine, I ordain and command that the works shall be lined and secured with large solid timber of known durability, and such as is least liable to decay under ground, cut and prepared according to the rules of art; or with good mason work of stone and mortar, if the value and other circumstances of the mine permit or require it: for which purpose there must be in all the mining places, towns, and districts, a certain number of those artificers, carpenters, and masons, who are called liners, (*ademadores*), and these must have journeymen and apprentices, in order to preserve and continue the exercise of this important business, which ought to be well paid and encouraged.

SECTION V.

In order to prevent the introduction of artificers who have not the requisite experience and intelligence in subterranean architecture, none shall be admitted (*in any place*), who have not been examined and approved by the Mining Prefessor of that place, or of some other.

SECTION VI.

If any mine-owner, in censequence of the great richness of the metallic substance in his vein, is desirous of substituting for the pillars, beams, or sufficient and necessary supports, made of the metallic substance itself, others constructed with mason-work of stone and mortar, he may be permitted to do so, under the inspection of one of the deputies of the district, assisted by his clerk, and with the approbation of the Mining Professor.

SECTION VII.

I strictly prohibit any one from taking away, or in any degree weakening and diminishing the pillars, beams, and necessary supports of the mines, under pain of ten years' imprisonment, to be inflicted according to the form prescribed by Chapter III. of these Ordinances, by the respective judge in each case, upon any workman, searcher (*buscon*), or investigator, (*cateador*) who shall have committed such offence, and the same upon the Miner or Mine-watcher who has permitted it; and the master of the mine shall lose the same, together with the half of his property, (*bienes*), and be for ever excluded from all mining employments.

SECTION VIII.

I ordain and command that the mines shall be kept clean and unobstructed, and that the works necessary or useful for the circulation of air, the carriage and extraction of the metal, or other purposes, although they may contain no more metallic matter than such as may remain in the pillars and partitions (*intermedios*), shall not be encumbered with rubbish (*atierres*), and clods of earth (*tepetates*), but that all these must be carried out, and thrown by each person on the earthmound of his own property, but on no account upon that of another person, without his express leave and consent.

SECTION IX.

In the mines there must be proper and safe steps or ladders, such and as many as are considered necessary by the Mining Surveyor, for the purpose of ascending and descending to the farthermost works, so that the lives of persons employed in the mines may never be endangered by their being weak, insecure, rotten, or much worn.

SECTION X.

In order to avoid the violation of the provisions of any of the Sections contained in this Chapter, it is my sovereign will that the Deputies of the Miners, accompanied by the Mining Professor of the district, and by the clerk if there be one, or, in default of him, by two witnesses in aid, shall once in every six months, or once in every year, (in places where the former is impracticable) visit all the mines in their jurisdiction which are in a course of actual working; and if they find any failure in the points referred to in the above-mentioned Sections, or in any others whatever, which regard the security, preservation, and better working of the mines, shall provide immediately a remedy for such defect, and take means to assure themselves that such remedy is carried into effect. And if the remedy be not applied, or if the same failure shall occur again, the proper penalties must be exacted, multiplying and aggravating them even to the extent of dispossessing the person so offending of the mine, which shall then belong to the first person who may denounce it; provided the Deputies proceed in the form prescribed by Chapter III. of these Ordinances.

SECTION XI.

I most rigorously prohibit all persons from piercing through adits or cross levels (*cruceros*), or other subterraneous passages, from works which are higher and full of water, or from leaving between them and others such slight supports as may allow the water to burst through; on the contrary, persons owning such works, must have them drained by engines before they shall attempt to communicate with new ones, unless the Mining Professor should judge that such piercing through will not be attended with danger to the workmen engaged in it.

SECTION XII.

Also I prohibit all persons from introducing workmen into any works containing noxious vapours, until they have been properly ventilated, according to the rules of art.

SECTION XIII.

Whereas the mines require incessant and continual working in order to procure the metals, certain operations being indispensable, which cannot without much time be accomplished, and which, if interrupted, generally require as great expences in their re-establishment, as they did in their original undertaking; wherefore, to remedy such inconvenience, and also to prevent masters of mines, who either cannot, or will not, work them, from keeping them in an useless state for a length of time, by pretending to work them, and thus depriving them of the real and effective labour which others might bestow on them, I ordain and command, that whosoever, during four successive months, shall fail to work any mine with (at least) four paid workmen, (*operarios rayados*) occupied in some exterior or interior work of real utility, shall, by so doing, lose all his right in the said mine, which shall belong to any person denouncing it, upon his satisfatorily proving, according to the provisions of Chapter VI. such act of desertion on the part of the owner.

SECTION XIV.

Experience having shewn that the provisions of the preceding Section have been eluded by the artful and fraudulent practice of some owners of mines, who cause their mines to be worked during some days in each (interval of) four months, keeping them in this manner many years in their possession; I ordain that whosoever shall fail to work his mine in the manner prescribed by the said Section, during eight months in the year, counting from the day of his coming into possession, even though the said eight months should be interspersed with some days or weeks of labour, shall by such labour forfeit the mine; and it shall be adjudged to the first person who denounces the same, and satisfactorily proves this second species of desertion; unless for this, or the one mentioned in the preceding Section, there be just cause assigned, such as pestilence, famine, or war, in that same mining place, or within twenty leagues thereof.

SECTION XV.

Considering that many Mine-owners, who have formerly worked their mines with ardour and diligence, expending large sums in shafts, adits, and other undertakings, may often be obliged to suspend their operations, while soliciting supplies, or from want of workmen, or necessary provisions, and other just and sufficient causes, which, combined with their former merit, render them worthy of equitable consideration; I declare that any such Mine-owner, keeping his mine in disuse in the manner and for the time above mentioned, shall not forfeit it at once in the manner described above, but his mine shall nevertheless be liable to denouncement before the respective new Tribunals of Miners, in order that both parties having been heard, and alleged merits and causes considered and proved, justice may be done between the parties.

SECTION XVI.

Since many Mine-owners abandon their mines, either for want of the capital necessary for carrying on operations therein, or because they do not choose to consume that which they may have already acquired from them, or because they have not spirit to venture on the difficulties of those undertakings, from which they may have conceived great hopes, or for other causes ; and since persons are not wanting, who might be desirous of taking such mines, if they were informed of their intended abandonment ; and as it is much easier to maintain a mine when in a course of working, than to reinstate it after it has suffered the injuries of time, it is my will that no person shall abandon the working of his mine or mines without making the Deputation of the district acquainted therewith, in order that the Deputation may publish the same, by fixing a notification on the doors of churches and other customary places, for the information of all persons.

SECTION XVII.

In order to avoid the false or equivocal reports which are often spread concerning deserted mines, the consequence of which reports is to augment the distrust in which this profession is ordinarily held, deterring many persons from engaging therein, who do not otherwise want inclination to follow it, I ordain,—

SECTION XVIII.

That no one shall abandon the working of his mine without giving notice to the respective Deputation, in order that an inspection may immediately be had thereof by the Deputies, accompanied by the Clerk and Surveyors, who must examine and measure the mine, particularizing all its circumstances, and draw up a map describing its plan and outlines, which, together with all the necessary information, must be preserved in the Archives, with liberty of access to all persons who may wish to see it, or to take a copy thereof.

CHAPTER X.

OF DRAINS IN MINES.

SECTION I.

As in most of the mines springs and currents frequently occur, from whence the water issues continually, and in such abundance as might in a short time inundate and overwhelm the works, to the hindrance of all progress in the extraction of the 'metals ; I desire and command that the owners of such mines shall keep their works constantly drained and evacuated, so that at all times the operations may be carried on, and the metals extracted without interruption.

SECTION II.

As it is much the most convenient and least expensive method of draining to countermine (*contraminar*) the veins by means of adits, I ordain that in all those mines which require draining, and whose situation will admit of it, and where benefit is likely to arise therefrom, according to the judgment of the Mining Professor of the district, the owners be obliged to make an adit sufficient for the draining and clearing of the works, provided the riches and and abundance of the ores are likely to repay such expence.

SECTION III.

Whereas several mines may sometimes be drained and cleared by one and the same adit, though each of them singly might be insufficient to support the expence thereof, I declare that the adit-shall be made and completed, and the expence divided among all the proprietors in proportion to the benefit they will each derive from it : and if this proportion cannot at the time be ascertained, the expence shall be divided among them in the mean time in equal parts, such parts being fixed according to the sum which the poorest of them can afford to pay, and should this one improve in condition, then the said parts shall be regulated according to what the poorest of the others can pay ; so that the works of the adit may not be suspended ; and all these points must be estimated and regulated by the Deputation of the district, according to the judgment of the respective Mining Professor.

SECTION IV.

If any individual should offer to make an adit by which one or more veins, or the mines opened in them, might be drained and cleared, although he be not the proprietor of any of them, either entirely or in part, his denouncement shall be received in due form, and immediate notice given to the owners of the said mines, who, if they will undertake such work themselves, are always to have the preference ; but, on their refusal, it shall be assigned to the adventurer under the following conditions :

SECTION V.

That the adit be really useful, and its formation practicable, according to the judgment of the Mining Professor, who must be charged with tracing out and determining the plan of the work, and directing its execution in the manner above expressed.

SECTION VI.

That the countermine shall be drawn, as far as it is possible, in a right line, and at the least possible distance from the vein or veins intended to be drained and cleared, or in the line and direction of one of them.

SECTION VII.

That the necessary openings for the admission of air be constructed, or that a counterlevel (*contracanon*) be made, or some other means adopted to preserve a free circulation of air for the health and advantage of the workmen.

SECTION VIII.

That its size (the size of the adit) must depend on the judgment of the Mining Professor, which will be regulated by circumstances; but that it shall never exceed two yards (*varas*) in width, and three in height, and that it be properly secured and lined (*ademado*).

SECTION IX.

That if the adventurer, in the progress of his work, meets with one or more new veins, he shall therein enjoy the right of a discoverer, and the reward which is assigned to him as such by these Ordinances; but if they are already known and opened in other places, I grant him the liberty of acquiring one portion in each of them, and if there be not sufficient space remaining for that purpose, he shall have the enjoyment of all that may remain, until he enters upon the property of another.

SECTION X.

That if the work should pass through any deserted mines, the adventurer shall thereby become master of the same, and may denounce them as soon as he projects the work; it being understood that he should maintain these and his new portions during the progress of his operations as far as lies in his power. But I declare that as soon as his work is concluded, he must have them distinctly portioned out, under pain of losing them, as before enjoined.

SECTION XI.

And finally, that if the adit should pass through mines already occupied and situated in the direction of the vein, half of the metals thence extracted shall belong to the adventurer, and half to the owner of the property; but the costs are to be all defrayed by the adventurer; and he must not exceed in his adit the dimensions before prescribed, nor may he undertake any other works, unless with the consent of the owner, in which case the expences must be divided between them. But if the adit should pass across the vein, the adventurer may open other works in pursuit of the same, and the metals, as

well as the expenses, shall be divided equally between them, until there shall
be some communication established with the works of the master of the mines
and if the adventurer does not give notice immediately on discovering the
metal, he shall not only lose his right to the half thereof, but shall be obliged
to make restitution of all he may have already extracted, and to pay double
its value; proof of such fraud and malice having been previously made out,
according to the form declared by Chapter III.

SECTION XII.

All things contained in this present Chapter, from the fifth section inclusive, with regard to adventurers, is likewise to be understood, as far as it is
capable of being adapted, in cases where Mine-Owners shall be disposed to
attempt the clearing of their own mines or those of others, by means of an adit
or countermine in common, whether the work is undertaken by all jointly, or
by some without the rest, or in company with adventurers, in all of which cases the stipulations which they have made must be punctually observed, provided they do not interfere with the injunctions and objects of these Ordinances.

SECTION XIII.

The owners of mines which require draining, but are in a situation which
will not admit of the formation of an adit, must work them by means of a
general and continued shaft, which in New Spain is called *tiro*, and serves
by means of machines and engines to draw off the water, and extract the ore
and other materials from the mines; and which must be made in such situation, and of such dimensions, and be secured in such manner, as the Mining
Professor of the district may determine and direct. And the Territorial
Deputations are enjoined to take especial notice concerning this matter in
their visits, inflicting and increasing the corresponding penalties, in proportion to the offences which may be proved to have been committed.

SECTION XIV.

Inasmuch as experience has shewn the general utility of the above-mentioned works, as well as the omission and inattention by which they are
sometimes made of a less depth than the other works, in order to avoid the
expence of such undertakings, which become much more serious and expensive by the delay; and if the owners have not sufficient capital they are
obliged to clear the lower works by interior drains, carrying up the water to
the *tiro*, by means of engines moved by men, with great expence and little
effect, and at times with an intolerable waste of human strength, I ordain
and command that all owners of mines which require draining, shall be obliged to make the base or foundation of the *tiro* deeper than the lowest works,
so that sufficient support may remain for their being worked, and enough
room in the *tiro* for the water: the observance of all which must be watch-

ed with particular care in the visits of the Territorial Deputation, the proper penalties being imposed, as enjoined in the preceding Section.

SECTION XV.

If any owner of mines requiring drains does not choose to keep them up, contenting himself with working in the upper parts of the mine, which the inundation does not reach ; and any person shall denounce the said mine or mines, offering to drain and clear the lower works, immediate information thereof shall be given to the owner, in order that if he be either unwilling or unable to drain them effectually, within the period of four months, they may be adjudged to the denouncer, he giving security for the expences of the drain, according to the taxation of the proper Surveyors, and the satisfaction of the Deputies of the District.

SECTION XVI.

If the owner of any mine, of which the works are lower than those of the mines belonging to his neighbours, whether from its situation, or from the circumstance of greater progress having been made in the works thereof, should be put to extraordinary expence, by his neighbours not draining such higher mines, or draining them insufficiently, in such manner that the waters from the higher works shall descend upon the lower, I ordain and command, that the owners of the higher mines shall keep up all the draining which they require ; or, on failure thereof, shall pay respectively to the owners of the lower mines, in silver or good money, the value of all the damage they may have sustained, estimated by Surveyors, who shall first of all enquire and make all possible experiments to ascertain the real truth and circumstances of the case.

SECTION XVII.

To all persons who will take upon themselves the expence of draining and cleaning several mines, by making shafts (*tiros*) in common, or other works, and of constructing and maintaining costly machines (where an adit is not practicable), I grant the ownership of all the desert mines and portions which they shall effectually clear ; even though they may be contiguous, and upon one of the same vein ; and I command that the Viceroy, at the representation of the Royal Tribunal General of Mexico, shall dispense to them all the customary privileges, exemptions, and aids : but I declare that the owners of occupied mines, deriving benefit in any manner from such works, shall be obliged to contribute to the expenses of the same, only in proportion to the advantage their mines may have received, according to the valuation of Surveyors, with the approbation of the Deputies of the District.

CHAPTER XI.

OF MINES WORKED BY COMPANIES.

SECTION I.

INASMUCH as mines are often worked by Miners joined in companies, from the time of the denouncement of such mine, or according to contracts entered into subsequently in various ways, to .the great advantage and improvement of the operations in mines, since it is much easier to engage therein when many persons concur, each subscribing a part of his capital, and as where the wealth of one alone is not sufficient for great undertakings, that of an united company may be ample; in such cases, I desire and command that such companies, whether public or private, may be encouraged, promoted, and protected by all convenient measures, my Viceroy granting to those who may form themselves into such companies, every favour, aid, and exemption which can be granted them, according to the judgment and discretion of the Royal Tribunal of Miners, and without detriment to the public or my Royal Treasury.

SECTION II.

Although by these Ordinances I prohibit any individual Mine-Owners working within the ordinary limits, from denouncing two adjoining mines on the same vein, yet notwithstanding, to those who work in companies, although they be not the discoverers, and without prejudice to the right which they might derive from becoming discoverers, I grant the right of denouncing four new portions, or four deserted mines, even though 'they should be contiguous, and on the same vein, (*rumbo*).

SECTION III.

The accustomed usage in New Spain of dividing a mine into twenty-four imaginary equal parts, commonly called barras, subdividing also each of these into suitable smaller parts, shall continue to be observed, as heretofore, without any alteration.

SECTION IV.

By consequence, no one of the partners may claim, or have a right to work the part A, or any determinate part of the mine, or any other to work the part B, or place therein fixed number of workmen; but they must work in common, as far as it is possible, and make a division of the expences, by sharing the amount of the same in equal proportions among all the partners, and there shall be the like division of the produce in metals of all kinds and qualities, whether in a rough state, or after they have been wrought, as may have been agreed upon by the parties.

SECTION V.

In order to avoid the disputes and differences which usually occur in Mining Companies about the direction of the works, applications for supplies, the administration, and other points connected with the operations, I ordain and command that all the measures necessary to be taken shall be determined by plurality of votes, with the intervention of one of the Deputies of the District, who shall always endeavour to preserve harmony among the parties.

SECTION VI.

The votes shall be valued and counted according to the shares (*barras*) which each partner shall possess in the mine; so that if one or more shall be owners of one and the same share, they shall have only one vote, and he who holds two shares shall have two votes, and so on for the rest; but if one partner alone possesses twelve or more shares, the owner of such a number of shares shall have a number of votes less by one than half the number of such shares.

SECTION VII.

In all cases where any dispute may arise, either from an equality in the number of votes, or from any other cause, the Mining Deputy who shall preside at the Junta, or Meeting, shall decide the same as above declared, and I charge the said Deputy to attend always to justice, and the common interest of all the partners.

SECTION VIII.

If, in the course of operations, a mine should be worked which produces no profit, or which does not repay, either entirely, or in part, the expences which have been bestowed upon it, and any one of the partners does not chuse to contribute his share of the expense, in this case the others shall give notice to the respective Deputation, in order that the day may be noted down, on which he ceased to contribute; and if he persists in this conduct during the continuance of four months, I declare, thereby he forfeits, reckoning from the day on which he ceased to contribute, all his share in the mine, which shall go to increase the portions of those who have contributed their contributions, without any obligation on their part to denounce the same: but if, before the expiration of the four months, he shall contribute his share of the expences, he shall be still a partner, provided he pays all arrears that shall have accrued from the time when he ceased to contribute, to the satisfaction of the parties concerned.

SECTION IX.

If, while any mine is in a course of profitable working, any partner should refuse to concur in the expenses of the dead works (*faenas muertas*) (established according to the forms before prescribed), upon the ground that such dead works would consume a part or the whole of the produce of the mine, the rest of the partners may retain and devote to this purpose a part or the whole of the produce which falls to his share..

SECTION X.

If one or more mines are worked by two partners, and they desire to break up the partnership, on account of disagreement, or other cause, they shall not be reciprocally obliged to sell or buy their shares to or from one another, but each of them has the right of selling his share to a third person, giving his partner, however, the first offer thereof.

SECTION XI.

The company is not to be considered as broken up by the death of one of the partners ; but the obligation devolves on his heirs, who have, however, the privilege of selling their share, according to the terms prescribed in the preceding section.

SECTION XII.

If any share in a mine, or any entire mine, should be sold, after having been appraised and valued by Surveyors, according to its condition at the time of the sale, and it should afterwards become of great value ; I declare that the sale shall not on that account be rescinded, on allegation of the great loss sustained, nor on demand of being restored to his former situation, (*i. e.* on the part of the seller) nor of any similar privilege.

CHAPTER XII.

OF THE LABOURERS IN MINES, AND IN THE WORKS OR ESTABLISH·MENTS FOR THE REDUCTION OF THE METALS.

SECTION I.

Forasmuch as it is a notorious and well established fact, that the working Miners are a very poor class of people, and very useful to the state, and that they ought to be adequately remunerated for the severe toil they undergo, I ordain and command that no Mine-owner shall presume, on any ground or pretext whatsoever, to alter the rate of wages established by long usage, and adopted in all the mining districts, but that the same shall be observed, as well in regard to persons employed in the works and machinery, as to the labourers in the mines, under the penalty, if at any time any Mine-owner shall diminish the established wages, of paying the said labourers the double thereof ; and the labourers shall be obliged to work according to the said established rate of wages.

SECTION II.

The workmen in the mines must be registered by their own proper names and must mark with plain and distinguishable strokes, each occasion of their leaving their work; so that they themselves may know and recognise the same, even when they are not able to read; according to the forms hitherto adopted in New Spain.

SECTION III.

The amount of the wages are to be paid every week to each workman, according to his tallies, (*rayas**), and with the greatest punctuality delivered in ready money and into their own hands, in current coin or in silver or gold bullion of good quality, if there be not ready money, or by part of the metal which may have been extracted, if it shall have been so agreed between the parties. And I strictly prohibit their being compelled to receive such payments in merchandize, effects, fruits, or provisions.

SECTION IV.

At the time when their wages are paid, they (the workmen), shall not be forced to satisfy the debt and charges for which they may be liable, even though they be such as are usually termed privileged, without a judicial order for so compelling them, except as to those which they may have contracted with the Mine-owner, with an understanding that the same should be paid out of their labour, and even in these cases, not more than a fourth part of their wages shall be so retained.

SECTION V.

I prohibit the making demands upon the workmen for alms, charity, collections for brotherhoods, (*cornadillos de cofradias*), or any similar purposes, until they have received their dues, and these being settled, such donations shall be left entirely to their free will and disposition.

SECTION VI.

Where the workmen are paid by weekly rations and monthly salaries, the rations supplied must be of good wholesome meat, wheat, maize, Indian corn, pinole, (a fruit of the country), salt, red pepper, (capsicum), and such other articles as may be usual, according to fixed and exact measures and weight, to all which particular attention must be paid in the visits, (of the Territorial Deputations).

---

* Literally, the strokes or tallies which represent the wages due to them. In future, wages will be used in the translation, as being a more familiar expression.

SECTION VII.

Each workman or servant of the mines, referred to in the preceding Section, must keep in his possession a paper, in which shall be marked the parts of his monthly salary which shall have become due, as well as every thing which he may have received on account, all written by the accountant, (*Rayador**), or paymaster of the mine and establishment and the dollars and reals distinguished by circles, lines and half-lines; so that each workman may adjust and understand his own account, and have·a proper statement thereof in his possession.

SECTION VIII.

The duties or tasks (*tequios o tareas*) of the workmen shall be assigned by the captain of the *Barras*†, who must attend to the hardness or softness of substance, the abundance, scarcity and other circumstances of the work, proceeding with the greatest justice and equity in moderating the said tasks, in allowing good pay to those employed in such tasks, and in encreasing the same, under any change of circumstances; and in case any party should complain of any particular grievance the respective Mining Deputation shall proceed to redress all injuries by a verbal decree, or by judicial process, if the parties cannot otherwise be brought to an agreement, all which shall be done in the form prescribed by Chapter III. of these Ordinances.

SECTION IX.

It is also my Royal will that no supplies shall be afforded to the Indians of allotment‡, (*repartimiento*), in order that immediately on concluding their tasks they may return to their villages and habitations, and others be employed in their stead as the law requires. And that the free Indians alone may receive supplies, as far as five dollars to each, conformably to an act granted by my Royal Audiency of Mexico; although in cases of any peculiar urgency, such as the celebration of their marriages, or the funerals of their wives or children I permit that on the same being proved to the satisfaction of the Mine-owner. Administrator, or Overseer, (*Mandon*), by a certificate from the curate (of the parish of an Indian so circumstanced), he may be furnished with what is necessary for such purpose.

---

* *Rayador*, literally, the inspector or settler of the rayas or tallies, alluded to and explained in Section III. of this Chapter; as it evidently means accountant, in future that expression will be used for Rayador.

† These *Barras* are the shares, twenty-four in number, into which every mine is divided.

‡ *Indios de repartimiento*, the Indians who are lotted in division from time to time, and sent to work in the mines; in opposition to free Indians.

SECTION X.

Both the Mine-owners and the workmen shall be entirely at liberty to agree between themselves whether they shall be paid for their work by the task, by a share of the profit, (*a partido*), or by salary and share of the profit. Supposing this mutual liberty understood, when the mine is not worked by share of the profits merely, the owner or administrator shall pay the workmen such wages or salary as shall be conformable to the First Section of this Chapter ; and if, when the arrangement is for task-work, any one of the labourers, called *Barreteros**, having finished his task, shall continue voluntarily for all or part of the time remaining, to extract further ores, the Mineowner shall not be obliged to pay otherwise than in money, and in proportion to his daily rate of wages, for all such ore as may be extracted. But if in order to promote and stimulate the exertions of the workmen, the Mineowner or administrator should agree to pay them at a certain rate for every sack or bag (*tenate*) of metal which they may extract beyond their task, or to pay them for the same with a part of such metal, all such contracts shall be fulfilled according to the engagements on both sides, provided the circumstances shall not have materially changed in the opinion of the respective Mining Deputies ; and if these should disagree, the respective Substitutes shall decide according to the rule already established in such cases ; but in all that regards the terms on which labourers are to work in the mines, whenever there shall arise any dispute between them and the master or steward of the mine, (*Mayordomo*), which may occasion injury to its working and progress, and consequently to the State, and either of the parties shall make an appeal, the respective Deputation shall decide the same, and eventually if necessary, the said Substitute, conformably to the practice established in the mine in question, or, if it be a new mine, then in conformity with the practice of the district.

SECTION XI.

The ore extracted in the course of the task-work, and that extracted in working for a share of the ore, shall be received and attested by the accountant, or inspector, or other person, appointed for that purpose by the Mineowner ; and if he thinks the ore delivered by any labourer as his share-work, better or purer than that of his task, they shall both be mingled together in the presence of the workman interested, and shall be stirred about as much as he may desire, in order that he may chuse, from whatever part of the heap so mingled he may prefer, as many sacks, bags, or measures as there were in his share before such mixture was made : it being understood that no Mine-owner, his steward, overseer, or other servants shall, on any pretence whatever, prevent the labourers interested from being present during all these proceedings, or cause the sacks to be filled from any other part of the heap than that which the said labourers shall choose.

* *Barretero*, literally, a person employed in such barras or shares as are explained above, Section VIII. Note.

SECTION XII.

The Inspector may examine all those who go in and out of the mines, observing, with the greatest care, whether they are in a state of intoxication, or whether they carry with them any intoxicating liquors; and he may also register all that comes in or out of the mine under the head of breakfasts, dinners, &c.; and if he should discover any stolen metal, tools, gunpowder, or any thing of the like kind, he shall preventively apprehend, confine, and secure the thief; and thereby give notice to the Territorial Deputation, in order that due proceedings may be instituted, conformably to the regulations established by Chapter III. of these Ordinances.

SECTION XIII.

Idle persons and vagabonds, of whatsoever cast or condition they may be, who shall be met with in the mining districts, or the neighbouring villages, may be seized and compelled to work in the mines, as well also as the labourers who from mere idleness shall have withdrawn themselves from this employment, without engaging in any other; for which purpose the Mine-Owners may appoint proper officers, (*recogedores*) by licence of the Courts, and the Territorial Deputations of the districts, as usual in such cases; but it is to be understood, that no Spaniard, or Spanish Mestizo,* the latter being considered as a Spaniard, can be included in such regulation, as both one and the other are by law exempted; and when such persons have incurred punishment by their idleness or offences, other penalties must be inflicted on them, by the proper judge, according to the nature of their offences.

SECTION XIV.

In the distribution and allotment of the Indians of the Villages near the mining districts, commonly called the Indians of the Quatequil, or Mita,† to the reducing establishments, the rights and pretentions, acquired at different times by the proprietors of such establishments, shall be maintained and observed in those which are in a course of working, and have continued so without interruption; but in the establishments which have been deserted and abandoned, and whose allotment of Indians may have passed to others

---

* Mestizos are a mixed race, the offspring of an European and Indian: they are mentioned by Robertson as the third class of inhabitants in the Spanish Colonies.—*See Rob. Amer.* Vol. iv. p. 33.

† The Mita, or compulsory labour in the mines, by chosen bands of Indians, so many out of every hundred, is by Humboldt said to be wholly abolished in New Spain.—*Humb. New Spain*, Vol. i. p. 124.

I can find no account of the word Mita. Perhaps the number of Indians taken for this purpose out of every hundred may have been originally the half, (*milad*); this conjecture is rendered more probable from the circumstance of the final *d* being often omitted in the Spanish pronunciation.

more recently established, the latter are to be maintained in the possession of the same; and, in case the former should be re-established, they shall only be entitled to the quatequil of such villages as shall have before belonged to them, and shall not have since passed to other establishments; and the same is to be observed in respect of the working companies (*quadrillas*), both of mines and of reducing establishments: but in neither case shall such distribution and allotment of Indians exceed the proportion of four out of every hundred, according to the established practice in New Spain, and in order that the Mitas may be regulated as much as possible in favour of the Indians, I ordain and command, that in the execution and fulfilment of the law, Article 1, Chap. 15, Book 6, and Article 4, Chap. 15, Book 7, the negroes and free mulattoes, who wander about as vagabonds, and the mestizos of the second class, who are without occupation, may be compelled to work in the mines; and that criminals condemned to hard labour, and not excepted by the preceding section, may be taken to work in the mines, with the consent of the Mine Proprietors, who are to be in that respect entirely free, either to admit such criminals to work in the mines, according to the greater or less degree of facility which there may be of guarding them during the intervals of their occupation.

SECTION XV.

Working Companies belonging to deserted establishments shall not be allowed to establish themselves in villages, even though they may construct a chapel and erect a belfry, because by so doing they appropriate to themselves the earth and water intended for the supply of such establishment; thus impeding and wholly preventing its re-establishment; to avoid which I desire and command them always to bear in mind that such situation may be at any time denounced, and in case of works being re-established there, they are again to become part of the working company, and to be dependant upon the proprietor of such establishment.

SECTION XVI.

The labourers belonging to working companies of mines or establishments, shall be obliged to work on the establishment to which they are attached, rather than elsewhere, and shall only be allowed to work elsewhere by the consent of the proprietor of such establishment, or in case he shall have no employment for them.

SECTION XVII.

As it is found by experience, that in unproductive mines there is generally a default of workmen, by reason of their all flocking to those mines which are in a course of working, particularly where the proprietors allow them a share of the produce, thereby interrupting and impeding the working of the other mines; for remedy thereof I ordain and command that the Territorial

Deputations shall cause such workmen as are in a vagabond state, and not attached to any establishment, to be alternately employed in each of these classes of mines, so that they may enjoy the benefit of being employed in those which are in a course of profitable working, and not deprive the others altogether of their service ; with the same view, it is my sovereign will that no workman going from one mine into another, shall be admitted by the proprietor of such other without producing a certificate of good behaviour from the master he has left, or his administrator ; otherwise such mine proprietor so admitting him, as well as the workman himself, shall be punished in proportion to the evil intention with which they appear to have acted ; the observance of all which things shall be strictly attended to by the Territorial Deputations, as pertaining to their jurisdiction.

SECTION XVIII.

Workmen who, having contracted debts while working in any mine, shall engage themselves to work in another, may be compelled to return to the former, with a view to the discharge of such debt by their labour therein, according to the fourth Section of this chapter, unless the creditor shall consent to accept security for his debt from the proprietor of such other mine.

SECTION XIX.

In cases of thefts committed by the workmen of mines on the establishments, whether of metallic ores, tools, gunpowder, or quicksilver, punishments shall be inflicted according to the nature and circumstance of the offence, and the repetition of the same ; imposing whatsoever is by law established, and measuring the punishment due to the offences of the Indians by the damage sustained, and the malice evinced ; the respective judges in the cognizance of such causes, regulating themselves by the rules laid down and declared by Chapter III. of these Ordinances.

SECTION XX.

Workmen who, for slight offences, debts, or other causes, are imprisoned according to custom, and remain there a long time to their own destruction, and to the distress of their families, may be removed from prison, and placed to work, provided that in the mine or establishment where they are employed, there may be the means of securing them during the intervals of their labour to the end that, after setting apart a proportion of their gains for their own support, and that of their families, the rest may be applied to the discharge of their debts, the confirmation of their marriages, the payment of pecuniary penalties, and the satisfaction of parties whom they may have aggrieved, and of all this the proprietor or administrator of the mine or establishment must keep a clear and distinct account.

SECTION XXI.

If any barretero, or other workman, or person serving in the mines, shall work improperly, leaving any metal adhering to the surface of the mine, or in any other manner maliciously concealing metal, he shall be punished in the manner prescribed by Section XIX. of this present Chapter.

CHAPTER XIII.

OF THE SUPPLY OF WATER AND PROVISIONS TO THE MINES.

SECTION I.

THE supply of water for drinking being an object of the greatest importance in mining districts, I ordain and command that its introduction thereto, the preservation of its source, and the good condition and cleanliness of the conduit pipes be particularly attended to, and that no water be used that is impregnated with mineral particles.

SECTION II.

I prohibit most rigorously the emptying of any water from the mine drains, and from the washing places of the works and smelting-houses, into the streams or aqueducts by which the population is supplied; and I command that the said water be carried off by canals or otherwise.

SECTION III.

I desire and command that in the immediate neighbourhood of mining districts, there may be a sufficient number of grazing places and watering places for the cattle which work the machinery, necessary to the reduction of the metal from the ore, or which are employed in the transportation thereof, or who shall be paid for the same, if their possession be lawful, according to the valuation of a surveyor appointed on each side, and of a third in case of disagreement; with the express understanding, however, that such sales shall only happen in cases of lands which can lawfully be granted, and to the extent which may be necessary for the above-mentioned purpose, and, as to any excess over and above, that shall only take place with the free consent of the owner of such lands.

SECTION IV.

All persons are permitted to go with and drive the said cattle through all common and public lands, meadows, or pastures belonging to other mining districts, or through places not possessing any mines, without paying any thing on that account, although their masters may not reside in such district; and they shall enjoy the like exemption from such payments on lands belonging to individuals where it is not the custom for other passengers or mule drivers to pay; but where it is the custom for others to pay, then they also shall pay what is usual and just; and I declare that persons going about to search for mines shall be allowed to have one beast to ride on, and one to carry their luggage, without paying any thing for their pasture, either on public or private property, and whether it be customary or not to pay for the same; but, in order that this privilege may not be abused, any excess shall be watched with the greatest care, and if such be committed, to the prejudice of a third person, application shall be made to the respective Royal Court, for the proper remedy.

SECTION V.

In order to restrain any extraordinary rise in the price of provisions and clothing in the mining districts, when they are in a flourishing state, and that the same may be equitably regulated according to the circumstances which ought to influence it, the Territorial Deputations shall make proper representations thereupon to the Courts of the District, according to what is laid down in Section xxxv. of Chapter III. of these Ordinances; and also for the restraining and punishment of monopolies, extortions, usuries, and all unfair or fraudulent contracts or practices whatsoever.

SECTION VI.

All persons shall be at liberty to carry to the mines maize, wheat, barley, and other provisions and necessaries, such as charcoal, wood, tallow, hides, &c.; more especially when they have been sent for them by the miners themselves; and for this purpose I grant them permission to bring such provisions from all cities, towns, villages, and establishments whatsoever, even if situated in other districts, provinces, or governments, provided there be just cause for so doing; and therefore I command all governors and magistrates of the different places not to obstruct them in so doing, nor to allow the price of such articles to be improperly raised, but rather to assist and favour them, in order that the mines and the persons employed in them, may be always sufficiently provided with what is necessary.

SECTION VII.

Without prejudice to the jurisdiction and cognizance granted to the Royal Courts by Section xxx. of Chapter III. of these Ordinances, the Territorial Deputations are to be allowed frequently to visit and inspect the fountains and sources which supply the waters for putting the machinery of the mines

in motion, in order that they may be able to make representations thereupon
to the said Courts as occasion may require, and in order that all persons may
be prevented from cutting down any of the woods in the neighbourhood which
serve to protect them, or clearing them away for tillage, or otherwise reducing them ; as also from making any hollows in the neighbourhood lower than
the waters, or doing any other thing by which they may be drained off, or
diminished ; but on the contrary that they may be cleansed and purified with
all the precautions of scientific practice.

SECTION VIII.

The said Deputations shall likewise take care that the rivers and streams
preserve their ancient courses and beds, representing to the Royal Courts in
proper time, and before the said evils shall have become irremediable, the
impediments which have occurred, either from the current leaving islands,
or banks which change the direction of the stream, or from the overflowing of
the banks, or from other causes, which might be remedied by proper diligence
in many cases ; and, to the end that the provisions of this and the preceding
Section may be carried into effect, the Deputies and the Surveyor of each
mining district shall twice in every year visit the fountains and springs, within their boundaries, once just before the rains, and once immediately after,
carefully examining them, and if they find that they require any cleansing,
repairing, alteration, or amendment, in order to preserve their proper channel and direction, they shall make representation thereof to the Royal Courts,
who shall, with the intervention of the said Deputies and Surveyor, order the
same to be repaired at the expence of the owners of the estates and others
interested in such waters ; and in case of there being no such interested
persons, or their contributions not being sufficient, the said Deputies shall
appoint such arbitrators as they shall consider competent and impartial, who
are to determine according to the provisions of Section XXXVI. of Chapter
III. of these Ordinances, whether or no such repairs shall be undertaken at
the public expence.

SECTION IX.

To the end that the high roads and private ways necessary for the intercourse of villages in the neighbourhood of mines, with the rest of the district
on which they depend for supplies, may be kept in as good and secure a condition as possible, considering, that generally those in the immediate neighbourhood of the mine districts are much broken up, difficult, and dangerous,
particularly during the rainy season, I ordain and command that the Territorial Deputations shall promote this important object by all the means in their
power, before the respective Royal Courts, by carrying the same into effect,
either at the expence of the owners of mines or establishments, or by imposing a toll upon passengers and mule drivers, if this be agreeable to the

practice of such place, or in any other manner, provided only, that the Court be guided in this respect by the provisions of the said Section xxxvi. of Chapter III.

SECTION X.

For the better preservation and security of private roads between villages and mines, between mines and mines, and also between mines and establishments, the provisions of the preceding Section shall be acted upon, even though such works ought in the particular case to have been effected by the owners of the respective mines or establishments; moreover, the Territorial Deputations are enjoined to visit the said roads frequently, with the utmost attention and care, inasmuch as the said roads and ways, being in general narrow and broken, are rendered still more dangerous by the constant traffic, carelessness, and negligence of those who frequent them.

SECTION XI.

As to rivers, streams, and currents, which it is necessary to pass over, in order to go to or from the mining districts, there shall be built substantial bridges of stone and lime-work, or at least of timber, on solid foundations of stone and cement, which are more proper for such rivers, as those which run between high grounds, at no great distance from each other, are generally deep and rapid, rather than of great width; for the necessity of their construction, the amount of their expence, and the ascertaining of the parties upon whom such expence is to be levied, proceedings are to be had according to Section xxxv. and xxxvi. of Chapter III. of these Ordinances.

SECTION XII.

The mountains and woods in the neighbourhood of mines, are to be used for the purpose of providing them with timber for their machinery, and with wood and charcoal for the reduction of the ores, and the same is to be understood with regard to those which are private property, provided a fair price be paid to the owners; and I hereby prohibit all persons from exporting or removing their timber, wood, or charcoal from their respective districts, to others which might be more properly supplied elsewhere.

SECTION XIII.

The cutters and carriers of wood shall not cut at any other time nor deliver in any other manner than shall be prescribed by the particular regulations which are to be drawn up by the Royal Tribunal General of Miners, by which they are to be regulated, provided that these regulations shall in the first instance be approved by the Viceroy, and authorized by my Royal approbation.

SECTION XIV.

All dealers in wood and charcoal are strictly prohibited from cutting young shoots for fire-wood or charcoal, and I ordain that plantations of young trees shall be formed, where there are none; particularly in those places where there have been such plantations formerly, as from the consumption and failure of re-production, the two species of wood most necessary in the working of mines and reduction of metals have become scarce; and be it understood, in order to attain this important object the Royal Tribunal of Miners shall draw up particular instructions and directions, which must be observed under certain penalties, to be named therein for that purpose, there being the same necessity for the approval of the Viceroy, and my approbation as in the preceding Section.

SECTION XV.

Wells of salt water and veins of rock-salt, which are frequently met with in some mining districts, may be denounced, the greatest care being used to authenticate such discoveries, and no impediment being thrown in the way thereof by any judge or individual; provided however, that notice thereof, and of such denouncement, be given to the superior Government, in order that they may take account of and determine as to the working, and distribution and price of the salt, so that no injury shall accrue to my Royal Revenue, and that the miners, and more particularly the discoverer and denouncer, may derive the utmost benefit therefrom; observing, however, that the Indians, are by no means to be deprived of the salt works which are conceded to them by law, nor prevented from the use thereof, in the same manner as is now permitted to them.

SECTION XVI.

The judge and deputies of each mine-establishment shall take particular care that in the prices of timber, wood, charcoal, hides, tallow, cordage, salt, magistral, (sulphate of iron) (chalk), ashes, barley, straw, and other things of indispensable necessity in the working of mines, the sellers thereof shall not act with extortion; for which purpose the said judge, acting in concert with the Territorial Deputation, shall fix the prices of the said articles, with due regard to justice and equity, so that neither the seller shall lose the regular profit of his trade, to which he is justly entitled, nor fall into the other extreme of demanding exorbitant prices, which would paralyse the labour of miners, who, generally speaking, are not in flourishing circumstances.

SECTION XVII.

The distribution by retail or parcelling out of quicksilver in small quantities, shall be provided for in the manner directed by my Royal Orders of the 12th of November, 1773, and 5th of October, 1774.

SECTION XVIII.

Whoever shall work mines in a different district to that in which he resides, and shall derive considerable advantage from such working, shall be obliged either to build a house in that village which is in the neighbourhood of his mine, or to construct some work of public utility to be estimated by the Deputies of Miners, and shall also be liable to all the charges which are or ought to be paid by the miners of the said district.

SECTION XIX.

No dealer or miner shall, under any pretence, whatsoever, intercept on the roads, the sellers of fruit, grain, or other commodity, even though they pretend that they are buying for their own consumption, and not for the purpose of selling such articles again; but I grant the mine-owners liberty to purchase such articles in other villages, and to conduct them, on their own account, to the mines, and I permit the sellers generally to carry them thither without obstruction.

CHAPTER XIV

OF THE MILLERS, (*MAQUILEROS*) PERSONS WHO REDUCE ORES FOR THE MINERS BY AGREEMENT, AND PURCHASERS OF THE METALS.

SECTION I.

CONSIDERING the measures which may best promote the advancement of the mines, as well the increase and support of the mining population, and observing the customs which have hitherto prevailed in New Spain, by which it is permitted to all persons to buy and sell ores, and also to erect establishments for reducing the same, although they may not themselves be the possessors of mines, I will and ordain that both these customs be kept up and encouraged, provided that in so doing, the strictest attention be paid to the enactments of the eleven following Sections.

SECTION II.

All persons are prohibited from purchasing ores, otherwise than in the outer courts of the mines, or in some public place adjoining thereto, within the view, and by the permission of the owner, administrator, er accountant of the mine, from whom such purchaser must receive a ticket, expressing the day on which the metal is purchased, its weight, quality, and price, and whether it be the property of the master, or of any person working or serving in the mine.

SECTION III.

If any miner shall lay information of any of his metal, which has been stolen, being in the possession of a purchaser, and such purchaser, on examination and comparison of the metal, cannot justify himself by the production of such a ticket as is mentioned in the preceding Section, the same shall be considered as having been stolen, without the necessity of farther proof, and shall be restored to the miner; but if the latter by any other means shall clearly prove it to have been stolen, and there shall have been a repetition of the offence, the offending party shall not only restore the stolen property to the miner, but such penalties shall be inflicted on the offender, by the proper judge, as are directed by Section xxix. of Chapter III. of these Ordinances, with attention to the nature and all the circumstances of the offence.

SECTION IV.

No one shall be allowed to purchase from persons working or serving in the mines quicksilver, either fused, or in a crude state, metallic grains, gunpowder, ashes, chalk, or lead, under a penalty to the buyer of paying double the amount thereof on conviction; and to the seller, of being severely punished, according to the nature of the offence, even though no one should come forward expressly to convict him.

SECTION V.

In order that the owners of establishments for reducing the metals may not exorbitantly raise the price thereof, to the prejudice of the miners; and on the other hand, may not fail to realize a fair profit, I ordain and command that the judges of the respective mining districts shall every year, acting in concert with the Territorial Deputations, establish and fix the proper dues to be taken during that year for every quintal of ore, regulating the same according to the price of timber, of iron, and of labour, and of whatever else ought to be considered for the purpose; and shall establish the same by a table of fees, which is to be prepared under the authority of the said judges, and to be affixed to and exhibited in public places, and to be kept in every establishment where metals are reduced in the manner here mentioned, and its provisions to be strictly complied with.

SECTION VI.

The said reducers are on no account to charge the owners of the metals a higher price for quicksilver than is paid for it in the same district by those Mine-owners, who procure it on their own account, and for their own consumption.

SECTION VII.

In the article of salt, magistral, chalk, powder of lead, charcoal, wood, and other ingredients, used in the reduction of metal by quicksilver, or by fire, the said reducers shall not be allowed to take more than twelve per cent. profit on the actual price at which they may be bought at first cost by those who purchase them on their own account, and for their own consumption.

SECTION VIII.

The tickets which are usually given to owners of metal, containing an account of the expences and produce, are not only to express the same generally, but are to particularize the reducing expences, the price of each ingredient, the price of the labour, the consumption of quicksilver, and the produce of gold, etc. and must be signed by the owner and administrator of the establishment, and by the amalgamator or smelter, and in the event of any of the preceding Sections being transgressed, proceedings shall be had by the production of such ticket against the owner or administrator of the establishment, so as to identify the owner of the metal; and if intentional fraud shall be proved against them, they shall pay him three times the value.

SECTION IX.

No reducer of metal shall compel the owner of metals to pay the costs of reduction with the silver or gold so reduced, but only in money; but if there shall have been an agreement to pay in bullion, the same is to be taken at its full value without any premium or reduction; and the same thing is to be observed with respect to the amalgam, (*silver and mercury combined*), which it may be sometimes necessary to leave at the establishment as a pledge during the continuance of such agreement.

SECTION X.

In order to prevent the frauds and impositions which frequently arise from the uncertainty of the reduction by quicksilver and by fire, sometimes to the injury of the owners of the metal, by taking away part of the silver or gold produced; sometimes to the injury of the reducers, when the metal is not sufficient to pay the costs of its reduction, I order and command, that, until the establishment of a Public Office in the Mining Districts, which ought to be done as soon as possible, for the reduction by way of assay of one or more quintals of metal, for the purpose of ascertaining its intrinsic richness, either the owner of the metal, or of the reducing establishment, when he shall entertain any doubts concerning the results of the reduction, may choose out and have deposited one or more quintals of the metal, to be reduced afterwards for his satisfaction, by surveyors appointed in the usual manner, one on each side, and a third in case of their disagreement.

SECTION XI.

With the same view that directed the preceding Section, no owner of metal, who sends it to be reduced by such an establishment, belonging to another person, shall be prevented from attending either personally, or by a confidential agent, all the operations of the reduction, from making trials, from assaying any part of the mass in various ways, and doing every thing else that he may think conducive towards the better reduction of the metal, or the satisfying himself of the manner in which it is done.

SECTION XII.

The amount of carriage to be paid to the mule drivers, upon metals taken from the mines to the establishments, whenever any excessive charge is made, shall be settled by the judge of the district, acting in concert with the Territorial Deputations, having a due regard to justice and equity, and making a difference between the dry and rainy seasons.

SECTION XIII.

And if any of the said mule drivers shall be proved to have stolen or sold any of the metal on the roads, replacing the same by other materials, they shall be proceeded against accordingly, by the proper judges, and Section XXIX. of Chapter III. of these Ordinances, shall be observed in the infliction of penalties on such persons ; and also, in case of the offence being repeated, always with due regard to the nature and character of the offence, deciding the same according to law, and in the form prescribed in said Chapter III. and be it understood, that if any of the cases comprised in Section XIII. of this Chapter, the imposition of penalties, or the loss of property, beasts of burthen, or other thing whatever, come under consideration, proceedings shall be had according to Section XXXII. of Chapter III.

CHAPTER XV.

OF THE CONTRACTORS FOR SUPPLYING MINES, (WITH MONEY AND OTHER ARTICLES,) AND OF THE DEALERS IN (GOLD AND) SILVER.

SECTION I.

It often happens that Mine-owners carry on the works in their mines with the capital of other persons, either because they have not at first sufficient funds of their own, or from having exhausted their own funds in various operations, before the extraction of sufficient metal to make them a return, and in such cases they are in the habit of agreeing with contractors for supplies,

(*Aviadores*), in one of two methods; either by letting them have the gold and silver which they may extract, at a price somewhat below the real value, leaving the said contractors the benefit of the difference, which method is called *allowing a premium upon the metals*, (*aviar á premios de platas*), or by giving the contractor a share in the mine, making him a perpetual proprietor thereof, or of the metals for a certain time, *by a species* of partnership; and whereas, the necessities of the Miners, and the facility of some of the contractors often lead to contracts, which, being unjust or usurious, or ill understood from the beginning, or appealed against by one or other of the parties, give rise to litigation, which suspends the supplies, and occasions injury to the mines, and the loss of the capital laid out upon them; it is my sovereign will and pleasure, that no Mine-owner shall conclude any agreement for supplies without a regular signed contract, leaving it at his option to complete the same, or not, before a notary or witnesses; and no agreements that may be entered into without such signed contract shall be capable of being enforced, but such cases to be determined according to the general rules.

SECTION II.

In all agreements of the first mentioned kind, (*á premios de plata*), attention and consideration must be given to the number of marks* in each delivery, and how often such deliveries take place, so that if, through any accidental circumstances in the mine, the number of deliveries should increase or diminish considerably, either of the contracting parties may be allowed to increase or diminish the premium upon the metals, without violating the original contracts in other respects; for which purpose in the instrument as originally drawn up, the number of annual deliveries shall be specified, and the number of marks in each delivery; or the parties, if they please, may renounce altogether any right to avail themselves of such accidents as are above mentioned, in which cases the original contracts shall remain in force for all purposes.

SECTION III.

If the Mine-owner shall secure to the Mine-contractor, a certain sum for the supplies, either by deposit, or security, to the satisfaction of the contractor, the latter shall not receive in the way of premium more than would amount to five per cent. per annum on the capital advanced.

SECTION IV.

The contractors shall furnish the supplies in ready money, or in bills payable without discount or loss, or, if the Mine-owners should prefer having goods and effects such shall be delivered to him of a good quality, and in a good condition; and at the price at which they could be bought for ready

* Eight ounces to a mark.

money, at the place where the contractor resides, and in no other manner whatsoever.

SECTION V.

Risks and accidents happening upon the road in the transport of supplies, and the freight and (excise) duties payable upon the supplies, shall be at the expence of the Mine-owner, where the contract is by premium upon the metals ; but where the contract is in the way of partnership, such costs shall be at the expence of both, unless any other mode be particularly expressed in the deed of agreement.

SECTION VI.

In case of the capital supplied being entirely expended, or of a part of it not being covered by the remaining effects, the Mine-owner shall not be responsible for the same, in his person, nor in any other property which he may possess, excepting only that connected with the mine, and the reducing establishment, supposing this latter to be erected out of the capital advanced ; but the mine, and the effects and profits thereof, after deducting the expences, shall go to the payment of the contractors one after another, beginning with the last or most recent ; be it understood, however, that this being a privilege granted by the law only to creditors who advanced second supplies for the restoring and refitting of mines, it is necessary that the three qualifications should all concur, in order to its being enjoyed ; but if the Mine-owner, from actual necessity, shall abandon the mine, without any fraudulent intention, and having given notice thereof to the creditors, it shall not remain liable for former claims, when it is in the hands of the new possessor ; and it is further declared, that if the capital supplied to such mines, and in regard to which such deficiency occurs, has not been furnished in the way of partnership, between the contractor and Mine-owner, in which case, the profit or loss is to be in common between them, but in the way of loan, and the Mine-owner shall have made his property answerable, either by choice, or because the contractor required it for greater security ; under such circumstances, the said obligation shall remain complete in all its parts, notwithstanding the general provisions of this section.

SECTION VII.

If no agreement shall have been made at first, as to the mode of securing the advances contracted for, when they are supplied in the way of premium upon the metal ; the contractor shall not require the same in any manner prejudicial to the Mine-owner in the working of his mine, by cutting off the supplies : nor shall he be obliged to receive back from the Mine-owner in small sums, the supplies he may have advanced.

SECTION VIII.

Although the Mine-owner may not have observed at any time that his silver contains a mixture of gold, the separation of which from the silver would be expensive; or that there be silver amongst the gold of a baser quality, and the contractor should have discovered the same, either by assaying or other method; be it understood that the profit thereof shall not go to the said contractor, but shall be placed to the credit of the Mine-owner, or proprietor of the metal, in the account kept between him and such contractor.

SECTION IX.

When the contract of supply is made in the way of partnership in the property of the mine, be it understood that the capital invested, until the time when there shall be a surplus profit over and above the expences, is not to be immediately deducted from the profits, with preference to the contractor, but the profits are to be divided,* the capital remaining so invested during the continuance of the partnership, (*mientras no se separe la compama*).

SECTION X.

The Merchants or Dealers in silver who receive it without having advanced any thing to the owners, or encountered any risk, shall pay for it at the full value, and if they give in exchange for it any goods, the latter shall be charged at the regular price, and shall be of good quality; and I strictly ordain and command that the said Merchants or Dealers in silver shall receive it from the Mine Owners, being assayed, and the fifth part deducted therefrom (as Royal duty) conformably to law, and as repeatedly enacted by Royal Decrees, in order to prevent its being illegally disposed of in any of the different ways in which my Royal rights are infringed: And I further declare that in those districts where such assaying or deducting of the fifth part cannot conveniently be managed, on account of their distance from the Royal treasuries or marking offices, the Merchants or Dealers shall bind themselves before the Royal Court and Territorial Deputation, to take the metal forthwith to the office (*caxa*) of the district, in order to fulfil the said obligation of paying any Royal dues, and to verify the preformance of the like as regards quicksilver, according to the establised custom in New Spain, the said court and Deputation, allowing them a certain time for carrying all this into effect, and giving notice of the said obligation to the Royal officers whom it may concern, so that if the said persons should fail to fulfil the same, such silver shall be deemed to be confiscated, and the said officers shall take steps to obtain possession of it, and to inflict the other penalties imposed by the laws upon the defrauders of my Royal rights.

---

* It must be understood, I presume, that the profits are to be divided in proportion to the number of barras or shares so held in partnership by the supplier.

SECTION XI.

All the Merchants of the mining districts shall keep a correct and light balance and scales, in which only all the silver and gold shall be weighed; and they shall never use for this purpose steel-yards, however large the masses or quantities of the metal may be; and they must also keep weights marked and properly adjusted according to those which they have received from the proper Royal authorities; and I permit the respective Deputies to inspect the same from time to time, (without prejudice to the regular inspection by the Royal Court and public Magistrate), and to take care that the weighing be always justly and correctly performed, to the end that, in case any fraud should be discovered, and also in case of the repetition of such fraud, proceedings may be had before the competent Royal Court for the imposition of penalties proportioned to the nature and character of the offence, the said Court hearing and receiving information on the subject from the Deputies of the District.

SECTION XII.

All the working Miners must keep their tools and utensils marked, and if any one shall purchase them from any workmen, or receive them in pledge, he shall pay for them double the value.

SECTION XIII.

The aforesaid merchants and contractors may, for their satisfaction, and that of the owner, heat the blocks or ingots of silver (mixed with quicksilver) over a charcoal fire, but not over a flame, or in any manner by which it might be reduced to a state of fusion, except in crucibles; and they may also be allowed to separate them so as to examine them within, but this must be done as well as trying its quality, by heating it upon a counter, or in such manner that the owner may be able to collect and carry away all the waste and refuse fragments of his silver.

SECTION XIV.

Every contractor has the right of appointing at any time an inspector (*interventor*) to any Mine-owner whom he contracted to supply, although it be not so expressed in the contract; but be it understood, that such interventor is only to attend to the correctness of the accounts, and to have power over the money and effects; but not to interfere with or obstruct the working of the mine, which belongs entirely to the mine owner; he may, however defer the carrying on of the operations, by presenting an account to the Deputies, requesting the Appointment of surveyors, but this only in cases which will admit of such delay.

SECTION XV.

Whereas the operations of mines in a course of working, particularly where they relate to the draining thereof, cannot be impeded without great injury, I command that if the contractor for furnishing supplies from time to time shall neglect to provide them in such manner that at the proper time of paying the wages (*rayas*), there shall not be sufficient to pay them, and the Mine-owner foreseeing this event, shall have called upon the contractor accordingly, and given notice thereof to the Deputation, then not only the wages shall be paid with the best furnished part of the mine, and even with the very implements and utensils, but the Mine-owner shall be entitled to demand immediate execution against the contractor for what is due to him, and to apply for money to any other person, or treat with a new contractor, whose claim shall be preferred to that of the preceding one, whenever the mine begins to yield a profit.

SECTION XVI.

Those who under pretence of obtaining supplies of mining operations, shall in any way misapply the capital and effects furnished to them for that purpose, shall not only be bound in their persons, and all their property, for the repayment of the same, and for all damage done, or interest due to the party, without being allowed the privilege of miners, or any other whatsoever, but shall be punished in manner suitable to the nature, heinousness, and circumstances of the offence; more particularly so, if they shall have received the advances in confidence or trust, all this being regulated by the dispositions of Section XXIX. of Chapter III.

SECTION XVII.

The searchers, (*cateadores*) workers who are paid by receiving part of the metal, (*buscones*) and labourers in general, and other persons who shall offer stones and specimens, falsely pretending that the same are the produce of a mine, thereby soliciting supplies for such supposed mine, with intent to defraud and deceive the unwary, shall be punished with all the rigour of the law, according to the circumstances, heinousness, and maliciousness of the offence, to be proved before the proper court, according to the provisions of Section xxix. of Chapter III. of these Ordinances.

CHAPTER XVI

OF THE FUND AND BANK OF SUPPLIES.

SECTION I.

WHEREAS by my above-quoted Royal Decree, of the 1st of July, 1776, I was pleased to relieve the body of miners of New Spain from the double duty of one real in each mark of silver, formerly paid to my Royal Treasury, under the name of Seigniorage, granting them, at the same time, the right of imposing upon their silver the half, or two third parts, of the said contribution, for the purpose of aiding and promoting the new and respectable establishment to which these Ordinances have reference ; and considering at the same time that the destination of the same, most conformable to my beneficent intentions in this respect, would be the formation of a fund for advancing supplies to the mines, the present insecure and fluctuating state of the mines in general being, for the most part, occasioned by the want of capital, with the aid of which there is no doubt they would be put in a more secure and flourishing condition, to the great advantage of my Royal Treasury and of the public. For these purposes, and keeping in view the proposition laid before me by the Royal Tribunal of the important body of the said miners, I have thought proper to decree and command, that all the silver entered in my Royal Mint in Mexico, or in any other that may be established in the Kingdom of New Spain, and all silver that shall be remitted to those in Spain on account of individuals, (and which must at all times have been at first assayed, and the fifth part deducted) shall henceforward pay two thirds of a real (*probably per mark*) towards the formation, preservation, and increase of a fund for the mines, and that no Mine-owner whatever, shall be exempted from such contribution, not even those to whom for any just cause I may have granted, or may in future grant, a remission or diminution of the duties on metal, which appertain to my Royal Treasury.

SECTION II.

The management, collection, and custody of the monies to be raised in this manner, shall be always at the disposal, and under the controul, of the said important body of miners, to whom they belong, by means of their Royal Tribunal General in Mexico, which represents them: after deducting from these monies whatever may be necessary for the support of the said Royal Tribunal, and of the college, and for the instruction of young persons intended for the mining business, of which mention will be made hereafter ; and all extraordinary and particular expences which may be incurred for the common interest and advantage of the said body of Miners, all the rest, and the successive augmentations thereof, shall be entirely devoted to furnishing supplies for the working of the mines throughout the kingdoms and provinces of New Spain, a bank being established for that purpose, according to the regulations laid down in the following Sections.

SECTION III.

For the management and business of the said bank, there shall be one principal factor, or more if necessary, a person of intelligence and experience in the method of supplying mines by contract, who shall be subject to and dependent upon the Royal Tribunal General of the Miners, and be appointed

by them in the election, by a majority of votes; they also having the power
to remove him at pleasure, and without being obliged to assign any reason
for such removal.

SECTION IV.

Such factor either may be paid by a per centage on the property of the
bank, or by a fixed salary, or in both these ways, as may be deemed expedient by the Royal Tribunal, according to circumstances; but he must give
bail and such securities for his conduct, as shall be satisfactory in the opinion
of the chiefs of that Tribunal.

SECTION V.

The gross amount of the capital of the bank, which shall be in money, or
in gold and silver bullion, shall be preserved in chests, of which there shall
be four keys, which shall be in the possession and keeping of four of the
principal persons belonging at the time to the Royal Tribunal; but the goods
and merchandize for the supplies of the mines, and such part of the capital
as shall be necessary for the current business and operations, shall be in the
possession and at the disposal of the said factor, he and the said persons
above-mentioned, being respectively responsible for what may be entrusted to
his and their care.

SECTION VI.

The Royal Tribunal General of Miners shall cause to be made out in the
factory every year, in the month of December, an account of the contents of
the warehouses and stores, and a cash account and balance; two of the said
principal persons of the Tribunal assisting at such operations; and moreover,
they shall take the accounts of the factor without prejudice to their right of
inspectisg the said accounts at other times, whenever they shall think it proper and prudent to do so.

SECTION VII.

The Royal Tribunal shall keep an account and correspondence with the
Mine-owners, who have their supplies by contract from the bank, and shall
receive and reply to their letters, and give the necessary orders to the factor
for these purposes.

SECTION VIII.

For carrying on the business of the factory there shall be such writing
clerks engaged as the factor shall think proper, he having the power of proposing them; but they are to be appointed, and their salaries are to be fixed,
by the Royal Tribunal, and they are to be paid by the bank; and the factor
is to have the power of diminishing them, on giving verbal notice thereof to
the Royal Tribunal.

SECTION IX.

The factor shall receive all silver which is remitted by Mine-owners contracting for their supplies with the bank, and shall exchange it for coined money at the mint in Mexico, paying in the first instance into the principal treasury all duties on the metals which may not have been paid in the provincial treasuries; with this understanding, however, that, before it is remitted to Mexico, the said mine-owners shall make declaration at the treasuries, or marking offices, in their respective districts, of the quantity of silver intended to be remitted without paying the duties on metals, and shall take out the proper permits for its removal, under an obligation to make a return afterwards to the said treasuries, shewing that the said duties have been paid, so that all frauds may be avoided, and the necessary quicksilver properly purified, under the penalty of confiscation of all that shall be sent in any other manner, and of incurring the punishments imposed by law upon defrauders of my Royal rights; and the officers in the districts shall give notice to those in Mexico, in order that the latter may take care that the provisions of this present Section be complied with.

SECTION X.

The said factor shall pay the interest (*réditos*) on the capital received at the bank, the salaries of persons employed, and all other sums whatsoever, upon warrants from the Royal Tribunal, by means of which, and the corresponding receipts, he shall make out and justify his accounts; but for the purpose of remitting supplies, whether in money or in effects, to persons with whom an account current is kept, no particular warrants shall be necessary, but it shall be sufficient for him to act under the general orders of the said Tribunal, given conformable to Section VIII. of this present Chapter, as to whatsoever shall be at his disposal, according to Section VI. of the same.

SECTION XI.

It shall be the duty of the factor to buy the goods and merchandize necessary for the supplies of the mines, according to the best of his judgment, and agreeable to the orders of the Royal Tribunal, entering them in a separate book, and preserving the invoices.

SECTION XII.

All goods delivered on account of the bank in the way of supplies to Mine-owners, must be of the best quality; and when in Mexico, at the current prices of Mexico; and when in mining districts, at the current prices in those districts, if the bank shall have a warehouse or magazine in the same, or the **goods be carried thither on account of the bank.**

SECTION XIII.

To qualify all proposals or demands relating to the supply of mines, the Royal Tribunal shall require the owners to produce their titles of property and possession, and such certificates, informations, and further proofs, as may be necessary to establish whatever they may have asserted concerning the actual state and condition of the mine ; in order that, after the papers have been properly examined by the assessor, the required credit may be given, if the proposals appear to be fair and well founded ; in which cases the Royal Tribunal is to make all necessary enquiries, both officially and secretly, with the greatest prudence and circumspection ; taking, or causing to be taken, such measures, judicial or extra-judicial, as shall appear to them necessary for regulating their conduct with regard to such supplies ; and all these documents are to be kept in their archives.

SECTION XIV.

During the time that the funds of the bank shall be sufficient to furnish all the mines for which there shall appear to be a fair and well-grounded claim to be supplied, the claims of those Mine-owners shall be first attended to, who are most in want thereof, without any distinction of persons, and without any preference being shewn, except on the score of the necessity and urgency of the case, the Royal Tribunal in such cases acting with that justice and impartiality which ought to be observed in all their transactions.

SECTION XV.

When the claim is thus ascertained to be proper and admissible, the terms and conditions, under which the supplies are to be furnished, shall be settled with the Mine-owner, and before the contract is concluded, it shall be laid before the Royal Tribunal, conformably to the provisions of Chapter XV. of these Ordinances ; the great bank of supplies not enjoying any privileges to the prejudice of other banks, or of individuals who supply mines ; and afterwards the contract, thus approved of, shall be executed in writing before the clerk of the Tribunal, and orders shall be given for furnishing the supplies accordingly.

SECTION XVI.

In mines which are thus supplied by the bank, Interventors shall be appointed, who shall be trust-worthy persons, of good character ; and they shall, jointly with the Mine-owner, receive and keep, the money and goods supplied by the bank, in cellars and chests, whereof there shall be two keys ; they shall apply them in a manner they think best, and they shall be present at the payment of the wages, shall sign the accounts, shall watch and inspect the workmen as they go into and out of the mines, and also the metals that are taken thereout, and shall be present at the reduction of the metal from the ore ; and, in short, shall concern themselves in all that is done in the name of the bank, agreeable to the instructions given them, until the time when the supplies shall have been repaid.

SECTION XVII.

The Interventors shall not oppose any arrangements that are made by the Mine-owner or administrator, in regard to the economy and management of the labour, or any works which may have been determined on in the mine ; provided, however, that in cases where considerable expence must be incurred, the Royal Tribunal shall first of all be consulted.

SECTION XVIII.

The interventors shall not interfere in the appointment of persons employed in a subaltern situation in the mines, but they may observe the conduct of such persons, in order to represent to the Mine-owner any thing which they may think requires amendment ; and if the same be not amended, they shall inform the Royal Tribunal thereof, in order that this latter body may make provisions for its amendment, and may do all in its power to keep the Interventor and the Mine-owner upon good terms, acting in concert together, and uniting their services towards the advancement of the operations.

SECTION XIX.

The Interventors shall be paid weekly the salaries that are allowed them, on account of supplies ; and when these shall have been repaid, their services shall be rewarded in proportion to the benefit which the bankers receive from them, and to the time and labour which they devoted to the cause, and their good conduct : but if, on the contrary, any fraud, concealment, or other improper practice shall appear on their part, whether to the prejudice of the bank, or to the Mine-owner, they shall be severely punished in proportion to their offences, by the proper judge, according to the provisions of Chapter III. of these Ordinances.

SECTION XX.

In case of any competition arising between any individual and the said bank, as to the supplying of a mine, I declare that the individual contractor shall have the preference, provided, that the proposed terms of supplying the mine, are the same in both cases ; and in order that the said bank may not throw any impediments in the way of a free supply of the mines, I declare also, that this kind of business shall continue to subsist as before, the bank having no other object but to remedy the scarcity of supplies, and to promote as much as possible, the flourishing condition of the mines.

13

CHAPTER XVII.

OF SURVEYORS FOR THE OPERATIONS OF THE MINES, AND THE REDUC-
TION OF THE METALS FROM ORE.

SECTION I.

IN order that the mines may be worked with stability and good effect, and that the full attainment of riches they contain may be accomplished, it is desirable that their operations should be directed by persons well acquainted with the principles and rules of the natural and practical sciences, and arts connected therewith, and who understand the best means of applying such knowledge, in consequence of their own experience ; for which purpose, and in order that Mine-owners may not be misled in the appointment of persons whom they shall take into their employment, accounting perhaps some persons to be well informed who may only possess a superficial knowledge, or choosing others who may be no otherwise qualified than by having resided a certain time in the mining Districts, without possessing either judgment or science, and without any claim but the recommendation of their friends ; and observing how much difficulty there is in correcting such errors, be they voluntary or involuntary, all which leads the Mine-owner into placing a blind and dangerous confidence upon important points, in persons unworthy of such confidence, and has occasioned them very serious losses ; in order to guard against these evils, and that the surveyors may be worthy of public confidence in all things connected with their art, 1 ordain and command that in every mining district there shall be one or more intelligent persons, who are well instructed and particularly acquainted with geography, subterraneous architectures, and hydraulics, and also, with mechanics, and the arts of carpenters, smiths, and masons, as far as such arts are necessary in the operations of mines, which persons are to be called Mining Professors ;* and also other persons well skilled in the science of minerals, commonly called mineralogy, and in the modes of extracting metals from ore, and reducing them to a state fit for use, commonly called metallurgy, which persons are to be called Surveyors of reduction ; (*Peritos Beneficialos*) ; and these latter, as well as the former, are to be examined, approved, and appointed by the Royal Tribunal General of Miners, and without such qualification they shall not be entitled to any credit, in causes which may arise, or otherwise, but shall be considered as intruders, and shall be excluded and fined whenever they shall interfere in any thing which relates to the surveyorship of mines, although they may

---

* Literally, practical Surveyors, (*Peritos Facultatioos*), but I have used the expression Mining Professor, as most consistent with the duties assigned to them.

offer themselves as bachelors of arts, land surveyors, architects, or masters of works, or as having been administrators of mines, or as having been in any way employed in the same.

SECTION II.

The said Mining Professors shall have in their possession the necessary and proper instruments for measuring mines, whether subterraneously or on the surface, which instruments must always be true and correct, and made according to rule, so that there may be no failure, or irregularity in the performance of such operations ; for which purpose they shall be inspected and examined at the time when the said persons are appointed, and afterwards on the occasional visits (*of the Deputies.*)

SECTION III.

The Surveyors of reduction shall have a suitable public laboratory, provided with furnaces and machines for grinding and washing the metals, as also with the proper ingredients, utensils and correct balances and weights, and every thing that may be necessary for making assays, on a small scale, and also for reducing by smelting, one, two, or three quintals of ore.

SECTION IV.

The Mining Professors are to examine at the proper time, and to give certificates of examination to all persons desirous of being employed as miners, or mining-captains, to direct the under-ground operations, and to persons employed in the lining of mines, and in the brick-work, and to the carpenters and smiths ; and I prohibit all persons from exercising such offices, or from employing themselves in the quality of masters in any place, where such business shall be going on, without having the above certificates of examination, under the penalty of three months imprisonment for the first offence, and of being banished from such place for the second, which punishments are to be imposed by the respective Territorial Deputies.

SECTION V.

The Surveyors of reduction of each mining district, shall examine, and give a certificate of approbation to all persons offering themselves as amalgamators, smelters, and refiners, without which certificate, no one shall be capable of being employed in any of these capacities, at any work, or reducing Establishment, under the penalties contained in the preceding Section ; and I ordain that, all these examinations, and all others, treated of in the present Chapter, shall take place, without any fees being received thereupon, and altogether gratis.

SECTION VI.

If any person shall pass from one Mining District to another, after having been examined and approved of by the proper authorities in that which he has left, there shall be no necessity for a further examination, but he shall produce his certificate, signed by the proper professor, and attested by the clerk, or in default thereof, by the Deputies of the District and two witnesses.

SECTION VII.

The said Mining Professors, and Surveyors of reduction, shall, at the time of their appointments, take a solemn oath before the Royal Tribunal, in due form, but gratis, that they will at all times, and in all cases, discharge their offices well and faithfully, to the best of their knowledge, without fraud, deceit, or any bad intention whatsoever; after which, they shall not be required upon every occasion which may arise judicially or extra-judicially to repeat the same; since, when the oath has been once administered, as above, they are ever afterwards to remain bound by it.

SECTION VIII.

The most perfect credit is to be given to the said mining Professors and Surveyors of reduction, in all matters connected with their office, but they may be objected to in case they have been appointed by the Judges; and when one has been appointed by one party in a suit, the other party may appoint another, and the Judge elect a third in case of their disagreeing, although they need not belong to the same District; but these objections and appointments of new Professors, shall not take place where there is reason to suspect that they originate in fraud or malice, or a wish to delay the determination of the case.

SECTION IX.

The Mining Professors and Surveyors of reduction, shall be present at all the visits (of the Deputies) to the Mines and Establishments, and shall observe and comply with every thing that is laid down in these Ordinances, and shall give their assistance in all cases properly belonging to their business, in which it may be required by the Judges and Deputies; taking on account thereof, such fees as shall be settled by a proper table of fees, which fees shall be proposed by the Territorial Deputations to the Royal Tribunal General; and when that body shall have gained information upon the subject, and consulted with the Viceroy thereupon, the said Viceroy shall, by means of such information, resolve and determine what fees are to be received, and without this previous authority the taking of fees shall not be carried into effect.

SECTION X.

In the interval that must elapse before the College for the education and instruction of young persons intended for the business of metallurgy, mineralogy, and other sciences necessary in the operations of mining, (the establishment of which college will be treated of in the next Chapter), shall supply a number of persons properly qualified, according to the provisions of the preceding Section, to fulfil the object of these Ordinances, I command that all persons at present employed in the operations of measuring mines, projecting shafts, and pits, and other important works, connected with the operations of the mines, whether appointed from having the name of land surveyors and measurers of mines, or from having been highly esteemed in the Mining Districts for their practical knowledge, shall present themselves before the Royal Tribunal General, in order to be examined, and to obtain the certificate of examination, without any fees being required, (as is provided by Section v. of this Chapter), and to exhibit the instruments which they use, in order that they may be examined and approved of; and in default thereof, they shall not be entitled to any credit either in causes which may arise, or otherwise; and if in any works directed by them any mischief should happen, the Mine-owner or Administrator who has employed them, shall not be excused from the responsibilities and penalties imposed by these Ordinances, and by the laws in general, upon all persons acting without the authority of surveyors, in cases where surveyors are required.

SECTION XI.

All persons to be appointed Mining Professors, or Surveyors of reduction must be either Spaniards, Mestizos derived from them, or noble Indians of known birth, parentage and education, and of good life and manners; under which circumstances these employments are always to be accounted honourable and meritorious, and persons who have served in them with fidelity, shall enjoy all the privileges of miners, and shall be eligible to higher occupations either in the mines or otherwise, having their seat in the public sittings next to the Judge and Deputies of the District, in the order of the seniority of their appointments, and without any distinction being made between the Mining Professors and Surveyors of reduction, who are to be treated with like and equal honours and distinctions.

CHAPTER XVIII.

OF THE EDUCATION AND INSTRUCTION OF YOUNG PERSONS INTENDED FOR THE MINING BUSINESS, AND FOR THE ENCOURAGEMENT OF THEIR INGENUITY.

SECTION I.

To the end that there may never be wanting a supply of persons of good education, and instructed in all the learning necessary for carrying on the operations of the mines, and that what has been hitherto acquired by long and painful experience, in the course of many centuries, being the result as well of the progress of the different Mining Countries, as of the individual skill and industry of the American Miners, may be preserved in a more certain and effectual manner, than by mere tradition, which is usually scarce and fallacious ; I will and ordain that the College and Schools of Miners, which have been proposed to me for these purposes by the Deputies Genera of the said important body of Miners, shall be erected and established, or, i already established, that they shall be maintained and supported in the forr and manner contained in the following Sections.

SECTION II.

There shall be for the present maintained, and provided with board and clothing in a suitable manner, twenty-five children, either Spaniards or noble Indians of legitimate birth, the near relations, or decendants of Miners, having always a preference in such appointments, and particularly those whose ancestors have resided in the Mining Districts.

SECTION III.

I grant besides free entrance into the Schools, and gratuitous iustruction therein, to all children whose fathers or tutors may wish to bring them up to the mining business, such children being sent every day from their homes to attend the lessons ; and I further command that all children of the above mentioned quality and birth shall be admitted to live in the College as pupils upon paying the expences of their maintenance while they are in the College.

SECTION IV.

The necessary secular professors are to be appointed at the said College with proper salaries, for the purpose of teaching the mathematics and experimental physics, which are conducive to the carrying on and advancement of mining operations.

SECTION V.

There shall also be appointed masters in such parts of mechanics as are necessary for the preparing and working of timber, metals, stones, and other materials used in the construction of buildings, machines, and instruments for carrying on the operations of the mines, and the reduction of the metals, and there shall also be a master of the arts of drawing and designing.

SECTION VI.

The said College is to bear the Title of " The Royal Seminary of Miners," and two secular Priests of mature age are to reside in it, one as Chaplain-rec-

tor, the other as Vice-rector, who are to superintend the religious and political education of the children, to see that they devote a due proportion of
their time to these purposes, and to say Mass to them every day in the year.

SECTION VII:

The immediate controul and direction of the said Royal Seminary shall be
entrusted to the Director General of Miners, to whom I grant the privilege
of proposing to the Royal Tribunal the proper persons to be appointed to the
professorships, and to other employments; and also the nomination of the
children who are to be admitted as collegians, (*Colegiales de ereccion*), or
pensioners, supposing them to possess the necessary qualifications; and he
shall also, after hearing the opinions of the respective masters of the college,
propose the arts and sciences proper to be taught therein, and the method to
be pursued in teaching them, so that the Royal Tribunal may be able to determine upon what is most proper; and it shall also be entrusted to the said
Director to observe and take care that all persons employed in the college
fulfil the duties of their situation, and to form particular rules for the government in the detail of the said college, which he shall also lay before the Royal
Tribunal, by them to be submitted to the Viceroy, who after obtaining the
necessary information on the subject, shall lay them before me for my Royal
approbation, having obtained which the said regulations shall be observed
and carried into effect, with exactness and punctuality.

SECTION VIII.

The expences of erecting, perserving, and supporting the said Royal Seminary, shall be defrayed out of the general fund of Miners, according to the
provisions of Section III. of Chapter XVI. of these Ordinances.

SECTION IX.

The said seminary shall be under my Royal protection, and immediately
subject to and dependant upon the Royal Tribunal General of Miners, in all
its concerns and appurtenances.

·SECTION X.

For the election and appointment of master professors of the sciences,
which are to be taught in the schools of the college, there shall be issued,
at a certain fixed time and place, letters of convocation; and to those who
present themselves for the appointments certain problems in the respective
sciences shall be delivered by lot, which they are to return with their solutions within three days, on condition, however, that before the delivery of
problems to such persons, the director shall have presented to the Royal Tri-
unal the solutions of each of them separately folded and sealed up, which

are not to be opened till each candidate shall have delivered in his solution; when a due comparison shall be made between the sealed solutions and the solutions of the candidates respectively, and on the day when all this takes place, the candidate shall hold a public sitting of two hours, lecturing upon such points as the Director shall propose to him at the moment, in the presence of the Royal Tribunal, and its secretary, who shall attest all that has been done (*acto*) upon this occasion, and enter it in his register.

SECTION XI.

After the conclusion of the said public act, the Director shall propose three of the Candidates for each professorship, one of whom shall be elected by the Royal Tribunal by secret ballot, and in case of a difficulty arising by there being an equal number of votes, (for any two or three of them), he who was first proposed shall have the election.

SECTION XII.

The said master Professors of the College, besides lecturing every day theoretically and practically, shall be each of them obliged to deliver, once in every six months, a treatise or dissertation upon some useful subject connected with the mining business, and the sciences relating thereto; which dissertations shall be read to the Royal Tribunal, and preserved in their archives, in order to be printed and published at a convenient opportunity.

SECTION XIII.

The Collegians and Students of the Seminary shall every year hold public exercises in the presence of the Royal Tribunal, in order that, having shewn the progress they have respectively made, they may be rewarded and distinguished according to their merit.

SECTION XIV.

The above-mentioned young persons, when they have concluded their studies, shall go for three years to assist in the Mining Districts, and to practice the several operations under the Mining Professor, or the Surveyors of reduction, of that district to which they are attached, in order that, having received a certificate signed by such Professors or Surveyors, and by the Territorial Deputies, they may be examined before the Royal Tribunal, as well in theoretical as in practical knowledge, and on being approved of by the same, shall receive their diploma (*titulo*), without paying any fees whatever; and they may be then appointed Mining Professors, or Surveyors of reduction, of the Mining Districts, or Interventor, where the supplies are furnished by the bank, or to any other suitable situation.

SECTION XV.

In order, more effectually, to advance the cause of instruction and improvement in the several important objects of the said College, and in the manner most useful to the mines ; I ordain and command that, the Mine-owners and Mine-suppliers who bring their silver to Mexico, shall be obliged to deliver to the said College, specimens of their ores, in sufficient quantities to admit of their quality and properties being examined, and of the most advantageous method of reduction thereof being ascertained, in order that, the Royal Tribunal, judging by the result of these experiments, may determine what will be most conducive to the improvements which are the object of the present arrangements.

SECTION XVI.

Considering that industry and ingenuity will make the most common productions of nature useful to man, and that, on the other hand, without them, the great advantages and profits expected from productions naturally rich and abundant, are often altogether defeated ; I ordain and command that industry and ingenuity in the mining business, which is of such vast importance therein, be excited, encouraged and supported, with all possible activity, intelligence, and discretion ; and that, particular care and attention be bestowed in observing the use and effects of the machinery, and the operations and methods at present employed in the application of it ; in order, that whatsoever is really useful and complete in its kind, may be preserved in full perfection, without being gradually lost or depreciated, as often happens in such cases ; and that, whatsoever, by comparison with better or more complete methods, shall appear capable of reform, may be brought into practice with the greatest degree of perfection and efficacy, without either suffering ancient prejudices founded on ignorance and caprice, to obstruct the progress of ingenuity, or ill-founded innovations, to disturb what is good and perfect in its present state.

SECTION XVII.

All persons who shall invent or propose any kind of machines, engines, expedients, operations, or methods, for facilitating the working of the mines, which shall produce any advantage, however small the same may at first appear, shall have a fair hearing and attention ; and if, on account of their poverty, they are unable to make the experiments requisite for exhibiting their invention, the expense thereof, as well as the construction of the necessary machines, shall be defrayed out of the general fund of the Miners, provided that they shall demonstrate and calculate the effects of such projects ; and that, the Director General of Miners, and the Professor of the College, shall approve the same, and consider them capable of being carried into effect : but ill-founded projects, arising out of erroneous principles, or want of practical knowledge, and from which the deluded authors are easily led to expect vast and imaginary profits, shall be rejected as useless and contemptible ; and if, the authors of such projects shall renew their applications, they shall receive no attention, unless they make the experiments at their own expense, and establish themselves the utility of their inventions ; and in all cases, the papers relating to such inventions shall remain in the archives of the Royal Tribunal, in order to be referred to, if necessary.

SECTION XVIII.

All useful and approved inventions, which, after being established and put in practice generally for the space of more than one year, shall be found to succeed, are to be rewarded with a patent (*privilegio exclusivo*), to continue for the life of the author, in order, that no one may make use of his invention, without his consent, and without allowing him a reasonable share of the profits, actually derived from the use of such invention.

SECTION XIX.

Whoever from his experience, study, and observation, or from having travelled in other countries, shall offer for adoption any machine, expedient, or mode, employed in other countries, or in former times ; and the same on examination and experience be approved of in the manner laid down by Section XVII. of this Chapter, he shall be considered and rewarded in the same manner as if he had been the actual inventor ; since, although his ingenuity may be less, his merit and trouble may perhaps have been greater, and the public advantage will be exactly the same, whether such mode result from an invention absolutely new, or from the introduction and application of a practice never before adopted in the place where it may be proposed.

CHAPTER XIX.

OF THE PRIVILEGES OF THE MINES.

SECTION I.

Although the regulations laid down in these Ordinances for the discipline, economy, and method of working, which are to be adopted in the mines of New Spain, are calculated to diminish considerably the dangers and difficulties which have hitherto occurred in carrying on this most important business, rendering by their powerful co-operation the richest of the mines more accessible, and the lawful modes of acquiring them less hazardous ; nevertheless, considering the difficulties and uncertainties which usually attend operations of this kind, and that their precious produce is the especial grant and favour of Providence to my dominions in Spanish America, and is the chief source of the prosperity of my subjects, the support of my Treasury, and the spring and moving power of the commerce of all my dominions, and to a great degree of that of the whole world ; I have therefore granted and do grant to those persons who apply themselves to the working of the mines of New Spain, all the favours and privileges .which have been granted to the Miners of Castille and Peru, in all respects in which they are capable of being adopted to the local circumstances of Spanish America ; and are not at variance with any thing established by these Ordinances.

SECTION II.

Moreover, I award to the scientific profession of mining, the privilege of nobility, to the end that all persons who devote themselves to that important study and occupation, may be esteemed and treated with all the distinctions which are due to so honourable an employment.

SECTION III.

Mine-owners shall not be liable to be arrested for debts, neither shall the administrators, superintendants (*veladores*), keepers of tallies, (*rayadores*), nor other persons, serving in the mines or establishments be so liable, provided that each of these persons in every such case remain in confinement within the mine or establishment to which he belongs, with an obligation upon his master to apply the third part of his salary or dues to the payment of his debts, as long as he remains in the service of such mine or establishment, and if he quits the same without engaging himself in any other mine or establishment, then he may be imprisoned.

SECTION IV.

If a sequestration be laid on the Mines or Establishments of any proprietor, in the interval during which the silver extracted therefrom is being applied in satisfaction of the debt, he shall only receive out of the produce what is absolutely requisite for his support, according to the circumstances of his family and condition ; but always with a view to this circumstance, that the situation of the creditor be not prejudiced, instead of amended, by the sequestration.

SECTION V.

If an execution be levied upon the other property of a Mine-owner, there shall always be reserved to him, a horse, with bridle and saddle, a baggage mule, his arms, bed, and the clothes commonly used by himself, his wife and children, and absolutely necessary to their decent appearance ; but all costly dresses, ornaments, jewels, or trinkets may be seized under the execution.

SECTION VI.

The Royal Tribunal of Miners shall inform me, through the Viceroy, of all deserving persons belonging to the Mining profession, especially of such as may have quitted it on account of having consumed their capital therein, or being too old and infirm to pursue it ; pointing out also such of them as the Tribunal may consider to be the most deserving of my Royal favour, in order to their being appointed to the offices of judges in the Mining Districts or Establishments, if that should appear expedient ; as well for the purpose of rewarding them according to their merits, as of filling the said office with practical and intelligent persons, such as the law-requires.

SECTION VII.

Children and descendants (*hijos y nietos*) of Mine-owners, and Mine-suppliers, who have been extensively concerned in the Mines, deserve also particular consideration ; and for that purpose the Royal Tribunal shall also inform me, through the Viceroy, of the merits of their ancestors ; in order that my Royal favor may appoint them to civil, military, and ecclesiastical appointments in America, if I shall think proper to do so.

SECTION VIII.

I declare that Mine-owners and Administrators shall not be prevented, or in any way impeded by their said employments, from obtaining and serving the offices of magistrates and governors, (*justitia y regidores*), of the cities, towns, and places of the Mining Districts, or of any others ; but they are not compelled to accept such offices, nor to be fined for declining the same, during the time of their employment in the Mines, if they desire to excuse themselves on that account.

SECTION IX.

In the allotment of ground for the purpose of building houses, in renting such as may be already built, and in providing themselves in the squares and market-places of the Mining villages, towns, and districts, not only with the articles necessary for the Mines and Establishments, but also with the supplies and provisions which may be wanted for their homes and families, the Miners are to be preferred to other persons, and to be treated with that respect which is due to their important profession : and I grant them the liberty of hunting and fishing in the mountains, forests, and rivers, of cutting wood, and making charcoal, and of pasturing their cattle in the grazing places and watering places, (*exidos y aguages*), in the same manner as any other inhabitant is permitted so to do, supposing such mountains, forests, rivers, grazing places and watering places, to be public property ; for in all such as are private they must pay the proper dues, as before enacted : and, finally, they are to enjoy all the cus-toms and privileges enjoyed by the inhabitants of any Mine-town, although they (the Miners) may not reside therein ; provided only that, in order to entitle them to these privileges, their Mines or Reducing Establishments be situated in the same district as such Mine-town.

SECTION X.

The excessive profusion of Miners in the employment of their capital, and their extreme imprudence, and irregularity, whereby themselves and their families are speedily reduced to distress, and their capital is diverted from the operations of mining into other channels, being as notorious as they are destructive ; I will, and ordain, that the Judges and Deputies of the Mine-towns and Districts shall advise thereupon, and in cases of necessity, expostulate with the Miners, particularly with those who are in prosperous circumstances, cautioning them against extravagant expense or idle profusion ; and if this should be found insufficient, then that they shall make a report to the Royal Tribunal General of Miners, in order that the latter, after satisfying themselves of the reprehensible conduct of the Miner, concerning whom such report is made, may appoint a person to watch over his interests (*curador*), or in some other manner, provide for the preservation of his property, as in the case of an incorrigible spendthrift.

SECTION XI.

In order to avoid the evil and injury, spiritual as well as temporal, occasioned by games of stake (*envite*), and hazard, and even by those which are permitted, when carried to excess, and also by other public diversions and festivities ; I prohibit most rigorously, in all Mine-towns and Districts, among masters as well as workmen, all those games at cards which have been before prohibited by Royal Edicts and Decrees, and also all playing at those games which are permitted, for a larger stake than is compatible with fair and moderate relaxation and amusement. And with equal rigour, I prohibit all playing at dice or tabas, and also cock fighting, and all other shameful diversions ; since they not only occasion the loss of time which might otherwise be devoted to labour, but lead to vast loss of property, and sometimes even to outrages and murders. Wherefore, I strictly enjoin the Judges and Deputies of all Mine-towns and Districts, to enforce with the utmost vigilance, the provisions of this present Section, on pain of being themselves wholly responsible for the neglect of the same, and of being liable to the penalties imposed by the said Royal Edicts and Decrees against all transgressors.

SECTION XII.

The Royal Tribunal General of Miners, shall observe, and carry into effect, whatsoever is contained in the present Ordinance, and shall cause them to be observed and fulfilled by all the subalterns, dependents, and inferior persons of all their body, each in his particular department, without any injurious evasions which might alter and corrupt their true spirit and intent, maintaining them always in their full vigour, and causing others to do the like. And the Territorial Deputations of Miners shall also observe, and carry into effect, whatsoever relates to them in these Ordinances, and shall cause them to be observed and executed with the utmost punctuality and correctness; and they shall not, any more than the Royal Tribunal General, act, or permit others to act, in contravention of their real tenour and meaning, in any manner whatsoever; and I only allow, in case of any point arising, which is not comprehended herein, or provided for in the Royal Orders which I have issued upon this subject, that both the one and the other (the Royal Tribunal General and the Deputations) should regulate themselves, in the decisions thereof, according to the form and practice of the Consulates of Commerce of my European and Spanish Dominions, as far as the same shall be practicable in such cases; but all doubts which may at any time arise, as to the true meaning of any one or more of the Sections of these Ordinances, shall be proposed by the Royal Tribunal General to the Viceroy, in order, that he, after obtaining the necessary information thereupon, may transmit them to me for my Royal determination.

SECTION XIII.

Finally,—I order and command, the Governor and persons composing my supreme Council and Chamber of the Indies, the Royal Audiencies and Tribunals of New Spain, the Viceroy thereof, the Captains and Commandants General, the Governors, Intendants, Ministers, Judges, and all other persons whatsoever whom these enactments may in any degree concern, to conform themselves precisely to these Ordinances, observing and fulfilling them, each in his respective department, with the most rigid exactness; regarding their contents, as positive and perpetual Laws and Statutes, and maintaining them, and causing them to be maintained inviolably, notwithstanding any other laws, ordinances, observances, customs, or practices, which might militate against them; since, if any such there be, I revoke them expressly, and declare, that they shall be of no effect, prohibiting, as I hereby prohibit, that they (the present Ordinances) should be explained or interpreted in any manner whatever, since it is my will, that they shall be understood literally, as they are written. And, in like manner, I most strictly enjoin all Tribunals, Magistrates, and Courts, comprehended in this and the preceding Section, to give their most effectual aid and assistance to the provisions and enactments of these my Royal Ordinances; preventing, as far as it is possible, all kinds of disputes and contentions, which will always incur my Royal displeasure, as being prejudicial to the administration of justice, and to the good government, tranquillity, and happiness of the important body of Miners of those my Dominions; for which purpose, I have commanded the dispatch of this present Decree (*cédula*), signed by my Royal hand, sealed with my private seal, and countersigned by my underwritten Secretary of State, and of the general Department of the Indies, and which shall be entered in the General Office for the dispatch of the affairs of the Indies, and in the several offices in New Spain, which it may concern. Done at Aranjeuz, the twenty-second day of May, in the year one thousand seven hundred and eighty-three.

I, THE KING.

JOSEPH DE GALVEZ.

Entered in the General Office of the Indies, Madrid, the twenty-fifth day of May, in the year one thousand seven hundred and eighty-three.

D. Francisco Machado,
A true Copy.

JOSEPH DE GALVEZ.

TRANSLATION OF THE LAWS OF SPAIN,

"CONCERNING MINES OF GOLD, SILVER, AND OTHER METALS,"

CONTAINED IN THE

18th Title of the " Novisima Recopilacion"

PUBLISHED IN 1806,

With Translations from the "Commentaries on the Mining Ordinances of Spain."

BY DON FRANCISCO XAVIER DE GAMBOA.

NOVISIMA RECOPILACION, Vol. iv., p. 366.

TITLE XVIII.

CONCERNING MINES OF GOLD, SILVER AND OTHER METALS.
Laws 47 and 48, tit. 32 of the ordinamiento de alcalá.

LAW I.

*The right of the King in mines of gold, silver, and other metals, salt springs
and wells, and the prohibition to work them without royal licence.*

All minerals of gold, silver, lead and every other metal whatsoever in
our realms belong to us ; therefore no one shall presume to work them without our especial licence and command ; and in like manner salt fountains,
reservoirs and springs, which are for the manufacture of salt, belong to us ;
wherefore we command that the rents derived therefrom be paid to us and
that no one presume to intermeddle with them, except those to whom former
kings our predecessors, or we ourselves shall have granted the privilege or
who shall have acquired them by immemorial possession. (Law 3, tit. 13,
book 6, R.*)

LAW II.

Don John I. at Birbisca in the year 1387.

*Concerning the right of searching for mines by a person in his own lands
and those of other persons, and to work them, with the premium which is
assigned.*

Inasmuch as we are informed that these our kingdoms abound and are
rich in minerals ; therefore as an act of grace and favor to our said kingdoms
and the inhabitants and residents of the cities and incorporate villages and

---

* This reference and subsequent similar ones are to a previous compilation of Spanish law
entitled " Nueva Recopilocion" also called the " Collection of Castile," (T.)

other places and to persons connected with the church, notwithstanding that by ourselves and our royal ancestors in those privileges which have been granted as a matter of favour there has been reserved by us minerals of gold, silver, and other similar metals; it is our pleasure that henceforth all said persons and all others whomsoever, of these our said kingdoms, may search for, examine, and may excavate their said lands and estates and remove from them said minerals of gold, silver, quicksilver and tin, stone and other metals; and that they may search and excavate for minerals in all other places whatsoever, not prejudicing in their searches and excavations, the rights of other persons, and acting with the permission of the owner; and all the minerals which shall be thus found and extracted shall be divided as follows: First, there shall be delivered and paid therefrom to the person who extracted the mineral all expenses of excavating and extracting, and of the remainder, the said expences having been deducted, the third part shall belong to the person extracting the mineral, and the other two parts to ourselves.—(Law 3, tit. 13, Book 6, R.).

LAW III.

Don Philip II. and during his absence, the Princess Donna Joanna at Valladolid, January 10, 1559.

Concerning the incorporation of mines of gold, silver, and quicksilver in the Crown, as Royal Patrimony, and the mode of working them.

It being very well known and understood, that great benefit and advantage as well to ourselves and our royal patrimony as to our subjects and native citizens, and the public good of our kingdom has followed the discovery, opening and working the mines of gold, silver and quicksilver and other metals in which these our kingdoms, as we learn from very ancient periods, are very rich and abundant; and although by the law which was enacted by king John First (see previous law) the right was granted to all persons to seek for, excavate and work the said minerals and metals, and by the same law is designated the mode of apportionment, yet experience has shown and we now perceive that there are very few mines which have been or will be discovered and worked; and yet it is said that there are some persons who have knowledge of rich mines, and for gain keep them concealed and will not make known their discovery, which, as we are informed, has arisen, among other causes, from the fact that the greater part of said mines have been and are sold to noblemen and other persons in the kingdoms, and from the grants by bishoprics and archbishoprics and provinces, so that in relation to said mines almost the whole kingdom has been thus distributed and divided up. And considering that the mines were granted to particular persons, and that no others should interfere with or embarrass them in the discovery or working of them, and especially that in many of the said grants it is expressly and par-

15

ticularly provided, that without the licence and consent of the first grantees, no one could seek for or work them, and the noblemen and persons who hold the said property so purchased, either in order to avoid the expence and labor, or to relieve themselves from attention to the business, have bestowed, and now bestow very little care and diligence in the discovery, occupying and working said mines ; and as very little advantage has followed to them or is now received from estates so purchased, and the benefit which we ourselves and our subjects and citizens might receive has been and continues to be generally impaired ; and it being represented that others will not engage in the discovery, occupation and working of said mines, because although by the said law of King John, the portions which each party is to have are designated, yet, as it is so ancient and has been so little in use and practice, and as neither in that nor in other laws of the kingdom have the many doubts and difficulties which may occur been determined, and which have thus occasioned disputes and lawsuits, they are apprehensive and fearful of expending their money and labor in such discovery and working of the mines ; and principally having doubts whether the said law and its provisions is to be understood to embrace the mines which were rich, and from which great and excessive interests might have been expected and obtained ; and in order in relation to all the matters aforesaid, to make such provisions that the obstructions and difficulties aforesaid may come to an end, and effectually to secure the rewards and advantages so that many persons of wealth may invest their property in the discovery, occupation and working of the mines, by whose diligence and labor God will permit the developement of the riches and bounties which are hid and covered up in the earth, and our own royal patrimony will be increased, the condition of our subjects ameliorated and our realm enriched ; and having commanded some of our principal accounting officers (*contadores*) to confer with some of the members of our council, and in a matter of so great importance, we having ourselves conferred with and been consulted by them ; it was resolved that we should direct the issue of this our ordinance, and adopt the provisions hereinafter written ; and we have approved of the same, and will that it shall have the vigor and force of law in the same manner as if it had been done and agreed to in the Cortes on the petition of the representatives (*Procuradores**) of the cities and villages of these kingdoms.

First, we reclaim, resume, and incorporate in ourselves and in our crown and patrimony all mines of gold, silver and quicksilver in these our kingdoms in whatever parts or places they may be or be found, whether the estates of the crown or of the nobility or clergy, or belonging to the public or the town-

---

* The general meaning of the term "procurador" is the agent or representative of another in the execution of a power entrusted to him. Anciently the "Procurador de Cortes" was a person deputed by the cities or villages having a vote in the Cortes to represent them and to agree in their name to the services asked by the king. (T)

ships or vacant lands, or in the estates and portions and lands of individuals, notwithstanding the grants which by ourselves or by the kings, our ancestors have been made, to any and all persons whatsoever of whatever state, rank and dignity they may be, and for whatever causes and reasons, as well grants for life or for years, and on condition as those perpetual, free, and without condition ; all which said grants, in view of the facility and generality with which they have been made, and the prejudice which to ourselves and our crown and royal patrimony has ensued and still continues, and the damage and injury to the public good, and the well being of our subjects and citizens which have resulted and may continue to result, and for other just causes thereto moving us, we revoke, annul and vacate, and it is our will and pleasure that the said minerals now and henceforth without any other act of seizin or possession, belong to our said crown and patrimony in accordance with, and as by the laws of these our kingdoms and ancient usages and customs properly belong to us in the same manner as if said sales and conveyances or any of them had not been made and granted ; and that the same shall alone continue as binding and in full force in relation to the mines of silver and gold in which the persons aforesaid, to whom said grants were made, or others in their name, and by their consent, have commenced working and are actually now at work at the date of these presents ; and moreover, it is our pleasure to recompense and indemnify the noblemen and other persons to whom the said grants which we have thus revoked, have been made, according as upon the examination of their conveyances of title, the causes and reasons of their being granted, their conditions and limitations and the extent to which they have been performed and complied with, on their part may appear just and reasonable. And to this end we order that those who hold the said grant, and claim the said recompense, shall present their claims within one year, in order that in view of the matters aforesaid, they may receive the recompense which is their due.

Second, inasmuch as the reducing and incorporating in ourselves and our royal patrimony, the said minerals as above stated is not with the view that we alone, or others in our name alone may seek for, discover, and work the said minerals, but rather that it is our purpose and pleasure that our subjects and native citizens shall participate in and have a portion of said minerals, and may employ themselves in the discovery and working of them ; therefore, by these presents we give permission and full authority to our said subjects and citizens, that they may freely without any other licence from ourselves or any other quarter, examine, seek for and excavate the said minerals of gold and silver, in all parts whatever of the estates of the crown, or of the nobility or clergy, and all other persons whatsoever, as well in public territory, common and unappropriated lands, as in the estates and lands of individuals, on paying the damage to the owners ; and that no person or persons shall interpose any obstruction or embarrassment neither on account of the said grants which have been made, and which as above stated we have revoked, nor for any other cause or reason whatsoever. And moreover, we grant the free privilege and full permission to all our said subjects and citizens, that in relation to the mines of gold and silver which they shall have discovered and have had registered in the manner hereinafter declared, to excavate and extract the said metals, and operate and work them, and employ all the machinery, labor and diligence which may be necessary, without being obstructed or embarrassed by ourselves or any one in our name, nor by the occupation of any other person, and that the within limits and boundaries of the mine which has been so discovered and registered, no other person be allowed to excavate and seek for, nor to work and labor upon the same. The said discoverer complying with the provisions hereinafter stated and ordained. It being understood that they may hold, explore and discover said mines in said regions and places except in the mines of Guadalcanal and one league around them, and in the mines which are discovered within the limits of Cazalla, Aracana, and Galarroca and a quarter of a league around each of them. All which shall have full and complete effect notwith-standing any leases which we may have ordered to be made of any of the minerals of our kingdom. (Chapter 1, 2 and 3 of the law 4. Tit. 1, Book 6, Recopilacion.) (a)

LAW IV.

WITH GAMBOA'S COMMENTARIES.

Don Philip II. at San Lorenzo, Aug. 22, 1584.

New ordinances which are to be observed in the discovery, occupation and working of the mines of gold, silver, quicksilver and other metals.

CHAPTER I.

OF THE NEW CODE OF MINING ORDINANCES, THE OLD ORDINANCES RE-MAINING IN FORCE, SO FAR AS THEY ARE NOT REPEALED BY THE FOR-MER, AND HOW FAR THEY ARE TO BE OBSERVED IN THE KINGDOM OF NEW SPAIN.—A NOTICE OF THE ORDINANCES FRAMED BY SOME OF THE VICEROYS, AND OF THE ORDINANCES IN FORCE IN PERU.

ORDINANCE I.

WE revoke, annul and make void the edicts issued at Valladolid, and all

(a) (Note (a) to the original text.)—The sections from the 3d to the 7th of this law as con-tained in the former compilation, treat of the portion which shall be received by persons discov-ering and working the mines in conformity with the second law ; concerning the forms and modes of proceeding in their discovery and registry, and of the powers and rights of the discoverers ; which sections are omitted as they will be found to have been repealed in the new ordinances contained in law 4th of this title published in 1584 ; and for the same reasons are omitted those comprehended in 78 sections in the royal edict of Madrid, of the 18th March, 1563, contained in law 5, Tit. 13, Book 6, of the Recopilacion.

laws of the Ordinamiento, Partidas, and all other laws, edicts, common law, and customs whatsoever, so far as they are in opposition to the provisions of this law: and it is our will and command, that they shall, in such respects, be void of all force or authority whatsoever, except only that the 3d law of this title, so far as it relates to the annexing to our royal patrimony the mines of gold, silver and quicksilver, in these our dominions, of which grants had been made to individuals, by departments, bishoprics and provinces, shall remain in force and authority; in conformity to which law, and to these our laws and ordinances, exclusively of all others, it is our will and command that the said mines shall be worked, and all suits and disputes be determined, which may in any manner arise concerning the said mines, or any matter annexed to, touching or relating to the same.

CONTENTS OF THE COMMENTARY ON THIS ORDINANCE.

1. Why called ordinances of the new code.
2. The old ordinances are repealed, so far only as they are at variance with the new.
3. They remain in other respects in full force and authority, and are to be referred to as rules in the decision of suits at law, and contain matters of much importance.
4. An objection to this doctrine refuted.
5 and 6. By the laws of the Indies, the ordinances of Castile are to be observed in New Spain, when not contrary to the laws framed for each province in particular.
7. An account of the ordinances of Peru, issued by the viceroy Don Francisco de Toledo. They are very important in certain cases, as affording rules for New Spain.
8. The ordinances of the new code, are the great authorities for all mining suits in the kingdom of Mexico.
9. No new system has been found necessary during the term of 176 years.
10. An account of the ordinances framed by the viceroy Don Luis de Velasco and the Marquess de Montesclaros, and which are not observed. Reflections on the idle desire of some persons for new ordinances.
11. The Viceroys are not at liberty to alter the ordinances, and no new ones can be set up, unless confirmed by the Council, after having been submitted to the consideration of experienced and intelligent persons.
12. and 13. There is no need to have recourse to Germany and France for ordnances, our own being sufficiently copious.

COMMENTARY.

1. The eighty-four heads into which this law is divided, are denominated ordinances of the New Code, and were originally appended to the old Collection, into the body of which they are introduced, in the edition printed at Madrid, in 1642. The name of *New* is conferred upon them in contradistinction to the old ordinances contained in the 5th law, of the same title and book, and to other laws of older date, relating to the working and supplying of mines; which,—

2. Are totally repealed by this 9th law, " so far as they are in opposition to its regulations;" so that the repeal applies to those points and in those cases only, wherein the former laws and ordinances are opposed to the 9th

law and no further ;* it being clearly the intention of the legislator to confine the repeal to the case of their being found to conflict: wherefore he wills
and commands, that the former laws and ordinances shall, " in such respects,"
be void of all force or authority whatsoever.

3. Whence it follows, that the rules and ordinances of the 5th and other
laws of this title, are still in force and authority, so far as they are not contrary to the regulations subsequently established by this law; and that they
are to be referred to and observed as rules for the decision of suits, and for
the working of the mines, as in fact the course and practice of the Courts of
New Spain. And this is confirmed by the consideration, that it is a rule
that the alteration or repeal of a law, is not to be presumed ; † combined
with the indisputable fact, that there are many very essential and necessary matters in the old ordinances of law 5, which are omitted and passed
over in silence in law 9, evidently to avoid repetition, and not with the intention of repealing or altering the other laws, in points as to which nothing contrary is ordered. And by a comparison of these several ordinances, which
we shall take care to institute in every instance, it will appear in what cases
the old ones, being at variance with the others, are repealed ; and in what
cases they are not repealed, no contrary regulation being established by
law 9.

4. And although, according to the wording of the ordinance, which says,
" except only that the 3rd and 4th law of this title, which relates to the annexing to our royal patrimony the mines of gold, silver and quicksilver, in
these our kingdoms, &c. shall remain in force and authority ; in conformity
to which law, and to these our laws and ordinances, exclusively of all
others, it is our will and command that the said mines shall be worked, and
all suits and disputes be determined," it might seem (from the expressions
" except only" and " exclusively of others"), that the other laws and ordinances are repealed, yet the fact is, that the repeal is to be taken with the
qualification " so far as they are in opposition," and extends no further ; and,
therefore, the old as well as the new ordinances, still equally form parts of
the body of the collection, so that the old ordinances are to be referred to
and followed, in any case omitted or passed over in the new code, for in such
cases there can be no variance or opposition between the former and the
latter. And the object of giving new authority to the fourth law, was to prevent so important a matter as the annexation of the mines of all metals to the

---

Leg. 28. ff. de legibus, " sed et posteriores leges ad priores pertinent, nisi contraria sint,"
puod multis argumentis probatur.

† D. de Luca, de jurisd. disc. 107, n. 10. " Legum correctio non est præsumenda, sed vitanda."
Et in decis. Sicil. sub. tit. de feudis, u. 214. " Statutum semper debet interpretari, ut minus
corrigat jus commune." Paris, cons. 110, n. 6, and cons. 84, n. 3, vol. 3. Et legum correctio
vitanda est, imo nec præsumitur ; neque in dubio facienda est ; nec ex paritate rationis." Tuschi, liter. c. concl. 1036. Velasco, in loc. comm. liter. c. concl. 229. 8 lib. 1, n. 37. Castillo,
Controv. lib. 5, p. 2, cap. 125, n 7.

crown, from being interpreted to be at variance with, and therefore repealed by, the second ordinance of this 9th law, whereby a grant of the mines is again made to the subjects of the crown, generally. It was therefore necessary to declare that the 4th law still remains in force and authority; but it must not be inferred as a consequence, that such of the old ordinances as relate to points and matters passed over in law 9, are repealed.

5. It appears then, that the working, denouncement and registry of mines, all disputes and questions at law which may arise concerning them, and all other matters incident or annexed thereto, are to be governed and determined by these ordinances of the new code, and by the old ordinances where not at variance with them. And that the former are the fundamental laws by which this important business is to be regulated, not merely in regard to the kingdom of Castile, for the mines of which they are framed, by Philip II. who promulgated them on the 22d of August, 1584, but also for the Indies, and for the kingdom of New Spain, in particular. By one of the laws of this latter country it is provided,* "That the viceroys shall confer with persons of intelligence and experience, upon the laws of Castile which relate to mining; and that if they shall be found suitable, they shall cause them to be observed, practised and enforced in the Indies; provided they be not at variance with the laws framed for each province in particular; and that they shall render a due report of those which are not put in practice for directing the observance of those which they may consider necessary to be enforced."

6. And by the other law† concerning the discovery and working of mines, the viceroys, presidents, and judges of audiencies, are commanded to maintain and enforce the precise and punctual observance of the ordinances of the new code, and not to enlarge the period of four months, after which a mine is liable to be denounced, if not sufficiently worked.

7. In obedience to the laws above-mentioned, the viceroy, Don Francisco de Toledo, drew up, for the kingdom of Peru, certain mining ordinances, a compendium of which is given by Don Gasper de Escalona, in his *Gazophilacio Real de el Peru*,‡ and which he illustrates with his usual erudition. And these ordinances (the observance of which is directed by a special law of the Indies, referring to the laws drawn up by this illustrious viceroy on every subject),§ together with the laws of Castile, where not at variance with the former, are to be looked to as the rules for deciding suits at law concerning mines, and for their economy, government and working, in that kingdom. And they are at the same time very useful to the judges, ministers and miners of New Spain, for their guidance in regard to certain questions and matters not touched upon in the ordinances of the new code, nor in the laws of

---

* Law 3, title 1, book 2, of the Collection of the Indies.
† Law 6, title 19, book 4, of the Collection of the Indies.
‡ Lib. 2, part 2, cap. 1, page 104.
§ Law 37, title 1, book 2, of the Collection of the Indies.

the Collection of the Indies.   For it is most reasonable, that in cases not noticed in the proper law of any country, the law or custom of the nearest province should be referred to; particularly where so close an affinity exists as between those of Peru and New Spain."

8. Still, however, the ordinances of the new code, and the laws of title 19, book 6, of the Collection of the Indies, are the fundamental authorities for all suits at law and other matters concerning mines, in the kingdom of Mexico, and the judges, advocates, mining deputies and miners of that kingdom, must conform to the spirit of these laws in every case that may occur.   And accordingly, it is usual with them, in their several proceedings, to say, that they act in conformity with the ordinances of the new code, or that the practice of such and such persons, is contrary to these ordinances, in such or such respects.

9. And although, in the space of 176 years, since 1584, the date of their promulgation, the disputes concerning mines, which the thirst for gain has excited, have been most frequent, and although the mining districts of this kingdom are very numerous, it does not seem that any want of a new system has ever been felt, or that any of the viceroys or ministers of audiencies, zealous as they are, have ever recommended any new plan or set of rules.

10. It is true that there were some ordinances drawn up by the viceroy, Don Luis de Velasco, and subsequently, some others framed by the Marquess de Montesclaros, the latter dated the 13th of March, 1606, and countersigned by Pedro de la Torre, and which were submitted to the king, and proclaimed at the mines; but all the thirty-six chapters they contain, with the exception of the 28th and 29th, which concern the bankruptcy of miners, relate to the distribution of quicksilver, salt and maize, among the miners, on account of the crown, with respect to all which the course now pursued is different, salt and maize being no longer distributed at all; and the distribution of quicksilver being conducted upon a new system: the ordinances in question, therefore, furnish no rules for the working of mines.   And the same remark applies to the five *ordinances of government,* an account of which is given by Don Juan de Montemayor,† and which merely give rules for certain particular cases, but do not regulate the mode or system of supplying or ascertaining the boundaries of mines, nor any other matter relating to their working.   And although there are some persons who would wish to have a set of rules more explicitly adapted to the circumstances of particular cases, in reference to the varieties of situation, ground or other details;

---

* L. de quibus 32. ff. de leg. and Jason, n. 6, in Card. de Luca, de servit. disc. 2, n. 19. "Licet autem istud sit statutum diversæ ditionis, nullamque vim legis habeat extra proprium territorium, et cum non subditis; nihilominus, stante præsertim regionum vicinitate, recte attendendum videtur pro argumento seu præsumptione: cum in his casibus, qui non habentur in jure expressé determinati, sive pro interpretatione juris dubii recte deserviant leges, vel consuetudines aliarum præsertim adjacentium civitatum vel provinciarum."

† Montemayor, Ordenanzas de Govierno, from the 77th, fol. 44.

yet these are, in fact, matters which the law cannot descend into ; * whilst the exercise of a sound discretion will suggest rules for the determination of omitted cases. And that our ordinances, if regard be had to their sense and spirit, are sufficiently copious, is proved by the experience of so long a period, in a country where there are so many mineral districts as in New Spain. And were distinct ordinances framed for each separate mining district or province, endless confusion would be the consequence ; whilst, as the case now stands, all the most general and important points are defined by the laws of the new code.

11. And the viceroys can on no pretence alter the laws ; their power, however high, not being absolute, nor extending to legislation, but merely authorizing them to advise with and report to the sovereign ; but the existing laws and ordinances must be observed with exactness, until the confirmation of other new ordinances by the council.† And if necessity or convenience require that others should be framed, the office of preparing them is not to be entrusted to any individual, but to several persons, selected from among the many disinterested and intelligent men who may be found in each province ; and who will be enabled, by their practical knowledge, to throw the strongest possible light on the subject ; and such is the direction of the law of the Indies cited above.‡

12. There is no need to have recourse to other nations for mining ordinances ; our own are amply sufficient. In framing them, recourse was had to the laws of Germany, as stated and explained by Agricola, although the mines of that country, differ from ours in the dimensions assigned to them, and in the mode of managing them when held by partners.§ It cannot be denied that the laws of the State of Hesse are very copious, little less so indeed than those of the Palatinate, as illustrated and stated by Krebs ;‖ but almost every contingency is comprehended in, and provided for, by our own.

---

* L. 10. ff. de leg. "Neque leges neque senatusconsulta ita scribi possunt ut omnes casus qui quandoque inciderint comprehendantur, sed sufficit ea quæ quandoque accidunt contineri." L. 12. ff. ead. "Non possunt omnes articuli sigillatim aut legibus aut senatusconsultis comprehendi, sed cum in aliqua causa sententia eorum manifesta est, is qui jurisdictioni præest ad similia procedere atque ita jus dicere debet." Franciscus Baconius, de justit. univers. aphorism 10. "Angustia prudentiæ humanæ casus omnes quos tempus reperit non potest capere. Non raro itaque se ostendunt casus omissi et novi. In hujusmodi casibus triplex adhibetur remedium sive supplementum. Vel per processum ad similia. Vel per usum exemplorum licet in legem non coalureint, vel per jurisdictiones quæ statuunt ex arbitrio boni viri et secundum discretionem sanam, sive illæ curiæ fuerint prætoriæ sive censoriæ."

† Law 1, title 19, book 4, Coll. of the Indies. "And with respect to the discovery of mines, and the taking possession of and forming establishments in them, the laws and ordinances framed for each province are to be observed, being confirmed by us."

‡ Law 3, title 1, book 2, Coll. of the Indies.

§ Agricola, de re metall. lib. 3.

‖ Philip Helfric Krebs, de ligno et lapide, tom. 2, class. 3, de metall. et mineralib.

13. As to those of France (as is remarked by Helot, in the preface to his translation of Schluter*), the only circumstances worthy of remark are, the great care with which they provide for an investigation into the situation and arrangement of the mines, and their facilities as to water, so necessary for mining purposes ; and above all, for an inquiry, whether the person who registers the mine, has sufficient capital for the undertaking, and has provided a proper director for the mine, without which he is not to be allowed to work it.   As to all other matters, however, such as smelting, amalgamation, the registry and denouncement of mines, the keeping a proper number of hands at work in them, the measurement and alteration of their boundaries, and their economy and management, our ordinances are very copious ; and if they are not acted up to, the fault is not in the law, but in not enforcing it.

<hr>

CHAPTER II.

OF THE SUPREME RIGHT OF THE PREROGATIVE, IN THE MINES OF GOLD, SILVER, AND OTHER METALS.—OF THE RE-ANNEXATION TO THE CROWN OF ALL THE MINES, HERETOFORE THE SUBJECT OF GRANTS BY PROVINCES AND BISHOPRICS, IN ORDER TO GIVE AN INTEREST IN THEM TO THE SUBJECTS OF THE CROWN GENERALLY, WHEREVER SITUATE.—OF THE VERY AMPLE NATURE OF THE GRANT AS REGARDS THE INDIES.—OF THE PERSONS WHO ARE PROHIBITED FROM WORKING MINES.—OF FOREIGNERS, ECCLESIASTICS AND CURATES.

ORDINANCE II. LXVII.

II. AND in order to benefit and favour our subjects, and the natives of these kingdoms, and all other persons whatsoever, though strangers to these our kingdoms, who shall work or discover any silver mines whatsoever, discovered or to be discovered, it is our will and command that they shall have them, and that they shall be their own, in possession and property, and that they may deal with them as with any thing of their own, observing, both in regard to what they have to pay to us by way of duty, and in all other respects, the regulations and arrangements, ordered by this edict, in the manner hereinafter-mentioned.

LXVII.—Also, we ordain and command, that our administrator-general, and the administrators of departments, and such persons as may be appointed by them or their successors, to attend officially at the mines, and the justices, and notaries, and sworn clerks, who have been or may have been appointed by us, and who shall hereafter be appointed to use or exercise their offices thereat, shall not be at liberty to hold, and shall not hold, any mine,

---

* Schluter (Christophe Andre), De la fonte des mines, traduit par M. Helot. Paris, 1750.

or share of a mine, in any department in the kingdom, either by themselves or through any person acting for them, directly or indirectly, during all such time as they shall hold the said offices, under pain of being for ever deprived thereof, and of forfeiting the mine or mines they may hold, which shall go to any person who shall inform against them; and under the further penalty of forfeiting a moiety of their property to our exchequer: and that any person who shall take a part in any of the matters so prohibited, shall incur the like forfeiture of property and mines.

CONTENTS OF THE COMMENTARY ON THESE ORDINANCES.

1. By the civil law, mines, when in public ground, belonged to the sovereign, and when in private ground, to the owner of the land.
2 and 3. From their great value, universal custom has made them a right of the prerogative.
4. Upon this point regard must be had, in each kingdom, to its own particular custom.
5, 6, and 7. By the law of the *Ordenamiento*, that of the *Partida* and those of Castile, mines are made a royal seigniory.
8. John II. allowed them to be worked, subject to an acknowledgment of two third shares of the produce.
9, 10, 11, and 12. Philip II. revoked various grants of the mines, which had been made, by provinces and bishoprics, and vested them in the crown; and his meaning was to grant an interest therein to his subjects, wherever situate, under the regulations of the old ordinances, and those of the new code.
13. The grant, as respects the Indies, is most ample, and extends generally to all the subjects of the crown.
14 and 15. Whence Lagunez and the Cardinal de Luca infer, that the mines of the Indies are not vested in the crown.
16 to 20. This opinion refuted.
21, 22, and 23. The reasoning of Lagunez answered.
24. The mines, in the hands of the subject, are liable to all the incidents of property, as objects of alienation or other dealings.
25 and 26. The grant of the sovereign to his subjects is a qualified grant, being accompanied with the obligation of obedience to the ordinances.
27 and 28. The extension of the grant to foreigners, is to be understood as applying to those only who are naturalized.
29 and 30. The clergy, and religious persons, and curates in particular, are prohibited from working mines, except such as descend to them.
31. A contrary practice prevails in New Spain.
32. Decisions of the councils of Lima and Mexico on this point.
33. Conclusions of Friar Juan de Paz, in favour of the curates of New Spain, upon the construction of a decision of the council of Mexico.
34. Recorded fact of a church mine being leased and worked, in the mining district of Zimapan.
35. The Indians were particularly named in the grant, because even the Spaniards were originally prohibited from working mines.
36. The mines of the marquisate of el Valle are common to all.
37. Of other persons prohibited to work mines.

SECTION I.

38. The working of quicksilver mines is permitted.

39. It does not appear that any such were worked in New Spain, in early times after its discovery.

40 and 41. Two royal orders, confirming certain directions for stopping up quicksilver mines in Quernavaca, and in the Sierra de Pinos.

42. Another precedent, to the same effect, from the office of the superintendent of quicksilver at Mexico.

43. The reason for not allowing the mines of this mineral to be worked in New Spain, is, that the quicksilver of el Almaden is disposed of on account of the revenue.

44 and 45. It was directed, by orders of the 4th of March, 1559, and the 22d of January, 1565, that the quicksilver should be sold at the greatest possible profit.

46. It was directed, by another order, of the 3d of June, 1567, that all quicksilver shipped on board the convoy, on account of individuals, should be seized.

46. The dealing in quicksilver otherwise than on account of the revenue is prohibited, and liable to a penalty.

48, 49 and 50. Because it would be prejudicial to the revenue, and injurious to the expensive establishment at el Almaden; and would give opportunity for much fraud and contraband dealing in bullion.

51 and 52. The merchants are prohibited from selling it, because if permitted, they would raise the price to an excessive rate, and this prohibition was obtained at the solicitation of the miners of New Spain and New Galicia.

COMMENTARY.

1. By the civil law, all veins and mineral deposits of gold or silver ore, or of precious stones, belonged, if in public ground, to the sovereign, and were part of his patrimony; but if on private property, they belonged to the owner of the land, subject to the condition, that if worked by the owner, he was bound to render a tenth part of the produce to the prince, as a right attaching to his crown; and that, if worked by any other person, by consent of the owner, the former was liable to the payment of two tenths, one to the prince and one to the owner of the property.[*]

2. Subsequently, it became an established custom in most kingdoms, and was declared by the particular laws and statutes of each, that all veins of the precious metals, and the produce of such veins, should vest in the crown, and be held to be part of the patrimony of the king or sovereign prince. That this is the case with respect to the empire of Germany, the Electorates,

---

[*] Lagunez, de fructib. 1. p. c. 10, n. 51, usque ad 54. Gutierrez, Pract. p. 4. quæst. 36. n. 59. Petrus Barbosa, in 1. divortio, §. si vir, ff. de solut. matrimonio, n. 18. Antunez, de donat. regiis part. 3. cap 12. per tot. Alfaro, de offic. fisc. gloss. 20. n. 101. aliique innumeri apud istos, et communiter DD. in d. §. si vir: qui omnes dictam distinctionem firmant: et pro jure fisci in fodinis repertis in loco publico, text. in C. unic. verb Argentariæ. Quæ sint regaliæ, Horatius Montanus de regal. verb. Argentariæ. Afflictis in tract. Quæ sint regalia, tit. 3. à num. 1. et pro jure privati in metallis fundi proprii, d. §, si vir, L. quosdam, Cod. de metall. lib. 11.

France, Portugal, Arragon and Catalonia, appears from the laws of each of those countries, and from the authority of various authors.[*]

3. And the reason is, that the metals are applicable to the use of the public, who ought not to be prejudiced by any impediments being thrown in the way of the discovering and working of their ores ; besides which, their products rank, not amongst those of an ordinary description, but amongst the most precious the earth affords, and therefore, instead of being appropriated to individuals, are proper to be set apart for the sovereign himself, whose coffers being thus enriched, he will be enabled to lighten the burdens of his people ; all which is set forth at length by the authors above referred to.[†]

4. This question, as is observed by the great Cardinal de Luca,[‡] has not received any general or uniform determination, but is decided by the laws and customs of each particular kingdom or principality. For upon the breaking up of the Roman Empire, the princes and states, which declared themselves independent, appropriated to themselves those tracts of ground, in which Nature has dispensed her more valuable products, with more than ordinary liberality ; which reserved portions or rights, were called rights of the crown. Among the chief of the valuable products, are the metallic ores of the first class, as those of gold, silver and other metals proper for forming money, which it is essential for sovereigns to be provided with, in order to support their warlike armaments by sea and land, to provide for the public necessities, and to maintain the good government of their dominions. And such is the course mentioned in the first book of the Maccabees, to have been pursued by the Romans, with regard to the mines of Spain ; such also is the plan adopted by our sovereigns, with regard to those of the Indies, some of which they have reserved to themselves, and the remainder they have left to their subjects, charged with the payment of the fifth, tenth or twentieth part of the produce. The above author, also, in the place cited, distinguishes the metals into those of the first, second and third class, by which means he determines several very important questions, without prejudice, however, to the laws, ordinances and statutes of each particular kingdom, which in each case claims the first notice.

---

[*] Antunez de donat. reg. lib. 3, cap. 12, n. 10. " Sed quamvis prædicti juris traditio et distinctio ab omnibus communiter sit recepta, tamen reges et principes in omnibus ferè orbis partibus eam non admiscrunt, imo peculiaribus legibus statuerint venas metallorum ubicunque inventas in locis publicis sive privatis ad se partinere et de regalibus esse ;" cum Rebuffo, Barbos Pereg Cabedo et aliis qui testantur de legibus Neapolis, Valentiæ, Cataloniæ, ut ipse de statuto Lusitaniæ. De Imperio, Arumæus, Discurs. Academicor. de jure publico, cap. 3, de regal. fisci, discurs. 15, §. 59, et seq. ubi etiam testatur de regno Hungriæ.

[†] Antunez ubi supr. n, 12, Solorz. de jure Indiar. lib. 1, c. 13, n. 12, et omnes sup. citati sub. n. 1.

[‡] Emin. de Luca, de regal. disc. 147, n. 17, usque ad finem.

5. In Spain, under the law of the *Partida*,* the property of the mines was so vested in the king, that they were held not to pass in a grant of the land, although not excepted out of the grant; and even though included in it, the grant was valid, as to them, only during the life of the king who made it, and required confirmation by his successors.

6. And by another rule of the same law,† the metals, amongst other things, were reserved to the sovereign, for maintaining him in honour, for defending his territories, for supporting his wars against the enemies of the faith and for relieving the people from taxes.

7. Afterwards, by a law of Don Alphonso XI. in the *Ordenamiento Real*,‡ copied in the collection of Castile,§ all mines of gold, silver or any other metal whatsoever, and the produce of the same, were declared to be the property of the crown, and no one was to presume to work them, except under some especial licence or grant, previously obtained, or unless authorised by immemorial prescription.

8. This rule was moderated by John I., and the law, as established by him,‖ permitted any person to dig or work mines, in his own land or inheritance, or with the permission of the proprietor, in that of any other individual: and to retain to himself, after deducting the expenses, one third of the produce, rendering the other two-thirds to the king. Whence it is evident, that the owners of private property, might prevent all other persons from searching therein for mines; and that the permission only extended to the searching for them on their own estates, the mines of which had, originally, been excepted by the sovereign out of his grants and charters.

9. Philip II.¶ acting under the authority of the council and chief ac-

---

* Law 5, title 15, Partida 2. "And mines, if there be any: and although it be not mentioned, in the grant, that the king retains to himself the things above-mentioned, yet it is not, therefore, to be understood that he to whom the grant is made, acquires a right to them: moreover, if the king should make over all these things to him by the grant, even then he cannot hold or use them, except during the life of the king who made the grant, and of any other who may please to confirm it." And see Gregor. Lop. at that place.

† Law 11, title 28, Partida 3. "The returns from the port, salt works, fisheries and iron works, and from the other metals, belong to the emperors and kings; and all these things were granted to them, that they might have wherewith to support an honourable establishment, to defend their lands and kingdoms, and to carry on war against the enemies of the faith; and that they might have no need to load their people with great or grievous burthens."

‡ Law 8, title 1, book 6, of the *Ordenamiento*.

§ Law 2, title 13, book 6, Collection of Castile. One of the most remarkable among the grants, is the *Privilegio rodado*, of Ferdinand the fourth, dated at Toro, the 13th of October, 1297, whereby, in consideration of the services of Don Alfonso Perez de Guzman, Governor of Tarifa; and particularly those displayed in the conquest of that town, and during its defence (on which occasion he threw the Moors a knife to kill his own son with, rather than surrender the town), the king made a grant to him of the town of San Lucar de Barromeda, with the thirds, and other things, including the mines. The grant is preserved in the house of the dukes of Medina Sidonia, his successors.

‖ Law 1, title 13, book 6, Collection of Castile.

¶ Law 4, same title and book.

countants, and considering, first, the benefits that his subjects, generally, would derive from working the mines of Spain, which had from of old been deemed to be both rich and abundant; second, the small number of mines actually worked, notwithstanding the grant of John I.; and, third, that though not worked by the proprietors, the exclusive grants that had been made by provinces and bishoprics, prevented any other person from presuming to work them; and considering also, that the above-mentioned law of John I., had not been enforced, and that there were various doubts and difficulties, not provided for by that or any other law; vested the mines, wheresoever situate, and whether in public or private ground,* in the crown; revoking the former grants thereof, the parties interested under which were to receive a compensation, upon exhibiting their claims within the term of one year.†

10. The object of so vesting them, was not that the right of searching for them should be limited to the crown alone, but that it should be freely extended to all the people, generally in such manner that they should be at liberty, without any licence from the crown or any other party, to try for mines in all places whatsoever, whether the ground belonged to the crown or any other lord, to abbeys or municipal corporations, wh ether it were public or waste ground, or whether it were the inheritance or soil of a private person, in which latter case, the owner had no power to put obstacles in the way of such search, provided he received a compensation for any damage done to his property, and were paid his third part of the produce, as directed by the law of John I. Besides these various other regulations were promulgated, which, with the above, are known by the name of the old ordinances, and to which we refer.‡

11. All which, as has been observed,§ are repealed by the new law of Philip II. except as to the vesting in the crown the mines of gold, silver and quicksilver, of which grants had theretofore been made to private persons, by districts, bishoprics and provinces; as to which they remain in full force and authority.

12. And by his second ordinance, which is now under consideration he grants permission to all persons, whether natives or foreigners, to search for mines, and declares that they shall be theirs in right of possession and property, and that they may dispose of them as of any thing of their own; provided

---

* "*Hæc et si quæ pari fuerant obnoxia juri,*
  Prælati proceres missisque potentibus urbes,
  Libera Romano liquerunt omnia regno."

  Ex Gunther, lib. 8. in Ligurino.

† Idem factum fuisse in Hungaria ex const. regis Mathiæ testatur Arumæus, de jur. public. disc. 15, §. 61. "Ut si aliquæ mineræ auri et argenti, salis vel aliæ fodinæ in possessionibus nobilium reperirentur, non auferrentur per regiam majestatem absque debita recompensatione."

‡ Law 5, title 13, book 6, Collection of Castile.

§ Above, ordinance 1, chap. 1, n. 2.

that they observe the rules of that edict, concerning the payments to be rendered to the crown, and the other matters regulated by it. And a similar provision was made by the first of the old ordinances.*

13. By the laws of the Indies, the Emperor Charles and King Philip II. made a similar grant to all their subjects, whether Indians or Spaniards, and of whatever station, condition, rank or dignity (except the governors, ministers, mayors, alcaldes and notaries attending at the mines, and some others who are also especially prohibited), authorising them to work the mines freely and without impediment, and making them common to all persons, wheresoever situate, provided that the Indians be not injuriously treated, and that no other parties be prejudiced ;† and likewise granting various immunities to the discoverers, whether Spaniards or Indians, as may be seen by reference to the municipal laws of the Indies.‡

14. From the very ample terms of this grant, as contained in the second ordinance, and in the laws and orders of the Indies, a doubt arises, whether the mines of those kingdoms are still to be regarded as the peculiar right of the crown, or whether they are to be considered as the absolute property of the subject : upon which point, Don Matheo de Lagunez,§ judge of the audiency of Quito, observes, that gold and silver, and the veins of all other metals whatsoever, in the Indies, are declared common, and that all persons are at liberty to try for them, wheresoever situate ; and that they are invited to do so, by the order of their catholic majesties, Ferdinand and Isabella, and by many other orders mentioned by Don Juan de Solorzano ; provided that they pay the fifth, and bring in the bullion to be stamped ; whence he infers, that the mines are not vested in the crown, and that consequently, so far as the Indies are concerned, all the rules of the civil law will apply, in reference to the question he is there treating of (which is simply, whether the metals are to be considered as products or not), and he conceives that the effect is precisely the same, as if the mines had been made private prop-

---

* Law 5, title 13, book 6, chap. 1. of the Collection of Castile.

† Law 1, title 19, book 4, Collection of the Indies. See ordinance 67 and 68, title 13, book 6, Collection of Castile, concerning prohibited persons.

‡ Title 19, book 4, Collection of the Indies.

§ Lagunez, de Fruct. 1. p. cap. 10, n. 63, 64, and 65. " In Indiarum tamen regnis auri argentive fodinæ, et similium metallorum venæ, communes diu sunc declaratæ, omnibusque permittitur ubicunque metalla quærere, et eruere : quinimo, et magnis prœmiis, et privilegiis, ad id. omnes invitantur per regiam schedulam regum catholicorum Ferdinandi, et Elizabeth, et alias pluries relatas per eruditissimum D. D. Joannem de Solorzano de jur. Indiar. tom. 2, lib. 5, cap. unic. à n. 22. ita tamen ut quintam partem omnium metallorum quæ extraxerint, regio fisco reservare teneantur : ex quibus ut ad supradictam nostram quæstionem redeamus circa metallorum, venarum et aliorum fructuum acquisitionem ; cum in Indiarum regnis mineralia dicta regio patrimonio non sint incorporata, sed potius libera, et omnibus cum dicto onere quinti obvia sint, absque dubio in Indiis locum habebunt omnia supradicta ad dict. L. divertio §. si vir, ff. de solut. matrim. et ad d. leg. item si fundi, §. sed si metalla, ff. de usufr. et ad cognitionem principalis nostræ quæstionis quando metalla fructus dicantur, et ad maritum, vel ad alium fructuarium pertineant ?"

erty, as they may be, by a particular grant ; and this he says is established by one of the laws of the Collection, and by the opinion of those who have treated of fiscal rights.

15. The Cardinal de Luca puts the same construction upon Solorzano's observations, for he says,* that upon the conquest of the new world, some of the mines of gold and silver were vested in the crown, whilst others remained the private property of the subject, who, however, was bound to render to the sovereign, a fifth, a tenth or a twentieth part of the produce, according to the nature of the mines and of the ground.

16. But with all the respect which is due to the judgment of so learned a minister as Lagunez, corroborated as it is by the opinion of the Cardinal de Luca, we cannot help regarding the mines of the Indies as a right of the crown, and construing them to be annexed to the royal patrimony, by the laws and orders above-cited : for Escalona, when considering these laws and orders, enumerates the mines as among the rights, and the most valuable ones,† of the crown, for which he cites the law of the *Partida*, and the copies of the letters of our sovereigns, to the viceroy, Don Francisco de Toledo. These letters always reserve this right, and were the viceroy's guide, in preparing the mining ordinances which he framed for Peru,‡ wherein he several times inserts a saving of this right of the crown.

17. Don Juan de Solorzano, supports§ the existence of this right of the crown in the Indies, as well as in Spain, referring to the order of their catholic majesties, giving permission to work mines, subject to the payment of a fifth, and also to other orders ratifying that order. And Alfaro, who refers to the same orders,|| confirms the opinion that the mines are vested in the crown, particularly in the Indies, where the gold and silver mines are found in rocky and cavernous places, not appropriated to any person, and conse-quently, belonging to the prince, as lord of the territory. Besides which, he considers all room for doubt removed, by their having been so vested by the law of Castile. Whence it is evident, that he considers that this law has

---

* De Luca, de regal. disc. 147, n. 22. " Quod moderno tempore quoque practicatum est in acquisitione novi orbis Indiarum, nam reliquis bonis in suo primo consueto statu relictis, aliquæ fodinæ argenti et auri regis effectæ sunt, atque regiæ coronæ incorporatæ ; reliquæ autem relictæ in dominio privato sub obligatione præstandi regi quintam partem, quandoque decimam vel vigesimam partem, juxta fondinarum, et regionum qualitatem, ut per Solorzanum, dict. tom. 2, lib. 5. part 2. c. 1, et unic. n. 23, et seqq.''

† Escalona, in his Gazophilacio, book 2, part 2, chap. 1, n. 2. " This duty (the fifth), is levied by virtue of the supreme right and seigniory universally vested in the princes, in right of their crown, over the minerals which Nature yields." So Gutierrez, Amaya, and others. Et ibid. verb. Quintos de cobre, fol. mihi 100. " All minerals and veins are rights and jewels of the crown." And see the margin of the ordinances of the viceroy, Don Francisco de Toledo, and several chapters of letters on the same subject.

‡ Escalona, ubi sup. page 101, book 2, part 2, chap. 1, Gazophil.

§ Solorzano, lib. 6, Polit. Ind. cap. 1.

|| Alfaro, de off. fisc. gloss. 20, s. 6, n. 103.

the same authority and force in the Indies, as in Spain, and that the municipal laws of the former countries have not severed the mines from the royal patrimony.

18. A further argument is drawn from a reservation made by the ordinances of Peru,* which (following the old law of Castile†) require a mine to be set out for the crown, of 60 varas in length in veins of silver, and 50, in those of gold, and contiguous to the discoverer's mine, who is to swear that it is on the richest part of the vein, although it is advisable, as the ordinance provides, to sell or lease this mine, from the risk of the ores proving poor.‡ And although it is not the practice, in New Spain, to set out such a mine for the crown, yet the payment of the fifth or tenth operates as an acknowledgment of the sovereign's right,§ and is a sufficient proof that all metallic ores are originally part of the royal patrimony.

19. Our opinion is further confirmed, by the circumstance, that no newly-discovered mine can be worked until registered, and that no old mine, once abandoned, can be worked again, until denounced and registered before the justice ; and that the boundaries of the mines cannot be assigned or the working conducted in an arbitrary manner, but according to the rules of the ordinances and laws, only ; so that an acknowledgment of the right is in fact made to the king, or to the justice in his name. And by the laws of the Indies, a licence must be obtained, previous to searching for mines or pearl banks ; and an oath must be taken that all discoveries shall be duly reported, for the better levying of the revenue.‖ And an additional corroboration of this opinion is derived from the circumstance, of permission being given to try for mines in the ground of any other proprietor, and of the latter being disabled from making any objection, provided a compensation be made to him for any damage to his property. For this, as we have already seen,¶ would not be tolerated by the civil law, were it not authorized by the crown, in the exercise of its supreme right of property over the mines, and were it not a consequence of their having been reserved for the general benefit of the subject, so that all persons should be at liberty to search for and profit by them. But after all, the strongest ground of argument is afforded by the laws of Castile and of the Indies themselves ; which give the subject an interest merely,** and not a separate, and absolute property in them, and which

---

* Escalona, Gazoph. book 1, chap. 15, and book 2, part 2, chap. 1, at the word Minas de S. M. page 99, in the 18th ordinance of the viceroy, Don Francisco de Toledo, title 1, concerning discoveries, page 108.

† Law 5, title 13, chap. 22, book 6, Coll. of Castile.

‡ Law 2, title 11, book 8, Coll. of the Indies. Escalona ubi sup.

§ Don Joseph Saenz, Tratad. de medidas de minas, cap. 3.

‖ Law 2, title 19, book 4, Collection of the Indies.

¶ Ubi sup. n. 1.

** Law 4, title 13, book 6, Collection of Castile, chap. 2. " That our natural-born subjects

authorise him to deal with them in such maner only, as shall be consistent with the regulations of the ordinances. And thus, although the grant gives a right of property, yet it only amounts to the cession of a partial interest, and not to an absolute transfer; the supreme right of property remaining vested in the crown.

20. The correct opinion then seems to be, that the property of the mines remains vested in the crown, and that as the sovereign cannot work them on his own account, he has given his subjects a partial interest in them, under various restrictions, and subject to various liabilities. And as a proof of this, it may be observed that, at first, the law made the quicksilver mines, amongst others, common;* that, subsequently, it was left to the discretion of the viceroys, to allow the discoverers of these mines such advantages as they might think proper;† but that finally, they were reserved for the use of the crown only,‡ and are not allowed to be worked in New Spain; all which is evidence of the supreme right of the crown.

21. Nor is Lagunez's opinion supported by his reasoning. For as to his first argument, founded on the declaration that the mines of the Indies are to be considered common, subject to the payment of the fifth; the fact is, that the acknowledgment of right implied in the payment of the fifth, and the performance of the other obligations to which the miners are subject, furnish an inference to the very contrary, namely, that the mines are vested in the crown.§ As to his second argument, although it is very true that private persons have a right of possession and property in the mines, yet the acknowledgment implied in the payment of a certain proportion to the treasury, is of itself sufficient to compel us to treat them as within the rights of the crown; and such, according to Arumæus and many other authors, is the light in which they are regarded in the empire of Germany, and in Hungary.‖ As to his third argument, we have only to observe, that by the laws of Castile,¶ the mines are granted to the subjects, *in possession and property*, with power to dispose of them, as of any thing of their own, and to search for them wheresoever situate, which goes much further than the mere saying, that they shall be *common to all*, which is the expression of the law of the Indies;** but yet all the mines of Spain, whether in public or private ground, are vest-

shall participate and have part." Law 1, title 10, book 8, Collection of the Indies. "For it is our will to make a grant of the other four parts, that every one may have power to dispose of the same."

* Law 1, title 19, book 4, Collection of the Indies. "Gold, silver and other metals."

† Law 4, title 19, book 4, Collection of the Indies.

‡ Montemayor, lib. 5, tit. 5, summary 8, concerning quicksilver, and the levying the duties thereon.

§ Vide sup. n. 20, marg.

‖ Arumæus, de jur. publ disc. 15, § 60.

¶ Laws 4 and 5, title 13, book 6, Collection of Castile.

** Law 1, title 19, book 4, Collection of the Indies.

ed in the crown; this vesting, as the law observes,* not being insisted on, with a view to their being worked on the sovereign's account, but for the sake of giving all his subjects an interest in the advantages derivable from them, subject to the payment of a third, a fourth or a fifth part of the produce· And viewing the subject in this light, the existence of this right and the annexation of the mines to the crown, are easily reconciled with the principle, that the mines are free and common to all; and with the exercise of a right of property over them, on the part of the subject.

22. And the laws and orders cited above, under which immunities are proposed, to incite the people to search for and work the mines, by no means prove that they are not still a right of the crown, for they undoubtedly are so in Portugal, where offers of similar immunities are nevertheless held out.† And this fact can at most only amount to evidence of an earnest desire for the promotion of the public good, by procuring the mines to be worked; which was the very object for which they were vested in the crown. So that the making them common to all and the giving permission to search for them, wheresoever situate, are proofs of the gracious disposition of the sovereign, who, in his desire to promote this object, has annexed the mines to the crown, has revoked the grants heretofore made, by provinces and bishoprics, and has rendered private property liable to a service, by disabling the proprietor from objecting to the mines being searched for or worked (provided a fair compensation be made to him for any damage to his property), and by establishing the principle, that the mines are excepted out of the grant of land under which such proprietor may hold.‡ And hence we may conclude, that the immunities thus offered in the Indies, the making the mines common, and the giving free permission to all persons to search for them, are evidences of the right of the crown, and not, as contended for by Lagunez, proofs of its non-existence.

23. It seems too, that he went out of his way, to involve himself in this question, for it has no bearing upon the principal point discussed by him, namely, whether the metals are products or not. For although they are not such, strictly speaking, since they do not reproduce; it is enough that they are emoluments or civil products, to make all the effects of the civil law attach;§ that is to say, to give an interest to the usufructuary, to the husband (when the wife has a mine for her portion), and to the tutor, who is entitled to the tenth part of the produce of the minor's property; all which may

---

* Law 4, title 13, book 6, Collection of Castile, cap. 2. "For the vesting the said mines in ourselves and in our royal inheritance, is not to the end nor for the purpose, that the said mines should be searched for and worked by ourselves alone, or in our name only; on the contrary, it is our intention and will that our natural-born subjects should participate and have part in the said mines, and should engage in discovering and working them, Wherefore, &c."

† Lagunez, de fruct. 1. part. cap. 10, n. 6, cum Acevedo et aliis.

‡ Antunez de Portugal, de donat. lib. 3, cap. 12, n. 14. in fin.

§ Lagunez, de fruct. part. 1, dict. cap. 10, per tot. cum multis juribus, et AA.

very well take effect, although at the same time it may follow, from the acknowledgment of right implied in the payment of the fifth, and the submission to the ordinances, that the mines are a right of the crown. For as the proportion which remains, after satisfying the demands of the ordinances, is strictly a product or emolument to the owner, the metals must in any case be regarded as products, either natural ones, if the fact be that they do reproduce, or civil ones, if they do not ; and an interest in them must therefore pass to the usufructuary, the husband, the tutor and others.

24. It being then established that the mines of the Indies are a right of the crown, and that this right is quite consistent with the property granted to the subject, therein, it must follow, beyond dispute, as a consequence of their being made over to the latter, with power to dispose of them as of any thing of his own, that all the incidents of property must attach in favour of the proprietor, and that they may therefore be exchanged, sold, leased or alienated, by contract, donation or inheritance ; may be given as a portion in marriage, or may be charged with a rent ; and that interest may be demanded for the purchase money, whilst remaining unpaid. For it is clear, that this class of property is to be regarded as bearing produce, and this is insisted on by the Cardinal de Luca, by Garcia, Petrus Barbosa, Molina, Castillo and Gutierrez, who speak with reference to those mines and veins of known and tried permanence, the ores of which, although not actually reproduced, are still to be regarded in the light of products.* And in the place cited, De Luca also deduces very sound rules, establishing the justice of reserving rent, on a lease of mines. But all the above qualities are to be understood as being governed by this essential condition, that those to whom the property devolves, by universal or particular succession, must conform to the ordinances, and fulfil the obligations thereby imposed, such being the law.

25. The grant of the sovereign, therefore, conveys to his subjects, a direct and beneficial right of property ; and is to be regarded as a qualified gift, which will appear, upon considering the rules by which that species of gift is defined in law ; that is to say, that it be a free and complete act, which being perfected, a charge attaches on the donee from that time forth (and the

---

* Luca, de regalib. disc. 117, n. 18. "Et licet in stricta juris censura id quod ex hujusmodi fodinis singulis annis percipitur, potius pars sortis quam fructus dicatur : quoniam fructus vere, et proprie dicitur ille qui renascitur, ac singulis annis, vel temporibus, salva rei substantiâ, seu causâ productivâ, percipitur; nihilominus, ubi non agitur de parvis et superficialibus mineriis modico tempore duraturis, sed de hujusmodi magnis, atque juxta tot sæculorum experimentum indeficientibus; tunc earum fructus consistere dicitur in ipsius substantiæ annuali, seu temporanea consumptione, et extractione : Unde propterea in eis cadit usufructus, ordinantur fideicommissa; dantur in dotem pro matrimonio carnali, seu pro dote ecclesiæ, vel beneficii, imponuntur super eis census, atque intrant pro pretio termini textus in Leg. curabit, Cod. de act. empt. cum similibus." Ut per Garciam de expensis, cap. 22, n. 47. Barbosa, in Leg. divortio, §. si vir, n. 9 and 10, ff. de solut, matrim. Barbatia, de divisione fructuum, part 1, cap. 17, n. 39. Molina, de primogeniis, lib. 1, c. 23, n. 8, in fin. Castill. de usufructu, cap. 37, n. 16. Gutierrez de gabell. de. q. 36. n. 11, te seq.

being worded as a condition makes no difference), and that upon the failure of the modification, limited by the donor in his own favour, or in that of a third person, or of the kingdom or republic, the gift determines ; as will be seen by reference to various texts, and doctors.*

26. And these rules are precisely applicable to this second ordinance : for his majesty thereby gives " and makes a grant to his subjects of the property and possession of the mines discovered, or to be discovered, with power to dispose of them, as of any thing of their own:" which amounts to a complete act of gift, no price being paid for the grant, nor for the registry or denouncement of the mine : " but," proceeds the ordinance, " observing, both in regard to what they have to pay us by way of duty, and in all other respects, the regulations and arrangements established by this edict, in the manner hereinafter-mentioned :" which is the charge or qualification, and which refers to the payment of the fifth, from that time forth, and to the observance of the ordinances which regulate the mode of working the mines, the number of hands to be kept at work in them, their boundaries and the other matters required to be observed, upon the omission or non-performance of which, the gift determines, and the mine becomes liable to be denounced by any one.†

27. The 2d and 16th ordinances, and the 1st of the old ordinances, make it lawful, not only for the subjects of the crown, but also for foreigners, to search for mines. The law of the Indies, under the title " Discovery of Mines," does not make any such particular mention of foreigners ; for their residence in those parts being prohibited‡ by the municipal laws and statutes of the country, unless specially permitted under letters of naturalization, they consequently, cannot apply themselves to the working of the minerals of that country ; on the contrary, our sovereigns have ordained by express laws, that those persons who are prohibited from going to, or residing in the Indies, shall not be at liberty to raise gold, silver or any other metal ;§ and the ordinance of the viceroy, Don Francisco de Toledo, in Peru,|| which makes it lawful for all foreigners to discover and take possession of mines, to stake them out, and to apply for the unappropriated space of ground, in the same manner as natural-born subjects, must necessarily be understood to apply to those only who have been naturalized by royal grant, and not to those otherwise circumstanced.

28. As to those foreigners who may have actually applied themselves to

---

* Law 1, Cod, de his. que sub modo. L. cum vos, Cod. de donat. Antunez, de donat. lib. 1, præl. 2, §. 1, a. n. 1, 10, et per totum, cum Gomez, Menochio, Mantica, Gregor. Arias a Mesa, et aliis.

† Law 5, title 13, book 6, cap. 1, Collection of Castile.

‡ The whole of title 27, book 9, of the Collection of the Indies.

§ Law 1, title 10, book 8. Law 6, title 27, book 9, of the Indies.

|| Ordinance 7, of the viceroy, Don Francisco de Toledo, in the Gazophil. of Escalona, book 2, p 2, chap. 1, page 106.

the working of mines, although it would be unjust, not being suspected persons, to deprive them of property upon which they have laid out their money, with beneficial effects to the public, yet it would be proper to compel them to sell their mines at a reasonable price, and then to send them out of the country. And this is the object of the law in directing that justice be done,[*] with reference to which, all such circumstances ought to be taken into the account, as the audiency may fairly, in justice, have regard to. But it is otherwise where such persons, so possessed of a mine, which is real property, shall have been established for twenty years, or shall be married, or have a family of children, or where other circumstances, under which they are tolerated by the laws of the Indies, shall enter into the case. As to all which matters, Veitia, Solorzano, Hevia Bolanos and Escalona,[†] and the laws above-cited, may be referred to. Regard must, however, always be had to the just, approved and notorious reasons, for prohibiting foreigners from all access to the Indies, for the purpose of trading, or of purchasing gold and silver.[‡]

29. Since the ordinance renders it lawful for all the subjects of the crown, of what station or condition soever, to work the mines, it might be inferred that this liberty is extended to the clergy; and, in fact, several very excellent works have been produced on these subjects, by the industry of ecclesiastics, such as the learned works of Barba and Ordonez,[§] on the subject of ores and smelting. And there is nothing indecorous in their acquiring knowledge or skill in these matters; but the certain orders of Philip II. and Philip IV., an abridgment of which may be found in the collection of Don Juan Francisco Montemayor,[||] it is directed, that neither the monks nor the clergy shall be allowed to employ themselves in working mines, as being indecorous and scandalous, and of bad example. And this rule is particularly proper, if the parties are charged with the religious superintendency of Indian districts.

30. Similar regulations are strictly enforced by the law of the Indies,[¶] and Solorzano cites various prohibitory orders, grounded on the avarice, cruelty and vexations which prevail in the management of the mines, under such circumstances; the only case excepted being that of a clergyman

* Law 26, title 27, book 9, Collection of the Indies.

† Law 10. 13, 15, 19, 22, 27, same title and book; see Veitia, Norte de la contratacion, lib. 1, cap. 31. Solorz. Polit. lib. 3, cap. 29, n. 46. Bolanos Cur. Philipp. part 2, lib. 1, cap. 27. Escalona in his Gazophil. lib. 1, cap. 29, page 156.

‡ Law 8, title 27, book 9, of the Indies.

§ Don Alvaro Alonso Barba, (in his Arte de los Metals) curate of Potosi in Peru. Don Juan Ordonez Montalvo, presbyter, and director of the mines of the Marquis de Valle-Ameno, in the mining district of el Monte, in New Spain, in his Cartilla, o arte nuevo de beneficiar los metales de Oro y Plata por Azogue, printed at Mexico, in the year 1758, at the press of the Bibliotheca Mexicana. See chap. 22, § 13, n. 55.

|| Montemayor, Sumarios de Cedulas Reales, lib. 5, tit. 4, sumario 14.

¶ Law 4, title 12, book 1, Collection of the Indies.

becoming entitled to a mine by inheritance, in which case he is allowed to work it until he has an opportunity of selling, leasing, or disposing of it to advantage.*

31. The contrary, however, is common practice in the Indies, where the clergy not only work mines on their own account, and at their own risk, and pay the duties like all other persons, without ever having their mines denounced ; but they also occupy themselves in the administration and management of the mines of others, in the very face of their superiors ; relying on the prevalence of the custom, and on the fact, that the business being conducted by servants, has nothing indecorous in it, and is by no means against conscience.†

32. The council of Lima,‡ prohibits curates and incumbents from working mines (amongst other lucrative occupations), under pain of excommunication, *ipso facto incurrenda ;* forbidding other ecclesiastics from engaging in actual trade only ; but the council of Mexico,§ setting forth that many curates and incumbents undertook the ministry in the Indies, more from a lust of gain, and in the expectation of having the services of the Indians in agriculture or mining, than from a desire to guide and enlighten their minds, orders, that no secular or regular curate, shall cultivate land within his jurisdiction, nor within the space of ten leagues around ; not excepting even the land of his own patrimony or of the church, if he has an opportunity of letting it : but that if no person can be found willing to take such land on lease, then he may employ the Indians who are so disposed, in cultivating it ; but that no compulsion shall be used towards them, and that they shall be paid for their labour, and be kindly treated ; and that if any such person as aforesaid shall act otherwise, the bishop shall deprive him, if he be a secular clergyman, of his benefice, and if a regular, of his cure, and shall suspend his right of electing, or being elected to any office.

33. From the decision of this council, friar Juan de Paz infers in his *Consultas y Resoluciones*, that the ecclesiastics‖ and curates of the kingdom of

---

* Soloiz. Polit. lib. 2, cap. 18, n. 53.

† Cap. Ejiciens, distinct. 88. Paz, Consultas y Resoluciones varias Theologicas, class. 1, cons. 59. per totam.

‡ Actione 3, cap. 5, Neque Indos ad mineralia sibi curanda mittere.

§ Lib. 3, tit. 20. "Ne clerici, vel monachi negotiis sæcularibus se immisceant, §. 5. Quia vero multi curati et beneficiati Indorum, hanc curam suscipiunt, magis lucri cupiditate (ut videlicet Indi sua colant prædia, aut minas effodiant), quam ut ipsi rudium Indorum animas instruant ; hæc synodus præcipit, ut nullus curatus Indorum, sive sæcularis, sive regularis, possint intra suam jurisdictionem, nec intra decem leucas in ejus ambitu, prædia (etiam si patrimonialia, aut ecclesiæ fuerint) colere, si sint qui ea conducere velint. Quod si conductores minime reperiantur, ea ipsis colere liceat, etiam per 'Indos, quos tamen ad id volentes tantum adhibeant, debitamque eis operum et laboris mercedem persolvant, benigneque, et comiter se gerant, si secus fecerint, episcopus curatos sæculares beneficio privet ; regulares autem, a regimine ecclesiæ amoveat, et voce activa et passiva perpetuo suspendat."

‖ Paz, ubi proxime.

Mexico are at liberty to work mines, whether they be church property, part of their own patrimony, or newly-discovered mines, subject to two conditions; first, that they do not compel the Indians to work in them against their inclination; and second, that they make those who do work, a just compensation for their labour; and that he conceives the object the council had in veiw was, that the Indians who might work in the mines should be induced so to occupy themselves, by good treatment and good pay, and not by contrary means: remarking, that where it prohibits the clergy from employing the Indians within their jurisdiction in working their mines, except under the circumstances above-mentioned, it enforces the regulation by threats, not of ecclesiastical censures, and the consequent punishment, but of forfeiture of their benefices.

34. Agreeably to these rules, we recollect an instance of a church mine at Zimapan being let on lease; but we also recollect other instances of church mines being managed direct by the curates; and as it is, generally speaking, difficult to find persons willing to take such hazardous property on lease, there is nothing to prevent the clergy from working mines at pleasure. Finally, as the laws of the Indies* direct that the councils of Lima and Mexico shall be obeyed, and their decrees be enforced, it follows, beyond a doubt, that the prohibition from working mines issued against curates, under pain of excommunication, by that of Lima, and the permission given to them to work mines, subject to the aforesaid conditions, by that of Mexico, are, by the laws of the Indies, made the standing law of each kingdom respectively.

35. As to the question, whether the Indians are at liberty to work mines, it cannot be matter of surprise that a special declaration to that effect,† besides the general one which would of itself have embraced them, should have been deemed necessary in our laws of the Indies; for they were in the habit of concealing the veins of silver and gold, to prevent their being worked, imagining perhaps, that if discovered they would be taken from them. In order therefore, to induce them to communicate their discoveries, it was directed by several orders, that they should be given to understand that they were to be entitled to all the mines they might discover; and further inducements were, at the same time, held out, by the offer of various immunities: for instance, the Indian who should discover a considerable mine or treasure, was promised exemption from tribute for himself, his sons, and his grandsons;‡ and all Indian discoverers of mines were authorised to work them in part payment of the taxes and tribute imposed on them, and for their own further benefit.§ And it was also ordered that the rules for ascertaining the bound-

---

* Law 7, title 8, book 1, of the Collection of the Indies.

† Law 14, title 19, book 4, Collection of the Indies.

‡ Law 15, same title and book. Order directed to Don Martina Henriquez, viceroy of Mexico, the 23d of December, 1574, in the revenue office of that city.

§ Montemayor, Sumar. 3, tit. 5, lib. 4.

aries of the mines so to be discovered by the Indians, should be the same for them as for the Spaniards*, without distinction.   And it is no great matter of surprise that it should have been thought necessary to frame especial statutes for these wretched Indians, whom we consider that, originally, permission was not even extended to the Spaniards to raise gold, silver or other metals, unless by particular licence from the governor.   The governors, however, in this respect, contravened orders which had been before issued, and in so doing they acted prejudicially for the interest of the kingdom at large, the revenue, and the subject individually.   At length, the order of the 9th of December, 1526, was issued by the Emperor Charles, upon which was founded the law of the Collection,† which gives absolute permission to all persons to work mines.

36. It is to be observed, that by an order of the 1st of September, 1530, it was provided and commanded, that the mines of the marquisate of el Valle should be common to all persons, under the penalty of 100,000 maravedis ; the object of which was to prevent its being supposed that the grant of towns and people made to the marquess, carried with it the right to the mines, which were to be common to all persons, in all parts and places.‡

37. Besides the classes of persons above-mentioned, the administrators general, and the officers particularised in the 67th ordinance are prohibited from working mines ; as well as the presidents, judges of audiency, alcaldes and fiscals,§ and all justices, notaries and sworn clerks, either by themselves or through any other person acting for them, directly or indirectly, wholly or in part, under pain of being deprived of their offices, and forfeiting their mine or mines.   And the law of the Indies‖ ordains, that the permission generally given to work mines, shall not be extended to the ministers, governors, mayors, chief or deputy alcaldes, lawyers, ordinary alcaldes and notaries attending at the mines, nor to any other person specially prohibited. And by three other laws,¶ the chief alcaldes are prohibited from purchasing ores or silver, and also from dealing with the miners, under colour of any contract of supply, or other pretence ; and they, as well as the notaries attending at the mines, are prohibited from entering into partnership with the mine owners, under the penalty of forfeiting their mines and being deprived

---

* Law 16, title 19, book 4, Collection of the Indies.

† Law 1, same title and book, which was taken from the order directed to Herman Cortes, the resident judge, dated 9th of November, 1526, and given by Don Vasco de Puga, fol. 12, of his Provisions Cedulas y Instrucciones ; " And you prohibit and forbid it and give no licence, except to such persons as you please, &c." The law and the order differ only in the date, but are the same in substance.

‡ This order is in our MS. index to the book of orders of the city of Mexico, which was preserved from the conflagration mentioned in a note to chap. 3, n. 23.

§ Law 60, title 16, book 2, Collection of the Indies.

‖ Law 1, title 19, book 4, Collection of theIndies.

¶ Laws 1, 2 and 3, title 21, book 4, Collection of the Indies.

of their offices. All hired servants also are prohibited, which will be seen, in the proper place, when we come to treat of the registering of mines by servants on the part of their masters.[*]

SECTION I.

The working of quicksilver mines was at first permitted in New Spain but was subsequently in several instances prohibited, it having been made unlawful to sell quicksilver in New Spain, except such as is remitted and distributed on the account of the crown.

38. The supreme right and authority in and over the mines, vested in and exercised by the crown, cannot be better illustrated than by giving an account of the mines of quicksilver, and of the manner in which that metal is sold and distributed. By our new ordinances, and by orders of the 19th of June, 1568, and the 19th of January, 1609, upon which the corresponding laws of the Collection of the Indies are founded,[†] permission was given, not only to raise gold, silver and other metals, generally, but likewise quicksilver in particular, and all possible activity was recommended in promoting the discovery and working of the mines of that metal, the viceroys, the audiences and governors, being directed to extend to the discoverers, every advantage that might seem reasonable ; provided, as is expressed in the above order of the 19th of June, 1568, that the interests of other parties should not be prejudiced, and that the duty of a fifth part should be paid in pure and clean quicksilver.[‡]

39. We are not informed, nor have we with all our industry been able to ascertain, from any of the curious histories and accounts of the mining districts of the Indies, or from any of the official reports or orders, whether any quicksilver mines were worked in New Spain during the period immediately subsequent to its discovery ;[§] but the probability is that none such were worked, and that even the existence of the metal was unknown. And this we infer from its great scarcity at that time, it being sometimes procured from the celebrated mines of Guancavelica in Peru, sometimes from those of

---

[*] Chap. 15, numb. 1 and 2.

[†] Laws 2 and 4, title 19, book 4, Collection of the Indies.

[‡] This and other orders stated by us, are compiled entire by Montemayor, in his 5th book, title 5, concerning quicksilver and the collection of the duties thereon, to which we refer.

[§] Don Joseph Villa-Senor, Theatr. Americ. tom. 1, cap. 48, relates, that the mining district of San Gregorio, in the jurisdiction of Acazuchitlan, or Tetela del rio, had been worked on his majesty's account for quicksilver and copper, and that it was in his time gone to decay. And that there were veins of quicksilver also in Halchicapa, but it does not appear when they were worked.

el Almaden in Spain, sometimes from Germany, and sometimes from China, by way of Acapulco. But three instances have occurred, during the present century, of private persons having proposed to work mines of quicksilver, and of orders having thereupon been issued to close the mines, which orders, in two of the instances, were expressly approved by the king.

40. The first instance is recorded in the recital of an order, dated at San Lorenzo, the fifth of July, 1718, and countersigned by Don Andres de Corobarrutia y Zupide, and which runs as follows: "To my viceroy and president, and the judges of my audiency of the city of Mexico, in the province of New Spain. By a dispatch of even date herewith, I have been pleased to give my commission and instructions to Don Juan Joseph de Veitia, to take certain measures for stopping up and preventing the working of the mines or veins of quicksilver discovered in the jurisdiction of the city of Quernavaca; in which matter, and in all that concerns the business of distributing the quicksilver for that kingdom, which I have entrusted to his care he is to proceed and act independently and exclusively of you my viceroy and you, the judges of my said audiency; and you are not under any pretext to interfere by taking cognizance of this matter, or any part thereof, of which I have thought proper to advise and instruct you, as I hereby do, for your government, and that you may not put any hindrance or impediment in his way, forewarning you, that any proceedings you may take in contravention of this order, will incur my displeasure, and will induce me to take the severest measures against you; and I desire you on the contrary, to shew him any favour or assistance that he may require of you, or that may be necessary for executing and carrying into full effect the matters aforesaid; and you shall give me an account of the receipt and execution of this order, through the office of my general superintendent of quicksilver, the first opportunity that may offer."[*]

41. The second instance is recorded in another royal order, dated the 24th of November, 1730, from which it appears, that Don Pedro Manzano having discovered two quicksilver mines, in the jurisdiction of the Sierra de Pinos, in the district of the audiency of Guadalaxara; one of which was in the Cerro del Carro, and the other in the Cerro del Picacho, he reported the same to the judge, charged with the exclusive cognizance of all affairs relating to quicksilver, who ordered that the works should be stopped, as being prejudicial to the mines of el Almaden, and as likely to give occasion for fraud: the king, being advised of these proceedings, was pleased to approve the prohibition so issued. And this is related by Don Mathias de la Mota, in his history of New Galicia.[†]

42. The third instance occurred in the year 1745, whilst Colonel Don Fermin de Echevers was president of the royal audiency of Guadalaxara.

---

[*] In our MS. of orders, tom. 2, fol. 162, back.
[†] Mota, Historia de la Galicia, MS. cap. 62, n. fin.

Another quicksilver mine was this year discovered in the Cerro del Carro, information whereof being given to the Marquess de Altamira, superintendent of quicksilver, and judge of the royal audiency of Mexico, he ordered that the works should be stopped. The order is extant in the office of the superintendent of quicksilver, and at Guadalaxara.

43. These three instances demonstrate that the working of quicksilver mines in New Spain, has been prohibited by the crown, because the quicksilver from the mines of el Almaden is distributed on account of the revenue ; but it appears, nevertheless, that there are such mines at Quernavaca, in the kingdom of New Spain, and in the Sierra de Pinos, in the kingdom of New Galicia ; and some are of opinion that quicksilver is to be found at la Pimeria, and that the Indians used to describe a lake of this metal, which must be something like la Gran Quivira in New Spain, or el Dorado in Peru.

44. The grounds of this prohibition are stated in several orders. The first of these was issued by the Princess Regent, and is dated at Valladolid, the 4th of March, 1559, and directed to the royal officers, and runs thus :— " To our officers of New Spain. Having considered what you, and our viceroy of that country have written to us, concerning the great necessity which exists for sending a quantity of quicksilver thither, for reducing the silver raised from the mines of New Spain aforesaid, and concerning the great advantages that would follow from our sending it thither to be sold by our officers ; by which means, over and above the great benefit that would be conferred on the inhabitants of the country aforesaid, we ourselves should derive great advantage, and might make a profit on the said quicksilver, of twice what it cost here ; we have provided, that all the quicksilver that is raised, and that may henceforth be raised, from the mines of el Almaden, shall be sent to you ; as well as a further quantity, which our factor-general has now purchased by our command, in order that you may sell the same ; and our officers of the *Casa de Contratacion* of Seville will therefore send you the quicksilver aforesaid, by virtue of the order that has been forwarded to them ; and we have prohibited the sending any quicksilver to the parts aforesaid, unless in our name, and by our command. Wherefore, I command you, that you provide some person at the city of Vera Cruz to receive and forward to you, at the city of Mexico, all the quicksilver that our said officers of Seville shall so send to you, and that when and so often as you shall receive it, you shall sell it at the greatest possible profit, and make as much by it as you conveniently may, which we expect from our confidence in your fidelity and care ; and our treasurer shall charge you with the money which you may thereby make, and you shall always render us an account of the quantity you receive, and of the price at which it is sold. And, forasmuch as the quicksilver costs here, from 55 to 58 ducats per quintal, you are to take an account thereof and of the freight and other expenses, of which the said officers of Seville will advise you, and to sell it at as much profit as

possible. Dated at Valladolid, the 4th of March, 1559.—The Princess. —In the name and by the command of his majesty.—Ochoa de Luyando."*

45. The second order is dated at the Pardo, the 22d of January, 1565,† and is directed to the viceroy and royal officers : It provides and charges, that great care be taken to sell the quicksilver at as much profit as possible, having regard to its influence on the working of the mines, and on the amount of the fifth, levied by the crown by way of duty.

46. The third order is dated the 3d of June, 1567, and is also directed to the royal officers, and after stating, that it had been ordained by divers laws and edicts, that no quicksilver should be sent to New Spain, except by licence and permission of the king, and that a great quantity had been carried over in the late convoys without such licence, and that a further quantity might probably be going over by that year's convoy ; it directed them to investigate and ascertain the fact, either personally, or through some one of trust, and if they should find any, to set it apart, and to report from whom and to whom it was being conveyed, that proper measures might be taken accordingly, on account of the great loss to the revenue from such proceedings.‡

47. Upon these and several other orders, is founded the law of the Collection of the Indies,§ which commands, that there shall be no trading in quicksilver, except on account of the revenue, and that all quicksilver shipped on any account shall be forfeited, together with double the value, one-third to go to the informer, and two-thirds to the exchequer ; and the merchants and miners are forbidden to retail even what has been distributed to them on account of the revenue.

48. From all which it is to be inferred that the principal reasons for maintaining this prohibition are, first, that the taking it off would involve the crown and the revenue in great loss, whilst under the present system, the quicksilver department produces a considerable profit.

49. Second, that as great expense is incurred at the mines of el Almaden, in the slow and tedious process of reducing this mineral (as appears from the ordinances of those mines, dated the 31st of January, 1735), it is not to be endured that any person should trade in it, except under a licence from the crown.

50. Third, that it has the effect, not only of preventing the frauds that would attend the wholesale and retail trade in quicksilver, but also of circumscribing the opportunities of withholding the silver from being stamped ; for if the miners had other means of procuring quicksilver, distinct from the

---

*In our old MS. of orders, fol. 98, back of the first part.

†Fol. 117 of said old orders, first part.

‡ Fol. 122, of said old orders, part 1st.

§ Law 1, title 23, book 8.

supply furnished by the crown, they might dispose of their silver clandestinely, to the great diminution of the tenths and other crown dues.

51. These considerations led to another royal order, dated at Aranjuez, the 8th of May, 1572, and countersigned by Antonio de Erasso, and which prohibited selling quicksilver to the merchants for the purpose of resale, even though it were in the first instance shipped by the king, and distributed on his account. This order was also one of those upon which was founded the law of the Indies, cited above, directing that the quicksilver should be forfeited, with double its value, and ordering further discretionary penalties to be regulated by the particular circumstances of the case. The reasons for this order appear upon the face of it, and it runs thus :—" To Don Martin Enriquez, our viceroy, governor and captain-general of New Spain, and president of our royal audiency thereof. Know, that both from what you and our officers of the country aforesaid have at divers times written to us, and from the relation, petition and earnest request of the miners of that country, and of the province of New Galicia, concerning the sale of the quicksilver shipped to the said country, on our account, and from the provinces of Peru, we are advised of the disadvantages that attend the system now followed in the sale thereof, as well as of the poverty of the miners, the low standard of the ores worked, the consequent diminution in the quantity of silver reduced, and the prejudicial effects that attach upon the miners themselves, upon the tenth duty, and upon the trade and commerce of that country in general, from the miners having to obtain the quicksilver at second-hand from the merchants ; and we are also aware of the other inconveniences that you have reported and represented to us in regard to this subject. Upon consideration whereof, and of other representations made to us here, and seeing that we desire to promote the interests of the country aforesaid, and to lend every aid to the said miners, we have commanded that some remedy against these evils should be looked for and considered of ; and that which at present appears to us the most practicable and proper is, that all the quicksilver that is conveyed to the country aforesaid, both from these kingdoms, on our own account, and from the provinces of Peru, should be deposited in our stores in the country aforesaid ; that a list should be made of all the miners in your government of New Spain aforesaid, and in that of New Galicia, and that one moiety of such quicksilver should be distributed to them on credit, in such manner that the proceeds thereof may be returned to this kingdom by the same convoy by which it is carried out ; and that the other moiety should also be disposed of in like manner, but so that the proceeds thereof may be returned by the next convey, good security being taken for the same ; and that the price to be given for the quicksilver aforesaid should be fixed by you and our officers of the said country aforesaid, and should be such as may be most beneficial to our revenue. Wherefore, I command you to provide for the observance and fulfilment of the

above arrangement, respecting the sale of such quicksilver as aforesaid, and for the better carrying the same into effect, you shall, in our name, prohibit every merchant or other person from purchasing quicksilver in the country aforesaid for the purpose of resale, under the penalty of forfeiting the same, and twice the value thereof; inasmuch as we do, for the present, prohibit and forbid such dealings, and we do from this time forth condemn those who shall act to the contrary hereof, in the penalty aforesaid."[*]

52. We may hence collect, that it appears, both from the reports of the government and from those of the miners of New Spain and New Galicia, that it would be very prejudicial to permit the merchants to deal in quicksilver; and the reason is, that they would be disposed to furnish it to those persons only with whom they might have contracts of supply, and would raise the price according to the demand; so that whatever precaution might be taken for binding the suppliers or merchants to return a proper quantity of silver to be stamped, in proportion to the quicksilver furnished them, much silver would remain unreduced; and as these parties would intercept all the profits, the miners would be totally ruined. And it follows therefore, that no remedy could have been applied, more beneficial to the miners, than the plan of distributing the quicksilver at the superintendent's office and district stores, by the officers of the crown, at such credit, and upon such security, as may be prudent, having regard to the greater or less need of the miners, the condition of their mines and reduction works, and the character of the purchasers. There are some who lament that quicksilver is not sold in small quantities, for the reduction of small parcels of ore; but in this and other matters of importance, regard is not to be had to small considerations: and it must answer better to sell such small quantities of ore, than to expend more than their value in reducing them.

CHAPTER III.

OF THE DIFFERENT TERMS UNDER WHICH THE CROWN HAS, FROM TIME TO TIME, PERMITTED ITS SUBJECTS TO WORK THE MINES.—OF THE RICHNESS OF THE MINES OF NEW SPAIN IN FORMER TIMES, AND THEIR SUBSEQUENT DECAY.—OF THE GREAT NUMBER OF MINES THE INDIES CONTAIN, AND A DUTY OF A FIFTH, A TENTH OR A TWENTIETH, RESERVED TO THE CROWN UPON THE GOLD, SILVER AND OTHER METALS RAISED FROM THEM.

ORDINANCES III. IV. V. VI. VII. VIII. IX. X. XI. XII. XIII. XIV. XV. LXXVI.

III. If the ores which shall be raised from the said mines shall yield at

[*] Fol. 104, back of said old orders, part 2.

the rate of a marc and a half, or 12 ouncee, per quintal of silver-lead, or under, they shall pay us the tenth part of the silver which shall be raised from such mines and ores, without any deduction whatsoever, for expenses, or on any other account, all which matters shall be at the charge of the persons who shall discover and work the said mines ; and all that remains after deducting such tenth part, they may have and retain to themselves.

IV. From the mines, the ores of which shall yield more than a marc and a half, and up to 4 marcs per quintal of silver-lead, they shall pay us the fifth part of the silver raised, without deducting expenses ; and the persons who shall work such mines and ores, shall have the remainder, as afore-said.

V. From the mines, the ores of which shall yield more than 4 marcs, and up to 6 marcs per quintal of silver-lead, they shall pay us the fourth part of the silver raised, without deducting expenses, and the persons aforesaid shall have the remainder, as aforesaid.

VI. From the mines, the ores of which shall yield more than 6 marcs per quintal of silver-lead, whatever their quality or richness may be, or may attain to be, and whether expected or not, they shall pay to us one half of the silver raised, without deducting expenses ; and the persons before-mentioned may take the remainder, as aforesaid.

VII. From the mines of gold, whatever the quality, quantity or richness of their ores shall or may be, they shall pay us one moiety of the gold raised, without any deduction for expenses, and the persons who shall discover and work them may retain the other moiety to themselves. And this is to be understood of every description of gold ore, however worked, and in whatever · manner procured, whether from mines, from streams, or elsewhere.

VIII. And forasmuch as there are some old mines in these our kingdoms, which were in work before the time of the promulgation of our decree of the 10th July, 1559, (Law 3) but which are not now worked by their proprietors, and were not in fact worked by them at the time of the issuing of that decree ; and forasmuch, also, as some other mines have been subsequently discovered and worked, from all of which, heaps of rubbish and slag have been raised ; we ordain that such persons as may be disposed to work such mines, or such heaps of rubbish or slag, without prejudice to the right of the proprietor, shall be at liberty to do so ; and that out of the ores which they shall raise from such mines, they shall pay us as follows.

IX. As to the mines which were abandoned, and had ceased to be worked before the promulgation of the said edict, and have since been again explored and worked, having been sunk to the depth of ten or more *estados*, if the ores raised from such mines shall yield 2 marcs or under of silver per quintal, they shall pay to us the twelfth part of the silver raised therefrom. And if they shall yield more than 2 marcs per quintal, they shall pay in the proportion provided above for newly-discovered mines, without deducting anything for expenses.   But it is declared that any mines whatsoever, whether old or new mines, being less than ten *estados* in depth, shall be regarded as new mines, and shall pay duty as such, in the same manner and form as is mentioned in the ordinances which refer to new mines.*

X. And if the heaps of rubbish or slag belonging to the mines mentioned in the preceding ordinance, shall be smelted alone and unmixed with other ores raised or to be raised, subsequent to the accumulation of such heaps of rubbish or slag, they shall pay to us the tenth part of the silver produced from such heaps of rubbish or slag, being smelted alone as before mentioned ; but if mixed with other ores, the proportion of silver to be paid, shall be regulated upon the same scale as the duty levied on the produce of the mines generally, having regard to the nature of the ores mixed therewith.

XI. And the lead, litharge, impregnated cupels and sweepings, and any thing else that may result from the process of refining, after the separation of the silver (of which they are to pay us the proportions above declared, free of all expenses), may and shall remain for the owners of the said mines ; such lead, litharge, impregnated cupels and sweepings, not being liable to pay us anything, and no impediment or hindrance shall be interposed in respect thereof.

XII. And forasmuch as the poor lead, which from its containing little or no silver, will not bear refining, is required, together with antimony and copper, for reducing the produce of mines of silver ; we ordain, that the mines of such lead, or of antimony and copper, now subsisting, or hereafter to be found in places where no grant of the mines and ores has been made, may be sought for and worked by all the persons above-mentioned, and they shall thereout pay to us, of copper the thirtieth part, and of antimony the tenth part, and of the poor lead (which is to be understood to be such as will yield more than 4 reals of silver per quintal), the twentieth part, all clear of expenses; provided that if such copper should contain gold, they shall pay us the sixth part of the gold, besides the duty on the copper ; and if it should contain silver, they shall pay us thereout, half the duty above declared to be payable upon the produce of silver ores, according to the number of marcs it may yield per quintal, and over and above the duty on the copper above-mentioned.

<hr />

(* Note 1 to § 9.)—By the first section of the royal cedula of the 18 August, 1607, in reference to the subject matter of this and the six preceding sections, his majesty determined that for the period of ten years only, there shall be paid by those working the mines of gold and silver in the mountains and worn out mines, one fifteenth, and after the said period of ten years the one tenth of the gross amount without deducting expenses, with the declaration that at the end of twenty years, his majesty might order the said duties to be raised, provided that they should not exceed one fifth, entrusting it to the charge of the council of the treasury, and the chief auditor of accounts. After the expiration of said twenty years in view of the condition of the mines, to determine on consultation as to how far the duties might properly be raised, provided that in no event should it exceed one fifth. (Law 10, tit. 3, lib. 6, Recopilacion.)

XIII. And it is to be understood, that all the proportions above declared to be payable to us out of the produce of the mines above described, both new and old, and of the heaps of rubbish and slag, are to be paid to us at the refining houses and smelting works which we shall establish for the purpose of refining, in silver, and not in ore, nor in silver-lead ; and that our proportion of the poor lead and copper shall be payable in ingots, and of the antimony in ore ; all of the same kind and quality as the proportion remaining to the owners, and clear of all expenses.

XIV. And because, according to the said edict of the 10th of January, 1559, those who have grants of mines are to enjoy all that is not gold, silver or quicksilver, according to their grants, and are also to enjoy the mines of gold and silver which were begun to be worked and were actually worked by them, or by other persons in their name, before the issuing of the said edict, and forasmuch as some doubts have been raised respecting these words, it having been said, that it might happen that the mines had been discovered and set to work one, two, or more years before the issuing of the said edict, but had ceased to be worked some time before the issuing thereof, and that such mines were therefore excluded by the said edict, as not having been actually at work at the time of issuing the same ; it is therefore declared, that the mines of gold and silver which are to be so enjoyed by such grantees, shall be such as were actually in work at the time of issuing the said edict, or within four months previous, and no others.

XV. Moreover, whereas we have ordained by the said edict of the year 1559, that no person shall search for or discover mines within one league around the mine of Guadalcanal, or within one quarter of a league around those of Cazalla, Galaroza and Aracena, respectively ; and whereas it has since been found to be expedient, and for our greater advantage, that the said limit of a quarter of a league should be extended, and that it should be declared from what points it is to be measured :—We do ordain, with respect to the three last-mentioned places, as well as that of Guadalcanal, that no person whatsoever shall take or hold mines for the space of a league around any of those places ; such league to be computed and measured in the following manner. As to Guadalcanal, from the house which is built there for the workshop of the said mines ; as to Cazalla, from the house over the mine of Pedro Candil ; as to Aracena, from the house built at the mine of el Cerro de los Azores ; and as to Galaroza, from the first mine which was discovered there, and which is near the town ; and that such leagues are to be lawful leagues of 15,000 feet, each foot being one third of a *vara*, and are to be measured along the surface ; and that all the mines which shall be found within those limits shall be appropriated to our use. But if, previous to the date of this our letter, any mines shall have been found beyond such space of a quarter of a league, and within the space of one league now limited, the discoverers thereof shall enjoy them according to the aforesaid edict.

LXXVI. Also, forasmuch as when the old mines reach the depth of thirty, forty or more *estados*, the expense of raising the water, rubbish and ore, and of letting down the timber and other requisites, is much greater than in mines of less depth, and frequently amounts to more than the produce, under which circumstances the owners being unable to pay so high a duty as is fixed by these ordinances for such old mines, it is reasonable that some moderation should be observed in respect thereof:—We therefore ordain and command, that when this shall be the case, and it shall appear to the satisfaction of our administrator-general, that any old mine is become, from its depth or from other causes, so expensive as to be of little or no profit to the owner, he shall transmit to the council of finance, a particular account of the case, together with his opinion on it, and the enquiries which he shall have made thereon; and we command that the matter shall thereupon be considered and determined, in as summary a manner as possible.

CONTENTS OF THE COMMENTARY ON THESE ORDINANCES.

1. Edicts of Alphonso the Wise, and John I. as to the king's duty on, and share of, the produce of the mines.
2. Another of the Princess Joanna.
3. Another of Philip II., dated 1568.
4. Another of the same, dated in 1584.
5. Another of Philip III.
6. The ancient richness of the mines of Spain inferred from these edicts.
7. A variety of evidence establishing this fact at different periods.
8. Their subsequent decay demonstrated from the reduction in the price of provisions.
9. Regret expressed by Bernardo Perez de Vargas, on account of the abandonment of the mines of Spain.
10. The mines were leased to the Counts de Fakares, who worked out their produce, and left them in a state of ruin.
11. They were again leased, in 1725, to the Swede, Liebert Wolters.
12, 13, and 14. By applying themselves to working the mines of the Indies, the Spaniards enrich, and by no means cause the depopulation of Spain; reflections on this subject, and on the causes of this depopulation.
15. Opinion, apparently unfounded, of a learned critic, that the richness of the Indies is the cause of the poverty of Spain.
16. Of the advantages, both spiritual and temporal, derived from the richness of these mines.
17. Of the zeal of Philip II. and Philip III. in promoting their working.
18. Calculation of the amount which Spain has drawn from the Indies, since 1724. It is shewn that the Spaniards certainly derive profit from these sources, even allowing for what unavoidably passes to foreigners in exchange for their manufactures.
19. The richness of the mines of Peru referred to. Considerations on the benefits derived by the kingdom of Spain, and by the commercial interest of that country, from the mines of the kingdom of Mexico, upon the coasts of which there is no contraband trade.
20 and 21. The title to the possession, and the mode of working our mines, are more consistent with justice at present, than in earlier times, from the regular course these matters have now assumed.

22. Application of all that has been said to the subject of the fifth or tenth duty payable to the crown.

23. A fifth, tenth, or twentieth part of the produce of the mines of the Indies, has been levied at different times, and under different circumstances.

24. Purchasers continued liable to pay a fifth, but subsequently have been charged with a tenth only.

25. A gracious concession to the kingdom of Guatemala, in respect to the fith duty upon gold.

26. Reasoning in justification of this deviation, and shewing how frequently an abatement of duty becomes necessary.

27. The tenth is levied upon gold and other metals, without any distinction of persons ; practical course of proceeding in respect thereof ; where, how and when, a fifth ought to be levied ; of the penalty for transgressing these rules, and the mode of estimating the amount of the duty.

28. For the prevention of fraud, the nonpayment of the fifth is not corrected by bringing in the bullion to be stamped at any of the ports, except that of Vera Cruz ; and why ? The markets of the fleet, now re-established at Xalapa, tend to prevent contraband dealings.

29. Gold and silver being wrought without having paid the fifth, are liable to confiscation ; but this penalty is usually dispensed with.

30 and 31. The Duke de la Palata prohibited the exportation of wrought silver from Peru to Spain. A statement of the order, which was confirmed by the king, with the qualification that it was to be only temporary.

32. Old silver, and such as is procured by burning silver tissues, does not pay the fifth.

33. The exercise of the business of a silversmith was prohibited in Mexico, in the year 1551, but was permitted again in 1559. It is advisable to pay the fifth upon table services of plate taken in execution, or enumerated in inventories.

34. Plate used for the service of the church, or the pontifical ornaments of a bishop, are exempted from the payment of the fifth, but none other.

35. A determination of the crown, as to bullion and worked plate, being the property of a deceased prelate, which had not paid the fifth.

36. An estimate of the amount this department brings in to the crown.

37. The fifth is payable on lead, and the other metals.

38, 39 and 40. Saltpetre, copper, alum and gunpowder are the subjects of monopolies, and the duty is included in the rent reserved.

COMMENTARY.

1. All these different heads of the ordinance relate to one object, namely, the right of the crown and the subject, respectively, to the ores produced from the mines, and the proportions which they ought severally to take ; the rules on which subject we are about to trace briefly from their source. By the edict of Alphonso XI., in the year 1345, the ores of all mines in common ground belong to the crown.* After this, John I. by an edict,† dated

* Law 2, title 13, book 2, of the Collection of Castile. " Wherefore we command that they shall pay us the proceeds of the whole of it."

† Law 3, title 13, book 6, of the Collection. " First, that he who shall raise it, shall deduct all the expenses he may have incurred in digging and raising it, and after deducting such expenses, the third part shall be for him who shall have raised it, and the other two thirds for our selves."

in the year 1387, ordered, that the expenses being first deducted, two third parts of the produce should go to the crown, and one third to the proprietor.

2. By an edict issued in the year 1559, by the Princess Joanna, in the absence of Philip II.* this last rule was established generally and without distinction; but if, after deducting the expenses, the miner's third part amounted to 100,000 ducats, he was thenceforth allowed the fourth part only; and if he realised 200,000 ducats, then he was to have the fifth part only; to which proportion he was to continue entitled, without further reduction, however profitable the mine might prove to be.†

3. About four years afterwards, in the year 1563, this rule was totally altered by an edict of Philip II. in which the subject is divided into several heads.‡ When the produce of the mine gave a marc and a half per quintal, or under, the duty was rated at one eighth, without deducting expenses;§ thence to 3 marcs, at one fourth;‖ above 3 marcs, and up to 6 marcs, at one third;¶ and above 6 marcs, at one half, whatever the produce might be, and whether expected or not.** The produce of the gold mines was charged with a duty of one half, without deducting expenses.†† The produce of old silver mines, which had been once abandoned (having been sunk to the depth of 20 or more *estados*), if amounting to a marc and a half per quintal, was charged with an eighth part. If yielding more, they were to pay as new mines‡‡. The produce of the heaps of refuse belonging to such old mines, was made liable to pay one fifth;§§ and the silver from the heaps of slag, one twentieth part; all clear of expenses.‖‖ The lead, litharge, impregnated cupels and sweepings, resulting from the process of refining, were declared free of duty.¶¶ Poor lead, which would not bare refining, and not yield more than 4 reals of silver per quintal, was charged with a fifteenth part; copper was charged with a twentieth part, and if it contained gold, one fourth part of the gold was payable over and above the duty on the copper; if it contained silver, such silver was liable to one half the duty payable on silver produced from the mines, over and above the duty on the copper, and antimony paid an eighth part.***

4. By the new edict, and the ordinances of the new code, issued by Philip II. in the year 1584, twenty-one years after, an abatement of duty was made, upon the following scale.††† The produce of mines yielding from 1 to 12 ounces, was decreed to pay a tenth part; from 12 ounces to 4 marcs,

---

* Law 4, title 13, book 6, of the code.   † Cap. 3, same law.
‡ Law 5, title 13, book 6.   § Ordinance 2, of the old ones, in the same law.
‖ Ordinance 3.   ¶ Ordinance 4.
** Ordinance 5.   †† Ordinance 6.
‡‡ Ordinance 7 and 8.   §§ Ordinance 9.
‖‖ Ordinance 10.   ¶¶ Ordinance 11.
*** Ordinances 10 and 11.
††† Law 9, title 13, book 6, ordinances 2 and 13 inclusive.

a fifth part; from 4 to 6 marcs, a fourth part; and above 6 marcs, one half. The produce of gold mines was charged with one half. The produce of old mines, abandoned before the issue of the edict, and worked to the depth of 10 or more *estados*, if yielding 2 marcs or under per quintal, was charged with a twelfth part; if yielding more, then with the same duty as the produce of new mines. The produce of old heaps of refuse and slag, was decreed to pay a tenth part; but if smelted with an intermixture of other ores, then (in consideration of the intermixture of new ores), such produce was made liable to pay in the same proportion as the produce of other mines. Lead, litharge, impregnated cupels and sweepings, and every thing else resulting from the process of refining, were made free of duty. Copper was made liable to pay a thirtieth part, besides which, if it contained gold or silver, the gold was decreed to pay a sixth part, and the silver one half the usual amount of duty payable on that metal. Antimony was charged with a tenth part. Lead, yielding not more than four reals of silver per quintal, a twentieth part. And these duties were to be paid in silver, and not in ore; and without deducting anything for expenses.

5. Afterwards by an edict of the 18th of August, 1607,* Philip III. premising that experience had shewn that it was necessary and expedient for the crown, and would be advantageous to the kingdom and its inhabitants at large, to extend more grace and favour to the discoverers of mines, than had been granted by the aforesaid ordinances of his father, in order to facilitate the payment and recovery of the said duties, and other matters; ordered, that during the next ten years, one fifteenth should be paid by way of duty; during the ten years next subsequent, one tenth; and thenceforth, one fifth.

6. From the alterations which appear, by these laws, to have been made in the rate of the duties in the space of so few years (and which were doubtless ordered with the view of stimulating the subject to work the mines, by leaving him a large return for his anxiety, expense and labour), the richness of the mines of Spain, in early times, is apparent; for the one third remaining after the payment of two third parts to the king (first deducting the expenses), must have given a profit; and it appears to have been regarded as no unusual thing for this one third part to amount to 100,000 or 200,000 ducats. And a similar remark will apply, even after the promulgation of the last edict, whence it is to be inferred, either that the ore was very rich (or at least of very fair quality), or that the important items of quicksilver, iron and steel, being produced within the kingdom of Spain, the expenses were smaller on that account, and admitted of a larger profit.

7. In the history of the Maccabees, where the great power of the Romans is described, it is mentioned as one of their mighty acts in Spain, that they had

* Law 10, title 13, book 6, Collection of Castile.

made themselves masters of the rich ores of gold and silver.* From no other country (according to Fray Juan de la Puente, who cites Solinus, Pliny, Lucius, Florus, Strabo, Posidonius, Polybius, Aristotle, Diodorus Siculus, Herodotus and other Greek and Latin authors), could so great an abundance of these rich ores be procured.† He states, upon the authority of Strabo,‡ that during a conflagration on the Pyrenees, streams of gold and silver flowed down their sides ; that all the mountains and hills of Spain afford the materials for money, and that that country is an inexhaustible source of metallic ore ; that Plutus, the god of riches, holds his habitation beneath its surface, and that the Carthaginians, on their landing there, found the basins and even the mangers made of silver. And he likewise asserts, quoting Aristotle, that upon the ancient Phœnicians§ navigating to Tartessus, the Spaniards gave them, in exchange for oil and other ordinary merchandise, more silver than the ships were capable of conveying ; and that upon setting sail, they not only made their common utensils, but even their anchors, of silver. But of all the writers on this subject, Don Antonio Carrillo Lasso is the most deserving of attention, he having collected, with admirable erudition, many most remarkable and wonderful instances,‖ in reference to all the different provinces of Spain, and with the view of shewing, that as they yielded, in former times, such immense riches, so might they in these times be rendered equally productive. This subject has, in fact, been treated by so many authors, that it would be easy to compile volumes¶ of such observations.

8. It is, however, quite enough to look at our laws and ordinances, by which it appears, that the reason of Philip II. annexing the mines to the royal patrimony was, that it had been understood from of old, that they were very rich and abundant.** But the same laws also tell us, that these riches had, many years before their time, vanished into empty air, and that in later times, the greatest scarcity of money had been experienced. According to the laws of the title concerning *provisions*, in the year 1433, the expense of the king's provisions, when he came in person to any city,

---

* Machabeon, 1. c. 8, v. 3. "Et quanta fecerunt in regione Hispaniæ, et quod in protestatem redegerunt metalla argenti et auri quæ illic sunt."

† Fr. Juan de la Puente, Conveniencia de las dos Monarquias, lib. 3, cap. 6, §. 4, in cap. 16, §. 3.

‡ Lib. 3, de situ orbis.

§ Lib. 1, de mirabilibus auscult. ad fin.

‖ Carrillo Lasso, Descripcion de las antiguas minas de Espana, in all his three chapters.

¶ Carranza Ajustamiento y propercion de moneda, p. 1, cap. 1, per tot. P. Pineda, in Salom. lib. 4, cap. 14 and 15, Malvenda, de Antichrist page 333, Duarte, in Monarch. lib. 3, et cum bis Solorz Pilot. lib. 6, cap. 1, n. 3, and tom 2, de jur. Indiar. lib. 1, cap. 13, n. 47 and 48, and cap. 16, n. 77, and lib. 5, cap. unic n. 10. P. Mariana, de reb. Hispaniæ, D. Pedro Peralta, Historia de Espana vindicada, lib. 1, cap. 2, page 59 and 60. Blasius Caryophil. de antiquis aur. argentique fodinis, part 10, et seq. et ex antiquis innumeri apud hos.

** Law 4, tit. 13, lib. 6, of Castile.

amounted to 600 maravedis,* or at most to 1200, those of the queen to 800, and of the prince to 600.† In the year 1368, John I. under the advice of all the great men and nobles of the kingdom, issued an edict, fixing the price of provisions and other articles at rates so low, as to shew, that a great want of specie must have been experienced before the discovery of America. This edict may also be seen in Mariana and Bordazar, and in the Memorial of the imperial city of Toledo, upon the equalisation of weights and measures, lately printed.‡

* A maravedi *de plata* is *d*. 0, 143 British ; a maravedi *vellon* is *d*. 0, 076 British. *Kelly's Cambist*, vol. 1, p. 318. It is presumed the former are meant.—*Trans.*

† Laws 1 and 2, tit. 12, book 6, Collection of Castile.

‡ P. Mariana, de ponderic et mensur. cap. 23. "Ex ea pecuniæ varietate, sed et minori copia argenti, factum est ut superioribus temporibus pretia rerum multo minora quam notro fuisse videantur, quod in historiis nostratibus maxime observavimus rerum gestarum in Hispania ante ducentos circiter annos, fanecam hordei, hoc est modios sex, duobus tantum maravedinis emi consuevisse, at vero in summa caritate annonæ ad maravedinos triginta crevisse ; cu-pretio aliarum rerum pretia respondebant proportione quadam." And he proceeds to insert the decree in Latin, verbatim. Antonio Bordazar de Artazu, Proporcion de monedas pesos, y me-didas, trat 1. de monedas, pag. 96, n. 258, recites the decree and says :—"I shall make a short digression in order to shew, in the varying condition of mankind, how great the value of gold and silver was in former times, compared with the present, if measured by the amount of goods given in exchange for them ; which change of value may be explained, either upon the ground of the scarcity of the precious metals in former times, before the discovery of America, or by taking into view the calamities of the present times, the price of provisions having been in-creased by war and famine, or by reference to both these considerations. Father Mariana, in his work de ponder. et mensur. cap. 23, sets forth a law issued by John I. of Castile, in the year of our Lord, 1368, whereby, under the advice of the nobles and other great men, he fixed the price of provisions and other articles of trade, as follows ;—The bushel of wheat to be sold at 15 maravedis ; of *farrago* at 4 ; of barley at 10 ; of oats at 8 ; 4 half gallons of old wine at 3 maravedis ; of new wine at 2½ ; and when sold by the cask, a fourteenth part to be taken off. French cloth at 60 maravedis a yard ; that of Flanders or England at 50. The purple cloth of Flanders at 100 maravedis ; that of Ypres at 110 maravedis. And none but ladies were to dress in London, Brussels, Montpellier or Valencia cloth, without permission from the king. A day labourer was to have, from November to March, 3 maravedis per day ; and a female 10 dineros, working from sunrise to sunset ; from March to November, 4 ; and a female 2. For ploughing a whole day, each team, 10 maravedis. For getting in the vintage, a man and ass, 7. A domestic servant, 100 maravedis per annum ; a female domestic servant, 50 ; and a housekeeper, 40. Shoes of goat hide, 6 maravedis. A horse's sad-dle, 100 maravedis ; a mule's saddle, 20 ; a bit, 1 maravedi. To a silver-smith, for working plate, 15 maravedis per marc, or if very neat workmanship, 20. A shield or double target, 20 maravedis ; if painted, 25 ; if gilt, 30. For grinding wheat, 2 maravedis per bushel. 1000 tiles, 60 Maravedis ; 1000 bricks, 55. A bushel of plaster of Paris, 6 ; of lime, 5 maravedis. An ox, 200 maravedis, and a yearling calf, 180. A pound of good mutton, 2 maravedis. Huck-sters were to sell a sucking pig at 8 maravedis, a hare at 3, a rabit at 2, a hen at 4, a goose at 6, a pigeon at 3; and a partridge at 5 ; but journeymen mechanics, and even master workmen, were not permitted to purchase them, except on the occasion of a wedding, or at Easter." The report of the imperial city of Toledo, on the equalization of weights and measures, page 109, sets forth the same decree, and mentions that Father Mariana must have been mistaken either in the date or in the name of the king, or in both ; for that this edict or ordinance is one of Henry II. ; and it gives, at page 113, a precise description of the king's banquets.

9. There can be no doubt that at the time of issuing our ordinances, very few mines were worked, many of them being kept concealed, as is set forth in the law itself.* And at a period subsequent to this, Don Bernardo Perez de Vargas, in the dedication of his famous treatise, *De re metallica*, inscribed to Philip II., laments deeply, that through the want of good master-workmen among our countrymen, we should be put to the expense of engaging foreigners, notwithstanding the great number of mines which had been discovered, both on account of the crown and its subjects,† which he considers a proof of the inferior industry of the natives of the peninsula.

10. In confirmation of this opinion it is known, that a lease was granted by Phillip II. to the Counts de Fakares (natives of Germany), of the celebrated mines of Gaudalcanal, Rio Tinto, Cazalla, Aracena and Galaroza, which were crown property, and within a certain distance of each of which, under the new and old ordinances, now under consideration, no other mines were permitted to be opened or worked.‡ By this contract, these foreigners became the richest subjects in Europe.; but afterwards, under a suspicion that the government meditated the resumption of the mines, they allowed the water to overflow them.§ An iniquitous piece of revenge, even had their suspicions rested on the most solid grounds. Don Joseph de Veitia Linage assures us, that in the space of five years, from 1557, there passed through the *Casa de Contratacion* of the Indies, 497,246,204 maravedis *de plata*,‖ raised from the mines of Gaudalcanal.¶

22. Considering it therefore, to be established, by the ordinances under consideration, and as an inference from the payment of the eighth, fifth and fourth respectively, to the crown, that the quality of the ores of Spain was high we also infer from the same ordinances that the crown being entitled

---

* Law 4, tit. 13, book 6. " The mines that have been discovered and worked are few in number. The rich and profitable mines are kept concealed, and they will not discover or point them out."

† Bernardo Perez de Vargas, de re metallica. Madrid, published in duodecimo, by Pierres Cosin, 1569.

‡ Ordinance 15.

§ Savary, Dictionnare universel de commerce, tom. 2, Let. Mines, fol. 1374. " L'experience a fait voir qui'i'l n'y a point en Europe de mines d'or, d'argent, ou autre metal qui surpassent celles qui ont eté trouvees dans la presqu' isle d'Espagne, tant par rapport a l'abondance qu' a la richesse de la matiere, surtout celles de Gaudalcanal, Rio Tinto, Cazalla, Aracena et Galaroza, dans les provinces d'Andalousie, et Estremadure. Les Comtes Alemans de Fakares aiant passé un contrat avec Filipe II. touchant ces cinq mines, ils firent de profit si considerable par l'or et l'argent qu'ils tirerent de celles de Gaudalcanal, la seule qui ait eté ouverte qu'ils y etoient devenus les plus riches sujets e l'Europe : mais aiant ensuité soupçonné que le dessein du gouvernement etoit de reprendre ces mines, ils les mirent sous l'eau, et priverent par la·le roy et ses sujets, du profit qu' on en auroit peu tirer.

‖ About $1,433,971.—*Trans.*

¶ Veitia, Norte de la Contratacion de Indias, lib., cap. 33, in fine.

to the produce of the mines, has made them common, subject to the liabilities above-mentioned.[*]

23. Our sovereigns first commanded, that a fifth should be levied on the gold, silver and other metals of the Indies, without deducting expences, leaving the other four parts free, as a return for the costs and expences of working.[†] At first, according to Solorzano, the privilege was granted, in some mining districts, of paying a tenth, more or less, or even a twentieth only; in consideration of certain of the mining districts being recently discovered, or being poorer,[‡] a privilege which ought still to be maintained, being especially sanctioned by the law.[§] Afterwards, by orders issued respectively from Valladolid, the 17th of September, 1548, from Aranjuez, the 25th of May, 1569, and from Madrid, the 26th of October, 1572, directed to the kingdom of Mexico, a tenth was ordered to be levied on the silver raised from the mines, instead of a fifth; but these abatements would appear to have been temporary, for besides that the first of the aforesaid orders expressly limits the privilege to the term of six years, the very repetition of the order at different periods, shews that it must have been temporary in its operation.[||] But, as we have already observed in Chap. II., n. 71, it appears, from the report of the meeting, consisting of the viceroy and ministers of Mexico, that by an order of the 30th of December, 1716, a tenth was ordered to be levied on the miners of New Spain generally; and it is stated by Don Francisco Ramiro de Valenzuela, in his additions to the *Politica* of Don Juan de Solorzano,[¶] that a like abatement was afterwards made, in 1735, with respect to the mines of Peru.

24. The purchasers of ores, however, still continued liable to pay the fifth, until by an order dated at Balsain, the 19th of June, 1723, it was ordered, that a tenth should be levied generally upon gold and silver, throughout the government of New Spain, whether reduced by smelting or amalgamation; and that not only the miners, but also the suppliers, the purchasers by auction or contract, and others, should be liable to the same reduced duty; the object being, by this reduction of duty, to prevent the fraudulent and clandestine embezzlement of the precious metals.

---

[*] Vide sup. cap. 2, n. 16 to 23. Lagunez, de fruct. 1. p. cap. 10, n. 63 and 64. Solorzano, de jur. Indiar. tom. 2, lib. 5, cap. unic. n. 22 et 25. And in the Polit. lib. 6, cap. 1, n. 21. Antunez de Portugal, de donat. lib. 3, cap. 12 throughout, particularly n. 10. Escalona, in his Gazoph. lib. 2, p. 2, cap. 1, n. 2 and 5.

[†] Law 1, tit. 10, book 8, Collection of the Indies.

[‡] Sclorz. lib. 6, Polit. cap. 1, n. 21.

[§] Law 55, tit. 10, book 8, Collection of the Indies.

[||] These orders are at pp. 34, 91 and 98 of a book in the city of Mexico, under the care of the secretary, Don Gabriel Mendieta Rebollo, who certified that it was perserved from the conflagration and tumult of that city, on the night of the 16th of August, 1692, together with another book of the ordinances of the city, an index to which we possess, in our MS. orders, vol. 1. p, 219.

[¶] Solorzan, lib. 6, Polit. cap 18. n. 125, and lib. 6, cap. 1, n. § 1.

25. And by another order, dated at San Ildefonso, the 10th of August, 1738, the unexampled privilege was conceded to the kingdom of Guatemala, for the term of ten years, of paying only five per cent. duty on gold (as is now done in Peru), the object of which concession was, to encourage the working of the mines of that kingdom, as we have observed in the proper place.*

26. It is evident from these laws and orders, and from those of Castile, that it had been found to be for the advantage of the treasury to make these considerate abatements, the expences of the subject being very great, and the standard of the ores too low to admit of reduction. If then, these and other motives operated in regard to the kingdom of Castile, in causing the reduction of duties observed to be sanctioned by the later ordinances, where the depth of the mines and the scantiness of the produce of the heaps of rubbish and slag are noticed as circumstances entitling the proprietors to a relief of duty, a privilege extended also, as appears by the 76th ordinance, to the owners of mines much flooded with water, and requiring works of drainage; how much more strongly ought similar motives to be afforded, by the circumstances which so notoriously prevail in the Indies, where the depth of many of the mines is incredible, the heaps of refuse ore of low standard immense, and the price of quicksilver, iron, steel, salt, magistral,† and other stores, and of utensils, and the rate of wages, twice or thrice as high as in Spain; circumstances which ought all of them, unquestionably to be taken into the account, and which are therefore much relied on by Solorbano, as giving a just claim to relief.‡ And in New Spain in particular, the price of quicksilver is still higher than in other parts of the Indies, from its being supplied from Europe or Peru. Besides all this, the water is, in many mines, too abundant to be overcome by the efforts of an individual; as for instance in Zacatecas, Pachuca and Real del Monte, where the most substantial men have broken down, and the largest fortunes have been absorbed.§

27. Returning to the subject of the tenth, the same amount of duty is also to be paid on gold and precious stones captured in war,|| on the produce of ores purchased,¶ and on what is set apart for the churches and monasteries.** The duty is also to be levied on what is paid by the Indians by way of tribute,†† which cannot be conveyed from one province to another, nor to Spain, without paying the duty,‡‡ under the penalty of forfeiting four times the value of the silver, together with the mules and beasts of burthen or slaves.§§ Nor is it lawful to be possessed of gold or silver, pearls, precious

---

* Cap. 2, n. fin.

† Roasted sulphuret of copper : a re-agent employed in the reduction of the ore by amalgamation.—*Trans.*

‡ Solorz. dict. lib. 1, n. 29.

§ Villa-Senor, Theatr. Americano, page 25, cap. 3, edition printed at Mexico in 1746.

|| Law 2, tit. 10, book 8, Collection of the Indies.

¶ Law 4, ditto.   ** Law 5, ditto.

†† Laws 6 and 7, ditto.   ‡‡ Laws 8, 9, 10, ditto.

§§ Law 11, ditto.

stones or pieces of plate, which have not paid the duty, under the penalty of the forfeiture of these articles, and of the goods of the silversmith who shall have made them.* Besides these, there are various other precautionary regulations, for preventing fraud as far as possible ; thus, if there be no refining establishment in the mining district, the bars or pieces, after being registered before the justice and royal officers, are to be conveyed direct to the nearest establishment of the kind ;† and the silver which ought to be taken in to pay the duty at one particular office, is not to be allowed to pay the duty at any other.‡ The duty is to be levied upon the real value of the gold or silver,§ and the one and a half per cent. ought to be first deducted, for the principal assayer, melter and stamper, and then the fifth, which is to be of gold or silver of the same quality as the piece stamped.|| Various other economical arrangements are also established by the laws of the Indies for the advancement of this important department.¶

28. Here we must notice three laws, two of which are the 16th and 18th laws of title 10, book 8, and relate to the gold and silver seized for not having paid the duty, at Cabit or any other port where there is no refining establishment ; such gold or silver is, by these laws, declared forfeited, because it is here evident that the object can only have been to export it clandestinely to foreign countries, to the great prejudice of the crown. But it is nevertheless conceded by the 25th law of the same title and book, with respect to the port of Vera Cruz, that gold or silver seized there for non-payment of the duty, shall be returned without further delay or impediment, upon payment of the proper duties. But the rule is not altered as to the other ports,** for this regulation being made for a special case, is merely a subordinate one, and has no repealing force ; and it was in fact made upon consideration of the great number of bars, both large and small, clandestinely sent to foreign countries. And here we may observe an exercise of the greatest benignity, in that this very extreme of irregularity, instead of calling forth a more severe and rigorous punishment, is met by free pardon and forgiveness, upon payment of the usual duties alone. And the injury to the revenue arising from this practice, has in great measure been remedied, by the establishment of the markets held at Xalapa on the arrival of the convoys, and by the Flotistas (as the agents and traders from Spain are called), being prevented, by the facilities afforded for purchasing the metals in the mining districts,

* Laws 47, 48, 49, book 8, Collection of the Indies.

† Law 11, ditto.   ‡ Law 12, ditto.

§ Laws 22, 23, and 24, ditto, and Laws 1 and 2, title 22, book 4, of Collection of the Indies.

|| Laws 19 and 21, title 10, book 8, Law 13, title 22, book 4, Collection of the Indies.

¶ Book 8, title 10, of the Collection of the Indies, on the royal duty of the fifth, and book 4, title 22, on the assaying and smelting of gold and silver.

** Argument, cap. si. Papa, 10 de privil. in 6, " et quia jam per alias leges provisum erat, quæ non sunt superfluæ nec abrogatæ," cap. si Romanorum, dist. 19.

and by other means, from penetrating into the interior of the kingdom, or establishing themselves at Mexico, the inhabitants of which kingdom, in fact, make more profit by selling the silver to the crown at a just price, according to its quality, at the same time paying the duty, than by selling it to the silversmiths or Flotistas, who always pay them less than the value ; and this may be said with still more truth, now that all the business of the mint, as well as of the Apartado,* is conducted with so much openness and fidelity,† a small rate of interest being all that is demanded for the advance of money to the owners, should it happen that they are urgently in want of it, during the tedious operation of parting the bars in which silver and gold are combined.

29. We should also notice laws 47, 48 and 49, by which all wrought gold and silver, pieces of plate, chains, &c., not having paid the duty, are declared forfeited (two parts to the exchequer, and one part to the judge and informer), as well as the goods of any silversmith who shall have any such in his possession, for the purpose of being worked.   The crown however, as observed by Escalona,‡ generally waives the benefit of these laws, and allows the forfeited property to be brought in to pay the duty.   But an order granting a special exemption of this kind, expires at once,§ and cannot be renewed from time to time, or enforced by the viceroy.

30. In the year 1682, the Duke de la Palata, in obedience to an order issued the 13th of October, 1680, prohibited the exportation of wrought silver from the kingdom of Peru, on account of the irregularities experienced at the markets of Portobello.   For it being unlawful to export unwrought silver, it was the practice to make it into heavy masses, which, after receiving half a dozen blows of a hammer, passed as wrought silver, and dealings were carried on in this way at that port to the amount of at least two millions : whereupon the duke issued an edict prohibiting the exportation of wrought silver, but permitting ornaments intended for the use of the churches or for presents, or plate required for use on the voyage, to be exported to Spain, by licence from the government.   And upon the silversmiths shutting up their shops, declaring that they could not work silver which had paid the duty, because they had always been accustomed to purchase it free of duty, the duke ordered that the law on this subject should be enforced, and issued an edict, directing that the assayers's mark should be added to that of the silversmith ;|| but leaving it still lawful to work old silver, and such as should

* Establishment for parting gold and silver.—*Trans.*

† Dispatch is directed by the 10th ordinance. "With as much dispatch as the state of the funds of the establishment will permit, it being of the utmost importance both to the mines and to the trade in general, that the value of the metals should be returned to the owners without delay ; to which therefore, my superintendent is to pay proper attention."

‡ Escalona, in his Gazophil. lib. 2, p. 2, cap. 1, n. 10. "These orders being dispensatory and a matter of favour, are exhausted by once operating, and cannot be renewed or made perpetual."

§ L. mortuo bove, §. hoc sermone, ff. de v. s.

|| Instructions of the Duke de la Palata to his successor, Count de la Monclova, num. 616.

be obtained by burning silver cloth, lace or other tissues, which might be presumed to have paid the duty.

31. After this, the council, by a report, dated the 1st of October, 1731, and submitted to the crown through the secretary's office for Peru, stated that the viceroy of that kingdom, having been advised by the board of finance, of the inconveniences attending the strict observance of the above laws, had suspended the operation of the edict of the Duke de la Palata (of which he had sent a copy), and had, in the meantime, given leave to export wrought silver from the market of Portobello as formerly; which report being referred to the board of trade and coinage, who advised upon it on the 8th of Nov. 1736, his majesty by a royal decree, of the 26th of Nov. 1738 (qualified by a clause making it temporary), ordered that the regulations of the Duke de la Palata should be observed, until his majesty, upon a consideration of the duke's edict, and of the reports of the viceroy of Peru and the board of finance, should determine upon the manner and form in which laws 47, 48 and 49, above-mentioned, should be interpreted and enforced, and until the proper order for that purpose should be issued. And although it is not known what course was subsequently taken, it is most natural to suppose that the excellent plan of the above-mentioned viceroy, whose mode of government was marked by so much discretion, should have been followed up, as the only plan that could be devised, for preventing contraband exportation.

32. It appears then, that old silver, and such as was obtained by burning silver tissues, was left free from duty; but that all other silver was made subject to duty, agreeably to the laws; whereupon the silversmiths shops were again opened, after being closed six months; and this prohibition remained in force after the time of the Duke de la Palata,[*] who observes, however, in the instructions to his successor, mentioned above, that he had good reason to believe that the silver wrought by those artificers did not pay the duty, although the impossibility of applying a remedy, made it necessary to connive at the evil.

33. As to New Spain, it was commanded, by orders of the 9th of Nov. 1526, and the 7th of April, 1551, under pain of death, and of the forfeiture of goods, that no person should exercise the business of a silversmith, on account of the frauds practised by them, in mixing the metals, and in eluding the payment of the duty; a remedy, which cannot be denied to have been an effectual, although a severe one. It appears however, from the collection of orders compiled by Don Vasco de Puga, judge of the audiency of Mexico,[†] that it was provided, by an order of the 23d of May, 1559, framed with a view to the general good, and to prevent the exportation of

[*] Instructions of the Duke de la Palata, num. 649.
[†] Don Vasco de Puga, Cedular. pag. 16. and 208.

jewelry from Spain, that these artificers should be tolerated, provided they observed the ordinances made for their government. But notwithstanding the above-mentioned laws and ordinances,* nearly the same difficulties are experienced as in Peru, from its not being possible to exercise equal vigilance, in all the numerous towns of that country. Old silver, that is to say, such as has already paid the duty, is entered in a book, called the *Libro de remaches*, that it may not be liable to be charged a second time.† But with respect to services, or separate pieces of plate, it has been found necessary to relax considerably. The zeal of the viceroys has gone no farther than the promulgation of an edict, issued by Count Fuenclara in the year 1745, allowing wrought silver to be brought in to pay the duty, free of penalty; from which measure the revenue has derived considerable benefit, as it also has from the order issued to the royal, public and provincial notaries, to bring in to be stamped, all such wrought silver seized upon executions or sequestrations, or enumerated in inventories, as should not have paid the duty; an order which it will be very important to renew from time to time.

34. But according to Escalona, who cites Lasarte and others, the silver used in the pontifical ornaments of the archbishops and bishops, and such as is employed for the service of the church, is exempted from the payment of the duty, (in analogy to its exemption from the duty on sales‡); this not being in opposition to law 5, tit. 10, book 8, of the Collection of the Indies, which orders the fifth to be levied on the gold and silver, raised by working on holidays or at any other time, though appropriated to the use of a church, monastery or ecclesiastic; for charitable gifts of this kind must be so limited as not to prejudice the revenues of the crown; and if these institutions interfere in the working of the mines, they must submit to the royal charges, such as the fifth, or tenth; and such is the tenor of the law and the authorities, in reference to cases of this description.§

35. Upon this point, we may notice an order, dated the 8th of Nov. 1681, directed to the audiency of Mexico, wherein his majesty approves the original and reviewed decrees of the 26th of April, 1679, and 22d of Jan. 1680; under which, 328 marcs, 4 ounces, and 4 tomins of unwrought silver, found among the property of Fray Thomas Monterroso, bishop of Oaxaca, deceased, were confiscated. And with respect to 416 marcs, 5 ounces of wrought silver, which had not paid duty, found amongst the same property,

---

* Laws 47, 45 and 49, tit. 10, book 8, Collection of the Indies.

† Law 13, tit. 7, book 8, Collection of the Indies. Escalona, in his Gazophil. lib, 2, p. 2, cap. 1, n. 18.

‡ Escalona, Gazophil. real de el Peru, lib. 2, p. 2, cap. 1, n. 17. Lasarte, de decima venditionis, cap. 19, n. 60, cum. Barthol. et aliis.

§ Cap. abbates, de decim. cap. tributum, 23. q. 3. Auth. item prædium, Cod. de sacros. eccles L de his, Cod de episcop. et cleric. Joan. Andr. in cap. 1. de censib. Imola, Baldo et alii. apud Fragoso, de regimin. republicæ, tom. 1, p .1, lib. 2, disp. 4, 83. a. n. 223, et seq. P. Molina, de just. et jur. tom 2, disp. 383, vers. ex his, L. 55, tit. 6, p. 1. et ibi Greg.

his majesty advised the audiency, that the question was under his consideration in council, and that his determination should be announced to them ; and he ordered them to deposit the plate in the royal treasury, in the mean-time. This order is stated by the fiscal, Don Martin de Solis, who mentions the great quantity of silver which was wrought without paying the fifth.

36. The amount of the duties of the one and a half per cent. and tenth, and the coinage dues, levied on silver in the kingdom of New Spain, although liable to be affected by the fluctuations in the produce of the mines, exceeds upon an average, 700,000 dollars annually ; and that of the duties on gold, 60,000 dollars. It is mentioned, however, by Don Joseph de Villa-Senor, in his *Theatro Americano*,* that the duties on the two metals together, amounted in the year 1743, to 821,974 dollars, 7 tomins and 3 grains. And they would reach a much higher amount, were proper observance paid to the laws of the Indies,† which prohibit all dealing or trading in silver in *pinas*,‡ ingots or any other form, or in gold, in dust or ingots, not having paid the fifth ; for in the remote provinces, from the want of coin notoriously experienced there (of which we shall treat in the proper place, under ordinances 58, 72 and 73, in chapter 22), all dealings without exception are conducted in current or leaf silver.

37. The fifth is also levied on all ores of lead, copper, tin, iron, &c. ; in place of which however, a tenth only is to be charged, during the first ten years. And these metals are to be brought in to be stamped, under the same penalties and regulations as are in force regarding gold and silver.§ But, as is observed by Escalona, the levy of these duties in the Indies, has been neglected, from the great expense attending it, and the smallness of the amount‖ when collected : which is, in fact, the case in New Spain : and although those who work and reduce the ores of these metals, do so by permission of the government only, which they are bound to obtain ; yet they do not attend to any of the regulations concerning boundaries, or the other formalities observed with respect to the silver mines ; which however, according to Escalona and Don Joseph Saenz, ought to be enforced.¶ And the moderate course thus adopted, of not exacting the duties upon these metals in the Indies, with so much strictness as those upon gold and silver, is in accordance with the spirit of the ordinances under consideration,** which

* Villa-Senor, Theatro Americano, cap. 5, page. 40 and 41.

† Law 33, tit. 10, book 8, Laws 1 and 2, tit. 23, book 3, Collection of the Indies.

‡ Silver, in the state in which it remains upon the completion of the process of reduction by amalgamation, after the quicksilver is driven off by heat.—*Trans.*

§ Law 51, title 10, book 8, Collection of the Indies.

‖ Escalona, in his Gazophil. lib. 2, p. 2, cap. 1, pag. 100, §. 5, de cobre, &c. where he collects together many royal orders, directed to the viceroys of Peru, and establishing the right of the crown.

¶ Escalona, loc. proxim. citat. Don Joseph Saenz, cap. 3, Tratad. de medir minas, MS.

** Ordinances 10 and 11.

fix the duty on poor lead and copper, at one-twentieth part ; and the latter metal also, being required for the other mines, should therefore be less heavily rated.

38. Gunpowder, into the composition of which saltpetre and sulphur enter, is the subject of monopoly, and returns to the crown more than 70,000 dollars per annum. The contractor purchases the sulphur and saltpetre at prices stipulated. The saltpetre is prepared at all the saltpetre works around Mexico, in the jurisdictions of Chalco, Tezcuco and Ayotlan.

39. There is a monopoly of copper in Mechoacan, which returns to the revenue, 1000 dollars per annum ; the mines which are the subject of it, are situated in the township of Santa Clara del Cobre, in the jurisdiction of Pascuaro.* And the monopoly of alum is farmed out, at the capital of Mexico, for more than 6500 dollars per annum.†

40. These contracts contain special conditions for preventing the articles to which they relate from being otherwise procured. As to sulphur, the contractors are regarded as owners of the mines, and, as appears from the 18th condition of the last contract made with Don Rodrigo de Neira,‡ in 1747, the transaction between the contractors and those who work the materials, partakes of the nature of a letting and hiring. Without their permission, no other articles of the same kind can be prepared, nor can the mines from which they are procured be worked ; such being the usual stipulations of the contract. And the rents which they respectively pay to the crown, under these contracts, include all the duties which the revenue can claim upon the articles to which they relate, it being stipulated by the contractors, that these rents are to be regarded as compensating for the duties of the fifth or tenth.

CHAPTER IV.

IT IS PERMITTED TO TRY FOR AND WORK MINES, WITHOUT RESTRAINT, IN PUBLIC AND ALSO IN PRIVATE GROUND, SUBJECT AS TO THE LATTER, TO THE RIGHT OF THE PROPRIETOR TO BE COMPENSATED FOR THE DAMAGE DONE TO HIS PROPERTY, ACCORDING TO AN ESTIMATE TO BE MADE BY SURVEYORS.—THE OCCUPYING AND REGISTERING OF THE MINE GIVE ANY PERSON A RIGHT AGAINST THE OWNER OF THE SOIL.

ORDINANCES XVI. LXV.

XVI. Also, we ordain and command, that it shall be lawful for all persons

* Villa-Senor, Theatr. Americ. lib. 1, cap. 5, pag. 41, and lib. 3, cap. 1, pag. 22.
† Idem, lib. 1, cap. 5, pag. 41.
‡ Conditions, printed at Mexico, 1747.

whatsoever, even foreigners, to search for mines of gold and silver, and such other mines as are the subject of these our ordinances, and to make trial-pits, and to take all the requisite measures for the discovery of the aforesaid metals, throughout the whole of the kingdoms and domains of the crown of Castile (except such places as are excepted),' in all fields, woods, waste places and threshing floors,† in pasture grounds, whether belonging to our-selves, to any town, or to individuals, and in any inheritance whatsoever, without any hindrance or interruption from the owners of such pasture grounds or inheritance, or from any other persons whomsoever. And that if it should be necessary to dig or sink in such pasture ground or inheritance, it shall be lawful so to do ; provided, that if any damage be committed, the mining justice shall appoint two persons of trust, who shall make personal inspection, and declare their opinion on oath, and that if they shall not agree in their declaration, the said justice shall appoint one or more other person or persons upon oath, until they shall agree, and what the major part of such persons shall so agree in declaring, he shall command to be paid and done accordingly. And that if ore shall be found, and it shall be thought proper to follow it out, and to set up an establishment and a work shop, and to make the other arrangements necessary for working the mine or mines and reduc-ing their ores, the **damage** such pasture grounds or inheritances shall have thereby sustained **or may** thereby sustain, shall be inspected by such two persons, who, upon a due consideration of the whole matter (under their oaths as aforesaid), shall estimate the amount of the damage, which the said justice shall command to be paid as aforesaid.

LXV. Also, we ordain and command, that when and so often as cases shall arise in which arbitrators shall be nominated by the parties, or by the said mining justice, such arbitrators shall, in the first place, take an oath that they will speak and declare their opinion truly and faithfully, and that if such arbitrators shall not agree together, then, in such case of disagreement, another person shall be nominated, either by agreement of parties, or by the mining justice, and that if such last-mentioned person shall agree in opinion with either of the aforesaid arbitrators, such opinion shall be observed and carried into effect. And that, if no two of them agree, but they differ in opinion, either wholly or in part, other persons shall be successively nomi-nated, until the major part agree in opinion upon the whole matter ; which being the case, what such majority shall pronounce and declare, shall be observed and carried into effect.

---

* This appears to refer to the mines of Guadalcanal, &c. mentioned above, chap. 3, ord. **xv.** —*Trans.*

† A plot of ground, on which the corn is trodden out of the ear by horses and mules.—*Trans.*

CONTENTS OF THE COMMENTARY ON THESE ORDINANCES.

1. It is freely permitted to search for mines in all parts, even in the ground of another proprietor.
2. This is a deviation from the civil law.
3. Nothing is now payable, as formerly, to the owner of the ground.
4. Answer to an objection grounded on one of the old ordinances and on one of those of Peru.
5. The mines are not to be considered as included by the sovereign in the grant of the land.
6. It is to be understood that this right of searching freely for mines, is not to be exercised to the damage of other persons; and that any such damage is to be estimated by surveyors, to be nominated by the justice; together with an umpire, in case of their not agreeing. Allusion to the bad qualities of these surveyors.
7. An enumeration of the various kinds of injury which the owners of the ground, and the Indians, may sustain.
8. It is to be borne in mind that every right is to be exercised within moderate limits, and so as not to prejudice other parties. And consequently, the power of setting up buildings, smelting works and furnaces, granted to the miners, is not to be regarded as extended to others.
9. Any person desirous of searching for a mine or treasure in cultivated ground, must give security for the damage.
10. There are very few mines in New Spain, worked in the ground of any other than the miner.
11. The owner of the ground is, for various reasons, not to be preferred before the party who has registered the mine.

COMMENTARY.

1. It appears from these ordinances, that both subjects of the crown and foreigners (taking this word with the limitation above stated),[*] have an absolute right to search for mines, in all places whatsoever, whether the ground be public or private property, and in the latter case without hindrance from the proprietor, provided they compensate him for any damage done, according to the estimate of experienced persons. Similar provisions are contained in the 15th of the old ordinances.[†] The corresponding ordinance of Peru, adds a penalty of 1000 dollars, to be imposed, without appeal, upon the mere proof of the act of resistance.[‡] And the general law of the Indies permits subjects to try for mines wherever they may think proper, and to work them freely and without any sort of impediment,[§] it being for the public benefit that it should be so. And this, according to Antunez, Alfaro and Gregorio Lopez,[||] who refer to Cepola, Paulo de Castro, Pedro Barbosa,

---

[*] Sup. cap. 2, n. 25, 26.

[†] Law 5, tit. 13, cap. 15, book 6, Collection of Castile.

[‡] Ordinance 1, of those issued by the viceroy, Don Francisco de Toledo, published by Escalona in his Gazoph. lib. 2, p. 2, c. 1, page 104.

[§] Law 1, tit. 19, book 4, of the Collection of the Indies.

[||] Antunez, de donat. lib. 3, cap. 12, n. 15, Alfaro, de offic. fisc. gloss. 20, §. 6, n. 114. Gregor Lopez, in gloss. 2, L. 27, tit. 11, partid. 4.

Horatius Montanus and others, is the reason for giving permission to try for a vein of ore on the ground of another, against the will of the owner. The same rule holds as to treasure, found either in Spain or the Indies, as to which the same forms of law must be observed, such treasure belonging by right to the crown.*

2. By these regulations, the civil law and the old law of Spain have been altered.—First, mines in public ground could not formerly be worked without a licence, as belonging by right to the sovereign, whilst those in private ground were regarded as the property of the owner of the soil, being the proper produce thereof. This is stated by Solorzano, Antunez, Gutierrez and Lagunez, who make copious references to the text of the common law; and cite the authority of many Doctors.† But according to our new ordinances, no licence to try for mines, either from the sovereign or the proprietor of the ground, is required.

3. Secondly, by the civil law, if any person discovered a vein by permission of the owner of the ground, he was liable to pay one tenth to the latter, and one tenth to the exchequer.‡ And according to the 15th of the old ordinances, the owner of the land, besides being compensated for the damage, was entitled to be paid one per cent. before deducting the payment to the revenue ;§ and this payment of one per cent. likewise obtained under the ordinance of Peru.|| But by the 16th ordinance of the new code, no part of the gold or silver raised, is to be paid to the owner of the inheritance or estate, and the payment to the revenue of the fifth or tenth, or whatever may be imposed, is the only payment required.

4. And although some persons would perhaps hold, that the omission in this 16th ordinance ought to be supplied from the 15th of the old ordinances, and from those of Peru, so as to establish the payment of this one per cent.

---

* Law 1, tit. 13, book 6, of the Collection of Castile. Law 1, tit. 12, book 8, of the Collection of the Indies, " As a revenue which of right belongs to us." This law gives the form of the security to be entered into for the damage ; and of the agreement as to the portion to be taken, first deducting the duties and fifths. And by the second law of the same title, the treasure found in sepulchres is to go, after deducting the fifth, one half to the king and one half to the discoverer. Amaya, in Cod. tit. 15, a. n. 49, usque ad 52, cum Valenzuela, Gutierrez, Castillo, Mastrillo, Covedo et aliis.

† L. 3, de jur. fisci. L. divortio §. si vir. ff. de reb. oer. Vide innumeros apud Solorz. de jur. Indiar. tom. 2, lib. 5, cap. unic. n. 27. Antunez, de donat. lib. 3, cap. 12, n 1, usque ad 10. Gutierr. Practicar. lib. 4, quæst. 36, n. 59. Lagunez, de fructib. 1, p. cap. 10, n. 52, et seqq. Amaya, in Cod. L. unic. de thesaur. n. 30, qui omnes cumulant jura et AA.

‡ L. cuncti, Cod. de metallar lib. 11. " Cuncti qui per privatorum loca saxorum venam. laboriosis effosionibus persequuntur, decimas fisco, decimas etiam domino repræsentent."

§ Cap. 15, of law 5, tit. 13, book 6, of the Collection of Castile. " Provided that, besides making a compensation for the damage, the owner of the pasture ground or inheritance where the mines shall be found, shall be paid one per cent. upon all the silver raised from such mines, clear of all expenses, and before the deduction and payment of our duties, it being our will and command that such one per cent. shall be paid out of the whole."

|| Ordinance 2, in Escalona's Gazophil. lib. 2, part 2, cap. 2, p. 104.

in New Spain ; it is impossible that this can be a correct opinion, for the intentional omission of this charge, whilst all the rest of the old ordinance is repeated verbatim in the new, is the same thing as if an express clause to the contrary had been inserted ; such an obvious omission on the part of the sovereign, to state what he might so easily have expressed, proving that it was not his will that the regulation he had previously made in the old ordinance should be enforced ; besides which, it is evident that the principal object of this and the other heads of the new ordinance, is to benefit and relieve the subject, by abating the charges previously payable to the crown.   And the ordinance of Peru is confined in its operation to that kingdom alone, and does not extend to New Spain, where the ordinances of the code are to be observed, until others shall be confirmed by the council.*   And the general laws of the Indies merely contain a proviso against injuring third persons, or the Indians ; the meaning of which is, as we have shewn in Chapter II., that compensation is to be made for the damage,† but not that any further charge should be imposed, beyond the fifth or tenth payable to the crown. Another argument, bearing with considerable force on the question, is derived from the words of the law, which, when provided for the payment of the fifth, declares that no other deduction shall be made, and that it is the will of their catholic majesties to grant away the other four parts, so that every person may have power to dispose of them, as of anything of their own, free, quit and clear, as a return for their costs and expenses.‡   And again, as they are to be common in all places, and to every description of persons, free and discharged from every kind of impediment,§ it follows, that they can be subject to no other charge except the fifth.

5. As a consequence of this liberty to seek for mines, extended absolutely to all persons, it follows, that they must be regarded as not having passed with the grants of land from the sovereign, unless particularly mentioned in the grant, or unless a case of immemorial prescription be made out.|| But, except in these two cases, no person of whatever condition, rank or dignity, can prevent their being searched for in his farms, pastures, inheritance or other place.   For they have been made everywhere common by royal authority, in favour of those subjects who shall first discover or take possession of them.

6. But this permission, it is to be understood, is to be so exercised as not to prejudice third persons ; and the amount of any damage that may be done, is to be estimated by surveyors (who are to be nominated by the justice and not by the parties), together with one or more umpires, in case of

---

* Laws 1 and 6, book 4, tit. 19, Law 3, tit. 3, book 2, Collection of the Indies.
† Law 1, tit. 19, book 4, Collection of the Indies.
‡ Law 1, tit. 10, book 8, Collection of the Indies.
§ Law 1, tit. 19, book 4, Collection of the Indies.
|| Law 2, title 13, book 6, Collection of Castile ; et ibi Acevedo.   Lagunez, de fruct. 1. p. cap. 10, u. fin. cum Horatio Montano, de regalib. verb. Argentaria, n. 5.

their not agreeing; and in default of payment of what the surveyors shall estimate upon oath, as the amount of the damage, execution shall be levied. Such are the provisions of our 16th ordinance, and they are more plainly laid down in the 65th, which prescribes the mode in which umpires are to be nominated, until they agree in opinion, directing that when the majority agree, their award is to be observed and enforced; which is also agreeable to the rules of the civil law, as we may learn from the Cardinal de Luca, and from Bichio, Burato and Gregorio.* And as we before remarked, the ordinance provides (probably with a view to dispatch), that the justice shall nominate the surveyors; for if they were to be nominated by the parties themselves, they would be prejudiced and inclined to the interest of those who had appointed them, and would be liable to be influenced by partiality or regard; which is so much the case, that the greatest inconvenience the judges experience in this and other matters, wherein it is necessary to have recourse to the aid of surveyors, arises from their obstinate disagreements, wherein they display, not their intelligence and skill, but their corruption, prejudice and partiality. And these evils are lamented by the most judicious writers,† who give rules for preventing the delays and vexatious objections interposed by the parties; one of which is, that a list should be previously given in, that there may be an opportunity of challenging any persons who are suspected, after which, no objection should be made to any person who may be appointed, but their judgment, or that of the umpire, in case of disagreement, should be final. And therefore, the ordinance directs, that they be persons in whom the judge can place confidence, and men of due probity, judgment and rectitude, so that they may form their estimate upon a fair consideration of all the damage attending the setting up of the mining establishment, and the other arrangments necessary for carrying on the works.

7. The damage may arise, not merely from the digging and excavating, the soil, but from the setting up and building houses and smelting furnaces‡ in pasture grounds required for cattle, or from any other inconvenient circumstance affecting the owner of the soil, and arising from the mines; as for instance, if, after the soil has been reduced into cultivation, the culture should be interfered with by the denouncement of the mine. And were the law otherwise, it would be unjust, as we are told by Acevedo and Antunez who follow Afflictis, Rolando del Valle and others.§ But by this means in

* Luc. disc. 33, de judic. n. 21. Bich. decis. 261 et 564. Burat dec. 56. Gregor. dec. 271, 177, p. 10, recent.

† Luca in various places in his Theatro, and especially in disc. 33, de judiciis, n. 19, usque ad 37; ibi. n. 33. " Circa propriam artem, vel peritiam, frequenter neque suum officium bene exercent; ut præsertim contigit in peritis estimatoribus." Et n. 24, " Quilibet est defensor vel patrocinator illius partis quæ ipsum elegit."

‡ Chap. 21, ordinance 52.

§ Acevedo, upon law 4, tit. 13, book 6. n. 1. Antunez, de donat. regiis, lib. 3, cap. 12, n. 17.

jury to third persons is prevented. Injury done to the Indians is particularly noticed by the law, which directs that regard be had to their wretched condition, and that compensation be made to them for the land taken from them, and for all other damage done to them;* and that no one presume to intrude wantonly into their ground.

8. And as every right, the exercise of which may indirectly operate to the prejudice of third persons, is to be used with as much moderation as may be, and so as to produce the least possible damage,† it will be proper that the justice should confine the right, and prevent the damage, as much as possible. That is to say, that he should permit no persons to erect smelting houses, furnaces or other works, except the owners of mines, of whom the law makes express mention,‡ and who require them, as accessary to the principal object of working the mines; and the purchasers of ores in the large way, who require them for the same reason. I recollect a case where, under pretence of setting up litharge works, certain inhabitants of the place, by name Castorena, were about to set up grinding and stamping mills, on part of the farm of Reoyos, in New Galicia, belonging to the Count de Santiago; but the royal audiency of that district, upon the representation of the Count, ordered them to quit the place, and to make good the damage done to the land by them and their cattle, as well because theirs was a case to which the ordinances did not apply, as because their works might have been carried on upon land of their own, without intruding into that of others.

9. This licence is also restricted by the second of the ordinance of Peru,§ which provides, that if the discoverers of mines wish to search in vineyards or plantations of trees, either from malicious motives, or because they are, as they allege, certain that ore is to be found there, they shall give security, before making any trial, to repay to the owner of the soil whatever damage they may occasion. And this is agreeable to the civil law,‖ which has for its object to prevent, by this precaution, the opportunity which would be presented for the exercise of malice, and to guard against the damage which might otherwise be suffered in buildings and cultivated ground,¶ in which, according to the law, it was not permitted to dig, under pretence of there being

---

* Law 1, title 19, book 4, Collection of the Indies.

† Odia restringi, favores convenit ampliari.

‡ Cap. 26, ord. 52. "The owners of them." "The owners of the mines." "The owners of the said mines."

§ Escalona, in his Gozoph. lib. 2, part 2, cap. 1, page 104.

‖ L. 15, §. 2, ff. de damno infecto, ibi: "Cum autem in alieno fiat, satisdationem prætor injungit."

¶ "Damnum infectum est damnum nondum factum, quod futurum veremur." Leg. 8, ff. de damno infecto.

ore.* And as to the object of these laws is to secure indemnity to third persons, namely, the owners of the soil, but at the same time not to restrain the right of searching for mines, it would be extremely agreeable to justice, in all cases where objections are made, upon a reasonable apprehension of damage, that the discoverer should give security to make it good, in analogy to the regulation of the law of the Indies, respecting those who are desirous of searching for treasure.†

10. In New Spain however, from the immense extent of those regions, and from the great abundance of mineral treasure which may be found in the common and waste places, there are no instances of mines being registered in the ground of other proprietors. By the 17th ordinance, mines are not allowed to be registered without producing ore, and indicating the place where it has been found.

11. The question may be raised, whether, upon the discovery of a mine in another proprietor's ground, the owner of the soil is entitled to claim precedence of and oust the discoverer? To which we reply, on the authority of Baldus, Paulo de Castro, Rosenthal, Petrus Barbosa, Bartholo and Cepola, all of whom are cited by Antunez,‡ that the discoverer is to be preferred before the owner of the ground, provided he comply with the directions of the ordinances concerning registry. First, because he who first takes possession according to law, is in a better condition.§ Second, because the mine or vein is not part of the estate, nor did it pass with the land, but is common, and falls to him who first takes possession of it. Third, because he who first sets about exploring and working the vein, is in a situation to claim the preference, both by rules of justice,‖ and by the ordinances of the new code, which confer upon the first discoverer the right of making the first registry, and of taking a large space of ground, with other privileges which we shall notice hereafter.¶ In Peru, a mine is to be allotted to the owner

---

* Leg. 6, Cod. de metall. "Quosdam operta humo esse saxa dicentes, id agere cognovimus, ut defossis in altum cuniculis alienarum' ædium fundamenta labefactent. Qua de re, si quando hujusmodi marmora sub ædificiis latere dicantur, perquirendi eadem copia denegetur."

† Law 1, tit. 12, book 8. "Binding themselves personally, and their property likewise, with sufficient sureties, to satisfy and make good to the owner, the damage or injury which the searching for treasure may occasion to the houses, cultivated grounds and possessions, where they shall assume the treasure to be, according to the estimate of intelligent and experienced persons."

‡ Antunez, de donat, lib. 3, cap. 13, n. 16.

§ Leg. 32, ff. de procurator. "Pluribus procuratoribus in solidum simul datis, occupantis melior conditio erit," Larrea, Decis. Granat. disp. 43, n. 3, and 31, cum pluribus.

‖ Antunez, de donationib. lib. 2, cap. 12, cum Barth. Cæpola, Barbosa et Rosenthal, n. 16. " Quia prius in cæpit quærere venas, et laborare facereque ea que pertinent ad inveniendam rem de cujus prælatione agitur."

¶ See chap. 8 and 9, and ord. 22 and 23. Law 9, tit. 13, book 6, Collection of Castile. Larrea, dec. 44, n. 3. " Et in minis argenti, auri, et in reliquis metallis pretiosis legibus nostris adeo jus adquiritur invenienti, ut illud extendat primus inventor in 120 ulnas longitudinis, et 60 latitudinis."

of the soil, after setting out one for the discoverer, and one for the crown.* But in New Spain there is no law to this effect, although the owner of the soil, as well as any other person, may afterwards register a mine if he pleases. Fourth, because it is to the advantage of the public, that ores should be searched for, and that mines should be explored and worked by the people generally,† and the owner of the soil has therefore no right to prohibit them from doing so, nor can he have any right to deprive another of the fruits of his diligence. And this applies not only to mines of the precious metals, but also to any mineral deposits, as was determined by the senate of Granada, in a decision which is illustrated by Larrea, in his collection, where he shews, that upon the ground of utility to the public, any other person may work upon the continuation of the original vein. And Corradini, in his *Tratado de el derecho de prelacion*, puts the question in express terms, and comes to the conclusion, that the proprietor of the ground has no right of priority, if the veins belong to the sovereign, but that, if they belong by right to the private owner, he is to have the benefit of them, unless some other person have commenced digging, or have laid out money on them, in which case such latter person shall be preferred, upon the ground of his having taken earliest possession.‡

CHAPTER V.

OF REGISTERING MINES OF GOLD AND SILVER, AND OF ENTERING IN THE REGISTER THE SALES, TRANSFERS AND ALTERATIONS OF THE BOUND-ARIES OF SUCH MINES ; HOW AND BEFORE WHOM SUCH REGISTRY IS TO BE MADE ; AND THAT THE DIFFERENCE BETWEEN REGISTRY AND DE-NOUNCEMENT IS ONLY IN FORM, AND NOT IN SUBSTANCE.

ORDINANCES XVII. XVIII. XIX. LXIX.

XVII. Also we ordain and command, that whoever shall discover a mine of gold, silver or other metal whatsoever, shall be bound, within 20 days after discovering or finding the ore, to register such mine before the mining justice within whose jurisdiction it shall be situate, and in the presence of a notary, producing the ore which he shall have found. And that the regis-ter shall describe the person who has made the discovery and registry, and also the place where the mine is situate, and where the ore produced was found. And that the person making such registry shall, within sixty days

---

* Ordinance 2, of the viceroy Don Francisco de Toledo, in Escalona, lib. 2, cap. 1, page 105.

† Larrea, dec. 44, n. 21. "Quasi publicæ utilitati quæ in metallorum indagatione consistit, maxime expediat a pluribus metalla perquiri et effodi." L. 1, Cod. de metallariis.

‡ Corradini, de jur. prælat. q. 67 per totam.

from the making thereof, be bound to send, and shall send an authenticated copy of such registry, to our administrator-general, if there be one in the district, and if not, then to the administrator of the department, within which the mine may be situate, in order that the interest which each person may have in such mines, may be noted and entered in the book of registry, and so that all the mines which shall be discovered, may be known, and an account thereof taken. And that in case such registry be not made in the manner and within the time aforesaid, any person may register such mine, and shall thereby have and acquire the right which such discoverer or other person, who might have required the registry, would have had, if he had caused the registry to be made as aforesaid.

XVIII. Also, forasmuch as many new and old mines which have been discovered and registered previous to the time of issuing these our ordinances are occupied, but are kept at a stand and unworked, and there is no complete information as to these mines, the registries of which have been made in an irregular manner :—We ordain and command, that all persons who, previous to the issuing of these our ordinances, shall have explored and registered old or newly-discovered mines, shall be bound to renew and make such registry again, within the term of two months, according to, and in the manner prescribed by the last ordinance, with respect to such as may hereafter be discovered. And that they shall be bound, within the further period of 60 days, to send, and they shall send such registries to our administrator-general aforesaid, if there be one within the district, and if not, then to the administrator-general of the department within which the mine shall be situate ; and that if they shall fail to do this, and to procure an authenticated copy of such registry, they shall be deemed to have forfeited, and shall forfeit the right they may have acquired or may claim, to such mine, and that any person who shall take the proper steps, agreeably to this our edict, shall have the mine.

XIX. Also, we ordain and command, that the mining administrators of each district shall keep a book, in which shall be entered all the registries made in such district, concerning all the mines already discovered, or which may be discovered, taken, sold, or dealt with in any other manner, and such administrators shall send to the office of our principal accountant, each for his own district, a report of the state of the mines of these our kingdoms, and of what shall have been done concerning them, signed with his own name ; and that after having sent the first report, they shall send, every six months, a like report of all that may have taken place, or been done in respect of the same.

LXIX. Also, we ordain and command, that all persons who shall seek for, find and take, mines or streamworks of gold, as well the first discoverers as others, shall, in regard to the taking possession of, registering and staking out the boundaries of such mines, observe the provisions of such of these ordinances as relate to the taking possession of, registering and staking out the boundaries of silver mines, and under the same penalties as are therein imposed ; and that they shall be bound, in conformity with the last-mentioned ordinances, and under the like penalties, to transmit the registries to our administrator-general, or to the administrater of the department, and that the last-mentioned officers shall keep books of registry, for the mines of gold, in like manner as is provided in regard to those of silver.

CONTENTS OF THE COMMENTARY ON THESE ORDINANCES.

1. Of the necessity of registering the mines, and the time prescribed for that purpose.
2. What registry is.
3. It is the basis of the title to the property of the mine.
4. Arguments showing the advantage and necessity of such a proceeding.
5. One object amongst others, is to furnish the respective governments with information concerning the mines.
6. Of the book of registry, its object and advantages. It is to be kept by the administrator of the department.
7 and 8. There being no such officers in the Indies, these books are to be kept by the governors and chief alcaldes, to prevent mistakes or false entries. A notice of a very strict order to this effect, issued by the Marquess de Casa Fuérte, in the year 1727.
9 and 10. There must be a new registry for every change of owner, and the like upon an alteration of the boundaries.
11. In Peru there is a mining notary in each province.
12. The hour of making the registry must be entered, and why ?
13. Several questions on the subject of registry proposed and answered.
14. The registry is not to be made before the officers of the crown.
15. Practice of the government in the case of new discoveries. Of the authority of the viceroys, and of the right of the presidents and governors to arrange matters concerning the government of the mines.
16 and 17. Delay in making registry is corrected, provided no other person shall have made registry in the mean time.
13. Of the facility with which the registry may be made, and which renders its omission inexcusable.
19. In Peru, the discoverer of a mine, not making registry within the time prescribed by the ordinance, loses the privilege of a discoverer.
20. Two exceptions to this rule, one when it is found impossible to do so, and the other in cases where the Indians are concerned, their ignorance being a sufficient excuse.
21 to 25. Registry and denouncement are substantially the same, although differing in form ; which is proved by several arguments, and by inference from several of the ordinances.

COMMENTARY.

1. The three first of these ordinances agree with the 16th, 17th and 18th of the old ordinances,* with the 4th chapter of the edict of the year 1559,†

---

* Law 5, tit. 13, book 6, Collection of Castile, cap. 16, 17 and 18.
† Law 4, cap. 4, eod.

and with the ordinances of Peru,[*] in this respect, that all these laws direct that newly-discovered mines of silver shall be registered. The like provision is made with regard to gold, by the 69th ordinance. The ordinances of Peru, however, allow 30 days for making the registry; but in New Spain, the law of Castile is followed, which fixes 20 days.

2. Registry is nothing more than a public description of the person who has found the mine, and the place where it is situate, and an exhibition of the ore, to be made before a justice and notary. The practice in the mining districts of New Spain is, to present a written document stating the particulars above mentioned, and the signs by which the mine may be known, setting forth the mines and stakes of other proprietors contiguous to it, and mentioning the name by which it is to be distinguished. All the trial pits, whether large or small, pits, trenches and other works within the boundaries, are to be likewise registered. The justice then declares the mine to be registered, and gives permission to work it; after which the miner must sink it to the depth of three *estados*;[†] subsequently also, he prays to have possession given to him, and the boundaries assigned.

3. The registry is the basis of the title to the mine, and the attributive cause of the subject's right of property in it; the crown having subjected the proprietor to this obligation when he made the mines common.[‡] And no mine can be lawfully worked, until registry is made, without which it is liable to be registered by any other person, the form of the ordinance not having been complied with.

4. The reasonableness of this regulation is evident. First, because the mines are not allowed to be worked without permission from the crown, or from the justice in the king's name;[§] which permission is granted at the time of making the registry. Second, because, as the revenue is interested in a share of the produce, it is incumbent on the discoverer to give information of his discovery, and by the civil law, concerning treasures, if he suppressed the discovery, he was liable to forfeit the whole of the treasure found, and double the value:[||] and therefore, the discoverer, if he would preserve his right, should give notice of the discovery of the mine, and make himself known. Third, because, by another of the ordinances, no one can register another person's mine, or a mine which any other person has discovered and registered;[¶] and therefore the person who has discovered the mine, ought to declare himself. Fourth, because, as is provided by another of the ordinances, no mine is allowed to be worked, unless both a vein and metallic ore be actually present,[**] on which account the ore must be

---

[*] Ordinance 4. Escalona, Gazophil. lib. ii, p. 2, cap. 1, pag. 105.

[†] See chap. 16. ord. 35 and 36.

[‡] Law 1, tit. 19, book 4, Collection of the Indies.   [§] Gutierr. Pract. q. 37. n. 63.

[||] L. 3. §. fin. ff. de jur. fisci. Law. 1, tit. 13, book 6, Collection of Castile.

[¶] See chap. 6, ordinance 20.   [**] Chap. 14, ordinance 30.

produced, and an oath must be taken, as provided by the ordinance of Peru, cited above, that it was found at the place described, in order that it may appear that the pit, which is proposed to be opened and worked, is not so proposed under a false or malicious pretence. Fifth, because, as all the mines, whether those taken by the first discoverer, or ordinary mines, must have some determinate* limits and boundaries assigned to them, their sight to be made known and pointed out for that purpose. Sixth, because, as a preference is given in measuring out the boundaries of the mines, according to the longer or shorter time which has elapsed since making the registry,† it is requisite that it should be made in due form, and consequently, if no registry be made, the title is defective. Seventh, because it frequently happens, where a communication is made between the workings of two mines, that it is alleged that one or the other. of them was commenced upon dead ground, not containing a vein or ore. And although, under certain circumstances, which will be noticed in their proper place, the registry is not conclusive evidence to the contrary, yet it may be of much assistance in establishing that the mine was properly commenced, if, as is generally the case, no clearer proofs of malice or fraud be adduced.

5. Besides the above-mentioned, another important object is attained by means of the registry, namely, that of having an account of all the mines which exist, or which may be discovered, as the ordinances express it ; by which means, not only the rights of individuals in relation to the mines, are assured, and this important class of property preserved in a regular course of succession ; but the withholding of the tenths or fifths payable on the silver which may be raised from them is prevented, and the government is furnished with authentic information concerning the mines, and is enabled to make proper arrangements in relation to their economy and government. With this view therefore, it is ordered, not only that the mine owners shall transmit their registries to the administrator-general, but that the mining administrator of each district shall keep a book, in which he is to enter all registries which may be made of mines already discovered, or to be discov- ered, taken, sold or dealt with in any other manner within his district ; and that he shall send a report to the office of the principal accountant every six months.

6. Properly speaking, the register is the book in which deeds and grants are entered, for the perpetual remembrance thereof; so that if they be lost, torn or defaced, or if any question be raised as to their identity or authority, recourse may be had to the book of registry, as appears from the law of the *Partida*,‡ agreeable to which all gifts and grants are registered in the public

---

* Chap. 10, ordinance 23.   † Chap. 11, ordinance 25.
‡ Law 8, tit. 19, part 3. " And we declare that the register is, in other words, a book to pre- serve the remembrance of the deeds and grants which may be made. And it is of much use for if the grant or deed be lost or torn, or if the writing be effaced, by age or by any other means

archives; and in cities and corporations, registry is made of the rents reserved upon houses and inheritances, and of all hypothecations of such property, in order to guard against the inconvenience which follows from the evidences of such transactions being wholly in the power of individuals, who may falsify, alter or lose them, to the prejudice of the public and of private interests.

7. But inasmuch as there are not any general or particular administrators in the Indies, although there are governors, mayors and chief alcaldes in the mining districts, and likewise mining and registering notaries, the provisions of these ordinances ought in this, as in all other respects, to be maintained and observed in that kingdom, agreeably to the rules of its municipal laws, as stated by us above.* For it is a great object to guard against the serious consequences which might otherwise ensue, from the importance of the interests which are involved in mining; the litigation being principally concerning mines yielding rich produce. And these considerations induced the viceroy, Marquess Casa Fuerte, to issue an order, dated at Mexico, the 28th of June, 1727, countersigned by Don Antonio de Aviles, commanding the royal officers and justices to send, as speedily as possible, an account of the mines within their several districts, whether at work or abandoned, and what means there might be of supplying them; and in case they should have no book of registry for the mines which might have been registered in all the departments of each district, then to form one with all possible dispatch, that an account might thus be obtained of all the mines in the kingdom, from which a general book might be made up, shewing all the mines which have been discovered, those which were then at work, and those which had been abandoned; and that the causes of their abandonment being ascertained, the proper arrangements might be made; such general book to be under the eye of the viceroy. But we are not aware that this order, so agreeable to the spirit of the ordinances now under consideration, and so important to the interests of the revenue, in a public, and of the subject, in a private point of view, was ever carried into effect. It would certainly be very desirable to compel the royal officers and chief mining alcaldes to observe it.

8. The original grants then, ought not to be given into the custody of the owners, until the registry be made in the proper book, under the direction of the mining notary of the department; for otherwise, these important instruments will be exposed to the contingencies alluded to above, and very serious difficulties may arise in subsequent dealings, in ascertaining whether the reg-

---

or if any question should be raised concerning it, from its being erased or upon any other ground; the loss may be repaired, or the old deed renewed, by reference to the register. And moreover, any question raised concerning deeds, of which suspicions are entertained, may be put at rest, &c." Law 3, tit. 3, book 5, and law 12, and the whole of tit. 15, book 2, of the Collection of Castile.

* Law 3, tit. 1, book 2, Collection of the Indies, and the whole of tit. 21, book 4, of the same.

istry or denouncement was made with due solemnity, the time and manner of making it, the greater or less antiquity of the mine, or the clearness with which the title of the owner is deduced; all which are avoided, if the registry or denouncement, the sales, contracts and other documents of title, under which the new possessor. proceeds to work the mine, and to enrol himself in the list of miners, are made to appear in the book or archive.

9. This is repeated in plainer terms in another ordinance,* which prohibits the sale of a mine, unless it be sunk to the depth of three *estados;* directing also, that the purchaser shall give notice of the sale, in order that it may be entered in the register book, under pain of forfeiting the mine and its value; "And the like if there be a change in the ownership of the mine, under any other title." By *title,* is to be understood a contract of any description, whether onerous or lucrative, or succession by testament or otherwise, in all which cases it is necessary that the registry should be made, " both for the sake," as is stated in the ordinance above-cited,† "of making it appear upon whom the share is to be levied," that is to say, from whom the royal duties are to be demanded; and also to guard against all the inconveniences which flow from the want of the proper formalities in the first registry, or in the subsequent deeds of transfer.

10. And not only ought the purchase deeds of mines to be entered in the register, but the alterations which the miners make in their boundaries, which we shall see, in the proper place, is provided by another ordinance.‡

11. In reference to this subject, the laws of the Indies and the ordinances of Peru§ have provided, that there shall be a mining notary in each province, before whom all the registries shall be passed, and who shall reside at the principal mining district, and that the registries of the discoveries made in other places shall be made before his deputies, and shall be ratified before the principal within 60 days, under pain of avoiding the registry. And he shall keep all the registries in one place, and in a clear manner.

12. And, as is stated by Escalona, in the margin of the ordinance above-mentioned, on the authority of a passage in Agricola, the notary ought not only to enter the particulars above-mentioned, but also the hour of making the registry.‖ And the reason is evident, for should any question of preference arise, in regard to the measuring or altering the boundaries, regard must be had to the priority of the registry, agreeably to the ordinance.¶ And the like reason applies in the case of bankruptcy, and in other cases

---

* Infr. chap. 16, ordinance 42.   † Ubi sup. n. 7, proxime antecedenti.

‡ Chap. 13, ord. 29.

§ The whole of tit. 5, book 8, concerning the mining and registering notaries, and the whole of tit. 21, book 4, concerning the principal mining alcaldes, and notaries. Order 5, tit. 9, Escalona, Gazoph. lib. 2, p. 2, cap. 1, pag. 112.

‖ Agricola, de re metallic. pag. 66, " Scriba fodinarum in codicem infert." And p. 97. " Primo signat nomen ejus qui petit jus fodinæ, deinde quo die quâve horâ," &c.

¶ Cap. 8, ord. 22.

where the right to preference may be contested, to confer which a priority of a single instant of time is sufficient.*

13. Having shewn what are the solemnities with which the registry ought to be made, several questions occur on certain points in these ordinances.

14. First, whether, in reference to our laws of the Indies,† the registry should not also be made before the royal officers of the district? The answer to which is, that it ought not to be, nor is it so in practice; for, although the laws direct that the discoverers shall make oath that they will bring in to be stamped all the gold, silver or pearls, respectively, which they may find in mines, rivers or oyster banks, this has reference to the levying of the revenue, which is a distinct object from the denouncement or registry of the mines, the latter being the office of the justices of the departments alone, many of whom have the title of chief mining alcaldes. And the oath above referred to is administered, in the case of a new discovery, in order to ensure the due levying of the duties, but not upon the registry of a mine, the title to which comes under the cognizance of the justice, as has been already shewn.

15. It often happens, that the discovery of some new mining district occurs, the richness of which calls attention to it. When this is the case, the governors, each in his own province, ought to make the best arrangement they can for settling such district and supplying it with provision, and for levying his majesty's share of the produce; these being, amongst others, the purpose for which the government of the provinces has been confined to them, and concerning which the royal laws address them, both personally and in their official character.‡ It is very true that, from the particular circumstances of some of the mining districts, such as their position, remoteness or richness, it is often necessary to form an establishment of royal officers, with assaying and smelting houses, and a treasury; but these arrangements are the province of the viceroy (subject to the approval of his majesty, if he should think proper to confirm them, upon consideration of the reports submitted to him); for the forming of these establishments, and the salaries and expenses to be allowed, depend, provisionally, upon the viceroys alone. So all other matters of government depend on the presidents and governors, in their respective districts, agreeable to the laws above-cited, and to royal orders issued since their promulgation. But judicial matters, such as registry, denouncement, the giving possession and so forth, are the province of

---

* Tot. tit. ff. et Cod. qui potior in pignor. cap. qui prior, de r. j. in 6. Salgado, in Labyr, 2 p. cap. 13, n. 6, cum pluribus ibi: " In his enim quæ momento temporis perficiuntur momentum sufficit, ut operentur; et ideo ad prælationem sufficit prioritas in puncto temporis," &c. Olea, de cess. jur. tit 8, quæst. 3, n. 3. Crespi, observe. 46.

† Laws 1 and 2, tit. 19, book 4, Collection of the Indies.

‡ Laws 1, 2, 9 and 10, tit. 19, Law 4, tit 20, book 4, Collection of the Indies.

the justices, and (by way of appeal) of the royal ordiencies, as we shall shew more particularly in the proper place.*

16. The second question which arises upon these ordinances is, whether the discoverer can make the registry after the expiration of the 20 days assigned for that purpose ?   In regard to which, it is necessary to bear in mind the following distinction.   If, after the expiration of that period, no person should register the mine, the discoverer may register it; for it is a common rule, that whilst circumstances remain unaltered, delay may be corrected, and even penalties avoided, as is shewn by Tapato and Pichardo, upon the authority of Osacius, Bellamera, Eneo Roberto, Acursius, Bartholo and others.†   And the 17th ordinance merely ordains, " that if the discoverer do not observe the proper form and time, any other person shall be at liberty to register the mine, and shall thereby have and acquire the rights which the discoverer would have had, if he had made the registry in due form ;" but it does not deprive the discoverer of the right of registering, if no other person have registered the mine.

17. If, after the expiration of the term of 20 days, some other person should come forward and register the mine, the discoverer loses his right, this being the penalty he is liable to pay for his culpable default, in neglecting the register his mine, and thus frustrating the ends of the ordinances.   For a mine which is worked without being registered, is not properly to be called a mine, and does not merit the name, even though it should yield good ore. The ordinances give the name of *mines* to such only as are registered, because the registry is the basis of the title to every mine, and because the omitting to make registry, evidences a vicious intention to dispose of the ore or silver clandestinely, in fraud of the right of the crown, and to put impediments in the way of other individuals, who might wish to take mines upon the same vein or at the same spot.

18. Nor ought any pretence of being impeded by illness, distance or the like, to be admitted by way of excuse ; for such impediments as these may always be overcome by diiigence.   And as servants are employed to raise the silver, so a servant may be sent with the ore, being furnished with an authority ; or if no notary is to be found, then, without such authority, and with a written note merely, or even without that, if the owner should happen not to be able to write.   For, as neither the ordinances nor the laws of the Indies require, as a necessary circumstance, that the owner should appear in person for this purpose, it follows that a servant may make registry in the name of his master,‡ because all acts which do not require personal attend-

---

* Chap. 25, infra, per tot.

† Tepat. Variar. juris sententiarum, lib. 1.   Ubi de moræ remissione, et purgatione, page 208, et seq. Pichardo, in Manuduct. ad Praxim, disp. de mora, a. n. 93, et n. 148.

‡ Chap. 15, ord. 32.   " Unless under a power, or by a servant receiving wages from the person for whom he shall take the mine."   Law 5, tit. 19, book 4, of the Collection of the Indies.

ance, may be performed by a deputy, under the authority of a power or letter or by some person appearing and giving security in the name of the owner of the mine, more particularly in a matter which is for his benefit.

19. This is in part confirmed by the 4th and 5th ordinance of Peru,[*] according to which, if the 30 days elapse without any registry being made, and no good cause of delay be shewn, the rights of the discoverer are lost. And to prevent disabilities arising from infancy, old age, infirmities or the like, being alleged as legitimate causes of delay, it is provided, that the registry may be made by virtue of an authority or letter directed to the nearest judge, who is to take a note of it, as a minute of the registry, until it can be formally ratified, which it must be within 40 days after.

20. There are however, two cases of exception :—First, supposing some person should apply to make registry, in opposition to the right of the discovery, when it happens that the latter is prevented by hostile force[†] from coming to the spot, the situation of the mine being at the same time very remote. And second, when the parties are Indians, in which case allowances are made for the natural ignorance of these people. The second ground of exception is noticed by the ordinances of Peru,[‡] which direct that the Indians shall not be limited to the term of 30 days, allowed to the discoverer in that kingdom for registering his mine, but that if they do not make registry within three months, then, even although the mine should be in actual work, it shall be open to any other person to acquire to himself, by registry, the rights of a discoverer. The ground of the first exception is this, that impediments of the description to which it applies, cannot be overcome, except at the risk of life ; but in case of non-observance of any positive rule, a fair and equitable inquiry should be made, whether the omission was a culpable one, or whether impediments existed which could not be got over ; and it should also be noticed, that there is a degree of malice and covetousness in applying to register a mine to which another party, who had been embarrassed by insuperable obstacles, has a claim. If however no impediment of this nature exist, or be made out, the general rule of the ordinance will operate with full force.

21. The third question is, what constitutes the difference between *denouncement* and *registry* ?[§] The reply to this question is, that there is substantially no difference between them, although there is a difference in form. There is in form, because registry generally applies to newly-discovered mines ; and denouncement, to mines which have been discovered before, but which, having been forfeited under the ordinances, as a penalty for being kept

---

[*] Escalona, Gazoph. lib. 2, p. 2, cap. 1, page 105.

[†] Cap. 3, ext. de præscript. et ibi DD.

[‡] Ord. 16, apud Escalon. ubi sup. p. 108, tit. 1.

[§] What the miners call denouncement, is the same as that which the law and ordinances denominate denunciation. L. 3, §. fin. ff. de jur. fisc. Ord. 38, and 39, chap. 18.

insufficiently worked for more than four months, or for certain other reasons,* are ordered to be adjudged to the first person who shall apply for them. In making registry, the person, the place and the ore, only, are required to be manifested ; but upon the denouncement of a mine for not being sufficiently worked, a summary judgment upon the question is requisite, and it is sometimes necessary to proceed to edicts or proclamations. They appear therefore to be distinct in form.

22. But they by no means differ in substance. First, because the object of both is to make a public mention of the mine, and to define its situation, for the purpose of obtaining a title to it. Second, because denouncement alone, gives no title to the property of the mine, but is merely in the nature of an accusation against the former owner, charging him with having allowed it to remain unworked, or with having come within some other ground of forfeiture ; after a summary cognizance of which, the mine should be entered in the register, together with the adjudication of the magistrate, and this more clearly appears from the 37th ordinance, which says, in reference to mines remaining unworked, " In such case he shall have forfeited, and shall forfeit the same, and thenceforth he shall have no right to it, unless upon making a registry thereof anew ; and such mine shall be adjudged to any person who shall denounce it for being insufficiently worked, provided he go through the same proceedings," that is to say, provided he register it. Hence it is evident, that with respect to an old mine, which has been discovered before, there must be a new registry after denouncement.

23. Third, the 27th ordinance, when describing the mode in which the pits of two *varas* deep and one wide are to be made, for the purpose of having a stake placed in the middle of them, so that it shall not be liable to be fraudulently displaced, imposes the forfeiture of the mine as a penalty for not doing so, and declares, " that any other person whatsoever may apply for it and register it as his own." Fourth, it is provided, by the 17th ordinance, now under consideration, that if the registry be not made in the manner and within the time prescribed, and the other formalities be not observed, any

---

* See the ordinances. The 17th and 69th impose this penalty in case of the proper forms not being observed in the registry; the 21st, for not declaring the names of a partner or partners ; the 27th, for not setting up permanent and fixed stakes ; the 32d, for taking a mine by the intervention of a third person, who has no authority for the purpose, not being a hired servant; the 35th, for not having sunk three *estados* after registry or denouncement ; the 37th and 71st, for keeping the mine unworked for a longer period than four months; the 38th and 39th, for not sinking three *estados* after denouncement ; the 43d, for purchasing a mine which is not sunk to the depth of three *estados*, in which case the mine and its value are declared forfeited : the 59th, for not giving information whether the ore is proper to be reduced by amalgamation, or otherwise ; the 67th, on account of certain persons being prohibited from holding mines ; and the 58th, for the same reason. And the chief alcaldes, royal officers, mining notaries, judges, governors, ministers and others, who are not permitted to purchase mines, are liable to forfeit them under law 1, tit. 19, book 4, and laws 1, 2 and 3, tit. 20, book 4, of the Collection of the Indies.

other person whatsoever " may register such mine," which must be supposed to have been discovered before. Fifth, it is declared in the 35th ordinance, that all those who may " take, hold or acquire mines, whether already discovered or hereafter to be discovered, shall be bound, from the time of their registering such mines, if new ones, to deepen one of the trial pits they may have made in them, and if old ones, then one of the pits, &c." so that the word registry is applied alike to both new and old mines. Sixth, the 42d ordinance prohibits the sale of mines, until they are sunk three *estados*, and directs that the justice shall be advised of the sale, in order that it may be entered in the book of registry, and the like whenever there is a change in the ownership of the mines.

24. Independent of these considerations, our position may be sufficiently made out, by reference to the etymology of the word registry, which in the Latin tongue, is commonly called *registrum*, but more properly *registum;* which is as much as to say *res gesta*, and signifies any judicial order or proceeding, affording certain evidence and testimony of some judicial act ; as may be seen in the Thesaurus of the Latin tongue, and in Quintilian, and as is also shewn by Solorzano, when treating of the registry of merchandise, upon the authority of Vopiscus, Prudentius, Petrus Faber, Cujacius and others ; and the like explanation is also given by Dufresne.* And there can be no doubt but that the justice and notary give as certain evidence and testimony of the proceedings concerning new mines, as of those concerning denounced mines, for they are all entered in the same register.

25. The above is sufficient to prove, that there is no substantial difference between denouncement and registry ; and that if a mine be denounced upon any of the grounds enumerated in the ordinances, it must be registered in the same manner as a mine newly discovered upon the surface of the earth ; and that the proceedings had, whether in regard to the new or old mines, must alike be made to appear upon the record, which is called a register, for the security of the discoverer and denouncer respectively. And if the judge or miner be well advised of these sound principles, deduced from the ordinances themselves, several irrelevant grounds of dispute may be avoided, as we shall notice by and by, when treating of priority of registry, one mine

---

* Albertus Burerus, Thesaur. ling. Latin. tom. 3, lit. R. Regerere; in librum referre quæ audiendo accepimus. Regestum Latine dici potest quod vulgo registrum vocamus teste Budeo, de rhetor. Ciceronis. Quintil. lib. 3. cap. 8. Sunt enim velut res regestæ in hos commentarios. Solorzan. Polit. lib. 6, cap. 10, u. 6. L. illicitas, §. veritas, ff. de off. præsid. Vopiscus, Prudentius et alii apud Petrum Fabrum, in. L. si librarius, 92, ff. de r. j. Cujacius, lib. 15, Observ. cap. 17, &c. Dufresne, Glossarium ad scriptores mediæ, et infimæ latinitatis, tom. 5, lit. R. verbo Regestum ; liber in quem regeruntur commentarii quivis. Regesto scribarum, apud Vopiscum in Probo. Regesta, quasi iterum gesta, Registrum pro registum : liber qui rerum gestarum memoriam continet, unde dicitur quasi rei gestæ statio. L. 8, tit. 19, part 3. The registraries are the other notaries aforesaid, who are employed in the king's palace, and whose office is to make entries in the books which are called registers.

being entitled to be measured out before another, or otherwise, according to the greater or less time elapsed since making the registry.*

---•·•---

CHAPTER VI.

A MINE, NOT THE PROPERTY OF THE PARTY, CANNOT BE REGISTERED BY HIM.

ORDINANCE XX.

ALSO, we ordain and command, that no person shall presume to register, or to enter in the register, a mine which is not his own property, under the penalty of 1000 ducats, to be imposed upon the person so offending; one half to be applied to the purposes of our exchequer, and the other half to be divided between the informer, and the judge who shall pass sentence; and over and above this, such person as aforesaid, shall forfeit the right he may have acquired to such mine.

CONTENTS OF THE COMMENTARY ON THIS ORDINANCE.

1. A difficulty occurs in the construction of this ordinance.
2 and 3. The meaning is, that a creditor, holding a mine by way of pledge, cannot register it as his own ; that no person can register a mine during the term of four months, in which it is allowed by law to remain insufficiently worked, and that a tutor or curator cannot register in his own name, a mine not belonging to him in his own right.
4. The question put, whether the real owner can enter the registry in a feigned name.
5. First argument in favour of the affirmative, that the substitution of a feigned name is sanctioned by law.
6. Second, that the same thing is done in many other transactions.
7. Third, that the reason of the ordinance does not hold in this case.
8. And that a penal regulation is not to be extended by construction, from one particular case to another distinct from it.
9 to 13. The question resolved in the negative, on the ground that such substitution of a feigned name, is contrary to several of the ordinances, to public order and to the regular form of mine proceedings.
14 and 15. Reply to the arguments on the other side.

COMMENTARY.

1. This ordinance is in accordance with the 19th of the old ordinances,† except that the latter imposes a penalty of 200 ducats, upon any person who shall register a mine not his own, which penalty the new ordinances increase to 1000 ducats ; besides declaring that he shall forfeit the *right* he may have *acquired* to such mine. The construction of this ordinance appears to be attended with considerable difficulty, particularly if we refer to the marginal

---

* Infra, cap. 11.
† Cap. 19, law 5, tit. 13, book 6, Collection of Castile.

note in the old collection, which runs thus, "no person shall register the mine of another, although he have a right to it," for if he have a right to it, and *a right already acquired*, it cannot be said to be the mine of another. Besides, if the mine be one in actual work, the owner will surely oppose the registry, whilst if it should be a mine which has been unworked for a longer period than four months, then, any person being at liberty to denounce it, there can be no impropriety in the party's doing so, and registering it as his own. But notwithstanding this appearance of difficulty, the sense of the ordinance admits of being clearly made out, as applying to more than one case.

2. The first case to which the ordinance applies, is where a creditor holding a mine by way of pledge, or claiming a lien upon it in respect of supplies furnished, pretends to register the mine, in satisfaction of what is due to him ; there can be no doubt that he has in this case a right to do so, by virtue of the express or implied pledge ; but as the mine is, in effect, the property of the debtor and under his dominion, the creditor cannot, upon his own authority merely, register it as for himself, nor acquire a right to it ; he can only demand payment of his debt, or apply to the justice to have execution levied. Another case is, when some person makes a new registry of the mine, before the expiration of the term of four months, during which it may by law remain insufficiently worked ;* for under these circumstances the owner may object within the term, in which case the registry so made will be rendered void. A third case is when one person having discovered the ore, some other person comes in to make registry within the term of 20 days, allowed by the ordinance for registering the mine.† In any of these three cases, the person who has registered the mine, such mine being the property of another, shall forfeit the right which he may claim to have acquired thereby, besides the penalty above-mentioned.

3. The like is the case, if a tutor, curator, *defender*‡ or agent, should register in his own name, a mine lawfully belonging to a person under age, an absentee or other party, each of whom shall have his proper action to annul the registry, which shall be annulled accordingly, in all cases of this nature that may arise, on account of the improper and fraudulent conduct of the party, in doing that in his own name which ought to have been done in the name of the lawful owner, or of the minor or ward ; all which is abundantly demonstrated by Salgado.§

---

* Chap. 17, ordinance 37.

† Chap. 5, ordinance 17.

‡ A person appointed to defend the interests of a debtor's estate, upon his giving up his property in favour of his creditors.—*Trans.*

§ Salgad. Labyr. p. 2, cap. 24, n. 45, ibi : " Hoc fundamentum exacte exornat per jura et DD Gutiérrez, de tutel. 2. p. cap. 10, per totum, qui n. 1, apponit, quod licet actus in dubio præsumatur factus nomine proprio, limitat non procedere, in tutore vel curatore faciente id quod nomine

4. But the principal question which arises upon this ordinance is, whether the registry of the mine will be good, supposing it be made in a foreign name, the real owner being some distinct person ? or whether the penalty of the ordinance will be thereby incurred ? On which point the following arguments appear to favour the opinion that the registry is valid, and that the penalty does not apply.

5. First, because the assumption of a feigned name, or the substitution of the name of one person for that of another, in contracts of purchase and sale, involves no impropriety, it being very usual for one person to be nominally concerned, whilst the person actually entering into the engagement is distinct ; or for one person to be the real owner of property, whilst another lends his name for convenience and in confidence. Hence the emperors Valerian and Galienus issued rescripts, to the effect that although an instrument of purchase should run in the name of the father-in-law, yet if the husband were the real owner, the wife should have no claim, upon a divorce, to the property which was the subject of the purchase, even although the deed should be in her own possession. The same rule is expressed in two other texts of the emperors Diocletian and Maximian, it being proper that the real intent of the transaction should be carried into effect, rather than the mere sense of the writing ; and the title of that head of the civil law must be sufficient to satisfy us, that the real meaning of the transaction shall prevail over any fictitious suggestions assigned.*

6. Second, because it is a matter of course, in the case of a contract of purchase and sale, to have regard to the person for whom the thing is really purchased, although some other name should appear in the instrument ; so that the real intention is not liable to be varied in consequence of some pretended fact, or of the substitution of some feigned name, but on the contrary, all the obligations and effects resulting from the contract, attach on the secret party and not on the fictitious or suppositious one. If a person holding the office of mayor, purchase lands with money destined for that purpose, he acquires them for the corporation, although his own name may appear in the instrument. If a rent be charged on property, by a party whose name appears as the feigned purchaser, the real owner will not be liable to it, for the party so named

---

alieno est obligatus, et ideo licet faciat nomine suo, præsumitur tamen nomine pupilli, per L. Lucius, §. tutorem, ff de admin. tutor. et per plurimes DD. et n. 3, post Cavalcanum et Mascardum, cons. 1393, n. 4, extendit ad quemlibet rerum alienarum administratorem, licet actum, et emptionem fecerit nomine proprio, nihilominus facere tenetur nomine minoris, et alieni, et isti non illi adquiratur. Quamplurimos DD. congessit Mangillius, de evictionib. q. 188, ex n. 13, cum seq. omnino videndus.

* L. 4. ff, si quis alt vel sub alter. nom, vel aliena pecun. emer. " Quamvis in instrumento emptionis socrus nomen inscripseris ; tamen si possessionem tenens dominus effectus es, ob eam rem frusta calumniam mulieris. quamvis ipsa contractûs tabulas habeat, reformidas," L. 5. et 6. ff. eod ; " Quia res gesta potior quam scriptura habetur." Tot. tit. Cod. Plus valere quod agitur. quam quod simulate concipitur.

fictitiously is a mere trustee or agent, and not the lawful owner. And the party actually in contemplation at the time of the transaction, shall prevail against the fictitious nominee; for the lawful owner not wishing his name to appear, is at liberty to insert that of some other person, provided he do so in good faith and without fraud, and with. some honest motive; as may be learned from Salgado, Vela, Barbosa, Menochius, Gratianus, Casaregis, Tuschi and many others.* It may therefore be inferred that the same thing may be done with regard to the registering of mines, without incurring the penalty.

7. Third, because the objects of this ordinance are twofold; the one to prevent injury to the lawful owner, and therefore to disable any other person from usurping possession of the mine, by registering it for himself; which object no longer exists when the owner consents to the act: and as it is, in such case, incumbent on him to secure himself by taking a declaration of trust from the nominee, he must, if he omit to do so, suffer the consequences. The other object of the ordinance is, to have it made known what persons, being the owners, are liable to the payment of the duties, and to the observance of the ordinances, which object may be attained, notwithstanding the insertion of a fictitious name in the registry.

8. And, finally, because a penalty limited in one particular case, ought not to be extended by construction to a different case, even though within the reason of the rule.† And as the case to which this penal ordinance applies, is that of one person usurping the mine of another, when he has a right to it by way of pledge only or in some other manner, as explained above, the penalty ought not to be extended to the distinct case which we have put.

9. Notwithstanding all these arguments, our opinion is, that if the tenor and purport of the ordinance be well considered, it will be deemed to extend to this case. First and principally, because the feigned name being entered in the register, the nominee would be entering in the register as his own, a mine which is not properly his, and the penalty must consequently be inevitably incurred; for there can be no doubt that when the nominee presents the ore, and makes the registry in his own name, upon the suggestion that the mine is his, while it really is not so, the document is publicly and notoriously made applicable to him; and if the rule of the ordinance does not hold in

---

* Salgad. Labyr. 2, p. cap. 24, per totum. et signanter a. n. 35. fundat majoratui ad quiri emptum pecunia ad emptionem prœdiorum destinata, quamvis possessor emat proprio nomine. Vela, dissert. 38, a n. 19, copioce illustrat senatus Granatensis decisionem qua reditum regium *Juro* emptum nomine Michaelis, et gravatum ab ipso; ad Franciscum fratrem, et ipsius hœredes pertinere declaratum fuit. Et n. 20, ibi : "Veritas in quolibet actu duntaxat inspicienda est, quam simulatum factum non immutat." Et prosequitur multitudine legum et AA. Barbos. in L. 4, Cod. Plus valere quod agitur, &c. Menoch. lib, 3, Præsumpt. præs. 125 Gratianus, Discept. c. 131, n. 17. Casaregis, de comm. tom. 1, disc. 43, n. 33 et 39. Tuschi. lit. S. conclus. 257, n. 38, et concl. 265, n. 20.

† Cap. renovantes, dist. 22. Cap. odia, de r. j. in 6. L. cum quidam, ff. de lib. et posth. Tiraquel. de retract. in præf. n. 62 et 63. Menoch. cons. 900, n. 13. Tusch. lit. R. conc. 31, n. 43.

a case like this, it will be impossible to find one to which it can more reasonably apply.

10. Second, because if the substitution of the name of one person for that of another were permitted, there would be much opportunity for fraud : one consequence would be, that the penalties would be avoided, by alleging that some other person was the actual owner ; another, that the payment of the duties would be eluded ; another, that one person would be enabled to hold more than two mines upon the same vein, all acquired by the denouncement or registry, contrary to the ordinances,* which permit an ordinary miner (not being a discoverer) to acquire mines beyond that number, by purchase and sale, or some other such mode, only ; but by assuming a feigned name, one person might obtain possession of any number of mines at pleasure ; and various opportunities of fraud would be let in, which, to an evil disposition, readily suggest themselves. But protection should never be extended to craft or fraud.†

11. Third, because the law ordains,‡ that any person who shall discover a mine of gold, silver, &c. shall be bound to register it within the term of 20 days, at the same time exhibiting the ore, and stating who is the person that has made the discovery : all which requires that the true and lawful owner should himself come forward. And this rule is broken in upon by substituting a feigned name, which is therefore sufficient to make the penalty attach. And as we have observed, in explaining the 17th ordinance above-cited, the objects of this exactness in regard to the forms of registry are various, embracing both the attainment of greater certainty as to the ownership of the mine, and the enforcing the duties of the registered miners ; all which would be alike frustrated, if the assumption of a fictitious name were permitted.

12. Fourth, because it is provided by another of the ordinances,§ that no person, of whatever condition, may take a mine for another, except by virtue of an authority, or unless he be a hired servant or the person for whom he shall take the mine ; and that if either of these qualifications be wanting the mine shall be considered as forfeited, and liable to be denounced, without any appeal on the part of the person who takes the mine, or of him in whose name it may be taken. If, then, this be the case, when there is no disguise or assumption of a fictitious character, there is still more reason that it should be so, when such a course of proceeding is resorted to.

13. Besides which, the principal object of the ordinance is, to forward the administration of justice, and to promote the general good, by establishing a registry of this valuable and important description of property, upon

---

* 31 and 32, of the old ordinances, of law 5, tit. 13, book 6, Collection of Castile. Chap. 8, infr. ordinance 31.

† Salgad. de retent. p. 2, cap 20, a n. 69. Gonzal. in cap. super literis, de rescript. n. 10, qui jura cumulant.

‡ Chap. 5, ordinance 17.

§ Chap. 15, ordinance 32.

the basis of regularity and correctness ; and to leave no opportunity for the exercise of fraud, which would be let in, by allowing a feigned name to be assumed, or the name of one person to be substituted for that of another. On this ground it is, that in the registery of shipping, which is a parallel case, it is made unlawful to enter another person's vessel in your own name, or your own vessel in another person's name ; but in such case the vessel is declared forfeited, together with three or four times the value ; as will be found on reference to our laws of the Indies, and to the illustrations of those laws given by Don Joseph de Veitia.* From all which it is to be inferred, that the registering a mine in another person's name is altogether to be discountenanced, and incurs the penalty of the ordinances.

14. And there is no weight in the arguments which have been stated on the other side of the question. Not in the first and second, which are founded on the civil law, and other authorities, making it out to be lawful to make a purchase in the name of another person, one party being named as the owner, whilst some other is so in fact ; for there is an evident difference between this case, and the case we are considering, namely, that in all other transactions the assumption of another person's name is a matter which passes between individuals, who adopt this course for their own private ends, and with a view to the accomplishment of some reasonable object, and generally without any fraudulent intention ; as when a husband makes a purchase in the name of his wife, or the chief officer of a corporation in his own name ; and in a word, any confusion in the title which it may occasion, will result to their own individual loss alone, and therefore the laws consult the rights of the real and lawful owners ; but the assumption of a fictitious name in the case of the registry of mines, and in reference to the right of ownership in them, is, as we have shewn, prejudicial to the interests of the public and of the revenue, and is a fraud upon the ordinances.

15. For the same reason, there is as little weight in the third and fourth arguments, for although the assumption of the name of some other person in the registry be consented to by the owner, although such person be not guilty of any encroachment or fraud upon the rights of the owner, against his consent, and although he may pay the duties, as the real owner might otherwise have done ; yet it must be borne in mind, that the ordinances are framed for public objects, some of which, amongst others, are, to guard against fraud, to prevent the holding more mines than are allowed by law, and to maintain a proper regularity in all that concerns mining property. And again, although the less important reasons above-mentioned should fail, yet the stronger and more forcible arguments which are founded on the fact of the registry being declared void, and the penalty imposed by the ordi-

---

* Law 34, tit. 33, law 69, tit. 35, book 9, of the Collection of the Indies. Veitia, Norte de a contractacion de Indias, lib. 2, cap. 17, u, 10.

nance, are not so easily to be got over, and render it impossible to allege, that by the construction contended for, a penal rule, applying to one particular case, is extended to a distinct case ; the case under consideration, of one person entering in the register, a mine which is not his own, being expressly comprehended in the ordinance, and being the precise case against which the fine and penalty imposed thereby, and by the other ordinance above-cited and agreeing with it, are directed.

———— ❖•❖ ————

CHAPTER VII.

OF MINES HELD IN PARTNERSHIP—OF THE NUMBER OF HANDS REQUIRED TO BE EMPLOYED IN THEM—OF THE MODE OF REGULATING THE WORKS AND DIVIDING THE PRODUCE—OF THE DIFFERENT KINDS OF AGREEMENT APPLICABLE TO PARTNERSHIPS IN THIS SPECIES OF PROPERTY—OF THE MODES IN WHICH SUCH PARTNERSHIPS ARE DETERMINED—AND OF THE NUMBER OF MINES THEY MAY LAWFULLY HOLD.

ORDINANCES XXI. XLIII. XLIV. XLV.

XXI. Also, we ordain and command, that when any person shall register a mine or mines not wholly his own, he shall be bound to declare what share or shares he holds in them ; and if he hold them in partnership, what share his partner or partners may hold in such mine or mines ; under the penalty (if he do not do so), of forfeiting the share or shares he may hold, which shall go to the partner or partners, the share or shares held by whom, he has so omitted to set forth.

XLIII. Also, we ordain and command, that when two or more persons shall hold a mine in partnership, for the purpose of working it and raising ore therefrom, if any one of the partners shall require the other partners to set on hands, they shall be bound to set on twelve persons in the whole, if there be ore enough for the purpose, and if so many can work conveniently ; or otherwise, as many as can conveniently work at once, according to the disposition of such mine, and the ore it may contain ; and if any one of them, being required so to do, shall not set on his proportion of hands, then the mining judge shall examine into the disposition of the mine, and shall set on, at the expense of the owners of the mine, such number of hands as the partner was bound to set on, to make up his proportion of the number of twelve persons ; in order that the working of the aforesaid mine may not come to a stand in consequence of such disputes.

XLIV. Also we declare and command, that if any one of the partners shall wish to set on more hands to work the mine, than such twelve persons, he shall be at liberty to do so, provided he give notice thereof to his partner or partners, in order that if they are willing to set on more hands, it may be done accordingly ; and if he shall not give such notice, he shall forfeit the ore he may raise, which shall belong to the partners aforesaid. And if, when he shall have given them notice, they shall not think proper to set on more hands, they shall not be bound to do so, because enough is done by setting on such twelve persons between all the partners ; but if, nevertheless, any one of the partners should still wish to set on more hands, giving notice as aforesaid, he shall be bound to give the other partners their share of the ore raised, as if the supernumerary hands he may have set on, and by whom such ore may have been raised, had been set on by all of them ; and the justice aforesaid shall compel him to do so.

XLV. Also, as to the ore which may be raised from mines held in partnership, if they shall not be disposed to smelt it in partnership, and to divide the produce when smelted and refined, according to their respective shares in the mine, they shall divide it in ore, in like proportion to their said respective shares ; and until so divided, it shall be kept all together, in a place of security, and none of them shall presume to take away any part of it, under pain of forfeiting his share, which shall go to the other partner or partners, and as much more as the value of such share, one half to go to our exchequer, and the other half to the informer and judge. And if they smelt it in partnership, they shall also refine the produce together, so that each person may afterwards receive the share belonging to him, un'er the penalty to which those persons are liable, who do not take the produce of the ore they have smelted, to be refined, but sell it or deal in it unrefined.

CONTENTS OF THE COMMENTARY ON THESE ORDINANCES.

1. Mining partnerships admit of a variety of different agreements.
2. A mine is divided by law into 12 or 24 bars, for the better regulation of the partnership.
3. It is obligatory on him who registers a mine held in partnership or in common, to state who are entitled in common with him, and in what shares.
4. The penalty for contravening this rule.
5. The penalty is not incurred by one who does so with the consent of his partner.
6. The penalty may be incurred, even before the three *estados* are sunk, as required by the ordinance.
7. To obtain the penalty, the partner suing for it must make it appear that a partnership exists, either express or implied.
8. Reflections on the unhappy case of the miserable discoverers, whose partners often deny the existence of a partnership.
9. Of the number of hands required to be kept at work in mines held in partnership, and the mode of working them.
10. They are sufficiently worked by setting on four workmen, in like manner as a mine belonging to a single individual.
11. Upon the requisition of any one partner, the whole together are bound to set on twelve workmen, and no more.
12. If any of them object to do so, the justice causes the full number to be set on, that there may be no stoppage in the works.

13. Any person setting on additional workmen, without giving notice to his partner, forfeits the ore which such workmen may raise.

14. If he give notice, then he must give his partners their share of the ore, deducting expenses.

15. Recapitulation of what has been stated.

16. An ordinance of the government of New Spain, on the subject of the number of hands to be set on.

17. What ought to be done by a partner who shall have found ore in a mine theretofore unproductive, he having set on an additional number of hands on his own account.

18. If he shall not, by this means, find ore, he shall not be paid his expenses.

19. Ordinances of Perú, as to the number of workmen to be employed in a mine held in partnership, which does not return profit.

20. In New Spain, a partner who omits, during a period of four months, to contribute to the expenses of four workmen, forfeits his share.

21. Discord is the bane of mining partnerships : prudent regulations of the German partnerships.

22. The overseers are the cause of much discord amongst partners ; but an *interventor** might be appointed.

23. Mode of dividing the works into regions.

24. The produce may be divided either in ore or in silver ; and any one taking from the common stock is liable to a penalty.

25 and 26. Agreements amongst partners, to contribute in different proportions, are lawful.

27. What number of mines partners may lawfully hold.

28. Don Joseph Saenz's opinion on this point. The contrary conclusion come to.

29. Namely, that they may hold as many contiguous mines as there are partners, and then, after an interval of three *pertenencias*, as many more.

30 to 33. This opinion supported upon the letter of the ordinances, and by several considerations arising out of them.

34. A man may hold a mine in partnership with others, contiguous to one belonging to him in severalty.

35 and 36. The partnership is determined by renouncement, sale or forfeiture, under the penalties of the ordinance.

37. And likewise by the death of a partner ; but the property is still held in common, and the shares remain distinct.

38 to 46. The partnership may be determined by an actual partition in measured *varas;* an opinion which is confirmed by the tenour of several of the ordinances of Peru, and by the expressions of those of the new code.

47. Whether the mine will conveniently admit of partition or not, is left to the judge to decide.

COMMENTARY.

1. Every occupation which offers a fair and honest profit, may be the subject of a partnership,† a kind of contract which is very often entered into, in reference to the working of mines, which, while they offer, on the one hand, great prospects of success, frequently, on the other hand, bring ruin

---

* A person appointed to watch specially over the interests of one or more of the partners in a mining concern.—*Trans.*

† Law 2, title 10, part 5. Law 5. L. 57, ff. pro. soc. Gutierrez, de juram. confirm. 1. p. cap. 48, n. 7. Felicius, de societ. cap. 9, a n. 3, usque ad 22, princ. tit. Instit. de societ. et ibi Institutar.

on the parties concerned in working them. The reason of partnerships being so often entered into in reference to mines is, that a mine (as is commonly said) requires a mine, that is to say, demands a large capital, and the owners or discoverers not being always able to undertake the expense, call in the aid of others, to whom they cede a partial interest in the mines, to be enabled to work them and raise the ore.* The transaction therefore, at its outset, involves a complete and gratuitous gift, which is however to be construed with reference to the partnership, the object of which is to carry on the work of the mine at the common expense. At other times, different parties enter into an agreement, to become partners in all the mines they may find in the course of their search. At other times, mine owners dispose of shares in their mines; and, finally, mines may be acquired and transferred for the purpose of being worked in common or in partnership, by every mode in which the right of property may be transferred, whether onerous or lucrative.

2. An entire mine consists of 12 bars; and although twice that number, or 24, are reckoned, in some mining districts, yet 12 is the more usual number in the principal districts, in analogy to the division of the inheritance into the parts of an *As*. These bars and the profits arising upon them, may be subdivided amongst a number of partners, according to the quantity of ore raised.† Each partner therefore, contributes to the expenses, and receives the produce, in proportion to the number of bars belonging to him; the owner of six bars, in the proportion of one half; of three bars, in the proportion of one fourth; of two bars, in the proportion of one sixth, and so on, as in the division of the inheritance; so that a due proportion exists between the capital subscribed and the profit or loss, derived or sustained, agreeably to the rules of the civil law.‡ But the partners are at liberty to enter into a variety of agreements amongst themselves, by virtue of which one partner may receive a larger share of the profits, or contribute less to the expenses, than another, as we shall explain by and by; in like manner as, in other cases of partnership, agreements introducing such inequalities are permitted.§

3. Having premised thus much, and proceeding to investigate the meaning of the ordinances which treat of partnership mines, we shall find that it is provided by the 21st ordinance of the new code (which agrees with the 20th of the old ordinances),‖ that a person registering mines which are not wholly his own, is bound to declare what share or shares he holds in them,

---

* Agricola, de re metall. lib. 4, p. 60.

† Idem, ibid.

‡ L. si non fuerint, 29. ff. pro socio, §. 1, et 3. Instit. de societ.

§ Ex iisdem jurib. num. præced. et §. 2. Instit. de societ. et ibi DD. Felicius. de societat. d. c. 9. à n. 22. latissime, usque ad n. 41.

‖ Law 5, tit. 13, book 6, Collection of Castile, cap. 20.

and if he hold them in partnership, then what share his partner or partners may hold. Here we must notice the distinction which is raised by these words, between mines held in common, and in partnership, as there may be a holding in common, without a partnership; although there can be no partnership without a holding in common. Thus in the instance of one and the same thing purchased by several persons jointly, or of an undivided inheritance, and in several cases noticed in the laws,* there is a holding in common, without a partnership; for the latter requires a special agreement or contract, which a holding in common does not, as it may arise from the very nature of certain acts performed. Our ordinance, therefore, in order to make mines held in common, and also those held in partnership, liable to the obligation of being registered, ordains first, that any person who shall hold mines which are not wholly his own, shall declare what his share is (and here it refers to mines held in common), and next, that if he shall hold them in partnership, he shall declare what the shares of his partners are. And, in consequence of this precept, it is the usual practice, at the time of presenting the petition of registry, to declare the names, and the bars or shares of the partners, before the justice; for the register being the basis of the title to the mine, and serving various ends, it ought to appear with certainty who the owners are, which we have seen when considering the other ordinances.†

4. Any partner who, in contravention of this precept, shall register the whole mine as his own, is subjected by the ordinance to the penalty of forfeiting the share or shares he may hold, in favor of the partner or partners whose shares he has omitted to set forth. A very reasonable and proper punishment, for the avaricious and fraudulent act of suppressing the right of another person, and appropriating to himself what is common to others with him; and for infringing the rules of the 20th ordinance, by registering as wholly his own, a mine which is only partially so. It is a very common practice of wicked and avaricious persons, to rob the poor and wretched individual who has discovered the vein, by thus depriving him of the share he is entitled to, merely because they know he is unable to defend his rights; and we have met with instances of this nefarious proceeding, in the case of mines of considerable richness. Although by the civil law, the action *pro socio* lies, to recover a share of the profit, and to establish the party's right, without going so far as to seek to make the party setting up a claim to his partner's interest,

---

* Felicius de societ. cap. 11, n. 2. " Et quia licet communio possit esse sine societate, tamen societas non posset esse sine communione. L. hæredes, §. non tantum, ff. fam. hercisc. L. 31. ff. pro. soc. Ut sit pro socio actio societatem intercedere oportet ; nec enim sufficit rem esse communem, nisi societas intercedit   communiter autem res agi potest etiam citra societatem : ut puta cum non affectione societatis incidimus in communionem : ut evenit in re duobus legata : item si a duobus simul empta res sit : aut si hæreditas, vel donatio communiter nobis obvenit, aut sia duobus separatim emimus partes eorum, no socii futuri. Et L. 32, cod." Ex DD. pene innumeri apud eundem Felicium.

† Chap. 5, above, ordinances 17, 18 and 19.

forfeit his share in favour of the injured party ;* yet as the observance of the ordinances, and the penalties inflicted thereby, are the conditions under which the sovereign has made the mines common, they ought to be observed, as laws peculiarly applying, rather than the civil law, which is of no weight where there is a law or determination of our kingdom, on the same subject.

5. The penalty is incurred, when the partner's share is concealed maliciously and fraudulently, and this is the reason of the offending party's share being given to him; but if the mine be registered in the name of one partner alone, by consent of all the partners, no injustice† is done, and the penalty does not attach, on account of the privity and consent of the other parties. And although the 20th ordinance might be cited to prove the contrary, that ordinance directing that he who enters in the register as his own, even with the consent of the discoverer, a mine which is not so, shall forfeit his right to it, as we have shewn in the proper place ;‡ yet the fact is, that this does not apply to a mine held in common, the property in which is vested with equal certainty, in each and every one of the partners; and if it be made to appear with certainty, who has the right of property, all that the ordinance requires is performed. And if any one partner is willing to take upon himself the obligation of keeping the mine at work, and the other duties annexed to the management of a mine, he is at liberty to do so; and he does not thereby act in opposition to the ordinances, but merely avails himself of an alternative which is open to him to adopt, and by which he confers a benefit on the other partners, who, of course, will not fail to keep a due watch over their own interest, or in any case, if they do not do so, they must take the blame of the omission upon themselves.

6. To make this penalty attach, it is not necessary to wait till the time of giving possession, that is, till the mine is sunk three *estados*, agreeably to the 35th ordinance; for although the title to the mine and the act of registry are made complete by the giving possession, yet, the time when the shares of the other partners are to be declared, is that of making the registry; such being the strict letter of the ordinance; " When any person shall register," &c. Between the times of making registry and giving possession, a great deal of ore may be raised, in fraud of the other part owners, for by the 36th ordinance, ore may be, and as experience proves, often is raised, before sinking the three *estados ;* and therefore the partner who contravenes the partnership rights, by working the mine on his own account alone, after making registry, will incur the penalty of the ordinance, even although the three *estados* are not sunk, nor the 90 days, within which they

---

* § 4, Inst. de societ. " hære ditatem solus lucri feceret, cogitur hoc lucrum communicare." Law 12, tit. 10, part 5.
† Cap. 27, de r. j. in 6, " Scienti, et volenti, non fit injuria, neque dolus."
‡ Cap. 6. per tot.

must be sunk, expired, and although the possession has not been judicially made over to him, for the fraud and injury towards his partner are complete.

7. The latter, in prosecuting his action for the penalty, must prove the subsistence of the partnership, either by an instrument in writing, or by witnesses, or in some other of the legal modes by which an express or implied contract of partnership may be established; that is to say, if the partnership be an express one, it must be proved by instruments, confession or witnesses; and if an implied one, by acts from which a partnership can be inferred, according to the clear doctrine of the law and the authorities.* And, in a word, as the contracts by which the partial property in a partnership mine may be transferred, are of various descriptions, as we have explained above, that which is relied on in bringing the action for the penalty must be proved.

8. With respect to suits concerning the right of possession or property in mines, the order and method to be pursued are regulated by others of the ordinances,† to which we refer, observing, in the mean time, with respect to the action *pro socio*, that proper regard should be had to the circumstances of the parties, and the miserable condition of the discoverers; who being the lawful owners of mines which Providence has permitted them to discover, are generally compelled to part with a share in them, in order to obtain some pecuniary assistance, or in consideration of the expenses being undertaken by some other party; and being sunk to the lowest scale of wretchedness, and often idiots, the consequence frequently is, that they are ousted altogether. As cases then, of this discription, afford many special circumstances in favour of these unfortunate persons, regard ought to be had to all the particular circumstances of the transaction, which being private, confidential and of difficult proof, demand the greatest discretion and tact in the judge.‡

---

* Felicius, de societ. cap. 10 et cap. 11, ubi plane de causa instrumentali societatis : et quod expressa probatur verbis, consensu, stipulatione, vel pacto, tacita vero per actus sociales : sive sit generalis, sive particularis societas ; et apud eum ex antiquis innumeris : juraque ad satietatem cumulat. Idem, cap. 11, n. 9. "Ubi adest conventio verbis declarata, opus non erit investigare conjecturas, quia id ex verbis, et conventione probabitur, et sic dictum, et sic conventum fuisse ; et fuisse contractam societatem poterit probari per instrumentum, vel aliam scripturam super inde confectam." Et n. 11. "Poterit etiam probari per literas alicujus socii alteri socio scriptas, et ratio est, quia literæ alicujus, præsertim sigillatæ, probant, et præcipue contra scribentem. L. Publia, ff. deposit. L. cum de indebito, ff. de probat. Bald. in L. ult. Cod. si cert. petat. Mascard. conc. 626. Et quod scriptura privata probet societatem tradit Paris, Decianus Rubæus." Et n. 12. "Probatur etiam fuisse inductam communionem, et societatem, per testes. Ruin. cons. 92, lib. 1. Etiam si sint singulares deponentes de diversis actibus, cum Gabriel. Corn. Bald. et Alex. debent deponere de actibus socialibus." Et n. 13, "Probatur societas quando extrajudicialiter socii fassi fuerunt se esse socios." Hebia Bolanos, in Cur. lib. 1. Commercio terrestre, cap. 3, n. 2. Castillo, de usufr. cap. 3, Gratian. tom. 2, discep. cap. 336; et apud hos quam plures.

† Chap. 23, ordinances 63 and 64.

‡ Super probatione in casibus difficilis probationis. Valenzuel. cons. 18. Vela, dissert. 38, a. n. 20. Solorz. Polit. lib. 3, cap. 26. Julio Clar. §. fin. quæst. 24. n. 19. Gomez, in L. 9. Taur. n.

9. Having thus investigated the mode of making registry of partnership mines, we proceed to investigate the rules under which they must be worked, as indicated in the 43d, 44th, and 45th ordinances of the new code, and the 46th, 47th, 48th, and 49th of the old ordinances. To avoid confusion, from the variety of points which these ordinances embrace, we shall distinguish the rules of law deducible from them into the following :—

10. First, that whether a mine belong to a single individual or to a partnership, the number of four persons at least must be kept at work in it ; which is provided by the 37th ordinance of the new code, and by the 40th of the old ordinances. And whatever be the extent of the partnership, four persons will be sufficient ; for the ordinances of Peru,* noticing that regard is to be had, not to the number of owners, but to the number of mines they possess, decide, in consequence, that if several persons hold one mine amongst them, they will satisfy the rule of law by setting on the same number of hands which an individual would be required to employ, were he the owner ; and that if they hold two or more mines, four persons must be kept at work in each mine.

11. Second, that if one partner require the others to set on more hands, they are compellable to set on twelve persons in all, if there be ore and space enough to admit of it ; or a smaller number, if the quantity of ore and disposition of the mine will not admit of more. The 43d ordinance of the new code and the 46th of the old ordinances, agree on this point.

12. Third, that if one of the partners, being required thereto, shall omit to set on his proper number of hands, the judge, after inspecting the disposition of the mine, shall cause to be set on, at the expense of the owners of the mine, so many hands as such partner was bound to supply, to make up his proportion of the number of twelve persons, that the works may not be impeded. Such is the direction of the 43d ordinance of the new code. The 46th of the old ordinances provided, that in this case such partner should not have any part of the ore, but this is altered by the ordinances of the new code, which direct the judge to set on twelve persons, at the expense of the owners, in order to put an end to all disputes. If however, the partner be not required to set on more hands, the 46th of the old ordin-

---

7 et 25. Bobadill. lib. 4, Polit. cap. 5, n. 39. Krebs, de lign. et lapide. set. 11. §. 43. "Similiter in dubio pauper, qui semper quiete vivere velle creditur, arg. L. 3. Cod. de defensor. civit. quando agit contra potentiorem, præsumitur justam causam fovere ;" quamvis hanc præsumptionem per se solam non sufficere, asserit, et §. 44. "In defectum probationum juramento deferendum."

* Ordinance 4, tit. 7, concerning mines insufficiently worked ; Escalona, Gazophil. lib. 2, p. 2, c. 1, page 115. "That when several persons shall be possessed of a mine in undivided shares, regard shall be had, not to the number of owners, but to the number of mines they shall be possessed of ; so that if they are possessed of a mine of 60 *varas* in extent, it will be sufficient to employ such number of Indians or negroes, as is aforesaid ; and if of greater extent, then more in the same proportion."

ances, directing that he shall have his share of the ore or silver clear of expenses, will apply, the 43d ordinance of the new code not touching upon this point.

13. Fourth, that if any partner should wish to employ more than twelve persons he may do so, signifying the same to his partners; but if he omit to give them notice, he shall incur the penalty of forfeiting the ore in their favour, without their being liable to contribute any thing to the expenses; on which point the 44th ordinance of the new code and the 47th of the old ordinances agree. The ore which he may raise by means of the barmen whom he shall employ, over and above the number of twelve; but what the other men raise is common property, there being no impropriety in raising that, nor is any penalty incurred thereby.

14. Fifth, that if the partners, being required to set on more than twelve persons, shall refuse to do so, they are justified in their refusal, the ordinances being satisfied by the number of twelve being employed. But if the partner who makes the requisition choose to set on more, he is at liberty to do it, but he must allow his partners their share of the ore raised, as if they had all joined in furnishing the hands he has employed above the number of twelve, and the justice shall compel him to do so; and herein the 44th ordinance of the new code and the 47th of the old ordinance agree. But in this case the expenses must first be deducted, for it is only in the case of his not giving notice, that he loses both the expenses and the ore.

15. These five rules may be reduced to this one general rule, that a partnership mine must be kept worked by four persons at least; and, if any one, partner shall require it, by twelve, or a smaller number of persons, according to the extent of the ore and the space for working. That if any partner shall wish to employ more than twelve persons, he may do so, giving notice to his copartners, to whom he must allow their proportion of the produce, deducting expenses; but if he shall set one more than four persons, or more than twelve, without notice to his partners, he shall forfeit the ore raised by such excess of hands beyond the regular number, and shall likewise lose his expenses. This is a summary of the above mentioned old and new ordinances, as far as they relate to mines yielding ore, the prosperous or profitable state of which may induce one or more of the partners to require more hands to be employed in working them.

16. A municipal law and ordinance of government, for New Spain, stated verbatim by Montemayor,* directs that the partners shall employ such number of hands or laborers as is directed by the ordinance, according to the

---

* Montemayor, Sumario de cedulas de Indias. Ordenanzas de Govierno, ord. 78, fol. 74, 7th September, 1578, at which time the ordinances of the new code were not issued, they having been proclaimed the 22d of August, 1584, and he therefore refers to the regulations of the old ordinances, namely, the 46th ordinance of law 5, tit. 13, book 6, as is stated in the 2d rule in this chapter.

depth of their mines : and that if any one of the partners shall not set on his proper number, he shall not receive a larger share of the ore than is proportioned to the number of hands he shall have furnished. But it declares that if he is unable to furnish the number of labourers required, and the other partners shall furnish them, they shall give him his proportion of the ore, after deducting the costs and expenses, without withholding any part on account of his not having furnished the full number of hands. This regulation is agreeable to what we have stated above, in the third and fifth rules ; and it is very reasonable, that when the property of the mine is vested in several persons, they should all enjoy the profit, after deducting the expenses, and that, while the other partners are at liberty to employ as many hands as they please, and have a right to be repaid their expenses, the omission of one to furnish a proportionate number of hands, should not, under these circumstances, afford a pretext for depriving him of his share. We find then, that due regard is had to equality, which is the rule most accordant with the nature of a contract of partnership.

17. What has been thus far stated, holds, as we have already observed, in regard to mines which are in produce, or in ore ; but the question, as it concerns mines not in produce, is not touched upon in the ordinances of the new code. The law must therefore be looked for in the 48th of the old ordinances, which directs, that if the other partners or their stewards, upon being required thereto, shall refuse to furnish more hands than the necessary number of four persons, any partner who is desirous to employ more, may do so ; and if he shall find ore which is worth prosecuting (that is to say, a vein or branch, which will admit of being worked, and promises a profit), he shall, on the following day, give notice to his partners to set on more hands, and the latter shall, within two days, elect between the two following alternatives, that is to say, either to pay for the work already done at the rate of four *reals* (or whatever may be the current rate of wages in the mining districts), or to allow the partner to raise ore enough to cover the expenses of the work already done, the amount of which is to be taken upon his oath, or that of his steward ; so that until he is satisfied, in one of these ways, for the amount of so much of the expenses already incurred, as ought to have been contributed by his partners, they cannot take any part of the ore ; and when he is so satisfied, they must employ twelve persons, agreeable to the third and fourth rule above-mentioned. But if the partner should fail to give notice of his having discovered ore, the day after his meeting with it, he must allow the other partners a share, from the time of making the discovery ; and as a punishment for his fraudulent concealment, he shall not recover from them the expenses of the work already done, either in ore or in money ; but from that time forth, twelve persons shall be employed, agreeable to the rule above-stated.

18. Hence it may be inferred, that although one partner may employ

additional hands, when in quest of the vein, and shall, if he find ore, be satisfied for the expenses he may have incurred, yet if he do not find ore, he shall not recover from his partners the expenses of such work ; for as they cannot be compelled to furnish hands, beyond the number of four, whom it is obligatory upon them to keep at work, it is evident that the other partner, in adding to the number of labourers employed, must have contemplated taking the risk upon himself alone, and ought therefore alone to bear the loss, should no ore be found ; but if ore be found, he must, in equity and justice, be repaid his expenses, as his copartners would otherwise be taking an unfair advantage of his labour and outlay.

19. All that has been said applies to New Spain, being agreeable to the laws of Castile. But for Peru, it is provided by two of the ordinances of that kingdom, that if there be a mine not yielding ore, and the partners being required to furnish more hands, decline to accede to the request, or be absent, and one partner shall work it alone, for the term of two months, it shall become his sole property, unless the other or others of them shall, before the expiration of that term, require him, in the presence of the justice, to accept his share of the expenses, or shall deposit such share of the expenses ; and he is to be put to his oath as to the amount of the expenses, no evidence in confirmation of his statement being required, except such as may be furnished from the inspection of the work done during the two months, by two or three witnesses. And if the mine contain ore, it may be worked at the expense of one partner, although one or more of the other partners should object.* These ordinances agree in substance with those of Castile, except in adding, that the partner who shall not concur in furnishing additional hands, when required, is, after the lapse of two months, to lose his property in the mine, and the like if he absent himself for such term of two months.

20. But hence arises the question, whether, in the kingdom of New Spain, a partner shall lose his part interest in an unfruitful or unproductive mine, if he fail to contribute his share of the expenses of keeping four persons at work ? Upon which point there is no clear or special rule laid down by the ordinances of Castile. It might be argued, that he ought to lose his interest at the end of the two months, as in Peru, and that being obliged, by the 37th ordinance of the new code, and the 40th and 48th of the old ordinances, to set on four persons, the act of withholding his contributions to the expenses of such four persons, is one which tends to dissolve the copartnership, in the same manner as all other partnerships are dissolved, by one partner withdrawing from the business for which they are constituted.† And

---

* Escalona, Gazoph. lib. 2, p. 2, cap. 1, tit. 7, concerning insufficient working, ordinances 4 and 6.

† Habia Bolanos, in Cur. Philipp. lib. 1, Comm. terrestre, §. 3, n. 43. "And if they should withdraw from their original occupation by which means it is evident the partnership is dissoved." Dec. cons. 86, n. 53, lib. 1, Ludov. concl. 53, vers. 2 et 5.

in other kingdoms, a partner loses his share by the lapse of a single month, as may be seen in Agricola.* But our opinion would be, that as the judge and the partner cannot exact a greater penalty than the law itself imposes, therefore, as by the 37th ordinance, the mine is only made liable to be forfeited for being kept unworked four months successively, a partner cannot be considered to have forfeited his share, except by omitting to contribute for the term of four months; after which period it must, by the same rule, be considered as forfeited, and he himself as having lost all right to it, unless he, before the expiration of the four months, repay to his partner his expenses, or deposit them, agreeable to the ordinance of Peru, cited in the last paragraph.

21. Although a partnership confers rights almost fraternal,† it generally proves a nest of discord,‡ and the case where mines are concerned, by no means forms an exception; which is indeed much to be lamented, as partnerships afford the only practicable means of carrying on adits and general works of drainage, so much require l in many mines which have yielded countless riches in former times, or of exploring and working the infinite number of mines with which New Spain is shewn, by Don Joseph de Villa-Señor,§ and proved by experience, to abound. Many mining districts which are not now worked, might be brought into a flourishing state, by means of the united funds and combined strength of several persons in partnership; but as it is, they remain unworked, by reason of insufficiency of individual means on the one hand, and the disagreements of the miners on the other; there being very few partnerships which do not end unfortunately. For where directions are given by a variety of persons, the affairs of the partnership must necessarily run into disorder and confusion, unless the authority of the sovereign interpose to regulate them, as is the case in the great partnerships of Saxony, at Friberg, and Sneeberg, and in the valley of Joachimica, where it is the rule to divide partnership mines into 122, 126 or 128 shares, one of which is to be set apart for the church, and another for the poor, with the greatest regularity, and under public authority; the methods of dividing the produce and the rules of contribution to the expences being at the same time most excellent, as may be seen in Agricola.‖ But a too eager thirst for gain is unfortunately the universal bane, so that, instead of unity prevailing amongst the partners, as with brothers, it is some-

---

* Agricol. de re metall. lib. 4, page 86. "Cujusque fodinæ non fecundæ metallo, præfectus symbola dominis schæda in foribus publici ædificii fixa indicit, magna, vel parva, prout magister metallicorum et duumviri jurati de his decreverunt, quæ siquis mensis spatio non dederit, eum eximit e dominorum numero, ejusque partes reliquis dominis communes facit."

† L, 63, ff. pro soc. "Cum societas jus quodammodo fraternitatis in se habeat."

‡ Law 1, title 15, partid. 6.

§ Villa-Senor, Theatro Americano, lib. 1. cap. 3, pag. 24, 25.

‖ Agricol. de re metallic. lib. 4, pag. 62 and 63.

times impossible to bring them to any understanding at all, without dissolving the partnership, or without their separating and giving up the business.

22. In our mines of New Spain, discords arise from the conduct of overseers and administrators, who being, as it were, placed to superintend the management of the concern, whether a mine or smelting work, are always obsequious to, and conduct the works according to the wishes of the party who, holding the largest share, is the most powerful; which is evidently a great injustice, as all the parties contribute to the salaries of these officers, in proportion to their shares; and it is one of the commonest principles, that what concerns all, ought to be done to the approbation of all. In a case of this kind, therefore, if the partners do not agree as to the plan of working, or as to any of the necessary operations for that purpose, the justice ought to determine, under the advice of surveyors, which of the plans proposed by any of the owners is the best,* and should keep the administrator to his duty, or, if he be incorrigible, dismiss him from his office; for the appointing an *interventor* at the expense of the party complaining, which we have sometimes seen done, is a severe measure, and burdens him with an additional expense; unless, indeed, it happen that his suspicions are unfounded, for then he ought to be made to pay for his want of confidence.

23. In deep mines, admitting of a variety of works, we have occasionally met with instances where the partners have agreed to work the mine by regions; so that one should work in one direction, and the other in another; or where they have taken it in turn to work upon the vein at alternate periods of time. Neither of these plans is free from inconvenience; the first being inconvenient from the thefts and disputes of the workmen and labourers; and the second, from the parties being apt to work out the vein, and cut away the pillars of support, in order to make the most of their time; yet they serve to quiet disputes between the owners; and the latter plan, that of working alternately, is a correct and legal one, as may be seen by the text of Ulpian ;† for as the result is uncertain, and the chances of each party are equal, there can be no objection to its justice or legality.

24. Proceeding now to illustrate the mode of dividing the produce, we find it referred to by the 45th ordinance of the new code, which agrees with the 49th of the old ordinances,‡ and from which it appears, that the partners may either divide the ore in specie, or divide the silver when smelted and refined. If the former plan is adopted, the division should be made by weight or measure, the ore being mixed up together and thrown into a round heap, and each party being allotted his share, according to the number of bars he holds in the mine. But if the ore be smelted on the partnership

---

* Felic. de societ. cap. 28, n. 44, 45 et 48, et cap. 27, n. 29. "Opinio ejus sequenda erit, qui magis idoneam refectionem proponat. L. in reficiendo, ff. de damno infecto."

† L. 23, ff. comm. divid.

‡ Law 5, tit. 13, book 9, Collection of Castile, cap. 49.

account, each partner ought to take his share of the silver, upon the same principle. The ore, until divided, should be kept in a safe place, called a *galera* (a shed), and no one of the partners is to presume to take away any part of it, under pain of forfeiting his share of the ore to the other partner or partners, and as much more as the value of that share, which is to be one half to the exchequer and the other half to the informer. If it be smelted on the partnership account, it must also be refined on the same account, under the penalty decreed against those who shall smelt ore and sell it, or deal in it, unrefined. The penalty or forfeiture of the ore above-mentioned, is merited, not only because the offence is that of stealing what is common property,* but also because it is to be presumed that he who commits such a fraud in regard to the ore, would also commit a fraud upon the duties. And although the penal action which according to the rules of law,† will hold against a partner, who by craft and fraud takes what is common property, without the consent of his partners, will not generally hold, if he has done so in the exercise of his right as owner, which is also a rule of the *Curia*, and founded on one of the laws of the *Partida* ;‡ yet the contrary is the case with regard to the mines and their produce, both because such an act is prohibited by the ordinance, and also because it is desirable to prevent one partner from taking the rich ores, and leaving those of worse quality for the others, and to remove a fruitful source of dispute and altercation.

25. We have already hinted, that although the share of the expenses to be borne, and of the produce to be received by each of the partners in the mine, ought to be proportioned to the number of bars or parts he holds, yet that agreements may be lawfully made to a different effect, as in other kinds of partnership. Whence it follows, that it is lawful for one partner to agree to substitute his labour, in the place of his contribution to the expenses, the other partner contributing the whole of the capital, and the produce being equally divided. And should any question be raised on this point, the proper reply would be, that it is to be presumed that the industry and labour of the one, are equivalent to the money of the other; but if it should be rejoined that they are unequal, and that the money is more than equivalent to the labour, or *vice versa*, the question, if fairly considered, will appear to be set at rest, by referring to the different nature of the two things contributed, and that it is a more serious thing to hazard life than property, as is laid down by Felicius, upon the authority of Petrus Ubaldis, Nata, Ludovicus, Fachineus, Baldus, Romanus, Menochius, and Socinus. And so, if one

* L. 45, ff. de furt. " Si socius communis rei furtum fecerit (potest enim communis rei furtum facere), indubitate dicendum est furti actionem competere."

† L. 45 et 51, ff. pro socio ; " Merito autem adjectum est *si perfallaciam, et dolo malo amovit,* quia cum sine dolo malo fecit, furti non tenetur, et sane plerumque credendum est eum qui partis dominus est, jure potius suo uti quam furti consilium inire."

‡ Curia Philipp. lib. 1. Commercio ter estre, §. companeros, n. 21.

contributes authority, another labour, and a third money; for the voluntary
choice of the parties must measure the fairness of the agreement, and it is
impossible to lay down any more precise rule.* The labour of attending at
the mine and smelting works, and looking after the management of the concern is great, is combined with hazard, and is very anxious; and a partner
employing his labour in that manner, renders the mine more profitable, and
becomes entitled to receive the same compensation which would be allowed
an administrator, and thus he brings an equivalent for the capital which another partner may contribute in money. And as is remarked by the laws,
the labour contributed by one partner is sometimes so considerable in amount
as to be more valuable to the partnership than money; as for instance, when
one partner alone undertakes the voyages and journies, and encounters all
the perils in his own person.†

26. So also it is lawful to agree that one partner shall bring the mine
into the partnership, and another take upon himself the expenses, dividing
the produce equally between them; so likewise if one furnishes the mine,
and another the labour or industry;‡ in which latter case the property of
the mine is not transferred, but remains in that partner who has brought in
the mine for the purpose of working it. And the reasonableness of such an
agreement is evident from this, that the profit may prove to be very considerable, and that the party who furnishes the capital may possibly make much
more gain from the silver produced from the mine, than by any other means;
as is the case in a partnership between the owner of the soil and the
cultivator.§

27. After these considerations on the division of the produce, the next
point is to inquire how many mines the partners may hold upon one vein,
acquired by means of registry or denouncement. The ordinances of the
new code pass over this point in silence, and therefore, as they lay down no
rule contrary to the 32d of the old ordinances, the force and authority of the
latter still remain.‖ It is provided by this ordinance, "that if there be a
partnership consisting of two persons, they may take two mines upon one

* Felicius, de societ. cap. 9, n. 39. Petrus Ubald. in tract de duobus fratr. p. 4, n. 3. Nata,
cons. 403, n. 5. Joseph Ludov. in comm. conc. 53, n. 156. Bald. in L. si non fuerint, n. 2, ff
pro soc. Menoch. de arbitr. cas. 125. Socin. consil. 265, lib. 2. Idem Felicius, cap. 15, n. 44,
cum aliis inuumer. ubi plenissime Covarr. Var. lib. 3, cap. 2, n. 2. Gomez, Var. res. cap. 5,
n. 5.

† Law 4, title 10, part 5. L. 29, ff pro soc. "Ita coiri societatem posse, ut nullius partem
damni alter sentiat lucrum, vero commune sit, Casius putat : quod ita demum valebit (ut et
Sabinius scripsit) si tanti sit opera quanti damnum est : plerumque enim tanta est industria
socii ut plus societati conferat, quam pecunia : item si solus naviget, solus peregrinetur. peri-
cula subeat solus." §. 2, Instit. de societ.

‡ §. et ita, Inst. de societ. L. Societas, L. cum duobus, §. si incoeunda. ff. pro socio. Sotus.
de just. et jur. lib. 6, quæst. 6, art. 1. vers. quin vero.

§ Felicius, de societ. cap. 27, n. 43. cum pluribus.

‖ Law 5, tit. 13, book 6, ord. 32.

stake, and may also take two other mines upon one stake, upon the same vein, provided they leave three *pertenencias** between the first two and the other two, as provided by the ordinance next preceding this," that is to say the 31st of the old ordinances ; " and if there be more than two partners, they may take such mines in partnership, in the same order, and if they shall have purchased them, they may hold them agreeably to what is stated in the said ordinance," that is to say, all contiguous, although they be several in number.

28. Don Joseph Saenz de Escobar,† in reference to these two ordinances, says, that a space of three mines must intervene between each of the partnership mines, and that each of the partners is bound to leave this interva of three *pertenencias*, it being a sufficient privilege that the partners should be allowed to hold three or four more mines, leaving these three *pertenencias* between each. He was quite sensible of the difficulty in the construction of these two ordinances, and with submission to any better interpretation, stated the opinion he had formed, which we respect and venerate as that of a very learned, practical and experienced man, and one of whose great acuteness on this subject we are well aware. Notwithstanding this, the letter and spirit of the old ordinances, now under consideration, compel us to give the following as our opinion.

29. That is to say, that two, three, four or more partners, may hold two, three, four or more contiguous mines ; and that then, leaving a space of three *pertenencias* after the last of them, they may take two, three, four or more other contiguous mines, according to the number of persons forming the partnership. This is no new doctrine, but is according to the strict text of the ordinance, which permits two partners " to take two mines upon one stake, and then two other mines upon one stake upon the same vein ; and if there be more than two partners, then to take such mines in the same progressive order." And it is putting a forcible construction upon the ordinance, to say there must be a space of three *pertenencias* between each of the partnership mines, in opposition to the expression " take two mines upon one stake and then two other mines upon one stake," and also contrary to the title or inscription in the margin of this ordinance in the old Collection, which runs thus : " That two contiguous mines may be taken in partnership, and then two more, leaving the space of three *pertenencias*, and if there be more than two partners, they may take them in the same order." And it would be impossible to have two mines upon one stake, and then two more upon one stake, or to take two contiguous mines, and then two more contiguous mines, if three *pertenencias* must be left between each of the partnership mines ; for if these three *pertenencias* were left between, the two mines would not be contiguous, agreeably to the title or inscription above-mentioned, nor would they be upon

---

* A set or parcel of mining ground, of dimensions assigned by law. See chap. 9.—*Trans.*

† Saenz, Tratado de medidas de minas, cap. 2, n. 13 and 17.

one stake, as the text of the ordinance has it, but they would be separated from each other by the intermediate space of three *pertenencias*.

30. When, therefore, the ordinance says, " Provided they leave three *pertenencias* between the first two mines and the other two, as provided by the ordinance next preceding this ;" it must necessarily be understood that three *pertenencias* are to be left between the two mines which are contiguous and upon one stake, and the other two which are contiguous and upon one stake, precisely in the same manner as it is incumbent on an individual miner, who cannot hold more than two mines, to leave that space between them ; and so, if there be three, four, five or more partners, observing the same order progressively ; that is to say, they may take three, four, five or more mines upon one stake, and contiguous ; and then, leaving the intermediate space, they may take as many more, according to the number of partners. Besides, if it had been the meaning of the 32d ordinance, that such an intermediate space was to be left between each of the mines, it might easily have been so expressed, as in the 31st, which refers to a single miner ; instead of which, what the ordinance declares is just the reverse, namely that the intermediate space must be left between the two first and the other two, as if each two mines were to be taken collectively.

31. Neither is the allowing two partners to hold four mines, or three partners six mines, or four, eight mines, and so on progressively, by any means to be considered a privilege, as Don Joseph Saenz would have it ; being in fact no more than a fair and ordinary right ; and, in effect, each partner has but two mines, a number which any person may hold, leaving three *pertenencias* between them. Now, if one person may hold two mines, it is plain that each of the partners may hold that number ; and therefore, if the partnership consist of two, they may hold four mines ; if of three, six mines ; if of four, eight mines, and so on, allowing two mines for each partner ; and there can be no *privilege* in this, nor in the mines being permitted to be contiguous, leaving the space of three *pertenencias* between each two, three, four, &c. For if the ordinance allows the partners, when two in number, to hold two contiguous mines, and two more, also contiguous, leaving the space of three *pertenencias* between each two, then may three, four, five or more partners hold a proportionate number of mines, observing the same rule of arrangement. And although the ordinance, in reference to the case of there being more than two partners, says, " that they may take such mines in partnership, in the same order," which might appear to indicate that three partners can take but two mines, namely, those before mentioned and previously referred to ; yet the expression, " such mines," must be understood in a distributive sense, according to the number of persons concerned, and increasing progressively as that number increases.

32. It should also be borne in mind, that the object of the provision, directing an intermediate space of three *pertenencias* to be left between the two

mines, which any person is allowed to take upon one and the same vein, is to restrain excessive covetousness, and to allow of other persons registering mines upon the vein. Now, the copartners themselves are such other persons, and they are not, by reason of their being partners, to be regarded as in a worse situation than any other parties; nor can the taking more mines be treated as the covetous act of one of them alone, when others are joined in partnership with him. Another object of the ordinance is, so to arrange, that the mines shall be worked to a greater advantage, and that the vein shall be explored at intervals; and also that the miner shall be prevented from altering his boundaries at several points, which might be done, if each person could take two contiguous mines. But there can be no doubt that partners may work to much more advantage than individuals, and that they will work upon the vein at intervals; and it will also be their business to keep the boundaries of each mine correct according to law.

33. Finally, as each partner may hold, in his own person, two mines, and as the partners, if they be two, three or four in number, are owners, *per modum unius*, of four, six or eight mines, they ought not, when combined, to be compelled to do more than is required of an individual miner. If then, a single miner is bound to leave the usual space between his two mines, all the partners together, who are interested *per modum unius*, need only leave the space of three *pertenencias* between each four, or each six, or each eight of the mines they are allowed to hold, according to the number of individuals.

34. The question may also be raised whether, supposing five persons have registered, separately, that number of mines, they can afterwards form a partnership together, and enter the contract in the register, the mines being contiguous. This question is answered by referring to the last point; for, if five individuals, separately, may register five mines, contiguous to each other, why may they not do so when partners? Or, why should the five, as partners, be in a worse condition than as independent individuals? Much more, when we consider that partnerships are so much privileged and so much to be encouraged; such combinations having been entered into in working the most celebrated mines of Europe, and affording the best means of promoting the active working of the mines, and, immediately, of benefiting the commonwealth and the crown. Add to which, that if any miner may, by purchasing the three intermediate mines, hold five contiguous mines, without infringing the ordinance, why should not the partners be allowed to hold half their mines contiguous, and then, leaving the usual space between, to hold an equal number also contiguous? Don Joseph Saenz assures us, that it is the practice of the miners to invite some one who appears likely to be an easy neighbour, to take the mine adjacent, that they may get possession of so much of the intermediate space.* With how much more reason then, may

---

* Saenz, loc. ubi proxime, n. 19.

one partner hold a mine contiguous to that of his fellow-partner, leaving the proper space between those two mines, and the two others which they are allowed to take ? We shall notice in its proper place, the artifice resorted to by miners who have made discoveries, or others, to get possession of two contiguous mines ; for the consideration of which, as well as of the question whether the copartners can hold several mines contiguously, when acquired by inheritance or donation, as they can when acquired by purchase, we refer to the place alluded to.*

35. Having considered the modes in which a mining partnership may be constituted, and the rules as to the number of hands necessary to be kept at work, the division of the produce, and the number of mines the partners may hold, we proceed to consider the mode in which a mining partnership may be dissolved or determined. First, then, it is determined by one of the partners renouncing his share, and not choosing to proceed with the works, or to continue his contribution to the expenses ; in like manner as other partnerships are determined by renouncement.† Second, it is determined by one partner selling his share or interest ; for although the law is, that the partnership interest cannot be ceded or transferred, yet this is to be understood of partnerships where the personal services of the party are looked to for the purpose of trading,‡ or in business, the secrets of which it is not proper to reveal, as that would deprive the other of the profits ; but it does not hold, where there is a common subject matter, of which each party may cede or sell his share.§   And in practice, in all the mining districts, shares in mines are sold, both judicially and extrajudicially : and there was an instance not long ago, at the time when so much noise was made in New Spain, by the *bonanza* at Bolanos, of the one third share in a mine being sold for 90,000 dollars, the whole of which sum was returned in six months, from the extraordinary richness of the mine. This mine was called *la Conquista*, and was the first discovered upon the vein ; and shares in many other mines were sold at the same time, in that mining district. And the use of the mine being common to several owners, it follows of necessity, that they must be interested as partners, in working it, and in sharing the ore or silver.

36. Third, if the mine be left insufficiently worked, or be forfeited under any of the penalties of the ordinances, then, as the business is at an end, the partnership is determined.‖

37. A partnership also determines, in general, by the death of any of the

---

* Chap. 8, ordinance 31.

† §. 4, Inst. de societ.

‡ L. 19, ff. pro soc. " Cum enim societas consensu contrahitur, socius mihi esse non potest, quem ego socium esse nolui." Hebia Bolanos, in Cur. lib. 1, comm. terrest. §. 3, n. 39. "It being evident that the partner is chosen on account of his trustworthiness and industry."

§ L. 14, §. 3, ff. comm. divid. Leg. 68, ff. pro soc. L. 66, ff. de reb. cred. L. penult. Cod. de præd. et aliis rebus minor.

‖ §. 6. Instit. de societ. Felicius de Societ. cap. 34, per totum.

partners, their personal services being looked to, as observed above, on admitting them into partnership :* but as the use and property of the mine being common, the heirs must, of necessity, succeed to the possession, as the mine cannot otherwise be worked ; and this is the case with regard to part-nerships in the collection of the public taxes or other public offices, which Baldus calls (according to Felicius), *partnership of necessity :*† so that the heir, although he be not a partner, not having been chosen such, yet, as the law observes,‡ necessarily succeeds to the emolument, or responsibility. And it is not to be doubted but that the heir succeeds also to a share in the common subject matter, and that with regard to mines, the impossibility of their being enjoyed otherwise than in common, necessarily involves a tacit continuance of the partnership with the heirs, and has the effect of constitut-ing a partnership amongst all the partners.

38. The partnership or common holding is determined by partition, for no one can be compelled to continue in it. Whereupon will arise the question, whether the mine can be divided into material parts, allotting a number of *varas* to each partner, in proportion to his interest in the mine ; whether, for example, supposing that there are three partners, each may have allotted to him the space of 40 *varas*, which is the third part of the 120 *varas*, consti-tuting the whole length of the mine ; and so that each may work his own share. And it would seem that there is no difficulty in this. First, because this is the manner in which the estates of miners are divided, if one of those who are jointly interested call for a partition.§ So a tree or rock situated upon the confines of two estates, and whether fixed to the soil or unattached, belongs in respective shares to the two proprietors ;|| and in case of dispute, a partition must be resorted to.¶ Secondly, Escalona, when considering three of the ordinances of Peru, advocates the reasonableness of this plan of making a partition in mines, upon the authority of Jason, Ayora and others.**

39. By the first of these ordinances it is ordained, " That when there is a partnership between persons interested in undivided shares, and one partner being desirous of a partition, demands to have one made, then, whatever may be the subject matter, the other shall be obliged to accede to the request, and the judge shall compel him to do so ; provided that he who makes the

---

* §. 5. Instit. eod. " Cartam personam sibi elegit."

† Felicius, de societ. cap. 32, n. 19. " Conclusio supra posita, et ampliata, quod societas non transeat ad hæredes, et morte extinguatur, declaratur non procedere in societate vectigalium, seu aliarum publicarum functionum ; et ista appellatur societas necessitatis, a Bald. in L. tam diu, n. 2. Cod pro soc. &c."

‡ L. verum, 63. §. in hæredem, ff. pro socio.

§ L. inter omnes, Cod. de præd. minor.

|| L. arbor. 19, ff. comm. divid. L. 83, ff. pro socio.

¶ L. 26, ff. de servit. urban. præd.

** Escalona, Gazoph. lib. 2, p. 2, cap. 1, page 116, tit. 7, concerning mines sufficiently worked, ordinances 5 and 6 ; and tit. 3, concerning measurements, ordinance 2.

demand shall make the partition of partnership property, and that the other party shall, within six days, make choice of which share he will have : and in such partition no more shares shall be made than there are partners ; and when the choice is made, each shall hold his share, and the partition shall serve him for a title, and there shall be no further suit on the subject, nor shall any such be entertained or admitted ; and if the partnership shall consist of more than two, he who demands to have the partition made, shall make it, and the other two shall make their choice ; and if such others shall not agree, the mine shall be divided, and these others shall draw lots for the choice ; and he who has demanded to have the partition made, shall take the share which remains ; and if either of the other two shall prefer it to that which has fallen to him, he may take it the same day, but not afterwards ; and the share which remains shall always be for him who has demanded to have the partition made."

40. By the next ordinance it is provided, "That when there shall be partners, who shall hold a mine in undivided shares, and one of them being absent, he who is present shall work the mine with the number of Indians prescribed by the ordinance, and shall find no ore, the ordinance shall be observed which provides, that after the expiration of two months he shall have it for his own absolutely. In this case, no one can apply to have the mine adjudged to him for being insufficiently worked. If however he shall work the mine with the number of Indians proportioned to the share he may possess in it, and no more, he will thereby fulfil his obligation, as far as concerns his own share, but the share of his partners may be applied for by any person, as insufficiently worked : and if it shall be adjudged to such person, the partner shall be obliged to make his election whether he will have a partition, within ten days ; and if they shall agree to divide it, it shall be divided, and the original partner shall choose which share he pleases, and having once chosen, neither of them shall be at liberty to change, and there shall be no deceit, nor shall any complaint of the party so having made his choice, be listened to ; and if he shall not make his choice within the term prefixed, they shall both possess the mine, *pro indivisio*."

41. The third of these ordinances directs : "That when it shall happen that a mine has to be divided amongst many, by reason of descent or purchase, the measurement shall be made upon the surface of the earth, and shall be reduced to a plane, by means of a level. And that as soon as the partition is made, on whatever account it be, the shares shall be marked out with land marks, in the manner directed, &c."

42. It is evident, from these three ordinances, that a mine may be the subject of partition, and that it may be worked in part, and in part denounced for being insufficiently worked ; and also, that the shares into which it is divided upon a purchase or descent, ought to be defined and marked out with land marks, so that each party may work his own share separately ;

and as the law of the *Partida* says,[*] each is better satisfied with his share when he has it to himself, and he arranges it better and makes more advantage of it.

43. The question, moreover, is put beyond a doubt, by two other ordinances of Peru, one of which sanctions the taking a mine of 15 *varas* in width, if it be a waste space between other mines ;[†] and the other fixes the number of hands to be kept at work in a mine of 60 *varas*, at eight Indians or four Negroes ; and in a mine of 30 *varas* or under, at four Indians or four Negroes ;[‡] whence it is to be inferred beyond question, that the mine may be divided by *varas*.

44. And the point is still more clearly established by one of the ordinances of Castile, according to which, any person may apply for the waste spaces remaining between two mines,[§] which are often of a smaller number of *varas* than a regular mine, for these waste spaces may be of 100, 80 or 20 *varas*, or more or less, according as the number of *varas* to spare is more or less. And it is well known, that in practice, the waste spaces are taken possession of in this manner, as we have ourselves witnessed in the mining district of Bolaños, where the title of *Zapopan* mines was given to them ; and also in other mining districts.

45. The old ordinances allowed 80 or 100 *varas* only, for the length of a silver mine.[||] The gold mines, also, are *mines*, and yet, under the ordinances of the new code, those taken by the discoverer can only be 80 *varas*, and the ordinary ones only 60 *varas* in length, and one-half, respectively, in width ;[¶] and by the old ordinances they were of still smaller dimensions, that is to say, 50 and 40 *varas* respectively,[**] so that a mine may be really such, although it be not 120 *varas* in length. And if the law itself sometimes assigns a less extent to mines, so may their dimensions be diminished upon the division of a partnership, agreeably to the law. And finally, the length of 120 *varas* is fixed as a matter of favour, and the object is, that that number should not be exceeded ; but this does not prevent the miner from contenting himself with less, and renouncing the rest.

46. Nor can it be urged, with any effect, that this would occasion confusion, or that as different fixed stakes would be set up in the mines, thus rendered, by division, less than the regular size, it would be easy, by entering these pits, to gain access to the ore belonging to the adjoining mine owner ; for the same thing might be said of the waste spaces which are allowed to be taken

---

[*] Law 1, tit. 15, part 6.

[†] Ord. 1, tit. 2, concerning the spaces allotted for mines, in Escalon. ubi. sup.

[‡] Ord. 3, tit. 7, concerning mines insufficiently worked, apud eund.

[§] Chap. 13, ordinance 29.

[||] L. 4, tit. 13, book 6, ord. 22.

[¶] Chap. 9, ordinance 70.

[**] Ordinance 75, law 5, tit. 13, book 6.

between the different mines, and yet these inconveniences are not found to occur, for if a party registers a pit upon a vein and upon ore, and follows it up, then, even supposing that he does carry on his works within the limits of some other owner, he becomes entitled, by his diligence, to the ore he may raise.* And there is no fraud in a case of this kind, fraud being imputed only in the case of a party working where there is neither a vein nor ore, nor any appearance of it, and with a view merely to take advantage of the ore of a neighbour, by mining within his boundaries. But if those who make partition of the mine proceed with regularity, and measure out the ground in *varas*, so as to ascertain what is the share of each, each of them registering a pit upon ore, or leaving the entrance common, it is precisely the same thing whether the mine contain 8 *varas* or 80, provided the limit of extent fixed by law, be not exceeded.

47. And above all, as it is impossible to lay down rules for all cases and in all matters, the aspect of which, from the various combinations of qualities, persons and incidents which occur, varies with the most trifling variations in the circumstances, the subject must be left, after laying down the above rules, to the sound direction of the judges, in the exercise of which, it must be determined whether, under such or such circumstances, the metalliferous estate will conveniently admit of division, or not ; as is laid down by Felicius, upon the authority of Baldus and Decianus ; and if it will not admit of such division, then it should be adjudged to one of the partners, and, in preference, to him who holds the largest share. Or, according to a better opinion, for which he cites Tiraquelo and Capicius,† they should be admitted to bid for it, giving a preference to the partner who holds the largest share ; by which means the inconvenience of obliging the parties to continue the common holding or partnership is avoided, whilst the adjudication, or the better plan of a judicial sale, preserves the interest of the partner who calls for a partition, without rendering it necessary to divide the property. This rule is likewise laid down in the *Curia*, being founded on the law of the *Partida*, and the civil law, and it is also illustrated by Ayora.‡

* Chap. 14, ordinance 30.

† Felicius, de soc. cap. 39, n. 86. " Secundo consideravit, au res, puta fundus, commodam patiatur divisionem, quod quando sit declarat Baldus, in L. sancimus, Cod. de donat. et in cap. 1, in princ. de duob. fratr. de nov. benef. invest. et Decian. cons. 15, n. 38, lib. 1, et erit ista declaratio judici arbitraria, cum certa regula dari non possit, et si videbit commodam non pati divisionem uni erit adjudicanda, ut per Barth. in L. ad officium, Cod. comm. divid. Contra hanc Barth. opinionem faciunt tradita a Bald. in L. sancimus, Cod. de donat. nam vult, quod si res commode dividi non possit, præferatur ille qui in re habet majorem partem Verum a Barth. opinione non est recedendum, et est intelligendum, Baldum loqui quod in par licitatione solummodo præferatur ille qui in re majorem partem habet, ita tradit Tiraquel. de jure primogen. q. 60, n. 16. Capicius, dec. 36."

‡ Curia, lib. 1, comm. terrest. §. companeros 3. n. 49, L. fin. tit. 15, p. 6. L. ad officium, Cod. comm. divid. Ayora de part, p. 1, cap. 3, n. 30.

CHAPTER VIII.

OF THE FIRST DISCOVERERS, AND THEIR PRIVILEGE OF HOLDING SEVE-
RAL MINES, AN ORDINARY MINER BEING CAPABLE OF HOLDING TWO
ONLY, UNLESS ACQUIRED BY PURCHASE OR INHERITANCE, UNDER
WHICH CIRCUMSTANCES HE MAY HOLD AN UNLIMITED NUMBER.

ORDINANCES XXII. XXXI.

XXII. ALSO, we ordain and command, that the person who shall first find
or discover a mine, shall, as the first finder or discoverer, be the first to make
registry, and shall enjoy all such mining *pertenencias* as he shall stake out,
or choose to stake out, upon the mines and veins he shall discover, or shall
have discovered, provided that he shall, within ten natural days from the time
of his making registry of such mine, stake out, declare and distinguish such
pertenencias as he may be desirous of having ; and that he shall enjoy the
extent of space which properly belongs to each portion staked out, throughout all the *pertenencias* which he shall so stake out and distinguish, as such
discoverer ; and that he shall be obliged, within the aforesaid term of ten days,
to stake out all the *pertenencias* which he shall so choose, to be performed
in such manner as he shall think fit, although he should include and take
within his boundaries any trial pit or trial pits which other persons, coming
after him, may have made, or may make ; provided he first set up a fixed
stake in each of the *pertenencias* he shall so distinguish and take, which he
shall not be at liberty to leave, nor shall leave, when he shall stake out or
alter his boundaries, however he may stake out or alter the same. And
that such persons as shall come after him, shall proceed in their order, to stake
out or alter their boundaries, as they shall from time to time discover ore.
And that when they shall have made registry, as they are bound to do, they
shall proceed to set up a fixed stake in each of the *pertenencias* they may
choose to take and distinguish, within the term of ten days, as aforesaid, but
after the expiration of the first ten days allowed to the first discoverer ; for
those who stake out a mine, are always to have ten days to view the ground,
and to take all such *pertenencias* as they shall wish to have, and to set up a
fixed stake ; but they cannot disturb or enter upon the *pertenencias* which
shall have been already staked out, because all the *pertenencias* and boundaries which shall have been taken and marked out by those who shall have
first set out stakes, are to be preserved. And if two or more persons shall
apply to have their boundary stakes set out, it shall be ascertained, in a short
and summary manner, which of them applied first ; and he who shall be ascertained to have been the first, shall be preferred, saving the right of the
other party, if he shall, nevertheless, claim to have first made application
to have such stakes set out, as aforesaid.

XXXI. Also, we ordain and command, that the first finder and discoverer
of such mines may take as many stakes and *pertenencias* as he chooses, ob-

serving, in respect to the same, all that is contained in the ordinances relating to this matter; and that he may also hold and possess all mines and *pertenencias*, how many soever they be, which he shall purchase or inherit, or which may appertain to him under any title or cause whatsoever.

CONTENTS OF THE COMMENTARY ON THESE ORDINANCES.

1. Of the regard which ought to be paid to the dicoverers of mines.
2. The discoverer is the person who finds ore in the vein, although he may not open the first pit on the ground.
3. If it be a question who was the first discoverer, it shall be ascertained in a summary way, the right of the losing party being reserved.
4. If two different persons find ore upon the vein at the same time, it might appear that they would reciprocally prevent each other from being discoverers.
5. This perplexity, however, is easily got over, with regard to the mines.
6, 7 and 8. For it is inferred, from two of the ordinances of Peru, that each party acquires to himself the privilege of a discoverer, although some preference is shewn towards him who first applies to the justice.
9 and 10. The same rule prevails in New Spain, except that no preference is given to the party applying first; arguments establishing this doctrine.
11. The discoverer may take as many mines as he pleases, under certain conditions.
12, 13, 14 and 15. The old ordinances are altered by our text, as to the number of mines the discoverer is allowed to take, and the mode of taking them, as he may, by the present law, take as many contiguous mines as he pleases, taking care to keep a proper number of hands at work, and observing the other rules of the ordinances.
16. Other miners, as well as the discoverer, to be entitled to register a mine, must have discovered ore, and must set up a fixed stake within ten days.
17. Of the order to be observed amongst these parties in granting mines; the preference being given to the party who first applies to the justice.
18. What is to be donewhen several parties apply, at the same time, to have the boundary takes set out.
19. No ordinary miner can take two contiguous mines, but any person may hold two or more, if acquired by purchase.
20, 21 and 22. It is resolved and proved, that any person may also hold several mines, if acquired by inheritance or any other lucrative title.

COMMENTARY.

1. If the inventors of arts tending to the common benefit of society,[*] are justly entitled to reward, the discoverers of mines, the precious metals produced from which are the main spring of arts, and the animating spirit of commerce, are surely still more proper objects of such encouragement. For rewards so bestowed, besides being a proper return for the labour and anxiety of the discoverers, have the further effect of stimulating others to search for veins and mines, on which the general prosperity of the state mainly depends.[†]

---

[*] Solorz. tom. 1. de jur. Ind. lib. 1, cap. 16, a n. 35. Polydor. Virgilius, de rerum inventoribus.

[†] Agricola, de re metall. lib. 3. page 56. "Ut primo venæ inventori meritam referat, et cæteros metallicos excitet ad studium quærendarum venarum."

2. The subject to which these ordinances, from the 22d to the 31st inclusive, relate, is that of the privileges of the first discoverers. In which the first thing to be noticed is, that the first discoverer is " he who shall have first found or discovered the mine ;" or, as the ordinance of Peru has it," " he who has first found ore in the vein, notwithstanding that some other person may have been the first to commence making trial pits ;" (trial pits made by way of trying the vein.) And our own ordinance contains a like provision, directing that the first discoverer shall take out such *pertenencias* as he shall choose to have, within the term of ten days, " although he should include and take within his *pertenencias* any trial pit or trial pits which other persons coming after him may have made :" for the first discoverer is not the person who opens the first pit, but he who first finds ore. He who opens the first pit may not find ore, and even if he should have opened the pit after discovering ore, yet he cannot anticipate the discoverer, or divest his right of making registry previous to any other person, within the 20 days fixed by the ordinance.†

3. Supposing that two or more persons should find ore at different parts of the vein at the same moment, it may be asked, which of them is to be considered the first discoverer ? This question is not touched upon in the ordinances of the new code ; and all that is contained in the old ones‡ in reference to it, is a declaration, that if two or more persons should apply at the same time, it shall be ascertained in a short and summary manner, which of them was the first finder or discoverer ; and that he who shall be ascertained to have been the first shall be preferred, saving the right of the other, if he shall nevertheless insist that he was the first finder. But this is a distinct case from that which we have supposed ; for if it can be ascertained which of them was the first finder or discoverer, the preference must be given to him, whether upon a summary or plenary trial, and even although they should simultaneously make application to have their boundaries marked out. But the case we have suggested, is that of their having both found ore at the same moment, so that it cannot be made out who was the first discoverer, which, although of frequent occurrence, is within possibility.

4. Did we depend on the civil law for a solution, we should adopt the opinion, from analogy to what takes place under similar circumstances, that each would prevent the other from becoming entitled to the privileges of a first discoverer, and that neither of them ought to be so considered. Thus a legacy given to him who shall first ascend the Capitol, is prevented from taking effect, if two persons ascend at the same time, so as to make it impossible to ascertain which of them was the first. So if given to him who

---

* Ord. 9, tit. 1, concerning first discoverers; Escalona, Gazoph. lib. 2, part. 2, cap. 1, page 106.

† Chap. 5, sup. ord. 17.

‡ Ord. 21, law 5, tit. 13, book 6, Collection of Castile.

shall raise a monument, and several persons raise monuments ; and so, if given to the eldest, where there are two persons of the same age ; or to the greatest friend, where there are two persons who have equal claims of friendship : as may be seen by reference to the text of Ulpian, and those who follow him.* It would follow therefore, that, supposing two different persons to make the discovery simultaneously, neither of them would be entitled to the privileges of a discoverer.

5. But the solution is not to be sought amongst these subtilties of the Roman civil law. For the reason which prevents the legacies from taking effect in the above instances, is the testator's not having fully comprehended the effect of the condition, he having had one single person only in contemplation. But the object of our laws is to promote the working of the mines, as of the utmost importance to the public, not regarding whether the discoverers be several, or one only ; and it would be very far from reasonable to determine, that the mines shall remain untouched, and the labour of the discoverers be disappointed of its due reward, merely because they have happened to discover the vein at one and the same time. We must therefore look for some other principle, more direct in its application, and harmonising better with the intention of the ordinances, upon which to ground the decision of this question.

6. Such a principle may be found in the ordinances of Peru, by which it is provided : " That if two or more persons shall find ore together upon the same occasion, he who shall first produce the ore before the justice, having previously made an assay, as directed by the ordinances, shall be deemed to be the discoverer ; and if the dispute concern a single vein, the other party shall be at liberty to set up his stake next to the mine allotted to the crown ; but if it also concern another vein, he may make his choice in the manner to be declared."†

7. This declaration is made in another of the ordinances, which establishes : " That whoever shall discover a vein, more than one league from any other mining district, shall enjoy the rights of a discoverer, upon that vein , but if he shall discover another vein on the same ground within that distance, he shall have a mine of 60 *varas* at any part of it he pleases, and if he shall discover other veins, he shall be entitled to have that space upon all, until he has six mines of sixty *varas* each ; and every one who shall discover new veins shall have the same privilege, although he be not a discoverer of a new mineral tract, up to the number of five mines ; and as to such others as he may acquire by staking out or by purchase, regard shall be had to the subsequent ordinances, which treat of taking more than the allowed number of mines. But if he should discover other mines beyond the said

---

* L. si fuerint, ff. de reb. dub. L. duo sunt Titii, de testam. tutel.

† Ordin. 9, tit. 1. concerning first discoverers ; Escalona, Gazoph. lib. **2.** part. **2,** cap. 1, pag. 106.

space of one league, in which he shall be entitled to enjoy the rights of a discoverer, such mines as he may take there, or may be granted to him in that character, shall not be reckoned in the aforesaid number, either with regard to him, or to any other persons who may discover veins in such new mineral tract; except that they shall be obliged to keep them properly worked, and if they neglect to do so, the ordinances relating to mines left insufficiently worked, shall be applied to them."[*]

8. These two ordinances serve to shew, that if there be different veins at less than one league distance from some other mining district, one mine may be taken upon each vein, to the number of six mines; but if two or more persons find ore upon different parts of the same vein, he who first produces the ore before the justice, is the discoverer, and the other may have a mine next to that which the ordinances of Peru direct to be set out for the crown;[†] so that they have between them, the two mines which one alone would have been entitled to, had he been the sole discoverer; but he who exhibits the most diligence in producing the ore before the justice, enjoys the discoverer's mine, exceeding the ordinary ones by 20 *varas* in length and 10 in width, according to the dimensions assigned to the mines in that kingdom.

9. By analogy to which, it may be inferred, that in New Spain, where a single discoverer is at liberty to take as many mines as he pleases, measuring out the boundaries in whatever direction he thinks best, the same right ought to be enjoyed to an equal extent, by each of the two persons who should have discovered ore upon different parts of the vein, at the same time; which may be done, without any necessity for making a common or partnership concern, as equality may be attained by making their choice separately, each taking his principal mine upon that of the vein where he may have found the ore. And although one should use more diligence than the other or others, in producing the ore before the justice, the latter ought not to be prejudiced by his being thus beforehand, provided the application be made within the term of 20 days, allowed by the ordinances of Castile[‡] for making the registry, as no delay will be occasioned thereby. And although, under the ordinances of Peru, the party who applies first, is entitled to an additional space of 20 *varas*, this circumstance is of little moment; for in New Spain, the discoverer, as we shall explain in its proper place in the next chapter, is entitled to an equal extent in all the mines he selects. And in the case of their disagreeing in making the choice, the judge must bring them to an understanding, either by drawing lots, or in some other way.

10. This doctrine harmonises well with the grand object of encouraging the working of the mines, and stimulating the subject to discover them, for

---

* Ord. 14, apud eund. ubi proxime, pag. 107.
† Ord. 18, apud eund. pag. 108.
‡ Chap. 5, ord. 17.

the general benefit of the revenue and the nation at large. And the extending the right, in this manner, to both discoverers, is an easy means of
providing for the interest of each, and makes the case analogous to that of
two creditors having instruments of the same date, by virtue of which they
require (according to several authors, who rely on some important texts*),
an equal right to priority in respect of their several debts, against the thing
pledged, so as to come in in equal shares, or in proportion to the amount of
their debts. This is also agreeable to the course pursued by Scipio, in giving to two persons the mural crown, which he had promised to the first who
should ascend the walls of Carthage; and to other instances of a similar
kind which might be cited, of persons enjoying some dignity, patronage or
office, in common, and dividing and enjoying the emoluments equally.

11. Dismissing this topic, we proceed to observe, that the 22d ordinance
directs, that the first disoverer shall enjoy all the mining *pertenencias* which
he may stake out and distinguish, but subject to the following conditions;
first, that he shall make registry agreeably to the ordinances on that subject;
second, that he shall distinguish the *pertenencias* he is desirous of having,
within ten ten days from the time of making registry; and third, that he shall
set up a fixed stake,† in each of the *pertenencias* he shall so distinguish and
take. These are conditions which it is indispensably necessary to observe, as appears from the word *provided*, in the ordinance, which imports a
condition, and that the party is not to enjoy the rights of a first discoverer,
nor to have the *pertenencias* he fixes upon, unless he fulfil the conditions par-
ticularized.‡ He must therefore, within ten days, set up a fixed stake in
each of the mines he may be desirous of taking, distinguishing and staking
out each *pertenencia*; and he cannot claim to have ten days for each mine,
or for setting out the limits of each separate mine, for the ordinance says,
"within which (ten days) he shall stake out, declare and distinguish;" and
it again repeats:—" he shall be obliged, within the aforesaid term of ten days,
to stake out all the *pertenencias* which he shall so choose;" and further on,
it adds: " after the expiration of the first ten days allowed to the first discoverer;" in enforcing which provisions, the object of the ordinance is to reap
the benefits derivable from setting the mines to work, and to provide for the
interests of those who, coming afterwards, may be desirous to make registry;

---

* L. si fundus, §. si duo. ff. de pignor. L. idemque, ff. qui potiores in pignor. hab. Peregrinus
de jur. fisci. 2, lib. 6, tit. 6, n. 35. Gomez, in L. 45, Taur. n. 3. Carrasco, in LL. Recop. cap.
11, n. 182. Barbosa, in L. 1, p. 2, n. 8, ff. de solut matrim. apud ques innumeri: et apud
Acosta, de priv. cred. in præf. ad reg. 3, n. 3, 4, 5 et 91.

† The *fixed stake* is the denomination given to the principal pit of the mine, from which the
works are commenced, and which is never to be abandoned upon any subsequent demarcation
or alteration of the boundaries.

‡ Juxta ea quæ cum pluribus tradit Antunez, de donat. lib. 1, præl. 2, § 1, a n. 26. Salgado,
de reg. protect. p. 4, cap. 12, n. 39 et 40. Conditio inducit formam in lege: Molina, de primogen lib. 2, cap. 11, n. 12, Tiraq. de retract. §. 37, gloss. 2, n. 28. Gutierr. Pract. lib. 3, quæst.
52, n. 5.

and therefore, in order to prevent their being delayed by the first discoverer, it fixes that period for the whole.

12. With respect to the preference given to the first discoverer, this ordinance follows the 21st of the old ordinances, altering the 31st of those ordinances, under which, neither the first discoverer nor any other person could take more than two mines upon one vein, and even those were not to be contiguous, but must have a space of *three pertenencias* between them, unless acquired by purchase ; in which case, the owners might hold several, even though contiguous.* As then, the ordinance under consideration authorises the discoverer to take as many mines as he thinks proper, it follows that the 31st ordinance above-mentioned, is varied, both in respect to the number of mines allowed to be taken, and to their relative situation, namely that they may now be either contiguous or apart, at the pleasure of the discoverer.

13. That the rule of the old ordinance is varied as to the number of mines allowed to be taken, appears from this that a grant is made to the discoverer, of any number he pleases, and therefore, by one of the first rules of law,† he is not excluded from any one *pertenencia* upon the vein. And he is, therefore, at liberty to take the whole vein, and to work it, provided he set up a stake in each mine, keep the requisite number of hands to work in each, and attend to the other directions of the ordinances ; for if he lay out his money upon mines, and work them on his own account, he is likewise fairly entitled to enjoy all the benefit himself ; and such is the manner in which Agricola treats this question, in two places where he considers the subject.‡

14. It follows also, that it is varied as regards the relative situation of the mines ; for the observation incidentally made by Don Joseph Saenz,§ that the first discoverer may certainly, under the 31st ordinance of the new code, take more than two mines upon the same vein, but that he must leave the three *pertenencias* between, is evidently contrary to our 22d ordinance, which in an ample and almost redundant manner, grants to the first discoverer, " all such mining *pertenencias* as he shall stake out, or choose to stake out," and entitles him " to distinguish such *pertenencias* as he may be desirous of having," " as he shall think fit," without requiring him to leave any intermediate space between one mine and another, but leaving it to his own choice

---

* Law 5, tit. 13, book 6, Collection of Castile, ord. 21 and 31.

† Qui dicit omne nihil excludit.

‡ Agricola, de re metallica, lib. 4 page 60. " Alicubi denique jus totius alicujus loci, rivulis, valleculis aliisque terminis definiti tribuitur uno domino." Et pag. 62. " Uni autem domino licitum est possidere unam integram fodinæ aream, duas, tres, pluresve : unum integrum cuniculum ant plures : modo jussis legum metallicarum et decretis magistri metallicorum obtemperet, quia qui solus facit impensas in fodinas, si fuerint metallis fecundæ, solus ex eis fructam capiet."

§ Saenz. Tratad. de medidas de minas, cap. 2, n. 18 " Hence it follows, that the 31st ordinance of the new code has repealed the old ordinance concerning new discoverers, by authorising them to take more than two mines upon one vein, leaving three *pertenencias* between."

to select them, and therefore authorising him to take them either contiguous or separate, as he pleases.

15. It is true, that the 31st ordinance of the new code says, that the first discoverer may hold as many mines as he pleases, observing all that is contained in the ordinances relating to this subject; whence Don Joseph Saenz seems to infer, that the 31st of the old ordinances ought to be observed with regard to the intermediate space to be left, although not with regard to the number of the mines allowed to be taken; but this is contrary to the letter of our 22d ordinance, which uses the most extensive and redundant form of expression.   And as this and other ordinances of the new code, treat of the larger number of mines and priority of choice allowed to the first discoverers, it is, no doubt, to these, and the observance of their provisions, that the 31st refers, and by no means to the 31st of the old ordinances, which is wholly repealed by the 22d ordinance, now under consideration, in favour of the first discoverer, whom it empowers to take a larger number of mines, by means of registry, and also to take them contiguous, without being obliged to leave the intermediate space of three mines.

16. The ordinance next proceeds to speak of the other persons who may come after the first discoverer, and directs that they shall set up stakes, or alter their boundaries in their order, " as they shall discover ore ;" which implies, that they cannot take mines, or set out or alter their boundaries, unless they shall have discovered ore in the pit registered as the principal pit.* The ordinance also imposes on them the same obligation of setting up a fixed stake in, and measuring out, each mine, within ten days, but does not authorise them to trespass upon *pretenencias* already staked or measured out by other persons; for the very object of defining the boundaries of a mine, is to prevent disputes of this kind between neighbours ;† and he who has first measured out and occupied a particular spot, is in a better situation than the other.

17. After the first discoverer has measured out his boundaries, the rule to be observed with regard to all other persons, as to such new discoveries, is, that they shall have their boundary stakes set out in the order in which they make application for that purpose, so that it is the diligence of the party in applying first, which entitles him to a preference over the others; which is as proper a mode of apportioning out the vein as could be adopted.   In Peru,‡ the rule is, that the discoverer shall declare upon oath, what persons were sinking trial pits on the ground, at the time of his discovering the vein; and if any of them apply within 30 days, the judge is to give them a mine

---

* See chap. 5, ord. 17, as to registry.

† Agricol. de re metall. lib. 3, pag. 60.   "Area cujusque fodinæ ideo terminis describitur, ne lis oriatur inter fodinarum vicinarum dominos."

‡ Ord. 6, tit. 1, concerning discoverers ; Escalona, Gazoph. lib. 2, p. 2, cap. 1, pag. 105 and 106.

of sixty *varas* in extent, in the order in which they shall make application. And if the discoverer shall have forgotten any one of them, who shall prove, by two witnesses, that he was making trials at the time, he shall enjoy the same rights as the others.

18. If two or more persons (proceeds our ordinance), shall apply to have their boundary stakes set out, it shall be ascertained, in a summary way, which of them applied first, and he shall be perferred; saving the rights of such others as shall nevertheless claim to have made the first application, to be determined upon a plenary trial. This case appears to involve some difficulty, and can only occur when the application to set out boundaries has been made verbally, for the proper way of making it is by petition to the justice in writing; the question, who has made the first application, will therefore be determined by referring to the time of presenting the petition, the day and hour of which should be noted in the register,* as the standard determining the order of priority, in which different parties may measure out their mines.† This case differs from that proposed in the 21st of the old ordinances, which speaks of two persons, both of whom claim to be the first discoverers; in which case it is to be ascertained, in a summary way, which of them was first; saving the right of the other, to be determined upon a plenary trial,‡ as before observed in n. 3.

19. We have stated above, that the 31st of the old ordinances is repealed in favour of the first discoverer, by the 22nd ordinance of the new code; and we now add, that it is also annulled, as respects him, by the 31st of the new ordinances, which authorises the discoverer to take all such stakes or *pertenencias* as he pleases, observing the rules of the ordinances. But as to other persons, not being first discoverers, the 31st of the old ordinances still applies; its effect being, that no person shall hold more than two mines upon the same vein, acquired by registry or denouncement, and that such two mines must have an intermediate space of three mines between them; but not so as to mines purchased, which may be held contiguous, even though several in number. The reason is this, that if the party purchase them, they are, necessarily, regular mines, and sunk to the requisite depth; and it is evident, that his object in taking them is to work them and raise the ore, and that he is not merely instigated by an avaricious desire of occupying a large space, to exclude others altogether from the ground.

20. The first discoverer being capable of holding several mines, either contiguous or apart, when acquired by inheritance, it has been made a question, whether any other miner can hold such mines under the same circumstances. The opinion of Don Joseph Saenz is to the contrary;§ but we

---

* Chap. 5, u. 12.
† Chap. 11, ord. 25, infra.
‡ Law 5, title 13, book 6, Collection of Castile, ord. 21.
§ D. Joseph Saenz, Tratado de medidas de minas, cap. 2, n. 16.

have not been able to make out the grounds on which this opinion rests, nor can we discover any: for although, in the 31st ordinance we are treating of, the words " shall inherit," apply to the discoverer, to whom alone the ordinace refers, it does not follow that other miners are incapacitated from hold. ing any mines that may descend to them; for if they can take them by way of purchase or exchange, or other onerous title, why should they be disabled from taking them by way of legacy, donation, inheritance or any other lucrative title?

21. The 31st of the old ordinances does not contain the words " shall inherit," in reference to the first discoverer, and yet we do not hesitate to say, that even when this ordinance was in force, incapacitating the discoverer from holding more than two mines, and those separately, like any other person, unless acquired by purchase, our opinion would nevertheless have been that he might still have held them, if acquired by inheritance; and so of any other miner. For were it not so, parties would be deprived of the benefit they might derive from a gift or bequest of the mine, if made to them; descendants would be rendered incapable of taking what they would otherwise inherit from their ancestors, and parents what they would succeed to from their children; and all this without any ordinance expressly ordering it so. The same reasoning then, will apply to this ordinance of the new code, for neither that nor any other ordinance prohibits the holding several mines, if acquired by descent; nor does it intend when laying down rules for a discoverer, to make the permission granted to him operate to exclude all others.

22. This therefore being a *casus omissus*, the construction most favourable for the miners should be adopted; and if a mine, transferred by a lucrative title, have been sunk to the depth of three *estados*, as required in a mine when sold, or if the obligation to sink to that depth be a concomitant of the transfer, the object of the ordinances, so far as they seek to promote the exploring and working of the vein, is accomplished; and their other aim, that of restraining covetousness, cannot here come in question: as the transfer, if by gift, is a liberal act; and if by inheritance, either a necessary or a liberal one. And there is, in fact, more covetousness in accumulating a number of mines by purchase, than by inheritance; for in the case of a purchase, the money is laid out in the anxious desire to obtain more, but where property is acquired by a lucrative title, there is no motive but the liberality of the donor or testator, or the necessity of the legitimate heir succeeding, by reason of his consanguinity. We see that the miners, to avoid encountering unpleasant neighbours, persuade some other person to register the ground adjacent to their mine, which, when sunk to the depth of three *estados*, they purchase at a small price. This is a very common practice, and there is nothing to prevent it, for the vendor and purchaser respectively, merely avail themselves of the rights they are entitled to under the ordinance, which permits the selling a mine when duly registered and sunk

to the proper depth. There is no doubt, however, that through this device of making purchases at a small price, an opportunity is afforded for the indulgence of covetousness, which is not the case when the mine is acquired by donation, inheritance or bequest. Besides, there is no prohibition against giving, bequeathing or leaving a mine to descend to the heir ; nor are the miners who have more than two mines upon one vein, prohibited, either expressly or by implication, from acquiring others by a lucrative title ; particularly as transfers of the latter class generally proceed from the ties of blood, affection or merit.

CHAPTER IX.

OF THE LENGTH AND BREADTH OF MINES, AND IN WHAT MANNER THEY MUST BE TAKEN.—OF THE FIXED STAKE, WHICH ALL PERSONS ARE BOUND TO ADHERE TO IN THEIR MINES.—OF THE DISCOVERER'S RIGHT TO A LARGER EXTENT OF GROUND IN ALL THE MINES WHICH HE SHALL ORIGINALLY FIX UPON.—IT IS SHEWN THAT THERE MAY BE DIFFERENT FIRST DISCOVERERS IN RESPECT OF DIFFERENT VEINS IN ONE AND THE SAME MINERAL TRACT.

ORDINANCES XXIII. LXX.

XXIII. Also, we ordain and command, that any person who shall have discovered, or shall discover any new mine, and shall have made registry, as directed by the last ordinance, shall enjoy a space of 160 *varas* in length upon the vein, and 80 in width ; and if he shall wish to measure out the said space of 160 *varas* and 80 *varas*, crosswise upon the vein, he shall be at liberty to do so, in such manner as he may find most convenient. And it is declared, that after the first discoverer shall have distinguished the *pertenencias* he chooses to take, within the aforesaid ten days allowed him for that purpose, no other person shall be entitled to have the boundaries set out, nor to set out their boundaries, until after the expiration of a further period of ten days, that he may define the limits of the *pertenencias* he chooses to take, as first discoverer ; in doing which he must not leave his fixed stake, and must not prejudice any other person or persons, on either side of him, who may occupy mines which they have sunk and registered before him ; and those who shall have taken after the first discoverer, or shall thenceforth take mines, may proceed to take and work their mines and *pertenencias ;* and each of the mines taken after those of the said discoverer, shall be 120 *varas* in length, and 60 in width, which space may be taken crosswise upon the vein, or as it shall seem best, provided they do not leave their fixed stake, and do not prejudice other persons.

LXX. Also, we ordain and command, that the first discoverer of such mines or streamworks of gold, shall take and have a space of 80 *varas* in length, and 40 in width, which they may take as they shall deem best ; and those who shall come after them shall take and have a space of 60 *varas* in length and 30 in width, which they shall also take as they shall deem best ; and in every other respect they shall observe all that is contained in the aforesaid ordinances, with regard to silver, under the penalties thereby limited.

CONTENTS OF THE COMMENTARY ON THESE ORDINANCES.

1 and 2. Of the length and breadth of the mines in New Spain and Peru.

3 and 4. The privilege of taking a larger space of ground, allowed to the discoverer, extends to all the mines he may take.

5. The right to this privilege has not been weakened or destroyed by the omission or neglect to exercise it.

6, 7, 8 and 9. An instance from the mining district of El Monte, confirming our opinion ; with a statement, in substance, of the petition presented by the discoverer, and of the superior government of Mexico.

10. This privilege applies to the mines which the discoverer takes as such, and not to those he may acquire by any other title.

11. Privileges of the discoverer in Peru.

12 and 13. The length of the mine may be taken either upon the course of the vein or across it.

14. This doctrine confirmed by the opinion of Saenz.

15. The diversities noticed in the course of different veins, make it necessary that this liberty should be allowed.

16 and 17. Of the varieties in the course of different veins, some being deep, some spreading, some curved, &c.

18. In Peru, the length of the mine must be taken along the course of the vein : and why?

19, 20 and 21. A *fixed stake* defined. and its importance in preserving order amongst the different mines, shewn.

22. The mode in which land is measured, differs from that pursued in measuring mines.

23. The discoverer, in tracing his boundaries, must not prejudice his neighbours.

24 and 25. There may be several discoverers in the same mineral tract, each upon his own vein.

26. Modification of this doctrine as to Peru.

27, 28 and 29. It is not the practice in New Spain to set out a mine for the crown, nor does it seem for the interest of the sovereign to do so ; he is at liberty however, as supreme lord, to take any number he pleases.

COMMENTARY.

1. Having illustrated, under the preceding ordinances, the preference allowed to the first discoverer in registering and measuring out any number of mines he pleases, whether lying contiguous or apart, we next proceed to inquire what number of *varas* each mining *pertenencia* should occupy.

2. Under the old laws and ordinances, the discoverer, or any other per-

son, might take a space of 100 *varas* in length and 50 in width.[*] After-wards, the discoverer was allowed 120 *varas* in length and 60 in breadth, all other persons remaining entitled, as before, to 100 *varas* in length and 50 in breadth.[†] These laws are altered by our 23d ordinance, which assigns to the discoverer a space of 160 *varas* in length and 80 in breadth, and to all other persons 120 *varas* in length, and 60 in breadth. In Peru, the discoverer's mine is 80 *varas* in length, and that of an ordinary miner, 60 ; each of them being one half, respectively in breadth [‡] The above applies to silver mines, but as to gold, our 70th ordinance allows, for the discoverer's mine, 80 *varas* in length, and for that of an ordinary miner, 60 ; and one half, respectively, in breadth, for each of them ; our 70th ordinance herein altering the old ordinance, which confined them within more narrow limits.[§]

3. The first question which suggests itself is, whether each of the mines which the discoverer is empowered, by the 22d and 31st ordinances of the new code, to take, is to be 160 *varas* in length, and 80 in width, or whether the first mine only, chosen by him, is to be of these dimensions. The answer to which is, that the dimensions of 160 *varas* in length and 80 in breadth, may be assigned to all the mines which the discoverer may select at the time of registering the vein, or within ten days after, such a privilege being conferred by the express terms of the ordinances. This will appear from the words of the 22d ; " Provided that he shall, within ten natural days from his making registry of such mine, stake out, declare and distinguish such *pertenencias* as he may be desirous of having, and that he shall enjoy the extent of space which properly belongs to each portion staked out, throughout all the *pertenencias* which he shall so stake out and distinguish as such discoverer." And also from those of the 31st ; " That he may take as many stakes and *pertenencias* as he chooses, observing, in respect to the same, all that is contained in the ordinances relating to this matter." Whence it is plain that all the mining *pertenencias* he takes, are taken in the character of a discoverer, and that each may be of the dimensions allowed to the discoverer, by the 23d ordinance.

4. This ordinance, referring to the ordinance preceding, fixes the dimensions at 160 *varas* in length and 80 in width ; making no distinction whether one mine or several be taken. Since then, the matter referred to must be considered as included in that from which reference is made,[||] and since also, where the law itself makes no distinction, none such can properly be taken,[¶] it clearly follows, that the discoverer is entitled to assign these di-

---

[*] Law 4, § 4, tit. 13, book 6, Collection of Castile.

[†] Law 5, tit. 13, book 6, ord. 22.

[‡] Vide chap. 8, sup. n. 8 and 9, and Escalona, Gazop. lib. 2, p. 2, cap. 1, tit. 1, ord. 9, and ord. 1, tit. 4, concerning the spaces allotted for mines.

[§] Ord. 75, law 5, tit. 13, book 6.

[||] Relatum est in referente.

[¶] " Ubi lex non distinguit, nec nos distinguere debemus." Gutierrez, lib. 3. Pract. quæst.

mensions to all and each of the mines he may select. After indicating what these dimensions are to be, the ordinance adds, that no one shall require to have the boundaries set out, or set them out, until after ten days, during which time the discoverer shall have " defined the limits of the *pertenencias* he chooses to take as first discoverer" of the mine or vein. As therefore, he is at liberty to take several, the same rule of measurement must extend to all; for as there are several things to be defined, the manner in which they are to be defined under this direction, must be the same for one and all.* And it is evident from another provision, " And each of the mines taken after those of the said discoverer, shall be 120 *varas* in length and 60 in width," that those which the discoverer may have previously taken, are supposed to be of different and more ample dimensions.

5. The fact of its not being usual for the discoverer to take several mines of more than the ordinary dimensions, does not take from the authority of this law, which is general, and is not liable to be affected by the caprice of the subject; nor is it a sufficient ground to deprive persons of their legal rights, that other persons have omitted to exercise those rights, the omission depending on neglect, and not upon any defect of right; for had the ordinance been cited, with a demand to have it observed, no resistance could have been made to the claim. The non-usage of a beneficial law or privilege, does not annul it or weaken its force, unless, when an opportunity of exercising it has occurred, it have been formally renounced, or unless, when its fulfilment has been demanded, the contrary have been enforced. To maintain a right, it is sufficient that there be capability or power of exercising it; and such will be found to be the doctrine of Garcia, who lays it down nearly in these very words, upon the authority of Paulus, Angelus, Felinus, Platea, Jason and Innocencius.†

6. The reason of the practice having been, as it appears, not to apply for more than one discoverer's mine, is probaby to be found in the inability of the discoverer to undertake the expense of keeping a larger number at work; but it by no means follows, that his title to the privilege conferred upon him by the ordinance is weakened, should he think proper to demand it. We are not aware whether this right has ever been denied, when brought in question, but we do happen to know that, in the viceroyalty of the Archbishop Don Juan Antonio de Vizarron, Don Joseph de Bustamante having denounced the Vizcayna vein, in Real del Monte, as having been insufficiently work-

---

16, n. 47. Vela. dissert. 6, u. 1, et dissert. 29, n. 19. Garc. de nobilit. gloss. 3, §. 1, n. 25. Salg. de retent. p. 2, cap. 10, n. 32. L. non distinguemus, ff. de recept. arbit. L. præses, ff. de offic. præsid.

* " Determinatio respiciens plura determinabilia debet ea pariformiter determinare." Salgad. de retent. p. 2, cap. 20, §. 1, n. 9, cum pluribus. L. si legatarius, §. 1, ff. de r. j. L. jam hoc jure, ff. de vulg. et pupil. substit.

† Garcia, de nobilit. gloss. 6, n. 37. P. Suarez, de leg. lib. 8, cap 34. n. 6 et 7.

ed, permission was granted to him, upon application for that purpose, and under the advice and opinion of Don Domingo Vacarcel, minister of the chancery of Mexico, a person of great judgment and learning, and of known experience in these matters, to assign the dimensions of 160 *varas* in length and 80 in width, to each of the new mines which he should discover in driv-ing the adit of the Viscayna vein.

7. The order issued to Bustamante bears date the 1st of June, 1739, and is countersigned by Don Joseph de Gorraez; and it states the denounce-ment, and the second of the conditions proposed by Bustamante, which runs thus: " Secondly, that your excellency would be pleased to declare, and to grant me the use, property and benefit of all the veins which may be found throughout the whole length of the said adit by me, my heirs, or those who shall, through me, become possessed of, or work the said adit, agreeably to the rules governing this matter, in the 31st and 82d ordinances of the new mining code. For which purpose, and in reference to the time when it may please God that I should meet with them, in any part of the said work, I do hereby register the same before your excellency, conformably to the aforesaid ordinances, and so that it shall not be necessary to make a new denounce-ment, upon each occasion of my finding new veins, but that this denounce-ment shall serve for all veins that may be found there, from time to time; it being understood that no person shall, for the future, be at liberty to work any vein in the space extending from the commencement, or mouth of the adit, in a straight line, to beneath the pits of the Vizcayna vein (upon which vein I do hereby particularly denounce all the pits which shall not have been kept properly at work, as directed by the ordinance); and not only through-out the whole length of the aforesaid adit, but also for the space of 160 *va-ras* in length and 80 in width, in each mine which I shall discover, on either side of the said adit, and in which I shall set up a fixed stake; which di-mensions I set forth merely as a form, and as the proper extent of each mine, but without waving my right to the whole length of the said adit, from the pits of the Vizcayna vein aforesaid, agreeably to the ordinances above-men-tioned, providing, that the first discoverer (as I shall be in respect to the veins I may meet with) shall enjoy all the mines he may choose to take, and shall stake them out in such manner as he shall think best. As then, the adit aforesaid is to proceed in a straight line till it reaches a point beneath the pits of the Vizcayna vein, it will serve as a fixed stake for all the veins which may be found upon its course; and, as the first discoverer is permitted to place his fixed stake wherever he pleases, and to measure from it a space of 160 *varas*, it is evident, that for every vein which may be found, 160 *va-ras* may be measured off on one side of the adit, and the same number on the other, so that one mine shall be measured off upon each side," &c.

8. That part of the order which refers to the second condition is as follows: ' I also declare the aforesaid Don Joseph Bustamante, to be the discoverer

29

of all the new veins which he may find throughout the course of the said adit, and that he may therefore, agreeably to the 31st and 82d ordinances of the new code aforesaid, take as many *pertenencias* as he may think proper, observing in respect thereof, all that is contained in the ordinances which relate to that subject ; for which purpose, deeming them, as I do from henceforth deem them, to be registered and denounced, I do adjudge them to him : and I grant him authority to take such fixed stakes as he shall think proper, from the commencement or mouth of the adit, in a right line, to beneath the pits of the Vizcayna vein (which is the vein he most particularly denounces), and to measure out the aforesaid space of 160 *varas* in length and 80 in width, for each mine ; understanding that this is to be the case with respect to new veins only, which shall not have been previously discovered ; but not with respect to the abandoned mines upon the Vizcayna vein, the dimensions of which latter shall be 120 *varas* in length and 60 in width only," &c.

9. From this precedent (which unites all the qualifications required by the great Bacon,[*] being a deliberate decision of the viceroy, given under the advice and opinion of a minister of as much experience and understanding as any who have flourished in New Spain), it is to be inferred, first, that the ordinance was understood in its proper and extended sense, not only by the person making the application, who was a very experienced miner, but also by the judges ; and secondly, that as Don Joseph Bustamante claimed and was allowed, the privilege of assigning the dimensions of 160 and 80 *varas*, to each of the mines he might take upon the new veins, so, were other discoverers to asserts their claims, the privilege would be extended to them also ; and consequently, that all the mines selected by the discoverers within ten days from their first making registry of a new vein, ought to be of the full dimensions. That this is the meaning of the ordinances does, in fact, abundantly appear ; for not only is it so expressed in the new ordinance, but the old ordinance also, under which the discoverer could take but two mines, leaving an interval of three mines between,[†] permitted the dimensions then allowed to discoverers' mines to be assigned to each, without making any distinction, in that respect, between the first and second.[‡]

10. We must notice however, that this privilege is granted to the discoverer personally, in consideration of his diligence ; which appears from the words of the ordinance ; " Any person who shall have discovered, or shall discover, shall enjoy 160 *varas*, &c.;" shewing that the grant is made to him person-

---

[*] Bacon. de Verulamio. de justitia universali, aphorismo 27. " In exemplis plurimum interest per quas manus transierint, et transacta sint, si enim apud scribas tantum, et ministros justitiæ ex cursu curiæ, absque notitia manifesta superiorum obtinuerint, aut etiam apud errorum magistrum, populum, conculcanda sunt, et parvi facienda. Sin apud senatores aut judices, aut curias principales ita sub oculis posita fuerint, ut necesse fuerit illa approbatione judicum saltem tacita munita fuisse, plus dignationis habent."

[†] Ord. 31, law 5, tit. 13, book 6, Collection of Castile.

[‡] Ord. 22, law 5.

ally, and as a reward for the merit of the discovery. And as the ordinance assigns the term of ten days for selecting the mines, the right ceases at the expiration of that time,* after which, or in default of any other of the requisites enumerated in the preceding ordinances, any mines which he may acquire, whether by purchase or otherwise, must be of the ordinary extent, and no more.

11. All that we have stated applies to New Spain (where the ordinances of the new code are the laws by which the working of the mines is regulated) ; but by no means to Peru, by one of the particular ordinances of which kingdom it is directed ; " That the discoverer of a vein may take a mine of 80 *varas* in length and 40 in width, at any part he may choose ; and also another mine of 60 *varas* in length and 30 in width, provided there be one mine between them.†" Notwithstanding this, the discoverers are allowed several privileges in that kingdom, such as that of taking these two distinct mines, or altering their boundaries in the direction towards which the vein inclines, even after a year has expired,‡ with others, as may be seen by reference to the same ordinances.

12. Having ascertained the number of *varas* which the discoverer or other miners are respectively entitled to take, we will next observe, that the 23d ordinance declares, that " The discoverer shall enjoy a space of 160 *varas* in length upon the vein, and 80 in width ; and if he shall wish to measure out the said space of 160 *varas* and 80 *varas*, crosswise upon the vein, he shall be at liberty to do so, in such manner as he may find most convenient.—And the others may take the 120 *varas* in length and 60 in width crosswise upon the vein, or as it shall seem best ;" which are the same terms as are employed by the 22d of the old ordinances,§ in reference to the form in which the number of *varas* it assigns for the length and breadth of a mine are to be laid down.

13. Whence we perceive the error of those who conceive, that from the first words, " a space of 160 *varas* in length upon the vein," the length of the mine must be measured along the course of the vein ; for under all the ordinances above referred to, the space of 160 and 80, or of 120 and 60 *varas* is allowed to be taken across the vein, or as the miner shall find most convenient, or deem best. And the 26th expresses it still more plainly, " Each one taking the number of *varas* he ought to take, wherever he may think proper or deem best ;" which is equivalent to saying that the length or breadth may be taken in any direction, right or oblique, at pleasure.

14. Don Joseph Saenz, in his " *Tratado de medidas de minas*," establishes the same doctrine, shewing that this is one of the circumstances in

---

* L. mortuo bove, §. hoc. sermone, ff. de V. S.

† Ord. 9, tit. 1, concerning discoverers ; Escalona, Gazoph. lib. 2, p. 2, cap. 1, pag. 106.

‡ Ord. 8, Escalona, ubi proxime.

§ Law 5. tit. 13, book 6, ord. 22.

which the measurement of mines and of land, differ ; the latter being usually measured upon the four principal points of the compass, whilst mines may be measured upon any of the 32 points, at the pleasure of the miner, who is authorised by the ordinances to measure out the number of *varas*, allowed to the mining *pertenencia*, either upon the course of the vein, across the vein, or otherwise, as he shall think best ;[*] and he adds, that the course of the vein itself is generally subject to variation. In another place[†], he gives a mechanical illustration of the subject, by supposing a tambour frame to be taken, without any cross piece (*atravesano*), and made in the form of a parallelogram, twice as long as broad ; which is the form both of the discoverer's and of an ordinary mine, the length of these being 160 and 120 *varas*, and the width one half, respectively. He then fixes a nail in a table, to represent the fixed stake, and by changing or varying the position of the frame in every possible way, first to one side and then to the other, first towards one corner and then towards another, and alternately nearer or farther from the nail, but always keeping the nail within the frame, he shews the different ways in which the boundaries of the mine may be measured ; which may, in fact, be in any direction whatsoever, always preserving the fixed stake. It cannot therefore be doubted, that the miner may take the 160 or 120 *varas*, and the 80 or 60 *varas*, in any direction he pleases, either upon the course of the vein, or across it, as he shall find best.

15. The object of the ordinance in granting this privilege, is to benefit the owner of the mine. For as the treasure lies sometimes along the course of the vein, which will itself vary in direction, and sometimes upon the inclination or underlay of the vein, which is either inferred from various signs known to professors in the art, or ascertained from pits or other works, sunk upon the vein ; it has been made a rule, in order to facilitate the acquisition of the ore, which is the only object of engaging in such laborious undertakings, that the space may be taken either across or upon the course of the vein, as the miner may judge most expedient.

16. Upon investigating the nature of veins, a great diversity is found in them ; so much so, that the position or course of one affords no rule for determining that of others. And although this subject is abstruse and difficult, its secrets being concealed in the bowels of the earth, whence it is more proper for the natural philosophers, who have discussed and explored the mysteries of the subterranean world, yet it is very appropriate to our subject to consider the varieties, the different courses and directions of veins, as ascertained by professors and men experienced in the subject ; as this very diversity demonstrates the reasonableness of allowing the measurements of the mines to be taken in whatever direction may be conceived most favourable for the purpose. This subject has been exhausted by Perez de Vargas,

---

[*] Saenz, Tratado de medidas de minas, cap. 2, n. 22.

[†] Id. ib. cap. 5, n. 16 to 22.

in his famous and rare treatise,* in a passage which we have extracted, where he copies the illustrations which had been given very much at length,

* Bernardo Perez de Vargas, de re metall. lib. 5, cap. 5, concerning the differences in metallic veins. "Metallic veins generally differ in depth, width or length. Amongst these there is one sort of vein which, commencing at the surface of the earth, descends downwards into the depth, and this is called by the master workmen, a deep vein.

"There is another sort of vein, called a spreading or wide vein, which neither rises from below upwards, nor descends from above downwards ; but which spreads sideways, in the depth of the earth, like a long loaf or cake, or like a sole, a sea-fish.

" Another kind of vein is that which is described as an aggregation of several veins, making together one vein ; forming above, a hollow, like a dish, and spreading downwards. The space between two veins is called an *intervenio.* A deep vein widens downwards.

" Deep veins differ in themselves, some being a pace, some two cubits, some a cubit, some one foot, and some half a foot, in width.

" Some again, are a palm in width, some three fingers, and some two ; these, however, are narrow. In places where the veins are very wide, a cubit is considered narrow ; the veins of Oremnicio are said to be, in some parts, twenty paces wide.

" The wide veins vary in height (or thickness), for some are a pace in height, some two or more, some a cubit, some a foot, some half a foot, all which are considered thick veins ; others, being a palm, three fingers, or one finger in height, are considered shallow.

" The deep veins also differ in their dip, for some incline from east to west, some from west to east, some from south to north, others from north to south. The question whether the vein inclines from west to east, or from east to west, from south to north, or from north to south, is ascertained by observing the inclination of the rocks, between which the vein lies, noticing towards which part the rock and vein incline, or in what direction they lean.

" The wide veins differ also in respect of their width ; the part towards which they spread, is easily ascertained from the position of the rocks including them. There are some deep veins which proceed in an uniform direct line, whilst others are tortuous and curved ; some veins descend along the slope of a mountain, without passing out of it : others descend from the summit of a hill or mountain into the valley, and then again ascend up some opposite hill or mountain : others descend from the hills into the flats and plains, along which they take their course, others run for a great extent through the plains, mountains or hills : very often the deep veins, running in different directions, intersect and cross each other ; at other times they unite like branches or converging roads, forming a trunk, like that of a tree ; at other times, after uniting they again separate, in the depth of the earth, the right hand vein going off to the left, and the left hand one to the right. At other times, the vein, meeting with a rock, divides, and forms branches, which either subsequently re-unite, or continue separate like threads. To ascertain to whom these veins belong, when they thus unite and cross each other, the joints of the rock must be noticed, observing in what direction they point, and whether they incline to the east or west, north or south. A deep vein has a beginning and an end, a tail and a head ; the beginning is where it commences, the end where it terminates ; the head is the part which meets the surface, and the tail is that part in the depth of the earth. A wide vein has a beginning and an end ; but instead of the head and a tail, it has sides.

"An aggregated vein has a beginning, end, head and tail, like a deep vein. A deep vein will frequently intersect or cross a wide vein, or an aggregated and united vein.

" There are other small veins called fibres, which either traverse the principal veins, or accompany them, and add to their width, and these fibres frequently descend from the surface, and guide us to the deep vein. These fibres often disturb the position of the joints of the rocks, within which the vein lies, making them point to the east, instead of, as before, to the west, which ought to be known and borne in mind. These veins and fibres are either compact and solid, or hollow : the compact and solid ones do not contain water, but may contain some air ; the hollow ones now and then contain water, and frequently air, and water generally flows from them. Of the solid veins and fibres, some are hard, others soft, and others moderately soft."

many years before, by Agricola,[*] who gives plans of the veins, and of their junctions, by way of explaining their varieties of course.

17. Some are called *deep* veins, which take an inclined or downward direction; and of those, some proceed in a direct line from above downwards, and others in a convex or curved direction. Deep veins sometimes cross each other, afterwards taking different directions; at others they unite and form a trunk, in the manner of a tree; afterwards separating, the right hand vein going off to the left, and the left hand one to the right; at other times, when the vein comes upon a rock, it divides into branches, which either run on as separate veins, or re-unite. After the deep veins, there are others called wide, spreading or broad veins, which neither ascend nor descend, but spread sideways: in New Spain they are called *mantos*. Others are called *aggregated* veins, and consist of many veins united in one: others again are *fibres*, which sometimes cross the principal veins, and at others accompany them, and add to their width, and thus frequently serve as guides to the *deep* vein. All the space lying between two veins, whether *deep*, *wide*, or *aggregated* veins, or merely fibres, is called an *intervenio*. The course of the vein is ascertained by examining the leaning of the rock or barren ground, between which the vein lies, at its commissure· or junction with the vein, noticing what direction it takes. And the subject is illustrated in a compendious and plain manner, by father Athanasius Kircher, who when treating of his noble district of the subterranean world, gives a plan or map illustrating the *deep*, *wide*, *curved*, *shallow* and *transverse* veins, and their *intervenios*, or intermediate spaces. From all the above, it is evident, that as the vein is liable to such variations in its course, sometimes descending from the mountains to the plains, and then re-ascending; sometimes taking a direct, at others an oblique, at others a curvilinear, and at others a waving, serpentine, or tortuous course; sometimes inclining or underlying to one side, and sometimes to the other (whence the term *underlay* or *inclination* of the vein), it is requisite that the miner should have the opportunity of measuring out the length and breadth of his mining *pertenencia*, in whatever direction he finds it most expedient to follow, according as the vein extends itself downwards, sideways, or upon the underlay.

18. What we have stated on this subject, is to be taken as the rule for New Spain, being agreeable to the ordinances of Castile. But in Peru, the discoverer must take the 80 *varas* lengthwise upon the course of the vein, and he must take the 40 in width, 20 on one side of the vein, and 20 on the other; and so the ordinary miner must take 60 *varas* lengthwise upon the course of the vein, and 15 in breadth on each side, so that the vein shall be in the midst; but not including in this space the width of the body

---

[*] Agricola, de re metallica, per totum librum secundam, ubi typos, atque figuras fodinarum, cum venis profundis, dilatatis, cumulatis, humilibus, interveniis ponit ob oculis.

of the vein itself." The reason of this rule is, that it is provided by their ordinances,† that one or two pits shall be sunk upon the vein to explore and investigate it, and that the discoverer and those who may come after him, shall select their *pertenencias.*

19. Having ascertained the number of *varas* which may be taken by the discoverer, or an ordinary miner, the ordinance proceeds to declare, that in so doing, two conditions must be attended to ; first, that the parties do not abandon their fixed stake ; and second, that they work no prejudice to third persons. The first condition is thrice repeated by our ordinance. And the old ordinances enforce the same rule, as does the 24th of the new code ; the latter in these words :—"There must always be a fixed stake, which must be adhered to, and must not be abandoned in staking out or altering the boundaries." So the 26th : " The fixed stake shall be within the said oblong, and shall not be left outside it, each one taking the number of *varas* he ought to take, wherever he may think proper, or deem best." The 27th, treating of alterations in the boundaries, says, " without prejudice to the boundary stakes, he may have set out, and so that the fixed stake be not left outside." The 29th says twice, " keeping his fixed stake within his *pertinencia.*" And in reference to a party applying for a waste space of ground, " That he shall not leave his fixed stake outside." The 22d directs the discoverer, before all things, " To set up a fixed stake in each of the *pertenencias* he shall distinguish and take ; which he shall not be at liberty to leave, nor shall leave, in staking out or altering his boundaries, however he may stake out or alter the same." And as to other miners, it directs that, " Having made registry, and set up a fixed stake, &c." So that, as the nail remains within the frame, in the illustration suggested above, the fixed stake must always remain within the limits of the mine, whether in tracing out the boundaries originally, or altering the boundaries, or under any other circumstances whatsoever.

20. It is a sufficient reason for the observance and fulfilment of this rule, that it is one repeatedly enforced by the law, and as to which the will of the legislator is repeatedly declared :‡ but besides being a rule of law, there is another reason which renders its observance indispensable ; namely, that were there no such thing as a fixed stake, and were it permitted, from time to time, to take a new centre to measure from, abandoning the pit originally opened at the time of making registry, it would be impossible to place mining property under any tolerable system of regulation ; and that, if so important

---

* Escalon. Gazoph. lib. 2, p. 2, cap. 1. p. 111, tit 4. concerning the spaces allotted for mines, ord. 1.

† Apud eund. tit. 1, ord. 11 ct 18, p, 109 and 110.

‡ D. Barb. Axiomat. 105, n. 1. " Geminatio actus, seu verborum, majorem deliberationem, et enixam voluntatem manifeste inducit." L. Balista, ff. ad Trebellianum. Valenzuela, consil. 102. u. 102. Everardo, in topicis loco, 121, n. 1. " Verborum geminatio, seu actus reiteratio, denotat firmitatem propositi, voluntatus, et consensus."

and essential a rule were liable to be varied at the will or pleasure of the owners, in working, measuring or altering the boundaries of their mines, the whole scheme of the ordinances would be frustrated.

21. That this is so, is evident, for if it were allowable to alter the situation of the mouth or pit, an opportunity would be afforded of fraudulently obtaining access to another person's ground, for the purpose of getting at the ore, contrary to the ordinance* And an unlimited right would be conferred, of taking fresh points, from which to measure out or originate alterations, in the boundaries, to the destruction of all order, which requires that the limits of each separate estate or *pertenencia* should be defined, to prevent litigation or dissension.† But the principal point is this, that this class of property being highly valuable, from its rich and profitable nature, has vested in the crown, in order to give an interest in it to all the subjects of the crown generally,‡ whence it becomes necessary that the boundaries of the mines should be ascertained agreeably to the practice of all nations who work them,§ so that each proprietor being confined within his own limits and bounds, all his fellow-subjects may be admitted to their share of the benefit. As then, there must be a fixed centre to measure from, no point can be more appropriate for the purpose, than the principal pit of the mine, where the discovery of the ore is supposed to have been made, and which is taken to have been sunk to the required depth of three *estados*, and which is also usually made the entrance, by means whereof the vein is worked; for it affords an unchanging and perpetually enduring landmark; and being the foundation or base of the mine, and the way by which the entrance and exit to and from the works are obtained, it possesses many characters which tend to preserve its identity.

22. With regard to grants of land, the marks to which recourse is had to identify the subject of the grant, are different, and all questions as to the boundaries and produce, have relation to the surface only, it is sufficient to ascertain the identity of the boundaries, by marks of the description usually employed. We could wish indeed, that some better rule were devised with regard to the boundaries of these grants, such as the adoption of some kind of landmark, which should be invariable, whereby much litigation and expense, in inspections of the ground, which frequently, instead of clearing up matters, throw them into greater confusion, would be avoided. But the produce of a mine is derived from the vein, which is explored by means of the principal pit, the works for that purpose taking their rise from that pit; and

---

* Chap. 14, ord. 30.

† Agricol. de re metallica, lib. 4, page 60. Area cujusque fodinæ ideo terminis describitur, ne lis oriatur inter vicinarum fodinarum dominos."

‡ Vide chap. 2, sup. n. 10, 11 and 12.

§ Agricol de re metall. lib. 4, per totum ubi dimensiones aræ fodinarum describit: Et in principio inquit page 55. "Hæc autem mensura metallicis usitata ex Græcorum consuetudine videri potest defluxisse ad Germanos. Peru, ordin. 18, tit. 1, concerning discoverers, and tit. 3 and 4, concerning boundaries and the spaces allotted for mines, Escalona, ubi sup.

as an infinity of instances may arise, of communications happening to be made between different mines, in which cases it becomes necessary to survey and measure them internally, in order that each party may retire within his own *pertenencias*, it seems, that the only point suited for a centre of measurement, is the principal pit, which ought therefore to be fixed and invariable.

23. The second condition, that the boundaries to be set out by the discoverer or other person, " be," (as our ordinance expresses it) " without prejudice to any other person or persons who shall have dug and registered their mines before him on either side," is consonant to justice : the prior occupancy of these parties fairly entitling them to a preference. These words however, shew (as observed by Don Joseph Saenz)[*] that the newly-discovered vein may be so near some other vein, previously discovered, that their mines may interfere ; and hence arises the question whether every person who discovers a new vein, not at the distance of one, two or three leagues from other veins, but in the same mineral tract, shall enjoy the rights of a discoverer, or whether, to entitle him to those rights, the discovery must be made beyond that distance, and in a distinct spot or mineral tract.

24. The ordinance now under consideration, and the old ordinance,[†] which it follows as to this point, place it beyond a doubt, that a person who discovers a new vein, although in the immediate vicinity of another vein, shall enjoy all the privileges of the ordinances. The latter of these laws certainly still holds, as to this point, unaltered, there never having been, to our knowledge, any determination of the tribunals of New Spain, or any ordinance of any of the viceroys to the contrary ; nor are we aware that the case has happened, of the rights given by this ordinance having been claimed before the justices, and denied, and of the denial being confirmed by the royal audiency sitting in judgment : or in fact, that there has ever been any litigation upon the point. And therefore, however deeply the miners may have been impressed with the erroneous opinion, that two or more persons cannot enjoy the rights of discoverers in respect of veins lying near together ; the adoption of this erroneous opinion can work no prejudice to those who, insisting on their rights, demand to have the more extended space allotted to them, and claim the preference to which discoverers are entitled.

25. And notwithstanding Don Joseph Saenz[‡] considers that the rule should be qualified, in case any especial determination to the contrary should be found to have been made, yet he states, at the same time, that he is not aware of any such, although, with his experience and application, he certainly could not have failed to discover it, had any existed. For ourselves, we have never, during twenty years' experience in the management of very important mining affairs, heard of or seen any law, order, decree or ordi-

---

[*] Don Joseph Saenz, Trat. de medidas de minas, cap. 3, n. 6.

[†] Law 5, tit. 13, book 6, ord. 22.

[‡] Saenz, loc. ubi proxim.

nance in opposition to that to which we allude, nor have we ever been advised of or met with any precedent to the contrary; whence it follows that it must still be in force. And it would certainly be a great incitement to the discovery of new veins, to put this rule in practice, whenever the case might occur, to which there could be no objection, as the giving a greater number of *varas* is a trifling object, when compared with the benefits resulting from the discovery.

26. We have seen but one of the ordinances of Peru[*] referring to this point, and that we have set forth when illustrating some of the preceding ordinances.[†] It provides, " that whoever shall discover a vein more than one league from any place where there is a mining settlement," shall, as to such vein, " enjoy the rights of a discoverer ;" whence it would follow, that within a less distance than one league, he shall not enjoy such rights. But as this is a municipal ordinance, framed for Peru alone, it does not affect those of Castile, which are to be observed in New Spain ; besides, this ordinance of Peru proceeds to declare, that every person who shall discover new veins, shall have a mine of 60 *varas* upon each of them, until he has six mines, although not a discoverer of a new mineral tract ; which liberty of holding six mines ·is a privilege, as compared with the rights of an ordinary miner ; for by a preceding ordinance no person can hold more than three silver mines, although on different veins, and whether purchased or obtained by registry ; and if any person should take a greater number, any other person is at liberty to apply for the excess.[‡]

27. We stated, at the outset, that this ordinance has altered the 22d of the old ordinances, by allowing the miners a greater number of *varas ;* but it is to be observed, that the latter directs that a mine shall be set out for the crown, next to the discoverer's mine, and of the same dimensions ;[§] and as our ordinance does not notice this, and ordains nothing to the contrary, it seems that the old ordinance is not altered in this respect. This rule of allotting a mine to the crown, prevails in Peru ;[||] and Agricola states, that in Germany, it was the practice to set out six double mines, after the discoverer had taken his ; one for the king or prince, another for the queen, another for the master of the horse, another for the gentleman or cupbearer, another for the chamberlain, and another for the warden of the mines.[¶]

28. Don Joseph Saenz says, that our ordinance has altered the old or-dinance as to this point ; and that had it not intended to do so, it would not have passed over a matter of so much importance, and so directly affecting

[*] Escalona, ubi sup. tit. 1, concerning discoverers ; ordin. 14

[†] Vid. sup. cap. 8, n. 7, in marg.

[‡] Ord. 13, loc. ubi sup. apud Escalonam.

[§] Ord. 22, law 5, tit. 18, book 6, Collection of Castile.

[||] Ordin. 18, tit. 1, concerning discoverers ; Escalona, Gazoph. lib. 2, part. 2, cap. 1, pag. 108.

[¶] Agricol. de re metall. lib. 4, pag. 57. " Deinde magister metallicorum debatvenæ inventori demensum. Postea unum demensum regi, vel principi, alterum ejus uxori, tertium magistro quitum, quartum pincernæ, quintum cubiculario, sextum sibi ipsi. ''

the interests of the crown, as we have noticed in another place.* Without admitting however, that any such alteration is distinctly to be collected, we agree that the custom of New Spain has proceeded upon this hypothesis, for it is not the practice, in that country, to set out a mine for the crown. And such mines, even if set out, could not conveniently be worked on account of the crown, nor could they be leased or sold to advantage: for if the first course were pursued, the revenue would be exposed to risk; and if the second were attempted, it would be in vain, for all the other mines being made common, and liable to be registered at pleasure, no one would be found willing to purchase or take on lease, this particular mine; and in the mean time, the space occupied by this mine would remain unproductive, instead of benefiting the revenue by returning the fifths and other duties, as it might, if worked by an individual. Neither is it the practice in Peru, according to Escalona,† who refers to several royal orders, to work these mines on account of the crown; but they are directed to be sold or leased, which it must however be difficult to accomplish; and consequently, whilst the difficulty of finding a person willing to purchase or take the mine on lease, continues, it must remain unproductive.

29. The orders cited by Escalona, form the basis of a law of the Collection of the Indies, directing the viceroys and presidents to inform themselves of the quality of the mines of gold, silver or quicksilver, belonging to the crown, and to cause them to be worked, leased or sold,‡ which law extends to both the continents of America generally. Agreeably to this law, it cannot be doubted but that the king, as lord of the mines, and in exercise of the high and supreme right he enjoys over them, might take all or any proportion of the mines at pleasure; for, as we have stated in Chapter II., he has only admitted his subjects to a partial interest in them. But as the fifth, tenth or twentieth part of the produce has been fixed as a satisfaction for his interest in the mines of New Spain, and as it has never been considered expedient to work any of the mines on account of the crown (the only instance we know, being that of the copper mines of Santa Clara, in the jurisdiction of Pascuaro, in Mechoachan, which are leased out),§ it follows, from the evidence afforded by these customs and practices in New Spain, that the intention of the sovereign is that the mines of gold, silver and other minerals, should be worked by his subjects, and not on account of the revenue, not wishing to expose his finances to the hazards and risks of mining. And no mines of gold or silver have ever been taken in that kingdom, for the purpose of being leased or sold, on account of the crown, not only on account of their great abundance, but also because the viceroys sensible of the nature of

* Vide sup. cap. 2, n. 18.
† Escalona, locis ubi proxime.
‡ Law 2, tit. 11, bonk 8, of the Collection of the Indies.
§ Vide sup. chap. 3, n. 39.

this kind of property, which will sometimes rapidly advance to a state of prosperity, and at others as rapidly fall off and become barren (all which renders it difficult to sell or lease it), have not thought proper to do so.

CHAPTER X.

OF THE NECESSITY OF SETTING OUT BOUNDARY STAKES, AND OF THE TERM ALLOWED BY LAW FOR THAT PURPOSE, AS WELL WHEN THE OWNER OF THE MINE, WHO IS REQUIRED TO SET THEM OUT, IS ABSENT, AS WHEN HE IS PRESENT.

ORDINANCE XXIV.

Also, we ordain and command, whether with regard to mines heretofore discovered, or to such as may hereafter be discovered, that if any person shall require to have boundary stakes set out by the first discoverer or by any other persons who may have set out boundary stakes, after having registered their mines; such first discoverer, or such other persons as aforesaid, shall be obliged to set out such boundary stakes, within ten days from the day when they shall be required to do so, if they be at the mines. And if they shall not set them out, then, after the time aforesaid, the mining justice, who shall, under these our ordinances, have cognizance of such matters, shall set out such boundary stakes, taking with him persons who understand staking out mines, and who shall be sworn; and if the person of whom the request is made, be not at the mines, but be in the vicinity, within ten leagues of such mines, he shall be obliged to set out the boundary stakes within fifteen days; and if he do not set them out by the expiration of such fifteen days, the said justice shall set them out as aforesaid. And if the party be not in the vicinity of the said mines, nor within ten leagues thereof, notice shall be given to his steward, or to the person who shall have charge of the working of the mine, or be left at his house, if he have any, and public proclamation shall be made upon the first holiday which shall occur. And the term of fifteen days shall commence to run from the day of the notice being given to such steward or other person, or being left at his house; and such proclamation shall be posted upon the door of the church of the said mines; and if there be no church at the mines, then upon that of the nearest town. And when the said term of fifteen days is expired, the said justice shall set out such boundary stakes as aforesaid, observing in setting out the same, that there must always be a fixed stake, which must be adhered to, and must not be abandoned in staking out or altering the boundaries.

CONTENTS OF THE COMMENTARY ON THIS ORDINANCE.

1. What is meant by setting out boundary stakes, and applying to have them set out.
2. Of the term fixed by law for setting them out.
3. The time is peremptory, and the judge has no discretion.
4. A provision of the ordinance, in case of the owner being absent.
5. The propriety of allowing the steward, in such case, to set them out, is shewn.
6 and 7. Whether the term shall run against the proprietor when he is unavoidably delayed. Grounds for replying in the negative.
8. The contrary opinion proposed and established.
9. Refutation of the arguments on the other side.
10, 11 and 12. What is to be done, in case the owner of the mine should be absent at more than ten leagues distance.

COMMENTARY.

1. Having ascertained the number of *varas* the discoverer is allowed in his mines, and the common or ordinary miners in theirs, this ordinance which follows, proceeds to state the term within which boundary stakes must be set out, if required by a neighbour. It must be observed, in the first place, that an application to set out boundary stakes is said to be made, when a miner of longer standing is required to mark out the number of *varas* he chooses to extend his mine, in this or that direction, on the side on which the mine of the person who makes the requisition is situate ; and when his mine is so measured out, the rest remains for those who have not yet measured out their boundaries. The reason why it is necessary to apply to have the boundary stakes set out, is, that the miner of longest standing has a right to measure out his boundaries first ; and that after measuring them out, he is at liberty to alter them on that side on which he has not set out boundary stakes, as will be seen by subsequent ordinances.* The party who sets out boundary stakes, is he who first makes measurement ; and the party who applies to have them set out, is he who demands to have the boundaries of the oldest mine measured, that he may afterwards measure out those of his own.

2. This being the case, if the person or persons who are required to set out boundary stakes, are present at the mines, they must, according to the 24th ordinance, and the 22d, of which we have already treated,† set them out " within ten days ;" if they be absent from the place, but be in the vicinity, and within ten leagues, then within fifteen days ; and if they be not in the vicinity, nor within the distance of ten leagues, but at a greater distance, a proclamation is to be made on the first holiday, and is to be posted up at the church of the place, and if there be none, then at the nearest church ; notice is to be given to the steward, or person who may have charge of the mine, or a summons or notice is to be posted up at his house, from which

---

* Chaps. 11, 12, 13.   † Chap. 8, ordinance 22.

time fifteen days more are reckoned, within which he must set out the boundary stakes. And if it be not done by the expiration of that period, in each case respectively, the justice must do it, with the assistance of surveyors, who shall make the measurement upon oath. And the 23d of the old ordinances, granting a shorter time, is so far repealed.

3. These periods, being definitively fixed by law, cannot be enlarged, and are not subject to the discretion of the judge; just as the term of four months, after which the ordinance makes a mine liable to be denounced when insufficiently worked, cannot, according to the laws of the Indies, be enlarged by the viceroys or other judges; [*] in analogy to the well-established rule applied in regard to appeals, and other judicial proceedings, which cannot be resorted to after the lapse of the period allowed for the purpose.[†] Besides, it is reasonable, that if the neighbouring mine owners wish to have the boundaries of their mines measured out and ascertained, some fixed time should be assigned for measuring out or altering the boundaries of the older mine, and that the owners of the more recent mines should not be liable to be kept in suspense, and uncertain in what direction to measure their boundaries, until their neighbour should think proper to measure out or alter his limits, by deciding to take this or that particular direction.

4. And since it ought not to be in the power of one proprietor to prevent the owners of other mines adjoining, from ascertaining and measuring out their boundaries, or to frustrate and delay them in that object, the ordinance has made abundant provision, that in case of his absence, whether it be voluntary or of necessity, and whether upon just cause or otherwise, he shall, if within ten leagues, be summoned; and if he be at a greater distance, that the business shall be transacted with the steward or person in charge of the mine, or that a paper shall be left at the house of the owner, if he have one, a proclamation being made, which is equivalent to a public citation or summons.[‡]

5. The ordinances permit the steward to discover mines for his employer, and to set out boundary stakes, or apply to have boundary stakes set out in the mines he may discover during his absence :[§] but it is still more reasonable that a person in this station, who is supposed to be skilful and experienced in these matters, and appointed to his office for this amongst other purposes, should, in obedience to the directions of the judge, which he is bound to obey, set out such boundary stakes, in such directions, and to such extent, as he may deem most expedient. The practical importance of this ordinance has been very evident in various cases which we have witnessed; as for

---

* Law 6, tit. 19, book 4, Collection of the Indies.

† Law 1, tit. 18, book 4, Law 1, tit. 19, book 4, Collection of Castile.

‡ Law 10, tit. 7, book 3, Law 3, tit. 10, book 4, Collection of Castile. Infr. chap. 13, ord. 39, " It shall be good, and shall be deemed a sufficient citation."

§ Vide ordin. 34, infra, chap. 15.

instance, where it has become known that a *bonanza* has been met with, and the direction taken by the rich vein has been ascertained, in which case, all are anxious to measure out their boundaries upon that ground, immediately, whilst the party who happens to be the longest standing, or whose object is to alter his boundaries, is desirous to keep them all in suspense, contrary to the intention of the ordinances; whence it appears how important it is that the periods fixed by the 24th ordinance should be considered as peremptory.

6. Supposing the mine owner, whether in the vicinity, or at more than ten leagues distance, to be reasonably prevented from coming to the mines, it may be asked, whether the term of fifteen days shall run against him? In favour of the negative, we might refer to all those principles of law which establish that time shall not run against a person disabled by an impediment, which he cannot remove; that the whole time during which the impediment subsists shall be allowed; and that whether the impediment be judicial or extra-judicial, whether it depend on matter of fact or matter of law, the whole time during which it continues shall be left out of the account. Hence a person under impediment is not regarded as contumacious or disobedient; and for the like reason, whilst the question of nullity is under consideration, or whilst an application to the prince is pending, the term allowed for appealing does not run; so whilst the suspension of a bull is under cognizance, the time allowed for proclaiming the resignation of the benefice does not run; and with regard to peremptory edicts, when it appears that there is an impediment to their being carried into execution, the period fixed for that purpose is extended, and is shewn at length by Salgado in several places, upon the authority of a great number of texts, and many doctors.[*]

7. Add to which, that the owner, being the person who is best acquainted with the mines, may be apprehensive that his administrator may perhaps prejudice his interests by taking the boundaries in one direction, rather than in another, which might be more desirable; whilst there cannot be any great inconvenience in a little delay, particularly if no communication have occurred between the works of the different mines; as any person working on a vein, or immediately following up ore, is at liberty to carry on his works into the *pertenencia* of another miner.[†] If then, the mines be supposed to have actually communicated, it must be presumed that the course of the vein has been ascertained, and the administrator must consequently know what will be most for his employer's interest; but if the mines have not communicated, the delay can occasion no mischief, and therefore, upon a statement of the impediment being made on the part of the absent person, the term ought to be enlarged.

8. Notwithstanding these arguments, however, the contrary rule is that

---

[*] Salgad de reg. protect. 1. p. cap. 7. a n. 65, et p. 2, cap. 13, a n. 253; et plenissim de retent. bullar. p. 1, cap. 15, per tot. and 2 p. cap. 20, a n. 22.

[†] Chap. 14, ord. 30.

which ought to be observed, as being expressly decided by the ordinance, and therefore the justices, after the 15 days are expired, must proceed to set out the measurements, whatever pretence may be alleged against it. First, because the ordinance does not require the personal concurrence of the owner, neither his actual presence during the measurement of any importance, since he may appear by his steward or administrator; and therefore, although the owner be at a very great distance, it is sufficient to summon the steward, "under whose charge the working of the mine is," as the ordinance expresses it, and who will know in what direction it is expedient to measure the boundaries. Second, because it must be considered the owner's own fault that he did not measure out his own mine at the time of registering it, and taking possession. Third, because knowing that he might at any moment be called upon to set out the boundary stakes, by the neighbour on whose side he had not done so, he ought to have left proper instructions with his steward. And, mainly, because it is not right that the limits of contiguous mines should remain undefined, to the prejudice of the public and of the mine owners, merely on account of the absence of the proprietor of longest standing, whether such absence be voluntary or necessary. And were the judges to depart from the terms of the ordinance, the consequences of adopting such a course would be many and serious; for the uncertainty as to what ground might be left unoccupied, would interfere with the registering of pits upon the vein. The boundaries of the older mines remaining undefined, it would be impossible to ascertain those of the adjacent mines, and the litigation and dissension ensuing from the confusion thus introduced, as to the boundaries, would be highly prejudicial to the mine works and mine proprietors.

9. Nor do the arguments first advanced weaken this conclusion; for the rule that time shall not run against a person under an impediment, cannot apply, when the act to be done does not require personal attendance, and when the administrator, who must be presumed to know the course of the works, and the direction in which it is most expedient that the measurement should be made, may just as well perform it; particularly as the omission would be an infringement on the law, and would be prejudicial to the interests of the public and of the adjoining mine owners. The reason why, pending an application to the prince, or whilst the question of nullity is under consideration, the time allowed for other proceedings does not run, is plain, for the latter are put a stop to by the former; and so, when the act requires personal attendance, or when it is for the benefit of the public that a longer time should be allowed; but the effect in the case proposed is just the reverse, for although every one is at liberty, in following up the vein, to work into the *pertenencia* of another proprietor, until an intercommunication occurs, yet by having his mine measured out, he will avoid the risk of a heavy lawsuit, and he will, at the same time, afford the opportunity to others of measuring out

their boundaries also; by which means the different parcels of ground being ascertained, the mining district will become properly settled, agreeably to the laws and ordinances. And a public object of this kind ought not to be interfered with, by the absence of a single person, when his place may and ought to be supplied by that of the person in whom he reposes so much confidence as to entrust him with the charge of the works: besides which, several opportunities of fraud may be prevented by adhering to this rule; for the object of delaying the measurement of the boundaries, is to be in a condition to keep the adjoining proprietors in suspense, and to gratify the covetous desire of occupying the whole vein, if possible, instead of being confined within certain limits, as required by the ordinances.

10. It is also a question, whether in the third case provided for by the ordinance, that of the owner of the mine being absent at more than ten leagues, distance, supposing the proclamation to have been posted up, and published, and notice to have been given to the steward, or other person in charge of the mine, such person may set out the boundary stakes; or whether the justice must set them out himself, without the intervention of the steward?

11. The answer is, that the steward must advise his employer, that he may furnish him with a proper authority for that purpose, or come and set out the boundary stakes, in person. But should neither of these steps be taken, a distinction must be noticed; for the owner either has omitted to stake out his mine before his departure, and it yet remains to be done, which is the case supposed by the ordinance, "who may have to set out," or he has left the boundary stakes set out. If the latter be the case, the servant cannot alter them, or set out others; it being so provided by the 34th ordinance.[*]

12. If the former be the case, that is to say, if the employer have not left the boundary stakes set out, he must send an authority for that purpose, within the fifteen days, which is the object of his being summoned; and if, by reason of the distance, or from its not being possible to give him notice during that term, it is not practicable for him to send an authority, or to come himself, we are of opinion that the justice ought to set out the boundaries, having regard to the ordinances, and to the preference to which the earliest or senior proprietor is entitled; and if the absent person be the senior, his steward or servant ought to set out the boundaries, in the direction most suited to the rights and interests of his employer, in the same manner as he would be authorised to do, in taking a mine for his employer, under the ordinance last cited, to which, and to the illustration of this point, given in the commentary upon it, we refer,[†] that being the place to which it properly belongs.

---

[*] Infra, chap. 15, ordin. 34, "And the steward or servant shall not be at liberty to alter the boundary stakes which his said employer shall have set out, or left fixed, without any authority from his employer."

[†] Infra, chap. 15, n. 16 and 17.

CHAPTER XI.

THE MINERS OUGHT TO STAKE OUT AND MEASURE THE BOUNDARIES OF
THEIR MINES, ACCORDING TO THE ORDER AND STANDING OF THEIR
RESPECTIVE ENTRIES IN THE REGISTER.—THE QUESTION CONSIDERED
AND SOLVED, WHETHER IF A MINE BE INSUFFICIENTLY WORKED, OR
BECOME FORFEITED IN ANY OTHER MANNER, AND BE AFTERWARDS DE-
NOUNCED AND ADJUDGED TO SOME OTHER PERSON, REGARD SHOULD
BE HAD, IN MEASURING OUT THE BOUNDARIES, TO THE ORIGINAL RE-
GISTRY, OR TO THAT. MADE, SUBSEQUENTLY, UPON THE DENOUNCE-
MENT.

ORDINANCE XXV.

Also, we ordain and command, that if two or more persons simultaneously
make application to have the boundary stakes set out by such first discoverer,
or any other person whose mine shall yet remain to be staked out, such first-
mentioned persons holding mines on any sides of the mine, in respect of which
such application to set out boundary stakes shall be made, it shall be ascertained from the registries, which of them is entitled to have the stake set out
first, and which second ; and thus they shall go on setting out the boundary
stakes in successive order, observing, in regard to the dimensions and all other matters, the rules contained in these our ordinances.

CONTENTS OF THE COMMENTARY ON THIS ORDINANCE.

1. In measuring out the boundaries, a preference is given, according to priority of registry.
2 and 3. The mine cannot be measured out whilst any question as to the nullity of the registry, or the forfeiture of the mine under any penalty, is depending.
4. Any such question ought to be decided in a summary way.
5. When the registries are of the same date, the preference is to be decided by lot.
6. When a party who has registered, and another who has denounced, apply at the same
time, priority in date gives the preference.
7 and 8. If a mine, after being registered, is adjudged to some other person for being insufficiently worked, regard is to be had to the last entry in the register, and not to the
original one, which has become extinct.
9. An ordinance of Peru, confirming this opinion.
10. A party denouncing a mine must make registry anew ; it being the only title he has
to shew.
11. And so, although the party denouncing the mine be the same that has abandoned it.
12. A party denouncing a mine does not succeed to the rights of him who has abandoned
it, but takes it as a new mine.
13. A mine, when abandoned, loses even the name of a mine, in analogy to what takes
place when a son comes under his own authority, with regard to the *peculium quasi
castrense*, or property he is allowed to have at his own disposal before that period.
14 to 19. It is established, by analogy to the various cases of legacies, *emphyteusis*, fends,
immunities, and grants from the crown, that when a grant, after having failed, is made
anew, it has all the qualities of a new grant.

20. The point established beyond a doubt, by a determination of the royal audiency of Gaudalaxara.

21. It is inferred from this opinion, that in a question between registry and denouncement, regard is had to priority in point of date only, without reference to the original registry of the mine.

22. When an older mine is abandoned, the proprietor of a more recent mine is at liberty, in altering his boundaries, to carry them forward upon the ground of the former.

23. Even though the abandoned mine be the discoverer's mine. And the party denouncing such a mine cannot claim the larger number of *varas* which the discoverer had.

24. When a mine is lawfully transferred from one to another, whether by an onerous or lucrative title, regard is always had to the title conferred by the original registry.

COMMENTARY.

1. It being settled that one miner may make application to have the boundary stakes set out by another, the question arises who has the first right of measuring out his mine ? The 25th ordinance of the new code, following the 24th of the old ordinances,[*] directs, that it shall be ascertained by reference to the registries, which is entitled to set out his boundaries first, and which second, and so on successively ; so that the preference is regulated according to their several priorities in occupying the vein and in making registry ; and he who is first in point of time, even if only by an hour, or a moment, gains a preference in ascertaining his boundaries.[†] And although the ordinance, upon this point, seems plain and clear, some considerable difficulties nevertheless suggest themselves.

2. The first is, whether, supposing a question to arise on the validity or nullity of the registry or denunciation (usually called denouncement, as we have noticed elsewhere) ;[‡] the ascertaining of the boundaries should be deferred whilst the point is in dispute ? The answer to which must be in the affirmative, for the question whether the registry be valid, or whether the mine have been registered according to law, must be determined, before measuring it out, or setting out the boundary stakes ; the supposition upon which the arrangement proceeds, must be verified, before it can be carried into effect ; the mine must exist, before it can be measured out : for according to the plainest and simplest principles, that which does not exist, cannot have any qualities attached to it, and these observations will apply to every case in which there is a preliminary question to be decided, which must always be disposed of before the principal question depending upon is entered into.[§] Thus an appeal is suspended, by a

---

[*] Law 5, tit. 12, book 6, ord. 24, Collection of Castile.

[†] Chap. 5, n. 12. Cap. qui prior. de r. j. in 6. Innumeri textus et AA. apud Acostam, de privil. credit. in præf. ad regul. 3. per tot.

[‡] Chap. 5, a n. 21.

[§] L. 7, tit. 10, part. 3, et ibi Greg. L. 1, Cod. si quis alter. test. prohibuerit ; §. prejudiciales ; Inst. de act. et ibi DD. Salg. de reg. protect. p. 4, cap. 14, et o. 2, cap. 18, n. 4, cum plur. et de retent bullar. p. 1, cap. 11, a n. 33.

question of nullity being interposed; and the term allowed for making proof, by the question being raised, whether such or such interrogatories are to be admitted.* So that before the mine can be measured out or the boundaries defined, it must first be ascertained that the registry is valid; which is the same thing as saying that before the mine is measured out, it must be ascertained that it is a mine; for a mine unregistered is, as we have shewn at length, in the proper place, no mine at all, the registry being the fundamental ground of title.†

3. The same rule, we apprehend, will hold, if a question be raised judi-cially, upon any other of the many grounds upon which the ordinances make the mine subject to the penalty of forfeiture, and render it liable to be adjudged to any other person who shall apply for it; as to which, reference may be had to our observations in the place last cited, where we have gone through the penal ordinances at much length, and with much minuteness,‡ enumerating the circumstances under which the non-observance of the forms and indispensable requisites which they enforce, incurs the penalty threat-ened.

4. The second question is, whether the judicial investigation of the prelim-inary question, as to the nullity of the registry, or of the ground upon which the mine is supposed, agreeably to the ordinances, to have become the sub-ject of the forfeiture, and which is to have the effect of preventing the boundaries from being ascertained, until it is decided, is to be conducted in a summary or plenary manner. The reply is, that it must be decided summa-rily, and that as soon as the cause is determined by the justice, the boundaries of the mines shall be measured out according to his decision, saving the right of the party worsted in the cause. This doctrine is founded on the ordinance, which in another place directs that the trial shall be conducted in a summary way, that the business of measuring out the boundaries may not be retarded.§ By another ordinance also, it is directed, that upon a mine being denounced for not being kept sufficiently worked, the cause shall be determined within forty days, and if it shall be declared to have been insufficiently worked, the party denouncing it shall enter into possession, notwithstanding any appeal or question of invalidity or injustice which may be interposed or raised, keeping an account, which he shall render and satisfy if he be worsted in the appeal, and giving security for 1000 ducats.‖ A similar rule is laid down by the

---

* Salg. de retent, p. 1, cap. 15, n. 25 et 27.

† Supra, chap. 5. n. 17.

‡ Chap. 5, n. 21. in margin, where the grounds of forfeiting the mine are enumerated.

§ Sup. chap. 8, ord. 22; "And if two or more persons shall apply to have their boundary stakes set out, it shall be ascertained, in a short and summary manner, which of them applied first; and he who shall be ascertained to have been the first, shall be preferred, saving the right of the other party, if he shall, nevertheless, claim to have first made application to have such stakes set out as aforesaid."

‖ Chap. 18, ordin. 38 and 39

ordinance which treats of suits concerning the possession of mines, or in other words, suits founded upon some of the penal regulations of the ordinances.* Consequently, therefore, in cases of a similar class to the above, the trial should likewise be summary, so as not to interfere with working or measuring out the mines; and if, after the judgment is executed, it should be reversed upon appeal, the measurements must be rectified in favour of the party who gains the appeal, to whom also an account of the profits, after deducting the expenses, must be rendered.

5. The third question is, how the measurement of the boundaries ought to be regulated, in mines registered upon one and the same day, when it does not appear what was the hour of making the registry, or which of the mines was first registered. The answer is, that if it cannot be ascertained which of them had the priority, and the parties cannot be brought to agree, the question must be resolved by lot, which, according to the law and the authorities, is the course to be pursued in cases of this kind.†

6. The fourth question is, whether registry takes precedence of denouncement, or *vice versa*; or whether a registered mine is to be measured out before one that has been denounced? We reply, that if the registry is of earlier date than the denouncement, the party who has made registry should have his boundaries measured out before the party who has denounced; but if, on the other hand, the denouncement be of the earlier date, the party who has denounced should have the preference. For denouncement and registry do not differ in substance; and whether the person be the discoverer of a new mine, or the denouncer of a mine insufficiently worked, he is equally said to make registry, as has been fully shewn in the proper place, when treating of registry, to which we refer.‡

7. The fifth question is, whether, in measuring the boundaries of a mine, which, having been registered according to law, has afterwards been adjudged to some other person as insufficiently worked, regard should be had to the first registry, or to the adjudication made upon the denouncement? We reply, that the measurement should be regulated by the last registry made upon the denouncement and adjudication, and not by the original registry; which, although it seems rather a nice point, is plain enough, and may be deduced from more principles than one.

8. When the mine has been left insufficiently worked, or is become forfeited under any of the circumstances enumerated in the ordinances (which we have particularised in another place),§ the first registry is at an end, the mine

---

* Chap. 23, ord. 63, infra.

† Felicius, de societ. cap. 27, a n. 30, et cap. 28, u. 46 ; cum L. fin. Cod. commun. de legat. et cum Bald. in L. si major, Cod. comm. dibid. Tiraquel. de jure primig. quæst. 17 opposit. 1, n. 23. Felicius, cap. 39, ubi de divisione per sortem.

‡ Chap. 5, from n. 21 to 25.

§ Chap. 5, u. 21, in marg.

has ceased to be such, it is considered as waived,* and is liable, as is declared by the same ordinances, to be given to the first person who shall occupy it.† The right, therefore, of the party in possession being determined, and the mine having ceased to be such, the original title cannot be revived in the party who denounces it, and to whom it is adjudged anew; for it is one of the commonest principles, that a right once extinguished, cannot be revived; and that when the right of the donor is determined, that of the donee is determined also.‡

9. Amongst the ordinances of Peru, there is a very peculiar one, which directs, "that if those who shall have discovered a mining tract, shall abandon it altogether, none of them remaining upon it, and after the expiration of three months, any person shall register it, he shall enjoy the rights of a discoverer in respect of any veins which he may discover anew, and in those already manifested, as if such tract had never been registered." Consequently, when a mine is abandoned and forfeited, so that any person may register it, it is looked upon as if such mine had never been registered, the first registry being altogether put out of the case and extinguished.

10. A party denouncing a mine, and applying to have it adjudged to him as insufficiently worked, or upon any other ground under which the ordinances declare it forfeited, should make registry of it anew, and observe the conditions limited by the ordinance, as appears from the ordinances themselves in the places above cited.§ The old registry then is of no avail, for every thing is to be done anew,—the mine itself, under the new registry, is a new subject; the three *estados* must be sunk anew, the possession is given anew, and the possessor is new. *Recedant vetera, nova sint omnia.*

11. The first registry is, in fact, abolished, extinguished and annihilated so completely, that, as is clearly laid down in the ordinance,|| the very party who has abandoned the mine, having forfeited it by leaving it insufficiently worked, "has no right to it except by making registry of it anew;" so that even supposing no new party to interpose, a fresh registry is required, the original registry being of no avail, even to the same individual; but being

* Circa bona pro derelicto, quod statim amittatur dominium, quamvis alius non subintret in possessione, vid. Antun. de donat. lib. 3, cap. 13, cum innumeris. n. 108.

† Ord. 17, "Any other person whatsoever may register such mine." Ord. 37, "In such case he shall have forfeiteted it, and shall forfeit it, and it shall be adjudged to any person who shall denounce it as insufficiently worked." "Ord. 27, "Under the penalty of forfeiting the right they may have to such mine, and that any other person shall be at liberty to apply for it, and register it as his own." And many others, which we have referred to in chap. 5, n. 21, in margin.

‡ Resoluto jure dantis, resolvitur jus accipientis. Jus semel extinctum non reviviscit. L. lex vectigali, ff. de pignor. Luca, de donat. disc. 13, n. 4.

§ Chap. 17, ord. 37. and others to the same effect, which we have enumerated in chap. 5, n. 21, margin.

|| Infra, chap. 17. ord. 37.

merged and annihilated, without leaving a trace, even in favour of the party himself who originally made it.

12. To the arguments afforded by these rules of the new ordinances, so distinctly expressed as not to leave the least doubt upon the point, we may add the circumstance, that the party denouncing the mine, does not succeed to the interest of the former possessor, but on the contrary, informs against him, accusing him of having infringed the ordinances, and of having omitted to fulfil their conditions ; by which act, as he impugns the title and registry of the other party, he cannot be allowed to avail himself of it, for the purpose of measuring his boundaries. The new possessor comes in under the authority of the law, which makes him a new grant, and gives him a new investiture, and a new title, and consequently, a new mine ; and therefore, in measuring his boundaries, he should be regulated by the date of his own title, and not by that of the extinct and annulled registry, which can have no effect whatever. Nor is it possible that the old right of measuring out the boundaries, can be revived by the mine becoming the new acquisition of a different possessor, who does not come in under the first, but enters anew into the possession of the mine, as if it had never been measured out, or been a mine at all ; for properly speaking, it does not retain, under these circumstances, even the name of a mine.

13. The law directs that the will of a son, bequeathing the *peculium quasi castrense*[*] shall not be questioned nor attacked as inofficious, whilst he is under the authority of his father ; but that when he is emancipated from that authority, it shall be liable to be so questioned, because such property does not even retain the name of *peculium*, but is confounded with his other property.[†] So that a mine, when once the right to it is so extinguished that it may be taken and denounced by any other person, as if it were a new mine, ought not to retain even the name of a mine.

14. A bequest of a slave, who is afterwards manumitted during the life of the testator, will not be revived, though he should subsequently fall into servitude again, because he is as it were a new man.[‡] A decurion,[§] when banished or exiled, is no longer a decurion, but at the expiration of the term of exile, although re-eligible to the dignity, he does not necessarily take his former rank or place, for he comes in as a new man, and a new decurion ; and herein he differs from one who has merely been suspended from

---

[*] Under the civil law, property acquired by a son, whilst still under paternal authority, by the exercise of any liberal art, and which he was allowed to dispose of, in contradistinction to property otherwise acquired. See Vicat, jur. ut. vocab. at the word *peculium.—Trans.*

[†] L. fin. §. 1 et 2, Cod. de inof. test. " Cum neque nomen peculii permanet, sed aliis rebus confunditur, et similem fortunam recipit quem admodum et cæteræ res eorum," &c.

[‡] L. 27. §. 2, ff. de adimend. leg. " Nam et si rursus in servitutem reciderit, non tamen legatum ejus resuscitabitur, novus enim videtur homo esse."

[§] In the Roman colonies, a municipal officer ; in some measure analogous to a common-councilman in this country.—*Trans.*

his office for a certain time, for the latter, when the time is expired, is restored to the rank he held before, as a direct consequence of his restitution.* And thus a new title and a new registry make a new mine; and the rank and place it is to occupy are to be determined solely by the new title, without the possibility of the old title being recovered, for the law does not restore the mine, but makes a new gift of it.

15. If an *emphyteusis*† which has determined, be subsequently granted again under new terms, it is not the same, but another and distinct *emphyteusis*, and the same may be said with regard to a feud; for which see Menochius, who cites Baldus, Angelus, Croto and Oldrado.‡

16. With regard to a feud,§ Carleval‖ lays down, that when it reverts to the king, it is, in form, determined and extinguished, although the subject of the feud still exists in substance; so that if granted to another party, it is no longer the same feud, but a new one; for the identity and individuality of the feud depend more upon the identity of investiture, than of the subject matter of the feud; in like manner as the identity of a natural thing depends more upon the identity of the form than of the substance.

17. The like is also established by a celebrated opinion of Alexander,¶

---

* L. 2, ff. de decurion: " Qui relegatus ad tempus est, si decurio sit, desinit esse decurio. Alia causa est ejus qui ad tempus ab ordine removeter.—§. 1. Restitutus tamen in ordinem, arbitor eundem ordinem tenere quem pridem habuit. Non idem erit in eo qui relegatus ad tempus est; nam hic velut novus in ordinem venit."

† An agreement respecting real property, granted to another, on condition of his bringing it into cultivation, and paying an annual rent. See Vicat, jur. ut. vocab. at the word *Emphyteusis*—*Trans.*

‡ Menoch. de presumpt. lib. 3, præs. 93, n. 36. " Quando emphyteusis post caducitatem fuit denuo concessa, adjecta nova qualitate tunc dicitur emphyteusis nova; ut tradunt Bald. in 1, 1, column 4, ff. de rer. divis. in, cap. 1, an agnatus vel filius, et §. imperialem, §. insuper, de prohib. feud. alienat. Angel. in L. jus civile, ff. de just. Crot. in L. re conjuncti, n. 144, vers. secundo tamen, ff. de legat. 3. Ita etiam de feudo respondit Oldrad. in cons. 178, cum dixit feudum censeri novum ob novas qualitates in nova investitura adjectas."

§ " Sir Henry Spelman, after Cujas, defines a fief" (or feud) " to be ' a right which the vassal hath in land, or some immoveable thing of his lord's, to use the same and take the profits thereof, hereditarily, rendering unto his lord such feudal duties and services as belong to military tenure; the mere propriety of the soil always remaining in the lord.'" Coke upon Littleton, by Hargrave and Butler, 191. a. note.—*Trans.*

‖ Carleval, de jud. tit. 3, disp. 23, u. 14. " Sed tempore quo feudum est devolutum ad regiam curiam ob lineam finitam, non potest subjici hypothecæ a quondam utili domino; cum ipso defuncto, res feudalis remaneat libera ab ejus utili dominio, et contractus feudi, feudumque ipsum antiquum, formaliter loquendo (si licet uti metaphysicis verbis, aptissime tamen rem explicantibus), sit extinctum · tametsi res ipsa feudalis materialiter maneat eadem sub dominio directo. Ex quo fit, ut si alius ipsa reinvestiretur, non esset idem feudum cum antiquo, sed feudum novum, cap. 1, de succes. fratr. cap. 1, de fratr. de nov; benef. invest. Ad unitatem enim feudi, et individuationem (ut sic dicam) magis attenditur unitas investituræ quam rei feudalis: quemadmodum quoad unitatem rei naturalis, m gis inspicitur unitas formæ, quam materiæ."

¶ Alexander, lib. 5, cons. cons. 34, n. 5. " Dicitur de novo venire ad habitandum ex quo erat ex toto translatus et extinctus primus incolatus. Hoc comprobatur per ea quæ dicimus in feudo novo et antiquo Nam plures erant fratres habentes feudum antiquum, et ascendenti suo pro se et suis descendentibus concesso, et unus ex dictis fratribus feloniam commisit, propter quam ve-

upon the question whether a certain immunity granted for the term of 50 years, to those who should come anew to inhabit a certain place, should be enjoyed by one who had formerly been an inhabitant, and, after being six years absent, had returned again ? To which he gives an answer in the affirmative, on the ground of his being a new citizen and a new inhabitant, his former character of an inhabitant having been extinguished ; referring to the analogous case of a feud, which has escheated to the lord, in consequence of the treason of the feudatory, and which, when granted anew, is regarded as a new feud ; and observing that when any thing is become determined, a party who restores it is regarded in the same light as one who grants it anew ; which doctrine he supports by various texts, and upon the authority of the Glossary, and of Angelus, Isernia, Bartholus, Baldus, Tiraquelo, Afflictis, Decius and others.

18. But the doctrine which most favours our opinion is that of Solorzano,[*] with reference to grants from the crown for lives, as to which he suggests the important question, whether, if such a grant be determined, in consequence of the crime of rebellion, or by any other cause inducing a forfeiture, and be afterwards made anew, it is to be regarded as the same grant, and in the same condition as before ? which is an important point, in reference to determining the question, whether the two or three lives for the term of which these grants are made, are to begin to run from the time of the new grant ?

niebat privandus feudo, et debedat reverti ad dominum feudi, an si dominus feloniam illam, seu offensam remisit dicto fratri, feudum illud dicitur novum, vel antiquum ? Et concluditur quod si jus antiqui feudi fuit omnino extinctum, ut quia erat vassallus ex tali felonia ipso jure privatus feudo a lege, vel etiam corporalis possessio feudi sit ad dominum reversa, et denuo sit vassallo facta investitura, appellabitur feudum novum : alias appellaretur antiquum." Et n. 7, " Quando funditu aliquid est extinctum idem judicamus de restaurante, vel renovante extinctum prout judicamus de eo qui de novo facit," &c.

* Solorz. de jur. Indiar. tom. 2, lib. 2, cap. 27, u. n. 101, ibi : " Nam si duntaxat restituendi animum habuisset, dici non potest plus juris reo concedere voluisse, quam ante privationem habuerat : cum restitutio sit in statum pristinum reposito, et tantum reddat quod abstulit læsio. Cæterum sinon utatur verbo restitutionis, aut cum hoc alia verba involvat quæ novam gratiam factam esse significent, præsertim ubi sumus in casu in quo pœna privationis ipso jure incursa fuerat, ut in crimine læsæ majestatis contingit, vel sententia declaratoria præcesserat, cujus virtute dominus jam possessionem apprehendit ; tunc dicendum est tanquam novum concessum censeri, et sic ex eo die vitarum tempus incipere. Ut tenet Gloss. in cap. 1, §, insuper, de prohibit. feudi alienat. per Freder. quam sequuntur Baldus, Isernia, Afflictis, et alii scribentes ibidem. Curtius junior. cons. 18, u. 47. Sigismund. Gofred. icons. 52, n. 3, in feudalib. et commune testatur Duenas, reg. 323. Julius Clar. in § feudum, quæst. 8, u. 6, et juxta hanc distinctionem accipienda sunt, quæ disputat Jason, cons. 136, vol. 4. Ruin. cons. 12, vol. 2. Roland. cons. 60, n. 8, lib. 1. Villalobos, in Com. opin. lit. n. 5. Sforcia, de restit. q. 98, art. 2, n. 20, et seq. Rosenthal, omnino videndus, de cap. 2, conc. 18 et 19 ; et de emphyteusi loquuns Alvarus Valascus, 2. p. q. 4, per tot. et tetigi sup. 22, u. 7 ; et novissime D. Valenz. cons. 160, u. 75, et seq. vol. 2. Pro quibus facit text. in L. 2, §. si ab ære alieno ff. de pecul. L. inter stipulantem, 83, §. sacram, vers. et navis, ff. de V. O. ibi. ' Et navis, si hac mente resoluta est, ut in alium usum tabulæ destinarentur, licet mutato consilio reficiatur, tamen et perempta prior navis et hæc alia dicenda est.' L. qui res, 98, §. area, ff. de solut. ibi : ' Alia enim videtur esse posterior navis, sicut ille alius homo est.' "

19. The reply to this question involves a distinction. Either the sovereign uses the word *restitution*, in which case the grant is restored to its former state, or he only uses words denoting a new grant ; in which case the grant must be considered to have been made anew, and the lives will commence to run from that day, particularly if the case be one in which the forfeiture have been incurred *ipso jure*. This doctrine he rests on the authority of the Glossary, and of Isernia, Baldus, Afflictis, Curtius, Gofredo, Dueñas, Julius Clarus, Jason, Ruinus, Rolando, Villalobos, Sforcia, Rosenthal, Alvaro Valasco, and Valenzuela ; and also of two remarkable texts, which establish, that if a ship be taken to pieces, and then be reconstructed of the same planks put together, it is to be regarded as a different ship ; in the same manner as if a slave who has been made the subject of a bequest, and been afterwards manumitted, should subsequently return into slavery, he is not the same slave, but is, as it were, a new man.

20. In further support of the doctrine, we will cite an instance which occurred in the royal audiency of Guadalaxara. The mine of Loreto was registered at Zacatecas, in the year 1735, and being afterwards abandoned, its original owners denounced it again, in the year 1745. In the mean time, that is to say, in the year 1738, the mine No pensada had been registered. A suit arose in the year 1754, as to the right of measuring the boundaries, which was tried before the justice of Zacatecas originally, and before the audiency of Guadalaxara upon appeal, both of whom gave sentence in favour of the No pensada, and its proprietor, Don Joseph Juaristi, and against the mine Loreto, and its proprietors, Don Juan Tello de Albornoz and his partners, upon the ground of several precedents, and in reliance upon the current practice. From all which authorities, it is to be inferred, according to our view of the subject, that a mine adjudged anew, upon denouncement, is a new mine, and is considered distinct from that which had been originally registered, the former registry being determined. And that with regard to the right of measuring the boundaries, or any other question, reference is to be had solely to the date of the registry of the new grant last made, as the only title by which such matters are to be regulated. From this doctrine we deduce the following corollaries.

21. First, that if a person holding a mine which has been adjudged to him upon denouncement, and another holding a mine acquired by a registry, prior in date to the denouncement, although subsequent to the original registry of the mine denounced, should apply simultaneously to have the boundaries set out, the latter will be entitled to measure out his boundaries first.

22. Second, that when a mine has been left insufficiently worked, or the penalty of forfeiture has been otherwise incurred by the owner, the boundaries of a more recent mine may, notwithstanding that the other mine has been defined and staked out, be extended upon the site of the older mine ; and that when the pit of an abandoned mine has been occupied, under a new

denouncement, the proprietors of the adjoining mines may, if required to set out their boundaries, extend them upon the site of the newly-denounced mine. For a mine when abandoned, neither possesses definite boundaries, nor any other qualities formerly belonging to it; and other mines, which, had it not been abandoned, and deprived, in consequence of the forfeiture, of its character of a mine, would have been reckoned as more recent in point of registry, now gain a priority in that respect.

23. Third, that this takes place, not only with regard to ordinary mines, but also to those of the discoverer, or, as they are termed, *descubridora* mines: that is to say, that a party who denounces these mines, after they have been abandoned or become forfeited, does not enjoy the extra number of *varas* which before formed a part of them, but acquires the same number only, as would be allowed in any other mine. For the additional extent being allowed in consideration of the *person*, the right to it is lost by the abandonment of the mine. And even though the party registering the mine anew, should be the discoverer himself, it will make no difference; for the original right, as we have seen, is become totally extinct, without leaving a vestige which can be made effectual for any purpose.

24. Fourth, that when mines pass from one possessor to a variety of others in turn, by inheritance, bequest, gift or contract, the first registy is the title by which the right of measuring the boundaries must be governed. For the course of succession being supposed to be continuous, the mine thus transferred, whether by a lucrative or onerous cause or mode of transfer, still depends on the same original title, and consequently remains the same mine, and the universal or particular successor, acquires all the rights which that title can confer. In this case, therefore, the priority of the registry is not regulated by the date of the several parties becoming possessed of or succeeding to the mine, but by the first registry; the title conferred by which, we suppose to have been transferred from one to another, without any discontinuance or interruption, the mine having at no time been abandoned. And, as we have before observed, the name of the new proprietor is to be entered in the same registry,[*] that it may always, thereafter, appear that he had proceeded to work the mine, under the proper title and registry. It appears then, that parties who become possessed of, or succeed to the property in this manner, deduce their title one from the other; but that a person making denouncement, does not depend upon or deduce his title from him who has abandoned, or in some other manner incurred the forfeiture of the mine but derives all his rights from the last adjudication of the mine, under which he claims.

---

* Chap. 16, ordin. 42, and see above, chap. 5, n. 9.

CHAPTER XII.

OF MEASURING THE BOUNDARIES OF MINES, AND OF THE GREAT IMPOR-
TANCE AND NECESSITY OF A PRECISE OBSERVANCE OF THE ORDINAN-
CES UPON THIS SUBJECT.—OF THE SUBJECT TO WHICH THE MEASURE-
MENT IS APPLIED.—OF THE SURVEYORS EMPLOYED IN MAKING MEAS-
UREMENTS; AND OF THE MISTAKES OCCASIONED BY THEIR UNSKIL-
FULNESS, AND THE MISCHIEF TO WHICH THESE MISTAKES GIVE RISE.
—OF THE INSTRUMENTS REQUIRED FOR THE PURPOSE, AND OF THE
SURVEYING OF MINES, INTERNALLY AND EXTERNALLY.

ORDINANCES XXVI. XXVII.

XXVI. ALSO, we ordain and command, that when and so often as such
boundary stakes shall be required to be set out, or shall be set out as aforesaid, care shall be taken in setting out the stakes, to make an oblong, with
right angles; and the said fixed stake shall be within the said oblong, and
shall not be left outside it, each one taking the number of *varas* he ought to
take, wherever he may think proper or deem best, in the manner already
set forth and declared.

XXVII. Also, forasmuch as it might happen, when fixed stakes have
been set out between two or more persons, that some one of them might,
with a view to his own advantage, take up from its place one or more of
the stakes, as he might think fit, and remove them to some other place
which he might think more desirable for him, whence divers suits might
arise:—We declare and command, that when any person shall require another to set out boundary stakes, or shall himself without being required set
out, or wish to set out, boundary stakes in his mine, he shall be obliged, at
the places where he shall set out fixed stakes, on the side of his neighbours,
to make a pit for each of such stakes, of two *varas* in depth, and one in
width; and he shall set up a stake in the midst of each of such pits, and
shall not be at liberty to remove it except in the cases in which, under these
ordinances, the boundaries are allowed to be altered: and the stake or
stakes thus set up, shall be regarded as boundaries between the party setting them up, and his neighbours aforesaid; all which they shall do and
observe, under the penalty of forfeiting the right they may have to such
mine, and that any other person shall be at liberty to apply for it and register it as his own.

CONTENTS OF THE COMMENTARY ON THESE ORDINANCES.

1. The form in which a mine is to be measured out, is, according to the ordinance, that
   of a right-angled oblong.
2. The miner is at liberty to measure out his boundaries in what manner and direction he
   pleases, always adhering, however, to his fixed stake.
3. The boundary stakes set out between him and his neighbours cannot be altered.

4. Why they are here called fixed stakes.

5. An ordinance of Peru, concerning the setting out of landmarks, enacting a capital punishment against any one who contumaciously infringes it.

6. Reason for this severe provision.

7. Old method of making the boundaries of mines, and penalties enforced against those who disturbed them.

8. Of the negligence of the miners, in regard to measuring out their mines, and its prejudicial effects.

COMMENTARY.

1. These ordinances, which follow the 25th and 26th of the old ordinances,[*] direct, first, that the boundaries of a mine shall form an oblong, with angles; and as the breadth of a mine is half its length,[†] it follows, that the boundaries must form an oblong four-sided figure, or parallelogram; the opposite sides of which are parallel and equidistant.[‡]

2. Second, they repeat the precept, that in whatever direction the miner may choose to take the length and breadth of his mine, the fixed stake is always to remain within it; as, when the oblong tambour frame, in the illustration above suggested,[§] is placed around the nail, the nail always remains within it, however the position of the tambour frame may be changed.

3. Third, in order that no person may alter the stakes which he may have set out between his own mine and those of his neighbours, they ordain that the stakes shall be placed in pits of two *varas* in depth, and one in width; and that it shall not be lawful to remove them, except in the cases in which the ordinances[||] permit alterations in the boundaries to be made, under pain of forfeiting the mine, so that any other person may register it as his own (which is a just and merited penalty), besides the penalties incurred under the royal and civil law, by those who change or confound boundaries, and under which the parties are to be punished according to their rank.[¶]

4. These ordinances twice apply the term, fixed stakes, to the stakes which are set out and assigned between the proprietor and a neighbour; but they are fixed stakes in this respect only, that they cannot be moved forward to to the prejudice of such neighbour, although the position may be changed with regard to other parties, between whom and the mine owner of longest standing, the boundary stakes have not been set out; and he is at liberty, on the side of such latter parties, to remove his boundary stakes to any other

---

[*] Law 5, tit. 13, book 6, Collection of Castile, chap. 25 and 26.

[†] In New Spain, the length is, for a discoverer's mine 160, for an ordinary mine, 120; for a discoverer's of gold, 80 *varas*; for an ordinary mine, 60. In Peru, the discoverer's mine, 80; an ordinary mine, 60. And the width of each is one half the above length respectively. See cap. 9, n. 2.

[‡] Nolet, Leçons de physique expérimentale, tom. 1. Explications de termes de géométrie, pag. 54. P. Zaragoza, Geometría practica, proemial 14.

[§] See chap. 9, n. 14.

[||] Infr. chap. 13, ord. 28 and 29.

[¶] L. 30, tit. 14, part. 7. L. fin. tit. 15, part. 6, tot. tit. ff. de term. mot.

position, as we shall explain by and bye.* The *fixed stake*, properly so
called, is only so applied to the pit which has served as a basis for the registry
of the vein.

5. In Peru, the boundaries of the mines must be defined by landmarks,
under the penalty of 100 dollars ; and by removing the landmarks clandestinely, the forfeiture of the mine is incurred. For the second offence, the
punishment is capital. An inspection is to be made at the beginning of each
year, to ascertain whether the mines are secured by proper supports, with a
penalty of three marcs, if not found to be so.†

6. The anxious care evinced in these regulations, is no more than is due,
where so important a subject as the precious mineral deposits of gold and
silver is concerned, and is necessary, to restrain covetousness and prevent
litigation, and also to avoid the injury which may be done, by one proprietor
gaining access to the ground of another ; not superficially, where no fruits
are produced, but internally, where one or two *varas* or even half a *vara*,
wrongfully taken, will often, from the extraordinary richness of some veins,
give an enormous profit.

7. To define the limits of mines, and to prevent suits amongst the owners,
it was formerly the practice to set up stones at their confines ; subsequently
to which, trunks or timbers of oak or pine, bound with hoops of iron, to prevent their being cut down, were employed, as more conspicuously marking
the boundaries ; and these were not allowed to be removed, as appears from
Agricola.‡ The laws enacted by the Romans against transgressors of boundaries were various. Numa Pompilius dedicated these boundary stones or
landmarks to Jupiter Terminalis, and made a law that any person violating
them might be put to death with impunity. In Holy Writ, a curse is pronounced against such offenders. By the canon law, the punishment of
greater excommunication is inflicted ; and by the civil law, besides its being
open to bring an action for the damage, and for a restitution of the boundaries, a penalty is inflicted according to the rank of the party and the circumstances of the case. All which is stated at length by Don Domingo de
Zaulis, archbishop of Theodosia, in his learned and erudite observations,§
where he refers to various authorities.

---

* Chap. 13, ord. 28 and 29, infra.

† Ord. 1 and 3, concerning boundaries; Escalona, Gazophil. lib. 2, part. 2, cap. 1, pag. 111.

‡ Agricola, de re metall. lib. 4, p. 60. " Arca cujusque fodinæ ideo terminis describitur, ne
lis oriatur inter vicinarum fodinarum dominos : termini autem quondam metallicis fuerunt solum
saxa, atque ex eo nomen invenerunt, nam saxum terminale, nunc etiam terminus appellatur :
hodie vero stipites acervi, vel quernoi, vel picei, annulis ferreis superne muniti, ne mutilentur, ad
saxa terminalia affiguntur, ut sint magis insignes."

§ Dominicus de Zaulis, Observat. tom. 2, rubric. 10, lib. 5, ո. 11. " Variæ leges a Romanis
editæ fuerunt contra violatares et amoventes terminos, seu limites, ut ii sint pacis præsides, et
amicitiæ custodes : nempe Mamilia, Roscia, Peducea, Allinea, Fabia, Sempronia, Julia, quarum
dispositionem late refert Gibalin. de univers. rer. human. negotiat. lib. 4, cap. 4, artic. 4, consec-

8. The boundaries of land then, merely as such, being made the subject of so much anxiety, in regard to the benefits derived by the proprietors and the public, by the exchange of its produce for money ; those of the mines, whence are derived the precious metals, of which that very money is composed, ought surely to be deemed worthy of as much or still greater attention, and the keeping them duly ascertained and defined, should be made the object of the greatest vigilance. The practice, however, in the mining districts, will be found to be very much the reverse of this ; for, either from sloth and idleness, or from covetous and improper motives, the measuring out the boundaries of the mines is neglected, with the connivance of those whose duty it is to scrutinize into and punish the omission, until the discoverer of some great *bonanza*, or the occurrence of a communication between different mines, arouses the feelings of interest ; and litigation and contention, as to the boundaries, are the consequences, which would have been prevented, had the alternative, so properly directed by the ordinance, of measuring out the mines, and setting up regular landmarks at once, been adopted, as we shall hereafter explain more fully in its proper place, when treating of communications occurring between different mines.*

CHAPTER XIII.

OF ALTERING THE BOUNDARIES AND MAKING ADDITIONAL PITS, AND THE CIRCUMSTANCES UNDER WHICH EITHER OF THESE MAY BE DONE; AND OF THE UNAPPROPRIATED SPACES REMAINING AFTER THE BOUNDARIES OF THE MINES HAVE BEEN DETERMINED.

ORDINANCES XXVIII. XXIX.

XXVIII. Also, we declare and command, that when any person shall have been required to set out his boundary stakes, and shall have done so, and some other person shall again require him to set out boundary stakes on

tar. 5, n. 8, et Numa Pompilius Romanorum rex II. de lapidibus terminalibus legem sanxit, ut unusquisque sua sorte contentus esset, nec res alienas appeteret, cavit, lege determinandis praesidiis lata : hosque lapides Jovi Terminali sacros esse voluit, adjecta contra terminorum motores gravi poena, si quis vero sustulisset, aut suo loco movisset terminos, eum qui tale quid patrare ausus fuerit, huic Deo Terminali sacrum esse sanxit, ut cuilibet impune eum interficere tanquam sacrilegum liceret, et purus ab eo piaculo esset : ut tradit Dionys. Halicarnass. Roman. Antiquit. lib. 2, in fine, quem refert Mylerius, in ejus Metrologia, cap. 15, §. 1, n. 1, in fine, cum seq. In Sacris Literis etiam horrenda maledictionis poena imposita fuit, ut in Deuteron. cap. 19. n. 14, juncto cap. 27, n. 17, et Proverb. cap. 2, n. 28. De jure canonico, clericus finales terminos movens, majori excommunicatione punitur. Cap. tanta, 14, distinct. 86 ; et cap. tanta, 11, caus, 1, quaest. 7. De jure vero civili, variae poenae, secundum varietatem imperantium, et diversitatem temporum impositae, ut advertit Myler. in dicto tit. de poena termini motoris. §. 4 et 5, utrobique, n. 1.''

* Chap. 14, ordinance 30, infra.

some other side of his mine, he shall be at liberty to alter his boundaries, as between himself and the party so newly requiring him to set out boundary stakes, but without prejudice to the boundary stakes already fixed, and so that he do not abandon his fixed stake.

XXIX. Also, we ordain and command, that when any person shall have set out boundary stakes, as between himself and another, on any side of his mine, and shall wish to alter the boundaries, before any other person shall have required him to set out boundary stakes on some other side of his mine, where he has not yet set them out, he shall be at liberty to do so, provided he go before the justice having cognizance of such matters, to define such boundaries, and show what alteration he proposes to make in the then boundaries of his said mine ; and such justice shall allow such alteration of boundaries to be made, and shall note the same, in the margin of the entry which shall have been made in the register concerning such mine. Provided that it be done without prejudice to third parties, as is aforesaid, and so that he keep his fixed stake within his *pertenencia.* And the unappropriated spaces which he shall leave between his mine and that of his neighbour, shall be adjudged to the first person who may apply for them ; and if such neighbour should apply first, he shall be at liberty to take them, provided that, including the space he thus take in, he have no more than the proper extent of a mine, and that he do not leave his fixed stake outside ; and also that he give an account of such alteration to the justice aforesaid, that it may be noted in the register.

CONTENTS OF THE COMMENTARY ON THESE ORDINANCES.

1. What is meant by altering the boundary stakes.
2. The liberty of altering the boundary stakes is granted, subject to certain regulations, the principal of which is, that the fixed stake must be adhered to.
3. Pits opened for the purpose of working the mine, are not fixed stakes.
4. Nevertheless, such additional pits are not to be opened but upon good cause, and with the permission of the judge.
5 and 6. They may be opened on dead ground, and why? But they must always communicate internally with the principal pit. A reason given for this.
7. Executory decree of the royal audiency of Mexico upon this point.
8 and 9. A second condition to be observed in altering the boundary stakes is, that the boundaries already set out between the party and a neighbour whose mine is kept at work, are not to be prejudiced.
10. Three other conditions, which are indispensable in altering the boundary stakes, are, that the legal dimensions of the mine be preserved, the licence of the judge obtained, and the alterations registered.
11, 12 and 13. Advantages of having the boundaries of the mine measured out, and evils which ensue from neglecting to do so.
14. Unappropriated spaces : what they are. They are adjudged to the first person who applies for them, with the exception of the party who has left them unappropriated in altering his boundaries.

15. They will be granted to the owner of the adjoining mine, provided he do not abandon his fixed stake, that he register the alteration thus made, and that, including these waste spaces, his mine do not exceed the proper extent.

16. The owner of the adjoining mine is not preferred, in regard to these waste spaces, if he be not the first who applies for them.

17. A peculiar ordinance of Peru on the subject of altering the boundaries.

COMMENTARY.

1. The mine being defined and measured out, the owner is at liberty to alter the terminal boundary stakes, on any side of his mine. This is called *mejora de estacas* (a bettering of the boundary stakes), because he removes them to some place which he thinks more eligible, for the purpose of working the vein, either along its course, or upon the underlay. Alterations of this nature are mentioned in two of the old ordinances, the 27th and 28th,[*] which agree with those we have set forth, and according to which the miner may alter his boundary stakes, either when applied to by some other person, who requires to have the boundary stakes set out, or of his own free will and inclination, conceiving it to be advantageous to do so. Veins are subject to much variation in their course and direction ;[†] in one place they will yield treasure in abundance, whilst in others, the poverty of the ores will perhaps be such as to baffle the miner and supplier alike. It has therefore been found expedient, that permission should be given, to remove the boundary stakes to some part of the vein which may yield more produce ; and, likewise, that those who have been prior in point of occupancy, should also have a prior right of making alterations, according to the date of their registry, as we have explained in the proper place.[‡]

2. This right of altering the boundaries is not absolute, nor perpetual in duration, but is subject to the following rules. First, the fixed stake, or principal pit of the mine, must always be adhered to, in altering the position of the other stakes, in whatever direction they may be removed ; so that whether the number of *varas* be diminished in one direction, and increased in the other, or *vice versa*, the fixed stake must always remain within the boundaries. We have already shown,[§] how all the ordinances relating to boundaries, enforce the adhering, invariably, to this fixed stake, as a centre from which the measurements must always commence : and the ordinances now under consideration enforce the same rule three times.[||] And in fact, the engrossing disposition of some miners is such, that if it were allowable to remove the fixed stake, in measuring out the boundaries, they would never be kept within moderation, nor would the just and proper limits of the mines

---

[*] Law 5, tit. 13, book 6, Collection of Castile, ord. 27 and 28.

[†] Vide chap. 9, n. 16 and 17.

[‡] Supra, chap. 11, n. 22.

[§] Supra, chap. 9, n. 19.

[||] The 28th, "So that he do not abandon his fixed stake." The 29th, "And so that he keep his fixed stake within his *pertenencia*. And so that he do not leave his fixed stake outside."

ever be assigned ; as it would be possible, proceeding insensibly, to occupy the whole mineral tract.

3. The practice of the miners, in opening several additional pits within the limits of a mine, does not clash with this rule, for such pits are not at all regarded in measuring out the boundaries of the mine ; the original registered pit or fixed stake being alone to be observed and adhered to, whether in measuring out the limits of the mine, in altering the boundaries, or in any other proceeding. These other pits are intended for giving ventilation to the works, for raising the ores with more facility, or for some other purpose, having reference to the working of the mine ; but not for *termini a quo*, or points from which the miner is to originate his measurements at pleasure. For although the fixed stake should become choked, fall in, or be out of shape, the measurements must be governed by the position of that alone, and not by that of any of the other pits, which are called *bocas mejoras*.

4. We are now arrived at that part of our subject, in which it becomes proper to speak of these *bocas mejoras*, and to shew in what manner and under what conditions they may be opened. The term *boca mejora* is applied in the same manner as the term *mejora de estacas ;* that is to say, it signifies a pit opened for the better prosecution of the works of the mine. For instance, such an improved or additional pit may be sunk for the purpose of cutting the vein, and so communicating with the works driven from the principal pit, or fixed stake. The owner of the mine cannot open any number of pits at pleasure ; this would lead to intolerable abuses, and would give an opportunity for proceeding fraudulently : as for instance, a pit might be opened in the vicinity of a mine belonging to another party, with a view to get access to ore properly belonging to him, contrary to the ordinances, which prohibit such proceedings.* The judge must therefore be applied to for his permission, as in the case of making an alteration in the boundaries ; the necessity and advantage of opening such a pit, and the object for which it is intended, with regard to facilitating the works, being stated. An inspection is first to be had, and the opinion of two mining deputies, and of surveyors, being taken, and the contiguous mine owners being summoned to attend, the permission will be granted or refused, according to the merits appearing on the issue of the proceedings. If granted, an entry of the pit should be made in the registry of the mine, shewing the spot where it is opened, and its distance from the fixed stake, in order that no dispute may thereafter arise, instances of which we have known to occur, from a doubt as to which of the pits might be the principal one.

5. The necessity for these additional or improved pits, depends on the very constitution of the veins themselves ; and as the only object for which they are sunk, is to facilitate the interior workings, driven from the

---

* Chap. 14, ord. 30, infra.

principal pit, it is not required that they should, like the registered pit, or fixed stake, be opened upon the vein or upon ore ; but they may be opened upon dead or barren ground. They should, properly, be sunk straight down upon the workings, to give them air, and to afford the means of prosecuting them with more facility, in such manner, that it shall be practicable to enter by the fixed stake or principal pit and come out by the new or improved pit, or *vice versa*, as in a house with two or three doors, affording facilities for entrance or other purposes. But should the object or purpose of these new pits be different ; should the miner for instance, propose to turn aside and explore the vein in some new direction, or to work towards the adjoining mine, not making these new workings communicate with those driven from the principal pit, his fraudulent and malevolent intentions become apparent ; these new pits being permitted to be made, for the purpose of communication only, and for no other. They must therefore, in this case, be stopped up, as works fraudulently and malevolently designed, and opened with an improper view, and not for the purposes sanctioned by law, which are those of improving the means of access, promoting ventilation and facilitating the raising of the ore or water.[*]

6. The reason of this rule is evidently the same as that of the rule concerning adits, which must have a determinate height and breadth, the miner not being allowed to deviate by working other veins, even though he should meet with any, nor to extend the width of the adit, upon his own authority, beyond the dimensions allowed by the ordinance.[†] Besides which, a limited cause, and a limited permission, can produce only a limited effect,[‡] and if works might be followed up from each of the pits in *any* direction, without communicating with the principal pit, there would be several mines, instead of one mine only. And, to say nothing of the fraud and mischief which might arise from an opportunity being afforded of gaining an entrance into the ground of other mine owners, this inconvenience would follow, that if the works driven from the new pit, should happen to communicate with those of an adjoining mine (in which case it would become necessary to measure out the boundaries, commencing the measurements, not from the new pit, but from the fixed stake), it would be found impossible to ascertain the dimensions of the mine internally ; for the two pits not being supposed to communicate, the solid mass intervening between the works of the one pit and those of the other, would render it impracticable to pass from the former works or excavations to the latter.

7. In a suit agitated in the year 1748, between Doña Francisca de Sardeneta, proprietor of the mine of Cabrera, and Don Juan Moreno de Mesa, proprietor of that of San Antonio, in which the rights of the latter party

---

[*] L. 10. ff. de servit. "Licere fodiendo, substruendo, iter facere." Escalon. in Gazoph. lib. 2, p. 2, cap. 1, tit. 8, n. 2 et 11.

[†] Chap. 26, ord. 82, infra.

[‡] Salgad. de reg. protect. 1, p. cap. 8, num. 10. Tiraquel. in tractatu, Cessante causa, n. 147.

were advocated by the author, it appeared, that an additional pit had been sunk by Moreno, in exploring the vein ; by works driven from which, he had accidentally communicated with works driven from Cabrera, which latter had extended within the boundaries of San Antonio. But it being shewn, that the works of the latter mine were connected with the fixed stake, the royal audiency decreed the owner of Cabrera to withdraw within her own limits. And it seems, that after making this second pit, Moreno proposed to make another new pit, which he in fact did, so that he had three pits to his mine, but all communicating internally. We have known the same thing done in other mines, in various places ; in which instances, however, the fact of the pits having been connected internally, has afforded evidence that the object of sinking the additional pit was legitimate. Such a work is called a *barreno, boca mejora contramina*. From the above, we may infer, that although several pits may be sunk, if required for working the vein, yet it is necessary that good reason should be first shewn, and the permission of the judge obtained, and that they should all communicate with the principal pit ; which being the fixed stake, is the only pit to be regarded in measuring out the mine, or in altering the situation of the stakes bounding the oblong figure which defines its extent.

8. The second condition under which an alteration in the boundaries is permitted, is, that it be without prejudice to the boundaries already set out between the mine in question, and that of any adjoining proprietor, it not being lawful to advance the boundaries twice on the same side. When therefore an alteration has been once made, the right of advancing the boundaries in that direction, to the prejudice of the adjoining mine owner, who has defined his limits on that side, no longer exists. But if the latter have abandoned or left his mine insufficiently worked, and it have been adjudged to a new owner, or if the ground be not yet adjudged, but remain unoccupied, the mine owner may extend his boundaries a second time upon that side ; for a mine abandoned or left insufficiently worked, is no longer a mine, and a mine adjudged for having been left insufficiently worked, or for any other cause, is not the same mine as before, but a distinct and new mine, and held under a different title. And the presumption of injury to a third party no longer exists, for the party newly come into possession has never required to have the boundary stakes set out, nor have they been set out, as to him ; nor does he deduce his title, origin or cause, through the former owner, whom we suppose to have forfeited the mine by leaving it insufficiently worked, or upon some other ground, according to the ordinance. As to this point, all the arguments we have set forth when treating of priority of registry will apply, in a complete and convincing manner, and to them we refer.[*]

* Chap. 11, n. 21 and 22.

9. But if the miner on whose side boundary stakes have been set out, or those who succeed to him in the possession of the mine, whether by universal or particular succession, remain in possession of the ground, the party who has so set out his boundary stakes, cannot alter his limits again, on that side. But as to the other sides, he is at liberty to alter his boundaries, either for his own convenience, or upon being required to do so; as for instance, the number of *varas*, whatever it be, which he may have taken in an easterly direction from the fixed stake, he may now take in a westerly direction from it; and the space which is, in consequence, left unoccupied on the east side, is called an unappropriated space or *excess (demasia,)* of which we shall speak presently. He may do the same on the north and south side, or in any other direction in which he is required to set out boundaries; but when the mine is thus defined and staked out on all the four sides, he is no longer at liberty to alter the boundaries, whilst the adjacent mine owners or their lawful successors, retain possession of the property.

10. The third condition which must be observed in making any alteration in the boundaries, that the mine must retain the form of a right-angled oblong, similar to that in which it was first set out, the rules concerning which, laid down in the ordinances that treat of this subject, must always be invaribly observed.* The stakes must also be set up in pits, with proper firmness and security. The fourth condition is, that if the miner propose to make the alteration of his own accord, he must first obtain permission of the justice and both in this case, and in that of his being required by a neighbour to set out boundaries, he must define them within ten days, if on the spot, and within fifteen days, if absent; as directed by the ordinance, which we have explained in the proper place.† Fifth, the alteration must be noted in the register, as provided by the 29th ordinance, now under consideration, for perpetual evidence thereof, and to prevent any confusion between the bounds first assigned and subsequent alterations, and to afford the means of clearly distinguishing the *pertenencias* of the different mines, which is an object of very great importance to the public, and requires that the greatest precision should be observed, both in the original registries, and in the subsequent ones, upon charges occurring in the ownership of the mine, or upon additional pits being opened, or alterations made in the boundaries.‡

11. From what has been said, we may infer how important it is, that each mine owner should define the boundaries of his mine, at the time of possession being given to him. First, because the fixed stake is thus rendered at once distinct. Second, because the adjoining mine owner is thus kept under proper restraint, by having his boundaries assigned to him. Third, because, if they should be required to be set out on any other side,

---

* Chap. 12, sup. ord. 26 and 27.   ‡ Chap. 5, ubi latè.
† Chap. 10, Ord. 24, ubi plenè.

the miner will then have an opportunity of altering them, or he may do so of his own free will.   And fourth, because, if any communication should happen to be made with an adjoining mine, the dispute will be confined to a mere question of internal measurement, and no more.

12. But when the contrary course of omitting to measure out the bounds of the mine, is taken, mischief only can be expected to ensue ; for should any communication happen to be made, whilst the position of the terminal stakes remains unascertained, the oldest miner, having the right of setting out his boundaries first, and being now aware of the direction in which the richest part of the vein lies, takes the whole or the greater part of his ground on that side, which he probably would not have done, had he set out the boundaries between himself and his neighbour at first.   Hence follow endless litigations and disputes, in the course of which, the silver produced is wasted in the prosecution of law proceedings.   It is, therefore, much to be desired that a positive ordinance should be issued, directing that every one should set out his boundaries at the time of possession being given, even though the adjoining mine owner should not require it, under pain of incurring the forfeiture of the mine, and of being, *ipso facto*, deprived of it, even though not denounced by any other party.

13. It is melancholy to see the neighbouring mine owners summoned, pits registered immediately contiguous to each other ; the three *estados* sunk, and possession given, and all from an anxiety to extend the boundaries in the direction in which the treasure is found to lie.   Communications between the different works are the consequence, for whether through the centre of the earth, or through the air, men will make their way in pursuit of riches ; and conscience being easily blinded by the lust of gain, questions arise as to the registry, as to the identity of the fixed stake, as to priority of date, as to alleged nullity in the denouncement, or insufficiency in the summons, and the like ; the mines are stopped up during the time directed by the ordinance, and a train of mischievous consequences to the public and to private interests ensue, which would be prevented, were each mine measured out at the time of giving possession, upon regular notice to the neighbouring proprietors, and before the discovery of the rich points of the vein should have afforded a stimulus to avarice.   For when there is nothing to excite the evil passions, mankind are generally disposed to act with regularity and good faith.

14. We have already noticed, that the unappropriated space between a mine, the boundaries of which have been altered, and that of an adjoining proprietor, on whose side the boundaries had previously been set out, is called a *demasia* (*excess*), because such piece of ground is to spare, between the mines thus measured out.   The 29th ordinance provides, that these unappropriated spaces shall be assigned to the first who may apply for them ; but the miner who has varied his boundaries, being the very party who has

relinquished them, cannot be such *first* person, for that would be to relinquish and to retain them, at one and the same time, so that the extent of the mine would be greater than is allowed by law. Neither can he denounce or register such unappropriated space as a new mine; for besides that it is a fraud upon the ordinances to aim at having two contiguous mines upon one vein, acquired by denouncement or registry, an opportunity would be afforded for many other abuses, and a wide field laid upon for the exercise of covetousness. A miner, were this permitted, might alter his boundaries, by advancing along the course of the vein, with the certainty, at the very time of making the application to alter his boundaries, of being enabled also to apply for the waste space left. But it is the constant aim of the ordinances to restrain this eager and grasping disposition, with a view to the mines being more thoroughly and better worked, and to their produce being distributed amongst a greater number of persons.

15. These unappropriated spaces, then, are to be assigned to the first person who may apply for them; subject to the condition that he set up a fixed stake, make registry, sink a pit to the proper depth, and observe the other provisions of the ordinance. And if the proprietor of the adjoining mine, on whose side the boundaries had been originally set out, should be the first to apply for such an unappropriated space, it is to be adjudged to him, but subject to three conditions. First, that he do not abandon his fixed stake. Second, that he register the alteration made in his boundaries, before the justice, that it may be entered in the register. Third, that taking into the account, the extension of his boundaries over this unappropriated space, he have no more than the proper number of *varas* in a regular mine; that is to say, he is not to have two mines, his own original mine and a second, under the title of an unappropriated space, but one single mine only; and consequently, as many *varas* as he advances upon the unappropriated ground, so many must he relinquish in the direction, from which he is receding.

16. If, notwithstanding that the proprietor of the adjoining mine is desirous of advancing his boundaries, some other person should apply first for the waste space, the latter is to be preferred, as being first in point of time; for the express words of the ordinance are, " to the first person who may apply for them ;" and it is only conditionally, " if the neighbouring mine owner should apply first ;" that the preference is to be given to him. But should he contend that he is entitled, under the ordinance,* as being prior in point of registry, to extend his boundaries over that piece of ground, it will be proper to remind him, that that ordinance has reference to other and distinct circumstances; namely, to the case of two contiguous mines, the owners of which propose to alter their ground, no boundaries having as yet been set out between them, in which case the proprietor of longest standing is to be preferred. These waste spaces, however, having their limits already de-

* Chap. 11, ord. 25.

fined, namely, by the boundary stakes set out by the two adjoining mine owners, the party denouncing the waste space has no occasion to apply to have the boundaries set out at all. Besides, there is nothing to authorise a party, under the pretence of altering his boundaries, to occupy a *pertenencia* which is adjudged by the law to the first who may apply for it.* And the adjoining miner has nothing but his own neglect to complain of, as he might have applied for the unappropriated space, when summoned; add to which, that the law, under these circumstances, leaving the adjoining mine owner in the same situation as before, does him no injustice, whilst it is important to the public, that the greatest possible number of mines should be worked by different persons.

17. The alterations of the boundaries in Peru, are subject to the rules of their own peculiar ordinances.† Upon a vein being discovered, the first comers, after staking out their mines, are allowed a year for altering their boundaries; after the expiration of which, any persons making trial pits without the limits of the *pertenencias* staked out, and meeting with the same vein, may proceed to work it; and none of the former persons will be allowed to alter their boundaries, except the discoverer, whose two mines, together with that set out for the crown, contiguous to the first of them, may be taken upon any part of the vein at pleasure.

CHAPTER XIV.

OF INTERNAL COMMUNICATIONS OCCURRING BETWEEN THE WORKS OF DIFFERENT MINES.—A PARTY WHO, BEING IN THE IMMEDIATE PURSUIT OF ORE, MAKES HIS WAY INTO THE PERTENENCIA OF ANOTHER PROPRIETOR, GAINS A PROPERTY IN THE ORE HE RAISES, UP TO THE TIME OF THE WORKS COMMUNICATING AND THE DIMENSIONS BEING ASCERTAINED.—IT IS SHEWN, THAT THE PROPERTY OF THE VEIN IS NOT GRANTED TO AN INDEFINITE EXTENT UPON THE UNDERLAY; AND THAT IF TWO MINERS HAPPEN TO COMMUNICATE AT A POINT WITHOUT THE LIMITS OF EITHER PERTENENCIA, THEY ARE ENTITLED TO MAINTAIN THEIR GROUND, UP TO THE POINT WHERE THEY MEET.—OF THE IMPROPRIETY OF OPENING A PIT, MERELY FOR THE PURPOSE OF GAINING ACCESS TO THE ORE OF ANOTHER PROPRIETOR.—OF THE CASES WHERE NO FRAUDULENT OR WRONGFUL INTENTIONS ARE IMPUTED, THE GROUND OF SUSPICION BEING REMOVED BY THE GREAT DEVIATIONS FROM REGULARITY EXHIBITED IN SOME VEINS, AS WELL AS IN THE INTERMEDIATE SPACES BETWEEN THEM.

ORDINANCE XXX.

ALSO, we ordain and command, that if any mine shall be extended beyond

---

* From the terms of ord. 29, and from the ordinances of Peru, 1, tit. 2, concerning unappropriated spaces, in Escalona, Gazoph. lib. 2, p. 2, cap. 1, pag. 109. "For him who may have applied for such unappropriated spaces, for from the moment of his applying for them, he has acquired a right to them."

† Ord. 8, tit. 1. concerning discoverers, in Escalona, Gazophil. lib. 2, p. 2, cap. 1, pag. 106.

the boundary or limit, properly assigned to it under these ordinances, either in respect of the length or of the breadth, and the ore therein contained shall be continuous with the ore in the mine of some other party, and the two mines shall become one, in the depth; the miner who shall have first sunk, and made his way into the other mine, shall and may enjoy the ore he shall raise therefrom, until the owner of the other mine shall carry on his works to meet him in which case the latter may require the party who has anticipated him, to set out his boundaries; and if it should be found that he is within the limits of the other's *pertenencia,* he shall withdraw, and relinquish the vein to the miner within whose *pertenencia* he may have entered; and all the ore which he may have raised from the other's *pertenencia,* up to that time, shall belong to him who has raised it; and he shall not be obliged to give it to the other, inasmuch as he had acquired a right to it by the care and diligence used in working with more activity than his neighbour. But if any party shall take a *pertenencia* contiguous to the mine of another, either on the side of its length or of its breadth, where there is no vein, or, there being a vein, yet such vein shall not contain ore, nor exhibit any appearance of it, but he shall work the same merely with the intention of profiting by the ore of his neighbour, when he shall get within his boundaries: We command, that such person shall not have the power to acquire, and shall not acquire any right, even though his neighbour's ore should take its course within his *pertenencia;* and our mining judges and justices shall determine it so, and shall not allow or permit such mines, not being upon a vein or ore, to be worked.

CONTENTS OF THE COMMENTARY ON THIS ORDINANCE.

1. Of the difficulty and importance which the subject of this ordinance involves.
2. Whether a miner working beyond his boundaries, in the immediate pursuit of ore, shall make the ore his own.
3 to 7. The question is to be determined differently, according to circumstances, as appears from the ordinances of the old code, which are not repealed.
8. Several questions arising from the 30th ordinance of the old, and the 30th of the new code.
9. If two mines communicate internally, neither of them being measured out, which ought to be measured first? Reply, that the mine of the longer standing has the preference.
10, 11 and 12. Whether in such case, the miner of longer standing can extend his boundaries beyond the fixed stake of his neighbour? Reply, that he cannot, which is demonstrated.
13 to 17. Whether, if the miner of longer standing have measured out his boundaries, he can so extend them as against a more recent miner, who has not so measured them out? Reply, in the affirmative, the reasons for which are shewn.
18. When two or more mines communicate beyond the *pertenencias* of both, the proprietors are entitled to maintain their ground, up to the point to which they have worked.
19. An executory decree of the royal audiency of Mexico on this point, made in a suit

between Don Juan Antonio Carriedo, and Don Manuel de Aranda, two miners of Guanaxuato.

20 to 23. Another such decree, made in a suit between the Count de San Pedro, and Don Antonio Jacinto Diez Madronedo, and his partners, in the same mining district.

24. Another suit between the Count and the heirs of Don Joseph de Sardeneta, which was attended with a similar result.

25. A very well-considered order of Don Juan Antonio Vizarron, viceroy of Mexico, referred to, determining, that the property of the vein is not acquired to an indefinite extent on the underlay, but that the internal limits must correspond with the superficial boundaries.

26. Several arguments in support of this determination.

27 and 28. The subject concluded, and the doctrine supported, by a decision in point, reported by Larrea.

29. A party making his way within another's boundaries, in the immediate pursuit of ore, gains a property in the ore he raises, until he communicates with his neighbour's works; and why?

30. When the workings communicate, the mines must be measured out, a boundary wall must be set up, and each party must withdraw within his own *pertenencia*.

31. A party who makes his way into the *pertenencia* of a neighbour, when not in the immediate pursuit of ore, does not become entitled to the ore he may find, and the justices are to prohibit works so carried on.

32. Parties so acting are deceitful and wicked.

33. And they must restore all the ore they may have raised.

34. It is difficult to enforce this rule, without great zeal on the part of the judges.

35. Such parties do not gain a property, even in the ore raised from within their own *pertenencias*, and the pits opened with these improper views should be stopped up, and the parties be punished.

36 and 37. The improper views entertained in opening the pit should be established. How they may be proved.

38. The penalty is imposed upon the party opening a pit *solely* for the purpose of stealing the ore of another.

39. A level which deviates from the course of the vein, previously followed, being driven solely with the wrongful object of communicating with the works of a neighbour, should also be stopped up, as driven with improper views, although the whole mine is not to be stopped up.

40 and 41. The royal audiencies decide whether levels have been driven with correct or fraudulent views, according to circumstances.

42. The barrenness of the vein or the hardness of the ground, may render it necessary to alter the direction of the works; in which case the presumption of fraud does not arise.

43. The veins are frequently subject to become barren; or to deviate in their course.

44. A new vein, or a branch of a vein, discovered in the course of prosecuting the old vein, may lawfully be followed up.

45. And the consequences, in case of a communication being made with another mine, are the same as if the original vein were in question.

46. The qualification implied in the word *solely*, in the text, is to be taken strictly.

47. To justify working into a neighbour's *pertenencia*, it is necessary to be in the immediate pursuit of ore; but not so, to authorise making investigations in our own ground.

48. Of a particular case, in which the miner making such a communication with another mine, is cleared from any suspicion of entertaining a wrongful purpose, although not

in the immediate pursuit of ore   The discretion of the judges should be exercised in this case, according to circumstances.

49 to 53. Of the peculiar ordinances of Peru, concerning communications between different mines.

COMMENTARY.

1. Of all the ordinances contained in the new code, and in the old law, there are none more difficult, or which have been more frequently the subject of litigation in the courts, than this. Scarcely any important suit occurs, which does not turn upon a communication between mines, and a demand to have the ore accounted for; nor are any proceedings more anxious than those which are, in consequence, gone through upon the ground. It therefore becomes necessary, in illustrating the provisions of the 29th and 30th of the old ordinances upon the subject, and ascertaining how far they are still subsisting, and how far repealed by the 30th ordinance of the new code, to consider the subject at some length, pointing out, from time to time, the several distinctions which occur.

2. The question is, whether the proprietor of an older mine, who works beyond his boundaries, and makes his way into another mine, in the immediate pursuit of ore, gains a property in the ore raised, or is bound to restore it?

3. The 29th of the old ordinances distinguished the question into two cases. First, when the proprietor of the older mine *had not* set out the boundaries between his mine and that of the other proprietor, and the latter demanded to be protected in the possession of his mine. In which case, the justice was to afford him protection, and not to allow the other to proceed to raise any more ore; but all that the older proprietor had raised up to that time, belonged to him, and he might likewise alter his boundaries on that side, although not required to do so by the other.

4. The second case was, when the proprietor of the older mine *had* set out boundaries between his own mine and the more recent one. In which case he was to restore to the proprietor of the latter, all the ore he might have raised, deducting expenses.

5. These two cases are both provided for in the first case put by our 30th ordinance of the new code; under which however, the older miner, not having set out his boundaries, still retains the right to advance them. It is there determined, that even if both the mines should have been staked out, he who works with most activity, being in the immediate pursuit of ore, shall enjoy all that he may raise from the other's *pertenencia* (having acquired a right to it by the diligence he has exerted), until a communication be made internally between the two workings, when each shall withdraw within his own limits, to be ascertained by measurement.

6. The 30th of the old ordinances declares, in the case above supposed, that when the ore takes its course into a mine, the proprietor of which has

not applied to have the boundaries set out, the miner may follow it up, and avail himself of it, although he should work out of his own *pertenencias*. And should the later proprietor apply to have the boundaries set out, the older one, whether his mine be a discoverer's or an ordinary mine, may advance his limits in any direction in which the ore takes its course, taking either the length or breadth of his mine on that side ; provided he do not abandon his stake, and that his mine form a four-sided oblong with right angles. And the unappropriated spaces which he leaves on the side from which he withdraws himself, are to be assigned to any person who may apply for them.

7. This ordinance is not affected by the 30th of the new code, which speaks, in the first instance, of a communication occurring between two mines, both of which have been measured ; and in the second place, of a party opening a mine in ground where there is neither a vein nor ore nor any appearance of ore. The 30th of the old ordinances is therefore still in force, nothing opposed to it being contained in those of the new code.

8. Assuming then, that the 30th ordinance of the old, and the 30th of the new code, are both wholly in force, we shall consider, in order to come to a more complete understanding of these ordinances several questions which arise upon the manner of construing them.

9. First, if the workings of two mines, neither of which have been measured out, should communicate internally, which of them shall be measured first ? We reply, that which is prior in the date of its registry ; in the same manner as when an application is first made to set out boundaries ; for the party who has first registered or made denouncement is always preferred.* This is the practice of the courts of New Spain, and we recollect an instance of it in a case in which a communication had occurred between the mine of San Antonio, and that of Cabrera, in the mining district of Guanaxuato, the former belonging to Don Juan Moreno, and the latter to Doña Francisca Sardeneta, and of which we have spoken elsewhere : and likewise in another case, in which the mines of Don Antonio Davila, and Don Joseph Puebla, in the mining district of Sultepec, were concerned, in the year 1746 ; and another, where a communication had occurred between the mines Catafortuna and San Estanislao, belonging to Don Francisco de la Mora, and that of la Cruz, the property of Don Baltasar Delgado, and his partners, in the mining district of Gaudalcazar, in the Jurisdiction of San Luis, in the years 1753 and 1754. All these suits were carried up to the royal audiency of Mexico, which confirmed the proceedings : thereby establishing, that the older mine should always be measured first, upon the communication occurring, the ores raised up to that time being left to the party who had worked with most activity ; and that after the measurement is made, a division called a *quarda-raya* should be put up in the interior. The same rule was observed in a case where a communication had occurred between the two mines, Roldanera and

* Chap. 11, ord. 25.

Gaudalupe, the former belonging to Don Gregorio Zumalde, and the latter to Don Juan Alonso Diaz de la Campa, both inhabitants of Zacatecas, the suit arising out of which was prosecuted before the mayor of that mining district, and subsequently, before the royal audiency of Guadalaxara.

10. The second question is, whether, in the case proposed, the proprietor of the older mine can advance his boundaries on the side on which the communication has occurred, so as to take in the pit or fixed stake of the more recent mine ? We reply that he can take into his limits all the ground intervening between the two pits, or fixed stakes. He cannot do the first, because, by not objecting to the sinking of the pit, upon its being registered by his neighbour, or upon the possession being given to him, he has assented to its being made, and it would be a manifest injustice that he should be allowed to take the benefit of this pit himself, causing the loss of all that the owner has laid out upon it, and depriving him of the advantage he may derive from sinking and exploring the vein in other directions. But he may extend his boundaries over all the intermediate ground, being entitled, in consequence of his priority, to measure out his boundaries in whatever direction he may think, and to compell the proprietor of the more recent mine, to withdraw.*

11. Don Joseph Saenz resolves this question in these words :† " With regard to this question I have always been much struck with the objection the miners seem to have to getting their mines measured out, until called upon by other proprietors to set out their boundaries, as if they could not afterwards alter them. And yet such a course could involve them in no risk, and might produce much benefit; for should any other party apply subsequently to have the boundaries set out, they would then have an opportunity of altering them ; and should the two mines, as proposed in the 30th ordinance of the new code, happen to communicate at any future time, it would prove of the highest importance to both. And the mischief is, not only that one party will perhaps register a mine upon a vein where another party is at work, without applying to have the boundaries set out, and that the latter will assent to his opening a pit upon it; but that neither the one nor the other think of measuring out their boundaries, being satisfied with the assurance, that the pit, the opening of which has been so assented to, cannot be taken into the other mine, but taking no account of the ground lying intermediate between the two mines. If ore however, be found in this intermediate ground, and the workings happen to communicate, their eyes are opened to the mischief which has arisen ; the older proprietor having the preference, drives back him whose registry is of later date, and lays down his boundaries in a manner never calculated on by the latter, who complains of the hardship, he having perhaps been the first to find the ore. It is nev-

---

* See chap. 9 and 11. ord. 23 and 25.
† Saenz, Tratado de medidas de minas, cap. 6, n. 13.

ertheless just that he should lose the benefit of it, for having omitted, when he had his registry, to observe the rule of the ordinance, by applying to the older proprietor to set out his boundaries, and to define the number of *varas* he might choose to take on that side ; in which case perhaps, he would have left him more ground than would have included the spot where the ore was afterwards found."

12. Whence it is plain, that although the older proprietor may take the ground intervening between the two pits, he cannot touch the fixed stake of the other miner, the sinking of which he has assented to. For the pit having been occupied when the whole of the ground was vacant, and when no mine had been marked out or boundaries defined, and the neighbouring proprietor having assented to its being occupied, and not having, previous to the discovery of the ore, either made any objection, or required to have such boundaries assigned to him, as would include the space occupied by the pit ; but having omitted, whilst he had the opportunity, to assert his objection, to enforce his right of measuring out his boundaries in that direction, or to prevent the pit from being registered and opened, he cannot, after such discovery of ore, have any right to occupy it.

13. The third question involves a more serious difficulty ; it is, whether, when the older mine has been already measured out, the proprietor can alter his boundaries so as to take in the pit of another mine, the owner of which has not applied to have the boundaries set out ? It will probably be said, that a neighbour who has measured out his mine, has just as much assented to sinking the pit, as one who has not ; and that having so assented, the same answer must be given as in the last case ; so that if, in that case, it be determined that he cannot include the pit of the more recent mine within his boundaries, upon measuring them out, neither can he, in the present case, upon extending them. And that if he had been desirous of preventing the other from sinking the pit, and had wished to extend his own limits in that direction, he might have opposed the registry, and have objected to possession being given ; and, at the same time, have applied to have his own boundaries advanced ; but that he should not first assent to the opening of the mine, and lead his neighbour into expense, and then endeavour to deprive him of his mine, to turn his labour to his own advantage, and to make a profit of the ore discovered by the other.

14. We acknowledge the force of this reasoning, but it must yield before the express terms of the law, as stated in the 30th of the old ordinances, which is still in full force, and which ordains, that in such case the proprietor of the older mine, from whose ground the ore is found to take its course, may enlarge his boundaries in the direction in which the ore lies, taking the allotted dimensions of his mine on that side ; and it repeats, that he may do so on one side or sides on which the ore may take its course ; and what is more, even though he should have altered his boundaries one or more times ;

that is to say, although he may have taken on the south side ten *varas*, and afterwards ten more, and subsequently twenty more, making such alterations upon application to the justice; yet if he have not set out the boundary stakes, as between his own mine and that of the younger proprietor, he is at liberty to alter them again : and whether the latter require him to set out his boundaries or not, he may measure out the whole length or breadth of his mine on that side on which the ore takes its course. Consequently, as the pit so registered and assented to may fall within this space, it may be made the property of the older miner so advancing his boundaries.

15. This is laid down by Saenz in the following words :* " This is repeated in the 30th ordinance of the old code, which adds, that he may alter his boundaries on any side or sides where the ore may take its course, although he should have altered his boundaries once or oftener; and what appears most remarkable in this case, is, that the miner thus extending his boundaries, is authorised to take the whole length or breadth of his mine on the side where the ore takes its course; whence it may happen, that the boundaries thus taken may include the pits, to the sinking of which he has tacitly assented; the other parties being deprived of them, which would be a just punishment for their having registered the mine, without applying to have the boundaries set out."

16. This penalty, in short, being expressly imposed by the ordinance, must take effect, even supposing the sinking of the pit to have been tacitly assented to ; and the party who has made registry, without requiring to have the boundaries set out, may attribute his liability to the penalty, and the loss of the expenses he has incurred, to his own negligence ; particularly as the very reason of his opening the mine, without requiring to have the boundaries set out is, that he is aware that the vein takes such a course as to extend into his neighbour's *pertenencias*.

17. Nor is this inconsistent with the reply given to the second question, which determines, that if the older miner have not measured out his mine, he cannot take in the pit, to the sinking of which he has assented, although he may include within his boundaries all the intermediate space. For the reason is, not merely that he has so assented, but that he has omitted to measure out his own boundaries, probably in the expectation, that some other party may discover what course the rich part of the vein takes. Besides, the words of the ordinance authorise the older miner to alter his boundaries, to the extent of the whole length of his mine, and permit him, as a punishment to the younger miner for not having applied to have the boundaries set out, to take away his pit from him, if the dimensions allowed to his own mine will include it. Now, as this penalty applies to one particular case, namely, that the older miner, in whose favour it is made, having measured out his

* Saenz, de medidas de minas, cap. 7, n. 3.

boundaries, it is not to be extended to a different case, in favour of a party who has not fulfilled the ordinance, by measuring out his mine.

18. The fourth question is, whether, when the communication happens to be made beyond the *pertenencias* of both mines, each of the proprietors ought to withdraw within his own limits, or whether the works should be made over to him, upon the underlay of whose portion of the vein they are driven. This question was, to our knowledge, made a point of dispute in reference to several very important concerns, and occasioned extensive litigation, upon the result of which, it was determined by the royal audiency of Mexico, that each of the mine owners should be maintained in the possession of the ground he had occupied beyond his own limits, not being at the same time within the limits of any other mine, but being in common ground, unoccupied by any other party : and it was ordered, that whenever the workings should meet, a pillar should be set up as a *guarda-raya*, and that each should be at liberty to work freely through the virgin ground or the works already driven, upon the underlay of the vein.

19. Don Juan Antonio Carriedo, proprietor of the mine of Saucedo, instituted a suit against Don Manuel de Aranda Saavedra, proprietor of the mine of Mellado, in the mining district of Guanaxuato, concerning three works, called San Pedro, el Rebage and la Cocinera. The royal audiency, on the 19th of September, 1726, declared, that they belonged to Carriedo ; but the question being afterwards brought forward by way of supplication,* and various proceedings being had to ascertain whether the three works were within or beyond the limits of these mines, it was established that they were beyond the limits, both of these two mines, and of another called Quebradilla, which was also involved in the dispute. And it was consequently declared, by a decree of review, of the 4th of September, 1727, that the possession and property of three works belonged to Aranda and Carriedo, and their partners in the two aforesaid mines of Mellado and Saucedo, in consideration of the fair intentions of each in occupying them.

20. The Count de San Pedro del Alamo, proprietor of the mine of Santa Anita, in the mining district of Guanaxuato, as testamentary executor and heir of Don Manuel Gomez Corban, contested with Don Antonio Jacinto Diez Madroñedo and Don Alonso Zid Fernandez, proprietors of the mine of San Lucas de Atalaya, the property of certain works, which were ascertained by proceedings to which recourse was had, to be without the *pertenencias* of both mines. These proceedings were conducted by Don Joseph de la Borda, under the appointment of the viceroy of Mexico, Count Revilla-Gigedo ; the audiency of Mexico having deemed it requisite that the person employed for

---

* A supplication is a rehearing of the sentence of one of the supreme tribunals, from which there is no opportunity of appeal. See Institutes of the civil law of Spain, by Doctor Ignatius Jordan de Asso y del Rio, and Doctor Miguel de Manuel y Rodriguez, translated by L. F. C. Johnston, p. 347.— *Trans.*

the purpose should be a person of experience, such as Borda ; and their correctness was impugned by the count, whilst the other parties, on the contrary, maintained their accuracy.

21. The count insisted, that the underlay of the vein, which took its course from his mine of Santa Anita, was infinite it its extent, or that, at any rate, the vein was his property, as far as it extended upon the underlay, as being one and the same vein : and that as, when the vein, being what is called a deep vein, proceeds perpendicularly downwards, the miner may work on to the antipodes, or to the infernal regions, as Amaya says ;[*] so, if the vein be inclined, its whole extent upon the underlay is granted to the miner.

22. Zid Fernandez and Madroñedo contended, on the other hand, that by their prior occupation, the ground being common, they had acquired a right to it. That the property of the vein did not extend indefinitely upon the underlay, that the ordinances permit other veins to be registered in that direction ; and that all the ordinances prescribe a legal and definite extent to the mines, both in length and breadth ; that it is a party who is within another's limits only, who is to withdraw upon a communication occurring between the works within those limit ; but that if the communication happen beyond their *pertenencias*, each party should leave a space of two *varas* and a half, and that a wall of five *vàras* in thickness should be set up, to serve as a *guarda-raya* or boundary ; and that both miners should then be at liberty to prosecute their works upon the virgin ground, the same proceeding being repeated in the event of their again meeting.

23. The latter party, in the end, carried their point ; for by a decree of the royal audiency of the 24th of March, 1749, the proceedings of Don Joseph de la Borda, and the measurements of the mine of Santa Anita, and of the mine called San Lucas de Abaxo, were, amongst other things, confirmed, and it was declared that the work called el Purgatorio, belonged to and was the property of the count, and el Rosario and the other disputed works, to Zid and Madroñedo ; and that both of them should be at liberty to work freely, through the untouched ground, upon the underlay of the vein, until they should happen to meet, in which case *guarda-rayas* should be set up in the manner directed by the royal ordinances, the same proceeding being repeated whenever they might again happen to communicate ; which should be observed and fulfilled, notwithstanding any supplication : perpetual silence being enjoined. And although the count prayed leave to present a supplication, it was refused him, but he was allowed an authenticated copy, to enable him to apply to the council, where he in fact obtained a hearing ; but his heirs afterwards gave up the point, before it had been

---

[*] Amaya, in Cod. lib. 10, tit. 15, a n. 30, ibi : " Et ideo ipsius venditoris debent censeri quia in illo minerali habet dominium, sicut in toto fundo, et sicut illud quod superius respondet superficiei mei fundi, censetur meum usque ad cœlum, leg. altius, 8, Cod. de servit. sic etiam quod est sub fundo meo debet censeri meum usque ad inferos; ut notat Cœpola, de servit. rustic. cap. 21, a n. 4 ; et in leg. inter publica, §. 1, n. 10, ff. de V. signif.

declared whether a second supplication, which he had presented to the audiency, could be admitted.

24. The same count, as heir of Corban, and proprietor of the mine called Catilla, claimed to exclude the heirs of Don Joseph de Sardeneta, who were proprietors of the mine of Rayas, from another work beyond the limits of both mines ; but the latter were maintained in their possession by a decree of the royal audiency, issued about the same time. In this cause, the author was concerned in advocating the rights of the heirs of Sardeneta.

25. To the authority of these most respectable decisions, we may add that of an order issued by the Archbishop Don Juan Antonio de Vizarron, when viceroy, on the 26th February, 1739, which combines the special circircumstance, that it was issued under the advice of the deputies of the important mining district of Guanaxuato. Their opinion touched upon several points, and amongst other things noticed, that the miners maintained, that the prescribed number of *varas* had relation only to the exterior or surface of the mines, not allowing that the internal dimensions must correspond perpendicularly with those measured out externally, but insisting that the miner might work to an unlimited extent internally. Whereupon it was declared, after considering the opinion of the fiscal, and the opinion of the assessor-general, that the property of the vein is not granted to an indefinite extent on the underlay. And that the internal dimensions must correspond perpendicularly with, and be similar to, the external limits.

26. Were an indefinite extent of the vein upon the underlay, granted to the miner, the permission given to open pits, would extend to pits upon the course of the vein only ; and the permission to extend the boundaries upon the underlay, as granted by the 30th of the old ordinances, which, as before observed, is still in force, would be superfluous ; for the enlargement of the boundaries externally, is of no avail, if the whole underlay, internally, belongs to the miner ; and the absurd consequence would also follow, that no mines could be registered upon either side of the vein, contrary to the tenor of the 30th of the old ordinances, and also of the 30th of the new code, which refer to the case of a mine extending beyond its limits *breadthwise*, and being continuous with the ore of the mine of another, which beyond doubt, must be on one side of it. Finally, the rule that the internal dimensions must correspond perpendicularly with the external limits, and all that is provided by the old and new ordinances, for ensuring precision in the measurement, and certainty in the position of the fixed stakes, would be completely frustrated. And had the miner a right to the whole underlay of the vein, there would be no necessity for forming an oblong, nor for limiting the width to 60 *varas*, for as to the surface, which is not the source of profit, the measurements are of no importance ; whilst, as to the interior, it is ridiculous to talk of boundaries, if the right to an indefinite extent upon the underlay be admitted. Besides which, endless absurdities would follow

from such a supposition, insomuch that it would be necessary to expunge part of several ordinances, particularly the 30th, of which we are now treating, and which supposes that the communication may be made, either upon the course of the vein, or upon the underlay; and it being declared that each party must, in that case, withdraw within his own limits, it is evident, that as there is a limit to the number of *varas* to be taken upon the course of the vein, so is there upon the underlay: and that the number of *varas* allowed for the breadth being limited, it cannot, consequently, be infinite.

27. Whence it may be inferred, that if the works of two contiguous mines, should be carried beyond their limits, and a communication happen out of their limits, in ground unoccupied by any other party, the first occupant will acquire a right to that ground by his greater activity and diligence;[*] and as these parties, thus coming in opposite directions, are out of their limits, each of them having by his diligence, worked up to the point of meeting, and no further, they must be restrained by means of a *guarda-raya*, each remaining in possession of the ground he has been the first to occupy; but neither is at liberty, under the pretence that the underlay is but a part of the same vein, to claim a right to the whole of such underlay, or to drive out a party whom we suppose not to have made his way within the other's limits but to be in ground beyond those limits.

28. And although this is sufficiently demonstrated, from all the ordinances which speak of the longitudinal and lateral dimensions of mines, it is still further confirmed by a decision of the senate of Granada, stated by Larrea,[†] upon the subject of opening marble quarries; by which it was determined, that the marble quarries opened in a public place, belonged to the party who had opened them, but that he should not be entitled to prevent other persons from raising stone, from some other place, merely because the same vein might extend to that point: as an authority for which decision, reference is made to the mines of gold and silver, in which, although more precious, it is stated that the discoverer cannot prohibit or prevent the raising of the ore beyond his own limits or measured bounds, notwithstanding that the vein be continuous; it being for the public benefit that the mines should be explored

---

[*] L. 3. ff. de adquir. rer. dom.

[†] Larr. Decis. Granat. disp 44, a. n. 8. "Senatus decrevit solum posse prohiberi lapidem eximi in duabus lapidicinis quæ in publico loco apertæ, decreto civitatis, et istæ ad cum qui aperuit pertinere : in reliquis vero, et si ejusdem venæ lapides dicebantur, absolvendos reos qui lapidem eximebant, decretum est." Ibid. u. 7. "Quo fit, ut in venis metallorum, non conceditur inventori, ut possit ultra modum et mensuram prædictam alium prohibere ne metalla effodiat et vena utatur." Et n. 21. "Verum quamvis constiterit eandem esse venam, cum tamen in pretiosis metallis, quæ longe majori sumptu et labore perquiruntur, jure nostro limitatur, ne quis ultra limitationem termini præoccupatione totam venam adquirat, sed ad 120 ulnas longitudinis, et 60 latitudinis jus primi inventoris extandatur ; quasi publicæ utilitati, quæ in metallorum indagatione consistit, L. 1, Cod. de metallar. maxime expediat a pluribus metalla perquiri et effodi. Idem in lapidibus dicendum est, &c."

by a great number of persons. The decision also cites several other opinions, texts and doctors, bearing upon the same point ; so that, although the underlay be part of the same vein, the mine must be confined to its proper length and breadth ; beyond which the miner can only acquire so much of the interior as he may occupy before any other person, but he cannot prevent others from doing the same.

29. Having thus far been engaged in investigating the questions arising out of the 30th of the old ordinances, and the 30th of the new code, we now proceed to treat of the cases governed by the express terms of the latter. We have already observed, that the first of these cases is, when a mine is carried beyond its limits, either in length or breadth, the ore being continuous with the ore of some other mine. The ordinance directs, first, that the proprietor shall enjoy all the ore he may raise from his neighbour's *pertenencia*, until the latter intercept him by his works ; and in this point it repeals the 29th of the old ordinances. The first ground of this peculiarity is, that the prince has been pleased so to ordain it ; he, as lord, having power to impose this and other conditions and obligations, in admitting his subjects to an interest in the mines that were his by sovereign right.* A second reason is, that as the sovereign still retains his right, in regard to the fifth or tenth paid out of the mines, he has been desirous that this branch of income should not be reduced, but be increased by all proper means ; but it would be hard if, after discovering the vein, a party in the immediate pursuit of ore should be obliged to relinquish his object, merely because he has made way into the ground of another proprietor, who does not meet him by his works, or urge forward his operations. And a third reason, which is stated in the ordinance, is, that the benefits derived from raising the ores being general,† it is necessary to hold up a reward for him who may exert most care and diligence in exploring and working the vein.

30. It directs, in the second place, that when the works happen to communicate, the party who shall have advanced his works with the greatest activity, shall measure out his boundaries ; and that in case it be found that he is within his neighbour's *pertenencia*, he shall vacate it. This may be easily accomplished ; for, as it is known, from the external measurements, how many *varas* there are in that direction on the surface, the like number must be measured off internally, and a *guarda-raya* or pillar, spoken of in discussing the preceding questions, must be set up. This must be done in the form and manner described in treating of the internal dimensions, which must correspond, perpendicularly, with the external boundaries ; for the only use of measuring out the mines upon the surface is, that a like space may be enjoyed in the interior, where the silver and gold, the pure blood of the vein, take their course. Which completes the illustration of the first

---

* Antun. de donat. lib. 3. cap. 9, u. 10, et seq. et vide dict. cap. 2, per tot.
† Larrea, loc. ubi sup. L. 1, Cod. de metall. lib. 11.

case put by the ordinance, namely, when the miner working upon the vein, and in the immediate pursuit of ore, makes his way within the limits of another mine ; in which case, the ore which he raises before they meet, becomes his own, after which he is to define his limits, and vacate his neighbour's ground.

31. The second case is, when a party takes a mine where there is no vein, or where being a vein, there is neither ore, nor the indication of any, contiguous to the other side or extremity of some other mine, and works the former with the mere view of profiting by his neighbour's ore, when he can carry on his works so far as to get within his *pertenencia*. The ordinance here ordains, first, that such party shall not acquire any right to the ore, even should it be found to extend into his own *pertenencia ;* and secondly, that the justice shall not permit such mines, not being upon a vein or ore to be worked.

32. Those who open a pit, and take a mine or *pertenencia*, with the sole view of availing themselves of their neighbour's ore, are called by Saenz[*] pretended miners. Agricola calls them wicked men :[†] and they are doubtless to be regarded as making attempts upon the property of others, and should be banished from the mines ; being in truth, pilferers, though assuming the character of miners. Such persons cannot acquire a right to any thing raised from their neighbours' mines, for reasons exactly the converse of those we have given in reference to the first case. In that case, the party gains a right to the ore raised from his neighbour's *pertenencia*, because it is the will of the sovereign that he should be furnished with such an inducement to carry on his works, and because he is upon the vein, and in the immediate pursuit of ore ; but in the second case, such is not and cannot be the will of the sovereign, who would never authorise robbery or usurpation. In the first case, a reward is given for following up the ore, and using greater activity in carrying on the operations ; in the latter case, such a reward would operate as an encouragement, to a party working with the fraudulent view of taking the property of another.

33. This being the case, he is bound, in every point of view, to restore all the ore he may have raised ; for he cannot acquire any property in it, or make it his own, and it is a rule, that whatever is stolen or pilfered, in violation of the rights of the lawful owner of the mine, must be restored. And if the case be so established before the justice, he must give his decision accordingly, in agreement with the ordinance, the observance of which he must enforce with all the rigour of the law.

34. The misfortune is, that it is very rarely that restitution is actually

---

[*] Saenz, Tratado de medidas de minas, cap. 7, n. 22.

[†] Agricola, de re metall. lib. 1, p. 16. " Nam improbi quidam homines venulas proximas venis affluentibus aliquo metallo fodientes, in alienam possessionem invadunt. Itaque eos injuriarum accusatos, magistratus expellit atque exturbat ex fodinis."

enforced, or the property made good to the owner; for even supposing the difficulty of establishing the amount of the ore raised, to be got over, that of recovering the amount from the contending parties, is, from the extent to which fraud and collusion are practised, and the difficulty of detection, generally found to be still greater; the consequence of which is, that the party who gains the suit, besides having his property invaded and taken from him, has to bear a considerable further expense incurred in litigation. For these wicked intruders and pretended miners are prompted, by the consciousness of their evil intentions, to be as expeditious as possible in getting possession of, and concealing the property; and if the works are not promptly put a stop to by the justices, during the proceedings, or pending the various steps of appeal, they make the most of their time in realising the produce.

35. Hence it may be inferred, that if the intruder be proceeded against, whether civilly or criminally, he will, besides the ordinary punishment for the outrage, be liable to forfeit the mine, and to restore the whole of the produce. And this, not only when he has carried on his works into the *per-tenencia* of his neighbour, but even when he has remained within his own limits; that is to say, even supposing his neighbour should, in the immediate pursuit of ore, have made his way within the *pertenencia* of the pretended miner; " although his neighbour's ore should take its course within his *per-tenencia*." Consequently, he can acquire no property in the ore, and the fraudulent mine, or *boca ladrona*, as it is commonly called (and often with propriety), must be stopped up; for as the ordinance says, agreeing with others which we have set forth,[*] a mine " where there is no vein nor ore," must not be worked; it being a fair presumption that the object of laying out money in such a work, is to invade the property of others, and thus to commit two improprieties; the first, in laying out money unprofitably upon a mine; and the second, in redeeming this expence out of the produce of a neighbour's mine. And as the latter is supposed to be carrying on his works agreeably to the ordinance, whilst the other, knowing the course of the vein, opens a pit and takes a mine where there is no ore, solely in the hope of finding an opportunity to rob his neighbour, it is clear, that let them meet where they may, such a mine must be stopped up, as fraudulently designed.

36. This penalty, of forfeiting the mine and restoring the ore, can only be exacted upon a judicial hearing of the cause; and it must be established that the fraudulent mine was taken with the sole view of making advantage of the property of the other. The evidence of this intention may be furnished by an examination of the fixed stake, to ascertain whether it have been opened upon a vein and upon ore, and whether the pit sunk, according to rule, is upon the vein. We recollect an instance of a certain mine, in

---

[*] Vide chap. 5, ord. 17. "Or finding the ore." " And where the ore produced was found." Chap. 8, ord. 22. " As they shall, from time to time, discover ore."

which, after being registered, a blessing was pronounced upon the ore ; and yet, as it was afterwards seen, all this outward appearance was merely intended to cover the real object of the work, which was solely that of taking advantage ·of the ore of a neighbour; for upon the arrival of the commissary, appointed by the audiency of Mexico, he ascertained that this pit was an improper one, opened in ground where there was no vein, a level having also been driven, under similar circumstances. It was therefore ordered, that the mine should be closed up, together with some other mines which had been opened in the mining district and mines of Guadalcazar, with a view to benefit by the ores of the mines of San Estanislao and Marquesate, belonging to Don Francisco de Mora, of which we have spoken elsewhere.*

37. Another case in which fraud and wrong intentions are presumed, is that in which a person registers a small and almost barren vein or branch, and after sinking upon it, and taking possession, deviates from his course, and drives a level in some other direction, in order to intercept his neighbour's works, and get access to his ores ; for in such a case it is evident, that the pit or vein being such as could not return the expenses of working, could only have been opened with the view of benefiting by the property of the neighbour.

38. Fraud, as existing only in the mind, and not being obvious to the sight, is difficult of proof, and can only be inferred from the antecedent and concomitant circumstances of the fact ;† and therefore, it being difficult to establish that the mine has been opened, *solely* for the purpose of stealing the ore, such an intention must be inferred from the attendant facts and circumstances, having regard to the character of the parties, the means they have had recourse to, the fact of the pit having been opened by any party interested in the adjoining mine, for the purpose of ascertaining the course of the vein ; and every other circumstance which bears upon the question, or which affords any ground to argue, that the pit or mine would not have been pened, but from a covetous desire to gain access to the other's property.

39. Another case which may occur, is that of a pit, or fixed stake, being opened upon ore, and works being prosecuted upon a vein of medium quality, sufficient to pay the expences, and of a level being subsequently driven in a direction deviating from that of the vein ; it being known that a neighbouring mine owner has been working in that direction. In such a case, although the mine is not to be stopped up, the works, generally, being prosecuted upon the vein, and upon ore of a quality to pay the expenses, yet it cannot be doubted but that the level, if driven in a different direction from that of the vein,

---

* Vide chap. 12, n. 46 ; and ubi sup. n. 9.

† Escobar, de ratiocin. cap. 1, n. 24. Matheu, de re criminali, controv. 63, num. 39. Menoch. lib. 5. præsumpt, 3, num. 102. Farinac. de falsitate et simulat. quæst. 162, n. 105, et in Praxi, tom. 3, quæst. 89. Casfill. lib. 3, cap. 1, n. 84.

which may be ascertained by simple inspection, is a fraudulent work. And consequently, if a neighbour, in prosecuting a direct work, should make his way into the *pertenencia* of a party driving such a level, and be intercepted by the level, the party driving it cannot call upon his neighbour to withdraw : for in this case, the meeting or communication occurs, not whilst prosecuting the works upon the proper vein of his mine, but whilst wrongfully endeavouring to intercept his neighbour, and to prevent him from enjoying the return of his diligence and merit. The fraudulent and covetous motives, then, by which he is instigated, being apparent, he ought to be restrained, for no one should be allowed to profit by his own fraud and evil intentions.

40. We recollect cases, in which the royal audiency of Mexico has ordered the levels and pits of certain fraudulent mines to be stopped up, it having been established, from the opinion of the surveyors, and from inspection, that the object of driving levels was fraudulent, and that they had been opened, merely because it was known that a neighbouring proprietor was at work upon the vein, and raising rich ore. And we remember other cases, in which, on the other hand, we have succeeded in obtaining a decision in favour of the levels and workings, establishing that they have been driven with proper views. An instance of the former occurred, in regard to a level driven, in the year 1746, in Sultepec, by Don Antonio Davila, into the mine of Don Joseph de Puebla ; and of the latter, in regard to one driven, in the year 1748, by Don Juan Moreno de Mesa, from his mine of San Antonio, in Guanaxuato, into the mine of Cabrera, belonging to Doña Francisca de Sardeneta ; of which we have spoken elsewhere.

41. And although malice might be imputed, when the vein is lost, as occasionally happens, which is called *emborascarse*, and in which state it may continue for the space of half a *vara*, a palm, or a finger ; or when barren and rough ground has been worked upon at intervals, or when cross cuts have been driven ; yet if the mine have been regularly worked from the fixed stake, in the direct pursuit of the vein, the fact will appear upon inspection, and it will be evident, that being worked in conformity with the rules of the ordinances, it cannot have been opened with the mere intention of intercepting and profiting by the ore of a neighbour.

42. It is very common for veins to lose themselves and become barren in this manner, in consequence of their meeting with hard bodies of rock which they cannot penetrate ; and it is then necessary to work indirectly. Every miner, therefore, is authorized to drive, within his own ground, such dead works as may be necessary to enable him to follow up the vein, when thus lost or barren ; and were it not so, it would be necessary, in cases of this kind, in which the works cannot be prosecuted without such dead works as cross-cuts, pits and indirect cuts, to suspend the working of the mines. For between the different veins there are always interposed spaces of barren ground, which must either be cut away,—a work of great expense, and to be spared if pos-

sible,—or must be avoided by altering the course of the works; and consequently, if such works, being driven with a view to explore the vein in the regular way, should communicate with those of a neighbouring miner, who has
worked beyond his limits, he must withdraw, and leave the first miner to enjoy
the produce of his own proper *pertenencia* : for the works, in this case, being
planned by the miner with the legitimate object of realising his own property, and the usual mode of working having been pursued by him, there is no
room for the inference, that the works have been driven with any fraudulent
view, or solely with that of getting access to the property of a neighbour.

43. Veins are liable to become barren, not only from solid masses, or banks
of ground being interposed ; but also because the ore collects together in particular places, leaving the others destitute, according to the nature of the
matrix and the quality of the ground. We have heard from some practical and
very experienced miners of the district of San Phelipe, called Chiguagua, in
the kingdom of New Biscay, and of the mining district of Zimapan, in the arch-
bishopric of Mexico, that there are instances in those districts, of a very remarkable description of matrix, in which cavities, or vaults, called *bobedales*, of large
extent, are found at intervals ; and that they are guided to these cavities by the
colour of the ground. Thus it is in the subterranean world ; veins are found to
have more variations, turnings and returnings, than could possibly be conceived,
were not the windings of their course developed in the progress of the works, and
made evident by the tortuous direction they are found to have taken. And hence
it is, that the under ground surveys are so troublesome, it being generally necessary, in order to make out the direction required, to wind through a series of turns,
and to make frequent angles in the survey. Whether the vein then conceal
itself, become barren, divide, lose itself, or be cut off or intercepted by barren ground, the miner may follow in pursuit of it, regulating his works conformably to the ordinances ; and so long as he works upon his own ground,
and in search of his own vein, it shall never be said, that, in what he has done,
it has been his sole view to get access to the vein of another, even though he
should, in the course of his works, fall in with such a vein.

44. It is no less certain, as experience demonstrates, that in driving a
cross-cut, or working in pursuit of the lost vein, it is very possible to fall in
with another vein, which may either be a principal vein, or a branch of the
former ; and if the miner, in pursuing this new vein, should encounter the
works of a neighbouring miner, his conduct cannot be impeached. For there
are, between one mineral vein and another, intermediate spaces, as in the
human body, or in a tree, which are the types of a mine ; and as in crossing
from one vein to another, or from one branch to another, though not following
the course of a vein or branch, the intermediate space crossed is considered
part of the same body or the same tree, so it is with regard to mineral veins :
for although in passing from one to another, an intervening space of ground
be crossed, yet the whole is regarded as one mine, just as the hand is one

hand, although it have five distinct and separate fingers.   We have already observed elsewhere, upon the authority of Agricola, Perez de Vargas and Kircher, to which we refer,[*] that veins may be deep, wide, curved or transverse, and that there are, between them, intervals or spaces of dead ground, not containing ore.   Were it otherwise, were the whole mine one contiguous vein, or mass of ore, there would be no occasion for dead works ; but this is not the nature of mineral veins, which are divided and dispersed like the veins of the body, or the·branches of a tree.

45. From the above it may be inferred, that if a miner, in the immediate pursuit of a vein, happen to communicate with the works of another miner, it cannot be argued that his views were fraudulent, or that. his object was solely to occupy a neighbour's ground, and to·benefit by his ore, even although the vein should be a different one from that which he had at first pursued, the latter having become barren.   For there may be a great variety of dif· ferent veins contained in the same mine, some being principal veins, some branches, some cross veins, or what not ; and as the miner registers, not only the principal pit, but all the·trial pits, both great and small, veins, and everything else contained within his *pertenencia*, he may take the produce of one or more veins, at pleasure, provided he conduct his works according to the ordinance.

46. The word *sole* or *solely*, is a qualifying, restraining and limiting word ; it confines the rule to the particular case of which it speaks, and implies, that the rule for all other cases will be the reverse.[†]   So that if the intention of the miner be not *solely* to profit by the ore his neighbour is pursuing—if that be not his object, or if, being his object, it be not his *sole* object ;—if, in registering his vein, his intention has been to explore it in a fair and honourable manner, sinking his pits, and driving his cross-cuts and other works according to the rules of the ordinance ;—then, should he happen to meet with another vein, and whilst working upon that, or upon his own vein, to communicate with the works of a neighbour, he is exempted from the penalty, as being a legitimate miner, working with fair and honourable views, and not with the sole object of getting access to his neighbour's ore.

47. Don Joseph Saenz, in discussing the second case to which this ordinance[‡] applies, says, that to justify entering a neighbour's *pertenencia*, you must be in the immediate pursuit of ore.   That if a pretended miner fraudulently intercept a neighbour, even in his own ground, the latter shall not be obliged to withdraw ; but that if a party, working with fair and honourable views, abandon a vein which has become barren, and find another, and afterwards happen to make a communication with a neighbour in his own *pertenencia*, each shall retire within his own boundaries, there being no fraud on either side.   And he explains, according to this doctrine, a passage in a

---

[*] Chap. 9, n. 16 and 17.

[†] Salgado, de retent. p. 2, cap. 17, n. 13, et seq. et apud eum innumeri.   Barbosa, dict. 97.

[‡] Saenz Trat. de medidas de minas, cap. 7, n. 22, et seq.

letter of the first of April, 1635, cited by Escalona.* The letter ordered, that the workings should be prosecuted immediately upon the vein, and that no intercommunications should be made. As however, it may be necessary, from the nature of the different veins, to drive works in search of them, to drive across from one to another, and to make various other works, Saenz considers that the necessity of being in immediate pursuit of ore, must be understood to apply to the case of a miner working into the *pertenencia* of his neighbour; but that to be entitled to stop the works of a neighbour, who makes his way into the ground of another miner, the latter not being a pretended miner merely, it is sufficient to effect a communication, whether by working upon some new vein, which has been met with, or upon the original vein when re-discovered, after being lost.

48. In addition to the above cases, we will suggest another, which is very likely to occur. It is that of a legitimate and not a pretended miner, (the vein originally prosecuted by whom has fallen into *borrasca*), who happens, whilst driving dead works within his own ground, in search of the vein, to effect a communication with a work which his neighbour is prosecuting upon ore. Here it is to be considered, that the miner is working conformably to the ordinances, that he is in his own ground and within his own boundaries, and that the dead works he is carrying on are within those boundaries, and are driven in search of the vein, which is the object he actually has in view, so that it cannot be said that his *sole* object is to avail himself of his neighbour's ore; and therefore, the communication having happened when both miners were working in the regular way, without any fraudulent views, it would seem that each of them must withdraw within his own limits. As, however, it is impossible to be prepared for every case which may occur, the judges must, in their best discretion, decide upon the fairness and unfairness of the miner's object, according to the particular facts of each case, having regard to the character of the parties, the distance of the mines from each other, the greater or less activity with which the works have been carried on, and all the other attendant circumstances.

49. In Peru, it is the rule, under their peculiar ordinances, set forth by Don Gaspar de Escalona,† that no one shall make a trial pit within another miner's boundaries, and that no one shall enter his neighbor's ground, under the pretence that he is pursuing a branch which takes off from his own mine; but that he shall stop his works as soon as he reaches his neighbour's boundaries; and so likewise, if he is in pursuit of a vein, which, although distinct from his own neighbour's vein and beyond the boundaries, yet evidently takes such a course as to pass within them; it being his duty to stop as soon as he arrives at those boundaries.

* Escalona, Gazophil. part 2, lib. 2, c. 1, ord. 6, tit. 4, concerning the spaces allotted for mines, in marg.

† Escalona, loc. ubi proxime. ord. 2, 3, 4 and 5, tit. concerning the spaces allotted for mines.

50. But that, if the principal vein of a mine should take its course within another's limits, it may be followed up without any impediment; and that if the two principal veins should happen to meet, so as to form one body, uniting in a work in active prosecution, the ore shall be divided into five parts, one of which shall be assigned to the owner or owners of the oldest mine, and the rest be divided amongst the owners, in proportion to their respective shares. And that if these two veins should unite with a third, the like course shall be pursued. Veins of this kind, which divide and re-unite, are called *socias*.

51. Also, that if the vein divide into branches before taking its course within the boundaries of the neighbouring mine, the owner shall select one of them, which he shall take as the principal vein, and in working upon which, he shall be at liberty to enter his neighbour's ground; but that until such selection be made, he shall not enter it in the pursuit of any of the branches.

52. And finally, that if the party so working into his neighbour's ground, shall discover any vein which the other proprietor has not previously discovered, the latter shall have one fifth part of the produce, and the former the remainder, until the vein unites with the principal one; but that if such vein shall have been previously discovered, and shall unite with the vein of the party so working into the other's ground, one fifth part of the produce shall be appropriated to the older proprietor, and the remainder be divided amongst all the proprietors, in proportion to their shares; and that if such vein be merely a branch running in a cross direction, the proprietor of the *pertenencia* shall be entitled to take the produce of it.

53. These regulations are agreeable to the civil law, and to the practice in the mines of Germany, as stated by Agricola, in the passages cited by Escalona;* but as they rather interfere, under some circumstances, with the active prosecution of the works, by directing that they shall not be carried on into a neighbour's ground; and, under other circumstances, have the effect of constituting a partnership amongst the proprietors of different veins, which would generally be a source of discord, we feel justified in saying, that our 30th ordinance provides better in the two cases suggested by it, for the prosecution of the works, and for the interests of the owners.

CHAPTER XV.

TO AUTHORISE THE REGISTERING A MINE IN THE NAME OF ANOTHER PERSON, IT IS NECESSARY THAT THE PERSON MAKING THE ENTRY, SHOULD EITHER BE THE HIRED SERVANT OF THE OTHER, OR HAVE A SPECIAL AUTHORITY FOR THE PURPOSE.—OF THE POWERS OF SERVANTS REGISTERING MINES FOR THEIR MASTERS.

ORDINANCES XXXII. XXXIII. XXXIV. LXVIII.

XXXII. Also, we ordain and command, that no person, be he of what

* Escalona, ubi supra.

condition he may, shall be at liberty to take a mine for another person, unless he have an authority, or be a servant receiving wages of the person for whom he shall take such mine ; and in default of any of these requisites, the mine shall be forfeited, and shall belong to any person who shall denounce it, and the judge shall immediately give possession thereof to the party making such denouncement ; without allowing any appeal on the part of the person in whose name such mine shall have been taken, or of him who shall have taken it.

XXXIII. Also, we ordain and command, that no steward who shall be employed in working or carrying on such mines, nor any other person who shall live with the owner of the mines, even though he may have charge of the mines and hands, shall be at liberty to alter the stakes which his employer may have set up, without his permission and authority, even although he should be called upon to set out such stakes ; and that if he shall alter them, or shall set them out anew, it shall avail nothing, and shall work no prejudice to the proprietor of such mine.

XXXIV. Also, we ordain and command, that where any such steward who shall have charge of any mines or of any reduction establishment, shall take or discover a mine, such steward shall be at liberty to stake out the mine or mines he may so take, and to set out the boundary stakes on the side of any party who may apply for that purpose, until such time as his employer shall visit such mines. But that after his employer, the owner of such mine or mines as aforesaid, shall have arrived, he shall not be at liberty to apply for, nor to set out boundary stakes any further ; and the steward or servant aforesaid shall not be at liberty to alter the boundary stakes which his said employer shall have set out or left fixed, without an authority from him.

LXVIII. Also, we ordain and command, that all persons who shall be appointed to attend to the working and carrying on of the aforesaid mines, either by our appointment or that of our district-administrator or administrators, or who shall in any manner receive a salary or pay from us for that purpose, shall be disabled from holding mines, or any share in them, either by themselves or through any other person acting for them, directly or indirectly, in the districts where they shall be employed in or work mines, or within two leagues around the same ; and if they shall take or have any mine or mines as aforesaid, or any share in them, whilst they shall receive our salary or pay as aforesaid, they shall forfeit such mine or mines, or share of mines, which shall go to any person who shall denounce the same ; and shall, moreover, be banished from the aforesaid mines and the space of six leagues around, for the term of three full years ; and they shall not break in upon that term, under the penalty, if of noble rank, of the said term of banishment being doubled ; and if of lower condition, of serving such three years in the galleys.

CONTENTS OF THE COMMENTARY ON THESE ORDINANCES.

COMMENTARY.

1. We may register mines not only by ourselves, but also through other persons, for, under the 32d ordinance, which follows the old ordinance, this is an act not requiring personal attendance. There seems a difficulty, however, in comprehending these ordinances ; for if, to authorise registering for another, an authority be required ; and if the receiving wages does not operate as an authority from the master, it must follow, either that a servant ought not, merely as receiving wages, to be permitted to make registry for his master, or that any person whatever ought to be permitted to register mines for another, even without an authority. In support of the latter alternative, in particular, it may be argued, that the acquisition of such an interest cannot be prejudical, even supposing the mine should afterwards be abandoned, and may prove an advantage should it turn out to be rich ; and it may be alleged, as a case in point, that it is permitted, as we have observed elsewhere, to make registry upon the authority of a letter,* should the discoverer be unable to proceed to the spot.

2. Notwithstanding which, it is necessary, to authorise registering for another, either to be his hired servant, or his agent, lawfully empowered ; for although service and wages do not necessarily confer an authority, yet they give occasion to presume that the transaction is under the master's orders, it being notorious that a steward or servant employed in the mines, cannot

* Vide chap. 5, n. 18 and 19.

take a mine for himself, within two leagues around, under pain of forfeiting the mine and of being banished, according to our 68th ordinance, now under consideration, which however, it is to be observed, applies to mines belonging the crown. But neither can a servant employed in the mines of an individual, register mines for himself, within the space of *one* league around, until the expiration of two years from the time of his quitting service ; and this under the old ordinance, which is still in force,[*] and which is doubtless intended to prevent servants setting up in opposition to their masters, and to prevent other frauds and irregularities on their part.[†]

3. A servant can only register for his master, unless he be in partnership with him or have his licence and permission, in which cases he may register for himself. And if he act otherwise, he is liable, besides the penalty of banishment, to forfeit the mine in favour of his master, if capable of holding it, or otherwise, of the exchequer; so that the mines taken by slaves or servants, belong to their masters, and the former cannot authorise other persons to occupy them. This is the rule of the old ordinance, which is still in force, nothing being ordered to the contrary by those of the new code. And the audiency of Guadalaxara has, in two instances, declared, that Don Juan Alonso Diaz de la Campa and the Count de San Matheo were respectively entitled to two mines, which their servants had registered at Zacatecas, on the ground of the ordinance being still in force,[‡] and of its being ordered by the law of the Indies to be observed.[§]

4. Whence it is evident, that a hired servant is authorised by the law and the ordinances, to register a mine for his master. And, in fact, as any mines which he registers for himself, fall to his master, and become his property, without any other person being at liberty to occupy them, much more may he register them expressly in the name of his master ; as there can be no fraud in registering for the benefit of the person to whom the law itself would transfer the mine, were it registered in the name of the servant. It is, consequently, matter of demonstration, that the character of a hired servant carries with it an authority to register mines in the name of the master ; which is one of the excepted cases in our 32d ordinance.

5. The other exception is that of an agent lawfully authorised, who is permitted to register a mine for another ; but a general power is not sufficient, it must be a special one, as under the ordinances of Peru ; for although in case of necessity, or any other impediment, affording a reasonable excuse,

---

[*] Ordinance 34, law 5, tit. 13, book 6. Collection of Castile.

[†] Ad tradita per Antunez, de donat, p. 3, cap. 4, n. 17. Zaulis, observ. ad rub. 12, lib. 2, tom. 1, n. 14.

[‡] Ord. 34, law 5, tit. 13, book 6, Collection of Castile.

[§] Law 5, tit. 19, book 4, Collection of the Indies. "We ordain and command, that the particular laws and ordinances concerning mines shall be observed, fulfilled and enforced ; and that in fulfilling the same, that law shall be enforced which ordains, that servants shall register the mines they may discover, for their masters, and not in their own name."

the registry may be made upon the authority of a letter, yet it must be ratified within forty days.[*] Don Joseph Saenz observes, that according to the ordinances of Castile, the authority must be special, for many legal reasons, which he passes over, but which is evident enough.[†]

6. The first of the reasons is, that the act of registry not only gives a property in the mine, but renders the owner liable to the penalties of the law, which he may incur in various ways, as may be seen by referring to the penal ordinances.[‡] And there can be no doubt, that to charge a person with obligations, and to make him liable to penalties, a special authority is required, as is shewn by Pareja and Cyriac, upon the authority of several texts, and of Bartolus, Suarez de Paz, Rebuffo, Farinacius, Menochius and Gratianus.[§]

7. The second reason is, that besides being the rule in Peru, that the discoverer shall declare upon oath, what persons were engaged in the search with him, and that the ore he produces is the very same that he has raised from the mine he is desirous of registering;[||] it is required also, in New Spain, that the ore shall be produced in the same manner; and that, at any rate, an oath shall be taken, that no wrongful design is entertained; for each of which purpose, it is necessary, according to Pareja, in the place above-cited, and to Covarrubias, Solorzano and Rosenthal,[¶] to have a special authority.[**]

8. Third, the miner takes upon himself the expense of registry, of sinking the mine to the proper depth, and of keeping it at work; but his funds cannot be engaged, nor he himself be rendered liable to pay, without a special authority.[**]

9. Fourth, an authority of this kind is required for the purpose of receiving possession, according to the doctrine of Solorzano, in reference to grants of land from the crown; where he says that a general authority, with the

---

[*] Ord. 5. tit. 1, concerning discoverers; Escalona, Gazoph. lib. 2, part. 2, cap. 1, pag. 105. "The discoverer may make registry by means of a special authority, empowering the doing all. that is contained in the ordinance."

[†] Saenz, Trat. de medidas de minas, cap. 2, n. 20.

[‡] See chap. 5, n. 21, and in the margin.

[§] Pareja, de instr. edit. tit. 6, resol. 3, n. 51. " Sed sic est quod procurator nil potest facere absque speciali mandato, per quod dominus incidat in pœnam, ut tradit. Barth. communiter receptus in L. si procurator, n. 6 et 7, ff. de condict. indebit. Suarez de Paz, in Prax. 6, part. tom. 1, cap. unic. n. 1. Rebuff. in Tract. de accusat. art. 1, gl. 1, n. 2, and 3. Farinac. part. 2. Fragment. criminal. litt. J. n. 704. Jacob. Menoch. cons. 127, n 8, et cons. 718, n. 2. Steph. Gratian· Discept. for. cap. 105, n. 21." Cyriac. Controv. 239 et 327, n. 11.

[||] Escalona, Gazoph. lib. 2, part. 2, cap. 1, pag. 106.

[¶] Pareja, ubi sup. n. 51 et 52. Covarrub. in C. quamvis pactum, de pact. in 6. 1, part. §. 5. a n. 19; et 1, var. cap. 6, n. 2, post med. Solorzan. in Polit. lib. 3, cap. 14, n. 19, in fin. Rosenthal, de feud. cap. 3. conc. 9.

[**] Cap. qui ad agendum, de proc. in 6, ubi Gloss. verbo *Pacisci:* et inibi enumerantur casus in quibus speciale exigitur mandatum.

clause, *cum libera*, is not sufficient, although Rosenthal, in his work on feuds considers it sufficient.*

10. The fifth, and principal reason is founded on its being the great object of the ordinances to prevent fraud, to distibute the mines amongst a variety of persons, and to assure the right of each proprietor ; for the person making registry might be induced to make use of some other person's name, from his being himself one of those who are prohibited from taking mines, or, being capable of taking mines, he might yet, under cover of another person's name, take a greater number of mines than is allowed ; and it might also happen, even supposing the mine to be really taken for another person, that the latter might elude his obligations, and avoid the penalties of the ordinance, by alleging that he had given no order or authority for taking the mine.

11. And as the object of the 32d ordinance is to guard against such frauds as these, and others of a like nature, which might be practised, it requires an authority to be given, which must be special, to shew with certainty in whom the right is vested, and to shut out every opportunity of fraud : but the law is satisfied, if the registry be made by a hired servant in the name of his master, to whom, all mines taken by the servant, in any other name, are made over by the law. But if he be not an agent especially authorised, or a hired servant, the mine is liable to be denounced, and shall be adjudged and given in possession to the party denouncing it, and shall by no means revert, either to the party who has taken it, or to him in whose name it may have been taken ; such being the penalty imposed, if the requisite that the party registering shall be furnished with an authority, or be a hired servant, be wanting :—" In default of any of these requisites."

12. And although there is an ambiguity in these words, which convey the idea, that it is necessary that the party should be a hired servant, and should likewise have an authority, to enable him to make registry for the other ; yet they must evidently be construed with reference to the disjunctive sentence preceding, " Unless he have an authority, or be a servant receiving wages ;" for the rule, sometimes sanctioned, of construing a disjunctive as a conjunctive, and *vice versa*, clearly cannot apply in this case, where the subject matter will not admit of it, as it is impossible to entertain a doubt, that any person may, by virtue of a special authority, make registry for another, without being a servant, and that, under the 33d of the old ordinances, a servant may register a mine for his master, without a special authority for that purpose.

13. A question might be raised, whether a mine can be registered for another person, security being given, that the transaction shall be ratified, and whether it would be liable to be denounced during the term, under the penalty declared in the 32d ordinance ? We reply, that although

* Solorz. ubi proxim. sub eod. n. 19.

the ratification of an act is regarded as equal to a previous authority to perform it,* and security is very commonly allowed to be given in other matters,† yet it must be observed that this is the case with regard to matters which require a general authority only, and not a special one, such as is required for the purpose of registering a mine ; for, as is shewn by Covarrubias, from several texts and authorities,‡ the law will not presume the special assent of the absent party.

14. The judge therefore, must not allow registry to be made in the name of another person (unless a third servant or slave, who must necessarily acquire the property for his master), without a special authority, this being a formality required by the ordinance, and thereby made so essential, that its omission incurs the penalty of irrecoverably forfeiting the mine. But if the judge do in fact, and contrary to law, allow the registry to be made, it will be good, provided it be ratified whilst the transaction is still unimpeached ; that is to say, provided no one have denounced the mine in the interim : but should any one, in the mean time, denounce it, he has a just right to do so ; and the law and the ordinance, being framed for this particular case, and imposing certain terms and conditions which ought to have been fulfilled in the specific form directed, and at the specific time prefixed,—which is that of making registry,—must take their course. This however, will not apply in case of any evident and reasonable impediment, which exception we have noticed when treating of registry.§

15. The question may also be raised, whether a general authority, with a clause for free and general administration, is sufficient for the purpose of registry ? We reply that it is not ; for although many authors are of opinion that in matters requiring a special authority, a general power, with a clause, *cum libera*, is sufficient, yet others consider this clause merely as a form of the notaries, and conceive that, not being a disposing clause, it has no enlarging operation ; insomuch, that it is subject to many limitations, thirty-two of which are enumerated by Barbosa, and some also by Fragoso, as may be seen in the places cited by Pareja.‖ And there being a penalty in question, and the law requiring the greatest certainty in the party making registry,¶ the clause of free and general admission is not sufficient ; but a special power is necessary, as removing all doubt, and not leaving room for any kind of

---

* L. 10, tit. 34, part. 7. L. 1. §, si ratum, 6, ff. quod jussu, cap. ratihabitionem, 10, de r. j. in 6. Innumeri apud Vela, dissert. 38, n. 50.

† L. 10, tit. 5, part. 5, L. sed et hæ, in princ. ff. de procur.

‡ Covarrub. 1, var. cap. 6, u. 5. L. patri pro filio, ff. de minor. L. filius, Cod. de pact. L. qui hominem, §. gener. ff. de solut. L. non solum, ff. de solut. mat. L. qui aliena, §. quamquam, ff. de negot. gestis.

§ Chap. 5, n. 20.

‖ Pareja, de instr. edit. tit. 5, resol. 10, n. 66.

¶ Chap. 5, ord. 17, " The person who has made the discovery and registry." And chap. 6, ord. 20, " No person shall presume to enter in the register a mine which is not his own."

uncertainty, which, as we have before observed, is agreeable to the opinion of Solorzano, in reference to grants of land from the crown.*

16. Having established then, that a mine may be registered by an agent specially authorised, or a hired servant, the 33d and 34th ordinances (which follow the 35th and 36th of the old ones,) proceed to enact three provisions. First, that the steward may measure out and set out boundary stakes for such mines as he shall take, until his employer shall visit the mines. And this is reasonable, for a person who has authority to perform the precedent act that is to say, the registry, must have authority to perform the act necessarily consequent, that is to say, to measure out the mine, and set out boundary stakes; † and since a servant is authorised to make registry, he is also authorised to apply to have the boundaries set out, or to set them out as he may think proper.

17. Secondly, they provide, that after the arrival of his master, the servant can no longer apply for, or set out boundary stakes, nor, without his master's authority, alter the position of such as the former may have set out, or left set out. The reason is, that the master being the lawful owner, his acts cannot be impugned or varied by the servant or steward, without a special authority; and that the latter being bound to obey, has no power or right to act in opposition to his master, much less in a matter of so much moment as that of altering the boundaries; for it may happen that the greater number of *varas* are taken in the more barren direction, and the smaller number, or none at all, in the more fruitful one; on one side the ground may happen to be barren, on the other it may produce the richest ores of silver and gold; and if, in the alteration in the boundaries, it should turn out that barren ground has been taken, and silver and gold relinquished, the mischief is considerable. The owner then, alone, as arbiter and manager of his own affairs, is competent to do this; but if he himself, or a party who has his special power and authority to do it, should act erroneously, he must take the whole blame upon himself. Without such an authority therefore, the steward cannot alter the boundary stakes which his employer may have set out or have left set out, on his absenting himself a second time, after visiting the mine.

18. The third provision is, that even if required to set out the boundary stakes, neither the steward, nor any other person living with the owner of the mines, even though he have charge of the mine and hands, can vary or alter the boundary stakes, without a licence and authority; the master being at liberty to insist on the nullity of such an act, and being by no means prejudiced in consequence of it. And the reasons are the same as set forth in the preceding section; with this further reason, that the steward not being the owner, is not the party who should be required to set out the bounda-

* Vide ubi supr. n. 4.
† Ex trita regula, qui vult consequens, vult antecedens.

ries.   The master himself therefore, ought to be called upon to do this act, and he ought to be summoned personally, if he be on the spot, or within the distance of ten leagues, agreeably to the ordinance,* and any thing done, without summoning the lawful owner, is void, and cannot operate to his pre-judice.   And the master being the person who ought to be called upon and summoned, the steward cannot act for him without a special power and authority; the right of altering the boundaries, and of taking a greater or less number of *varas,* in this or that direction, upon which may depend the acquisition or loss of great riches being one which is not to be given up or relinquished, except under his special licence and authority.†

19. But hence arises the following difficulty, namely, supposing the mine to be staked out, and the owner to be absent at a greater distance than the ten leagues limited in the 24th ordinance, can the steward alter the bound-ary stakes, if required to be set out on some side or sides, on which the owner has not set them out?   The answer is, that he cannot do so without a special licence and authority, and that he must advise his employer within the term of fifteen days, allowed by the same ordinance; but that if he shall not do so, then the owner of the mine must take the blame upon him-self, for not having left him an authority to vary the boundaries, when he must have been aware that the boundary stakes might be required to be set out on any side.   Besides, if, having the opportunity of leaving such an au-thority, he has chosen to absent himself at a great distance, without doing so, it is a sign that he did not think it worth while.   And finally, it being quite clear that the 33d and 34th ordinances prohibit his altering the stakes which his employer may have set out, he can have no authority to change them, without a special order for that purpose.

20. Neither is this opinion affected by the 24th ordinance, according to which, when the owner is absent at more than ten leagues distance, the applica-tion to have the boundaries set out is to be notified to the mayor, and a procla-mation is to be posted up and published; for this ordinance applies to the case when the owners of mines not yet staked out, are called upon to set out their boundaries, in which case a summons is served upon the steward, at his employer's house, or at the church, and proclamation is made, that he may be informed of it, and may set out the boundaries within fifteen days, in de-fault of which they are to be set out by the justice.   In this case, the mine not being staked out, it is reasonable that the steward should, during the absence of his employer, set out such boundaries as he may think proper, and afterwards advance or alter them, either under his authority, if he can procure it within the term, or without such authority, if, from his employer

---

* Chap. 10, supra, ord. 24.

† Vela, dissert. 38, n. 84, ubi juribus et D D. probat non posse fieri novationem absque speciali domini mandato.   Olea de cess. jur. tit. 2, q. 6, n. 24 et 25.   Quod procurator etsi liberam habeat administrationem, cedere non potest, neque donare.

being at a great distance, or from any other serious impediment, it be impossible to procure: and the owner not having left the boundaries set out, the steward does not, in this case, undo anything his employer has done, or alter or vary the boundary stakes after their position has been approved and inspected by the latter (which is what our ordinance prohibits), but he sets out the boundaries originally, for the benefit of the mine, and he is served with the notice and summons, that he may advise his employer and defend the rights of the mine. And it is reasonable, that a party allowed to register a new mine for his master, should also be at liberty to set out the boundaries, when the latter has not done so; it being irregular, when a mine is registered, to leave the boundaries undefined, and it being impossible that any one can be better qualified to defend the rights of the miner, or to assign the most desirable boundaries, than the steward or curator of the mine: and the act of the steward, in thus staking out the boundaries of the mine, can never be impugned by his employer, when done in compliance with the ordinance, and upon the requisition of another party.

21. But in the case in question, the circumstances are the very reverse; for it is there supposed, that the owner has left the boundaries set out; and if, being aware that the surrounding miners might require the boundary stakes to be set out on the other sides, he has not left any authority to alter them, he must take the blame upon himself, and it must be considered as an indication, that he is satisfied with the boundaries he has left regularly set out: and therefore the steward cannot alter them, without an order or authority: nor can he counteract the will and act of his master, on pretence of his being under any impediment, either real or alleged. In a word, when the mine has not been staked out, it may be interpreted to be the will of the owner that it should be staked out; but when he has left the boundary stakes set out, his will must be interpreted to be the very reverse, unless he leave some further order for the purpose. Upon which point we have already touched, in treating of the 24th ordinance, to which we refer.*

CHAPTER XVI.

OF THE DEPTH OF THREE *ESTADOS*, TO WHICH THE MINES ARE REQUIRED TO BE SUNK, AND OF THE TERM ALLOWED FOR SINKING IT.—OF THE CASES WHICH ARE EXEMPTED FROM THIS OBLIGATION—A MINE CANNOT BE SOLD UNTIL SUNK TO THIS DEPTH—OF THE FORMALITIES REQUIRED IN SELLING MINES SUNK TO THE PROPER DEPTH.—WHETHER THERE BE ANY REMEDY IN CASE OF *LESION ENORME*,† IN

---

* Supr. chap. 10, num. 7.

† *Lesion enorme* is a fraud to the amount of somewhat more or less than one half the just price of the thing sold; and which, in ordinary cases, renders the sale liable to be annulled.

SALES OF THIS CLASS OF PROPERTY.—OF THE OTHER CONTRACTS WHICH MAY BE MADE CONCERNING MINES, ESPECIALLY THE PRECARI. OUS GIFT OR LOAN.*

ORDINANCES XXXV. XXXVI. XLII.

XXXV. Also, we ordain and command, that all persons whatsoever who shall hold, take or acquire mines, whether already discovered or hereafter to be discovered, shall be obliged, within the term of three months, reckoning from the day on which they shall register such mines, to sink in such mines, if they be new, one of the trial pits which they shall have made therein, or if old, then one of the pits therein, which shall contain a vein or ore, to the depth of three *estados*, each *estado* being seven thirds of a *vara* in length; under the penalty, if they shall not sink, or have sunk the aforesaid three *estados*, at the expiration of such three months, of forfeiting the mines, which shall be for any person who shall denounce them; and our mining justice shall immediately put the party so denouncing, into possession, subject to the same obligation of sinking the aforesaid three *estados*, within the term aforesaid, notwithstanding any appeal or question of nullity or injustice that may be interposed or raised.

XXXVI. Also, forasmuch as it is provided and commanded by the ordinance preceding this, and by some others of these our ordinances, that such persons as shall take or hold mines, or purchase or become possessed of them in any other manner, shall be obliged to deepen such mines according to what is contained in said ordinances; and whereas our intention and will is, to prevent suits and differences, and to obviate fraud:—We declare and command, that it shall be understood that they are obliged, if they can, to deepen the aforesaid trial pits or other pits, or otherwise to incur the penalties of the aforesaid ordinances. But if they should omit to deepen them, not through their own default, but from some accidental circumstance, or from its being more expedient to proceed in pursuit of the ore, which may take its course in some other direction, and should continue to work as may be most expedient and advantageous, they shall not become liable to, nor incur the penalties aforesaid, provided that, when this shall be the case, they shall be obliged to give notice thereof to the district-administrator, within whose district such mine shall be, that an inquiry may be made, whether their hav-

---

See Institutes of the civil law of Spain, &c. translated by L. F. C. Johnston, p. 220. *Lesion. enormisima* is a fraud to the amount of considerably more than one half the just price.—*Trans.*

* A precarious loan is a loan "of things to be used at the will and discretion of the person who lends." Institutes of the civil law of Spain, &c. translated by L. F. C. Johnston, p. 181. The definition of the *precarium* of the civil law, given in the digest, appears better adapted to the author's meaning, L. 1, ff. de precar. "Precarium est quod precibus pretenti utendum conceditur, tamdiu quamdiu is qui concessit patitur.—§. 2. Et distat a donatione, eo quod qui donat sic dat, ne recipiat, at qui precario concedit, sic dat, quasi tunc recepturus cum sibi libuerit precarium solvere —§. 3. Et est simile commodato, nam et qui commodat rem, sic commodat, ut non faciat rem accipientis, set ut ei uti re commodata permittat."—*Trans.*

ing failed to comply with the aforesaid ordinances, was on account of such circumstance as aforesaid, or of their having proceeded in pursuit of such ore as aforesaid; or through their own default. Whereupon, after making such inquiry, the administrator shall make such declarations and provisions as may be proper, in such manner that when the inconvenience is removed, the mines aforesaid may be deepened according to the provisions of the aforesaid ordinances.

XLII. Also, forasmuch as it might happen that persons taking mines might sell or deal with them, without working them, or ascertaining whether they contained ore, and might proceed to take others for the same purpose, whence divers inconveniences might ensue; to avoid the same, we command, that no one shall be at liberty to sell, deal with or purchase any mine, unless it have been sunk to the depth of three *estados* at least, under the penalty of forfeiting what may have been given for the mine, to be applied as is before mentioned, and likewise of forfeiting such mine, which shall be for the party who shall denounce it, subject to the same obligation of sinking to the aforesaid depth of three *estados*. And if the mine so sold or dealt with, shall have been sunk such three *estados*, then, in order to authorise such sale or dealing, the purchaser thereof shall be obliged to give notice of the same to the justice aforesaid, that it may be entered in the book of registry, and he shall send an authenticated copy thereof to the aforesaid district-administrator, that it may be noted in the book, and that it may be known from whom the duty is to be levied; which shall be done and performed under the penalty aforesaid; and the like, if there be, in any other manner, a change in the ownership of such mine.

CONTENTS OF THE COMMENTARY ON THESE ORDINANCES.

1. Of the depth of three *estados*, required to be sunk in mines; the term within which it is to be sunk, and the penalty for omiting to sink it.
2. Reasons for this provision of the ordinance; the object being, that the mines may be more completely worked.
3. The three months within which it is to be done, are one contiguous period.
4. The quality of the ore is generally ascertained within the depth of three *estados*.
5 and 6. It is not necessary to sink to this depth, when the vein is tortuous, spreading or inclined.
7. But recourse must be had to the justice, to obtain a declaration, that the obligation may be dispensed with.
8. Accidental and unavoidable circumstances, may also remove the necessity for sinking to this depth.
9. Such as the hardness of the vein, or the rising of spring water.
10. The falling of the pit or other works, famine, pestilence or war.
11. In such cases, possession is to be given by the judge, without this depth being sunk.
12. A mine of less depth than this cannot be sold, under pain of forfeiting the mine and the price.

13. Of the formalities attending the sale of a mine sunk to the proper depth. Whether the purchasers must sink afresh, like a party making denouncement?

14. Reply in the negative. Distinction between a denouncer and a purchaser.

15. Nor does the 42d ordinance require, that on the purchase of a mine sunk to the proper depth, it should be further deepened.

16. The value of mines is arbitrary, and is matter of opinion.

17. In such sales the remedy for *lesion enorme* or *enormisima*, does not apply. An ordinance of Peru, conclusive on the subject.

18. Because the profit and loss are eventual and contingent.

19. A mine may be given as a marriage portion, may be hypothecated, &c.

20 and 21. Whether a mine can be the subject of a precarious gift or loan? Reflections upon an executory decree of the royal audiency of Mexico, made in a suit instituted by Don Pedro Romero Terreros, against the Marquess de Valle-Ameno, in the mining district of el Monte.

22. A mine may be made the subject of a precarious gift or loan, if there be a special agreement to such effect.

23. An ordinance of Peru, as to sinking mines to a certain depth.

COMMENTARY.

1. These ordinances, which follow[*] the 37th, 38th and 45th of the old ordinances respectively, treat of the depth to which mines must be sunk, to prevent their being liable to denouncement or forfeiture. The law directed, originally, that they should be sunk to the depth of three *estados*, within six months from the time of registry.[†] This rule, however, has since been altered, the time having been reduced, by the 37th of the old ordinances, and the 35th of the new code, to three months. In mines newly registered, this depth is to be sunk in any one of the trial pits, upon which it may be convenient to the miner to set up his fixed stake; and in old mines which have been denounced, in any one of the pits, under the penalty, after the expiration of the term, of forfeiting the mine, which is to be adjudged and given in possession to the party making denouncement, notwithstanding any appeal; but subject, in his hands, to the same obligation of sinking to the depth of three *estados*, within three months from the adjudication.

2. The object of this most reasonable provision is stated by the law,[‡] in these words :—" Forasmuch as the discoverers of mines, after they may thus have discovered and registered them, might claim to have acquired, by these means alone, such a right as to prevent any other person from entering within the limits of such mines, or from trying or working the same, and might thus keep them in an unserviceable state; not working them themselves, and not leaving others at liberty to work them, whereby the principal benefits and advantages which are derived, both by ourselves and our subjects generally, would be counteracted, such benefits and advantages depending

[*] Law 5, tit. 13, book 6, Collection of Castile.

[†] Law 4, tit. 13, book 6, Collection of Castile.

[‡] Law 4, tit. 13, book 6, chap. 6.

mainly on the mines and ores being kept. at work, and not merely on their being discovered ; therefore, we declare, &c."

3. Whence it follows, that the object of the law, in limiting the term to three months, is, that the digging and working of the mines shall be more actively carried on. These three months must be reckoned continuously, and moment by moment, from the day of registry, as being a term defined by law, and not properly admitting of being interrupted or varied, as we have observed to be the rule in such cases. Were no precise term fixed, it would follow, that a discoverer or purchaser, might hold many mines without working them ; keeping some in reserve, until he had tried his fortune in others, contrary to the intention of the sovereign, who desires that the discovery and working of the ores should be conducted with as much activity as possible ; and so much so, that he grants to the miner who works beyond his limits, the ore he may raise from his neighbour's mine, until he communicates with his workings ; as we have seen in its place.*

4. The reason of directing that three *estados* at least, each of the length of seven thirds of a *vara*, making seven Castilian *varas*, shall be sunk, is, that at this depth the vein usually displays itself, and bears a decided character, the quality of its ore appearing with greater certainty than at first. This is found by experience to be the case, and is also mentioned by Don Luis Berrio de Montalvo, in his report to the Count de Salvatierra, where he observes, that this is the reason of the discoverer of a mine being obliged, by the law of the realm, to sink it to the depth of three *estados*.† For although the veins exhibit themselves on the surface, sometimes by their crests, sometimes by stripes of red, or of some colour different from that of the ground, sometimes by fumes of iron ochre and sulphur, and sometimes by white spar ; yet, in exploring the veins distinguished as deep veins, by means of a pit, the strength or richness of the vein is usually discovered, at the depth of about three *estados*.

5. This depth of three *estados* is very proper for deep veins, such as those above referred to in which the works may be carried on perpendicularly downwards ; but as veins of other classes, as tortuous, winding or spreading veins, often occur, the course of which latter is inclined or underlying, as we have elsewhere remarked,* whilst some form horizontal and superficial beds, which are, as it were, the overflowings of some principal vein, which has burst out at that part (and which, by tracing up the former, may often be discovered, but as often cannot, from masses of rock intervening,) it is evident that the miner would be spending his money in vain, were he obliged, when the vein is inclined, to sink a pit of seven *varas* di-

* Chap. 14. n. 29.
† D. Luis Berrio de Montalvo, Informe al Conde de Salvatierra sobre el beneficio nuevo de metales, cap. 6, pag. 10, circa fin.
‡ Chap. 9, n. 16 and 17.

rectly downwards upon it, as, instead of ore, he would be working upon dead ground, contrary to the object of the ordinances.

6. To provide for this case, the 36th ordinance of the new code and the 38th of the old ordinances establish, that if it be expedient to proceed in pursuit of the ore, from its taking its course in some other direction, as is frequently the case, the miner shall not incur the penalties enacted, both be-cause he is in no default in omitting to sink to the required depth, and because the vein, proceeding in an inclined or spreading direction, the law can-not compel him to sink in a manner repugnant to the very nature of the vein, whilst it is convenient and desirable that he should carry on his works in an inclined direction upon the underlay, the object of raising the ore, which is chiefly looked to by the law, being thus attained.

7. But in this case, the miner must have recourse to the justice, that after investigating the correctness of the fact, and ascertaining that the miner is in no default, in not sinking to the full depth, he may make such provision as may be expedient; which means no more than that he may en-large the term, so far as may be required, for carrying on the workings, in pursuit of the ore so taking its course as aforesaid;* until at length, either the obstacle itself cease to exist, or the workings of the mine begin to ex-tend in length and depth at the same time, agreeably to the example we have given in treating of the internal measurements of mines.

8. The 36th ordinance also provides, that the miner shall be exempted from the penalty, if the omission to sink to this depth, arise from any acci-dental circumstance; but he must give an account to the justice in the same manner, that after examining into the reality of the impediment, he may make such provision as may be proper; and whenever the obstacle is re-moved, the miner will be obliged to sink to the depth required, according to the usual rule in regard to acts, the performance of which is suspended; for when the impediment ceases to exist, the obligation is revived. The or-dinance merely says generally, "From some accidental circumstance, or because it may be more convenient to proceed in pursuit of the ore," with-out specifying the nature of the accidental circumstances to which it alludes. There are however, several circumstances, which being of occasional, though not frequent occurrence, must be regarded as accidental, and which require some consideration with reference to this question, for the govern-ment of the miner, and that he may be enabled to avoid the penalty.

9. The first is, when a vein of rare and extraordinary hardness is met with. Now as the pit is usually narrow, and the ordinance does not require a greater number of hands than four persons to be set on, as we shall see in treating of the next ordinance; this must be considered as a reasonable impediment, it being sometimes impossible to overcome such a degree of

---

* "Dilatio potest dari post primam, toties quoties opus est, causa cognita." L. oratione; et ibi Gloss. 2, ff. de feriis.

hardness, within ninety days. Secondly, where springs of water break out (whence, as some are of opinion, the name of vein is derived, from the resemblance to those of the human body) ; in this case, the lower levels become inundated, and it is impossible to work them, until the accomplishment of the draining by means of engines employed for the purpose ; which generally requres preparation, expense, and a longer period than three months : and it will often happen, that the draining, though commenced immediately upon denouncing the mine, is carried on for a long time, without its being found possible to sink to the required depth in any of the pits, from their being under water. In the mines of Porco and Verenguela, in Peru, the ground being porous, and the difficulty of carrying on the works in face of the water being very great, they are only allowed to be denounced, for insufficient working, in the months of December, January, Febuary and March, during which alone it is practicable to carry on the works.[*]

10. The third case is, when there is a falling in of the pit, or of the other works, or piillars of support ; during the timbering and repairing of which, the sinking upon the vein cannot proceed. The fourth is, the occurrence of war, mortality or famine, at the place, or within twenty leagues around ; for in such case, the ordinances do not even require the number of four per-sons to be kept at work ; and consequently the obligation to proceed in sinking, is no longer in force. And so in several other cases, which no foresight can provide for, and in which, if there be no fault or omission on the part of the miner, he should not incur the penalty ; and a person who should, in a case of this kind, denounce the mine, on the ground of its not being sunk to the proper depth, should be resisted, as being actuated by malice, upon the judge ascertaining, as required by the ordinances, that the circumstances were accidental and unavoidable, and that the miner had it not in his power to overcome the impediment. And although suits, upon denouncements of this description, for not sinking to the proper depth, rarely or never occur in the tribunals, it is by no means unnecessary to provide for such cases, their non-occurrence, at present, being attributable, either to the abundance of the mines, or the tolerance of the justices, who ought, in conformity with the so often repeated direction of the ordinances, to urge the works, in order to stimulate to a more brisk course of working in the mining districts.

11. We recollect to have remarked in another place, that upon its being ascertained that the mine has been sunk to the proper depth, possession may be demanded and given, at the end of three months from the registry ; so that it would seem that without sinking it, the miner acquires no right to be put in possession as lawful owner, having failed to comply with the condition imposed by the ordinance, when conferring the right of property and dominion. But, as in the case of the veins being inclined, or of the occurrence of

---

[*] Ord. 10, tit. 7, concerning insufficient working ; Escalona, Gazophil, lib. 2, p. 2 cap. 1, pag. 117.

any accidental circumstances, operating as obstacles, the law dispenses with, or suspends the necessity for sinking to the required depth, the miner may, in such cases, demand, and the judge must give, possession of the mine.

12. From all that has been said, we may collect how just and reasonable are the provisions of the 42d ordinance of the new code, and the 45th of the old ordinances, which prohibit the sale of a mine or any dealing in it, until the three *estados* be sunk, under the penalty of forfeiture of the mine, and of the vendor losing the price which might be given for it, the mine being open to denouncement. And this,—First, from his not having acquired a perfect right of possession and property, by sinking the required depth, which, as mentioned above, is a condition prescribed by the ordinance. Second, because the vendor should not be enriched with what is not his own. Third, because mines are not subject to be dealt in, or reckoned as the property of the subject, until sunk to the proper depth. Fourth, because, as the ordinance observes, it is the practice to sell some mines and take others, with a view to sale, without ascertaining whether they contain ore or not, which is a manifest fraud upon the purchaser, who incautiously falls into the snare, not seeing that he might denounce other mines of equally good quality, and demand to have them adjudged to him and forgetting that he may be giving either a very high, or a very low price, as it may turn out. And finally, because the ordinances being framed with great strictness (as is evident from the time being now limited to ninety days instead of the more enlarged term of six months, formerly allowed), it would be a fraud upon them to sell the mines within that term, without having observed the conditions which they require.

13. The 42d ordinance proceeds to provide, under the same penalty, that upon selling or dealing with a mine sunk to the proper depth, the purchaser shall give notice to the justice, that the transaction may be registered. And so, if a change in the ownership of the mine occur in any other mode. The object of this rule has been stated when treating of registry ;* it is, that it may appear with certainty in whom the right of property is vested, and from whom the crown dues are to be recovered : but the question here occurs, whether the purchaser of a mine sunk to the proper depth, is himself required to deepen it three *estados* further ? And whether a person succeeding to the possession of the mine, under other circumstances, is obliged to do the same ; in like manner as a person to whom it is adjudged for insufficent working, and who is bound to do it, notwithstanding its having been sunk before ? This question arises, particularly with reference to the opening of the 36th ordinance, where it is stated, that forasmuch as it is provided and commanded, by the 35th ordinance preceding, and by other ordinances, that such persons as shall take, hold or purchase mines, or become

* Vide chap. 5, u. 9.

possessed of them in any other manner, shall be obliged to sink, &c. From which preamble it might be inferred, that every new possessor is obliged to sink to this depth.

14. Notwithstanding this, the contrary must be taken to be the law; namely, that a purchaser or any other party, lawfully succeeding to the rights of the former possessor, upon acquiring a mine sunk to the depth required by the 42d ordinance, is not obliged to sink a further depth of three *estados*, within the term of three months from the date of his entry into possession, and of the registry of his title of succession; but that the depth that has been sunk by his lawful antecessor in title, shall avail for him, and that he shall be at liberty to proceed with the workings as he may find most convenient, the mine not being liable to denouncement, but being viewed as if it were still in the possession of his predecessor, to whose real and personal rights, in respect of the mine, he has succeeded. The reason of which is, that the priority of the registry is computed from the time of the first possessor, and through all the subsequent ones, who deduce their title from him, as we have explained elsewhere;* and therefore, the mine having been sunk to the proper depth by the predecessor, from whom the title is deduced, it is not proper that a new obligation to do so, should be imposed on his successor, who is not to be regarded, for this purpose, as a new person, but as one and the same with the person from whom he deduces his origin and title. But, with regard to the new denouncer of an old mine, which has been once sunk to the proper depth, the case is just the reverse; for such a party is by no means the lawful successor of the person who has left the mine insufficiently worked, or who has otherwise incurred the penalty of forfeiture, under the ordinances; but is a new possessor, under a new title, granted him by the ordinance, by virtue of his denouncement and registry, from the date of which the priority of his right is to be computed; the mine being considered as a new mine, in his hands, and he himself being regarded as a new proprietor, which we have before remarked in another place.†

15. Nor does the 42d ordinance make it obligatory upon the purchaser of a mine sunk to the proper depth, to sink it anew; on the contrary, it supposes that this requisite has been already complied with, before the sale is allowed. And had it meant to impose this, it would not have passed it over, any more than it has passed it over in the case of the new denouncer, whom it declares liable to the obligation. Neither is the preamble of the 36th ordinance opposed to this doctrine; for of the ordinances to which it refers, none of them impose the obligation of sinking anew, and that ordinance itself only imposes it in the case of mines purchased without having been sunk to the depth of three *estados*, from the ore having taken its course in some unusual direction, or from any of those accidental circumstances which we have explained above, having occurred; for there can be no doubt that, in

* Vide chap. 11, n. fin.   † Chap. 11, n. 12.

these cases, if the miner has done his best, in keeping the full number of hands at work, and has not been able to overcome the impediment, either from the ore taking its course in some other direction, or from some other reasonable cause, allowed by the justice, he is at liberty to sell the mine, the presumption of fraud and the other reasons for the prohibition, no longer applying ; and that it will be the duty of his successor, when the impediment is overcome, to proceed to sink the mine to the proper depth. And finally, all that the 42d ordinance provides, is, that an account shall be given of the sale, but it makes no mention of sinking anew ; on the contrary, it provides, that the sale may be made freely, subject only to the condition of registering the contract and the name of the successor.

16. Whilst upon the ordinances which touch upon the sale of mines, it will not be out of our way to inquire, First, how their price or value is to be regulated ? Whence we may also learn the price at which they may be taken on lease ; it being evident, that as they may be sold, so also they may be let on lease. To the question suggested, it may be answered, that the value of mines of gold and silver is, properly speaking, a matter of opinion, and can only be determined from conjecture, more or less probable, founded on the notions entertained of the vein, the quality of its ores, and other prudential calculations, the matter being in itself altogether uncertain. And the miner, properly speaking, purchases an uncertainty, which may be the means of enriching him or otherwise, as the quality of the ore may prove better or worse, and the more or less hard, and more or less constant. The nature of such purchases is illustrated by Cardinal de Luca, who refers to analogous cases, such as the taking of salt works on lease, and the farming of the public taxes.* We have known 90,000 dollars given for the third part of a mine in the mining district of Bolaños, and the whole sum returned by the mine, within a few days. And the case may be compared, as in the text of the civil law and the glossary, to that of one who purchases of a fisherman, the contents of a single haul of his net, in which case the price of the thing, in itself uncertain, is estimated upon probabilities.† So that there can be no fixed standard for regulating the price to be given upon selling or leasing a mine ; the fancy, experience and prudential calculations of the parties concerned, being the only guides.

17. The second question is, whether, upon the purchase and sale of a mine, a charge of *lesion enorme* or *enormisima* can be set up ? We reply, that it cannot. First, because it is so provided, expressly, by an ordinance

---

* Card. de Luca, de regalib. disc. 117, n. 6. "Ac propterea hujusmodi mineralium appaltatores, ad instar appaltatorum vectigalium et gabellarum, emere quoque dicuntur incertam aleam, ex qua ditari vel depauperari possint, juxta majorum vel minorum materiæ hæsitationem, in qua vere et proprie consistit valor seu substantia appaltus ; juxta dictum consil. Socin. 156, lib 2, cum aliis, sup. disc. 105 et 107."

† L. 12, ff. de act. empt. et vend. "Si jactum retis emero, et jactare retem piscator noluit, incertum ejus rei æstimandum est." Gloss. litt. C. in fin. "Vel æstimatur quantum est verisimile quod esset captum, quod inspicitur secundum quod consuetum est."

of Peru, which declares, that upon the purchase and sale of mines, no one shall be at liberty to charge deceit or *lesion enormisima*, even though he should offer to prove that the mines were worth more or less at the time of the contract; insomuch that even though persons under age or Indians, be concerned, yet, if the sale be made with the solemnities of the law, the same rule must be observed, and the judges must act accordingly, under a penalty of five hundred dollars.*

18. Second, because in purchasing a mine, the profit or loss is eventual and contingent; and in matters where the profit or loss depends on chance, no regard is had to *lesion;* nor would it be just, as is shewn by Olea, upon the authority of various texts, and of Noguerol, Barbosa, Guzman, Gutierrez, Hermosilla, Larrea, Leotardo and others,† that a deficiency of price should be made good to the vendor, when he would not have to make good any loss sustained by the purchaser, however great.   And nothing is so much exposed to great contingencies of profit and loss, as the working of mines, a business carried on quite in the dark, amongst alternations of *borrasca* and *bonanza*, and which is very commonly attended with great expense, continual theft, and ultimate loss.   As therefore, the value of a mine must be regulated according to fancy, the greater or less knowledge the parties have of the quality of the ores, or the probability it affords of giving produce, it must be impossible, whilst the value of the subject matter remains incapable of being ascertained, to fix the amount of damage suffered in respect of the price.

19. As the 42d ordinance also treats of every kind of dealing in mines, by way of sale, agreement or any other species of contract, this will be the proper place to notice that a mine may be given as a marriage portion, may be charged with a rent, may be granted by way of *emphyteusis*, or be hypothecated; and in a word, that mines may be made the subject of every species of contract applicable to the concerns of mankind : provided they be known mines, and be proved to be capable of yielding ore of a fair standard; as we have shewn elsewhere, upon the authority of Cardinal de Luca, and several others cited by him.‡

20. A further question, however, presents itself, namely, whether a mine can be made the subject of a precarious gift or loan ?   This question arose in a suit agitated before the audiency of Mexico, between Don Pedro Rome-

---

* Ord. 1, tit. 9, concerning the mode of trying suits ; Escalona, Gazoph. lib. 2, p. 2, cap. 1, p. 123 ; where he cites Barth. in L. verum, § sciendum, ff. de minorib.

† Olea, de cess. jur. tit. 6, q. 10, n. 16.   "Læsio in his contractibus qui lucro, et damno expositi sunt, non consideratur." L. 1, Cod. de pact. Noguerol, alleg. 37. u. 63.   Barbosa, voto 25, n. 94, lib. 2 ; et voto 62, à n. 6.   Guzman, de evict. quæst. 21, à n. 33, ubi n. 44, asserit incertitudinis ratione licitum esse contractum emptionis alicujus juris vitalititii, quamvis repitus percepti sortem acceptam excedant.   Larrea, alleg. 27 ;   " Nec audiendum esset cedens et venditor cum non recte meliorationem petat, qui deteriorationem non esset postulaturus." L. cum pro pecunia. pen ff. de solut.

‡ Vide chap. 2, n. 24.

ro Terreros, knight of the order of Calatrava, and the Marquess de Valle-Ameno, to whom Terreros and his partner, Don Joseph Alexandro Busta-mante, had given a mine in the mining district of El Monte, upon the under-standing that they might resume it any time they might think proper : de-siring him, at the same time, if he should cease to work it, from its not turn-ing out well, to advise them, that they might take it into their hands. This transaction took place in 1747, and in the year 1753, Terreros claimed to re-sume possession of the mine, alleging that it had only been granted by way of a precarious gift or loan, and that the grant was therefore revocable at any moment.[*]

21. But it was insisted by the author, on the part of the marquess, that the gift was a complete, and not a precarious one. That a precarious gift is re-vocable at any moment, even though there be a covenant not to revoke it[†] but that it was inconsistent with the nature of the transaction in question, to suppose that it could have been the intention of the parties concerned, that the marquess should take the mine, lay out money in timbering and draining it, and in driving a level and air holes for ventilation, as he had done, and yet that he should be liable to have it taken away from him at any moment ; particularly as the donors, in the letter in which they expressed their consent to his working it, had wished him the best success. In support of which view, the author referred to the doctrine of Paulo de Castro, who make a dis-tinction between the case where acts in their nature merely temporary, are permitted to be done upon the ground in question ; as throwing down sand, lime, or stones ; in which case the contract may be presumed precarious :— and the case where acts are permitted of a nature which cannot be regarded as merely temporary, but as permanent ;—as when permission is given to build or to fix up beams, in which case a gift is presumed :. so that the nature of the grant is to be collected by referring to the subject matter, and the cir-cumstances attending it, agreeably to the text of the civil law ; which is treat-ed as a proper direction by Angelus and Cepola.[‡] Upon the second branch of this distinction, we rested our argument in favour of the marquess ; as the working of a mine requires not only the erection of a shed, but the timbering of many yards of the pit and other works, which of themselves imply a per-manency of interest, incompatible with the nature of a precarious gift, and reconcilable with that of an absolute gift only. And it was so decided by the royal audiency of Mexico, overruling the arguments relied on by Terreros, as entitling him to resume the mine, either on the ground of the gift being a

---

[*] L. 1, et 15, ff. de precar.

[†] Hermosilla, in L. 9, tit. 2, partit. 5. gloss. 1, n. 11, ibi : "Non valebit pactum, quod nisi tem-pore non restituatur."

[‡] Paulus de Castro, in L. si precareo, § ult. n. 4. Angel. cons. 1, n. 7. Cæpola, de servit. ur-ban. præd. cap. 73, n. 6. L. si uno in principio, ff. locati, apud Mantic. de tacit. convent. lib. 13, tit. 5, n. 9.

precarious one, or of the mine having been left unworked, of which last point we shall take further notice elsewhere.*

22. But as every different transaction involves different agree nents and other circumstances requiring to be taken into view, so that it is impossible to regulate them all in the same manner, or by the same rules, it is evident, that if there be an express agreement to grant the mine by way of a precarious gift or loan, then, as the agreement of the contracting parties is that which gives laws to the contract, the use of the mine must be regarded as precarious, with regard to the time for which it is granted, although the ore raised must always be regarded as a gift ; for it is evident to common sense, and has been shewn by the Cardinal de Luca, when treating of salt mines,† that the only use of which a vein is capable, is that which consists in digging and working it.

23. Having seen what are the rules requiring observance in New Spain, under the ordinances of Castile, we proceed to state briefly, that it is provided in Peru, by the peculiar ordinances of that country, that the mine shall be sunk to the depth of six *varas*, and dug to the width of three, within sixty days, under pain of forfeiture ; so that it shall be liable to be adjudged to any other person, which person, however, will also be required to sink the pit four *estados* more, or make a new pit of that depth, under the like penalty of forfeiture ; and that mines cannot be sold or alienated, until sunk to the depth of ten *estados* at least, under pain of the sale being annulled, and of the mine being adjudged to any one who may apply for it, even should the purchaser be at work upon it ; and the judgment, both in this and the other cases, is to be made in a summary way, upon the truth being ascertained.‡ As to which the doubts, rules and limitations we have before suggested, as being agreeable to law and to the nature of mines, will apply.

---

* Chap. 17, n. 7 and 8.

† Luca, de regalib d isc. 117, u. 6, ibi : " Juxta majorem vel minorem materiæ hæsitationem, in qua verè et propriè consistit valor seu substantia appaltus." Et num. 17, ibi ; " Hinc proinde habemus, quod quando fodinæ dominus illam locat, aliud concedere non dicitur nisi facultatem utendi pro eo tempore, quo elapso cessat, ut bene Gutierr. de gabell. quæst. 36, u. 10 ; et conferunt quæ apud Socin. cons. 156, lib. 2, quod non importat aliud nisi jus, seu facultatem privativè venden di eam mercem statuto tempore, emendo aleam lucri, vel respectivè damni, resultantis a majori vel minori hæsitatione in tempore statuto." Et num. 18. " Tunc earum fructus consistere dicitur in ipsius substantiæ annuali, seu temporanea consumptione, et hæsitatione."

‡ Ord. 1 and 2, tit. 7, concerning insufficient working ; Escalona, Gazoph. lib. 2, p. 2, cap. 1, pag 115.

CHAPTER XVII.

OF THE NUMBER OF FOUR PERSONS REQUIRED TO BE KEPT AT WORK.
IN MINES OF GOLD AND SILVER, AND OF THE PENALTY OF FORFEIT·
URE WHICH ATTACHES UPON THEIR BEING LEFT UNWORKED FOR FOUR
SUCCESSIVE MONTHS, AFTER WHICH THERE CAN BE NO RESTITUTION
OR OTHER REMEDY.—OF THE DESCRIPTION OF WORK ABOUT WHICH
THEY MUST BE EMPLOYED, AND WHICH IS DETERMINED TO BE ANY
KIND OF WORK, WHETHER UPON THE SURFACE OR IN THE INTERIOR,
TENDING TO THE HABILITATION* OF THE MINE —THE ONLY GROUNDS
OF EXEMPTION FROM THE PENALTY ARE, THE OCCURRENCE OF PESTI-
LENCE, FAMINE OR WAR.—CONSIDERATIONS ON THE DEFICIENCY OF
HANDS FOR THESE MOST IMPORTANT WORKS.

ORDINANCES XXXVII. LXXI.

XXXVII. ALSO, forasmuch as it commonly happens, that there are persons who hold many mines which they have taken, discovered, purchased or
acquired in some other manner, and who do not work them or keep them in
activity, either because it is not in their power, or because they are engaged
in working others which they consider better, in consequence of which they
neglect to sink or explore the former mines, or to raise the ores from them,
although sometimes better than the ores raised from the-mines prosecuted by
them : and whereas the mines they omit to work as aforesaid, become filled
with water, to the injury of other adjoining and surrounding mines, which
are kept at work, and which become deeper than the former.   Wherefore,
to obviate these and other inconveniences which follow or might follow from
not working the mines,—We ordain and command, that all persons shall be
obliged to keep their mines worked by at least four persons in each mine or
pertenencia, whether they be sole proprietors of such mines or hold them in
partnership ; for however that may be, the setting on such four persons in
the whole extent of each mine, shall be sufficient to shew that such mines
are kept at work ; which four persons aforesaid· are to employ themselves
about the working of the mines in which they shall be set on, in raising water
or ore, or in doing some other work for its improvement, either within or
without the mine : under the penalty, if any mine whatsoever shall not be
kept worked by such four persons as aforesaid, during the term of four
months successively, that the person to whom it may belong shall, *ipso facto*,
forfeit it, and that he shall, from that time forth, have no right to the mine,
unless by making registry thereof anew, and going through the other pro·
ceedings, in conformity with these ordinances ; such mine to be adjudged to
any person who may denounce it as insufficiently worked, provided he go
through the proceedings aforesaid.   But if, from any reasonable impediment,

_____

* *Habilitation*, as applied to mining, is the bringing a mine, or part of a mine, into a working
state, or the maintaining it in that state.—*Trans.*

such as war, mortality or famine, occurring in the part or place within the jurisdiction of which the mine may be situated, or within twenty leagues around, it shall be impossible to keep it worked by such four persons : in these cases, the aforesaid term of four months shall not run. If, however, such impediments shall exist out of the jurisdiction within which such mine shall be situated, and beyond such twenty leagues around, this shall not be admitted as an excuse for not keeping the mine at work, according to and under the penalties contained in this our ordinance.

LXXI. Also, we ordain and command, that all who shall be possessed of mines or streamworks of gold, shall be obliged to keep them at work, as is commanded with regard to working the mines of silver, under the penalties hereinbefore declared.

CONTENTS OF THE COMMENTARY ON THESE ORDINANCES.

1. In case of neglecting to keep four persons at work in the mine, for the term of four months, the forfeiture thereof is incurred.
2. The ordinances of Péru were originally more strict, but were relaxed by the Marquess de Canete.
3. Difference between possessing a mine, and keeping it worked.
4. Any kind of labour, either internal or external, applied to the substance and soil of the mine, or having relation to the mine and its habilitation, is a sufficient working.
5. But not so the setting up machinery or reducing the ores.
6. By the law, the term of four months cannot be enlarged, even by the viceroy.
7. An important suit on the question, whether a mine had been kept at work, between Don Pedro Terreros and the Marquess de Valle-Ameno, before the royal audiency of Mexico.
8. An executory sentence was given in favour of the marquess, by the viceroy and audiency, and confirmed by the council, who declared a supplication to be inadmissible.
9. Of the strictness with which the keeping at work should be established.
10. Ground upon which the council refused to admit a supplication on the part of Terreros.
11. If the term of four months, during which the mine is omitted to be kept at work, be not continuous, the mine is not forfeited.
12. The plan of setting hands to work, merely to interrupt the period of four months, seems contrary to the ordinance.
13. But the ordinances must be observed, and the justices ought anxiously to endeavour to keep up the works.
14. A mine left insufficiently worked, and set to work again without a new registry being made, does not become the property of the person so working it anew, but is liable to be denounced.
15. Upon which it shall be adjudged to the denouncer, although the former owner be working it at the time.
16. War, pestilence and famine, prevent the term from running.
17. No circumstance which cannot be reduced to one of the above three, is admissible as an excuse.
18. Minority in age, absence on public affairs, &c. afford no excuse, and why.
19. There is no restitution after the lapse of the period of four months, but *re integrâ*, the mine may be registered anew.

20. *Re non integrâ*, it cannot be registered, nor will restitution be allowed, in opposition to the rights of third parties.
21. The law of itself divests the rights of the party who has abandoned the works, and transfers it to the party making denouncement.
22. There is a right to recover over, against a tutor or curator leaving a mine unworked. An ordinance of Peru, providing for the interests of absent heirs.
23. If the mine have not yet been adjudged to the party who has denounced it, and he have not laid out money upon it, it may be restored.
24. Extreme poverty affords no ground of exemption from the penalty for leaving the mine unworked.

COMMENTARY.

1. These ordinances, which follow the 40th and 76th of the old ordinances,* provide, that whether the mine belong to one proprietor, or to several in partnership, it must be kept worked by at least four persons. The objects looked to by the sovereign in imposing this condition, are important, as may be collected from the ordinances themselves; the chief of them is the raising of the ore, which cannot be effected without workmen: and as four persons are but a trifling number to employ in the whole extent of a mine, the works of which, upon ore or dead ground, generally require many more, there is no excuse for omitting to supply that number, except under the unusual and accidental circumstances provided for by the ordinances themselves. Under any other circumstances, it will be difficult to find a case where so limited a number of workmen as four, cannot be procured; and a miner leaving a mine insufficiently work for four months successively, certainly deserves to lose it, for his neglect. By the old ordinance, now altered, the term was only two months.

2. In Peru, the term fixed by the ordinances, after which a mine might be denounced for insufficient working, was very limited. In mines of 60 *varas*, eight Indians or four negroes were to be kept at work, besides the miner; and in those of 30 *varas* or under, four Indians or four negroes: and if this number was left incomplete during twenty days, or if no work was done for six successive days, during such twenty days, the mine was liable to be applied for and adjudged as unworked; but the viceroy, Marquess de Cañete extended the time to a year and a day. These ordinances also provided, that if any person had a space of 60 *varas*, at two or three detached points, or had several mines, he must set on that number of persons at each point; but this rule was afterwards annulled by the *supplement of Lupidana*, it being ordered, that a person having several mines, should keep up his right to the whole number, by carrying on one or two works; as is set forth by Escalona, citing Montesinos, in his *Politica de Mineros.*†

---

* L. 5, tit. 13, book 6, Collection of Castile, cap. 40 and 76.

† Escalona, in his Gasoph. lib. 2, p. 2, cap. 1, tit. 7, concerning insufficient working; ord. 3 and 4.

3. Whence it follows, that the mere keeping possession of the mine, is not sufficient to authorise saying that it is kept at work, possession being distinct from keeping at work; the former depends on receiving and having the custody of the instrument conferring the title, on the delivery and receipt of the keys, on some corporeal act, such as the tearing off boughs, throwing aside stones, or walking upon any part of the estate, or on some other symbolical act, performed with the intention of taking or maintaining possession of the whole, as may be seen in various texts and doctors.* But the keeping a mine at work, is the employing the labour of four persons, either within or without the mine, in some object tending to the working and habilitation of the mine. So that a mine may be in the possession of a party, though at the same time left insufficiently worked; it may have a guard and be under custody, and yet not be kept in sufficient work; it being an indispensable requisite to the latter object, that four labourers or workmen should be employed; and the performance of acts of possession, without observing the indispensable requisite of keeping the mine at work, is not sufficient to obviate the penalty.

4. The ordinance, however, may be satisfied, without absolutely employing barmen in digging ore; as by raising water, or performing any other useful work, either *within* or *without* the mine; *within*, by carrying on dead works, when the veins become barren, by forming pillars of support, making air holes, or channels for internal draining, or by timbering the pillars and works; that is to say, by lining them with timber, for their support: *without* the mine, as by driving an adit, sinking or timbering a pit, driving a level or *contramina*, or draining by means of machinery or whims. In fine, a mine in which four persons are employed, in any act tending to the hahilitation of the mine, and to its being more effectually worked, is considered as worked, according to law.

5. Whence it follows, that as the work done must tend to the improvement of the mine, either *within* or *without*, the reducing the ore in the amalgamation or smelting works, which tends not to the improvement of the mine, but of the ore, cannot be regarded as a sufficient working; neither can the arranging the machines or tools, or other necessary implements; for although the end of such operations is the working of the mine, yet they do not tend directly to its habilitation, the extraction of its ores, or the promotion of ventilation in the works; and when the ordinance requires four persons to be kept at work in raising ore, water or earth, or improving the mine in some other way, it of course takes for granted, that the means necessary for this purpose, the implements, machinery and tools employed in the art, are provided.

---

* L. 3, ff. de adq. possess. §. 4, Inst. de rer. divis. L. 1, Cod. de donat. Picler. de caus. poss. et prop. u. 6 et 17. Gomez. in L. 45. Taur. u. 32, 34 et 45. Covarrub. in reg. possessor. 2, p. a n. 1.

6. The royal audiencies have always regarded the punctual observance of this ordinance as indispensable, to ensure to the public the benefits derivable from working the mines. As a proof of this, we may observe, that it is commanded by the law of the Indies,* that although proprietors who have abandoned their mines should apply to the viceroys or presidents, to maintain their right of possession, by granting orders that the mine shall not be liable, during a certain time, to be denounced for insufficient working, yet the ordinances of the new code shall be punctually and precisely observed, and the appointed term of four months shall not be enlarged ; such being the most expedient course to pursue.

7. We have watched several suits, agitated before the royal audiency of Mexico, on the subject of the denouncement of mines for insufficient working, in the districts of Guanaxuato and el Monte, in all of which the greatest strictness was observed on the part of the person denounced, in establishing the fact of their having been kept at work ; and on the part of the person making denouncement, in proving that they had been insufficiently worked, during the term in dispute. In a suit prosecuted by Don Pedro Romero Terreros against the Marquess de Valle-Ameno, on the question of the abandonment of the mine of San Vicente, in the mining district of el Monte, which we have already noticed,† notwithstanding that the marquess had obtained a favourable decree from the viceroy, acting under the advice of an assessor, the audiency allowed the matter to be tried before them in the second instance, upon an allegation by Terreros, that the mine had been left unworked, and the author was under the necessity of going into interrogatories to prove that the marquess had timbered the pit, had sunk it many *varas*, had driven a level and air shafts to habilitate the mine, the works having become choked with vapour, and had also done many other acts, not merely indicating an actual possession, but strictly in the nature of working ; at the same time arguing, that there was no necessity to establish these facts, the gift of the mine made by Don Joseph Bustamante to the marquess, in January 1747, having been absolute, and having been ratified by the antecessor in title of Terreros, in November 1748, and July 1749, between which times, the abandonment set up by Terreros was alleged to have taken place ; and submitting further, that if Terreros could, by carrying on one single adit, maintain his right to 36 mines on the *Vizcayna* vein,‡ San Vicente being one of them, then the marquess, as a partner contributing to the work of the adit, in respect of the last-mentioned mine and others belonging to him, must also be

---

* Law 6, tit. 19, book 4, Collection of the Indies.

† See chap. 16, n. 20 and 21.

‡ This privelege was stipulated for by Don Joseph Alexandro de Bustamante, and was conceded to him by an order of the superior government of Mexico, of the first of June, 1739; and after his death, to his successor, Don Pedro Romero Terreros, by another order of the same superior government.

considered to have kept that mine sufficiently at work, agreeably to the or-dinance now under consideration, and to a conclusive ordinance of Peru, which, in reference to the keeping mines at work, declares, that this purpose may be satisfied by driving adits, which it makes sufficient to prevent the mines from being denounced as insufficiently worked.* Together with several other arguments which we adduced in support of his right.

8. Finally, upon the evidence being considered, the marquess obtained a sentence of review, confirming the decree of the viceroy; and Terreros having demanded an authenticated copy of the proceedings, that he might apply to the council, without presenting a supplication to the audiency, the audiency declared, upon the petition of the marquess, that their decree was to be considered as valid and definitive. The marquess however, having been summoned before the council, the authenticated copy of the proceedings having been laid before them, on the part of Terreros, and the petition of the fiscal having been considered, the claim of Terreros to present to the council the supplication which he had waived presenting to the audiency, was dismissed; as appears from the order, and from the certificate of Don Pedro de la Vega, the chief clerk in the office of secretary to the council, dated the 12th of August, 1758,† and given at the instance of the Marquess de Valle-Ameno and his heirs.

9. Whence it may be collected, that the audiency of Mexico enforces, with great strictness, the observance of this ordinance, concerning the keeping the mines at work; and also, that in the opinion of the audiency, not only the raising of ore, but the other acts proved on the part of the marquess, such as timbering, draining and driving a level or air shaft, for the

---

* Escalon. Gazoph. lib. 2, p. 2, cap. 1, tit. 7, concerning mines insufficiently worked. Ord. 9, "If any person shall possess mines upon any vein, and shall drive an adit to the vein, so long as he shall work the adit, it shall not be lawful to take away the mines from him, as insufficiently worked. The same privilege is granted to those who may possess mines upon such vein, if they shall contribute to, or drive such adit in partnership."

† "I, Don Pedro de la Vega, a member of his majesty's council, his secretary, and chief clerk in the office of the secretary to the council and chamber of the Indies, in relation to the provinces of New Spain, do certify, that after considering, in the council aforesaid, an appeal presented by Don Pedro Romero de Terreros, knight of the order of Calatrava, and an inhabitant of the city of Santiago de Queretaro, in New Spain, referred to the council by order of his majesty, and praying that, for the reasons therein stated, a hearing might be afforded to an ordinary supplication, which ought to have been prosecuted before the royal audiency of Mexico, from a sentence of review passed against him, and confirming another sentence to the same effect, pronounced by the viceroy of those provinces, in a suit which the appellant had prosecuted against the Marquess de Valle-Ameno, concerning the property of the mine of San Vicente, in the mining district of el Monte, in the jurisdiction of Pachuca, in the provinces aforesaid:—it was determined (amongst other things), on the 18th of February last, upon consideration of the above, and of what was set forth by the fiscal, that the aforesaid appeal of the above-mentioned Don Pedro Romero Terreros, could not be admitted. And that the same may duly appear, I hereby give the these presents, pursuant to a resolution of the council aforesaid, of the fifth of this present month, at the instance of the heirs of the aforesaid Marquess de Valle-Ameno. At Madrid, 12th of April, 1758."

purpose of habilitating the mine, or relieving the works from vapour, would constitute a sufficient working.

10. We have also a remarkable precedent, in the refusal of the council to admit the appeal of Terreros ; which, although foreign to the subject under consideration, is yet worthy of particular notice, for the instruction of litigating parties, and the prevention of the irregular proceedings to which they are induced to have recourse, to the injury, no less of the public, than of the parties concerned. Amongst the statements considered by the council, were the representations contained in the petition of the fiscal, which, after noticing the ordinary remedy of supplication to the audiency, and the extraordinary remedies of second supplication, and appeal for notorious injustice, the former allowed by the law, and the latter by a special order,[*]

* The order (*auto acordado*) was *verbatim*, as follows : " The council having taken into consideration, the abuses practised by litigant parties, in prosecuting suits before the audiencies and tribunals of the kingdoms of Peru and New Spain, by interposing appeals to the council, from the determinations of those courts, in matters of every description, although they most frequently fail in establishing any circumstances to justify such a course ; which is to the prejudice of the litigant parties and of the public interest, is derogatory to the authority of the tribunals subordinate to the council, and is the means of impeding the dispatch of the more important business of the latter tribunal :—His majesty, after considering. on the 25th of January last, what means might afford a convenient remedy for these evils, has been pleased to resolve that whenever, from this time forth, any person or persons shall resort to the extraordinary remedy of appeal to the council, on the ground of nullity or notorious injustice, against any proceeding which shall have a definitive force, or against a sentence executed of any of the inferior tribunals of this kingdom or that of the Indies, the party who shall propose to make such appeal, shall, upon merely applying for an order to have such proceedings brought up, or upon presenting the same, first deposit or give, legal, plain and sufficient security (to the satisfaction of the notary of the chamber of the council, and upon his account and at his risk), for five hundred ducats *vellon*, if the appeal be from any of the tribunals of these kingdoms subordinate to the council, and if from any of the tribunals of the Indies, one thousand crowns of silver ; and that unless this be done, the council shall not be at liberty to demand the proceedings, nor to admit such as may be presented to them ; and which sum, so deposited or secured, shall, if the sentence against which such appeal for invalidity or notorious injustice may have been interposed, be reversed by the council, be returned to the party who may have deposited it ; but if confirmed, shall, as a punishment for his termerity, be divided into three parts : one for the exchequer ; another for the judges of the audiency or tribunal, against the sentence of which the appeal may have been interposed ; and the other, for the party against whom the appeal may have been presented ; excepting only from this liability, the poor, who may have litigated as such, and who shall prove the same in the council, which latter shall give security on oath, and shall be liable to as heavy a fine as it shall seem fit to impose on them, regard being had to the nature or importance of the proceedings, and other circumstances, of which the council is the best judge. That no appeals shall be entertained against judgments given in possessory suits, of whatever nature or description they may be. That it shall not be lawful to entertain any appeal from any suit depending in the audiencies of the Indies, the ultimate determination of which ought, under the special laws of those kingdoms, to proceed exclusively by way of second supplication, to be presented to the chamber of fifteen hundred,[*] in the council. That no appeal shall be admitted from a sentence of review ordered to be executed, notwithstanding any

* A tribunal of appeal, so called because the appellant was obliged to deposit 1500 Castilian *doblas*, of 485 *maravedis* each, to abide the event of the suit.—*Trans.*

proceeded to observe, " That the application could not be admitted, because " the favour of the prince ought not to be extended to a party, who, having it in his power to apply to the ordinary civil law remedy, allowed by the laws of the country, has chosen to waive or renounce it, as had been done by Terreros, and that if the appeal were admitted, the greatest inconvenience would ensue; that every one would abandon the courts of first instance, and the ordinary remedies of the law, and would have recourse to new and extraordinary remedies, tending to bring the superior tribunals into disesteem, to detract from the authority of decisions, which ought to be regarded as definitive, to prejudice the interests of the public, and to bring irreparable injury upon the parties concerned:" which may serve to indicate that great circumspection and attention should be observed in preferring extraordinary appeals, on the ground of nullity or notorious injustice; and that the supreme council never sanctions the unjust means resorted to by litigating parties, for the purpose of annoying their adversaries.

11. To return, from this important digression, to our proper subject. Having investigated what number of persons must be employed, and what descriptions of labour prosecuted, to constitute a sufficient *working* in point of law, the ordinance proceeds to impose the penalty of forfeiting the mine, " *ipso facto*," upon leaving it insufficiently worked for four months successively, " and that he shall have no right to the mine, unless by making registry thereof anew, and going through the other proceedings in conformity with these ordinances." Whence it may be inferred, first, that if the owner abandon the mine for two months, then work it for two months, and then again abandon it, or leave it insufficiently worked for two or three months more, the first and last periods cannot be added together, so as to induce a forfeiture of the mine, the time of its having been left unworked not being continuous, as required by the ordinance, but interrupted; and this being a penal ordinance, and therefore to be confined to the cases to which it strictly applies. That which is continuous, is that which has no interruption, interval or intermission;* time is said to be continuous, when it is not interrupted

---

supplication, unless the parties proposing to present such appeal, shall establish before the council, that they have applied for permission to present a supplication against such sentence, and that the same has been refused. That all advocates who shall sign petitions of appeal which may be entertained by the council, agreeably to what is before provided in this royal order, upon the understanding that the statements which they contain are correct, and are supported by sufficient facts and reasons; and likewise, all advocates who shall appear to support such petitions of appeal, shall be fined in such a sum as shall be deemed reasonable by the judges who may determine them, if, in the proceedings had thereon, the contrary should be shewn. And likewise, that the determinations which may be made by the council, upon these appeals, shall be enforced, without admitting any supplication or other appeal against the same. Which I communicate to you by order of the council, that you may be advised of what will be required of you, so far as you are concerned. Madrid, 24th February, 1712 —Don Bernardo Tinajero de la Escalera.—Senor Juan Ortiz de Bracamonte."

* Calep. verb. *continuus*, Thesaur. Ling. Latin.

by any act of opposite or distinct tendency ; and the continuance is said to be civil or natural, according to the nature of the act. But with regard to time, there is no such thing as accumulation; five and five in philosophical understanding, are not ten, although when added together they amount to this number. He who has been a novice during two distinct periods of six months each, cannot, by adding them together, make them one year, so as to entitle him to profess ; one who has been incarcerated for two different periods of six months, cannot claim to be released from prison, upon the allegation that he has been confined one continuous year ; one who has given shelter to a banished person for ten days, at different intervals of time, is not to be punished, like one who has given him shelter for ten days continuously : and so in various other instances, which may be found in Angelus, Speculator, Cuneus, and Avendaño, as cited by Garcia.* If therefore, it be established, that work has been done, although at intervals, the continuity of the term of four months, during which the mine may have been left insufficiently worked, will be deemed to have been destroyed by such interruption, so as to prevent the penalty attaching. And in practice it is well known, that the owners keep up their right to the mine by working from time to time, until they find it convenient or practicable to apply briskly to the prosecution of the draining, or of the dead works ; which proceeds on this principle of alternately taking up and intermitting the work.

12. Notwithstanding this, it is worth while to consider, whether this plan of keeping up the working, by opening the mine a day or two before the expiration of the term of four months, and proceeding with some dead work or other, is not a fraud upon the ordinances, and contrary to their object; for the mine, so far from being improved, remains just as neglected, and just as much flooded with water as before ; the sole purpose answered being that of providing a cloak to shelter a miner, and to prevent denouncement. And as there can be no doubt that he who proceeds in opposition to the spirit of the law, notwithstanding he may keep close to the letter, is guilty of a breach of the law, and is not to be permitted to elude its penalties, by sheltering

---

* Garcia, de nobil. gloss. 12, n. 37, et gloss. 31. verb. *continuus*, a. n. 1, ibi : "Hoc verbum *continuus*, aliquando dicit continuationem civilem, aliquando naturalem; patet hæc distinctio ex text. in L. continuus, ff. de verb. oblig. ibi : "Ut tamen aliquod momentum naturæ intervenire possit ;" et rursum ibi : "Cæterum si post interrogationem aliud agere cæperit, nil proderit quamvis eadem die spopondisset ;" et n. 2, ibi : "Quia si respiceret solum tempus, tunc tempus in dubio deberet intelligi continuum ; pro quo est Angelus, in L. si idem cum eod. ff. dejurisd. omn. jud. ubi quærit utrum in tempore fiat coacervatio, et decidit, quod non : ponit exemplum in eo, qui stetit per diversa semestria in ordine meudicantium, quod non erit professus ; et qui stetit in carcere eodem modo, non dicitur stetisse per annum, si eum complevit per inter valla, ut sic amore Dei debeat relaxari ex forma statuti : allegat Speculator, tit. de stat. monachor. §. 1, vers. 38. Barth. in L. fin. §. quoties, ff. de publican. et Gulielmum de Cuneo ; in L. necnon, §, si quis sæpius, ff. ex quib. caus. major. Et n. 5, tradit Aristotle. lib. 3, Metaph. cap. 9 ; ubi quod numeri consistunt in individua, sicuti species ita ut quinque et quinque specifice non sint decem, licet coacervati ad summam decem adscendant."

himself under a sophistical interpretation of words, according to the cele-brated law of the code ;* it would seem that the penalty ought to be incurred by one who works his mine for three days only, or a little more, in the course of the year, at the beginning or end of each of the three periods of four months ; at the same time leaving it incumbered by water and otherwise neglected, contrary to the true intent of the ordinances, his only view being to prevent denouncement.

13. As the ordinances, however, have made no further provision than the above, and as from their requiring, to make the penalty attach, that the mine should be left insufficiently worked for the term of four successive months, it follows plainly, that the effect of the penalty may be avoided, by working for a few days at intervals ; and nothing remains but to hope that the legis-lature may make some other provision ; although the precaution is sometimes taken, under circumstances in which very few miners would be desirous of denouncing the mine, even if left completely unworked. It is part of the business of the justice to visit the mines, and by imposing fines and penalties, to enforce their being worked, according to the ordinances ; but as no one comes forward to insist upon this being done, irregularities are permitted, through the negligence and undue connivance of the justices, to pass unnoticed.

14. The second point established by the words of the ordinance, in pro-viding that by leaving the mine unworked for four successive months, " the person to whom it may belong, shall, *ipso facto*, forfeit it," is, that although the person who has left the mine unworked should again set it at work, before it has been denounced by any other person, yet he can claim no title to the mine, and any other person may denounce it, as not having been registered, and as merely held in the possession of the party, contrary to right ; in the same manner as, under the ordinance of Peru, when a mine has been sold without having been previously sunk to the depth of ten *estados*, it is liable to be denounced, even though the purchaser be at work upon it ; which, as we have already seen, is also the rule under the law of Castile, if the mines have been sold without being sunk to the depth of three *estados*.* And a party in actual possession of a mine, not having been registered, is liable, under another ordinance, to have it denounced, and to be charged with the penalty.‡ And as, under the circumstances last-mentioned, the party has the opportunity of registering the mine before any one else, so may a person who has forfeited his mine by leaving it insufficiently worked. But his original right is completely divested, and as it were annihilated, not a vestage of it remaining from that time forth ; so much so, that if he do not make registry anew, the old registry will avail him nothing, being lost by his neg-

---

* L. non dubium, 5, Cod. de legib.

† Chap. 16, per tot. et num. fin. refertur ordinat. Peruvica.

‡ Chap. 5, n. 17.

lecting the work. And it cannot be argued, that, *re integra*, the delay may be purged, for this rule only holds where the law has made no provisions to the contrary ; but there is such a provision in our ordinance, the mine being declared to be forfeited, *ipso facto*, without any occasion for an application to the judge. The point may be aptly illustrated by the doctrine of Acosta (supported by various texts and doctors), in regard to a person taking an *emphyteusis*, who, if he do not pay the rent, incurs a forfeiture.* The penalty of the law, therefore, cannot be avoided by any proceeding whatever, except that of making registry anew.

15. And such a provision, is, in fact, most beneficial and desirable, as the miners, acting under the fear of this most reasonable penalty, will be deterred from leaving their mines unworked, and taking them up again at pleasure, without renewing the registry, and they will thus be stimulated to carry on the works with more effect. If, then, the party making denouncement can establish, that the miner, although working the mine at the time, is nevertheless doing so without having renewed his title, and that he has previously abandoned the working for four months, the mine must, under the express terms of the ordinance, be adjudged to the party having made the denouncement. And however hard this may seem, such is the express law, and it is material to the public interest (which depends much on keeping up the working of the mines, and enforcing the observance of the forms of registry) that it should be so. By neglecting these points, therefore, the owners render themselves worthy of punishment ; besides they cannot possibly set up a claim to an interest in the mines, unless they choose to observe the forms and conditions under which the sovereign has been pleased, in his munificence, to make them common. And as the acts required to be done, depend solely upon the proprietors themselves, they cannot, if through carelessness or culpable negligence they omit to perform them, be admitted to plead an excuse, lest abuse, confusion and litigation should be introduced, to the great prejudice of the public.

16. The ordinance excepts the cases of just impediment, that is to say, war, pestilence or famine, to the intent that they prevail within the mining district, or for twenty leagues around and no further, the term of four months shall be suspended from running. Which provision is an addition of the new code, not being contained in the 40th of the old ordinances. The

---

* Acosta, de privil. credit. reg. 1. ampliat. 11, n. 16, 17 et 18. "Præterea his, quæ supra diximus, circa emphyteutam et similes non solventes pensionem, adjiciendum erit, quod prædicti in commissum cadent quantumvis nulla interpellatio judicialis, aut extrajudicialis interveniat ; nam tempore a jure præfinito decurso, causa dominii directi in concursu potior erit ; etenim dies interpellat pro homine ; quod procedit etiam si creditores moram purgare velint, et pensionem solvere." Et pluribus citatis prosequitur, ibi : " Quia ubi dies et pœna obligatione adjicitur, mora dilui non potest." L. magnam, Cod. de contrah. et committ. stipul. Pichard, in tract. de mora, ex n. 69 ; ubi infinitos citat Gomez, in L. 38, Taur. n. 3. Matienzo, in L. 7, tit. 4, lib. 5. Recop. gloss. 3, n. 2.

ground of the exception is clear, namely, that a term or prescription does not run against a person under impediment; the time during which the impediment continues being omitted in the calculation, according to the ordinary rules and principles, which we have noticed elsewhere.[*] And as the penalty is enacted against those only, who negligently omit to work their mines, whilst the omitting to do so in time of pestilence, famine or war, is no proof of negligence, but only an anxiety for the general safety, it follows that, in cases of this kind, as no blame attaches, the penalty does not take effect.

17. It might be asked, whether any other impediments, besides those of pestilence, famine or war, can be admitted to excuse the necessity of working, or to suspend the running of the period of four months? The reply is, that none such can be admitted; for the declaration of the law, that by just impediments are to be understood war, pestilence or famine, is evidently intended to convey a definition and limitation, and not an example or illustration. And, upon well considering the matter, it will be seen, that under no other circumstances can there be a difficulty in finding so small a number of hands as four persons. Schism, tumult or riot, and epidemic sickness, may be reduced to and are included under one or other of the above three cases, as different species of the same genus, and therefore constitute no new description of impediment.

18. Minority in age, absence on public affairs, banishment, and other cases privileged by the civil law,[†] will not, nor ought to authorise the maintaining a right to a mine without keeping it at work; the formality in the latter case, being required by the law, and being a condition the soveregn has thought proper to annex, in granting the right of property: to maintain which, therefore, on the part of the subject, it is absolutely necessary that this indispensable obligation should be observed. Nor is there a single ordinance giving any privilege of exemption from this rule; but, on the contrary, they all concur in urging the working and improvement of the mines, for the benefit of the crown (in respect of the fifth or tenth in which it is interested), and of the state, which ought to be preferred before that of individuals; notwithstanding that the latter may wish (disregarding the forms of the law, which, upon the very fact of their being left unworked, divests and extinguishes the right of the party who has neglected the working), to maintain their right to the mines, without keeping them at work.

19. It follows therefore, that neither a minor, nor any other privileged person, can demand to be indemnified against the lapse of this period of four months. For *re integra*, that is to say, if no one have denounced the mine, he may make registry anew, which will give him a new title, under a new grant of the law. It is clear that the law allows this to be done, for it says,

[*] See chap. 16, n. 10.

[†] Tit. 25, part 3; tot tit. 19, part. 6; tot. tit. Cod. quib. non obstet long. temp. præscrip.

that he shall have no right to it, "unless by making registry thereof anew, and going through the other proceedings in conformity with these ordinances;" and therefore the minor, community, church or other party, having the ordinary legal remedy of making registry anew, there is no occasion to have recourse to the extraordinary one of restoring the mine.*

20. But *re non integra*, that is to say, supposing the mine to have been denounced by, and adjudged to, some other person, in the form prescribed by the 38th and 39th ordinances; the matter cannot be restored to its former plight. First, because the ordinance excludes every remedy, after the matter has been determined in the mode which it prescribes.† Second, because the civil law never gives restitution when the effect would be to benefit one person at the expense of another, or to profit the one by the labour and toil of the other.‡ Third, because there is no restitution against an infraction of the precept, even of an individual; which must be observed, to give a right to any entail or trust founded by him: the cause must therefore be the same with one who infringes the precept or form of the law. For even in the case of a minor, no restitution is allowed against a breach of the forms or conditions of the law, but the trust will pass, by virtue of the law, to the next in order, and a right being thus acquired under the operation of the law, no restitution can be allowed in opposition to it; as is shewn by Larrea, upon the authority of Decius, Mieres, Caldas Pereyra and many others, and so by Garcia, Covarrubias, Felinus, Pareja and others, referred to by Ayllon.§

21. As the law, then, extinguishes the right to the mine, for the non-observance of the precept to keep it at work, and the mine is, by the operation of the same law, made over to the party who denounces and works it, having previously made registry according to the ordinance, the restitution of the mine would prejudice this acquired and vested right, whilst the party

---

* L. in causæ, ff. de minor. "Nam si communi auxilio munitus sit, non debet ei tribui extra-ordinarium remedium."

† Chap. 18, ord. 38, "And what shall be so determined, shall be observed and enforced, and there shall not be admitted any appeal, supplication, charge of nullity or injustice, or other remedy against the same."

‡ L. 18, ff ex quib. cujus major. "Sciendum est quod in his casibus restitutionis auxilium majoribus damus, in quibus rei duntaxat persequendi gratia quæruntur: non cum et lucri faciendi ex alterius pœna vel damno, auxilium sibi impertiri desiderant." L. quod si minor, §. Scævola, ff. de minor.

§ Larrea, Decis, Granat. decis. 59, a n. 12. "In quo opinionum conflictu, senatus restitutionem esse denegandum decrevit; ne voluntas institutoris primogenii illudatur: et contra legis dispositionem nulla minori conceditur restitutio, nec contra implementum conditionis legalis, ut ex Decio, cons. 161, vers. postremo, L. minoribus, Cod. de his quib. ut indig. L. 13, tit. 7, part 6, L. 11, tit. 8, lib. 5, Recop. probavit Mieres, dict. illat. 8, n. 164; et ex Gloss. in L. exigendi Cod. de procur. et ex consilio ejusdem Caldas Pereyra, in L. si curatorem habens, n. 79, vers. 4. Gomez, Var. resol. cap. 14, et ibi Ayllon, u. 45. Pareja, de edit. instr. tom. 2, tit. 9, resol. 5, ex n. 5. Cancer. 1, p. cap. 13, n. 58. Fachineo, lib. 8, cap. 49. Costa, lib. 2. Select. cap. 4, n. 2, et apud hos innumeri.

who has negligently left the mine unworked, would benefit by the labour of the other, and make a profit out of the loss of the rightful owner.

22. But it may be said, perhaps, iu some cases, that the blame of the neglect may be attributable to a tutor, steward or administrator. If this be the case, then, the remedy must be by an action against these parties, but not by a restitution of the mine, and an expulsion of the rightful owner, who has acquired a property in it by the operation of the law, and agreeable to the forms of the ordinances. It is with a view to provide for a case of this kind, that the laws of Peru* direct, that upon the death of the proprietor of a mine, his executors shall, if the heirs be in Spain, sell it, like other landed property, within thirty days; having it first proclaimed, and offered to the best bidder, and remitting the money to Spain; but that if the heirs be in Peru, the mine shall not be liable to be denounced, as unworked, within five months; after which, it shall: and that if the executors shall not perform all that is above directed, they shall be liable to make good any loss. By force of this ordinance, therefore, the mine is liable to be denounced for insufficient working, after the expiration of five months; even though the heirs be absent from the place, and be they under what circumstances they may—minors, or of full age, rich or poor; and an executor who gives occasion to the denouncement of the mine, by leaving it insufficiently worked, or who, by his default, occasions any other damage, is liable to make compensation; and therefore a tutor, curator, steward or administrator, of a mine belonging to a minor or other privileged party, is under the same obligation to work the mine; which, in case of his default, will become liable to be denounced, at the end of four months; and when once in the possession of a party who has registered it anew, restitution can no longer be admitted.

23. We say, *when once in the possession of a party who has registered it anew;* for if it have not yet been adjudged to him, and he have not yet expended money or labour upon the mine, it is equivalent to the matter being in the same condition: and we should not hesitate to say, under such circumstances, that a person under age, who might have omitted, from want of reflection, to keep the mine at work, ought to have it restored to him, no injury being thereby done to the person claiming to have the mine adjudged to him for insufficient working; and this being the express doctrine of the law,† and of various authors. But if all the proceedings have been gone through, and the adjudication be concluded, the expenses in course of disbursement, and all the previous arrangements made, equity will not permit the original owner to take advantage of the labour of the other. So that regard

---

* Ordinance 8, tit. 7, concerning mines left insufficiently worked: Escalona, Gazoph. lib. 2, p. 2, cap. 1, pag. 117.

† L. 2, tit. 19, p. 6, L. quod si minor, §. Scævola, ff. de minor. Larrea, decis 59, u. 21; ubi refert verba Mieres, et tradit Acostam, in L. gallus, §. et quid si tantum, ff. de lib. et posth. p. 2, u. 49. Covarr. 1, Var. cap. 5, n. 7. Caldas, in L. si curatorem, verb. læsis, n. 47.

must be had to the particular circumstances of the case, and restitution must be granted or refused, as the judge may, in his discretion, find meet.

24. Neither is extreme poverty treated as a sufficient impediment, to authorise the omission to work the mine, or to prevent the penalty of forfeiture from attaching ; notwithstanding the various privileges allowed to persons in poverty, on account of their wretched condition. For the ordinance expressly declares that this penalty shall be incurred, not only by those who abandon the working of the mines, in order that they may work others, but also by those who have not the means or ability to work them, as appears from the preamble, " and they do not work them, either because it is not in their power, or because they are engaged in working others which they consider better." He therefore, who cannot afford to pay for keeping them at work, must seek some other employment : for in carrying on works of this kind, money is every thing ; and a mine will always require a mine.

CHAPTER XVIII.

OF THE JUDICIAL COURSE OF PROCEEDING IN THE FIRST AND SECOND INSTANCE, UPON THE DENOUNCEMENT OF A MINE.—OF THE STRICTNESS REQUIRED TO BE OBSERVED IN BOTH INSTANCES, ANY OTHER APPEAL BEING DENIED ; AND OF THE SENTENCE OF ADJUDICATION OF THE MINE.

ORDINANCES XXXVIII. XXXIX.

XXXVIII. Also, we ordain and command, that for the purpose of having any mine pronounced or declared to have been insufficiently worked, the party who shall come to denounce it, shall appear before the mining justice, and shall make the denouncement, wherein he shall name the mine, describe the hill or place where it is situate, and upon whose boundaries (if any,) it abuts, and set forth its condition, in regard to depth, and whether it contain any ore or not ; and it shall be ascertained, within forty days, whether the mine have been left insufficiently worked for such four months, the party being summoned, if possible, in person, or at his house (supposing he have one at a mine in question or in the vicinity, or that it can conveniently be done,) by mentioning it or making it known to his wife, or servants, or nearest neighbour or neighbours, so that it may come to his knowledge ; but if he cannot be summoned in the vicinity, not having any house there, as is aforesaid, then by edicts and proclamation in the manner hereafter to be mentioned. And within forty days, to be computed from the day on which such denouncement shall be made, both parties shall be at liberty to allege and prove such matters as they may think proper ; and the cause shall be determined upon what shall be done within the term aforesaid, without any other termination or adjournment; and if such mine shall be pronounced to have been insufficiently worked, then it shall be adjudged as such to the aforesaid denouncer, and possession thereof shall be immediately given to him, notwithstanding any appeal, or question of invalidity or injustice, that may be interposed or raised against what shall be so pronounced; provided the party aforesaid, to whom such mine shall be adjudged, shall be obliged, within the term of three months, to deepen such one of the trial pits therein as he shall think proper, and to make it three *estados* deeper than it was at the time of his making the aforesaid denouncement, and for that purpose it shall be measured in the presence of our mining justice; all which he shall do and perform, under the penalty of forfeiting the mine, and of its being adjudged to any person who shall denounce it, subject to the same obligation and penalty. Provided he keep an account, to be entered in a book, of the ore and silver which may be raised from such mine, and of the expenses which may be laid out in working it, by the day, month and year; and that he give security in one thousand ducats, that if he be worsted upon appeal, and be ordered to render an account, and make satisfaction, he may have the means of doing so, and may do so. And if either party shall consider himself aggrieved, he shall be at liberty to appeal within three days, and justice shall be determined and done, upon what shall be stated, alleged and proved by the two parties, within sixty days, to be computed from the day of denouncing the decree, without any other termination or prorogation; and what shall be so determined shall be observed and executed, and no appeal, supplication, charge of nullity or injustice, or other remedy, shall be allowed.

XXXIX. Also, we ordain and command, that if it should happen that any mine is denounced for insufficient working, which does not appear to have an owner, or having one, he should be absent, and it should not be known where he is, or he should be in some place where notice cannot be given to him according to the last ordinance, the justice aforesaid shall, on some Sunday, when coming from mass at the church of the mines aforesaid, or if there be no church there, then at that of the nearest town, where there shall be at least eight persons present, cause such denouncement to be publicly proclaimed, that it may be known, and that information thereof may be given to the party to whom it may belong, or to some one who may answer for him, in order that he may, if he please, come forward and make his defence. And such proclamation being made, a transcript thereof shall be affixed on the principal door of such church, so as to appear publicly; and such proclamation shall be made on two other subsequent Sundays; so that altogether, there shall be three proclamations, on three Sundays, and the copies thereof shall be affixed as aforesaid, which shall be held and accounted a sufficient summons, in like manner as if it had been made personally; and if the owner, or some person competent to resist such denouncement, shall appear pending such three proclamations, or within forty days from the first of them being made, then the parties being heard, agreeably to the preceding ordinance, justice shall be done ; and if he shall not appear within such term of forty days, or before the proclamations shall have been made, such denouncer shall give evidence of the mine aforesaid having been left insufficiently worked during such term of four months as aforesaid, which being given, and such forty days having expired, the mine shall be pronounced to have been so insufficiently worked, and shall be adjudged to such denouncer, and possession thereof shall be given to him. Provided that he shall be obliged to sink three *estados*, agreeably to the aforesaid ordinances, and under the penalty thereof. And if, after such forty days are expired, and within the three days during which an appeal is allowed, the owner, or any party having authority, shall appear, he shall be at liberty to appeal, and justice shall be done, agreeably to the aforesaid ordinances.

CONTENTS OF THE COMMENTARY ON THESE ORDINANCES.

1. In procuring a declaration, that a mine has been insufficiently worked, the judicial proceedings commence by libel.
2. Of summoning the party denounced, to attend the investigation.
3. The term allowed for the proceedings is forty days ; and it cannot be extended.
4. Three days only are allowed for appealing. The appeal can have a devolutive* effect only, and in the mean time, the successful party must select some trial pit or other pit, and sink it three *estados* : must keep an account, and give security.
5. The appeal must be terminated within sixty days, and no further appeal is admitted.
6. The like is to be observed in case the defendant, being absent, should appear and appeal within the term of three days.
7, 8, 9 and 10. Several peculiarities in these ordinances and in the method they prescribe.
11. Their object is to expedite the proceedings as much as possible, in order to promote the more active working of the mines.
12. The rule of terminating the proceedings within sixty days, is not regarded in practice.
13. Whether the security for one thousand ducats, which is to be given by the denouncer when victorious, is also to be given when the other party gains the cause ? Answered in the affirmative.
14. The denouncer, when successful, must sink to the depth of three *estados*, the mine being now a new one, and the rights of the party denounced being extinguished.
15. Of the account to be kept by the miner.
16. Of the course of proceedings followed in Peru, in obtaining a declaration that a mine has been insufficiently worked

---

* " The suspensive effect is the cognizance which the superior court takes of the sentence or decree of the judge *a quo*, or inferior court, suspending the execution of it. The *devolutive* is the cognizance which the superior court takes of the decree or sentence of the inferior, without suspending the execution of it." Institutes of the civil law of Spain, &c. translated by L. F. C. Johnstone, p. 342, note 12 .—*Trans.*

COMMENTARY.

1. These ordinances, which follow the 41st and 42d of the old ordinances, regulate the course of proceeding to be observed judicially, in denouncing and declaring a mine to have been insufficiently worked. In the first place, the denouncer presents a libel to the justice, setting forth that the mine, situated in such a hill or place, abutting upon the boundaries of certain other mines (if any), of which Titius was the possessor, and which is in ruins, filled with water, or in ore, as may be, has been left insufficiently worked for more than four successive months, whereof he is ready to give proof; and having set forth so much of the evidence as is sufficient, he prays to have the mine adjudged to him, being ready to sink it to the proper depth, and to observe all the other provisions of the ordinances.

2. Second, the justice entertains the denouncement, and orders the depositions to be taken; the former possessor, against whom the denouncement is made, being summoned (or his wife, servants, or nearest neighbour, if he be absent, but in the vicinity) ; and if he have no house, and his place of abode be not known, or if it be unknown who is the owner of the mine, then three proclamations are to be made on as many distinct Sundays, in the presence of eight persons at least, and notices are to be affixed on the doors of the church of the place, or, if there be no church at the place, then of that of the nearest town, that it may come to his knowledge, and that he may make his defence, either in person, or by an agent duly authorised; and this, as we have observed elsewhere,* is esteemed a sufficient summons, being expressly made so by the 39th ordinance.

3. Third, the parties are to be heard, and to prove their allegations with regard to the mine having been sufficiently worked or otherwise, within forty days, to be computed from the date of the denouncement, which term is not to be enlarged. And the three proclamations must be made, and the notices be affixed, within the same term of forty days. And in the case above mentioned, of its being unknown who is the proprietor, or what is his place of abode, if the defendant do not appear, either personally or by some agent duly authorised, proof of the mine having been left unworked must be given, within the same period.

4. Fourth, upon the expiration of the forty days, judgment is to be pronounced ; and if the mine should be declared to have been insufficiently worked, the other party is to be as liberty to appeal within three days ; but the appeal is only to have a devolutive effect, and possession is to be given to the successful party, notwithstanding any appeal or charge of nullity or injustice, subject to three obligations. The first, to sink such one of the trial pits or other pits as he may select, to the depth of three *estados*, within the term of three months ; for which purpose, the depth of such pit is to be

---

* Chap. 10, n. 2.

measured before the justice, at the time of the adjudication, under pain of forfeiting the mine, if omitted to be done. The second, to keep an account, to be delivered in, if he should be unsuccessful upon appeal. The third to give security to the amount of one thousand ducats, to the effect that he will render an account in the above event.

5. Fifth, the appeal must be concluded within sixty days from the judgment being given, and what shall be thereupon determined, shall be observed and enforced ; and no appeal, supplication, charge of nullity or injustice, or other remedy shall be allowed.

6. Sixth, supposing the party denounced to have been absent during the proceedings, and that it has not been known where he has been ; if, after the proclamations have been made, and the notices affixed, the insufficient working established, and judgment given, he should appear within the three days allowed for appealing, either by himself, or by some authorised agent, he will be at liberty to do so, within that time ; the judgment however, being executed, subject to the aforesaid three duties of sinking, keeping an account and giving security for one thousand ducats. But, as declared in the last paragraph, no remedy is to be allowed against the sentence pronounced thereupon.

7. Several peculiarities, meriting observation and illustrating, are observed upon considering these ordinances. First, that although the term for appealing is generally five days, yet in a cause concerning the insufficient working of a mine, the appeal must be made within three days from the sentence.

8. Second, that although an appeal has generally both effects, yet an appeal from a decree declaring a mine to have been insufficiently worked, and adjudging the same, has only the devolutive effect.

9. Third, that the time for trying the appeal is limited to sixty days, although more is allowed in other suits.

10. Fourth, that no appeal, supplication, charge of nullity or injustice, or other remedy, is allowed against the sentence pronounced on the appeal ; whereas it is usual to present a supplication against the sentences of review of the royal audiencies, even though confirmatory of the judgment of the ordinary judge.

11. All these restrictions are founded on the great importance of expediting the suits in which miners are concerned ; it being an essential object to keep the working of the mines uninterrupted. For if a sentence adjudging a mine for insufficient working, were not carried into effect, it would remain unworked for a still longer time, to the prejudice of the public and of the revenue ; whilst the advantage of the denouncer and the denounced, are alike consulted by executing the decree, and giving possession, under the security of one thousand ducats, and subject to the obligation of rendering an

* Law 1, tit 18, book 4, Collection of Castile. Cur. Philip. 5, p. §. 1, n. 16.

account. These, then, are the reasonable grounds on which the legislature has deemed it right to abridge the ordinary periods.

12. Notwithstanding this, the observance of this term of sixty days, within which the proceedings upon appeal ought to be terminated, is not strictly attended to in practice, either from the nature of the proceedings themselves, or from the parties not having a proper regard to expedition, or from the great pressure of business, which is dispatched according to the order in which it stands. The business relating to mines is, however, generally dispatched in the audiencies with as much expedition as possible, and the reiterated injunctions of the laws and ordinances enforcing the speedy dispatch of the causes in which the miners are concerned,* as being of great importance to the public, are duly attended to.

13. Another matter demanding consideration is, that the 38th ordinance, in directing, that when a mine is pronounced to have been insufficiently worked, and is adjudged to the party denouncing it, the latter, besides taking possession and sinking three *estados*, shall give security for one thousand ducats, and keep an account, &c., does not provide for the case of its being declared that the mine has *not* been left insufficiently worked ; whence arises the question, whether the party against whom denouncement has been made, and who retains possession of the mine, must give the like security, and keep a like account ? The reply to which will be in the affirmative, for the rights of the plaintiff and defendant are upon the same footing ; and as the ore or produce of the mine is the object in question, if the party denounced is to be secured against the event of the sentence being reversed on appeal, the denouncer is entitled to be furnished with the like security against such an event. The security given, agreeably to the law of Toledo, by the plaintiff at whose suit execution is levied, upon enforcing a decree for a sale, under the executive mode of proceeding,† must in the same manner, be given by the defendant, if demanded, upon executing the decree when in his favour. And as the appeal has not the suspensive effect, against the person at whose suit execution is levied, giving security, the case is the same with regard to the defendant in execution, giving the like security ; the situation of both,

---

* Infr. cap. 25, ubi ex ipsius litera commendatur celeritas in causis metallicorum. Law 5, tit. 20, book 4, Collection of the Indies. " We charge and command our royal audiencies to dispatch, and cause to be dispatched, with much brevity, the causes, suits and matters relating to the miners and amalgamators, which shall be pending before them, that they may not have their attention distracted by suits, nor have to make long journeys, to the prejudice of the works of their mines and reduction establishments."

† The executive mode of proceeding is a process by which execution is obtained against the property of a debtor, and the debt levied by a sale, more expeditiously than in the ordinary course of justice. For the cases in which it may be had recourse to, and the mode of prosecuting it, see Institutes of the Civil Law of Spain, &c. translated by L. F. C. Johnstone, p. 251.— *Trans.*

with regard to the suit, being the same, according to Hyppolitus, Gutierrez and others, cited in the *Curia*.[*]

14. Another observation occurs, in reference to the direction of the 38th ordinance, that such trial pit or other pit, as the denouncer shall think fit, shall be sunk three *estados*, for which purpose it shall be measured in the presence of the justice ; and which shall be done and performed under pain of forfeiting the mine, and of its being adjudged to any one who shall denounce it. Whence we may perceive, that no vestige of right remains in the last possessor, no tenth part, as in some places ;[†] and that no regard is had to the depth he may have previously sunk, nor to the boundaries he may have previously set out or fixed ; and therefore the new possessor, to whom the mine is adjudged, must sink to the proper depth, and set up his fixed stake upon such trial pit as he shall so sink, which is a direction well worthy of attention, from the great importance of preserving the identity of the mine, and of its fixed stake.

15. These ordinances also direct that the miner shall keep an account, to be rendered, in case he should be worsted upon appeal. But as the question of restoring the ore, and keeping an account, is involved in the 63d and 64th ordinances, where the subject of suits concerning the possession and property of mines is considered, we refer the reader to that place.[‡]

16. With respect to the course observed in Peru, in obtaining a declaration that a mine has been insufficiently worked, we have already stated, in the last chapter,[§] that it must have remained unworked a year and a day, the ordinance which gave twenty days only, having been altered ; but the mode of establishing that it has been insufficiently worked for a year and a day, remains unaltered, and is as follows. If the party be upon the spot, he is to be summoned personally ; and if absent, he is to be summoned by three proclamations, one to be made upon the day of the denouncement, another on the fifth day after, and a third upon the ninth day after that ; and the evidence is to be given in within six days ; upon the expiration of which, the cause is to be determined : so that the whole term allowed is twenty days.

---

[*] Cur. Phil. 2, p. §, 21. u. 4. Law 2, tit. 21, book 4, Coll. of Castile, where it is held, that not only the plaintiff, but the defendant also, must give security ; cap. 2, de mut. pet.

[†] Vide supr. chap. 11. n. 10 11 and 12.

[‡] Infr. chap. 23.

[*] Vide supr. chap. 17, u. 2.

CHAPTER XIX.

OF THE DAMAGES TO BE PAID BY THE PROPRIETORS OF THE MORE EL-
EVATED MINES, THE WATERS OF WHICH FLOW INTO THE LOWER
MINES.—OF THE OBLIGATION WHICH ALL MINERS ARE UNDER, TO KEEP
THEIR MINES CLEAR AND FREE OF WATER; THE LOWER ONES NOT
BEING SUBJECT TO THE SERVICE OF RECEIVING THE WATER FROM
THE UPPER ONES.—IT IS THE DUTY OF THE JUSTICES ANXIOUSLY TO
PROMOTE THE DRAINING.—A DESCRIPTION OF THE PITS AND ADITS
USED FOR THIS PURPOSE; OBSERVATIONS ON THE GREAT NUMBER OF
MINES UNDER WATER IN DIFFERENT MINING DISTRICTS.

ORDINANCE XL.

ALSO, forasmuch as it might happen that some mines might be flooded by
the water flowing in from the neighbouring and adjoining mines of less depth,
by which means the working of such deep mines might be brought to a stand,
and the proprietors thereof damaged:—We command our administrator-
general and district-administrators, and each and any one of them, that they
take especial care to visit such mines, and to arrange that they shall all be
kept clear and free of water, and be worked and kept up. And if any mine
shall be damaged by the water of one or more other mines, our administrator-
general, or district-administrator aforesaid, shall, upon the request of the
party, inspect it, and shall cause two persons, named by the parties, and
approved of by him, to be sworn in his presence, and to ascertain the damage
and expense which such mine may require (*terná*) in clearing out and draining; and what shall be so ascertained, the mining justice shall order to be
paid, so that the damage may cease, and the working be proceeded in; and
so that the person who has sustained wrong may be redressed.

———————

CONTENTS OF THE COMMENTARY ON THIS ORDINANCE.

1. This ordinance, directing that the owner of a more elevated mine shall make amends
   for any damage caused by the water flowing into a lower mine, is of very difficult
   construction.

2 and 3. The lower ground being, as it were, naturally liable to the service of receiving
   the water from the upper ground.

4 and 5. The difficulty in the ordinance is not removed by the suggestion, that it is to be
   understood to apply to the water thrown out, and which has been submitted to human
   agency.

6 and 7. The ordinance justified, by the consideration, that the mines are, by law, to be
   kept drained; and it is explained as applying to damage caused by negligence in
   regard to draining.

8. The lower ground must, in general, submit to receive the water flowing from the higher
   ground, unless where there is some law to the contrary.

9. The situation of mines, being generally in hilly ground, renders it necessary to keep
   up the draining, and imposes a responsibility on those who neglect it.

10. These damages are to be levied, not upon an *ex officio* order of the judge, but upon the application of the party ; and are to be estimated by surveyors.

11. The lower mines are not liable to the service of receiving the water from the higher ones.

12. It is the duty of the justices to watch anxiously over the draining. Of the advantages which would attend this practice, if enforced.

COMMENTARY.

1. The rule of this ordinance, and of the 43d of the ordinances, which it follows, directing that the expenses of draining off the water which flows into a deeper mine, from mines of less depth in the vicinity, shall be estimated and made good, it would seem difficult to comprehend, or even to reconcile with justice. The difficulty consists in this, that the lower ground must always be liable to the service of receiving the water which flows naturally from the higher ;* in consequence of which, the action for removing or relieving from the effect of water, does not hold when the damage done is produced in the natural course, but only when confined, or let down suddenly, or turned into some new course, by the agency and operation of man.† And this is confirmed by the text of the civil law, where it is laid down, that the lower ground must, by law, by its position, and by custom, be subservient to the higher.‡

2. This is also proved by the law of the *Partida*, which declares,§ " That notwithstanding that water should flow from an inheritance which is situated higher, into one which is situated lower, or stones or earth should be carried down by the action of the water, or otherwise (so that it be not done maliciously by the hand of man), and damage should ensue ; yet he to whom the inheritance, which is situated highest, may belong, is not culpable, nor bound to make it good."

3. The authors who have treated of services, in particular, lay it down unanimously, that the lower ground must, as a natural service, receive the water from the higher ground, although it must necessarily receive an injury thereby, unless it be made, by the agency of man, to produce damage which it would not otherwise cause ; but that if it flow naturally, and take its course unimpelled by any external agency, nothing wrong attaches to the owner of the higher ground, who, being guilty of no fault, cannot be made

---

* L. 1, §. 22, ff. de aqua et aqua pluvia arcend. "Semper enim hanc esse servitutem inferiorum, praediorum ut natura profluentum aquam excipiant." Et §. 23. " Agri naturam esse servandam, et semper inferiorem superiori inservire "

† Dict. leg. 1, §. 1. "Hæc actio toties locum habet quoties manu opere facto, agro aqua nocitura est, id est, cum quis manu fecerit, quo aliter flueret, quam natura soleret, si forte immittendo eam, aut majorem fecerit, aut citatiorem aut vehementiorem, aut si comprimendo redundare effecit ; quod si natura aqua noceret, ea actione non continetur."

‡ L. 2, ff. eod. "In summa, tria sunt per quæ inferior locus superiori servit. Lex ; Natura loci : Vetustas, quæ semper pro lege habetur, minuendarum litium causa."

§ L. 14, tit 32, part. 3.

liable to any penalty ; as may be seen in Cepola, Pechio, Lagunez, and many others.* By the same rule, then, there shall be no injustice in the lower mine receiving the waters of the higher mine ; nor shall that circumstance afford any ground for rendering the owner of the latter liable to the expenses of draining the former ; the damage arising, not from any fault on his part, but from the natural constitution of the ground.

4. Nor is there any ground for suggesting that the ordinance may refer to such water as may be raised through the pit, by means of machinery, and thrown off into the neghbouring mines, although such a direction would be very proper. For the ordinance does not refer to such water, but to water finding its way from one mine to another, though fissures or veins beneath the surface ; whereas the water which is drained by machinery, does not flow from one mine to another, but is raised artificially, and thrown off by the draining apparatus.

5. It is evident, therefore, that the ordinance does not refer to the water thrown off by machinery, but to the subterranean waters : and this is proved by a passage in Agricola, from which the ordinance appears to have been taken. It is there said, " That if from the water not being drawn off from the pit of any mine, situated higher, it found its way through veins or fissures, into the pit of some other mine, the working of which became thereby impeded ; then, if the owners made application, complaining of the damage, and two surveyors declared on oath, that this was the case, he who had been the cause of such damage, forfeited his mine in favour of the injured party. In other places, the rule was, that he should contribute a proportion of the expense, to make amends for the damage, if it occurred in no more than two pits ; and if he did not do so, he forfeited the mine. But by draining the inundated works, he might recover the right to his mine."† Whence it appears, that neither the ordinance nor Agricola refer to water thrown off by machinery, but to such as finds its way through subterraneous veins and channels ; and consequently, we are still pressed upon by the difficulty, that as no blame attaches in allowing the water to take its natural course from above downwards, so neither can there be any ground for the penalty of forfeiting the mine, stated by Agricola to be enforced in some places, nor for

---

* Cepola, tract. 2, de servit. cap. 4, n. 71 et 77. Pechio, de servit. tom. 3, cap. 9, n. 118. Lagunez, de fruct. part. 1, cap. 5, n. 30 et 39 ; et plures apud eos.

† Agricol. de re metall. lib. 4, pag. 64, lin. 6. " Præterea, quondam si aqua non exanclata ex altiori alicujus fodinæ puteo. per venan aut fibram fundebatur in alterius fodinæ puteum, et labori erat impedimento ; tunc domini fodinæ damnum facientia adibant magistrum metallorum, et conquerebantur de damno, qui ad puteos mittebat duumviros juratos : hi si ita rem se habere comperissent, jus fodinæ damnum dantis, dominis damnum facientibus dabatur. Sed mos iste quibusdam in locis immutatus. Fam magister metallicorum si idipsum de duobus puteis compertum habet, dominos, putei damnum dantis juvet sumptum ex parte suppeditare dominis putei facientis damnum. Quod si non fecerint, tunc eos privat jure fodinæ : contra dominjus fodinæ obtinent, si fossores misserint in opera, et aquam et puteis exanclaverint."

the direction of our ordinance, that the draining shall be paid for, the damage stopped, and amends made to the injured party.

6. Notwithstanding the above remarks, the ordinance may be shewn to be reasonable and just. First, because by the rules of law, all the mines are to be kept clear and free of water ; for which purpose the justice is ordered to exert the greatest vigilance in inspecting them : which is one of the burdens the sovereign has thought proper to impose, in giving his subjects an interest in the mines, and to which mining property, and the owners of such property, are therefore necessarily subject by law. And it is to facilitate this object of drawing off the water, that pits, adits, and *contraminas*, are made. If then, the owner of a mine of less depth allow it to fill with water, omitting to draw it off by the pit, and the water, by its weight and pressure, flow into and inundate the deeper mines, he is doubly culpable : first, in not draining his own mine ; and second, in unjustly causing the inundation of an adjoining mine, and thereby preventing its works from being continued ; and it is, consequently, just, that he should be made liable to pay the expenses of draining, which is a less punishment than the forfeiture of the mine, stated by Agricola to have been sometimes imposed.

7. Second, because neither Agricola nor the ordinance, blame nature for making the water descend by its gravity from above downwards ; neither do they, in fact, refer to water proceeding from snow, springs or rain, independent of human agency, which is an inevitable evil : what the ordinance says is this ; " And if any mine shall be damaged by one or more others ;" that is to say, by water allowed to collect together, and which the owner does not drain off, as he is in duty bound to do. And Agricola expresses himself still more plainly, " Si aqua non exanclata ex altiori alicujus fodinæ puteo, &c. ;" that is to say, if water, which has not been drawn off as it ought to have been, shall inundate the adjoining property, the injury to the owner must be redressed, by paying him the expense of the draining, so as to remedy the damage of which the other, by not draining, was the culpable cause.

8. Third, because, although water descending naturally from the higher ground, must necessarily be received by the lower ; yet this is to be understood only, when there is no agreement or law to the contrary, as is proved by Cepola, from various texts,* one of which sets forth, that property is

---

* Cepola, de servit. rust. præd. tract. 2, u. 71, ibi : " Quæro nunc de alia quæstione quotidiana. Aqua ex fundo meo superiore descendit ad tuum inferiorem, et inundat totum fundum tuum, ex magna abundantia aquarum. Quæritur de duobus. Primo : numquid ego, qui sum dominus fundi superioris, cogar retinere aquam in fundo meo, puta faciendo fossam et aggeres, et in eo aquam recolligendo, ne discurrat ad fundum tuum ? Circa quæ dicas, imprimis, tria esse consideranda : primum legis conventio, ut si aliqua intervenit, illa sit servanda. L. 1, §. denique; L. 2, ff. de aqua pluv. arc. L. 1, §. si convenerit. ff. deposit. et aliis." Et sub eod. n. in fin. ibi : " Quando intervenet de retinenda in superiori, ne descendat ad inferiorem, vel de mittenda in fundum inferiorem, dicas illam conventionem esse servandam, et per eam, servitutem imponi, dict. L. 1 et 2, ff. de aq. pluv. arc. L. semper, ff. de reg. jur."

made subject to different laws and obligations, according to circumstances, and that when none such are imposed by law, they must operate according to the course of nature ;* but that if there be any express direction or law, the property becomes thereby liable to a service. Whence Cepola infers,† that if, by any law or agreement, the owner of the higher ground has become liable to the service of keeping in the water, or the owner, of the lower ground, to that of receiving it, each of them respectively, is bound to clear off the water, and to secure the dams, agreeably to the common rule, that he who is bound to perform any particular thing, is also bound to go through all the means necessary for accomplishing it; and that he who wills the consequent, must also will the antecedent. As then it is a provision of the law, that all miners shall keep their mines drained and clear of water, that they may be enabled to proceed with their own works, and may not impede those of their neighbours, they become liable, in complying with this rule, to the obligation or service of clearing and carrying off the water from their own mines, and they will be guilty, if they allow it to remain, of a great wrong, in allowing their own mines to fill with water, and of a much greater, in causing the inundation of their neighbour's mine.

9. Fourth, because the very situation of the mines calls for some law or regulation with respect to drainage : for they are generally found amongst hills and mountains, some in high ground, others in low, and the water usually takes its course freely, through all the mines upon the same vein. Such then being the state of things, were the owner of the lower mine bound to receive, and to draw off at his own expense, all the water from the higher ones, which would flow to him if not drawn off through their pits, he would be doubly injured; first, in his works being impeded; and second, in being made liable to the expense of draining. The ordinance proceeds with great equity, therefore, in making the owner of the higher mine liable to the expenses; for after all, no recompence is made for the damage sustained, in consequence of the works being impeded, contrary to the laws, which always urge the keeping up the works in an active train, and which provide (amongst other things,) with a view to this important end, that mines shall be drained by means of pits, adits or *contraminas*, directing that such works shall be executed wherever circumstances will admit of it; and even permitting adits and *contraminas* to be driven by individuals, independent of owners of the mines, as will be mentioned in the proper place.‡

---

* L. 1, §. 23, ff. de aq. pluv. arc. "Denique ait conditionibus agrorum quasdam leges esse dictas. Si tamen lex non sit agro dicta, agri naturam esse servandam."

† Id. ubi prox. n. 72. "Sed dubitare potest si simpliciter est imposita servitus, ut superior vicinus teneatur retinere aquam in fundo suo, vel quod inferior teneatur fossa eam recipere, nunquid superior, vel inferior teneatur purgare, vel aggeres facere, aut munire ? Et videtur, quod sic : quia qui tenetur ad unum, tenetur ad omnia per quæ pervenitur ad illud. Qui permittit consequens, videtur permittere necessario antecedens, &c."

‡ Vide infr. chap. 26, n. 26.

10. Having, by these arguments, overcome the difficulty which at first startled us, it is clearly established, that the damage caused by the overflowing of the water, must be estimated and paid for; but this is not to be done *ex officio*, but *upon the application of the party*. For if he remain silent, and make no application, but carry on the draining himself, he must be considered to have waived his right. If, however, he demand to be compensated for the damage, the justice must have an inspection made, and must determine the amount of the damage, upon the estimate of two surveyors upon oath; which damage he shall command to be promptly paid, agreeably to the spirit in which causes of this kind are conducted,* the injury being such as requires an instant remedy. And in determining the amount which will fairly cover it, must be estimated by experienced surveyors; that is to say, the quantity of water is to be computed, by comparing the state of the mine before and after the flowing in of the water, the expense required to draw it off being estimated according to the breadth and depth of the space the water occupies; wherein the practice of the district, as pursued by other miners, in the course of their draining, is the only rule to be observed.

11. From this ordinance, and the rule it enforces, it follows; that the inferior mines are not liable to the service of receiving the water from the higher mines, but that, on the contrary, by allowing the water to flow into the lower mines, an injustice is done to their owners, by impeding the works, and diminishing their profits, for which compensation ought to be made. And that all the mines, whether higher or lower in situation, must be kept drained by their owners, this service being imposed by the law. But the liability of the miner to allow a passage for the works of drainage, from other mines, is a service of a distinct kind, of which we shall speak when treating of *contraminas*, and is so far from being injurious to the mines through which a passage is allowed, that it is rather an advantage, in facilitating the draining of the latter, and the freeing them from rubbish.†

12. It follows also, that it is incumbent upon the mining justices to visit the mines in their respective districts, and to make arrangements, so that they shall all be kept free from water, in order that they may be kept regularly at work. Did the chief alcaldes zealously urge this object, and promote regular works of drainage, much injury might almost insensibly be prevented, and we should no longer have to witness the abandonment of many mining districts, which, although now overwhelmed with water, have, in their time, yielded riches to an incalculable amount. And were the visits they make directed to this important object, they would be attended with much advantage, instead of serving, as at present, rather as a pretext for extortion, than an incentive to labour.

* Agricola, ubi sup. ii. 5.   † Vide chap. 26, throughout.

CHAPTER XX.

OF THE RUBBISH HEAPS OF MINES, AND OF GIVINGS WAY IN THE WORKS OF MINES.—OF THE PILLARS OF SUPPORT, TIMBER-WORK, PITS AND CISTERNS.—OF THE ACTIVITY WITH WHICH THE JUSTICES SHOULD PROMOTE THE CONSTRUCTION AND PRESERVATION OF THESE WORKS.

ORDINANCES XLI. XLVI. LXXIV.

XLI. ALSO, we ordain and command, that persons who shall hold or work any mine or mines, shall be obliged to keep them clear, and timbered in such manner that they shall not fall in nor become choked ; leaving in such mines as shall produce ores of the quality of a marc and a half, or under, per quintal of silver-lead, such bridges, strengthenings or supports (*testeros*), as may be proper for their security and permanence ; and such mines as shall produce ores of better quality, shall, besides the above, be very thoroughly lined and secured with good timber ; and, in case of the contrary, the justice of such mine shall cause the work to be performed at the expense of the mine owners. And in order that this may be done and performed in manner aforesaid, our administrator-general, or district-administrator, is to observe, and shall observe, particular care in visiting and causing such mines to be inspected, taking with him persons who understand the subject, that he may make such provision as may be requisite, as is mentioned in this and the last ordinance.

XLVI. Also, we ordain and command, that no person, in working or digging his mine, shall be at liberty to throw the earth which he may raise from such mine, upon the mine, or within the *pertenencia* of another proprietor, under the penalty of ten ducats for every time he shall do so, to be applied as aforesaid. And the mining justice shall, whenever the party may require it of him, cause such earth to be removed and cleared from such *pertenencia*, at the expense of the party who may have thrown, or directed it to be thrown there, notwithstanding any appeal, or charge of nullity or injustice, that may be interposed ; but each person is permitted to carry out the earth from his mine through any *pertenencia*, provided that such earth be deposited out of the range of such *pertenencia*.

LXXIV. Also, forasmuch as we are advised, that much inconvenience arises from sinking pits in mines, very near each other at the surface, and likewise from sinking them continuously, without making any landing-places ; not only in regard to their permanence, but also because they cannot be worked or drained conveniently ; for a remedy hereof, we ordain and command, that when from henceforth any new mine shall be discovered, the pits continued shall be made ten *varas* from each other, and each pit shall be fourteen *estados* in depth ; and if they shall have to be sunk deeper, an excavation or recess (*mineta*), shall be made, before sinking any deeper ; from which the next pit shall be formed. But forasmuch as in many places, circumstances will not admit of this arrangement being adopted; in such cases, what shall appear in the opinion of the administrator of the district, and of other miners who shall understand this matter, to be most convenient, shall be done.

CONTENTS OF THE COMMENTARY ON THESE ORDINANCES.

COMMENTARY.

1. Of these three ordinances, the 41st agrees with the 44th, and the 46th with the 50th, of the old ordinances, but the 74th does not follow any other ordinance. They all look to the permanence and security of the mines. The object of the 46th, is to prevent rubbish from being thrown out upon the mine of another; of the 41st, to ensure the strengthening of the mines internally; and of the 74th, to regulate the arrangement of the pits and landing-places in the best possible manner, according to the judgment of the justice, and of experienced persons.

2. As to the first point, it must be remarked, that although the ordinances

have made the mines liable to various services, yet they do not intend that they should be burthened with the rubbish from other mines, lest they should fall in and be destroyed; their intention being, that each miner should make his rubbish heap in some convenient place, not upon the vein, nor upon the weak parts of the ground. But no question ever arises upon this point in New Spain, because, in that country, each person piles up his rubbish and builds his offices, upon his own ground, without inconvenience to others; and such rubbish is in fact useful, as it may be employed in erecting sheds and buildings to cover the pit, in furnishing earth for mortar, and in other ways.

3. As the mines are required to be kept free from rubbish, and their passages to be left clear, so that the works shall not be impeded, it follows necessarily, that it is incumbent on the miners to clear out and remove the rubbish and refuse. It may, however, be thrown aside within the mine, if there be any useless cavity in it; that is to say, the inutility of the cavity being first ascertained by the justices and surveyors, and it being shewn that the course of working will not be thereby interfered with, such cavity is allowed to be used as a depository for the rubbish; by which means the expense of raising it to the surface is spared, whilst, at the same time, the giving way, or falling in of the mine, may be repaired or prevented.

4. As to the second point, of the strengthenings, bridges and supports (*testeros*), it will be recollected, that the ordinance enforces particular anxiety on the part of the justice, in visiting the mines, and causing inspection to be made by experienced persons, to ascertain whether they are well secured, timbered and strengthened with pillars of support. Nothing however, is more neglected than the observance of this precept, although it is, above all others, that which it most behoves the district judge to enforce, on account of the great loss in which the falling in of the mine involves both the revenue and the public; and still more, from the melancholy effects of such a catastrophe, in overwhelming and burying the miserable workmen in its ruins, which are consequences of the very greatest moment. And as the cutting away of the pillars (as the miners express it), is a step generally prompted by the lust of gain, the owners should be fined, or subjected to some more severe mark of displeasure, as being the cause of these misfortunes, and of their attendant evils.*

5. Under the name of pillars, is included every thing which prevents the roof of the work, or the wall of the vein, from giving away. If the course

---

* L. 21, tit. 32, partida 3; "They should faithfully and with great earnestness command those who are placed over the works, to execute them, so that nothing wrong ensue through their fault or neglect; and if they shall not enforce the same upon their bodies, and all that they may possess, recourse must be had to the king thereupon." Concordat L. 25, eod. tit. et partit. ibi: "He must keep it up and work it, in such manner that it shall not fall in through his default or neglect." "Qui causam damni dat, damnum dedisse videtur." L. 21, tit. 24, part. 7. Krebs, de ligno et lapide, sect. 9. ubi domini tenentur quando damnum funium ac perticarum vetustate contingit. Et carpentarii tenentur de damno at ruina per negligentiam.

of the vein be inclined, or underlying, the support left between the two walls, so as to unite them, is called a pillar. If the course of the vein be perpendicularly downwards, the pillars are made in such a manner as to rest one upon another. And when the pillar is formed, the work is proceeded in; the roof being secured, so that it shall not give way or fall in.

6. This is not their only use in the perpendicular veins, for they likewise serve to fix and support the ladders, and to afford a resting-place for the workmen; so that if a workman slip, he will not fall to the bottom of the work, but will be intercepted by the pillar. They are also of important use in promoting the circulation of the air, so as to ventilate the works.

7. The distance between the pillars, whether in inclined or perpendicular veins, must be regulated by the firmness or weakness of the mine, and the constitution of the ground, which must also determine whether their thickness shall be two, four or five yards square. For greater precaution is required in some descriptions of ground than in others, so that the security of the mine, and what is more, the safety of the workmen, are consulted by making a pillar at every ten *varas*, or eight *varas*, according to the judgment of the surveyors, and the greater or less firmness of the ground.

8. The pillars are formed by leaving a mass of the rock or vein itself, and frequently consist of the very richest ore in the vein. In some places they are timbered; that is to say covered with wood, as has been mentioned before; in others, they are left bare. The object of the ordinance in providing, that when the quality of the ore exceeds a marc and a half per quintal, the pillars shall be covered with good timber, is merely for their permanent preservation; to prevent their being destroyed by the workmen, for the sake of the ore, which they contrive to steal with the greatest dexterity, without a pick, wedge or crow, and without making any noise which can lead to their detection. But if the covering them with timber be omitted, on account of the great expense attending it, a guard, at least, ought to be appointed to watch them, or they should be covered with the rubbish and loose stones, which may be substituted in the place of wood. In default of all these precautions, it becomes the duty of the justice to supply the omission, according to the judgment of surveyors, at the expense of the owners.

9. When the pillars are once formed, the owner cannot destroy them, even though they should consist of the richest ore, without being guilty of great breach of the ordinances; nor can the justice authorise their being cut away, either to the extent of destroying them completely, or merely of picking and weakening them; for the great object of the law, is to provide for the safety and permanence of the mines, and to prevent any giving way, which might lead to their total falling in, and endanger the lives of the workmen. And in case of its being proved and established, that such a catastrophe has been the consequence of the removal of the pillars, it would be proper that the

fault should be punished, not only by the forfeiture of the mine, but also by other more severe penalties, according to circumstances.*

10. No precautions should be dispensed with to ensure safety, where imminent danger to the life of man is involved ; and consequently, as neither the preprietor, nor even an engineer, can be morally certain that the ground will hold together without pillars, and as also the permanence of the mine is made by the ordinance an indispensable object ; neither the justice, nor any superior judge, be he who he may, can dispense with the precautions for that purpose, without rendering himself reponsible for the serious consequences which may ensue : but on the contrary, these officers are bound to punish the fault of removing the pillars, notwithstanding any pretext or excuse on the part of the owners. The chief alcaldes are bound to inform themselves, whether any impropriety has been committed in this respect, that an inspec- tion may be made, and the matter set right, by providing proper supports ; for it should be a primary object with them to provide for the security of the public, and the preservation and improvement of the mines. It would be very proper that these duties should be particularly noticed, when these justi- ces render an account of the discharge of their offices : as the present neg- lect of those duties is attended with scandalous and lamentable consequences, in the frequent deplorable instances of the falling in of mines, and the con- sequent loss of life experenced.

11. Nor can the removal of the pillars be permitted, under pretence of substituting pillars of stone and mortar, or any other material in their place ; for besides that this would be contrary to the meaning of the ordinances, the security of the ground is not sufficiently provided for by it, nor is it possible, by means of pillars of this kind, to maintain that perfect equilibrium which is preserved by pillars formed naturally out of the substance of the ground ; or to support the whole weight of a mountain, which will frequently give way upon removing a single stone from its natural bed, or upon weak- ening the support in the slightest degree : to say nothing of the great expense of putting up such supports, whether of timber or stone. But the princi- pal objection is, that the water and moisture which filtrate through the mines, prevent such works being constructed with stability.

12. Whence it follows, that if the owner of a mine should, in his eager- ness for gain, proceed to cut away the supports, he is, in the first place, to be punished by a severe fine ; and in the next place, inquiry is to be made, wheth- er the mine will admit of being made secure by substituting artificial pillars of support, in the place of such as have been cut away or weakened ; or whether, on the other hand, it will not admit of being so repaired, but threatens to give way altogether. If the latter be the case, the owner must be ordered, not only to remove all the workmen, but also to close up com-

* Vide supra, u. 4.

43

pletely, and at his own expense, all the levels which communicate with the unsafe cavity, to the satisfaction of the surveyors employed : for when a giving way occurs, the violence of the wind is so great, in its escape, as to carry every thing before it.

13. If, however, it be practicable to make the place secure by supplying pillars, it must be done, and as firmly as possible ; but at the same time, the owner is not to escape the penalty to which he has rendered himself liable by his criminal impropriety of conduct. In performing the work, prudence and discretion are to be observed, regard being had to the advantage of the public, without, at the same time, bearing hard upon the proprietor, or involving him in unreasonable expence. The works of support are therefore to be made upon a scale, not of magnificence, but of solidity, suited to the object in view.

14. It should also be ascertained, whether the ruin or falling in has been occasioned by the want of the pillar which has been so removed ; for if it appear, upon inspecting the nature of the ground, and of the vein, its walls, backs and roofs, and from there being other pillars of support to bear up the weight, that there would have been no impropriety in leaving a greater space than usual between the pillars ; then, no great blame will attach for having weakened or cut away a single pillar, rendered superfluous by the number of others around. The safety of the mine, however, which is the primary object of the ordinances, must never be lost sight of.

15. We have noticed elsewhere, the cutting away of the pillars of the mine Benitillas in the district of Zacatecas. And from this instance, in which the mayor, Don Phelipe Otadui y Avendano, taking upon himself to punish the offence, was supported by the decision of his majesty, in favour of his jurisdiction, and of that of the audiency of Guadalaxara, in opposition to the viceroy (who wished to take the cognizance of the matter into his own hands), it is evident that it would be highly commendable in the mining justices to direct great care and vigilance to this point ; and we are more particularly induced to enforce this, from our having been assured, by a person who saw and examined the mines, that in later times, such a falling in did actually occur in the above mine of Benitillas, to the great injury of the mines of Oyarzum and Urista.

16. In some places, natural vaults of extraordinary beauty and extent are found, exceeding even 100 *varas* in height and length. From their vaulted form, they are in themselves firm and strong by nature ; and although fearful places to enter, yet their firmness is well known, and the miners work in them with security. They are found to contain ore, loose sand or earth, which the miners gradually remove, leaving the vault, store or depository, empty and hollow. And after removing the whole of the contents, they frequently, upon breaking in further, discover other vaults, to which they are guided by indications derived from the colour of the ground, or from the

echo returned on striking with a crow or bar, as if from a hollow place. This is the description given of the mines of Chiguagua, by Don Mathias de la Mota,[*] and we have received information to the same effect, from several persons of great experience in that district, particularly with regard to a work called San Agustin, in the mine of Aranzazu, belonging to the family of Trasviña, which is an extremely firm and most beautiful vault, capable of containing the largest church in Madrid or Mexico. Such also is the case with regard to the mines of Zimapan where, according to the account of persons who have had much experience in working them, similar vaults are found. These caverns being formed by Nature, do not require pillars of support, and it would indeed, be a difficult matter to set about forming them. But when the hills are artificially undermined and cut away, it is impossible that they should sustain their own weight, unless supported by strong and firm pillars.

17. As to the third point, with regard to the pits; although the ordinance provides that they shall be ten *varas* distant from each other, and that each of them shall be fourteen *estados* in depth, it concludes by saying, that such course shall be pursued, as the nature of the ground will permit, under the authority of the justice, and according to the opinion of surveyors and miners. The usual plan is, to sink them three *estados*, and to make them six *varas* apart, the ladders being set up and secured firmly upon landing-places or rests, which serve to facilitate the descent, and to render the working more easy, and likewise tend, by their solidity, to ensure the permanence of the mine, which is the principal object of the ordinance. The word pit (*pozo*) is properly applied when working perpendicularly downwards, or in depth; but when the vein is inclined, or underlying, and the works gain in length and depth, they are said to be conducted *a chiflon*.

18. In like manner, the justices and mine owners should take care that there are formed, from time to time, cisterns or reservoirs, to collect the water from the infiltrations or springs in the upper works, so as to prevent its descending to the bottom, which would render it impossible to carry on the lower works. From these higher reservoirs, the water is to be conveyed in channels or conduits, as may be convenient, so as to be more readily carried off by the general channel of drainage, or through the pit, which may be more easily accomplished by this precaution; but if the water be allowed to find its way to the bottom, the draining is rendered difficult, and the works become filled with water. It is therefore of the greatest importance that the reservoirs should be inspected; and as it is an imperative duty to leave pillars of support at intervals, and not to cut them away or weaken them, even though they should consist of the richest ores of gold or silver, so likewise it is no less essential that proper reservoirs should be constructed, and that a

---

[*] Mota Historia MS. de la Galicia, cap. 62, n. 1.

prohibition should be enforced against weakening or destroying them, merely to gratify an avaricious desire of possessing the ore.

19. And although it may seem hard, supposing the vein to become barren, to be disabled from cutting into the pilla s or reservoirs, however rich in gold or silver, yet it would be still harder that the whole mine should be ruined by falling in, and that human life, the most precious gift of Nature, should in consequence be put in jeopardy. Indeed, this is a point upon which no precaution should be dispensed with, and those who servilely give way to the eagerness of the miners, and authorise them to remove or weaken the pillars of support, act in opposition to the dictates of conscience, and to the true interests of the mine, and render themselves gravely responsible for their conduct. All which is shewn by Agricola in a very few words.[*]

20. On the other hand, the greatest credit is due to those justices who rigorously visit with punishment, the removal of the pillars, and impose fines upon those miners and proprietors, who, allowing the suggestions of avarice to prevail over the dictates of conscience, are guilty of weakening the supports of their mines. When a considerable amount of ore is raised from any mine, it is soon known, from common report, and from the disclosures of the workmen and purchasers of the ore, whether it has been procured in a fair and successful course of working, or whether it is derived from the destruction of the pillars; and it is therefore an easy matter for the justice to proceed to an actual investigation of the fact, if he choose to take the trouble. And their interference is more urgently called for, when the proprietors, as they sometimes do, proceed to cut away the pillars of the deeper works, intending to conceal their offence, by allowing the water to rise, thus endeavouring to hide one offence, by committing a second. For must the justices be intimidated by the favour, wealth, interest or power of the mine owners; for if they perform their duty faithfully, they are sure to be justified by their superiors, who will be readily convinced that they have had no other object than to prevent the falling in of the mine, and the fatal accidents which might attend such an event, as well as the loss it would occasion both to the crown and to the public. If any party then, propose to relinquish a mine, he must not, upon doing so, act injuriously to the general interests of the crown and its subjects, none of whom will be found inclined to denounce a mine deprived of its pillars of support, and filled with water; as, even after drawing off the water, the person undertaking it would be exposed to the risk of still greater loss, by the falling in of the works; whilst, if the pillars of support be standing, any person denouncing the mine, will have the satisfaction of being assured of its firmness and security.

* Agricola, de re metall. lib. 4 p. 69. "Verum faber lignarius sit oportent, ut possit puteos extruere, columnas collocare, et facere substructiones, quæ montem subfossum susstineant, ne saxa tecti venarum non fulta, a toto corpore montis resolvantur, ruinisque opprimant operarios : fabricari, et in cuniculos ponero canales, in quos aqua ex venis, fibris, commissuris saxorum, collecta derivetur, ut effluere possit."

CHAPTER XXI.

OF THE PRIVILEGES OF THE MINERS, WHICH ARE EMPTY AND APPARENT
ONLY, AND CONTRIBUTE NOTHING TO THEIR RELIEF.—OF SEQUESTRA-
TIONS OF MINES AND REDUCTION WORKS FOR CROWN DEBTS, AND OF
THE SUPPLIER'S PRIVILEGE.—CONSIDERATIONS ON THE MINER'S THREE
GREAT ENEMIES ; THAT IS TO SAY, THE MINER HIMSELF, THE SUPPLI-
ER, AND CERTAIN OTHER PARTIES WHO DEAL WITH HIM.—COMMENDA-
TION OF THE PRUDENT MANAGEMENT AND NOBLE UNDERTAKINGS OF
TWO MINERS OF NEW SPAIN.

ORDINANCES XLVII. XLIX. L. LI. LII. LXXVIII. LXXXIII.

XLVII. Also, we ordain and command, that the washing places, which
may be necessary for washing the ores of the aforesaid mines, shall be taken
wherever most convenient to the miners, provided that if they would be injurious to any town, or to the cattle, and cannot be made without producing injury, the water shall be taken from the river, brook or pool, where such ores
may be washed, and shall be turned off, so as not to return to such river or
brook ; and if this cannot be done, enclosures or courts shall be formed, at
the expense of those who shall make such washing places ; and for better performing the above, the mining justice, within whose district such washing
places shall be made, shall cause the same to be complied with ; so that the
injury may be prevented.   And in taking such washing places, they shall be
staked out in the same manner as the mines aforesaid, and the dimensions of
each washing place shall be 60 feet in length (each foot the third of a *vara*)
and 12 feet in width ; but if the washing places shall be supplied with the
water drawn off from mines, and not from any river or brook, there shall be
no obligation to perform any of the matters aforesaid, but they may be made
wherever it shall seem best, near the mine, or the establishment where the
ores may be smelted.

XLIX. Also, we ordain and command, that for the purpose of working,
timbering and preserving the said mines, and constructing machines, buildings and huts, and for all other matters required for working and maintaining them, the owners of the aforesaid mines, and the persons employed about
them, shall be at liberty to make use, and may make use, of all the forests,
common ground, ground belonging to municipal bodies, and waste ground
nearest to the said mines ; and of the wood, timber and trunks thereof, and
to cut down such as may be dry, to the root, without paying anything for it.
And that they shall likewise be at liberty, for the purposes aforesaid, to
make use of the wood, timber and trunks, and to cut down such as may be
dry, to the root, in the pasture grounds of private persons and of municipal
bodies, which shall be nearest to the aforesaid mines, paying for what they
shall so cut down in such pasture grounds, the just value thereof to be estimated by the mining judge of the department ; the person or body to whom

such pasture ground shall belong, being summoned. And with respect to green timber and wood they shall also be at liberty to cut, in such public forests, and forests belonging to municipal bodies, as aforesaid, so much of the same as shall be necessary for the buildings and machines, and for timbering and supporting such mines, without paying anything for it, first obtaining a license for that purpose from the mining administrator of the department, but not otherwise. And if there shall not be, in such public forests, or forests belonging to municipal bodies, such green timber as shall be necessary for the purposes aforesaid, they shall be at liberty to cut the same in such pasture grounds belonging to individuals and municipal bodies, as aforesaid: first obtaining a licence for that purpose, as is aforesaid, from the administrator, and, before all things, summoning the body or person to whom such pasture grounds may belong or under whose care they may be, that they may be advised what may be so ordered to be cut. And the aforesaid administrator shall take particular care not to give such licences, except only for so much as may be necessary for working and keeping up the said mines, and no more, and that as little injury and damage as possible, shall be done to such forests and pasture grounds. And although we have commanded that the parties shall be summoned, previous to cutting such green timber, the aforesaid administrator may enforce the cutting of what he shall think ought to be cut, notwithstanding any opposition thereto; in consideration of the great loss which might ensue to the works and buildings of the aforesaid mines, from any delay being occasioned.

L. Also, we ordain and command, that all such owners of mines, and persons concerned in working them, as aforesaid, shall be at liberty to drive into such pasture grounds, meadows and threshing grounds, common grounds or forests, belonging to the public or to municipal bodies, as aforesaid, which shall be near such mines, or the establishments thereof, all their oxen and beasts, and those of their servants, being necessary for working the aforesaid mines, either for the machinery, or for draught, burden or riding, and likewise the oxen used in the waggons for bringing provisions, timber or other things to the aforesaid mines, establishments and buildings; provided that if the pasture grounds belong to municipal bodies or individuals, they shall pay for the herbage and pasture as the same are paid for in respect of other cattle. And those who shall be engaged in searching or trying for mines, or who shall be on their way to search for them, shall be at liberty to take with them one beast each, without paying anything for the grass which shall be eaten by such beasts.

LI. Also, we ordain and command, that all the proprietors of such mines, and their servants, and the persons who shall be concerned in working such mines and their ores, shall be at liberty to hunt and fish, freely, within three leagues around the place where the mining establishments aforesaid, in which they may reside, shall be situated, in the same manner as they might do, if they were inhabitants of the places situate within such space of three leagues, observing the laws and edicts of these our kingdoms upon that subject.

LII. Also, we ordain and command, that in any parts or places whatsoever, wherein mines have been discovered, or may henceforth be discovered, the owners thereof shall be at liberty to set up such establishments, houses, smelting houses, furnaces (*hornas, buitrones, fuslines*), and other works what soever, as may be necessary for working the mines, or smelting and refining the ores, when, how and in such manner and form, as they shall think proper, and even at a different spot from that where the mines are situated ; provided that if all the proprietors of a mine shall be willing and able to set up such buildings togetheer, in one place, the administrator-general, or administrator of the department shall take especial care that it shall be so done and performed, if it can be done without damage or injury to the owners of such mines and ores. And if, for the more convenient smelting and refining of the ores, the owners of the mines, or any of them, should wish to set up their establishments, and smelting and refining furnaces, in a place where there is a river or brook, for the purpose of working the bellows, they shall be at liberty to do so ; and may, for such purpose, freely make use of such river or brook, in such part, or at such place, as may be most convenient and least expensive to them, so that other persons be not injured, and that they pay for the space they may occupy, to be estimated and valued by two persons appointed by the mining judge of the department. And, that there may be no fraud in regard to the lead produced from such smelting works, we command, that each of the aforesaid mine owners shall keep an iron stamp, with which he shall stamp and mark the ingots of silver-lead, and all other ingots whatsoever produced from his mine or ore, and that it shall not be lawful to take them to be refined and that they shall not be refined, without such mark.

LXXVIII. Also we ordain and command, that all persons whatsoever, who shall be willing to carry provisions, maintenance and other things, to such mines, for the support of those who may abide or work in them, shall be at liberty to carry out, and may take and carry out the same freely, from all the cities, towns and places, of these our kingdoms and lordships. And that the justices thereof shall not prevent them, nor lay any embargo upon them, nor put any impediment in their way, nor enhance the price ; but that, on the contrary, they shall assist and favour them, that the aforesaid mines, and the persons who may be concerned in them, may be always provided and supplied therewith.

LXXXIII. Also, by way of benefit and favour to those who shall hold and work such mines, and to the administrators, assayers, smelters, refiners, accountants and paymasters thereof,—We ordain and command, that in the parts and places where they shall reside, at such mines, they shall be free and exempt from having guests or beasts of burden quartered upon them, and that they shall not be obliged to furnish beds, saddle-horses or mules, or waggons. And besides this, that they may, when at such mines, wear arms, offensive or defensive, at all times, by day or night, provided they be not such as are prohibited, and be not worn in prohibited places : which our justices shall observe and shall not oppose, during all such time as they shall be employed about the said mines, or the working thereof.

☞ The Commentary of Gamboa in relation to the ordinances in this and the three succeeding Chapters, is omitted, as adding nothing at present useful in the way of legal analysis or illustration to the ordinances themselves.

———— •·•————

CHAPTER XXII.

OF THE REDUCTION OF THE ORE, BOTH BY SMELTING AND AMALGAMATION WITH A MINUTE DESCRIPTION OF THE PROCESS IN EACH INSTANCE.—OF ALL THE OTHER METHODS, WHETHER ANCIENT OR MODERN, USED, FOR THE SAME PURPOSE.—OF THE ASSAYERS AND ASSAYS, AND OF THE PROHIBITION AGAINST DEALING IN SILVER, UNSTAMPED.—TWO PLANS SUGGESTED FOR PREVENTING THE FREQUENT EVASION OF THIS ORDER.—IN CONCLUSION, A HISTORY OF THE ERECTION AND REGULATIONS OF THE GREAT MINT OF MEXICO.

ORDINANCES XLVIII. LIII. LIV. LV. LVI. LVII. LVIII. LIX. LX. LXI. LXII. LXXII. LXXIII. LXXV.

XLVIII. ALSO, we ordain and command, that no person shall presume to search for, carry away or work ore, from the refuse heap, washing place or slag heap of any other person (the owner thereof being known), under the penalty of ten ducats for the first offence, and twenty for the second, to be applied as is aforesaid ; and for the third offence (over and above the payment of the aforesaid twenty ducats, to be applied as aforesaid), that he be banished for the term of three full years from the mines of that department, and that he do not shorten that term, under pain of completing twice the period. And moreover, all that he may have taken or may take, shall be for the owner of such refuse heap, washing place or slag heap : but we grant that the old slag heaps, which have resulted from ores of silver, copper, iron and other metals, and which, from having been made long since, have no owner, whereof there are many in these our kingdoms, may be made use of by such persons as shall work mines, because we are advised that they are good and necessary for the smelting of the ores ; and we ordain, that any miners whatsoever shall be at liberty to carry them away from any place whatsoever where they may be, and to make use of the same, without any person having the power to hinder them, under pretence that they are in his pastures or grounds, or that he has registered them, or upon any other ground whatsoever, if the owner who shall have accumulated such heaps do not appear.

LIII. Also, we ordain and command, that no person shall presume to smelt any ore, except in furnaces of his own, unless he shall have erected them in partnership ; and if any person, not having a furnace of his own, shall wish to smelt in that of some other person, he shall signify the same to our administrator of the department, with whose licence he shall be at liberty to smelt there, but not otherwise, under the penalty of forfeiting such silver-lead, one half to our exchequer, and one half to the denouncer and judge ; and also of forfeiting such mine, which shall be for the denouncer aforesaid.

LIV. Also, we ordain and command, that when, in smelting the ore from any mine, it shall happen to be expedient, in order to facilitate the smelting, to mix with it a proportion of ore from some other mine, this may be done, with the licence of the administrator of the department, provided that the quality of the ore into which such mixture may be introduced, do not surpass that of the ore, which may be so mixed and combined with it ; but if the former shall surpass the latter in quality, it shall not be lawful to do so, and it shall not be done, under the penalty of forfeiting the ore which may be so mixed, and the produce thereof, with as much more ; one half to our exchequer, and the other half to the denouncer, and the judge who shall pass sentence. And in order that what is contained in this our edict may not be contravened, we command our administrators, in each district respectively, to take particular care to inspect and assay the ores from such mines, which it may be so wished to mix together, that what may belong to us may be liquidated accordingly. And having done so, and made inspection, as in a matter of such importance is meet, and having ascertained what proportion we are entitled to, according to the quality of such ores, they may give such licence as aforesaid, such mixture being very advantageous for facilitating the smelting.

LV. Also, we ordain and command, that in each of the aforesaid mining districts or works, there shall be erected at our expense, a refining house, with furnaces of different kinds (*hornos, buitrones y fuslines,*) as may be most convenient, which shall have bellows, tools and such other things as are required for the refining of the silver-lead, which may be smelted in each mining district. To which refining house all persons shall be obliged to bring all the silver-lead which may be raised and smelted from such mine or mines, to be refined, and the same shall be there refined. And no person shall presume to refine such silver-lead, whether in large or small quantities, in any place except in such our refining house, nor to sell, give away or deal in such silver-lead, until it shall have been refined, under the penalty of forfeiting what he may so refine, sell, give away, or deal with in any other manner, with four times the amount, one half to be applied to our exchequer, and the other half to the person who shall in-

44

form against him, and the judge who shall give sentence ; which penalty aforesaid shall also be incurred by any person who shall take any part
in the above.   And where, from there not being any works established,
and from there not being mines sufficient to render it necessary, it may not
be convenient to set up such refining house, the said admimistrator of the
department shall provide and make such arrangements as may be expedient
and necessary, for collecting such lead as may be there, for the purpose of refining.   And the silver-lead, which shall be so collected, shall be
carried to the nearest refining house ; and when arrived there, such order
shall be observed in regard to the refining thereof, and in all other respects,
as is provided with respect to the ingots of silver-lead refined in such house
in the ordinary way.   But it is our gracious will, that such mine owners shall
be spared as much expense as possible in the conveyance of the silver-lead,
which, for the reason aforesaid, may not be refined at the mines aforesaid.

LVI. Also, we ordain and command, that there shall be, in each of such
refining houses at the several mines or districts, such refiners as may be requisite, to be appointed by our administrator of the department, to the satisfaction of the mine owners, who shall refine the silver-lead which may be
produced from such district or mine, at the expense of the parties, being
supplied by them with such charcoal as may be necessary ; and that no
other person shall intermeddle in such refining, under the penalty of receiving 100 lashes, and of serving three years at the oar in our galleys, without
wages ; and the administrator aforesaid, shall fix the rate at which such refiners are to be paid, for every quintal which they may refine.

LVII. Also, we ordain and command, that in each mining district, where
there may be such a refining house and in any other place where such may
be set up, under the orders of our administrator aforesaid, there shall be
a sworn clerk, who shall weigh the silver-lead which may be brought to be
refined, and who shall take an oath, upon being admitted into his office, that
he will discharge his duty truly and faithfully ; and likewise a notary, who
shall give certificates of the parcels of silver-lead which may be delivered
to the refiner, and all the parcels of silver-lead which shall be brought to be
refined shall be delivered to the refiner aforesaid, who shall have been selected by the aforesaid administrator of the department to refine the same.   And
the administrator aforesaid shall keep a book, wherein all such parcels shall
be entered, and the notary aforesaid shall keep another book, for the same
purpose ; which books, shall have an alphabetical index, with a separate
account for each of the persons who may bring silver-lead to be refined ;
and the sworn clerk aforesaid shall note, on a separate leaf, what is the
weight of such ingots, and they shall be delivered to the refiner ; and in
such book shall be entered, the day, month and year, the weight and number
of the ingots, the names of the persons who may have brought them to be
refined, what is the mark upon them, the name or names of the mine or

mines from which they may have proceeded, and the name of the refiner to whom they may be delivered, in such manner that a particular reckoning and account of the whole shall be kept. And the aforesaid administrator of the department or some person appointed by him, and the notary aforesaid, and the party, if he be able to write, and if not, then some other person for him, shall sign both the said books; and after all that is above-mentioned is done, the refiner aforesaid shall refine such parcel; but the silver-lead from one mine shall not be mixed with that from another mine, under the penalty, against the party so mixing them, of forfeiting such lead and silver, with four times the value, to be applied as is aforesaid; and if the refiner aforesaid shall mix them, he shall receive 100 lashes, and shall serve three years at the car in our galleys. And we charge our administrator aforesaid, to observe particular care and diligence in seeing that such refining is faithfuly performed, so that no fraud be practiced against our rights and no injustice be done to the parties.

LVIII. Also, we ordain and command, that, what is above-mentioned being done, and the silver being refined and taken out in the presence of our aforesaid administrator of the department, or some person appointed by him, and of the notary aforesaid, the sworn clerk shall weigh the silver, and take from it such part as we may be entitled to, agreeably to these our ordinances, and the same shall be delivered to the person whom we shall direct to be appointed for that purpose, who shall be charged with what may be so delivered to him, noting it in the books aforesaid, and in the book which our administrator aforesaid is to keep, with a record of the day, month and year, the mine or mines from which such silver proceeds, the name of the owner of the parcel, and of the person who has brought it to be refined, the weight of the silver in such parcel, and the proportion thereof which may belong to us, and may have been delivered to the aforesaid administrator; and all the persons aforesaid, and the party himself, shall sign the aforesaid three books, that the administrator may render an account accordingly, when required of him: and the remainder of the silver (after taking out our proportion, as aforesaid), shall be delivered to the owner, after impressing upon one, two or more places in each ingot (as it may require), the stamp of our royal arms, without which stamp aforesaid, no one shall presume to sell, purchase or deal in the silver raised from the aforesaid mines, under the penalty of forfeiting such silver, and what may be purchased therewith, and the half of all his property, to be applied as aforesaid. And over and above this, he shall be banished from the mines aforesaid, and the space of ten leagues around, for the term of six full years; and he shall not shorten such term, under pain of serving during the same period in the galleys, or wherever he may be ordered; which penalty aforesaid shall be incurred by the purchaser, or the person with whom dealings may be had in respect of such silver.

LIX. Also, forasmuch as many ores of silver are worked and reduced by quicksilver, at a less expense, and with more profit, and it might happen that some persons might propose to work with quicksilver, certain ores adapted for that method, in consequence of which, what is provided and commanded with respect to the ores worked and reduced by smelting and refining could not be observed, so as to make such silver, so reduced by quicksilver, pay to us the duty to which we are entitled, agreeable to these our ordinances, without any diminution therein :—We ordain and command, that any person who shall be desirous to work and reduce such ores by quicksilver, shall be obliged to give notice thereof to our administrator aforesaid, and to mention to him the mine or mines, the ores of which he shall wish to work and reduce by quicksilver, as aforesaid, that the same may be entered, and that it may be known, that the ores of such mine or mines are worked and reduced by quicksilver ; and during all such time as they shall choose to work and reduce such ores by that method, they shall not be at liberty to work, and shall not work or reduce the same in any other manner, unless upon giving notice thereof to the administrator, when they shall propose to do so, that the same may be noted, and that it may be known that they do not any longer work or reduce the ores of such mine with quicksilver, as aforesaid. And if they shall work and reduce the ores of such mines in any other manner, they shall forfeit the silver and ore, one half to our exchequer, and the other half to the informer and the judge who shall pass sentence, and they shall forfeit such mine or mines, which shall be for the informer. And the share or duty which we may be entitled to have, agreeably to these our ordinances, shall be ascertained by weighing the quintals of ore which may be mixed with quicksilver, in the presence of the sworn clerk, and notary, and of our administrator ; and when the quicksilver shall have been driven off from the amalgam obtained, so that the silver shall remain fine, it shall also be weighed, that it may be known and ascertained how much silver shall have been produced from the quintals of ore mixed with quicksilver ; and our duties shall be levied according to the produce, agreeably to these our ordinances as aforesaid : the same books, reckoning and account being kept, and the same order, form and manner being observed in this matter, as with respect to the silver to which the refining process is applied, as is above set forth, and under the same penalties, to be applied as is aforesaid.

LX. Also, we ordain and command, that it shall not be lawful to remove the silver from the place where it may have been put for the purpose of having the quicksilver driven off, except in the presence of our administrator of the department, or of the person whom he may appoint, but that it shall be weighed, and the duty which we may be entitled to, and which may belong to us, shall be taken from it, and be delivered to the person whom we shall command to be appointed for that purpose, in the presence of the said administrator and of the sworn clerk and notary, and the same reckoning and account thereof shall be kept as of the silver refined by fire ; and the remainder of the silver shall be delivered to the owner; and our royal stamp shall be impressed on each ingot, as aforesaid, and without such royal stamp, it shall not be lawful to sell or deal in such silver in any manner, under the penalty above limited, to be inflicted upon the owner of such silver, and the purchaser, or person who shall deal in it.*

LXI. Also, we ordain and command, that the proportion appertaining to us, of the poor lead which may be smelted, but which, from its not containing so much as four reals per quintal, will not bear refining, shall be stamped by the administrator of the department, or by the person whom he may appoint, in the place where it may be smelted; and upon its being found, by assay, to be poor lead, the person whom we shall have appointed for that purpose, shall receive the duty which may belong to us, agreeably to our ordinances: and it shall not be lawful to convey any lead, even though made from litharge, from one place to another, without such stamp, under the penalty, upon any person otherwise conveying it, of forfeiting the same, one half to the party who shall give information thereof, and the other half to the judge who shall pass sentence, and likewise four times the value to our exchequer; and the like with regard to copper, which, being first assayed, shall be stamped, that our proportion thereof, and of the silver and gold it may contain, may be paid; but this, with respect to the poor lead and copper, is to be understood to apply to places without the limits of the grants which have been made.

LXII. Also, we ordain and command, that all those who shall convey antimony out of the districts, where no grant has been made thereof, shall pay us the duty thereon, at the mines or veins from which it shall be raised; and that until paid, it shall be lawful to exchange or sell it in any other place, without the licence of our administrator of the department, or the person appointed by him, at the mining establishment nearest the mine, from which such antimony may have been raised; and that after such licence is obtained, no person shall be at liberty to carry or transport it without an order from such administrator, or from the person appointed by him; and that such vendor shall be obliged to advise the purchaser thereof, that such order may be taken out, and he shall so advise him, under pain of forfeiting the value of such antimony, and four times the amount, to be applied as aforesaid; and if any purchaser shall otherwise convey it away, it shall be taken from him as contraband, with four times the value, to be applied as is aforesaid;

---

* (Note 2, to §. 60, p. 383.) By the second section of the royal cedula of the 18 August, 1607, in relation to the subject matter of this section and of the precious ores from the 53d, his majesty thought proper to suspend to the extent above stated the enforcing these ordinances, and in relation to the mines which had been, and the places where they were worked until his majesty should otherwise provide, the commissary of the treasury and the principal auditor of the treasury should prescribe the form to be adopted in relation to all the matter aforesaid, taking particular care in the collection of the duties that they adopt such course as to impede as little as possible the working of the mines. (Section 2, of law 10, tit. 13, book 6, R.)

which is to be understood, as aforesaid, to apply to places where no grants have been made.

LXXII. Also, we ordain and command, that no person shall presume to treat for, deal in, sell or purchase, gold in dust, bars or ingots, unless stamped with our royal stamp, which we direct to be kept by the person who shall be appointed in our name in each district, to levy the share appertaining to us. And there shall also be a smelter, who shall smelt and make into bars (*vergas*), the gold which shall be raised, and who shall likewise be employed to check the weight; and he shall smelt, weigh, and stamp the same with our royal stamp aforesaid, in the presence of our administrator, or of the person appointed by him; and the share which shall belong to us, shall be given and delivered to the person who shall attend for that purpose in the district where the above shall be performed, and the remainder shall be given to the owner; and our administrator aforesaid shall keep a book, wherein he shall enter the parcels aforesaid, recording the day, month, and year, and he shall also note whose such gold is, and from what mine or streamwork it may have proceeded, and what proportion or share belonged to us, and was charged to such administrator, and what was taken by the owner of such parcel; which entry shall be signed by the administrator aforesaid, and by the party aforesaid, if he shall be able to sign his name; but if not, then by some other person for him; and also by the smelter, and the notary before whom the proceedings may have been had; which notary and smelter aforesaid, shall each of them keep another book, wherein the same entries shall be made, and which shall be signed, as aforesaid, by all these persons: and no person shall be at liberty to sell or deal in such gold, unless it shall have been smelted and stamped as is aforesaid, under the penalty limited in the ordinance touching this matter, in reference to silver; and the like penalty shall be incurred by the person purchasing or dealing for it, as is set forth in the aforesaid ordinance touching silver.

LXXIII. Also, forasmuch as it might happen, that the servants of the mine-owner aforesaid, or other persons, might sell or deal in gold or silver, which might not have been stamped with our royal stamp, contrary to these ordinances, but without the same being known to such owners:—We ordain and command, that any servant or person whatsoever, who shall sell or deal in gold or silver which shall not have been stamped with our royal stamp as aforesaid, without the owner knowing thereof, or being in fault; and likewise any person whatsoever, who shall purchase or deal in the same, shall, besides returning to the owner or paying him for what shall have been so sold or dealt in, forfeit the whole of his property, one half whereof shall be for our exchequer, and the other half for the informer and the judge who shall pass sentence, and shall also serve ten years at the oar, in the galleys.

LXXV. Also, forasmuch as we are informed that great negligence prevails amongst the smelters and refiners, in not assaying the ores previous to smelting, and the rich lead previous to refining, whence great damage results, not only to our revenue, but also to individuals ; besides which, many frauds may thence occur :—For a remedy thereof, we ordain and command, that our administrator-general, and administrators of departments, shall take great care in providing, that where there are many mines together, there shall be sufficient sworn assayers, both for the ores to be smelted and for the rich lead which may require to be refined, so that the smelter and refiners shall make the returns of the smeltings and refinings they may perform, correspond with the assays which may have been made.

CHAPTER XXIII.

OF POSSESSORY AND PETITORY SUITS* CONCERNING MINES : OF THE MIN-
ING INTERDICT† AND ITS PECULIARITIES.—OF THE FORM OF PROCEED-
ING AND TERMS ALLOWED IN EACH OF THESE SUITS, IN THE FIRST
AND SECOND INSTANCE.—OF THE SECURITY OF ONE THOUSAND DUCATS,
TO BE GIVEN, FOR RENDERING AN ACCOUNT ; AND OF PAYING OVER AND
ACCOUNTING FOR THE PROFITS, ACCORDING TO THE RESULT OF THE
ACCOUNT.

ORDINANCES LXIII. LXIV.

LXIII. Also, forasmuch as it is found by experience, that where suits and differences are raised concerning the possession of mines, their working is brought to a stand, or it is ordered that they should be closed un-till it be determined which party has the better right ; so that they fre-quently remain one, or two, or more years unworked : therefore, to prevent the damage that results from such mines being left unworked for so long a time ;—We ordain and command, that when and so often as such suits shall arise, the term of forty days shall be allowed, during which term and no lon-ger, the mine in dispute may remain closed, and within which time the par-ties shall state and allege the particulars of their claim before the mining justice, and shall exhibit to him such writings and documents as they may have ; and shall be at liberty to produce as many as twelve witnesses, and to examine each of them on every interrogatory, but no more ; and such jus-tice shall consider and make his determination upon what they shall state, allege and prove within the term aforesaid, without any further conclusion or adjournment ; saving to the party against whom he shall give judgment, the

---

* A *petitory* suit, in the courts of Spain, is a suit in which the right of *property* is controvert-ed, in opposition to a *possessory* suit, where the right of *possession* is alone in question.—*Trans.*

† An *interdict* (*interdictum*), in the civil law, was a summary species of action, principally applicable when the possession or *quasi* possession of a thing or right was in dispute. See **Vicat. Jur. ut. vocab.** at the word, *interdictum—Trans.*

liberty of prosecuting his claim to the right of property, as he shall think expedient, before the mining justice aforesaid: and he shall immediatly give possession of such mine to the party in whose favour he shall give sentence; who shall work it, keeping an account entered in a book, by the day, month and year, of the ore he may raise, and of the costs and expenses he may incur in working it: and he shall give security in the amount of one thousand ducats, for rendering an account and for the paying over the proceeds, if he should be worsted upon appeal, and if he should be ordered so to do: which shall be done and performed in manner aforesaid, notwithstanding any appeal or charge of nullity or injustice which may be interposed or set up. And if the party against whom sentence is given, should consider himself aggrieved, he shall be at liberty to appeal within three days, to our administrator-general of mines, and the term of sixty days shall be allowed for the appeal, or the question of nullity or injustice, during which term both parties shall prosecute their claims before such administrator, and shall exhibit to him their writings and vouchers, and produce their witnesses; and they shall be admitted to be heard in all that the law permits, as is aforesaid. And the justice of the case shall be determined, upon what they shall state, allege and prove, within the term aforesaid, without any further conclusion or adjournment; and if the sentence shall be in confirmation of the former judgment, such suit shall be at an end, as far as regards the right of possession, and there shall be no appeal therefrom. But the party in whose favour the suit shall be decided, shall nevertheless keep an account of the ore he may raise, and of such expences as aforesaid, in order that he may render the same, and make satisfaction accordingly, if he should be worsted as to the right of property, and should be decreed so to do. But if such sentence should not be confirmatory of the former judgment, and the parties should appeal therefrom, such appeal shall be made to the chief accountant of finance, and to no other court whatsoever. And if the parties, or any of them, should set up a claim to the right of property in such mines, the same shall be brought before the administrator of the district, or the administrator-general of the mines, and before no other judge, and he shall hear the parties concerning the same, and any appeal from the sentence which he may give, shall be made to the chief accountant aforesaid, and to no other court. And if a writ of execution should be issued, by virtue of which the possession of such mine or mines, together with the produce thereof, may have to be restored to some other person:—We command, that the person who shall have had possession, and the sureties whom he is to find, agreeably to this our letter, shall deliver in a certain and true account of, and make satisfaction accordingly for, all that may have been raised or produced from such mine, until the day on which it shall be taken from him, deducting the costs and expenses which may have been incurred in working the same; of which expenses he shall give in an account upon oath, signed with his name, and entire and explicit faith and credit shall be given to the same.

LXIV. Also, we ordain and command, that when and so often as any person shall make claim in a quiet and pacific manner, to a mine the possession of some other person, and shall also demand to have such mine closed ; then, inasmuch as, in a case of this kind, the principal object looked to is the ore raised from such mines, the justice aforesaid (to prevent the working of such mines from being put a stop to), shall command, that the party be summoned, and do, within the peremptory term of twenty days, give evidence concerning his right ; and that the other party do, if he think proper, give evidence to the contrary, or to such purport as he shall think proper. And immediately upon the expiration of the twenty days, if it shall appear that the party making the claim is right, he shall command the party in possession to keep an account, from that time forth, of the ore and silver produced from such mine, and of the costs and expenses incurred, as is mentioned in the last ordinance, in order that he may render the same, and make satisfaction accordingly, if he should be worsted ; which shall be observed, fulfilled and enforced, notwithstanding any appeal or any charge of nullity or injustice, which may be interposed or set up against it ; and this being done, the cause aforesaid shall be proceeded in, without allowing any delay or malicious procrastination, and justice shall be done.

CHAPTER XXIV.

OF THE FREQUENT THEFTS OF THE WORKMEN AT THE MINES, AND THEIR PUNISHMENT. —OF THE PURCHASERS OF ORE.

ORDINANCE LXVI.

ALSO, we ordain and command, that all thefts which may be committed in the said mines, mining districts and grounds, or in any place where there may be a mining establishment, for gold, silver, lead or ores of any class or description, the subject of such thefts being any thing relating to or concerning the working of such mines, shall be punished with the utmost rigour, and that any person who shall steal any such thing as aforesaid, shall, besides paying and restoring to the party the thing stolen, be condemned in seven-fold damages, to be applied, one half to our exchequer, and the other half to the person who shall give information, and the judge who shall pass sentence. And such thefts shall be subject to the cognizance of the administrator of each department, the sentence he may give being liable to an appeal to the administrator-general. But if he who shall have been so condemned in seven-fold damages, shall not have any property wherewith to pay them, the penalty shall be commuted for some corporal punishment, or for that of ban-

ishment, according to the heinousness of the offence ; from which commuted
sentence there shall be an appeal to our chief accountant of finance as
aforesaid, and to no other tribunal whatsoever, whether such commutation be
made by the administrator of the department, or the administrator-general.

CHAPTER XXV.

THE CIVIL AND CRIMINAL JURISDICTION IN SUITS CONCERNING MINES, BELONGS TO THE JUSTICES, SUBJECT TO AN APPEAL TO THE ROYAL AUDIENCIES ; AND THE VICEROYS HAVE NOT AUTHORITY TO TAKE COGNIZANCE OF SUCH MATTERS ; BUT THE ADMINISTRATIVE AUTHORITY IS, BY THE LAWS AND SEVERAL ROYAL ORDERS, VESTED IN THE VICEROYS.

ORDINANCE LXXVII.

ALSO, forasmuch as we are informed, that one of the causes preventing
the regular working of the mines heretofore discovered, and the search for
and discovery of new mines, is the occurrence of suits and disputes amongst
those who are concerned in and work them, and the inconvenience and vexation caused amongst the officers and workmen engaged in the mines, by the
justices and other persons, arising both from such justices not having had
proper practice and experience in mining affairs, and from the suits being
conducted in the ordinary deliberate manner ; in consequence whereof, the
property of the parties being expended and consumed, in the proceedings
had before the justices and the other tribunals to which they have recourse
by way of appeal, they are incapacitated from prosecuting the discovery and
working of such mines ; whence follows notable damage to ourselves, to
these our kingdoms, and to our subjects therein : Wherefore, for a remedy
thereof (as a matter of so much importance), and in order that all persons
may be encouraged to discover and work the aforesaid mines, we have resolved to appoint, and we shall appoint, an administrator-general, and such
other administrators as may be necessary for the departments and districts
which may be fixed upon, who shall be persons of practice and experience
in such matters, and who shall have government and jurisdiction over all the
aforesaid mines, and all matters relating thereto, and shall be superior to all
persons concerned about such mines ; and they shall take account and notice thereof, and shall take particular care that all the rules of these ordinances be observed and fulfilled, and they shall enforce the same, and cause
them to be observed and fulfilled, agreeably to the order and instructions
which we shall direct to be given to them accordingly. And they shall have
jurisdiction to take cognizance and shall take cognizance, in the first instance
of all suits, causes and matters, whether civil, criminal or relating to execu-

tion, which may be, arise or be agitated in each district, and they shall be at liberty and shall be bound, to take cognizance of the same, agreeably to these ordinances, in the following manner, that is to say :—If the administor-general be in the district of the department in which such suits may arise, he shall take cognizance of the same ; but if he be not in the district, the administrator of the department shall take cognizance of them ; and if the administrator-general shall leave such department, he shall refer the causes of which he may so have taken cognizance, in the state in which they may then be, to the administrator of the same department, who shall proceed with, and bring the same to a conclusion, agreeably to these ordinances: and if the administrator-general aforesaid shall return to such district, and shall find the causes which he shall have so referred, still undetermined, he shall be at liberty to resume the cognizance of the same whilst he may be there. And we command such administrator-general, and administrators of departments, to do and administer justice to the parties, in the cases and matters of which they may take cognizance, in a brief and summary manner, agreeably to these ordinances, so that the working of the mines be not hindered or embarrassed by reason of such suits. And we command our justices, both the ordinary justices, and those of the holy brotherhood, and also those appointed by commission, and all other justices whatsoever in these our kingdoms, and the other kingdoms under our dominion, that they do not intermeddle with the cognizance of such causes touching or concerning the aforesaid mines, or the persons, beasts, oxen or waggons which may be employed or work therein : and that they shall not proceed upon nor entertain, either *ex officio* or upon the application of the parties, any claim, petition, complaint or other matter, in all that is aforesaid, nor in any part thereof: and that if there be any such matters pending before them, they shall refer them immediately to such administrators of departments, that they may take cognizance of the same, as being the proper judges thereof, and may do justice to the parties. And for the present, we prohibit and hold prohibited, the said ordinary justices and judges, and those appointed by commission, and all others whatsoever, from taking cognizance, in any manner, of such causes and matters as aforesaid, concerning, proceeding from or in any manner depending on the aforesaid mines, or the persons working in, or clerks or officers of the same, as is aforesaid, notwithstanding any law, edict or other matter whatsoever to the contrary, which, as far as relates thereto, we dispense with, abrogate, annul and make void and of no force or effect, leaving them, nevertheless, in force, as to all other matters. And with respect to the persons who are to be appointed as administrators or receivers, or to any other office relating to the said mines, it is our pleasure that they should be appointed by our council of finance, under our letters and orders, signed with our hand ; and the like with regard to the orders and instructions, which are to be given them for their conduct in their several offices.

CONTENTS OF THE COMMENTARY ON THIS ORDINANCE.

1. This ordinance cannot be put in practice in the Indies.
2. Nor would it there have the desired effect of preventing delay.
3. Of the qualifications which the chief mining alcaldes are required by law to have.
4. There are numerous persons skilled in working mines, who might be made judges.
5. The proceedings, in the first instance, are subject to the cognizance of the justices, and the proceedings on appeal, to that of the royal audiencies ; and the viceroys or governors are not at liberty to challenge the cognizance of these causes.
6 and 7. The justices ought to visit the mines.   Of the inconvenience of sending visitors.
8. If, when the justices are called on to render their account, they were charged to visit the mines, many evils would by that means be prevented.
9, 10 and 11. In the case (which rarely occurs), of a visitor being sent by the viceroy, he should be instructed with reference to matters of government only, and not to questions of justice, whether civil and criminal matters, which belong to the justices and the audiencies.
12, 13, 14 and 15. A reference to several orders, establishing this point.
16. It is extremely important that the viceroy should have supreme power as to other points ; but questions of justice should be left to the tribunals.
17. Of the inconvenience occasioned by an application being made to the viceroy.
18. Of the ordinances of the viceroy of Peru, Don Francisco de Toledo, giving to the ordinary justices a more extensive jurisdiction than they are allowed, even in New Spain.

COMMENTARY.

1. This ordinance is not observed in the Indies, nor could it be enforced there, without great damage to the public, and particularly to the miners, who would have to maintain, at their own expense, a mining administrator-general, and particular administrators, in each department and in each mining district.   The investing these officers with exclusive jurisdiction, would have no influence in expediting the proceedings in mining suits, as we may learn from other analogous instances ; and were the right of appeal to the audiencies to be taken away, the remedy for judicial injustice would be cut off, and the parties would be robbed of a right of defence, to which they are naturally entitled.

2. The inconvenience arising from the delays of the ordinary judges, lamented in the ordinance, would not be prevented by the appointment of particular administrators.   The blame of the delay is, in general, attributable to themselves or their agents.   The remoteness of the places is another unavoidable source of delay.   The law has made abundant provision for ensuring dispatch in suits, and those who lament the delays which occur, must pray for a better spirit in the litigating parties themselves.   No lawsuit ever arises concerning a poor mine, but an anxiety to get possession of the rich mines, involves the parties in surveys, objections and new surveys, without

end, notwithstanding that the royal audiencies do all in their power to dispose of the mining business with expedition, agreeably to the law."

3. The other inconvenience lamented by the ordinance, that the ordinary justices have not the practice and experience required in matters relating to mining, might be obviated by appointing justices of intelligence, agreeably to the intention expressed, of appointing experienced administrators. The law of the Indies,† with a view to obviate this inconvenience. directs the viceroys and presidents to select and appoint sufficient and proper persons as chief mining alcades, who are to be capable and experienced in working mines. But if persons are appointed who are ignorant of the subject, the fault is not in the regulations of the law, but in the lamentable neglect with which they are regarded. What advantage can be expected from a soldier, a placeman, or a politician, who have probably never seen a mine? How are they to give judgment on questions concerning the interior works, timberings, pillars of support and fallings in? How to distinguish between different veins and their various courses? How to make nice and exact surveys? How to give judgment as to a shaft, or an additional pit? or to discharge numberless other duties?

4. There is no want of persons of worth, who are at the same time experienced in the working of mines. The viceroys and presidents, before whose eyes they are, know them. To appoint such persons to be mayors or chief alcades in the mining districts, would be reasonable in itself, beneficial to the mines, and a merited reward to the parties; their operations would be conducted with skill; the access to the mines would be easy, and justice would be distributed with dispatch, impartiality, knowledge and experience; we should no longer see the blind leading the blind; which, between judges and surveyors, is now very much the case, and the consequence would be, a saving of immense sums in costs, proceedings and journeys, all drawn from the pocket of the unfortunate miner, who bears the expense, and of the supplier, who furnishes the money.

5. The only plan then, for promoting dispatch in mining suits, and preventing the ruin of the miners, is to adhere to the law of the Indies, by leaving the proceedings, in the first instance, to the justices, and the appeals, to the royal audiencies; at the same time filling the offices of chief alcaldes and mayors, with persons experienced in the working of mines as provided by the law. And until the sovereign shall issue other laws, these must be inviolably observed, and the viceroys, governors and presidents are not to be at liberty to render them nugatory, by challenging the cognizance of such suits, or by nominating visitors or judges of commission, as to civil or criminal matters, where questions of justice between the parties are in litigation.

6. The justices are obliged, by their office, to visit the mines, and to investigate the state of the underground works, in regard to the pillars of sup-

---

* Law 5, tit. 20, book 4, Collection of the Indies.   † Law 1, tit. 21, book 4.

port, timber-work and pits, to fallings in of the ground, to the cutting away of the pillars of support, and every thing else affecting the working. If this well-established practice were adhered to, much expense and many errors might be prevented, arising out of the ignorance of those who are sometimes dispatched as visitors to the mines, of which they frequently conceive such a dread, that they will not even venture to look at them, but blindly resign their judgment to the opinions of the surveyors, whom it is usual to employ in those places ; upon which subject we have given our sentiments in the appropriate place.* We recollect one instance of a visitor, who (when about to descend into the mine), was made a jest of by the barmen and miners exaggerating the insecure state of the works, which impressed him with such violent apprehension, that he resumed his dress, which he had taken off, and left the inspection to be performed by some one else.

7. The discreet and experienced viceroys whom we have known, wishing to follow the best course of government, have refrained from appointing visitors (except in a very few cases), either for the mines or in other depart-ments, from the great inconveniences found by experience to follow, although not previously calculated on. As far as the mines are concerned, these inconveniences are indeed very great, when thoroughly understood.

8. If, when the mining justices render an account of their offices, the plan were adopted, of charging them to visit the mines at proper times, such a practice would not only be agreeable to the precepts of the laws and ordi-nances, in promoting the various ends they contemplate, as being advanced by the working of the mines; but it would also be the means of preventing the falling in of the ground and the consequent fatalities, the inundation of the works, and many other evils of serious moment, which arise from the licence of irregularities of the miners, and the connivance and thoughtless neglect of those who ought to keep strict watch over them.

9. We have observed above, that the cases are rare in which the viceroy proceeds to appoint a visitor ; but even when he does, the appointment must be in reference to questions of government only, or to the means of improv-ing the standard of the ore, or the methods of reducing by smelting or amalgamation ; as was done by the Count de Salvatierra, on the 22d of September, 1643, when he commissioned Don Luis Berrio de Montalvo, judge of the criminal court of the royal audiency of Mexico, under the title of administrator of the mines of the kingdom, to proceed to Tasco and other mining districts, to establish the method of amalgamation for reducing the silver in twenty-four hours, discovered by Pedro Garcia de Tapia and Pedro de Mendoza Melendez, and to take into consideration every thing relating thereto ; of which we have treated elsewhere.† But the appointment must not have reference to civil or criminal matters, which are objects of justice.

---

* Sup. chap. 12 and 22.   † Sup. chap. 22, n. 44, 45 and 46.

10. Such as denouncements, insufficient working, boundaries, questions of the right of possession or property, the proving of entries in the register, the removal of pillars of support or the embezzlement of bullion; all which belong to the chief alcaldes or mayors, and by way of appeal, to the royal audiencies. And it is not lawful for the governors or viceroys to challenge cognizance of these suits, nor to withdraw the proceedings in the first instance from before the justices; nor can they prohibit an appeal to the royal audiencies: all which, besides being clearly and explicitly laid down in the laws of the Collection of the Indies, is also repeatedly enforced by various orders. At the same time, the administrative department falls entirely within the province of these officers, as is declared by the same laws, in the following particulars: They are to cause the laws of Castile, concerning the mines, to be observed in the Indies;* they are to provide the mining establishments with provisions and to be careful of their interests, as likewise are the governors;† and they are to enforce the observance of the miners' privileges, to cause them to be provided with stores at reasonable prices, and to urge them to search for, discover, and work new mines;‡ because the abundance and richness of their ores is the chief strength of the kingdom. All these authorities concern the administrative department, and an equal right of exercising them is enjoyed by the governors in their several districts.

11. But as to questions of justice, it is otherwise: for instance, although it is the part of the viceroy, as a ministerial duty, to consider whether it will be proper to sequestrate mining machinery; yet when once seized, and judicial proceedings had before the royal officers, there is no appeal to the viceroy; but, being a question of justice, the appeal belongs to the audiencies:§ and although the proceedings do in fact depend on the exercise of the ministerial authority of the viceroy, he has no power to restrain them, nor can he delay or prejudge the appeal, by refusing to allow the proceedings to go on, or by stopping their progress in the first or subsequent instances.||

12. On several occasions, where it has appeared that an opposite course has been pursued in this delicate matter, orders have been issued with reference to it. The first we shall notice was on the 22d of March, 1708, in the viceroyalty of the Duke of Albuquerque, on occasion of complaint by the mayor of Zacatecas, that he had been impeded in trying and inquiring into certain improper dealings in the purchase of silver, and in the cutting away the pillars of support of the mine Benitillas. In this case, the council, after having advised the king of their resolution, declared, in a sitting of justice,

---

* Law 8, tit. 1, book 2, Collection of the Indies.

† Laws 6 and 9, tit. 19, book 4. Laws 1 and 4, tit. 20, book 4, Collection of the Indies.

‡ Law 1, tit. 11, book 8, Collection of the Indies.

§ Law 10, tit. 19, book 4, Collection of the Indies.

|| Laws 37 and 38, tit. 3, book 3, Collection of the Indies. Laws 35 and 60, same title and book. Laws 34 and 35, tit. 15, book 2, Collection of the Indies. Law 24, tit. 12, book 5. Solorzan. Polit. lib. 5, cap. 3.

that the jurisdiction, in all civil and criminal matters, belonging to the mayor, and in the second instance, to the audiency of Guadalaxara, to the express exclusion of the viceroy.

13. Another such order was issued on the 17th of March, 1738, in the viceroyalty of the Archbishop, Don Juan Antonio de Vizarron. That officer having conceived that he had the cognizance, as superintendent of the revenue (under law 3, tit. 1., book 2), of a question of justice concerning a mine belonging to Don Manuel Ginoecio, the audiency reported the case to the council, which directed that the above order of the year 1708 should be repeated, declaring that the proceedings in the first instance ought to be had before the justice of Sombrerete (where the mine was situate), and those on appeal, before the audiency of Guadalaxara, and that the viceroy must give way ; which they recommended him to do, and for the future, not to extend his jurisdiction beyond the regular routine of business, but to permit the audiency to exert its proper functions.

14. Another such order bears date the 25th of October, 1740, and was forwarded on occasion of the above-mentioned audiency having reported, that the viceroy last named, the Archbishop, had commissioned Don Francisco Antonio de Echavarri (now senior judge of the audiency of Mexico), to hear a suit then pending between Don Eusebio Sanchez de Ocampo, and Don Leonardo de el Hierro : whereupon his majesty directed that the above-mentioned order should be repeated, and that the viceroy should be advised, if he wished to maintain his station, not to intermeddle in questions of justice between parties, but to allow the justices to exercise their jurisdiction without interruption, and to leave the proceedings upon appeal to the audiencies, agreeably to the various laws and orders, entitling those courts to the cognizance of such matters.

15. By another royal order, of the 16th of September, 1756, his majesty confirmed an arrangement which had been made by the viceroy, Count de Revilla-Gigedo, for establishing a mayor at Bolaños, but disapproved of his having separated that district from the audiency of Guadalaxara, and annexed it to the jurisdiction of the viceroyalty of Mexico ; ordering that it should be restored to the jurisdiction of the first-mentioned audiency. And although the viceroy, Marquess de las Amarillas, represented that he had suspended fulfilling the order, at the same time forwarding documents on the subject, another royal order was issued in the year 1759, directing him to comply, without further delay, and ordering that the mayor and other justices of Bolaños, should be subject to the audiency, as the latter had been before.

16. The above by no means derogates from the lofty and eminent power of the viceroy, which is so important and necessary for the administration of the political, economical and military government of these kingdoms ; and so extensive, that he can with difficulty dispatch the immense mass of applica-

tions and other business he has to attend to, in reference to all these departments, besides the affairs of the revenue, the presentation to benefices, the superintendence of the military posts and missions, the providing supplies of provisions, the concluding contracts of hire, the reducing fresh tribes of Indians, and all the other matters which require the saction of his supreme authority. But as the supreme head of the kingdom, and representing the majesty of our sovereign, it is his duty to allow the other members of the body politic, and the tribunals appointed for the determination of questions of justice, to perform their functions without restraint. And he must not, by transgressing the proper limits of his jurisdiction, and assuming authorities which belong to other ministers, disturb the harmony and subordination which ought to exist in the functions of the different officers of the state, at the same time, in so doing, violating the laws (which are supreme above all), and working great injustice to the parties concerned.

17. It is indeed a grievous thing that the parties should, as they often are, and as we ourselves have witnessed in many cases, in not a few of which we have been concerned as counsel, be complled to proceed to Mexico, from Zacatecas, Bolaños, Sombrerete, Chiguagua, and other places, at the distance of two, three or four hundred leagues, to defend their rights. For to say nothing of the journeys to and fro, the expenses at Mexico, which are considerable, and those of the procurator, advocate, assessors and clerks, which must altogether be the ruin of the suitor, even if he should gain his cause ; the fact is, that it is impossible the truth can be made out at so great a distance. If the right of appeal be denied, there is an end of justice ; if it be granted, the whole matter is just where it was at first. But how can we speak in sufficiently strong terms, of the delays and objections, whether reasonable or groundless, interposed by the assessors ? The greater part however, of these evils (we do not say the whole, for expense must necessarily be attendant upon litigation), would be avoided, were the proceedings, in the first instance, left to the territorial justices (who have much greater facilities for going through the necessary preliminaries, the trials, surveys and inspections), and the appeals, to the audiency of the district, where no assessor is required, and where it is very rare indeed that any objection can be made to any of the officers : besides which, these courts being familiar with mining matters, from the various cases which come before them, bring the suit to a speedy end, which is of great importance to the public, and dispose of the business of the miners with the expedition so much insisted on by the laws.*

18. The viceroy, Don Francisco de Toledo, sensible of these truths, framed for Peru three special ordinances, directing that the registries should be made before the mining alcalde ; that that officer should visit the mines in dispute, and go through the preliminary operations in person, proceeding,

* Laws 2, 3 and 5, tit. 20, book 4, Collection of the Indies.

and enforcing his sentence in a summary way ; and that the appeals should be heard before the royal audiencies, which should likewise have cognizance of the cause, in the further stage of supplication. So that this great and celebrated viceroy did not think himself authorised to claim cognizance of these suits, but conceived it his duty to consider the public good, by leaving questions of justice to the courts.* It is to be observed, that when a question arises concerning a contract for the purchase or sale of a mine, the right of succession under a will or otherwise, or any other point of the like nature, it is competent not only to the mining judge and chief alcalde, but also to the ordinary justices of the territory, to entertain the suit ; and that it is only upon questions arising under the ordinances, that the jurisdiction, in the first instance, belongs to the mining judge. If there be no such judge, the question must be tried by the other justices, as may be noticed in the ordinances of Peru above referred to.

CHAPTER XXVI.

OF ADITS AND *CONTRAMINAS*, AND THEIR INPORTANCE.—OF THE OBLIGATION TO MAKE THEM, AND THE INCONVENIENCES WHICH FOLLOW FROM NEGLECTING TO DO SO.—OF REGISTETING AND MARKING THEM OUT, THEIR DIMENSIONS AND FORM, AND THE NUMBER OF HANDS TO BE EMPLOYED IN WORKING THEM.—OF THE APPORTIONMENT OF THE EXPENSE AND OF THE RIGHT TO THE ORES FOUND IN THE COURSE OF PROSECUTING SUCH WORKS, WHETHER IN UNOCCUPIED OR APPROPRIATED GROUND, AND WHETHER FOUND IN NEW VEINS OR IN A VEIN BELONGING TO SOME OTHER PARTY.

ORDINANCES LXXIX. LXXX. LXXXI. LXXXII.

LXXIX. ALSO, forasmuch as we are advised, that many mines are so situated as to admit of *contraminas* being made, and that mines newly discovered may possibly be similarly circumstanced, so that the water might flow out by the *contramina*, or be got out at less expense, which is of great importance, both in regard to the permanence of the mines, and their present working :—Wherefore, we ordain and command, that wherever there shall be opportunities for making such *contraminas*, the mine owners shall make them, and each shall contribute to the same, according to the nature and disposition of his mine, so admitting of being drained by a *contramina*. And that when the mine owners shall not agree amongst themselves to make the same, the administrator-general, having inspected and informed himself of the disposition of the ground, and the advantages which would attend the measure, shall arrange with them to do it. And that in such case (such mine owners being agreed,) he shall make such appointment of the expenses

* Escalona, Gazoph. lib. 2, p. 2, cap. 1, tit. 9, pag. 121, n. 1, 2 and 3.

as may be necessary, amongst the proprietors of the mines thereby benefit-
ed, assigning to each the contribution he is to make, according to the benefit he may thereby derive, and compelling him to pay and make good such
appointment for the purpose aforesaid. And the ore which may be raised in
the course of driving such *contramina*, shall go towards the expenses incurred about the same, and any deficiency which may be found, shall be apportioned according to the arrangement which the owners, or in default
thereof, the administrator shall have made.

LXXX. Also, we ordain and command, that if, in driving such *contramina* or *contraminas*, in pursuance of any such arrangement as aforesaid,
any new mines should be discovered, not previously discovered from the surface, such mines so discovered in the course of driving such *contramina*,
shall, notwithstanding that they may fall within the boundaries of other
mines discovered from the surface, belong to the mine owners who shall
have contributed to such *contramina*, and each of them shall receive a
share of the produce, proportionate to the share of the expenses which shall
have been apportioned to him as is aforesaid.

LXXXI. Also, we ordain and command, that if there shall be any mines
at a distance from the place where such *contramina* shall have been made,
for which reason the owners thereof shall decline to contribute to the expenses of the same, then, when and so often as it shall be ascertained that
the water in such distant mines is drained off or diminished, by means of
such *contramina*, or that the owners derive any other benefit therefrom, in
getting out ore, rubbish or any other matter whatsoever; they shall pay to
the owners of such *contramina*, so much as shall be rated and estimated by
the administrator-general, or the administrator of the department, or of the
nearest department as the amount of the benefit derived by their mines from
such *contramina*, having regard to the expense to which they would have been
put, had not such *contramina* been made, and which is thereby saved to them.

LXXXII. Also, we ordain and command, that if, in any of the mining
districts where it may be convenient to drive such *contramina* or *contraminas*, the mine owners thereof shall not be disposed to lay out money in driving the same, and any other individual should be willing to undertake the
work, the expediency of driving such *contramima* having been confirmed
by the administrator-general, and the commencement thereof having been
registered he shall be at liberty to drive and may drive the same to such an extent as he shall think proper, and without regarding any particular limitation of
stakes or boundaries. And all the ore and produce which may proceed from the
discoveries made in the course of such *contramina*, shall belong to the person who shall have made the same, observing however, that he shall not take
more of the ore of any other person's mine than shall be contained within
the cavity of such *contramina*, and that the party making such *contramina*
shall not be at liberty to extend it in depth, height or width, beyond the di-

mensions which shall have been assigned at the commencement of such *contramina*, and which it is to be eight quarters of a *vara* for the height, and five for the width. And he shall enjoy this preference with regard to the ore, so ·long only as there shall be no other deeper mine,* producing more benefit to the mines aforesaid, for this right is peculiar to the deepest *contramina* only.

CONTENTS OF THE COMMENTARY ON THESE ORDINANCES.

1. What an adit, or *contramina* is.
2. Of the advantages derived from adits.
3. It is, in certain cases, a duty to drive these works.
4. The disposition of the ground should be carefully examined by surveyors.
5. Of the fatal consequences of allowing these works to be conducted by incompetent persons.
6. Of the famous adit of the Vizcayna vein, in the mining district of el Monte.
7. Of the fearful depth of the mines in Pachuca, described with astonishment by Gemelli Carreri. The water has now overwhelmed these mines, burying immense treasures.
8. Of the poverty of the miners, which disables them from driving adits.
9. For want of works of this nature, the mines become irremediably sunk in water, as is the case in many of the mining districts of New Spain.. Of the anxious provisions of the ordinance.
10. It is probable that the water will be the ruin of the mines of New Spain, and the evil is to be apprehended with regard to both the continents of America.
11. It seems desirable that the crown should take a share in the expenses and profits of the adits, in the districts of most celebrity.
12. Of the injurious neglect of the justices, in not compelling the miners to open adits, where circumstances admit of it.
13. Of registering and marking out the adits. They may be opened in ground belonging to another proprietor.
14. A limited dimension is assigned for adits. The rule was dispensed with, as was just in the case of the adit of the Vizcayna vein.
15. Of the exclusive right of the sovereign and the viceroys, to dispense with the regulations on this point, and several considerations on the subject.
16. The adit must proceed in a direct line to the point in view.
17. The proper number of hands for an adit is four workmen.
18 and 19. In the course of the agreement for driving the adit of the Vizcayna mine, the viceroy determined, that it was unnecessary to set on hands in each separate mining *pertenencia*. Of the discussions which passed, and the modifications subject to which the permission was given.
20. Of levying the contribution to the expenses of the adit, amongst the mine owners concerned, and how it is to be estimated. The parties are compellable to pay the contribution.
21. Of the manner in which an agreement to forfeit all right to the mine, in default of contributing to the adit, is to be construed.
22. The ores found in the course of driving the adit, are to be divided proportionally among the contributors.
23. The 80th ordinance grants to the parties driving the adit the property of the new veins they may discover, although they be in the ground of another proprietor This ordinance reconciled with the 82d, and an explanation given of the course to be pursued in the case of a communication occurring.

---

* Evidently meaning *contramina*.—*Trans.*

24. The party driving the adit enjoys the rights of a discoverer, in respect to any new vein he may discover in driving it.

25. The parties driving the adit are to receive payment from those who derive benefit from the work.

26. Although the party driving the adit, be not a mine owner, the contribution must be paid to him.

27. This contribution is to be paid so long only as any actual benefit is derived ; but if another adit be made at a greater depth, the contribution becomes due to the proprietor of the latter.

COMMENTARY.

1. These four ordinances (which have none corresponding to them amongst the old ordinances), are of the first importance for keeping up the mining districts. They relate to adits, or *contraminas*, so called, because they are levels or galleries over against a mine. The pit or shaft of a mine is opened from the surface above, but an adit is opened from the foot or side of the hill, and driven to communicate with the pit. The pit therefore, descends from the surface towards the centre, and the adit ascends to meet the pit or pits of the mine. The arrangement of these works, thus explained, is sufficiently clear and intelligible, but may, if required, be seen in various plates given by Agricola.*

2. These *contraminas*, or adits, which are vulgarly called *canones* (levels or drifts), are subterraneous conduits or channels, and have for their principal object (amongst others, to collect together the water from several mines, affording one general means of drainage for all of them, and thus rendering it practicable to work parts of the vein, previously under water. This is the grand object of a *contramina* or work of general drainage. Pits are expensive works, and often become insufficient or unserviceable, either from variations in the course of the vein, or from the great pressure of the water in the deeper levels. But an adit, or *contramina*, whilst it is a durable and permanent work, provides an outlet to the waters, in their natural course,—affords a ready ingress and egress to the workmen, for the purposes of getting out ore and rubbish at a reduced expense, gives opportunities for exploring the principal vein of the mine, and the other veins connected or forming junctions with, or dividing and intersecting it, and by determining the course of the vein, and enabling the proper directions to be given to the different works, promotes the grand object of discovering and turning to advantage the metallic substances hidden in the bowels of the earth.

3. Upon all these grounds then, *contraminas* being works of the highest importance, both for giving permanence to the mines themselves, and for facilitating their present working, it is provided by the 79th ordinance (notwithstanding the rule that no one ought to be compelled to work his own property), that such works shall be driven, whenever there are conveniences

*Agricola, de re metall. lib. 5, p. 71. usq. ad 74.

for the purpose; the mine owners contributing thereto, according to the benefit they may derive from them; and that if they shall not agree, the justice shall apportion the expense, and compel them to make good the payment.

4. The first thing therefore, is to ascertain the disposition of the ground, and the advantages which may be derived from the mines being drained; in estimating which, not only the situation of the mines, but also the condition and depth of the lower works, subject to the water, must be taken in to the account, that it may be ascertained whether the water will flow out with facility. For if the lower workings be as deep or deeper than the point from which the mouth of the adit is to be commenced, little or no benefit can be expected, but on the contrary, much expense and loss will be incurred. In the first place then, the ground must be inspected, and a nice survey must be made by persons of skill and practice in geometry, to prevent any risk of failure in an undertaking of such extent and importance. For, if the depth of the pit internally, be equal to the external declivity, measured to the point at which the adit is proposed to be commenced, the expenditure of time and money will be in vain, and the object will fail of effect.

5. We alluded, when on the subject of surveys,* to the misfortunes which follow from entrusting works of this nicety to mechanical and ignorant miners, or to persons who, although of more intelligence, have not the skill in geometry required to enable them to form an opinion of the proper length, breadth and depth to be given to these works. And as it is an effort of extreme hardihood in a mine owner, considering the contingencies which arise, to hazard this property, even in works for obtaining ore, so is it a still bolder step to resign himself to the guidance of an ignorant miner, in sinking a pit or driving an adit, matters which necessarily involve considerable expense, and much dead work, without affording any certainty of discovering ore, to redeem the expense.

6. And here we must notice the distinguished merit of Don Joseph Alexandro Bustamante, and his fellow supplier and successor, Don Pedro Romero Terreros, of the order of Calatrava, in driving an adit for the mines of the Vizcayna vein, in the mining district of el Monte, and jurisdiction of Pachuca, from the spot called *Doña Juana*, or *Melgarego*. This work having been commenced on the 10th July, 1749, it was found, in the month of January, 1754, by surveys and inspections performed every four months, that the length driven was 856 *varas*; a work certainly worthy of commendation, and with more reason than some others of its class.† This adit was afterwards, by perseverence, activity and energy, carried to a still greater length, and found to be eminently useful: but not till nine years of fruitless labour

---

* Vide sup. chap. 12, n. 14.

† Qualis est illa cuniculi *de el Venino*, qui ducit ad venam ricam Potosiæ, qui improbo labore per 29 annos constructus, 250 ulnas non excedebat. Laet, Americæ descriptio, lib. 11, cap. 9.

had been spent in driving an adit from the place called Asoyatla, and after-wards another year in driving another adit from a place called Omitlan, or Guerrero, the two last being in different directions. What money must have been expended, and what patience exerted in these ten years! Bustamante, wearied of so much ineffectual labour, relinquished the prosecution of the work, and gave up his interest in the privileges granted to him by the superior government of Mexico, in the orders under which he had been authorised to undertake the adit; but the Marquess de Valle-Ameno, a partner in the work, and a proprietor of some adjoining mines, persisted in the enterprise, taking up the work from the extreme point of the adit driven from the place called *Dona Juana*, towards which the watercourses of the mining district of el Monte flowed, and he finally accomplished his object, although frustrated at the other two points, doubtless from not having taken a correct view of the disposition of the ground, of the distance between the mouth of the adit and the bottom workings, and of the depth of the latter below the former.

7. Gemelli Carreri, in travelling through that country in the year 1697, found the bottom workings of the mines of Pachuca to be of very great depth; the mine of Santa Cruz was more than 700 feet deep; that of Navarro, more than 600; and that of San Mateo, 400. Into the latter of these, with a miner's spirit, he descended, and he declares that it was the most foolish action he ever committed for the mere gratification of curiosity. The mine of Trinidad, consisting of the several mines of Campechana, Joya and Peñol, from which he assures us that forty millions of marcs of silver were raised in ten years, by means of as many as one thousand workmen, was so flooded with water, at the depth of 800 feet, that it required sixteen whims to drain it, and the expense of the timber alone, for preventing the falling in of the ground, was estimated at more than twenty thousand dollars.[*] In the early part of the present century, Don Isidro Rodriguez, of Madrid, of the order of Calatrava, sunk much money in these mines; but the irresistible force of the water overwhelmed the property he laid out in them, and the treasures of the mines themselves still remained buried in its depth. After all this, it is impossible to bestow too much commendation on the laudable energy displayed by Don Joseph de Bustamante, Don Pedro Romero Terre-ros, the Marquess de Valle-Ameno, Don Juan Varandiaram and Don Thomas Tello, and their partners, in undertaking and pursuing, during more than twenty years, from the year 1739, the great work of the adit, notwithstand-ing the depth of these mines, and the immense body of water contained in them. And the failure of the two first adits, combined with the success of the last, shews what mature deliberation should be bestowed, in planning works of such extent and expense as these; the failure of which is attended

* Gemelli Carreri, in his voyage round the world, 23d April, 1697. Histoire general des voyages, tom. 44, in 12. pag. 11.

with the most serious loss to the mine owner, who may, on the other hand, by the successful accomplishment of the work, be rendered both rich and powerful. The only way of effecting the latter object, is by having a practical survey of the ground made, under the direction of persons skilled in geometry.

8. In the second place, after considering the disposition of the ground, the attention must be turned to the arrangements required to be made amongst the mine owners, preparatory to driving the adit. This is the greatest difficulty experienced in carrying the 79th ordinance into effect, for although it directs that adits shall be driven wherever there are conveniences for the purpose, or that the owners shall be compelled by the justice to drive them ; yet the fact is, that the labour of these undertakings is so great, and the miners so necessitous and destitute of resources, that unless they happen to be men of very ample means, they are but rarely in a situation to undertake an adit of great length, or to expend many thousands of dollars in advance, upon the bare hope of reimbursement upon the draining being accomplished. On the other hand, if the business be made a partnership concern, the love of money becomes a great bar to its success, and the profit not being of a nature to admit of easy division, it so happens that very few instances occur, of agreements between different parties for undertaking these adits in concert. The miners, provided they have but some ore to work at for the time present, pay but little regard to prospects of a greater profit at a future period, and are alarmed at the idea of expense. They are satisfied with a small profit, and with the ordinary mode of drawing off the water by means of the pit, and they cannot find courage to form a combination for the purpose of driving an adit ; not calling to mind, that after a little time, when the works are carried somewhat deeper, their pits will become of little service, whilst an adit or *contramina* would provide for the permanent and continued working of the mine. And as the veins in mineral regions are found by experience[*] to incline towards each other, forming junctions at intervals, the consequence is, that having for a time, bread to cut, (as the saying is,) and other mines and veins to work, they are induced, in the hope of benefiting more by pursuing these, to neglect the old and tried mines, which would require an expenditure of money in works of drainage.

9. All these causes combined, render it difficult to put the directions of the ordinance in force, and will in time be the occasion of the ruin and abandonment of the principal mining districts, and indeed may now be observed to operate sensibly in some of them, more particularly in the rich veins of the mining district of Guanaxuato, which has been the Potosi of New Spain, and in those of Pachuca and Zacatecas, which have yielded riches beyond calculation. The productiveness of these veins is matter of notoriety, and has been long well established, and yet a vast number of their

* Vide infr. u. 12.

mines have been abandoned, on account of the force of the water, notwithstanding that the disposition of the ground is such, that the obstacle might have been overcome, had the owners been inclined to combine in the important undertaking of driving an adit, and so clearing the water from their lower works, which are more liable to be embarrassed by it, in proportion to their depth. And as the source of this water, being the rain which falls, is of permanent continuance, there is room to apprehend that the principal known deposits of treasure will in time cease to be worked, and that the very circumstance of there being such an abundance of mines, will be the cause of their becoming altogether unavailable. Such are the evils which may be anticipated from the non-observance of these ordinances, which are conceived with every view to the public benefit, as is evident from the clear authority given by the 82d, to any person, to drive an adit through the mine of another proprietor, and the express direction of the 81st, that the proprietors shall come to an understanding, or that the justice shall bring them to an agreement. But it is to be observed, that it is advisable that the miners should bring in their contributions, whether voluntary or compulsory, when the state of their mines is such as to supply them with funds for the purpose ; that is to say, when they are in a course of prosperity, although liable from their increasing depth, to be soon embarrassed with water ; for if they defer it till the water overwhelms them, the circumstance of their money being spent, and the works inundated, renders that difficult to be applied as a cure, which would have been easy as a preventive.

10. We have already noticed the lamentable neglect into which the working of the mines of Spain, the fruitful sources of immense treasure, has fallen. And there can be no doubt that one cause which contributed to the abandonment of the richer districts, was the embarrassment occasioned by the water, and the omission to drive adits and *contraminas*. This was the case with the rich mines of Guadalcanal and others, belonging to the crown ; in which, as well as in other mines of that kingdom, torrents of water broke forth, at a time when they were in most active work. The same misfortune happened with the mines of Carthagena, in the time of Hannibal : and, although one of the latter alone, named Bebulo, from its discoverer, returned him three thousand crowns per day, it was only in consequence of an adit having been driven by the Carthagenians with immense labour, through the mountains, for the length of 1500 paces, through which the water was let off, forming a complete river, as is testified by Pliny. Peru again, in its vast extent of surface, offers many deposits of gold and silver, as does New

* Plin. Naturalis historiæ, lib. 33, cap 31, ibi : " Mirum adhuc per Hispanias ab Hannibale inchoatos puteos durare sua ab inventoribus nomina habentes. Ex quois Bebulo appellatur hodieque qui tercentum pondo Hannibali subministravit indies, ad mille quingentos passus cavato monte, per quod spatium Accitani stantes diebus, noctibusque egerunt aquas lucernarum mensura, amnemque faciunt."

Spain, both in its cultivated and its remoter provinces; but there is reason to apprehend, that from the non-observance of these ordinances, the mining districts of the more populous and fruitful provinces will go to decay, although it would be easy to maintain them in their present flourishing state, and at the same time to make a considerable profit, merely by driving adits or *contraminas*, to drain the principal districts, such as, amongst others, Guanaxuato, Pachuca, Zacatecas, Tlalpujagua, and Sombrerete, the known and approved richness of which, promises the greatest advantage from such works. We know that the mine Quebradilla, in Zacatecas, when worked by a partnership, formed in the year 1741, yielded, in six days and a half, 260,000 dollars, after which a spring of water broke out in one of the ends, with irresistible force, and inundated the whole vein, which is about 22 *varas* in width; and hence it appears, how advantageous an adit, or work of general drainage would be, if undertaken. And the same may be said of other mining districts, where nothing but the water prevents the obtaining possession of the mineral treasure.

11. Considering the profit the crown derives from the duties on the silver and gold produced from the mines, which profit must diminish as the mines decay, it would certainly answer to the revenue, in districts of tried and approved richness, to assist the unfortunate miners, in providing means of drainage by *contraminas*. It has, it is very true, been found by experience, not to be desirable for the crown to undertake the working of mines, nor even to take on its own account, the mine which, under the old ordinances, was set apart for it, contiguous to the discoverer's mine, on account of the risks to which the revenue would be thereby exposed, and because, there being plenty of persons willing to work these mines, the crown is graciously pleased to be contented with the fifth, tenth, or other proportion justly allotted to it: but these reasons do not apply to the driving an adit in a mining district of notorious richness, where the presence of the water is the only obstacle to the working of the mines, the situation of the latter being such as to afford facilities for the purpose. For in such a case, there is, morally speaking, no risk at all, and the crown might have the benefit of two fifths, or tenths; one by virtue of its original right, and the other in consideration of the funds expended upon the work of drainage. So that the work being performed on the part of the crown and miners together, the loss could be but trifling, even supposing it to fail of effect; but if it should succeed, the advantages to both would be very considerable. Although this is a subject for the judgment of the sovereign and the discretion of his ministers, we think we should be wrong did we omit to place it in this point of view. And it has already been submitted to the sovereigns of Germany and France, as may be seen from the curious reflections in the *Journal économique*, upon the regulations to be observed in discovering and working mines. In that work, after noticing the ample funds required for this pur-

pose, the question is asked, whether it would be desirable that the sovereign should undertake the working of the mines, or whether it is better to leave them to the free agency of the subject; and it is suggested, that as, on the one hand, it is to the disadvantage of the sovereign that his subjects should sacrifice their fortunes, so it is to the disadvantage of the latter, that the sovereign should place his revenues in hazard; but that both these evils might be avoided by sharing the expenses and profits. By appointing then, an administrator-general of the smelting works, and constructing a grand work of drainage for the mines, the crown would gain a right to an additional ninth part, in return for such assistance, whilst the miners would be much aided in carrying through their works, and would find great advantage in being relieved from a part of their contributions thereto. And should the event not happen to answer the intention, the loss might be supported without any violent injury to the state.*

12. Having suggested these reasonable reflections on the important subject of executing the works of general drainage in the mining districts of approved richness, we proceed to remark, that although it is evidently very difficult, in general, to accomplish such works by the exertions of a set of individuals, both from their wanting the means, and from none but mine owners being willing to risk their money in adits, where there is no certain prospect of reimbursement; and that the water sometimes lies at such a depth, that it would be necessary to drive some leagues to give the adit a proper slope; yet it is notorious, that in many mining districts, where the circumstances are much less unfavourable, a great number of whims are often employed by different mine owners, in the laborious business of draining (raising the water through the pits,) a plan which is attended with the disadvantage of leaving the works always liable to be overwhelmed by a fresh influx of water, in consequence of which the property of

---

* Journal économique, Janvier, 1751, p. 122. "Il est d'une extreme necessité d'avoir des fonds très considerables lorsqu'ou se propose d'ouvrir un mine, car il devient également facheux de ne pouvoir faute d'argent, continuer les travaux commencés ou d'être obligé de les abandonner après que l'on en a fait toute la dépense. Gn demande à ce sujet s'il est plus à propos que le prince fasse une semblable entreprise, ou s'il convient qu'il la faisse faire à ses sujets? La difficulté de cette question consiste en ce qu'il est contre le bien du prince que ses sujets se ruinent, et contre celui des sujets de le prince porte toutes ses finances d'une côté au hazard de les perdre, et de laisser les autres parties des affaires publiques tomber dans la langueur. Mais cette difficulté fournit elle même sa solution. Il est visible en effet que le bien commun se trouvera en partageant les charges et les profits. Le prince peut établir une administration générale des fontes, et faire bâtir a ses dépenses la décharge principale des eaux de la mine, qui sert en même temps à faire écouler les eaux, et à donner aux mineurs un air sain et libre. Ce dernier point seul lui assure le droit de lever une neuvième sur tout le produit de la mine, et les avances qu'il fait à cette occasion soulagent beaucoup les compagnies particulières qui achevent plus aisément les bâtimens de la mine, et en font l'exploitation. Ainsi de part et d'autre on se sent du benefice que la mine peut rendre sans être dans le cas de faire de trop fortes contributions; et si l'entreprise n'a pas l'heureux succès que l'on s'en etoit promis, la perte devient plus facile à supporter, et l'etat en général n'en souffre que foiblement."

the miner is exhausted, and the public interest prejudiced by the necessity for repeated draining. But there are also places, where from the disposition of the ground, adits might be made at very little expense, and therefore, in these instances, it is evident that the only reason for the non-observance of these ordinances must be that the proprietors do not agree amongst themselves. And whether it be from connivance on the part of the justices, or from ignorance of their duty, it is very certain that they neglect to enforce the rules of these ordinances, insomuch that we never recollect to have heard of their resorting to compulsory measures for the purpose, or of their treating with the miners, in order to stimulate and encourage them to a better practice. By indulging in this neglect of their duty, they do injustice to the public, to individuals, and to the rights of the sovereign, who has made it a law, that the working of the mines shall be assisted by means of adits, as being works of great importance, and necessary for giving a permanent character to this valuable description of property. And if the mine owners can find sufficient capital and activity to work a number of whims, they might and ought to apply a part of the money thus expended, in permanent works of drainage; not omitting, however, to keep some of their pits at work in the mean time, which was the plan pursued in the mining district of el Monte, where, whilst contributions were making towards the completion of the adit mentioned above, the mines were kept in work by means of the pits. It usually happens, as a further encouragement to these works, that part of the expenses is covered by the ore found in their course, and by the discovery of new veins in the interior, which had not been explored from the surface; a result which is to be expected from the very nature of metallic ores; for wherever one vein has been discovered, it may be conjectured that others will be met with, as may be seen by referring to Saint Isidore and Pliny.[*]

·13. In the third place, registry must be made, and possession given; and the work must be defined and traced out from the mouth of the adit to the site of the vein or mine to which it is directed. The course thus assigned must be observed with precision, for otherwise it would be easy, under pretence of driving an adit, to deviate from the proper direction of the work, with a view to get ore belonging to other proprietors; the direction assigned must therefore not be deviated from, but must be pursued in a direct course. The possession given and registry made, confer a title to the work, the commencement of which may be opened in ground which falls within some other person's *pertenencia*, notwithstanding any opposition on his part; as appears from the ordinances of Peru,[†] and from our 79th ordinance, the

---

[*] S. Isidor. Etymolog. 16, cap. 17. "Metallum dictum oquod natura ejus ea sit, ut ubi una vena apparuerit, ibi spes sit alterius inquirendæ." Plinius, lib. 33, Hist. Natur. cap. 6, n. 20 " Et ubicunque una vena inventa ist, non procul invenitur alia. Metallum idem quod Vetallum, id est, quasi vena alia.

[†] Ord. 1, tit. 8, concerning adits. Escalona Gazoph. lib. 2, part. 2, pa . 118.

latter of which gives free power to make such works, wherever there shall be most advantages for the purpose.

14. In the fourth place, regard must be had to the width and height of the adit. In Peru, it must not exceed two *varas* and a half in width, and as much in height.* But our 82d ordinance assigns as a limit, eight quarters (of a *vara*) in height, and five in width, which are the dimensions to observed in New Spain. Don Joseph Alexandro de Bustamante, aware of this rule, prayed, on denouncing the mines of the Vizcayna vein, to be granted a dispensation from the observance of the 82d ordinance abovementioned, which was conceded to him, by an order of the superior government of Mexico, of the 1st June, 1739, the archbishop and viceroy, Don Juan Antonio Vizarron, availing himself, for that purpose, of the power given him by law 3, tit. 1, book 2, of the Collection of the Indies, to make such arrangments in mining matters as should be most expedient. Under this law, he referred the consideration of the height and width of the adit, to the judgment and discretion of the royal officers of Pachuca, with the advice of skilful and intelligent miners; which officers, after considering, under the suggestions of persons of experience, the distance between the fixed stake or mouth of the adit, and the *Vizcayna* vein; the circumstance that the workmen entering loaded with timber, and those going out, bearing rubbish, must meet; that men of more than two *varas* in height have to come in and go out, also loaded with burdens; that the ground is generally found to be very hard in the interior; that it would be advantageous to give more facility to the working: and that it would be necessary in some places to drive the *contraminas* side by side, and in other places, one above the other; agreed, that two *varas* and a half should be assigned for the width of the adit, and three *varas* for the height. For the second *contramina* or outlet, which was to run in some places parallel with the principal one, and in others, above or below it, being intended for the purpose of supplying air and giving a course to the water, they fixed two *varas* and a quarter for the limit of the height, and a *vara* and a half for the breadth.

15. All the above considerations however, must have been had in view, when the ordinance fixing the dimensions was framed; and the justices are therefore bound to obey it, and have no authority to dispense with its observance, such a power being reserved to none but the sovereign, or the high authority of the viceroy, upon a view of the circumstances of the case: as for instance, if the adit should pass through unoccupied ground, in which case, there can be no inconvenience in giving it larger dimensions; or if it merely pass through the ground of the parties concerned in the work, supposing them to consent to it; for in these cases, no one is injured by working the ore met with. But if it have to pass through the mines of other proprietors, great injury would be done by exceeding the dimensions of width and height

assigned by law, and taking the other party's ore,—it being a rule, that he who would improve his own property, must take care, in doing so, not to injure that of his neighbor ;* and the right of driving an adit, and opening a way through the ground of others, must be understood, like all other rights, to have the limitation annexed, that it operate as little injury as possible to third parties.

16. As a consequence of this rule, then, the adit must proceed in a direct line ; although, whenever the ground is found extremely hard, a cross-cut may be driven, to avoid the inconvenience, afterwards resuming the original direction ; but there is no right or permission to exceed the limited depth, height or width ; for not to mention the injustice of wrongfully taking another person's ore, as by making winzes or working perpendicularly downwards, the thing itself would be contrary to the very end of a general work of drainage, for the water would lodge in the hollows thus made, and both the footway and the water-course would be interrupted and obstructed.

17. In the fifth place, it is to be investigated, what number of hands are required to be kept at work, in adits and *contraminas*. As there is no ordinance which refers particularly to the number of men required to be employed in such works, it follows, that the number of four persons, required by the 37th ordinance for each mine, will be sufficient. That ordinance directs, that the four persons so set on to work the mine, shall be occupied in raising water or ore, or in some other beneficial work within or without the same ; but nothing can be regarded as more beneficial than a work of drainage to clear the lower levels of water. As adits, however, are works of great extent, it is expedient and indeed necessary, to urge them forward by employing a greater number of hands than four, under the arrangement which the miners, or in their default the justice, may have made ; for with so small a number as four persons, the work would be extremely tedious, and indeed might never arrive at completion.

18. But a considerable difficulty arises, upon the question whether supposing that there are, as is usually the case, several mining *pertenencias* in the superficial and external extent of the *contramina*, it is necessary to sink three *estados* in each of them, and to set on four persons, at least, to work in each, agreeably to the provisions of the ordinances ? This question arose in practice, on the occasions of Don Joseph de Bustamante denouncing the adit for the mines of the Vizcayna vein, of which we have before spoken, and was decided, in the resolutions of the order issued the 1st June, 1739 —" I also declare, that for the whole number of mines and veins denounced by the aforesaid Don Joseph (including the *Vizcayna* vein), throughout the whole length of the adit, and during all the progress of the work, until its final completion, it shall be sufficient to employ the regular number of hands at the end of the adit, so as to keep the work in progress, without its being

---

* L. 1, §. sed et si fossus, ff. de aqua, et au. pluv. arc.

necessary to set on hands, separately, in each of the pits contained in the ground denounced, or to sink the depth of three *estados* required by the ordinance ; for the reasons and on the grounds set forth by the petitioner. And for further security, modify the directions of the law in this respect, by virtue of the provision of the ordinance itself, dispensing with the setting on of four persons in each separate mine or *pertenencia*, if any reasonable obstacle prevent it ; particularly if the main object of draining can be attained in any other way, as in this instance, by means of the adit aforesaid."

19. The reasons set forth by Bustamante, the party who had made the denouncement, were grounded on the great expense of working so many pits ; and his argument was, that as they would all be restored to a work-ing state by means of the general work of drainage, the period of its ac-complishment would be the time to set on hands with advantage, as the pits would then be in a state to be worked with profit. Hence it appears, that it is only during the time of driving the adit, that the setting on four work-men in each mine is dispensed with ; the pits being construed to be kept sufficiently at work, so long as the adit is kept worked : but when that is completed, each mine must have a distinct set of workmen. It is to be ob-served however, that in order to prevent any fraud which might operate in-juriously to the public generally, and to provide for the due observance of the ordinances and the security of the tenths and other duties, and likewise to prevent the driving an adit being made a pretence, on the part of the sub-ject, for omitting to denounce, register or work the mines, it was provided, by the same order, that an inspection should be made every four months, to ascertain the progress and state of the work ; which was not to be abandon-ed without just cause, duly established by being submitted to the considera-tion of the superior government : for since the mine owners are liable to be compelled to drive an adit, it is evident that it cannot be optional with them to desist from proceeding in it at their pleasure.

20. In the sixth place, an adjustment must be made of the sums to be con-tributed by each of the persons who join in driving the adit ; in doing which, regard must be had principally, to any agreement which they may themselves have made, in reference to the situation of their respective mines ; and to the conditions under which such agreement may have been entered into. But if there be no such agreement, the estimate must be made by the justice, referring to the opinion of surveyors, and taking into the ac-count, the advantage each mine may derive from the adit, in respect of the drainage and means of access afforded by it, as provided by the 79th ordi-nance. It might be asked, whether, supposing any party should make de-fault in contributing his proportion, he should lose his interest in the adit ? As, however, the ordinance provides that he may be proceeded against for his contribution, it would seem that payment must be demanded and enforc-ed against him ; and if it cannot be obtained, the rules may be applied

which we have laid down in the proper place, in treating of partnership mines.*

21. It is to be observed, that although it be agreed that any party failing to contribute within such a time, shall forfeit his right, as was agreed by the partners in the above-mentioned undertaking of the adit of the Vizcayna vein, yet we should consider, supposing that the ore would cover the expenses, or that no means had been taken to compel payment, by summoning the party and proceeding judicially against him (which is the lawful remedy), that the right would not be actually lost by the time expiring; unless, indeed, the party upon being summoned, should renounce his claim: for it would be contrary to equity, to the rules of the ordinances, and to the public interest,† to deprive him of his right under any other circumstances.

22. In the seventh place, a devision must be made, of the proceeds of the ore found, and of the produce of the new veins, discovered in prosecuting the adit, in proportion to the share of the expenses contributed by each party: which is agreeable to reason and to the rules by which every partnership must be governed, and is likewise consistent with the directions of the 79th and 80th ordinances. The tenor of the latter of these is worthy of notice, for although no mine can be registered, or be acquired in property, except upon exhibiting the ore to the justice, and pointing out the site of the mine upon the surface, and no pit or fixed stake can be opened except upon ore (which is to prevent fraudulent practices in gaining access to, or working other persons' ore, as has been shewn under the proper ordinances);‡ yet it is provided by this 80th ordinance, that if in driving the adit, any new mines, not previously known, shall be discovered, they shall belong to the parties who may have contributed to the adit, in proportion to their respective contriputions. The reason is simply this, that there is, in this case, no room for the presumption of fraud or evil intent; the adit not being opened with the *sole* view,§ of getting access to the ore of another proprietor, but having for its principal object the draining of other mines already discovered, and rendering them fit for working: and the veins discovered being new ones, it would be unreasonable, and injurious both to the public and the private interest of the partners concerned in driving the adit, to make it a rule that they should remain unworked and unproductive of benefit.

23. The point which presents most difficulty in the construction of the 80th ordinance, is its giving the partners a right of property in the new mines or veins discovered, even though they should take their course within the limits of other mines previously discovered from the surface. For this shews that these veins may be followed up and worked within the limits

* Sup. chap. 7, n. 10, et seq.
† Arg. L. 6, Cod. si contr. jus, vel utilit. public.
‡ Vide supr. chap. 13, n. 4, and chap. 14, n. 36.
§ Vide supr. chap. 14, n. 36, et seq.

of another proprietor's ground; although according to the 82d ordinance, the parties concerned in driving the adit, can acquire no right to the ore of another person's mine, except so far as it falls within the space assigned for the width and height of the adit, that is to say, of eight quarters (of a *vara*) for the latter, and five for the former; as we have already seen. But this difficulty vanishes when it is observed, that the 82d ordinance has reference to ore found in another person's mine, such mine being merely liable to the service of admitting a passage, but without any deviation either upwards, downwards or sideways; lest any injury should be done to the owner, or to his property in the vein: whilst the 80th ordinance relates to new veins or mines, not previously discovered from the surface. As, however, the law, with a view to the general benefit, permits the driving of adits, their entrance being opened either in public ground, or in ground belonging to the party or to any other proprietor, and also permits the new veins met with, to be worked by the discoverers, it follows, that such veins may be worked, even though they should take their course within the limits of other mines. For if the law be, as we have already seen, that a miner in the immediate pursuit of a vein, may make his way within the limits of another proprietor's ground, until the two mines communicate together, after which the owners are to measure out their boundaries, and fall back within their respective limits, it follows, with still more reason, that where the vein pursued is a new one, and distinct from that which is worked in the other party's mine, the person in pursuit of the new vein may make his way into the ground of the latter. But if they should happen to communicate together in the course of their works, it would be reasonable, upon the grounds explained under ordinance 30, in chapter 14, that each should measure out his boundaries, according to his just right, and fall back within his own limits.

24. We must here call to mind what we have discussed more at length, whilst on the subject of first discoverers ;* namely, that every person finding a new vein, is entitled to the rights of a discoverer, and that consequently, the parties concerned in driving the adit will be entitled, as first discoverers, to assign to every one of the mines upon the new vein, the dimensions of 160 *varas* in length, and 80 in width, measured parallel to the adit; which were the terms of the grant made to Don Joseph Alexandro de Bustamante, by the superior government of Mexico, in the above-mentioned order of the 1st June, 1739.

25. In the eighth place, it must be ascertained what contribution is to be made to the proprietors of the adit, by parties whose mines may be drained or afforded access by it. The 81st ordinance leaves it to be estimated by the justice, who is to be governed by the amount of benefit derived from the draining, and the expense which the owner would be put to on that ac-

* Vide cap. 8. à n. 1. et seq. et cap. 9. à n. 3 et seq.

count, were it not saved to him by the adit. In Peru the ordinances direct that if the adit has merely the effect of draining the mines of other proprietors, they shall contribute a tenth of the produce, but that if they also use it as a thoroughfare, in working their mines, they shall contribute a fifth.* In New Spain, any agreement which the parties may have entered into, is to be observed, and in default of any such, a fair adjustment is to be made, as directed by the ordinance. The usual rule is to contribute a fourth part of the produce, which was the proportion stipulated for by Bustamante and his partners, in the adit of the Vizcayna vein, to be paid by those who did not join in contributing to the expences of the work. But considering the difference in the degree of benefit derived, and the amount of expense saved, under different circumstances, it would be most proper to follow the practice pursued in the mining districts, in other cases of a similar nature ; for the saving afforded, the advantages derived and the expenses laid out upon the work not being always the same, the *partido* (such is the name given to the share of ore contributed), should be regulated according to the circumstances of the case, and the practice followed in other similar cases, whether it be a third, a fourth or a sixth part of the produce.

26. A similar contribution must be made to a party who, not being a proprietor of mines, yet undertakes to drive an adit, or make a general work of drainage for the benefit of those who are proprietors of mines in work. A person undertaking the adit under such circumstances, must have the approval of the justice, and must make a formal registry of the work, and have it duly defined throughout the whole line of ground he may select. And the share to be contributed by the parties must be estimated according to the benefit they may derive, the expense they may be saved, and the amount they would have to expend in pits and independent works of drainage, were not a general outlet provided by the proprietor of the adit ; in favour of whom, regard must be had to the rules of these four ordinances, in respect to his being entitled both to the ore found in the course of the adit, and to the new veins he may discover.

27. The contribution will continue to be made, so long only as the mines shall be drained or worked through the medium of this adit ; but if another adit should be driven by different proprietors, at a greater depth, from which the mines derive more benefit, the contribution must be made to the latter, and not to the former. And if the depth of both should be the same, or nearly so, the share to be contributed, in respect of each mine, must be accounted for to the proprietor of the adit by means of which the mine in

---

* Ord. 10, tit. 8, concerning adits ; Escalona, Gazoph. lib. 2, part. 2. Antea solvebatur 5 pars Laet, Americæ descriptio, lib. 11. cap. 9, " Domini cuniculorum accipiunt quintam partem metalli quod educitur." Apud Germanos, pars nona solvebatur. Agricol. de re metall. lib. 4, p. 61

question is drained or worked ;* for this is a right which belongs to the adit of greatest depth ; and if the second adit be the deeper, it is sufficient to entitle it to the preference, provided the mines derive more benefit from it, which is also the rule under the ordinances of Peru.† The same rules will apply to pits by which the draining of adjoining mines is facilitated.

ORDINANCE LXXXIV

It is also our will and pleasure, and we command that the incorporation in our royal patrimony of the mines of gold, silver and quicksilver which we ordered to be made by said royal edict of the year '59 be construed without prejudice to the contract and agreement which we order to be made with Don Diego de Cordoba our Master of Horse, in relation to the mines which he has purchased, subscribed on the 15th day of the month of August in the year 1568.

By which said laws and ordinances, and by each one of them, we command that the said mines and all matters touching the same, and annexed to and concerning them shall be directed and governed ; and that all judges, justices and audiences in their several districts and jurisdiction, shall observe them and cause them to be observed, wholly and absolutely as to the provisions of all and each of them, that they shall be guilty of no act or omission, nor consent to any act or omission in violation of the tenor and form of the same, under the penalties contained in our said laws and ordinances, and under pain of our displeasure, and of a fine of ten thousand maravedis for each violation of the same ; and we command our principal auditors of accounts, that they record a copy of them in the books of our principal office of accounts, and cause them to be printed for the information of all.

And moreover, we command our said principal auditors of accounts, that the said books shall contain a statement and account of all proceedings by ourselves in relations to said mines, and of the reports and transcripts which the said administrators may have rendered of the condition of said mines, and of the cost and expense attending them.—(*Law* 9, *title* 13, *book* 6, *R.*) (3).

---

* Agricol. de re metall. lib. 4, pag. 61. " Quod si plures cuniculi in unam aream metallis fœcundam aguntar ; de metallo, quod quidem supra solum cujusque cuniculi effoditur, ejus domino datur nona."

-† Ord. 11, apud Escalon. ubi proxime.

(3) (Note. to the original text.)—By the resolutions of the General Council of Commerce, Money and Mines, of the 25th October, 1783, and 5th May, 1787, a citizen of Valencia having twice solicited a licence for the discovery of mines, it was denied him, and in view of it, it was ordered that in similar instances it should be borne in mind, that it is not expedient to grant individual permits for the discovery of mines, on account of the abuses which had attended the experiment, and because the power which they had under regulations and ordinances, of denounc-

LAW V.

Don Ferdinand VI. at Buen Retiro on the 19th of December, 1754.

Private jurisdiction of the Superintendent of the Mines of Almaden within the circuit of ten leagues.

It being of so great importance to preserve the mines of Almaden, and desiring that the arrangements which have been made to render them more productive might have due effect without those embarrassments occasioned by continued controversies, which have occurred on different occasions, between the Superintendent General of the Mines, the persons having charge of the royal herds, the waggoners, the justices of the villages included in the pasture grounds appropriated to the use of the towns and the "*Comendadores*" and owners of them, I have resolved on the subject and as a general rule, that within his circuit of ten leagues, computed from the four which are regarded as the mouth of the mine-enclosures and heaps of earth, the superintendent shall have private jurisdiction with regard to the pastures for cattle employed in their works, also for the cutting of timber and wood necessary for working the mines ; and that in regard to the jurisdiction above referred to it, shall not be competent for the sub-delegates aforesaid or the other subjects above mentioned to claim authority.

LAW VI.

Don Carlos IV. by resolution of October 19th, 1790.

Jurisdiction of the Superintendent of the Quicksilver Mine of Collado de la Plata.

The Commissioner or the deputy Commissioner of the quicksilver mine of Collado de la Plata in his stead—and the Superintendent of the mine according to the various articles of the royal ordinances concerning quicksilver mines, respectively have civil and criminal jurisdiction in the cognizance of causes and matters as well civil as criminal concerning the persons employed and the operations attached to the mine with appropriate judicial authority concerning them to the exclusion of other tribunals, except that of the gen-

ing the mines before the Judge in the several territories, and rendering an account of their admission, with proof to the council and with specimens of the minerals, was sufficient for all who were sincere in their intentions. And by another resolution of full council, of the 18th of August 1796, under the advice and approbation of his Majesty, another similar application from various citizens of Mexico, on account of the inconveniences experienced by the grant of a similar license, was denied.

eral superintendency; it being their appropriate duty with care and watch-
fulness to see that every one performs the obligation imposed, and punishing
severely every one who fails to fulfil it; that the aforesaid commissioner and
his substitute, or the person who shall be hereafter superintendent of said
mine, shall in all respects be subject to the general superintendency, giving
an account of whatever may occur and be worthy of being brought to their notice; not hereby conferring more jurisdiction in relation to the government of
the mines and the controversies connected with the management and business
of the same and its work-shops, and all matters which may incidentally arise,
than belongs to the general superintendency aforesaid: in such manner that
only their orders and not any others which may be issued by other tribunals
not sanctioned by the general superintendency aforesaid shall be complied with: being however, obliged to observe punctually the orders which
are communicated by my royal person; that the jurisdiction of the superintendent of the mine in virtue of the royal letter issued in the year 1685,
includes waggoners, carts and oxen, reduced to service and which are usefully
employed in the mine, having first, in relation to the security and licence,
complied with the formalities prescribed by the royal orders: that consequently they are the sole judges for the cognizance of the excesses which the
waggoners bound in the manner aforesaid commit in the pasturing of their
cattle and in the cutting of timber for farming utensils and every thing relating to it, and to the service of the mine, as well in relation to civil as to
criminal matters. That it is also their duty as judges, to preserve and defend
the aforesaid waggoners from every grievance, injury or violence which is
in opposition to their privilege of pasturage, and of cutting timber for their
waggons or other privilege pertaining to their jurisdiction, to which they may
be subjected; that the said superintendent of the mine is and shall hereafter be the judge and conservator exclusively of the forests and commons
appropriated, and which shall be appropriated for the service and benefit of
the aforesaid mine and its works, and shall have exclusive cognizance of
all causes and denouncements in relation to the destruction of trees, cutting
of timber, acts of incendiaries and all other acts and things besides, which may
be prejudicial to the mine: that no other tribunal except that of the general
superintendency shall hold cognizance in the way of appeal or any other legal
proceeding from the determination of the superintendent aforesaid as in relation to them all in this particular, I expressly prohibit it; that the orders
which the superintendent in the exercise of his jurisdiction, which is territorial
and extensive within the prescribed limits, for the execution of sentences,
for the exaction of penalties and the imprisonment of culprits being committed to the sub-delegate, *guarda major*, or other person other than the justices,
shall be observed by them; and they are bound to render corresponding aid
to the sub-delegate or special commissioner to carry them into effect, without
interposing any embarrassment, under the responsibility for all the damage

and injury arising from their default, in the fining and punishing of the offenders : that those employed with a fixed salary, or who constantly labor in said mine are and shall be free in their persons and cavalry horses from liability to military service and other assessments, and are not bound to contribute to them, nor are they subject to be drafted or enlisted in time of war, nor to pay money to supply others as their substitutes, nor are they liable to be coerced by the justices but are exempt from assessment for personal tax and services, from tribute, (moneda forera) (a), to the king, and money collected by the bull of the pope, nor are they bound against their will to accept and discharge the duties of those offices and other similar servile offices, being also exempt from the liability of giving quarters to soldiers, men at arms, or other military persons ; and finally, that in the above named superintendent or commissioner is reposed the authority of correcting and restraining any of our vassals whatsoever who disturb or in any manner impede the proper working of the mine, as it is also their duty watchfully to secure the observance of the privileges and exemption ; and if one or more wish or intend to innovate in this matter, and occasion vexation to any supplier engaged in the service of the said mines and works, or shall collect from him under the form of personal tax or other duty a few maravedis paid on account of the annoyance and expense of resisting, the superintendent shall proceed against them, and in case of resistance shall require restitution to be made, fixing the amount : which declarations as now arranged, and which first appeared in the royal ordinances of the year 1735, issued for the government and direction of the royal mines of Almaden, and communicated to all the tribunals of the kingdom, for their punctual observance. I will, shall form the rule and guide in that of Collado de la Plata, in order that those doubts and difficulties may come to an end, which only occasion disagreements between different jurisdictions : and in order that in relation to the exemption from town charges granted to the persons under salary and the regular labourers, frauds may not be committed, the sub-delegates for the time being shall make out a register, and shall transmit to the alcaldes of the rural towns, a statement of the inhabitants in each who are embraced in the list of labourers : and it is also my royal will that as well the Corrigidor as the deputy superintendent continue within their appropriate limits, and that with entire harmony they may mutually aid in the highest degree in all matters which belong to their respective jurisdictions the royal service and the faithful administration of justice, for otherwise I shall adopt such serious measures as each may deserve.

(a) A tribute payable to the king every seven years.

EXTRACTS

From the "Recopilacion de Leyes de Los Reynos de las Indias."

BOOK IV.—TITLE XIX.

Concerning the discovery and working of Mines.

LAW 1st.—Permitting all Spaniards and Indians, vassals of the Crown, to discover and work mines.

The Emperor Don Charles I. Grenada, December 9, 1526.—Don Philip II. Madrid, 19th June, 1568.

IT is our will and pleasure, that all persons, of whatever state, condition, rank or dignity, Spaniards or Indians, who are our vassals, may search for gold, silver, quicksilver, or other metals, either personally or by their servants or slaves, in all mines which they may discover or wherever they may choose, and peaceably hold and take possession, and work them freely, without any obstacle of any kind whatever, giving an account to the Governor and the fiscal officers in accordance with the provisions of the following law, so that the mines of gold, silver, and other metals may be common to all persons, and in all places and districts; provided, that no injury results to the Indians nor any third person, and that this permission is not to extend to the ministers, Governors, Corregidors, Alcaldes Mayores, and their substitutes, attornies, alcaldes and mining notaries, nor to those who have been specially prohibited; and concerning the selection and occupation of the mines, and the marking out the same, they shall conform to the laws and ordinances which have been adopted in each province, and which have been confirmed by us.

LAW 2d.—*That the discoverers of mines make oath to render an account of the gold, and first obtain a licence to discover such mines, and the beds of pearl oysters.*

We order that miners and all others who may have found gold in mines, streams or ravines, or in any other place, whatever shall appear before the Governor and royal officers, and swear that that they will account for the same and make a personal declaration thereof at the foundry, and the discoverers of mines and pearl beds shall obtain a license from the Governor who shall hold a special consultation on the subject with the royal officers, and they shall then agree upon what may be advisable for the proper collection of the duty.

LAW 3d.—*Concerning what is promised to the discover of a mine—that two parts shall be paid by the royal treasury and the other by those interested.*

Whenever it may so happen that money or other reward be promised to the miners who may discover mines of gold, silver, quicksilver, or other metals, there shall be paid by the royal treasury only two thirds of the amoun promised, and the other part shall be paid by those persons who extract the metal.

LAW 4th.—*To secure the discovery of Quicksilver mines.*

Don Philip 3d. at Madrid, 19th January, 1609.

We charge and command the viceroys, chancellors, and governors that they shall use all diligence in procuring the discovery and working of the mines of quicksilver, concerning which information has been received from some parts of the Indies, and bestow upon those who shall discover and work them such advantages as may seem to them and may be just—announcing to them they will not have any allotment of Indians for their work.

LAW 5th.—*That the mining ordinances be observed, and that which provides that servants shall register in the names of their masters those mines which they discover.*

Don Philip 4th, 7th June, 1630.

We order and command that the ordinances and particular laws in relation to mines be obeyed, observed and executed, and in the execution of them that that law be observed which ordains that servants shall register as their masters, the mines which they discover and not in their own names.

LAW 6th.—*That the ordinances in relation to the denouncing of mines be observed and the time limited not be extended.*

The decline in some of the mining districts results from the non-observance of our royal ordinances ;—especially in relation to those mines which have been deserted and abandoned; thence it results that after a period of four months without their being worked, any person may denounce them before the ordinary tribunals as abandoned, and that the requisite proceedings for a new grant of the mines being had, a decree is made in favor of the person denouncing, allowing him to work them as their real owner under the conditions which are prescrib. ed, that the mines shall not remain unworked and that he should discover new veins : and because orders having been given by some of our royal tribunals that the mining ordinances made for this purpose shall be observed and executed, the miners and those interested in the mines which have been abandoned have recourse to the viceroys or presidents, asking an order in their favor that for a certain period of time mines shall not be denounced as abandoned and consequently they continue deserted, and the ordinances cease to be executed. We command the viceroys, presidents and judges of our tribunals, that they observe and comply precisely and in every particular with the ordinances aforesaid which is fit and proper and our will, and that they shall not extend the prescribed period of time.

LAW 7th.—*That there shall not be wasted at the mines, the slag-heap, the rock removed from the sides and roof of the vein, the earthy matter taken from the vats in the amalgamation works, and the washings and sweepings.*

Don Philip 3d. at S. Lorenzo, Nov. 14th. 1603.

The rock removed from the sides and roof of the vein, the slag which remains after the assay and melting of the metals, the earthy matter taken from the vats in the amalgamation works, and the washings and sweepings which remain after the results to the proprietors arising from the mode of working in common use, shall be preserved and collected—so that they may be at hand for the public good, the advantage of the proprietors and the increased supply of our royal treasury.

LAW 8th.—*That the mining districts be furnished with provision, and that no monopoly be allowed.*

Don Philip 2d at Madrid, 5th March, 1571.—Toledo, 11th August, 1596.

We command the viceroys and judges that they make abundant provision of the necessary supplies for the towns and mining districts, and that the native Indians transport and furnish them in their districts at fair and moderate prices and that they shall require and oblige the muleteers to transport them, paying the freight, and that they do not consent to any monopoly of provisions.

LAW 9th.—*That the mines and working of them receive careful attention.*

Don Philip 3d at Aranda, 14th August, 1610.—See Law 1. Tit. 11. Lib. 8.

Inasmuch as the discovery, occupation, and working of the mines adds so much to the prosperity and increase of these kingdoms, and those of the Indies; We charge and command the Viceroys, Presidents, Governors and Alcaldes Mayores, that they bestow very particular attention in observing and having observed the orders which have been given and may be given in relation to the personal services of the Indians in those cases where by the laws of this book, it is permitted.

49

Law 10th.—*That the Viceroys and Presidents shall have cognizance in their executive capacity when it is expedient that execution should be issued
against the machines for working metals.—And the royal officers shall
have judicial cognizance with an appeal to the audiencies.*

Idem. at Pardo, 22d Nov. 1609.

Having experienced many inconveniences from the renting of the mills
for working the metals, from the practice introduced by which miners became
indebted to our royal treasury, and officers of the crown, in coercing the payment, are under the necessity of seizing the mills to secure the collection of
the debt : we declare, that when the day of payment arrives on which our
treasury, shall collect debs due, it belongs to the Governor and the officers of
justice to determine as to the expediency or inexpediency of issuing an execution against the mills belonging to the miners. And we order that the royal
officers before making their attachments, and making contracts for lease,
communicate with the viceroy or presiding governor of the audiency of the
district, and proceed in no other manner, and that the viceroy or president
declare what course shall be pursued as an administrative matter, and in
case the result shall be that execution shall issue and seizure and coercion of
payment against the mills, if petition is presented or defence made, which is
plainly of a judicial character, no recourse can be had by appeal either to
the viceroy or president, for being a judicial matter, it pertains to the audiency.

Law 11th.—*That Copper in the mines in Cuba be worked and remitted in conformity with the law.*

Philip 3d, Madrid, 22d December, 1608.—Philip 4th, 12th February, 1622.

We command that the persons who have the charge by commission from
us, agency, contract or in any other manner, of the copper mines of the
Island of Cuba, that they cause them to be worked with much care, in such
manner that the minerals may become ductile and maleable by roasting and
proper refining, and not in so hard and dry a state as that in which it has
been heretofore sent, in order that the foundries of Artillery may be more fitly
supplied, and that it be sent to Havana consigned to our royal officers, in
order that it may be sent to these kingdoms in the galleons, flag ships and
ships of the line belonging to the navy, registered and directed to the " Casa
de contratacion," all to be duly accounted for to us by the council of war of
the Indies.

Law 12th.—*That no one except the owner of mines can sell the metals.*

No Spaniard or Mestizo except the owner, shall be permitted to sell or shall sell any kinds of metals under penalty of forfeiting for the first offence one hundred dollars to be paid into our treasury; for the second, two hundred dollars, and for a third offence that he be banished forever from the mines and from a space of ten leagues around them, and the person buying the metals shall incur the same penalty.

LAW 13th.—*That Spaniards, Mestizos, free negroes and Mulattoes be persuaded to work in the mines.*

We order and command, that in order to secure the occupation and working of the mines, idle Spaniards who are able to work, Mestizos, free negroes, and mulattoes shall be required to hire themselves out and work in them and that the audiences and corregidors give special attention to this matter and that no idle people be permitted in the land.

LAW 14th.—*That Indians equally with Spaniards, may hold and work mines of gold and silver.*

Emperor Charles and Princess G., at Madrid, 17th Dec. 1551.—Philip 2d., 15th April 1563 16th March 1575.

We command that, in relation to the Indians, no restriction be imposed on their discovering, holding and occupying mines of gold and silver or other metals, or working them in the same manner as is done by Spaniards, in conformity with the ordinances of each province, and may extract these metals for their own profit and for the payment of their personal tax. And no Spaniard or Cacique shall have part or control in the mines which the Indians shall have discovered, held and worked.

LAW 15th.—*That to Indians who shall discover mines, there shall be secured the privileges which are specified, and that Spaniards and Mestizos shall be rewarded.*

Philip 4th., at Madrid, 28th March, 1633.—Don Carlos 2d., Regina G.

We ordain and recommend to the Viceroys, Presidents and Governors, that they exercise particular care and diligence in inquiring and ascertaining if in their districts, there are any mines of gold and silver and other metals to be found of which the Indians have or can obtain knowledge, and with sagacity and good counsel they compel to appear the most intelligent Indians, in order that these may communicate what they know by themselves or others of greater skill and understanding, as to the places and positions where it is supposed that there exist hidden mines which the Indians conceal, fearing to be employed in an industry really resulting in their benefit, being naturally inclined to idleness: and in our name assure them that for their care and trouble, if successful there shall be granted to them and henceforth is granted, many rewards and exemptions, and especially that they shall not be bound out to work in any mines, and that neither they nor their descendants for-ever be obliged to pay any personal tax : and if Spaniards or Mestizos they shall receive an appropriato reward.

LAW 16th.— *That as to the marking out by stakes of the mines, the same course to be taken, in relation to the Indians, as Spaniards.*

In some provinces of the Indies the practice has been introduced that if a number of Indians discover a vein, one only is selected who may apply for the staking out of the part which he selects to himself as the owner : where-fore and because we desire that the Indians shall have and enjoy all the benefit and profit to which they may be entitled on account of their diligence and industry : we command that in relation to the staking out of the mines which they may have discovered, they shall be treated in the same manner as Spaniards, with no difference whatever.

☞ That the viceroy shall cause to be observed in the Indies, the laws of these kingdoms of Castile touching mines which are appropriate, and shall forward a statement of such as are necessary.—*Law 3, Tit. 1, book 1.*

☞ That free negroes and mulattoes shall work in the mines, and may be condemned to such labour as a punishment for crimes committed by them.—*Law 4, Tit. 5, book 7.*

———— ●•● ————

TITLE XX.

Concerning Miners and workers in Quicksilver, and their privileges.

LAW 1st.— *That Miners shall be favoured, and that the articles employed in min-ing shall be exempt from execution.*

We order the Viceroys, Presidents, Governors, Alcaldes, Mayores, of the mines, Judges in our Indies, to favour the miners and workers in Quick-silver, and that they observe and cause to be observed the grants of privil-eges made by the kings our predecessors, and by ourselves as having the force of law, and especially that for no debts of whatever nature they may be, except debts due to us, may or shall be any execution issued against the slaves, tools, and necessaries of life and other things which may be required for the supplies, labour and provision of the mines, and the persons who may work in them, and we order that the executions which in confor-mity to law may be issued, shall be for the gold or silver which may be extracted and received from the mines from which creditors shall be paid in their order and grade in such manner as not to prevent or hinder the discovery, use and working of the mines, and may be satisfactory to the creditor.

LAW 2d.—*That miners who may be imprisoned for debts shall be imprisoned within the district and jurisdiction of the mines.*

It is important that the miners and workers in quicksilver should be favoured, and relieved in every possible way in order that the working of the mines be not stopped or suspended; and in order that from their absence no inconvenience may result, we think proper that persons imprisoned for debt of whatever kind, be imprisoned in the district and jurisdiction of the mines where they work, and that they be not removed from them.

LAW 3d.—*That the miners and workers in quicksilver of Potosi be not detained in Lima for the debts of the royal Treasury, having given security in that city.*

Philip 4th, at Madrid 9th Oct. 1635.

It is our will that when any miners and workers in quicksilver from the imperial city of Potosi, who are debtors to some extent to our royal treasury, and about to go to the city of the kings, and shall give security to present themselves within the period in which they are notified to appear before the royal officers of said Imperial city, they shall not on that account be detained or arrested, nor for any other civil cause, any decrees or ordinances to the contrary notwithstanding.

LAW 4th.—*That miners shall be provided with the materials which are necessary, at fair prices.*

Philip 3d., at Valladolid, 16th Nov. 1602.

In order to promote the good of the miners we direct the Viceroys and Governors to favor them and to cause them to be supplied with corn from our public stores, and all other articles besides which may be necessary for the supplies for working the mines and the reduction of the metals at fair prices, prohibiting the excessive charges which have been made.

LAW 5th.—*That the suits of the miners be quickly disposed of in the audiencies.*

We charge and command our royal audiencies that they summarily dispatch and cause to be dispatched, the causes, suits, and business of the miners and workers in quicksilver which are pending before them, that they may not be perplexed by suits nor subjected to long delays, to the damage and prejudice of the supplying of the mines and of their property.

LAW 6th.— *That the miners of the Philipine Islands enjoy the privilege hereby granted.*

Philip 4th., at Madrid, 16th April, 1685.

Whereas in the province of Cama Vines, of the Philipine Islands distant from the city of Monilla more than sixty leagues, there have been discovered mines of gold, the specimens of which are very rich, running from north to south nine leagues which have been tested by washing and quicksilver, and there have been discoveries of other mines and a commencement made by different persons in the occupation and working of them; it is our pleasure that the miners of the said Islands shall enjoy all the privileges which are conferred and established by the laws and ordinances. And we command the Governors and Captain General that they take special care that they be observed and that the mines be occupied and worked in such manner as may best promote our interest, the increase of our royal treasury, and the good of our vassals.

LAW 7th.— *That miners and workers of quicksilver of Potosi may be chosen corregidors, and to other public offices.*

Notwithstanding the provisions of the 17th and 43d laws, title 2, book 3d, we permit miners and workers in quicksilver of the imperial city of Potosi to be appointed corregidors and to other public and municipal offices, although they may be debtors to some extent to our royal treasury on account of quicksilver which may have been loaned to them or any other debt not connected with the office for which they are candidates or which they hold, and the exercise of which gives no jurisdiction in the matter in which they are debtors: and we grant to them if they have been admitted as councilmen that they may vote in the election of public officers, except when one desires to vote in virtue of an office which he may have purchased and not paid for, and the period shall have passed in which the price or any portion of it have become due and is unpaid.

TITLE XXI.

Concerning the Alcaldes Mayores, and Notaries of the Mines.

LAW 1st.— *That the "alcaldes mayores" of the mines shall possess the endowment and qualifications herein referred to, and shall not trade or make contracts.*

Inasmuch as it is very desirable that the " alcaldes mayores" of the mines be capable persons and skilled in the working of the mines, and possess those qualifications which are required for such offices : we command the viceroys and Presidents to whom pertain the direction of this subject, that they cause to be chosen and nominated, suitable persons and well fitted for the discharge and performance of the duties which they have to administer : and they are not to permit them to trade nor to contract with the miners under pretext of furnishing supplies or any other pretext, nor with any other persons which we hereby prohibit and forbid—and inasmuch as it has been claimed by the alcaldes mayores to have administration of territory with increased limits and jurisdiction, we order that our Viceroys, Presidents and Governors communicate with intelligent persons and determine upon that which may most promote our royal interests, the administration of justice, and the supply and working of the mines.

LAW 2d.—*That the " Alcaldes Mayores" of the mines shall not purchase or exchange silver.*

We command the Alcaldes Mayores of the mines, that neither personally nor through the medium of others shall they barter or purchase of the miners, gold, silver or other metals, either in advance or at the time of delivery, nor enter into any similar understandings and contracts, nor any contracts of whatever kind with the miners, under the penalty that the said Alcaldes Mayores be deprived of their offices and condemned to pay fourfold, and the miners be banished at the discretion of the judges trying the cause, and also subject to a fine of the amount of the contract, provided they shall not appear before the judge and disclose the transaction : and if information and proof be furnished of the contract, one half of the penalty shall belong to the minor who gave such information.

LAW 3d.—*That no Alcalde Mayore, Judge or Notary of the mines shall form a partnership with the owner of the mines nor be a discoverer of mines.*

We prohibit and forbid all Alcaldes Mayores, Judges and Notaries of the mines, forming a mining partnership with the owners of any mines, or engaging in the discovery of mines during their term of office, either personally or through other persons, under the penalty for said offence of being deprived of their office, and a fine of a thousand dollars to our exchequer and treasury.

LAW 4th.—*That the salaries of the Alcaldes Mayores and inspectors of mines be paid from the profits of the mines.*

The salaries which the Alcaldes Mayores and inspectors of the mines are entitled to receive shall be appropriated and paid to them from the profit received from the mines, and shall be taken from the profits of those mines which are under their administration, and not paid from the treasury, nor in any other manner.

BOOK VIII.—TITLE 11.—Law 2.

1573, 1575 & 1613.

That the royal mines may be worked, leased or sold, as may appear most desirable.

We grant to the viceroys and prætorial presidents power and authority, that if they consider that any of our mines of silver, gold or quicksilver discovered in those districts cannot be conveniently worked on our account, and find that for our own profit they may be more usefully and conveniently leased or sold, to make such lease or sale as may result favorably to our royal treasury, and to its increased income. And inasmuch as there are other mines which belong to us and which not being very rich cannot be worked, and if rented or sold we might be able to derive a profit from them; and it will be proper to adopt for this purpose some suitable means : We command the viceroys and presidents, that having informed themselves of the quantity and value of each mines, they shall proceed to work, lease or sell them as may best promote the increase of our royal treasury, and render an account of the whole to the Council of the Indies.

LIB. II.—TITLE I. Law 2.

The laws contained in this compilation to be observed in the manner and cases herein set forth.

Considering that it is of the utmost importance that the laws framed for the good government of our Indies, islands, and continent of the Northern and Southern Oceans, which have been promulgated in separate *cedulas*, enactments, instructions, and charters, be collected and digested into one body, and in the form of a code, and that the same be obeyed, fulfilled, and executed : We decree and command, that all the laws herein contained be fulfilled and executed as our laws, and in the manner set forth in the law prefixed to this compilation, and that they all have force of law and supreme authority in whatever they decide and determine ; and if it should be deemed expedient to enact others besides those contained in this book, the viceroys, presidents, tribunals, governors, and superior alcades, shall give us information thereof, through our council of the Indies, stating their motives and reasons for so doing, in order that, on due consideration, such measures may be taken as shall be thought proper and added in a separate book. We command that no addition be made to the municipal laws and ordinances of each city, nor in those which shall be made by any community or university, nor in the ordinances enacted for the good and benefit of the Indies, and confirmed by our viceroys or royal tribunals for their good government, when not repugnant to the laws contained in this book, which shall have the same force and operation as if they were confirmed by the tribunals (audiencias) until, after being seen by the council of Indies, they shall have been approved or rejected. And as regards what is not determined by the laws contained in this compilation, with respect to the decision of causes, the laws in the compilation, and *partidas* of the kingdom of Castile shall be observed in the manner set forth in the following law.

LIB. II.—TITLE 1, LAW 2.

For the observance of the laws of Castile, in cases which are not provided by those of the Indies.

We decree and command, that, in all cases, transactions and suits which are not decided nor provided by the laws contained in this compilation, nor by the regulations, provisions, or ordinances enacted and unrepealed, concerning the Indies, and by those which may be promulgated by our orders, the laws of our kingdom of Castile shall be observed, conformably to the law of Toro, with respect as well to the substance, determination, and decision of cases, transactions, and suits, as to the form of proceedings.

IBID.—LAW 4.

For the observance of the ancient laws in force for the government of the Indies, and of those which have been re-enacted.

We decree and command, that the laws and good customs anciently in force in the Indies, for their good government and police, and the usages and customs observed and retained from the introduction of Christianity among them, which are not repugnant to our sacred religion, or to the laws contained in this book, and to those which have been framed anew, be observed and fulfilled; and it having become expedient to do so, we hereby approve and confirm them, reserving to ourselves the power of adding thereto whatever we shall think fit and will appear to us necessary for the service of God our Lord, and our own, and for the protection of and christian police among, the natives of those provinces, without prejudice to established usages among them, or to their good and wholesome customs and statutes.

50

ARTICLES 144 to 147,
Of the " Ordinanza de Intendentes," of 1803.

ARTICLE 144.

The respectable body of miners has at all times deserved the greatest indulgence and attention, and having reduced for them to a tenth, the royal duty of a fifth which they have heretofore paid on silver and to three per cent. the duty on gold and other privileges in relation to the price of quicksilver, powder and provisions having been granted to them, and having been finally erected into a formal body like that of the tribunal of commerce under the ordinances for New Spain, approved on the 22d May, 1783, and which by royal order of the 8th December, 1785, were applied to Peru : and desirous that these provisions should produce the favourable effect designed by them, it is my wish that the intendant coerce exact compliance with them and apply themselves as their chief care, to encourage and protect the body aforesaid in like manner, causing the sub-delegates and ministers of the royal treasury to execute the same, who shall be severely punished if in the sale of quicksilver or of powder, they shall charge to or receive from the miners more than the just price, which shall be fixed for it, and although it be under the name of a gratification or of official and clerical fees it shall be immediately restored ;—the same being understood in relation to the ministers of the royal branch at Potosi, to whose charge pertains and should continue, the disposition of this material.

ARTICLE 145.

The Intendants shall be judges in appeal causes in their respective provinces without varying in other respects the provisions of Art. 13. title 3. of the ordinance " *de mineria*" above cited, and where the distance from the Capitol where they reside to the mine shall be so great as not to permit the prosecution there of the appeal without great delay and expense, they shall commission the sub-delegate to exercise said jurisdiction on adopting the most rapid dispatch consistent with justice, affording the preference to which the causes and judicial proceedings connected with this subject are entitled.

ARTICLE 146.

Nothing is more important to the mining interest than the providing of laborers and facilitating the abundant supply of quicksilver for the precious metals, and although at first there was in some places the practice of assigning Indians, who under the name of " Meta" (allotment,) took turns in such work, it will be very proper from the zeal of the intendents to consider the appropriate means by which it may be possible to relieve them from these labors, and to stimulate others to perform them voluntarily; therefore, it is their duty to provide that in relation to all, and especially the Indians, that they be kindly treated, and that they pay them their day wages punctually and in good money, without imposing upon them excessive labours or causing them other vexations which have been the means of withdrawing them from this service; and with regard to the abundance and price of quicksilver, they shall represent what they consider proper as well to the superintendent as to my royal person, through the officer of the Secretary of the Treasury; being advised not to incur my royal displeasure by any omission or neglect of·duty which may be marked against them.

ARTICLE 147.

There shall continue in Mexico henceforth the office of Comptroller of quicksilver which is already established there, the superintendent conforming to the instructions of the 15th January, 1709, by which he is to be governed according to existing circumstances; and in the other kingdoms where there is no such office established, the respective superintendents shall establish the appropriate regulations in order to furnish deposits of quicksilver for the supply of the towns near the mines, so that they may not experience the least failure, and with the concurrence of the Supreme Council of the government shall issue such orders as shall be general and conduce to the protection and increase of the mining interest, transferring to each intendent the special charge of adopting the same course in relation to the minerals in his province; and inasmuch as it is proper in all places to free the miners from the necessity under which they are of giving their silver and gold to the merchants who·pay for them less than their true value, and by this means also facilitating the concealment and fraudulent extraction of the metal; superintendents shall appropriate in the treasuries where the corresponding foundry is established, sufficient money for the prompt and full payment of those who offer to sell, and that said superintendent should keep a strict watch that the offices of foundry-man and assayer should be filled by faithful subjects instructed and examined according to law, and the superintendent on consultation with the tribunal of the miners shall promote if practicable the establishment of banks of exchange, where in imitation of that of the city of Potosi, in Peru, shall be purchased silver in mass, paying for it promptly and at a fair price, and granting to the miners other aid and supplies which at the time shall not be difficult safely to furnish.

DECREES

Of the Cortes of Spain, and of Ferdinand VII.

From the Printed Volumes, published by Authority.

THE general and extraordinary Cortes desiring that the important industry of mining in all the dominions of the Indies and Philipine Islands may receive all possible increase, and considering that the monopoly of quicksilver established by law 1, tit. 23, book 8, of the Recopilacion of the Indies, and the right that the crown reserved to itself according to article 22, tit. 7, of the ordinances of New Spain, of appropriating and working on its own account mines of this kind, whenever it might be thought proper, on making a previous arrangement with the discoverer or denouncer of said mines ; inasmuch as it thereby renders uncertain the interest of the owner, and checks the trade withholding people from the useful and expensive enterprise of discovering and working quicksilver mines, and likewise further employing themselves in the search for quicksilver, in its transport, and in creating a competition, all which would probably happen if this article were to be declared an article of free trade perpetually exempt from all taxes including the (cuinto) fifth or that part which the miner is bound to pay ; bearing in mind what was proposed and presented for consideration to the Cortes by the Council of regency on the 26th of December last in favor of the freedom of trade in so necessary an auxiliary for the working of gold and silver mines ; and bearing also in mind what has been presented and petitioned for on the subject by the deputies of the Indies in this Cortes, who have demonstrated with intelligence and zeal, the expediency of repealing the above mentioned provisions and any other in whole or in part of the same character, interfering with the freedom of trade in said article, and with the security of the perpetual and absolute ownership of the mines, *provided that in their discovery and working of said mines they shall observe the general regulations existing in the matter.* After a mature consideration, the Cortes have been pleased to decree and do decree the aforesaid repeal and grant of exemption from impediments as aforesaid, and at the same time do ordain that if in accordance with the former monopoly or otherwise, the Royal Treasury may have sent or shall send on its own account any quantity of quicksilver to be distributed at cost and charges as it has been the practice heretofore for the benefit of the miners, the distribution shall be precisely and exclusively made by the respective mining tribunals, as they are the best judges of the wants of the mines, and of every thing relating to the propriety and success of the object of those remittances, and consequently it shall be the duty of such tribunals, to cause the reimbursement to be duly made to the royal Treasury—the Cortes trusting to the honor, integrity and zeal of the above mentioned tribunals that they will correspond to the high confidence placed in them in a commission so interesting and worthy of the paternal views of the Cortes.

DECREE

Of the 12th of March, 1811.

Various Measures for the encouragement of Agriculture and Industry in America.

ONE of the principal cares, which occupies the attention of the general and extraordinary Cortes, being to furnish the inhabitants of the extensive provinces in America all the means necessary to promote and secure their real happiness, and being persuaded of the justice and utility of those proposed by the council of the regency upon the representations made by the Right Rev. Bishop of Valladolid de Michoacan, of the 30th May, 1810, with the interesting object of encouraging in those countries, the advancement and improvement of agriculture and industry, and to diminish, as far as practicable, the impediments and obstructions which at present retard their progress to the great injury of the state; they therefore decree:

1. That the tax upon stores known by the name of *pulperias* be abolished. 2. That it is permitted freely to make and to sell spirits of mezcal (*aguardiente mezcal*) in the viceroyalty of Mexico. 3. That six dollars in specie are to be paid on each barrel of said mezcal spirits, and that a reduction of two specie dollars be allowed on the tax imposed on each barrel of rum. 4. That the increase of two reals lately imposed on each pound of tobacco remains in force, as well as that of two per cent. over and above the six per cent. collected as excise duty, as well as the application of these duties to the payment of principal and interest of the loan of twenty millions of dollars opened in New Spain. 5. That in order to fill up this loan the more rapidly, it is permitted, out of the common funds belonging to the Indians, to invest so much in this loan at interest as the communities have the control of and may be willing voluntarily to contribute in the different towns, villages, and communities of that kingdom. 6. That the viceroy of New Spain, after consulting the fiscals and a (*junta*) board composed of the archbishop, regent, intendant, the contador mayor, the contador of tributes, a royal officer, the senior regidor, the procurator syndic, and a good man elected by the (*ayuntamiento*) common council of Mexico, will examine and reduce to its just value the duty to be in future paid on *pulque*, and cause the same to be carried into effect, rendering however account to his Majesty, through the council of the regency, for his sovereign sanction.

DECREE

Of the 14th of July, 1811.

The obligation of the Authorities to comply with the orders of their Superiors.

In view of the obligation to establish among all classes in the Monarchy absolute subordination to the government as the only mode of giving a uniform movement and direction to the machinery of State, and to direct to one end the exertions of all the general and extraordinary Cortes decree, as follows :

1. Every general, junta, audiency or other superior officer whose duty it is to secure compliance with the orders of their superiors, shall be responsible for their execution and deprived of their respective employments if by culpable omission, negligence or forbearance or by failure to impose immediate punishment on the disobedient, the same shall not be complied with.

2. Justices and inferior authorities to whom it immediately belongs to secure compliance with any law or order, shall, on failure to administer instantly the punishment prescribed by any law, be subjected to the same punishment as the offender.

3. The Council of the regency shall carefully enforce the observance of all laws, ordinances and decrees, exacting strict responsibility of the authorities charged with their execution and imposing the appropriate punishment which shall not be remitted; and it is the will of the Cortes that the Council of the Regency upon no consideration whatever shall repeat orders once given without having first imposed the appropriate punishment upon whomsoever shall in any culpable manner have impeded their fulfillment.

The Council of the Regency shall cause the foregoing to be made known and adopt the necessary measures for its observance, having first printed, published and circulated it. Dated at Cadiz, July 14, 1811.

The Mexican Secretary of the Treasury in a circular of the 5th June, 1839, refers to the foregoing decree of the Cortes of Spain as still in force. —See Diario del Gobierno of 10th June, 1839.

MANIFESTO

Of Ferdinand VII.

MANIFESTO of the King declaring the Constitution of the so called General and Extraordinary Cortes of the nation void and without force or effect directing at the same time what is to be observed in order that there may be no interruption in the administration of justice and the political arrangements and government of the people.

The King.—Since Divine Providence, by reason of the voluntary and solemn renunciation of my august father has placed me on the throne of my ancestors of which I was regarded already as the sworn successor by the representatives assembled in the Cortes, according to the usages and customs of the Spanish nation for a long time practiced; and since that auspicious day on which I entered into the Capital in the midst of the most sincere demonstrations of loyalty and affection with which the people of Madrid came out to receive me, making this manifestation of love to my royal person before the French army, which, under the guise of friendship had hastily advanced: being a presage of what this heroic people would one day perform for their king, and for their own honor, and giving an example which all other part of the kingdom nobly followed; since that day it has been my royal purpose to respond to sentiments so loyal and to fulfil the weighty obligations which rest upon a king towards his people to dedicate all my time to the discharge of such august functions and to repair those evils to which the pernicious influences of a Court favorite during the preceding reign gave rise. My first efforts were directed to the restoration of the various magistrates and other persons who had been arbitrarily deprived of their employments, but the unfavorable situation of affairs and the perfidy of Bonaparte, from the cruel effects of which I desired by going to Bayonne to preserve my people, scarce gave place for more. The royal family being then reunited there was committed in relation to it and in a signal manner in my own person an outrage exceeding in atrocity any furnished by the history of civilized nations, as well from the circumstances attending it as the series of events which then occurred; and in violation of the highest and most sacred law of nations, I was deprived of my liberty and of the enjoyment of the government of my kingdoms and carried to a palace with my beloved brother and uncle, and that mansion served as a prison for the space of almost six years. In the midst of these afflictions, the love and loyalty of my people was ever present to my memory, and the consideration of the infinite evils to which they were exposed formed a large part of these afflictions, surrounded as they were by enemies, almost deprived of the power of resistance; without a king and without a government previously established which could push forward any movement and reunite at its command the forces of the nation and direct their movements and apply the resources of the State to combat the large armies which simultaneously invaded the Peninsula, and were already most perfidiously placed in possession of the principal places.

In this deplorable condition I issued in the form in which being controlled by force, I could alone do it, and as the only remedy which remained, the decree of the 5th May, 1808, directed to the Council of Castile, and in their absence to whatsoever chancery or audiency should be found at liberty for the convocation of the Cortes, whose duty alone it should be by promptly arranging the necessary means and supplies, to secure the defence of the kingdom, and for that purpose remaining permanently in session to meet any emergency ; but this my royal decree unfortunately was then unknown, and although after this the provinces furnished supplies immediately upon their receiving notice of the cruel acts performed at Madrid by the commander of the French troops, on the memorable second of May, and by their government by means of the Juntas which they created.   The glorious battle of Bailen occurred at this time ; the French fled to Victoria, and all the provinces and the capital proclaimed me once more king of Castile and Leon, with all the formalities which have been practiced in relation to the kings, my august predecessors ; a recent event of which the medals struck at many different places bear true testimony, and which the towns through which I passed on my return from France confirmed by the utterance of those acclamations of joy which moved the sensibilities of my heart where they are engraved never to be effaced.   From among the deputies which they called the *juntas* the *central* one was formed which exercised in my royal name, the entire sovereign power from September 1808 until January 1810, in which month was established the Council of the Regency in which the exercise of that power was continued to the 24th of September of the same year, in which month were installed in the island of Leon the Cortes called general and extraordinary.   One hundred and four deputies, that is fifty seven Proprietaries and forty seven substitutes as appears by the act certified by the Secretary of State, of foreign affairs and Justice Nicholas Maria de Sierra, agreeing under oath to the act in which they promised to secure to me all my dominions as their sovereign.   But at this Cortes convened in a manner never practiced in Spain even on the most pressing occasions and in the most turbulent times of the minorities of the kings in which it had been customary to convene a more numerous body of representatives than the common and ordinary one, they were not called the estates of the nobility and clergy, although the central *junta* had so commanded, this decree having been artfully concealed from the council of the regency, and also that the *junta* had assigned to it the presidency of the Cortes—a prerogative of sovereignty which the regency would not have been deprived of at the discretion of Congress if they had had notice of the existence of the decree.   With this everything remained at the disposal of the Cortes, who on the very day of their installation and in the first of their acts deprived me of that sovereignty which but a short time before had been recognised by those very deputies, nominally ascribing the sovereignty to the nation in order to appropriate it to themselves and afterwards impose upon the nation, after such usurpation, the laws which they desired, placing a yoke upon the nation by which it was forced to receive those laws under a new constitution, which without power or authority from any province, town or *junta*, and without notice to those which are said to be represented by the substitutes of Spain and the Indies, the deputies established and they themselves sanctioned and published in 1812.

This first attempt against the prerogatives of the throne, abusing the name of the nation, was the foundation of much that followed; and in spite of the repugnance of many of the deputies and sometimes of a majority of them, what were called fundamental laws were brought forward and adopted by the means of the clamor, threats and violence of those who were present in the galleries of the Cortes, by which they were overawed and terrified; and that which was truly the work of a faction has been dressed up as the spurious representation of public sentiment, and as such obtained currency with those not seditiously inclined, so that in Cadiz, and afterwards at Madrid, they occasioned much trouble in those good cities.

These acts were so notorious, that scarcely any one is ignorant of them; and the very journals of the Cortes afford secret testimony of them all. A mode of making laws so foreign to the practice of the Spanish nation, gave rise to the alteration of those good laws under which at other times the nation had been respected and happy.—In a word, almost the entire form of the ancient constitution of the monarchy has been changed, and copying the revolutionary and democratic principles of the French Constitution of 1791, and omitting from the same what was assumed in the beginning of the constitution which was framed at Cadiz, they have sanctioned not the fundamenmental laws of a moderate monarchy, but those of a popular government, with a chief or magistrate, a mere executive delegate, but no king, although the title is preserved in order to deceive and mislead the inconsiderate, and the nation at large. The same want of freedom characterised the signing and swearing to this new Constitution, and it is evidence to all, not only what occurred in relation to the respectable bishop of Orense, but also the punishment threatened those who did not sign and swear to it. And in order to prepare the minds of men for these strange innovations, especially those relating to my royal person, and the prerogatives of the throne, they undertake, by means of the public papers, in some of which, some of the deputies of the Cortes were themselves interested, abusing the very liberty of the press established by themselves, to render odious the royal power, giving to all the rights of majesty, the name of despotism, treating as synonymous those of *king* and *despot*, and speaking of kings as tyrants; at the same time, cruelly persecuting whomsoever had the firmness to contradict or dissent from this course, regarding it as revolutionary and seditious; and this democracy prevailed in everything, and taking the title of *royal* from the army, navy, and all those establishments which for a long time had enjoyed that title, and instituting that of national, in order to flatter the people who, in spite of so many perverse acts, possessed with their national loyalty those sound opinions which always marked their character. In relation to all this, when I happily entered the kingdom, by enquiry I received a faithful account and full information, partly by my own observation, and partly through the public press of the same, from which, up to that time had been boldly scattered abroad, the gross and infamous matter in relation to my coming and my character, which, even with respect to any other person, would be a very grave offence and worthy of the severest notice and chastisement. These acts, so unexpected, filled my heart with bitterness, which was only in part alleviated by the demonstrations of affection from all those who hoped for my return, in order that by my presence they might put an end to those evils, and that oppression which those had suffered, who had cherished the remembrance of my person, and sighed for the true felicity of their country.

I promise and swear to you, true and loyal Spaniards at the same time that I compassionate the evils which you have suffered, that you shall not be defrauded of your noble expectations. Your Sovereign desires to be such for you and glories in being such over an heroic nation which by its immortal deeds has gained for itself the admiration of all, and preserved its liberty and honor.

I abhor and detest despotism ; neither the light nor the cultivation of the nations of Europe will now suffer it ; nor in Spain were there kings ever despots ; nor have the wholesome laws and constitutions of the kingdom ever authorized it, although unhappily, from time to time there have been some abuses of power, as in all other places and in every thing that pertains to man, and which no possible constitution can wholly prevent ; nor were these abuses in relation to the nation at large, but in relation to persons and property connected with unfortunate, but rarely witnessed circumstances, which gave the opportunity and occasion for them.—Nevertheless, in order as far as is given to human foresight to prevent these abuses, that is, by preserving what is due to the dignity and rights of the crown, since those which pertain to it and those which belong to the people are equally inviolable ; I will treat with the representatives of Spain and the Indies, and in a Cortes lawfully assembled, composed of both, and the more readily, because order being re-established and those salutary usages under which the nation has lived and which with their consent the kings, my august predecessors established, they may the more readily be united ; they shall be firmly and lawfully established so far as may be promotive of the good of my kingdoms, in order that my vassals may live prosperously and happily with one religion and empire, firmly united by an indissoluble bond, in which, and in which alone consists the temporal happiness of a king and a kingdom, which has, by distinction, the title of Catholic ; and henceforth I shall take in hand the preparation and regulation of what shall appear best for the re-union of these Cortes through which I hope may be secured the basis of the prosperity of my subjects in both hemispheres.

Liberty and security, individual and royal, shall be firmly secured by the means of laws which, guaranteeing public tranquility and order, leave to all that salutary liberty, in the undisturbed enjoyment of which, distinguishing a moderate government from an arbitrary and despotic one, those citizens who are its subjects ought to live. In the possession of this true liberty, all shall, at all times, enjoy the communications by the Press, of their thoughts and feelings, that is, within those limits which sound reason, sovereign and independent, prescribes to all, that it do not degenerate into licentiousness ; since the respect which is due to religion and government, and that which men mutually owe to each other for their own protection, cannot in any civilized government reasonably permit that it shall be trampled upon and destroyed with impunity.

All suspicion of the dissipation of the revenues of state shall be removed, by a separation in the treasury of that which may be assigned for those expenses which may be required from respect to my royal person and family and that of the nation which I have the glory to command, from the revenues which by the assent of the kingdom, is imposed and assigned for the maintenance of the state in all the branches of its administration. And those laws which may from time to time form the rule of conduct for my subjects shall be established with the assent of the Cortes. In order that this basis may serve as a sure presage of my royal intentions in the government of which I undertake the charge, and that I may be known to all not as a despot, or tyrant, but as a king and a father of his vassals. Therefore having learned by the unanimous information received from persons respectable for their zeal and knowledge and in relation to the matters herein contained, having received representations from various parts of the kingdom, in which are expressed the repugnance and disgust with which as well the constitution, formed by the general and extraordinary Cortes as the other political establishments recently introduced are regarded in the provinces ; the evil and prejudicial results which have followed from these and which would be augmented if I should add the authority of my consent, and should swear to support that constitution :—In conformity with such decided and general demonstrations of the wishes of my people, and because the same are just and well founded, I declare that my royal purpose is not only not to swear or accede to the said constitution or to any decree of the general and extraordinary Cortes, or the ordinary Cortes already issued, that is, such as deprive me of the rights and prerogatives of my sovereignty, established by the constitution and the laws under which the nation has for a long time continued ; but to declare that constitution and those decrees now and at all times void and of no force or effect, in the same manner as if such acts had never been passed, and that the same be abrogated, and with no obligation on the part of my people or subjects of whatsoever class or condition, to comply with or observe them.

And as he who should desire to sustain them and to contradict this my royal declaration, issued with the assent and approbation aforesaid, will assail the prerogatives of my sovereignty and the happiness of the nation, and occasion restlessness and disturbance in my kingdoms, I declare guilty of high treason any person who shall dare or attempt any such thing, and for such offence there shall be imposed the penalty of death, whether the offence be committed by acts or by writing, or verbally moving or inciting, or in any other manner, exhorting or persuading the obeying and observing said constitution and decrees : and in order that there may be no interruption in the administration of justice in the interval before the restoration of order, and of the observance in the kingdom of the system prevailing before the recent innovations, in relation to which, without loss of time, there will be suitable provision : it is my will that until such time, the ordinary justices in the towns which are found in office, the judges *de letras* [1] wherever they may reside, and the audiencies, intendants and other tribunals of justice in the exercise of their judicials powers ; and in relation to political and administrative matters the ayuntamientos of the towns shall remain as at present, and in the interim whatever is proper to be preserved shall remain, and until the Cortes, which I shall convene, shall, having examined into the matter and the permanent arrangement in this branch of the government of the kingdom, shall be established. And from the day on which this, my decree is published and shall be communicated to the President for the time being of the Cortes, then actually holding their sessions, they shall discontinue their sessions, and their acts, and those of their predecessors, and such records as there may be in their archives and those of their secretary, or under the control of any other person whatever, shall be taken by the person charged with the execution of this my royal decree, and be deposited for the present in the office of the ayuntamientos of the city of Madrid, shutting up and sealing the room where they shall be deposited ; the books of their library shall be passed over to the royal library : and I also declare to be high treason any act whatever, tending to the hindrance of the execution of this part of my royal decree, in whatever manner committed, and as such shall be subject to the penalty of death. And from that day the proceedings in any cause whatever, pending in any of the courts of justice of the kingdom for the infraction of the constitution, shall cease, and all persons who are imprisoned or in any manner arrested and not detained for any just cause known to the laws, shall be immediately set at liberty. Such is my will for the attainment in like manner of whatever pertains to the well being and happiness of the nation.—Dated at Valencia on the 4th May, 1814.—*I the King.*—

[1] *Juez de letras* or *juez letrado,* a judge who has the title of licentiate in the law or of counsellor at law, (abogado) and administers justice alone without the aid of an *asesor*—a lawyer appointed to assist the ordinary judge, with advice in the conduct of law proceedings.

As Secretary of the King in relation to decrees and hereto specially authorized.

PEDRO DE MACANAZ.

ROYAL DECREE,

Of His Majesty, re-establishing the *Chamber of the Indies* (Camara de Indias,) with the powers it possessed in May 1808, being composed, for the present, of the officers [ministros] herein described.

By my royal decree of this date, [see the following,] I have resolved to re-establish the royal and supreme council of the Indies, granting to it for the present the powers which it had on the 1st May, 1808, and with the number of officers expressed in the nominations which accompany the same, confirming and ratifying, for the future, its last organization, which limits to five the number of members entitled to wear sword and robes, and to fourteen those wearing robes, independently of the attorneys [fiscales,] also wearing robes [togados.] And whereas the good government, ecclesiastical as well as temporal of those dominions, requires that the chamber of the Indies, as anciently established, and with the enjoyment of equal dignity with that of Castile, should resume the exercise of its authority, without alteration of its former powers; I also have resolved to re-establish, as I hereby do re-establish, and confirm, the same. It shall consist, for the present, of the president and five ministers, three wearing robes, [togados,] and two wearing robes and swords, [de capa y espada,] who are designated in a list signed by my royal hand : but, when it shall have been reduced to the number required by the aforesaid organization, it shall only consist of the president, a minister wearing sword and robes, and three *togados.* You shall take notice of the above, and communicate the same to all whom it may concern.

Madrid, 2d July, 1814.—Signed with the royal hand of H. M.

To Don Miguel Lardizabal y Uribe.

ROYAL DECREE,

Re-establishing the Supreme Council of the Indies, with the same powers as it existed in the year 1808, declaring the number of ministers of which it is to consist.

The torrent of evils which afflict many of the provinces of my dominions in America ; the general subversion of the public administration prevailing in others, and the disorder and confusion introduced even in the administration of justice itself, called for my royal attention from the moment that, restored, through a special favour of Divine Providence, to the throne, I resumed the government of my kingdoms. The desire of restoring peace and happiness among my beloved vassals in those countries has induced me to reflect seriously and maturely upon the means of attaining that object ; and, after a long examination, it has occurred to me that one of the most expedient was the re-establishment of the supreme council of the Indies. That tribunal which in all times has professed love and fidelity for the kings, my ancestors, has always been distinguished for the zeal and correctness with which it has discharged the many and important trusts committed to it; whereby it has not only deserved their confidence, and been raised to equal honours and privileges with royal council, but also that of the natives and inhabitants of those countries who felt how much they were indebted to that body, created for their benefit and protection, almost at the time of the discovery of that immense section of the globe. Wherefore, moved by these considerations, and sensible of the importance to the good government of those dominions, that the ministers in whom I repose my confidence should possess the peculiar abilities and information which their administration requires, I have resolved to re-establish the aforesaid council, which, for the present, shall continue invested with the same powers it possessed on the 1st May, 1808. It will consist, as as formerly, of three permanent chambers, (salas,) viz. two of government and one of justice, which shall be composed of the ministers named in the list signed with my hand. And whereas it is not expedient that the number of places be increased, which was fixed to five ministers with sword and robes, by royal decrees of 13th of March, 1760, and 25th August, 1785, and to fourteen ministers, *togados*, two attorneys, [fiscales,} also *toyados*, two secretaries, and one accountant, established by the decrees of 29th July, 1773, 26th February, 1776, and 6th June and 11th March following : it is my will that these decrees be observed by completing the number of ministers of that class, and suppressing those who exceed the number of ministers of the other class, as the same shall become vacant; and that there be always among them some ministers who shall be natives of the Indies. As soon as the council shall have entered upon the exercise of its functions, they shall inquire into the changes which, in those extensive and valuable dominions, have originated from the great and extraordinary occurrences which have taken place in the mother country, and shall propose to me whatever they may think expedient for the restoration of order therein, and for the promotion of their welfare and prosperity. You will take notice of the above, and communicate the same to all whom it may concern.

Madrid 2d July, 1814.—Signed with the royal hand of H. M.

To Don Miguel Lardizabal y Uribe.

Names of the ministers who are to compose the three chambers [salas] of my royal and supreme council of the Indies, saving the right of seniority appertaining to each. [Names inserted and signed by the king.]

ROYAL DECREE

Of the 29th June, 1821, concerning the Protection of the Mining Interest.

Hicienda de Ultramar.

The king has been pleased to direct to me the following royal decree.   Don Ferdinand, &c.

The Cortes having complied with all the formalities prescribed by the constitution, have decreed as follows:

Article 1. The duties called the "fifth," the "one per cent" and the "seniorage," (quintos, uno per ciento, y Señorage) are abolished.

Art. 2. Instead of these is substituted a sole contribution of three per cent upon silver and the same upon gold, which shall be paid in the same form as has been pursued in relation to the "fifth."

Art. 3. Miners and persons interested in mining shall be subject to pay no other contribution except that of the mining fund of the tribunal general of the mines, when engaged in no other kind of industry, and concerned in no other kind of business : provided this is not to be understood as applicable to those general and municipal contributions, to which all other classes of citizens are subject.

Art. 4. There shall not be collected for coinage more than the actual expense of the operation, reducing the two reals which are now paid to what in the result shall be the true cost.   In order to the adopting of a rule on the subject, the mean expense of five years shall be taken, and this shall furnish the rate for the collections for the succeeding five years, this apportionment being renewed every five years.   In case of a new coinage of money being established, an estimate of expense shall be formed which shall govern for the first year, correcting it at the end of the year by the results furnished by the accounts, and being governed by this corrected estimate until at the end of the first five years, they may adopt the mean expense during that time.   To depositors there shall be returned in money the value of their metals in numerical order, without any other precedence or preference the one to the other, and with no unnecessary delay.

Art. 5. The collection of eight *maravadis* per marc of silver which has been paid as the expense of refining, and of twenty six *maravadis* imposed upon the same quantity of mixed bullion, which is introduced under the name of the waste of silver, shall cease.

Art. 6. The increase of silver, according to the laws governing it which results from the refining, and that which results from the reduction at the foundry from the loss of gold and silver, in order to alloy and reduce them to ingots, deducting the expense of the operation, also the product arising from the deficiency in weight or quality of the money, shall be passed over to the foundation fund of the body of the miners, and the income of gold and the actual waste of silver in the smelting house should be deducted from the cost of the operation.

Art. 7. There shall not be charged for expenses at the smelting house more than two reals of silver per marc, which is now what the operation costs, making the reduction indicated in the previous article, insuring to the depositors all the gold which their deposits of bullion contain. When by an improved process the cost shall be reduced, there shall be returned in the same proportion to the depositors the payments made by them on that account, securing to them the gold in the same proportion, and being ready to effect the arrangement either personally, or in such manner as may be most convenient.

Art. 8. All that has been stated in relation to silver is applicable to gold, there being collected in the same manner for coinage one marc of silver as of gold, dispensing with the duty called " bocado," and reducing that on the assay to the cost of the operation, as in the case of silver.

Art. 9. Having once made and verified the payment into the national treasury of the duty of three per cent upon silver and the same upon gold, and the seals which verify the payment having been placed on the bars and wedges of those metals, the owners are at liberty to sell them or apply them to such uses as they please, without any limitation fixing the price.

ART. 10. The royal orders of 13th January, 1783—12th November, 1791, and 6th December, 1796 relating to freedom from duty granted as to articles of consumption at the mines, as well as the order of the Cortes of the 13th January, 1812 in respect to salt, shall be punctually observed.

ART. 11. All duties established during the revolution, as well upon articles of consumption at the mines as upon the metals in mass, and coined under whatever name they may be called, are abolished.

ART. 12. The government will be careful to remit the largest possible quantity of quicksilver, consigning it to the deputations of the miners, in order that they may make distribution among the miners, and that from time to time there be a sufficient amount sent to supply the wants of the same, providing in Mexico a sufficient deposit, in order that they may never be in want of the material necessary for their work.

ART. 13. From time to time the offices of skill connected with the mints and the smelting house and those connected with the assay at the mints either in or without the Capital, shall be filled exclusively by persons who have the acquaintance with physical science, chemistry and mineralogy, necessary to discharge the duties, undergoing a private examination by persons skilled in those sciences, and as to those which are on the list in the said establishments, the alumni of the seminary of the mines shall be preferred in the priority of admission.

These provisions are to be understood as solely applicable to North America.

Madrid 8th June, 1821.—Wherefore, we command, &c.—At the Palace on the 29th June, 1821.

EXTRACTS

FROM

President Taylor's Annual Message to Congress, December 4th, 1849.

I also recommend that commissions be organized by Congress to examine and decide upon the validity of the present subsisting land titles in California and New Mexico; and that provision be made for the establishm offices of surveyor general in New Mexico, California, and Oregon, an the surveying and bringing into market the public lands in those territori; Those lands, remote in position and difficult of access, ought to be disposed of on terms liberal to all, but especially favorable to the early emig.nts.

In order that the situation and character of the principal mineral deposites in California may be ascertained, I recommend that a geological and mineralogical exploration be connected with the linear surveys, and that the mineral lands be divided into small lots suitable for mining, and be disposed of, by sale or lease, so as to give our citizens an opportunity of procuring a permanent right of property in the soil. This would seem to be as important to the success of mining as of agricultural pursuits.

The great mineral wealth of California, and the advantages which its ports and harbors, and those of Oregon afford to commerce, especially with the islands of the Pacific and Indian oceans, and the populous regions of Eastern Asia, make it certain that there will arise in a few years large and prosperous communities on our western coast. It therefore becomes important that a line of communication, the best and most expeditious which the nature of the country will admit, should be opened within the territory of the United States, from the navigable waters of the Atlantic on the gulf of Mexico to the Pacific. Opinion, as elicited and expressed by two large and respectable conventions, lately assembled at St. Louis and Memphis, points to a railroad as that which, if practicable, will best meet the wishes and wants of the country. But while this, if in successful operation, would be a work of great national importance, and of a value to the country which it wouldbe difficult to estimate, it ought also to be regarded as an undertaking of vast magnitude and expense, and one which must, if it be indeed practicable encounter many difficulties in its construction and use. Therefore, to avoid failure and disappointment, to enable Congress to judge whether, in the condition of the country through which it must pass, the work be feasible; and, if it be found so whether it should be undertaken as a national improvement or left to individual enterprise; and, in the latter alternative, what aid, if any, ought to be extended to it by the government, I recommend, as a preliminary measure, a careful reconnoissance of the several proposed routes by a scientific corps, and a report as to the practicability of making such a road, with an estimate of the cost of its construction and support. For further views on these and other matters connected with the duties of the Home Department, I refer you to the report of the secretary of the Interior.

———— ••• ————

EXTRACTS

From the Report of Hon. Thomas Ewing, Secretary of the Interior, Dec. 3, 1849.

PUBLIC LANDS IN OREGON, CALIFORNIA, AND NEW MEXICO.

No provision has yet been made to extend the laws for the disposition of the public lands into the territories of Oregon, California, and New Mexico. The public interest would seem to require that this should be done at an early day. To carry it into effect the negotiation of treaties with the Indian tribes who claim title to the lands, the creation of the office of surveyor general in each of those territories, and the establishment of land offices in convenient districts, will be necessary, accompanied with the usual appropriations for surveys. *   *   *   *   *   *   *

In California such commission will be more especially necessary. Many of the older grants in that territory, of considerable extent, have been resumed by the sovereign authority, and are now held under new grants which require examination. Many important and commanding points are claimed under very recent grants of a questionable character; and but a part of the public records were, at the time of our last advices, in the possession or within the knowledge of the proper authorities. There is, however, a large amount of land in this territory, held by grants of unquestionable validity, and some of them, especially those granted for pasturage, are large, covering many square leagues in extent. A considerable amount also is held by inchoate titles, regular and fair in their inception, but which have not been perfected. These titles, where commenced in good faith, by concession from the Spanish or Mexican authorities, ought to be favorably regarded, especially if followed by possession. In no case should the occupant of the soil suffer injury by the transfer of the sovereignty to the United States. This consideration has induced Congress to confirm inceptive grants, even where the conditions were not fulfilled, in all cases where it could reasonably be supposed that the government which made the grant would have waived or allowed further time for their performance.

This liberal consideration ought not, however, to be extended to doubtful grants of positions on the bays, islands, and headlands, which, when acquired, were known to be necessary to the United States as sites for forts, light-houses, or other objects of a national character. It is understood that titles of some kind, generally not valid without the confirmation of Congress, have been procured, and are claimed, to some of those points, which, if confirmed to and made the property of individuals, must be purchased back at a very large price. The right of the United States to such sites, where valid, ought to be at once asserted; and every spot necessary to the use of the government should be selected and separated from the general mass of public lands, and reserved from sale, and from the operation of the pre-emption laws, as they shall be extended to that territory.

MINERAL LANDS IN CALIFORNIA.

It is understood that a few of the larger grants cover, to some extent, the mines of gold and quicksilver.

By the laws of Spain these mines did not pass by a grant of the land, but remained in the crown, subject to be disposed of according to such ordinances and regulations as might be from time to time adopted. Any individual might enter upon the lands of another to search for ores of the precious metals; and having discovered a mine, he might register and thus acquire the right to work it on paying to the owner the damage done to the surface, and to the crown whose property it was, a fifth or tenth, according to the quality of the mine. If the finder neglect to work, or worked it imperfectly, it might be denounced by any other person, whereby he would become entitled.

This right to the mines of precious metals, which by the laws of Spain, remained in the crown, is believed to have been also retained by Mexico while she was sovereign of the Territory, and to have passed by her transfer to the United States. It is a right of the sovereign in the soil as perfect as if it had been expressly reserved in the body of the grant; and it will rest with Congress to determine whether, in those cases where lands duly granted contain gold, this right shall be asserted or relinquished. If relinquished, it will require an express law to effect the object; and if retained, legislation will be necessary to provide a mode by which it shall be exercised. For it is to be observed that the regulation permitting the acquisition of a right in the mines by registry or by denouncement was simply a mode of exercising by the sovereign the proprietary right which he had in the treasure as it lay in and was connected with the soil. Consequently, whenever that right was transferred by the transfer of the eminent domain, the mode adopted for its exercise ceased to be legal, for the same reason that the Spanish mode of disposing of the public lands in the first instance ceased to be legal after the transfer of the sovereignty.

Thus it appears that the deposites of gold, wherever found in the Territory, are the property of the United States. Those, however, which are known to exist upon the lands of individuals are of small comparative importance, by far the larger part being upon unclaimed public lands. Still, our information respecting them is yet extremely limited ; what we know in general is, that they are of great extent and extraordinary productiveness, even though rudely wrought. The gold is found sometimes in masses, the largest of which brought to the mint, weighed 89 ounces. They are generally equal to the standard of our coin in purity, and their appearance that of metal forced into the fissures and cavities of the rocks, in a state of fusion. Some, however, are flattened, apparently by pressure, and scratched as if by attrition on a rough surface. One small mass which was exhibited had about five parts in weight of gold to one of quartz, intimately blended, and both together bouldered, so as to form a handsome rounded pebble, with a surface of about equal parts quartz and gold. A very large proportion of the gold, however, is obtained in small scales by washing the earth, which is dug up in the beds of the streams, or near their margin. A mass of the crude earth, as taken at random from a placer, was tested by the director of the United States mint at Philadelphia, and found to contain 264¼ grains of gold (being, in value, a fraction over $10) to 100 lbs. of earth. It cannot, however, be reasonably supposed that the average alluvial earth in the placers is so highly auriferous.

No existing law puts it in the power of the Executive to regulate these mines, or protect them from intrusion. Hence, in addition to our own citizens, thousands of persons, of all nations and languages, flock in and gather gold, which they carry away to enrich themselves, leaving the lands the less in value by what they have abstracted ; and they render for it no remuneration, direct or indirect, to the government or people of the United States. Our laws, so strict in the preservation of public property that they punish our own citizens for cutting timber upon the public lands, ought not to permit strangers, who are not, and who never intend to become citizens, to enter at pleasure on these lands, and take from them the gold, which constitutes nearly all their value.

Some legal provision is necessary for the protection and disposition of these mines, and it is a matter worthy of much consideration how they should be disposed of so as best to promote the public interest and encourage individual enterprise. In the division of these lands regard should be had to the convenience of working every part of them containing gold, whether in the alluvion merely or in the fixed rocks. And, that such division may be made in the best manner practicable to promote the general interest and increase the value of the whole, a geological and mineralogical exploration should be connected with the linear surveys which should be made with the the assistance and under the supervision of a skilful engineer of mines.

The mining ordinances of Spain provide a mode of laying out the mines, which applies only to districts where veins of ore occur in the rocks, and where it is to be mined by following the metaliferous dike or stratum in the direction of its dip, and along its line of strike. But the gold which is found in the alluvion in California is continuous over a great extent of country, and it may be wrought upon any lot having surface earth and access to water. This district may be, therefore, divided into small lots, with a narrow front on the margin of the streams, and extending back in the form of a parallelogram. Where gold is found in the rocks *in situ*, the lots to embrace it should be larger, and laid off according to the Spanish method with regard to dip and strike. But so various are the conditions under which the precious metals may be found by a careful geological exploration, that the mode of laying off the ground cannot be safely anticipated, but must be left to the direction, on the spot, of a skilful engineer, whose services will be indispensable.

The division, disposition, and management of these mines will require much detail; but if placed on a proper footing, they may be made a source of considerable revenue. It is due to the nation at large that this rich deposite of mineral wealth should be made productive, so as to meet, in process of time, the heavy expense incurred in its acquisition. It is also due to those who become the lessees or purchasers of the mines that they should be furnished by the government with such scientific aid and directions as may enable them to conduct their operations not only to the advantage of the treasury, but also with convenience and profit to themselves. This scientific aid cannot be procured by individuals, as our people have little experience in mining, and there is not in the United States a school of mines, or any in which mining is taught as a separate science.

If the United States sell the mineral lands for cash, and transfer at once all title to the gold which they contain, but a very small part of their value will probably be realized. It would be better, in my opinion, to transfer them by sale or lease, reserving a part of the gold collected as rent or seignorage.

After mature reflection, I am satisfied that a mint at some convenient point will be advantageous to the miner, and the best medium for the collection and transmission of the gold reserved. Gamboa, a Spanish author of much science and practical observation, and at one time president of the Royal Academy of Mexico, strongly recommended the establishment of a mint in their principal mining district, as a means of collecting and transmiting the rents reserved by the crown, and especially to give a legitimate currency to the miners, that they might not be compelled, from necessity to barter their bullion, in violation of law. The same reasons would apply here with equal force.

When the land is properly divided, it will, in my opinion, be best to dispose of it, whether by lease or sale, so as to create an estate to be held only on condition that the gold collected from the mine shall be delivered into the custody of an officer of the branch mint. Out of the gold so deposited, there should be retained, for rent and assay, or coinage, a fixed per cent., such as may be deemed reasonable, and the residue passed to the credit of the miner, and paid to him at his option in coin or stamped bullion, or its value in drafts on the treasury or mint of the United States. The gold in the mine, and after it is gathered, until brought into the mint, should be and remain the property of the United States. The barter, sale, gift, or exportation of any portion of it before it shall have been delivered at the mint, and so coined, or assayed and stamped, or its concealment, with intent to avoid the payment of rent or seignorage, should involve a forfeiture of the gold itself, and also of the mine. The terms of lease or sale should be favorable to the miner, and the law should be st.ingent to enforce the payment of seignorage and rents.

So far as the surface deposits extend, I am of opinion that leases will, for yet a further reason, be preferable to sales of the lands. If sold, they will pass at once into the hands of large capitalists; if leased, industrious men without capital may become the proprietors, as they can work the mines and pay the rent out of the proceeds. But where gold is found in the rocks in place, the case is different. These must necessarily fall at once into the hands of large capitalists or joint stock companies, as they cannot be wrought without a heavy investment.

Some persons, whose opinions are entitled to much weight, apprehend difficulty in collecting the rents, if the mode of disposition which I suggest be adopted; but this, I think, is without a full consideration of the condition of the country and the means of enforcement. Gold, unless coined or stamped at the mint, could not circulate in California against a legal provision, and subject to a penalty such as is suggested. It could not be carried across the continent without risk of loss or detection, which would make the value of insurance equal to the rent. In any other direction it must pass the ports of California, and be there liable to detection.

Since the discovery of the mines, gold in California has not ranged higher than $16 per ounce: its actual value is a fraction over $18. The difference between its true value and the highest price at which it has sold, or would probably ever sell, except to houses transacting an open, regular and legal business, is therefore *one-ninth*, being more than half the amount that ought to be reserved as rent or seignorage.

If the penalty suggested above should be provided for an attempted evasion, and the ordinary advantages given to the officer or other person who should detect the fraud, as in case of smuggling, it would not be the interest of any one to become a dealer in the prohibited article at a small profit and great risk: nor would the miner risk a sale at a small advance of price, to be obtained at the hazard of a heavy forfeiture. The absolute security of the lawful business, the safety of the fund when deposited in the treasury of the United States, and the small profit and great risk of attempted frauds, would be reasonable security against them.

The property of the United States in the mines of quicksilver, derived from Spain through Mexico, with the eminent domain, is, as I have shown, the same as that to the gold, already considered. Indeed, the laws of Spain asserted more sternly and guarded more strictly the rights of the crown to that metal than to gold and silver. This arose from the scarcity of quicksilver, it being found in sufficient quantities to be worth mining in but few known places on the globe; while its necessary use in separating silver from its matrix, makes it an essential ingredient in silver mining operations.

The deposite of quicksilver, known to exist in California, is a sulphuret of mercury, or native cinnabar. The stratum of mineral, several feet in thickness, has been traced for a considerable distance along its line of strike. The specimens assayed at the mint range from 15.5 to 33.35 per cent. of metal; it is easy of access, and is mined and reduced without difficulty. So much of the mine as has been traced is situated on a ranch, to which the title is probably valid; and since the United States took possession of the country, an attempt has been made to acquire title to the *mine* by *denouncement*. This proceeding is, for the reasons that I have already given, invalid. It therefore remains for Congress to determine whether they will relinquish or assert the title of the United States in this mine.

EXTRACTS

From Executive Documents (H. of Rep.) No. 17, First Session, XXXIst Congress.

PRESIDENT TAYLOR'S MESSAGE, AND ACCOMPANYING DOCUMENTS.

To the House of Representatives of the United States :

I transmit to the House of Representatives, in answer to a resolution of that body passed on the 31st of December last, the accompanying reports of heads of departments, which contain all the official information in the possession of the Executive asked for by the resolution.

On coming into office, I found the military commandant of the department of California exercising the functions of civil governor in that Territory; and left, as I was, to act under the treaty of Guadalupe Hidalgo, without the aid of any legislative provision establishing a government in that Territory, I thought it best not to disturb that arrangment, made under my predecessor, until Congress should take some action on that subject. I therefore did not interfere with the powers of the military commandant, who continued to exercise the functions of civil governor as before; but I made no such appointment, conferred no such authority, and have allowed no increased compensation to the commandant for his services.

With a view to the faithful execution of the treaty, so far as lay in the power of the Executive, and to enable Congress to act, at the present session, with as full knowledge and as little difficulty as possible, on all matters of interest in these Territories, I sent the honorable Thomas Butler King as bearer of despatches to California, and certain officers to California and New Mexico, whose duties are particularly defined in the accompanying letters of instruction addressed to them severally by the proper departments.

I did not hesitate to express to the people of those Territories my desire that each Territory should, if prepared to comply with the requisitions of the constitution of the United States, form a plan of a State constitution and submit the same to Congress, with a prayer for admission into the Union as a State, but I did not anticipate, suggest, or authorize the establishment of any such government without the assent of Congress ; nor did I authorize any government agent or officer to interfere with or exercise any influence or control over the election of delegates, or over any convention, in making or modifying their domestic institutions or any of the provisions of their proposed constitution. On the contrary, the instructions given by my orders were, that all measures of domestic policy adopted by the people of California must originate solely with themselves ; that while the Executive of the United States was desirous to protect them in the formation of any government republican in its character, to be, at the proper time, submitted to Congress, yet it was to be distinctly understood that the plan of such a government must, at the same time, be the result of their own deliberate choice, and originate with themselves, without the interference of the Executive.

I am unable to give any information as to laws passed by any supposed government in California, or of any census taken in either of the Territories mentioned in the resolution, as I have no information on those subjects.

As already stated, I have not disturbed the arrangements which I found had existed under my predecessor.

In advising an early application by the people of these Territortes for admission as States, I was actuated principally by an earnest desire to afford to the wisdom and patriotism of Congress the opportunity of avoiding occasions of bitter and angry dissensions among the people of the United States.

Under the constitution, every State has the right of establishing, and, from time to time, altering its municipal laws and domestic institutions, independently of every other State and of the general government ; subject only to the prohibitions and guaranties expressly set forth in the constitution of the United States. The subjects thus left exclusively to the respective States were not designed or expected to become topics of national agitation. Still, as, under the constitution, Congress has power to make all needful rules and regulations respecting the Territories of the United States, every new acquisition of territory has led to discussions on the question whether the system of involuntary servitude which prevails in many of the states should or should not be prohibited in that Territory. The periods of excitement from this cause which have heretofore occurred have been safely passed; but during the interval, of whatever length, which may elapse before the admission of the Territories ceded by Mexico as States, it appears probable that similar excitement will prevail to an undue extent.

Under these circumstances, I thought, and still think, that it was my duty to endeavor to put it in the power of congress, by the admission of California and new Mexico as States, to remove all occasion for the unnecessary agitation of the public mind.

It is understood that the people of the western part of California have formed a plan of state constitution, and will soon submit the same to the judgment of Congress, and apply for admission as a State. This course on their part, though in accordance with, was not adopted exclusively in consequence of, any expression of my wishes, inasmuch as measures tending to this end had been promoted by the officers sent there by my predecessor, and were already in active progress of execution before any communication from me reached California. If the proposed constitution shall, when submitted to Congress, be found to be in compliance with the requisitions of the constitution of the United States, I earnestly recommend that it may receive the sanction of Congress.

The part of California not included in the proposed State of that name is believed to be uninhabited, except in a settlment of our countrymen in the vicinity of Salt Lake.

A claim has been advanced by the State of Texas to a very large portion of the most populous district of the Territory commonly designated by the name of New Mexico. If the people of New Mexico had formed a plan of a State government for that Territory as ceded by the treaty of Guadalupe Hidalgo, and had been admitted by Congress as a state, our constitution would have afforded the means of obtaining an adjustment of the question of boundary with Texas by a judicial decision. At present, however, no judicial tribunal has power of deciding that question, and it remains for Congress to devise some mode for its adjustment. Meanwhile, I submit to Congress the question whether it would be expedient, before such adjustment, to establish a territorial government, which, by including the district so claimed, would practically decide the question adversely to the State of Texas, or, by excluding it would decide it in her favor. In my opinion, such a course would not be expedient, especially as the people of this Territory still enjoy the benefit and protection of their municipal laws, originally derived from Mexico, and have a military force stationed there to protect them against the indians. It is undoubtedly true that the property, lives, liberties, and religion of the people of New Mexico are better protected than they ever were before. the treaty of cession.

Should Congress, when California shall present herself for incorporation into the Union, annex a condition to her admission as a State affecting her domestic institutions, contrary to the wishes of her people, and even compel her, temporarily, to comply with it yet the State could change her constitution, at any time after admission, when to her it should seem expedient. Any attempt to deny to the people of the State the right of self-government in a matter which peculiarly affects themselves, will infallibly be regarded by them as an invasion of their rights ; and, upon the principles laid down in our own Declaration of Independence, they will certainly be sustained by the great mass of the American people. To assert that they are a conquered people, and must, as a State, submit to the will of their conquerors in this regard, will meet with no cordial response among American freemen. Great numbers of them are native citizens of the United States, not inferior to the rest of our countrymen in intelligence and patriotism ; and no language of menace, to restrain them in the exercise of undoubted right, guarantied to them by the treaty of cession itself, shall ever be uttered by me or encouraged and sustained by persons acting under my authority. It is to be expected that, in Mexico, the people residing there will, at the time of their incorporation into the Union as a State, settle all questions of domestic policy to suit themselves. No material inconvenience will result from the want, for a short period, of a government established by Congress over that part of the territory which lies eastward of the new State of California ; and the reasons for my opinion that New Mexico will, at no very distant period, ask for admission into the Union, are founded on unofficial information, which, I suppose, is common to all who have cared to make inquiries on that subject.

Seeing, then, that the question which now excites such painful sensations in the country will in the end, certainly be settled by the silent effect of causes independent of the action of Congress, I again submit to your wisdom the policy recommended in my annual message, of awaiting the creation of geographical parties, and secure the harmony of feeling so necessary to the beneficial action of our political system. Connected as the Union is with the remembrance of past happiness, the sense of present blessings, and the hope of future peace and prosperity, every dictate of wisdom, every feeling of duty, and every emotion of patriotism, tend to inspire fidelity and devotion to it, and admonish us cautiously to avoid any unnecessary controversy which can either endanger it or impair its strength, the chief element of which is to be found in the regard and affection of the people for each other.

Z. TAYLOR.

WASHINGTON CITY, D. C., *January* 21, 1850.

Letter of Instructions of James Buchanan, Secretary of State, to William V. Voorhies, Esq. Oct. 7, 1848.

DEPARTMENT OF STATE,
Washington, October 7, 1848.

Sir: Previous to your departure for California, the President has instructed me to make known, through your agency, to the citizens of the United States inhabiting that Territory, his views respecting their present condition and future prospects. He deems it proper to employ you for this purpose, because the Postmaster General has appointed you an agent, under the " Act to establish certain post routes," approved August 14, 1848, " to make arrangements for the establishment of post offices, and for the transmission, receipt, and conveyance of letters in Oregon and California."

The President congratulates the citizens of California on the annexation of their fine province to the United States. On the 30th of May, 1848, the day on which the ratifications of our late treaty with Mexico were exchanged, California finally became an integral portion of this great and glorious republic; and the act of Congress to which I have already referred, in express terms recognises it to be " within the territory of the United States."

May this union be perpetual!

The people of California may feel the firmest conviction that the government and people of the United States will never abandon them or prove unmindful of their prosperity. Their fate and their fortunes are now indissolubly united with that of their brethren on this side of the Rocky mountains. How propitious this event both for them and for us! Whilst the other nations of the world are distracted by domestic dissensions, and are involved in a struggle between the privileges of the few and the rights of the many, Heaven has blessed our happy land with a government which secures equal rights to all our citizens, and has produced peace, happiness, and contentment throughout our borders. It has combined liberty with order, and all the sacred and indefeasible rights of the citizens with the strictest observance of law. Satisfied with the institutions under which we live, each individual is therefore left free to promote his own prosperity and happiness in the manner most in accordance with his own judgment.

Under such a constitution and such laws, the prospects of California are truly encouraging. Blessed with a mild and salubrious climate and a fertile soil, rich in mineral resources, and extending over nearly ten degrees of latitude along the coast of the Pacific, with some of the finest harbors in the world, the imagination can scarcely fix a limit to its future wealth and prosperity.

We can behold in the not distant future one or more glorious States of this confederacy springing into existence in California, governed by institutions similar to our own, and extending the blessings of religion, liberty, and law over that vast region.   Their free and unrestricted commerce and intercourse with the other States of the Union will confer mutual benefits and blessings on all parties concerned, and will bind us all together by the strongest ties of reciprocal affection and interest.   Their foreign trade with the west coast of America, with Asia, and the isles of the Pacific, will be protected by our common flag, and cannot fail to bear back to their shores the rich rewards of enterprise and industry.

After all, however, the speedy realization of these bright prospects depends much upon the wise and prudent conduct of the citizens of California in the present emergency.   If they commence their career under proper auspices, their advance will be rapid and certain ; but should they become entangled in difficulties and dissensions at the start, their progress will be greatly retarded.

The President deeply regrets that Congress did not at their late session establish a territorial government for California.   It would now be vain to enter into the reasons for this omission.   Whatever these may have been, he is firmly convinced that Congress feel a deep interest in the welfare of California and its people, and will at an early period of the next session provide for them a territorial government suited to their wants.   Our laws relating to trade and intercourse with the Indians will then be extended over them, custom-houses will be established for the collection of the revenue, and liberal grants of land will be made to those bold and patriotic citizens who amidst privations and dangers have emigrated or shall emigrate to that Territory from the States on this side of the Rocky mountains.

The President, in his annual message, at the commencement of the next session, will recommend all these great measures to Congress in the strongest terms, and will use every effort, consistently with his duty, to insure their accomplishment.

In the mean time, the condition of the people of California is anomalous, and will require, on their part, the exercise of great prudence and discretion. By the conclusion of the treaty of peace, the military government which was established over them under the laws of war, as recognised by the practice of all civilized nations, has ceased to derive its authority from this source of power.   But is there, for this reason, no government in California ?   Are life, liberty, and property under the protection of no existing authorities ? This would be a singular phenomenon in the face of the world, and especially among American citizens, distinguished as they are above all other people for their law abiding character.   Fortunately, they are not reduced to this sad condition.   The termination of the war left an existing government, a government *de facto*, in full operation ; and this will continue, with the presumed consent of the people, until Congress shall provide for them a territorial government.   The great law of necessity justifies this conclusion.   The consent of the people is irresistibly inferred from the fact that no civilized community could possibly desire to abrogate an existing government, when the alternative presented would be to place themselves in a state of anarchy, beyond the protection of all laws, and reduce them to the unhappy necessity of submitting to the dominion of the strongest.

This government *de facto* will, of course, exercise no power inconsistent with the provisions of the constitution of the United States, which is the supreme law of the land. For this reason, no import duties can be levied in California on articles the growth, produce, or manufacture of the United States, as no such duties can be imposed in any other part of our Union on the productions of California. Nor can new duties be charged in California upon such foreign productions as have already paid duties in any of our ports of entry, for the obvious reason that California is within the territory of the United States. I shall not enlarge upon this subject, however, as the Secretary of the Treasury will perform the duty.

The President urgently advises the people of California to live peaceably and quietly under the existing government. He believes that this will promote their lasting and best interest. If it be not what they could desire and had a right to expect, they can console themselves with the reflection that it will endure but for a few months. Should they attempt to change or amend it during this brief period, they most probably could not accomplish their object before the government established by Congress would go into operation. In the mean time, the country would be agitated, the citizens would be withdrawn from their usual employments, and domestic strife might divide and exasperate the people against each other; and this all to establish a government which in no conceivable contingency could endure for a single year. During this brief period, it is better to bear the ills they have than to fly to others they know not of.

The permanent prosperity of any new country is identified with the perfect security of its land titles. The land system of the general government has been a theme of admiration throughout the world. The wisdom of man has never devised a plan so well calculated to prevent litigation and place the rights of owners of the soil beyond dispute. This system has been one great cause of the rapid settlement and progress of new States and Territories. Emigrants have been attracted there, because every man knew that when he had acquired land from the government, he could sit under his own vine and under his own fig tree, and there would be none to make him afraid. Indeed, there can be no greater drawback to the prosperity of a country, as several of the older States have experienced, than disputed land titles. Prudent men will be deterred from emigrating to a State or Territory where they cannot obtain indisputable title, and must consequently be exposed to the danger of strife and litigation in respect to the soil on which they dwell. An uncertainty respecting the security of land titles arrests all valuable improvement, because no prudent man will expend his means for this purpose while there is danger that another may deprive him of the fruit of his labors. It is fortunate, therefore, that Congress alone, under the constitution, possesses " the power to dispose of and make all needful rules and regulations respecting the territory or other property of the United States." In the exercise of this power, the President is convinced that the emigrants will receive liberal donations of the public land.

Although Congress have not established a territorial government for the people of California, they have not been altogether unmindful of their interests. The benefit of our Post Office laws has been extended to them ; and you will bear with your authority from the Postmaster General to provide for the conveyance of public information and private correspondence among themselves, and between them and the citizens of Oregon, and of our States east of the Rocky mountains. The monthly steamers on the line from Panama to Astoria have been required " to stop and deliver and take mails at San Diego, San Francisco, and Monterey." These steamers, connected by the isthmus of Panama with those on the Atlantic, between New York and Chagres, will keep up a regular communication with California, and afford facilities to all those who may desire to emigrate to that Territory.

The necessary appropriations have also been made by Congress to maintain troops in California to protect its inhabitants against all attacks from a civilized or savage foe ; and it will afford the President peculiar pleasure to perform this duty promptly and effectively.

But, above all, the constitution of the United States, the safeguard of all our civil rights, was extended over California on the 30th May, 1848, the day on which our late treaty with Mexico was finally consummated. From that day its inhabitants became entitled to all the blessings and benefits resulting from the best form of civil government ever established amongst men. That they will prove worthy of this inestimable boon, no doubt is entertained.

Whilst the population of California will be composed chiefly of our own kindred, of a people speaking our own language, and educated for self-government under our own institutions, a considerable portion of them were Mexican citizens before the late treaty of peace. These, our new citizens, ought to be, and, from the justice and generosity of the American character, the President is confident that they will be, treated with respect and kindness, and thus be made to feel that by changing their allegiance they have become more prosperous and happy.

Yours, very respectfully,

JAMES BUCHANAN.

WILLIAM V. VORHIES, Esq.,
    Washington city.

Letter of Instructions of Hon. John M. Clayton, to Thomas Butler King.
April 3, 1849.

DEPARTMENT OF STATE,

Washington, April 3, 1849.

SIR : The President, reposing full confidence in your integrity, abilities, and prudence, has appointed you an agent for the purpose of conveying important instructions and despatches to our naval and military commanders in California. It is his desire that you should lose no time in repairing thither, by the best and most expeditious route, in the prosecution of the duties devolved upon you, which I shall proceed to explain in the following instructions.

The situation of the people of California and New Mexico has already, at this early period of his administration, attracted his attention. By the late treaty with Mexico, provision was made for the future admission of these Territories into the Union as States ; and, in the mean time, the government of the United States is bound to protect the inhabitants residing in them in the free and entire enjoyment of their lives, liberty, and property, and in the exercise of their civil and religious rights. Owing to causes with which you are fully acquainted, the Congress of the United States failed to assist the Executive by the passage of a law establishing a government in either of the new Territories. You are aware, however, that an act was passed, at the last session, to extend the revenue laws of the United States over the territory and waters of Upper California. This act creates a collection district in California. And you also know that, by another previous act, certain mail facilities have been extended to the same Territory. Whatever can be done, by the aid of the constitution of the United States, the treaty with Mexico, and the enactments of Congress, to afford to the people of the Territories the benefits of civil government and the protection that is due them, will be anxiously considered and attempted by the Executive.

You have been selected by the President to convey to them these assurances, and especially the assurance of his firm determination so far as his constitutional power extends, to omit nothing that may tend to promote and secure their peace and happiness. You are fully possessed of the President's views, and can, with propriety suggest to the people of California the adoption of measures best calculated to give them effect. These measures must, of course, originate solely with themselves. Assure them of the sincere desire of the Executive of the United States to protect and defend them in the formation of any government, republican in its character, hereafter to be submitted to Congress, which shall be the result of their own deliberate choice. But let it be, at the same time, distinctly understood by them that the plan of such a government must originate with themselves, and without the interference of the Executive.

The laws of California and New Mexico, as they existed at the conclusion of the treaty of Guadalupe Hidalgo, regulating the relations of the inhabitants with each other, will necessarily remain in force in those Territories. Their relations with their former government have been dissolved, and new relations created between them and the government of the United States; but the existing laws regulating the relations of the people with each other will continue until others, lawfully enacted, shall supercede them. Our naval and military commanders on those stations will be fully instructed to co-operate with the friends of order and good-government, so far as their co-operation can be useful and proper.

An important part of your duty will be to acquire, and to transmit to this department, the best and fullest information in regard to the population, the productions, and the resources of the country; the extent and character of all grants of land made by Mexico prior to the late treaty; the quantity and condition of the public domain, and especially of those portions which are rendered valuable by their metallic and mineral wealth; and the general fitness and capacity of these new acquisitions for the great purposes of agriculture, commerce, and manufactures. The development of the resources of this vast and interesting region, in all that concerns the interests and welfare of its present and future occupants, is a cherished object of this government; and all information which you can obtain in relation to these subjects will be most acceptable to this department.

It is desirable to know the numbers of the various Indian tribes which form a portion of the population of the Territories; their power, character, and modes of life; and the number of Mexicans held as captives there by any savage tribes, whose release and restoration to their own country this government is bound to exact by the 4th and 11th articles of the treaty: also, as nearly as may be, the number of Mexicans who, within the year after the exchange of the ratifications of the treaty, have withdrawn from the Territories; and the number of those who have declared their intention to preserve the character of citizens of the Mexican republic, agreeably to the 8th article of the treaty.

It is not credited by this government that any attempt will be made to alienate either of these portions of the Territories of the United States, or to establish an independent government within their limits. But should the existence of any such project be detected, you will not fail to bring it to the immediate notice of your government, that proper measures for the protection of the interests of the people of the United States may be promptly adopted.

You are fully authorised to confer with our military and naval commanders within these Territories, who will be instructed to assist you in the accomplishment of the object of your mission.

Your compensation will be at the rate of eight dollars per diem, from the time of your departure on the business of your mission until your return home ; and you will be allowed your travelling and other expenses during your absence, for which you will be careful to take vouchers in all cases where they can be obtained.

The sum of one thousand dollars is advanced to you on account.

I am, sir, very respectfully, your obedient servant,

JOHN M. CLAYTON.

Hon. THOMAS BUTLER KING,
    Appointed agent of the United States to California.

Letter of Mr. Ewing, Secretary of the Interior, to the Secretary of State, and instructions of the Commissioners of the Land Office to Wm. C. Jones, and Letter of Instructions of Mr. Ewing to Wm. C. Jones.

SIR : That I may be enabled to lay before Congress at their next session, something reliable as to the condition of land titles in California, it is important that the archives in that Territory and also in the city of Mexico (so far as they touch those titles) be examined and reported upon by a competent person.

To this end, I desire that such person be sent with official authority to make the necessary examination, to collect and secure the original archives in California, and to procure the necessary copies in the city of Mexico. This latter duty must necessarily be performed under authority from the State Department.

For this mission I propose William Cary Jones, Esq., well known to you as an adept in the Spanish language, and as a lawyer well skilled in the Spanish colonial titles. I propose, if it meet your approbation, that you commission him to visit the city of Mexico for this purpose, and that he be permitted to go by San Francisco, Monterey, and San Diego, and other places in California, and make at those points the necessary investigations.

For his goverment while engaged in California, I have caused the accompanying instructions to be prepared at the General Land Office ; and I propose, if you approve it, that he be governed by them, so far as they be applicable, in his examination at the city of Mexico also.

I am, very respectfully, yours,

T. EWING.

Hon. JOHN M. CLAYTON, *Secretary of State.*

GENERAL LAND OFFICE, *July* 5, 1849.

SIR : By a communication of the 29th ultimo, the Secretary of the Interior advised this office of your appointment as confidential agent of the government to visit Mexico and California, in order to obtain information, " as early as practicable, of the character and extent of the titles and claims to lands within the limits of the tract of country acquired by the United States by the late treaty with Mexico, purporting to have emanated from the former authorities of that country." At the same time, the Secretary has requested that such instructions and information may be given to you as the objects in view may render necessary. It is a principle of public law, now acknowledged and recognised by the usage of modern nations, that, though the sovereignty changes, private rights remain unaffected by that change; and consequently that the relation of the people to each other under such circumstances, and " their rights of property, remain undisturbed." This principle is explicitly recognised and sanctioned in the treaty between the United States and Mexico, as ratified on the 4th July, 1848, which in the most solemn form, and as the supreme law of the land, makes it obligatory upon our government to respect the valid and *bona fide* titles of individuals; and, in reference to the future management of the public domain within the limits of our newly acquired territories, to make it incumbent upon us to take such measures as will enable our government to separate from the mass of public lands all private property resting upon such titles derived from the former government. To this end, therefore, and in view of the directions from the Secretary, you are hereby instructed:

1. To proceed without delay to Upper California, and visit such places as Monterey on the Pacific, San Francisco, San Diego, or any other points you may deem necessary, in order to obtain full and authentic information to enable you to have access to all the provincial, departmental, or other records and archives connected with titles and claims to land in California, seeking facilities and aid from the United States military officers in command there, or from such persons as may be officiating judicially or in other civil capacities, for the time being, under the existing customs of the community.

2. Having gained access to those archives, you will then, after a careful and thorough examination of them, prepare a complete and perfect *abstract*, in such a form, as to arrangement and classification, as will exhibit the particulars—

First. As to all grants or claims in the territory derived from the government of Spain when her authorities held dominion over the country, showing the dates of such; the names of the original grantees; the area of each claim, with its front and depth; the name of the water-course, or other natural object indicating locality; whether or not surveyed; the date of survey, with the name of the officer making the grant, stating whether such grants have been sanctioned; and if so, when and by what officer or authority under the *Mexican* government, designating such as are in regular and legal form and appear *prima facie* to be *bona fide* valid titles, and such as are fraudulent or suspicious, reporting the reasons and grounds of the discrimination you may make.

Second. A similar abstract of such titles as were derived from the authorities of *Mexico* since the separation of that country as an independent republic from Old Spain, indicating the names of the granting officers in each case ; dates of, &c., of each element of title from the inceptive to the survey, and to the concession or title in form, showing whether the same emanated direct from the supreme government of Mexico, or from the departmental authorities, with information as to the titles and powers of the granting officers ; dates of their commissions and periods of incumbency, with such data as you may be able to procure touching their powers, and how derived, for alienating the national property ; specifying such grants as appear to be regular and valid, and such as are of an opposite character. You will be pleased to discriminate between such as are perfect titles, clothed with all legal formalities, and such as are inceptive or inchoate, and in all cases designating the names of the parties appearing in the archives, land or judicial records, as " present claimants," or whom, from authentic and reliable sources, you may find to be so, with a reference to the evidence you may have before you of present proprietorship.

Third. You will also make a separate classification and abstract of all grants or titles made about the time of the *revolutionary* movements in California— say in he months of June and July, 1846—and up to the period when actual hostilities between the United States and Mexico were known in California, and also of any which may have been subsequently made ; showing the dates of sales ; area of tracts ; names of original grantees ; when and by whom made ; whether surveyed or not ; whether to residents, non-residents, or foreigners ; whether or not clothed with the usual legal formalities, specifying such as may have been made without legal authority, with an abstract of the evidence of transfer by the grantors, and of such evidence to others from the grantees.

Fourth. You will obtain a copy of all the different authentic forms of title, from the first element up to the consummation of the grant—such as the petition, decree, order of survey, return of actual survey, concession grant, with the denomination of the various allotments, from a square league " *un sitio de granado mayor*," or square league of 4,428 acres, down to the smallest farm, or village, or town lot, with the ratios usual between the fronts and depths, and will prepare a comparative statement of the land measures formerly used in California under Spain and Mexico, and those now employed in the United States.

Fifth. You will direct particular attention to the extensive tracts or bodies of land covered by what are known as " *missions.*" You will ascertain as fully as possible the extent, locality, and value of each of them, and of the buildings or improvements thereon ; will trace out their early history, origin, and date of the establishment of them, respectively, and their transition, and under what authority from the ecclesiastical to the civil power, or national authorities; their condition as to the title and possession at the commencement of hostilities between the two republics; the dates of any sales made about that time, previously or subsequently; the circumstances under which, to whom and by whom made, and under color of what authority, with the dates of any subsequent sales by parties claiming under grants from the California authorities; with the particulars in each case as to date, consideration, &c., accompanied by plats or sketches exhibiting their actual location and relative position to places now laid down on maps of the country.

Sixth. You will carefully examine and report all the information you can obtain as to whether any titles were granted to " *mines,*" either of the precious metals, quicksilver, or other minerals; when and to whom made; the considerations; conditions; whether or not surveyed; localities; and all matters in regard to the same, particularly in respect to the validity or invalidity of any individual titles or claims which may be alleged to the same.

Seventh. You will also extend your researches so as to ascertain whether any claim has been set up or alleged to the *islands* or *keys*, or any of them, on the coast, or in the bays or harbors; and if so, the nature of such claims; whether or not in legal forms and from competent authorities of the former governments, or whether invalid, as against the title of the United States to all the public property under treaty—this inquiry being special, in view of the importance which some of these islands may be to the United States for fortifications and light-houses.

Eighth. You will make an inquiry into the nature of the "*Indian rights*" as existing under the Spanish and Mexican governments, and as subsisting when the United States obtained the sovereignty, indicating from authentic data the difference between the privileges enjoyed by the wandering tribes and those who have made " actual settlements" and established " rancherias," and will report their general form, extent, and localities; their probable number, and the manner and form in which such rights have been regarded by the Spanish and Mexican governments.

In returning you are authorized, if you can do so without protracting too long your stay, to proceed to Santa Fe, the capital of New Mexico, and there obtain access to the archives of that country, and to furnish similar information as to all titles which have emanated from the authorities when New Mexico was a province of Spain, and subsequently under the government of the Mexican republic.

Information has reached here that the perfecto at El Paso del Norte, since we acquired the country, had been actually engaged in disposing, for his own benefit, of the most valuable lands on the Rio Grande bottom, antedating titles to purchasers. You will, therefore, make a thorough inquiry and report in this matter, and prepare a complete abstract of such fraudulent grants.

An important object in your appointment is to obtain for our government reliable and authentic information in regard to the whole land system of the former governments while operating in the country comprised within the limits of our new acquisitions ; and to this end, you are authorized, either in going or returning, to visit the city of Mexico, for the purpose of examining the archives and obtaining the data desired, and will regard the points specified as intended to guide, but not confine your powers, which you will consider sufficiently expansive to accomplish all the purposes contemplated.

You will keep a journal of all your proceedings as the confidential agent of the government, noting the places in which the archives are deposited, and in whose custody, with minutes of every transaction or incident con_nected with the subject which you think would be important or useful to the government in determining upon an enlightened and just policy, not only in respect to individual titles, but in the management and disposal of the public domain.

Very respectfully, your obedient servant,

J. BUTTERFIELD,
Commissioner.

WM. CAREY JONES, ESQ., *Confidential Agent, &c.*

DEPARTMENT OF THE INTERIOR,
July 12, 1849.

SIR: I have examined and approved the instructions prepared for you in the General Land Office, and I desire information on all the matters therein named ; but it is important that your report should come in prior to the termination of the next session of Congress, and you are charged with duties so extended and deversified, that you will probably not be able to make, in time, the detailed examination contemplated by those instructions.

You will, however, obtain all the information in your power on all the subjects referred to therein ; but direct your attention, in the first place, to the mode of creating titles of land, from the first inception to the perfect title, as practised by Mexico within the province of California ; what kind of paper issued in the first instance, from what officer, when filed, and how and by whom recorded. So also with the subsequent steps, embracing the proceedings as to survey up to the perfecting of the title ; and if there be record books, files, or archives of any kind whatsoever, showing the nature, character, and extent of these grants, endeavour to find and secure them, so that they may be placed in the hands of the acting governor of the Territory for safe custody and future reference. In descending to details, you will examine chiefly the larger grants, as the missions, and find whether the title to them be in assignees, or whether they have reverted and vested in the sovereign.

It is also understood that there are large grants, and grants of islands, keys, and promontories, points of great value to the public, which purport to have emanated just prior to the occupation of the territory by the United States, but which are probably fictitious and really entitled to a later date. These you will examine carefully, and note down fully all the information which can be had on the spot which will throw light on those when they shall be hereafter the subject of investigation, stating the nature of the alleged title, whether purporting to be inchoate or complete. If there be any alleged grants of land covering a portion of the gold mines, you will also give to that your careful consideration. It will be a question worthy of examination when in the city of Mexico, whether in all grants in general, or in California in particular, there are not conditions and limitations, and whether there is not a reservation of mines of gold and silver, and a similar reservation as to quicksilver and other minerals.

It is also important in all large grants, or grants of important or valuable sites, or of mines, to ascertain whether or not they were actually surveyed and occupied under the government of Spain, or Mexico, and when publicity was first given to such grants, particularly as to such as are of a suspicious or doubtful character.

The department has no authority to pay you anything on account of your services; but you will be paid out of the contingent fund of the General Land office a sum sufficient to cover your expenses while in California, and also your necessary expenditures in procuring information, and finding and putting in place of security any books of records of land titles or other archives relating thereto, for which your drafts, not exceeding twenty-five hundred dollars in the whole, accompanied by a letter stating the special objects to which it has been, or is about to be, applied, will be duly honored.

You will be pleased to keep an account of your personal expenses, and also of the expenditures required in the execution of your duties, and make a rendition of the same to this department, to which, as to titles, &c., in California, you will make your report; and in reference to your examinations in Mexico you will make a separate communication to the State Department, a notice of which should be given in your report to this department. An application will be made by the department to Congress for an appropriation as an allowance to you of a fair compensation for your services.

Wishing you a pleasant voyage, and health and success in your arduous undertaking,

I am, very respectfully, your obedient servant,

T. EWING.

Wm. Carey Jones, Esq.

H. W. Halleck's Report on the Land regulations which govern the granting or selling. 2. Public lands in California, and the laws and regulations respecting the lands and other property belonging to the missions of California. March 1, 1849.

STATE DEPARTMENT OF THE TERRITORY OF CALIFORNIA,
Monterey, March 1, 1849.

SIR: In compliance with your instructions, I have collected together and examined all archives of the government of California which can be found, and have the honour to report as follows:

1st. On the laws and regulations which govern the granting or selling of public lands in California.

2d. On the laws and regulations respecting the lands and other property belonging to the missions of California.

3d. On the titles of lands in California which may be required for fortifications, arsenals, or other military structures, for the use of the general government of the United States.

The translation of the laws are made by Mr. W. E. P. Hartwell, the government translater, and are almost literal versions of the original.

Very respectfully, your obedient servant,

H. W. HALLECK,
Brevet Captain and Secretary of State.

Colonel R. B. MASON,
Commanding 10th military department, and Governor of California.

1st. Laws and regulations governing grants or sales of public lands in California.—The first authority for granting lands in Upper California is contained in the viceroy's instructions to the commandant of the "New Establishments of San Diego and Monterey," dated August 17, 1773. By articles 12, 13, 14 and 15 of these instructions, the commandant is empowered both to designate common lands, and to grant titles to individuals, whether Indians or new settlers, in the vicinity of the missions or pueblos. He might also if he deemed it expedient, change any mission into a pueblo, and subject it to the same civil and economical laws as governed the other pueblos of the kingdom.—(Vide appendix No. 1.)

On the 21st of September, 1774, the viceroy wrote to the commandant in Upper California, granting permission to the soldiers of the garrisons to marry the baptized Indian girls of the missions, and authorizing the assignment of lands to the soldiers so marrying. The first grant of this kind was that of a piece of land in Carmel Valley, of one hundred and forty varas, to Manuel Butron, who had married an Indian girl of the mission of San Carlos.

In order better to carry out the wishes of the Spanish government in reference to the establishment of depots of provisions, &c., in Upper California, for refreshing the Spanish vessels from the East Indies, and to furnish supplies to the garrisons of the presidios, directions were sent by the viceroy to Governor Neve in June, 1777, to establish two pueblos, one on the " Rio Guadalupe," and the other on the " Rio Porcincula," and to portion out ground to the new *publadores*, or colonists.

On the 1st of June, 1779, the governor drew up a set of new regulations for the government of California, which was approved by the King in a royal order of October 24, 1781. Title 14 of these regulations contains instructions respecting colonization, and the government of the new colonists. Each publador was to receive a bounty of $116 44 per annum for the first two years, and $60 per annum for the next three years; and also was to have the loan of horses, mules, cattle, farming utensils, &c. The streets, squares, municipal and common lands of the pueblos, and the *solares* or house-lots, and *suertes* of sowing lands of the *publadores*, were to be designated by the government.

Discharged soldiers were to receive building and planting lots, the same as the colonists. All the *publadores* were to possess the right of pasturing their cattle and of cutting wood on the common lands of the pueblos. Certain conditions were to be attached to these grants of land, such as the building of houses, planting of trees, &c., within a specified period of time.—(Vide appendix No. 2.)

These regulations with slight modifications, have formed the basis of the laws which have ever since governed the pueblos of California.

On the 22d of October, 1791, orders were sent to Governor Romeu authorizing the captains of presidios to grant and distribute house-lots and lands to the soldiers and citizens within the extent of two common leagues in every direction from the centre of each presidio square.—(Vide appendix No. 3.)

Immediately after the independence of Mexico, and during the government of Iturbide, a system of laws was established for colonization, dated April 11, 1823; but as these laws were suspended almost immediately afterwards, it is believed no grants of land were made under them in Upper California. On the 18th of August, 1824, the constituent congress passed a decree for the colonization of the territories of the republic, which decree was limited and defined by a series of regulations, dated November 21, 1828.

By these laws and regulations the governors (gefes politicos) of territories were authorized to grant (with certain special exceptions) vacant lands to contractors, (*empressarios*,) heads of families, and private persons. The grants to *empressarios* for colonies or towns were not to be valid till approved by the supreme government.

Nor were grants made to individuals or single families to be held as

definitively valid, till approved by the territorial deputation ; and if the ter.
ritorial deputation should not give its approval, the governor was to refer the
documents to the supreme government for its action.

But, without the previous approval of the supreme government, no territo.
rial governor could make grants of land within ten leagues of the seacoast, nor within twenty leagues of the boundaries of any foreign power.
Moreover, the general government reserved to itself the right to make use of
any portion of these lands for the purpose of constructing warehouses, arsenals, or other public edifices which it might deem expedient for the defence
or security of the nation. The maximum and minimum amounts of land
which could be given to any one person were specified, and also the circumstances under which the grant should become void.—(Vide appendix Nos. 4
and 5.)

These laws and regulations are believed to be still in force, as they are
referred to in the titles to lands granted in Upper California as late as July
8, 1846. The usual form of a confirmation of a grant of land by the territorial legislature, is as follows : " The grant made to N, of the place called
——, in the jurisdiction of ——, comprising —— sitios of large cattle,
(square leagues,) is approved according to the title given to him on the
—— of ——, 184—, in conformity with the law of the 18th of August,
1824, and the 5th article of the regulations of the 21st of November, 1828.
　　　　　　" A. B., *President of the Departmental Assembly.*
" C. D., *Secretary.*"

The restriction contained in paragraph 4 of the decree of August 18,
1824, is also fully recognised in the proceedings of the territorial legislature.
For example : in the instructions of the territorial junta to the deputy from
Upper California to the general congress of Mexico, dated July 25, 1836,
(paragraph 4,) it is expressly conceded that the general government of
Mexico alone had power to dispose of islands on the coast of California ; and
(paragraph 19) the deputy is directed to solicit from the general government an absolute confirmation of the grants of land made in California under
the colonization decree of August 18, 1824, and the regulations of November 21, 1828, releasing the proprietors from the restrictions contained in
these laws and regulations.

Again : in 1840 the territorial deputation made a representation to the
general government, asking that the law of colonization be extended so as to
include lands lying within ten leagues of the coast of California, and that
the grants already made by the territorial government within these limits be
confirmed by Mexico. It is believed, however, that the general government
never acted on this representation, and that the aforementioned laws and
regulations remain unchanged.

The restriction contained in paragraph 7 of the regulations of November

21, 1828, is also recognised in the proceedings of the territorial legislature, and has been announced and enforced by the supreme government. In 1845, when the supreme government confirmed the grant made to Don Esteban Smith of lands situated at and near the port of Bodega, orders were issued that no more grants of that kind be made by the territorial government, without obtaining the necessary authority from the supreme government of Mexico.—(Vide Governor Alvarado's certificate, appendix No. 6.)

Again this restriction is alluded to and recognised in a letter from the Department of Relations, dated Mexico, August 11, 1845, and signed Louis G. Cuevas; and in a letter from the Minister of Foreign Affairs, Government, and Policy, dated Mexico, January 19, 1846, and signed Costillo Lanvas—both of these letters having reference to the Macnamara colonization grant—and even in the grant itself, which was given by Governor Pico, and dated July 4, 1846, it is expressly stated that the approval of the supreme government is necessary to make it valid.—(Vide Senate Doc. No. 75, 1st session 30th Congress.)

The territorial governments were originally prohibited from making grants of public lands, of the islands of the coast, as well as of those in the bays, without the consent or approbation of the general government of Mexico; but the consent of the supreme executive power was given in 1838 to make grants of islands on the *coast* of California. The islands in the bays, however, are not included in this permission.—(Vide appendix No. 7.)

The general government of Mexico has also reserved to itself the right to take, and use for the purpose of fortifications or arsenals, lands belonging to any *State*, by indemnifying the State for the value of the lands so taken. This law was passed by Congress the 6th of April, 1830, and is in the following words:

" ART. 4. The executive may take such lands as it considers useful for fortifications or arsenals, and for the new colonies, indemnifying the States for the value thereof out of the amount due by them (the different States) to the federation."

This same law repealed the 7th article of the law of August 18, 1824, in the following words:

" ART. 11. In virtue of the power which the general Congress reserved to itself in the 7th article of the law of the 18th of August, 1824, foreigners belonging to nations whose possessions are bounded by the States and territories of the federation are prohibited from colonizing such adjoining lands; consequently, all contracts opposed to this law which may not as yet have been fulfilled, shall be suspended."

A large number of land titles in California are very indefinite with respect to boundaries, the grants being for so many " sitios," " creaderos," &c., lying between certain hills, streams, &c., as shown by rough sketches attached to the ·petitions. These sketches. frequently contain double the amount of land included in the grants; and even now very few of these grants have been surveyed or their boundaries definitely fixed.. The usual form of these titles is shown in appendix No. 8.

Some of the land titles given by the Californian government contain conditions respecting their sale, &c., which are not only onerous to the holders, but contrary to the spirit of our laws. These onerous conditions should be removed by act of Congress. A number of the grants of land made by the governors of California, have never been confirmed by the territorial legislature. In some cases that body has positively refused its approbation ; in other cases it has merely declined to act until furnished with certain information respecting the amount asked for, its boundaries, &c. ; in others again the petition, though before the legislature, was not reached previous to its final adjournment in July, 1846 ; and it is probable that some of these titles through carelessness were never submitted to that body for approval. Again : it has been alleged by very respectable authority, that certain titles to land were given by Governor Pico *after* the United States had taken possession of the country, and made to bear date prior to the 7th of July, 1846. These grants have of course never been confirmed by the territorial legislature, for that body adjourned on the 8th of July, the day after our flag was raised at Monterey ; nor have they been recorded in any book of records among the government archives, although it is said they purport to be so recorded. In settling land titles in this country, a broad distinction should be made between titles of this kind and those which were given in good faith by the California governors, previous to our taking possession of this country, but which have failed to receive the requisite confirmation for want of action on the part of the territorial legislature. In appendix No. 9, I have given a description of the different land measures adopted by the Mexican government. The description and table are translated from the " Ordenanzas de Tierras y Aguas," by Marianas Galuan, edition of 1844.

Where grants of land have been made by the territorial government for towns, (*fundos legal para pueblos,*) in conformity to the provisions of articles 10, 11, 12, and 13 of the regulations of November 21, 1828, the land lying within the limits of such grants may be disposed of by the founders or municipal authorities, agreeably to the general laws regulating the government of such towns. The spirit of these laws in California may be judged of by the following extract from an act of the territorial deputation, dated August 6, 1834 :

" ART. 1. The ayuntamientos will make application through the ordinary channels, requesting lands to be assigned to each pueblo for *eguidos* (common lands,) and *proprios* (municipal lands.)

" ART. 2. The lands assigned to each pueblo for *proprios* shall be sub-divided into middling-sized and small portions, and may be rented out or given at public auction, subject to an emphitennic rent or tax—*en senso enfitentico.*

The present possessors of lands belonging to the *proprios* will pay an annual tax, to be imposed by the ayuntamiento, the opinion of three intelligent men of honor being first taken.

" ART. 3. For the grant of a house lot for building on, the parties interested shall pay six dollars, and two rials for each lot of one hundred varas square, and in the same manner for a larger or smaller quantity at the rate of two rials for each vara front."

All grants, however, of land lying within ten leagues of the coast, whether made for towns, or for any other purpose, must be approved by the supreme executive power of Mexico in order to make them valid ; moreover, they are all subject to the reservation contained in article 5 of the law of August 18, 1824 ; that is general government has reserved to itself the right to make use of any portion of these lands for the purpose of constructing warehouses, arsenals, and other public edifices.

These town grants are usually not only definitively limited in their extent, but are made with certain conditions respecting the sale or division of these municipal lands, the price being fixed by law.

It appears from the documents and laws which have been referred to—

1st. That no grants of land made by the governors of California, after the 21st of November, 1828, are valid without the approval of the territorial legislature, or of the supreme government of Mexico.

2d. That the governor and legislature of California could, without the approval of the supreme government, make no grant whatever of land within ten leagues of the seacoast, nor within twenty leagues of the boundaries of any foreign power ; nor could they anywhere grant to any one person more than one league square (*una legua cuadrada*) of five thousand varas of irrigable land, (*tierra de regadio,*) four superficial ones of land dependent on the seasons, (*cuatro de superficei de temporal,*) and six superficial ones for rearing cattle, (*seis de superficei de abrenado.*)

3d. That where grants are made and properly approved for towns, all municipal lands lying within the limits of such grants may be disposed of by the municipal authorities in *solares* or building lots, in conformity to the laws applicable to such cases, except such lands as may be required by the general government for constructing warehouses, arsenals, or other public edifices, for the defence or security of the nation.

4th. That all lands in California not included within the limits of grants made in conformity to law, and prior to July 7, 1846, formed a part of the public domain of Mexico at the moment when the United States took possession of this territory.

Since the conquest no material change has taken place in the legal condition of land titles in this country.

Numerous applications have been made to the governor to decide upon the validity of these titles ; but all questions of this kind have been postponed until some competent tribunal shall be formed for their adjudication, the several claimants being advised in the mean time to have their lands surveyed by some competent surveyor

Soon after General Kearney became governor of this country, representations were made to him that it was important to the growth and prosperity of the town of San Francisco that the general government of the United States should immediately designate what land within the limits of that town was required for its use, (as pointed out in article 5th of the colonization law of August 18, 1824) the town being permitted to dispose of the remainder as municipal lands. General Kearney acting in the double capacity of civil governor of California and legal representative of the United States, made a decree, dated March 10, 1847, directing the selection of such land as was required for government purposes, and surrendering on the part of the United States, all claim to the remainder within certain defined limits.

If the beach and water lots " included between the points known as the Rincon and *Fort Montgomery*" are actually included within the original limits of the town, this decree of General Kearney can hardly be regarded as an ordinary *land grant* made by a territorial governor; it was rather the act of an agent of the supreme executive power of the general government, designating the lands required for the purposes contemplated in article 5 of the law of August 18, 1824, and releasing the remaining lands within such limits from the action of the general reservation contained in that article.—(Vide appendix No. 10.)

Representations having been made in 1847 to the governor, that the former alcalde of the town of Sonoma had been guilty of fraud in the grants and records of sale of municipal lands, a board of commissioners was appointed to examine into these charges, with powers to settle questions of title to these lands according to equity and justice. The proceedings and findings of these commissioners were approved by the governor; and on the 9th of October, 1847, returned to the alcalde of Sonoma for file in his office.—(See appendix No. 11.)

Representations were also made to the governor, that the municipal authorities of the pueblo of San Jose de Guadalupe had exceeded their powers in selling lands not belonging to, or at the disposal of, the town, and that they had divided up and granted or distributed to individuals all the common lands of the pueblo, the use of which had been conceded to the people of that place for the common purposes of pasture, wood, and sowing, but which had never been placed at the disposal of the municipal authorities either for distribution or sale. The opinion and action of the Executive on these proceedings are given in appendix No. 12.

It has also been alleged that the local authorities of other towns have not only disposed of municipal lands in a manner contrary to the provisions of the territorial laws, but in some instances have even gone beyond the limits of the town grants, and made sale of lands which properly belong to the national domain. But, as has already been said, there being no tribunals in this country competent to decide upon questions of this kind, they have been left for adjudication till the proper courts shall be established. And inasmuch as these questions touching the validity of land titles are exceedingly numerous, and as disputes are daily arising respecting the rights of the different claimants, it is deemed exceedingly important to the peace and prosperity of the country that measures be taken without delay for the speedy and final settlement of these titles upon principles of equity and justice.

2d. *Laws and regulations respecting the lands and other property belonging to the missions of California.*—The first law relating to the secularization of the religious establishments of the missionary priests in America was passed by the Spanish cortes the 15th of September, 1813. This law was made with respect to the missions of Buenos Ayres, and the first five articles refer merely to the transfer of these establishments from one class of priests to another. The final article is as follows :

" The religious missionaries shall immediately cease from the government and administration of the property (haciendas) of said Indians, it being left to the care and election of these (Indians) to appoint amongst themselves by means of their ayuntamientos, and with the intervention of the governor, persons to their satisfaction, capable of administering it, distributing the lands, and reducing them to private property, agreeably to the decree of the 4th of January, 1813, respecting the reduction of vacant and other lands to private dominion."

Basing themselves on the authority of this law, the governor and territorial deputation of California, under the pretence of ameliorating the condition of the natives, prepared a project for secularizing the missions of this province, and for converting them into pueblos or towns. Accordingly a *bando* or decree was issued on the 6th of January, 1831, designating the particular manner of parcelling out the lands and property of the several missions, and of regulating the government and police of the proposed towns. But the whole project (which, being without the approbation or authority of Mexico, was in itself illegal) was defeated by the new governor who had arrived at Santa Barbara the 31st of December, 1830. The latter immediately recalled the bando of his predecessor, and forbid all attempts to carry it into execution.

The question of secularization was afterwards agitated in the general congress of Mexico ; and on the 17th of August, 1833, a law for this object was passed by that body, and received the executive sanction. By this law the missions of Upper and Lower California were *secularized*, and became the property of the government. Each mission was to constitute a parish, and to be placed under the charge of a parish priest of the secular clergy, with a fixed salary. The churches of the several missions, with the sacred vessels, ornaments and other appurtenances, and such adjacent buildings as the government might deem necessary, were to be assigned for the use of the parish. The most appropriate building of each mission was to be assigned for the habitation of the curate, with a lot of ground not exceeding two hundred varas square. The remaining edifices were to be designated for court-houses, preparatory schools, workshops, &c. A lot of ground was also to be laid out in each parish for a burial-ground. All the expenses of this law were to be provided for out of the " products of the estates, capitals, and revenues, at present recognised as the pious fund of the missions of California."—(Vide appendix No. 13.)

The missions of both Upper and Lower California were thus made public property, and the lands which formerly belonged to these establishments could be disposed of after the date of this law only under the provisions of the decree of August 18, 1824, and the regulations of November 21, 1828. The case was anticipated and provided for in article 17 of these regulations.

Acting under the authority of these laws, the governor of California, (Figueron,) on the 9th of August, 1834, issued " provisional regulations," converting ten of these missions into pueblos. By these regulations, the duties of the priests were confined to the spiritual affairs of the missions, while the territorial government assumed to itself the administration of all their temporal affairs. To each head of family, and to all over the age of twenty-one years even when having no family, was to be assigned a lot of land not exceeding four hundred varas square, nor less than one hundred varas, out of the common lands of the missions. Common lands, (*egidos*,) and, when convenient, *municipal* lands (*propios*) also, were to be assigned to each pueblo. One-half of the stock, seeds, and agricultural implements of the missions was to be distributed to individuals in the same way; all other lands and property to remain at the disposal and direction of the governor. The fiscal affairs of these new pueblos were to be under the direction of ayuntamientos, while the legal matters were to be decided by the primary judges of the nearest towns. The emancipated Indians were to assist in the cultivation of the common grounds of the new pueblos, but were prohibited from selling any of the lots or stocks assigned to them by the government. All contracts made by them were declared null and void, and the property sold by them was to be reclaimed by the government as national property—the purchasers losing their money. If these Indians died without heirs, their property reverted to the nation.—(Vide appendix No. 14.) In the extraordinary session of the legislature at Monterey, November 3, 1834, these provisional regulations (except that relating to the personal services of the Indians to the priests) were confirmed, and others formed marking out the different curacies, defining the salaries of the priests, &c.—(Vide appendix No. 15.) The whole direction of the temporal affairs of these missions was transferred from the priests to civil officers, called administrators, who were stationed in the missions, and who, under the general direction of the government, were to manage the property of these establishments for the benefit of the Indians. They, however, were prohibited from making any sales of mission property without the express orders of the government.

On the 7th of November, 1835, a decree of the supreme government directed that the execution of the law of August 17 be suspended until the curates mentioned in article 2 should take possession.—(Vide appendix No. 16.)

Governor Alvarado's regulations of January 17, 1839, declare null and void all debts contracted by these administrators without the previous consent of the government. On the first of March, 1840, he made new regulations for the government of the missions—replacing the administrators by major-domos, and defining the powers and duties of the latter over these establish. ments. Both of these sets of regulations seemed designed merely to carry out the provisions of the previous laws and decrees.—(Vide appendix Nos. 17 and 18.)

On the 29th of March, 1843, Governor Micheltorena ordered twelve of these missions to be delivered up to the direction and management of the priests—the same as formerly. The mission lands which had been granted previous to that date, and in accordance with the law, were not to be re. claimed ; but all the cattle, property, and utensils of the missions which had been let out were to be restored to these establishments. One-eighth part of the total annual produce of these missions was to be paid into the public treasury for the support of the government troops and civil officers.—(Vide appendix No. 19.) By a decree of the departmental assembly, May 28, 1845, it was directed that certain missions (four in number) be considered as having already been converted into pueblos, and that their premises (except the reservations already mentioned) be sold at public auction. It was also directed that if the Indians of five other missions mentioned in the decree did not, after one month's public notice by proclamation, unite for the purpose of occupying and cultivating the said missions, the missions also, should be declared unoccupied, and be disposed of as the assembly and departmental government should deem best for the general good ; the remainder of the missions in Upper California (with the exception of the principal edifice at Santa Barbara) to be rented out at the option of the government —care being taken to secure their prosperity ; one-half of the total rent of the mission of Santa Barbara was to be invested for the benefit of the church and the support of its minister, and the other half for the benefit of its Indians. Of the rents of the other missions, one-third was to go to the priest and church, one-third to go to the benefit of the Indians, and one-third to be devoted to education and public beneficence, as soon as the legal debts of each mission were paid.—(Vide appendix No. 20.)

On the 28th of October, 1845, Governor Pico advertised for sale, to the highest bidder, five of the missions, and directed that, as soon as certain edifices of four other missions were selected for specified objects, the remaining edifices of these four establishments should also be sold at public auction. The day of sale and the manner of giving notice are specified in the regulations. Four other missions were to be rented to the highest bidder for the term of nine years. All the lands, vineyards, orchards, workshops, implements of agriculture, and other property of these missions, were to be included in the renting; but the principal edifice of the mission of Santa Barbara, and the churches, with the appurtenances, the court-houses, curates' houses, school-houses, and the small portions of land occupied by certain Indians in each of the missions, were excepted in the order for renting. The proceeds of these rents were to be divided into three parts, and disposed of as has already been mentioned.

The renters were to pay their rents punctually and quarterly; and, at the expiration of the nine years, were to deliver back, with improvements, and in a serviceable order, the property of the missions. They were to return the same number and description of cattle as received, and of such an age as not to embarrass the procreation of the following year. Before they could receive these establishments they were to give bonds to the satisfaction of the government, conditioned on the fulfilment of their obligations, and the payment of such damages as the government should find against them. The government reserved to itself the right of taking care that these establishments should prosper; in virtue of which right, it would take such measures as might be necessary to prevent their distribution, ruin, or decline, during the period of their renting. Six other missions, whose names are given, were to be rented in the same manner, as soon as their debts could be arranged.—(Vide appendix No. 21.)

A decree of the departmental assembly, April 3, 1846, authorized the application of the laws of bankruptcy to certain missions; and if necessary, to prevent their total ruin, their sale at public auction, the customary notice being previously given.

A portion of the lands and other property of these missions, were to be set apart for the maintenance of the priests, and the support of public worship. But this act was in no way to interfere with what had already been done under the previous decrees of the assembly. Six months at farthest were allowed for its fulfilment.—(Vide appendix No. 22.)

In 1846, after the adjournment of the departmental assembly, for want of a quorum, and the flight of Governor Pico from the country, Captain Flores, who assumed to be governor *ad interim*, organized a kind of provisional legislature, which body, on the 30th of October, passed a decree annulling the sales of missions made by Pico, and authorizing the governor *ad interim* to mortgage these establishments for the purpose of raising loans of money to carry on the war. But, as these proceedings took place several months after the United States had taken possession of the country, they were evidently illegal, and of no force.—(Vide appendix No. 23.)

It appears from the documents and laws to which I have referred—

1. That since the 17th of August, 1833, the missions of California have been regarded as national property, and held at the disposal of the government.

2. That, when thus made the property of the nation, they could be disposed of by the territorial government only in accordance with the colonization laws of 1824 and 1828, or under the authority of some special law of the Mexican Congress.

3. That the territorial or departmental legislature, basing its authority on the laws of the Mexican Congress, has authorised the governor, on specified conditions, to convert certain of these missions into pueblos, to sell some, and rent others.

4. That the territorial or departmental governors, acting under the authority of the legislature, has converted certain of these missions into pueblos, and sold and rented others, establishing certain conditions or regulations for the conversion, sale, or renting of these establishments.

5. That where any of these missions have been regularly converted into pueblos, the municipal lands, or lands lying within the limits of the town grant, (*fundo legal para pueblo,*) are to be disposed of in *solares*, or building lots, according to the provisions of the law applicable to such cases. The *common* lands, granted to these towns, must remain as such until the legislature converts them into municipal lands, or otherwise authorizes their sale; and all lands lying without these town limits can be disposed of only in accordance with the laws and regulations of 1824 and 1828.

6. That the land set apart for the priest, in each mission, could not exceed two hundred varas square; nor could more than four hundred varas square be granted to any one individual.

7. That the lands granted to Indians were merely for the use of themselves and of their descendants; that they could in no way be disposed of by them, but when abandoned they reverted to government.

8. That all sales of mission property by the Indians are null and void.

9. That no civil agent or administrator could dispose of mission property, or contract debts in the name of the missions, without the previous authority of the government.

10. That no lease of a mission or of mission property is made in conformity to law, unless bonds have been given to the satisfaction of the government, conditioned for the fulfilment of the obligations of the lessee.

12. That the renters of the missions are bound by certain regulations, respecting the care and preservation of the mission property.

13. That the rents are to be paid punctually and quarterly, one-third (in

Santa Barbara one-half) to the padres, prefects, or their authorized agents, and the other two-thirds into the public treasury, to be expended for certain specified objects.

14. That government has reserved to itself the right to take such measures as may be necessary *to prevent " the destruction, ruin, or decline" of the missions " during the period of their renting,"* and that, therefore, if the renters, previous to the expiration of their leases, be found injuring or destroying the mission property, the government may eject them.

15. That the mission lands and other property which have not been sold in accordance with the provisions of law, are still the property of government, and may be disposed of accordingly. Such was the legal condition of the missions of California when, on the 7th of July, 1846, the American flag was raised in Monterey, and the country taken formal possession of in the name of the United States. Nor has this condition been in any way changed by the American authorities since the conquest. Soon after General Kearney assumed the civil government in California, representations were made to him, from the most respectable sources, that the grants and sales of mission property by Governor Pico, just as he was leaving the country, were without the authority of law, and that, though actually made after the 7th of July, 1846, they had been antedated in order to give them the semblance of legality. These titles were not recorded in the usual book of records in the government archives ; but purported to be recorded in some other book, which, as yet, has never been found. Speculators had bought up these doubtful titles, and now demanded to be put in possession of their property. Under these circumstances, General Kearney issued a decree on the 22d of March, 1847, directing that certain missions, so claimed, be left in the hands of the priests until the proper tribunal should be organized to determine on the validity of these titles.—(Vide appendix No. 24.) In other cases, where the claimants were in actual possession, they were allowed to remain, but with the express understanding that this permission should in no way affect the legality of their titles. Those, also, who were found holding mission property on lease were left in quiet possession, except the renter of the mission of San Buenaventura, who, being detected in selling and destroying the property of the mission, to its injury and almost total ruin, was ejected by the commanding officer of the southern military district. Towards the close of 1847, it was reported to the governor that the priest of the mission of Sante Clara was selling the lands of that mission. He was immediately called upon for his authority for making such sales, and being unable to give any that was deemed satisfactory, the governor declared all sales made by him of mission lands to be illegal, null and void.—(Vide appendix No. 25.)

Again, in 1848, it being reported that the alcalde of Sante Barbara had attempted to give legal possession to some of the owners of doubtful titles to mission property, notice was given both to the alcalde and the claimants that this act of the alcalde was null and void; no alcalde in California having authority to give any legal force to claims to public lands in this territory.—(Vide appendix No. 26.)

APPENDIX NO. 1.

Extracts from " the instructions to be observed by the commandant appointed to the new establishments of San Diego and Monterey," given by El. Bailie Frior Don Antonio Bucareli y Urusu, dated Mexico, 17th August, 1773.

ARTICLE 2. The confusion which has reigned in the accounts, and the want of order which I have observed in everything else, have compelled me to establish this new method, and to appoint Captain Don Fernando Rivèra y Moncada commandant of San Diego and Monterey, because I am well informed of his good conduct or manner of proceeding, and of his knowledge of the new establishments, acquired in the employments and offices which he has therein obtained and in the presidios of California for many years.

ARTICLE 12. With the desire to establish population more speedily in the new establishments, I for the present grant the commandant the power to designate common lands, and also even to distribute lands in private to such Indians as may most dedicate themselves to agriculture and the breeding of cattle, for having property of their own, the love of it will cause them to radicate themselves more firmly; but the commandant must bear in mind that it is very desirable not to allow them to live dispersed—each one on the lands given to them—but that they must necessarily have their house and habitation in the town or mission where they have been established or settled.

ARTICLE 13. I grant the same faculty to the commandant with respect to distributing lands to the other founders (pobladores) according to their merit and means of labor—they also living in the town and not dispersed, declaring that in the practice of what is prescribed in this article and the preceding 12th, he must act in every respect in conformity with the provisions made in the collection of the laws respecting newly-acquired countries and towns, (*reducciones y poblaciones,*) granting them legal titles for the owner's protection without exacting any remuneration for it or for the act of possession.

ARTICLE 14. The commandant must be carefully attentive that the founders who go to the new establishments have the requisite arms for their defence and for assisting the garrisons of the presidios or missions in case of necessity, binding them to this obligation as a thing necessary for their own safety and that of all their neighbors.

ARTICLE 15. When it becomes expedient to change any mission into a pueblo, the commandant will proceed to reduce it to the civil and econominal government which, according to the laws, is observed in the other pueblos of this kingdom, giving it a name, and declaring for its patron the saint under whose auspices and venerable protection the mission was founded.

APPENDIX No. 2.

Extracts from the regulations for the government of the province of California, by Don Felipe De Neve, governor of the same, dated in the royal presidio of San Carlos de Monterey, 1st June, 1779, and approved by his Majesty in a royal order of the 24th October, 1781.

TITLE THE FOURTEENTH.—POLITICAL GOVERNMENT, AND INSTRUCTIONS RE-SPECTING COLONIZATION.

1st. The object of greatest importance towards the fulfilment of the pious intentions of the King, our master, and towards securing to his Majesty the dominion of the extensive country which occupies a space of more than two hundred leagues, comprehending the new establishment of the presidios, and the respective ports of San Diego, Monterey, and San Francisco, being to forward the reduction of, and as far as possible to make this vast country (which, with the exception of seventeen hundred and forty-nine Christians of both sexes in the eight missions on the road which leads from the first to the last named presidio, is inhabited by innumerable heathens) useful to the State, by erecting pueblos of which people, (*gente de razon—literally, people of reason,*) who, being united, may encourage agriculture, planting, the breeding of cattle and successively the other branches of industry; so that some years hence their produce may be sufficient to provide garrisons of the presidios with provisions and horses, thereby obviating the distance of transportation and the risks and losses which the royal government suffers thereby. With this just idea, the pueblo of San Jose has been founded and peopled; and the erection of another is determined upon, in which the colonists and their families, from the provinces of Sonora and Sinuloa, will establish themselves, the progressive augmentation of which, and of the families of the troops, will provide for the establishment of other towns, and furnish recruits for the presidio companies, thus freeing the royal revenue from the indispensable expenses at present required for these purposes; and it being necessary to establish rules for carrying all this into effect, the following instructions will be observed:

2d. As an equivalent for the $120 and rations, which hitherto have been assigned yearly to each poblador (founder or colonist) for the first two years, and the rations alone for the following one, calculated at a rial and a half per diem, free, for the three following ones, they will hereafter receive for each of the first two years $116 and $3\frac{1}{2}$ rials, the rations to be understood as comprehended in this amount: and in lieu of rations for the next three years, they will receive $60 yearly, by which arrangement they will be placed on more favorable terms than formerly, taking into consideration the advance that was charged on what they were paid with, and the discount on the rations furnished, which article they will in future receive at cost from the moment that these regulations be approved and declared to be in force, it being understood that the forementioned term of five years, as regards this emolument, is to be reckoned from the day on which the possession of the house-lots and pieces of land, (*solares y suertes de tierras,*) which are to be distributed to each poblador in the manner hereafter mentioned, be given; and the previous time, from the period of their enrolment, must be regulated according to the terms of their respective contracts, and, in order to avoid this expense, measures will be taken to have the new pobladores collocated, and put into possession immediately on their arrival.

3d. To each poblader, and to the community of the pueblo, there shall be given, under condition of repayment in horses and mules fit to be given and received, and in the payment of the other large and small cattle, at the just prices which are to be fixed by tariff, and of the tools and implements at cost as it is ordained, two mares, two cows and one calf, two sheep and two goats, all breeding animals, and one yoke of oxen or steers, one plow-share or point, one hoe, one *coa*, (a kind of wooden spade with a steel point,) one axe and one sickle, one wood-knife, one musket and one leather-shield, two horses and one cargo mule. To the community there shall likewise be given the males corresponding to the total number of cattle of different kinds distributed amongst all the inhabitants, one seed jackass, another common one and three she asses, one boar and three sows, one forge, with its corresponding anvil and other necessary tools, six crowbars, six iron spades or shovels, and the necessary tools for carpenter and cast work.

4th. The house-lots to be granted to the new pobladores are to be designated by government in the situations, and of the extent, corresponding to the locality on which the new pueblos are to be established, so that a square and streets be formed agreeable to the provisions of the laws of the kingdom; and conformable to the same, competent common lands (egidos) shall be designated for the pueblo and pasture grounds, with the sowing lands that may be necessary for municipal purposes, (proprios.)

5th. Each suerte of land, whether capable of irrigation or dependent on the seasons, (de riego de temporale,) shall consist of two hundred varas in length and two hundred in breadth, this being the area generally occupied in the sowing of one fanega of Indian corn. The distribution which is to be effected of the house-lots and pieces of land to the new colonists must be made in the name of the King, our master, by the government, with equality, and a proportion to the ground which admits the benefit of being watered, so that after making the necessary demarcation and reserving vacant the fourth part of the number which may result, counting with the number of poblado-res, should there be sufficient, each one shall have two suertes of irrigable land, and other two of dry ground, delivered to him; and of the royal lands (*realengas*) as many as may be considered necessary shall be separated for the proprios of the pueblo, and the remainder of these, as well as of the house-lots, shall be granted in the name of his Majesty, by the governor, to those who may hereafter come to colonize, and particularly to those soldiers who, having fulfilled the term of their engagement, or on account of advanc-ed age may have retired from service, and likewise to the families of those who may die; but these persons must work at their own expense, out of the funds which each of them ought to possess, and will not be entitled to receive from the royal revenue either salary, rations, or cattle, this privilege being limited to those who leave their own country for the purpose of settling this country.

6th. The houses built on the lots granted and designated to the new pobladores, and the parcels of land comprehended in their respective gifts, shall be perpetually hereditary to their sons and descendants, or to their daughters who marry useful colonists who have received no grants of land for themselves, provided the whole of them comply with the obligations to be expressed in these instructions; and in order that the sons of the possessors of these gifts observe the obedience and respect which they owe to their parents, these shall be freely authorized, in the case of having two or more sons, to choose which of them they please, being a layman, to succeed to the house and suertes of the town; and they may likewise dispose of them amongst their children, but not so as to divide a single suerte, because each and all of these are to remain indivisible and inalienable forever.

7th. Neither can the pobladores, nor their heirs, impose on the house or parcel of land granted to them, either tax, entail, reversion, mortgage, (*cento, vinculo, fianza, hipoteca*) or any other burden, although it be for pious pur-poses; and should any one do so in violation of this just prohibition, he shall irremediably be deprived of his property, and his grant shall *ipso facto* be given to another colonist who may be useful and obedient.

8th. The new colonists shall enjoy, for the purpose of maintaining their cattle the common privilege of the water and pasturage, fire-wood and tim-ber, of the common forest and pasture lands, to be designated according to law to each new pueblo; and besides, each one shall privately enjoy the pasture of his own land, but with the condition that as they have to possess and breed all kinds of large and small cattle, and it not being possible that each one can dedicate himself to the taking care of the small stock consigned to them—as by so doing they would be unable to attend to agriculture and the public works—for the present, the small cattle, and the sheep and goats of the community, must feed together, and the shepherd must be paid by such community; and with respect to collecting together the large cattle, and bringing them to the corrol, such as mares and asses, as may be required, this must be done by two of the pobladores, whom they must appoint amongst themselves, or as they may see fit, to look after this business, and thus the cattle of different kinds will be taken care of, and freed from the risk of running wild, at the same time that agricultural and other works of the community will be attended to; and each individual must take care to mark their respective small cattle and brand the large, for which purpose the records of the necessary branding irons will be made without any charge; but it is ordained that henceforth no colonist is to possess more than fifty head of the same kind of cattle, so that the utility produced by cattle be distributed amongst the whole of them, and that the true riches of the pueblo be not monopolized by a few inhabitants.

9th. The new colonists shall be free and exempt from paying tithes, or any other tax, on the fruits and produce of the lands and cattle given to them, provided that within a year from the day on which the house-lots and parcels of land be designated to them, they build a house in the best way they can, and live therein, upon the necessary trenches for watering their lands, placing at their boundaries, instead of landmarks, some fruit trees, or wild ones of some utility, at the rate of ten to each suerte; and likewise open the principal drain or trench, form a dam, and the other necessary public works, for the benefit of cultivation, which the community is bound particularly to attend to; and said community will see that the government buildings (casas kealas) be completed within the fourth year, and during the third a storehouse sufficiently capacious for a public granary, in which must be kept the produce of the public sowing, which at the rate of one almud (the twefth of a fanega) of Indian corn per inhabitant, must be made from said third year to the fifth, inclusive, in the lands designated for municipal purposes, (proprios) all the labor of which, until harvesting the crop and putting it in the granary, must be done by the community for whose benefit alone it must serve; and for the management and augmentation thereof, the necessary laws to be observed will, in due time be made.

10th. After the expiration of the five years they will pay the tithes to his Majesty, for him to dispose of agreeably to his royal pleasure, as belonging solely to him, not only on account of the absolute royal patronage which he possesses in these dominions, but also because they are the produce of uncultivated and abandoned lands which are about to become fruitful at the costs of the large outlays and expenses of the royal treasury. At the expiration of the said term of five years, the new pobladores and their descendants will pay, in acknowledgement of the direct and supreme dominion which belongs to the sovereign, one-half of a fanega of Indian corn for each irrigable suerte of land, and for their own benefit they shall be collectively under the direct obligation of attending to the repair of the principal trench, dam, auxiliary drains, and other public works of their pueblos, including that of the church.

11th. When the hogs and asses shall have multiplied, and the sufficient number of seed asses for covering the mares become adopted, and it be found practicable to distribute these two kinds of animals amongst the pobladores, it must be done with all possible equality, so that of the first kind each one may receive one boar and one sow, and of the second one ass, which the owner will mark and brand.

12th. Within the five years stipulated, the new pobladores shall be obliged to possess two yoke of oxen, two ploughs, two points or plough-shares for tilling the ground, two hoes, and the other necessary implements for agriculture; and by the end of the first three years their houses must be entirely finished, and furnished each with six hens and one cock; and it is expressly forbidden that any one shall, during the forementioned period of five years, aleniate by means of exchange, safe, or other pretext, or kill any of the cattle granted to them or the respective increase thereof, excepting sheep and goats, which, at the end of four years, it is necessary to dispose of, or else they would die; and therefore they may, at their discretion, dispose of as many of these animals as arrive at that age, but not of any younger ones, under the penalty that whoever shall violate this order, made for his own benefit and for the increase of his prosperity, shall forfeit *ipso facto* the amount of the rations granted to him for one year; and whoever shall receive one more head of such cattle during the same time, in whatever state or condition they may be, shall be obliged to return them.

13th. At the expiration of said five years, the female breeding animals of every kind, excepting swine and asses, of which each poblador is only obliged to possess one sow and one ass, male or female, being preserved; the yokes of oxen or steers designated for their agricultural purposes being provided, and they being furnished with a cargo-mule, and necessary horses, they shall be at liberty to sell their bulls, steers, foals or horses, asses, sheep, castrated goats, and pigs and sows; it being forbidden to kill cows, (except old or barren, and consequently unproductive ones,) sheep, or she-goats, which are not above three years old, and to sell mares or useful breeding females, until each poblador be possessed of fifteen mares and one stallion, fifteen cows and one bull, twelve sheep and one ram, and ten she-goats with one buck.

14th. No poblador or resident shall sell a foal horse or mule, or exchange said, except amongst each other, after they are provided with the necessary number, for the remainder must be dedicated solely to the purpose of re-mounting cavalry of the presidio troops, and will be paid for at the just pri-ces to be established, excepting all particularly fine horses or mules of said pueblos, under the penalty of twenty dollars, to be forfeited by whomsoever may violate this order. For every animal disposed of in any other man-ner than what is here stipulated, the half to be given to the informer, and the other half to be applied to municipal expenses, (gasto de republica).

15th. The Indian corn, beans, chick-peas, and lentils, produced by the pueblo, after the residents have separated what may be necessary for their own subsistence and for seed, must be bought and paid for in ready money at the prices established, or which may hereafter be established for provisioning the presidio, and from the amount of the same there must be de-ducted from the amount of each poblador such provident sums as may be considered proper towards refunding the royal revenue the advances made in money, horses, cattle, implements, seeds, and other articles, so that with-in the first five years the total amount must be paid.

16th. Each poblador and resident head of a family to whom house-lots or parcels of land may have been, or in future shall be granted, and their successors, shall be obliged to hold themselves equipped with two horses, a saddle complete, a musket, and the other arms already mentioned, which are to be furnished them at first cost, for the defence of their respective dis-tricts, and in order that they may (without abandoning this first obligation) repair to where the governer may, in cases of urgency, order them.

17th. The corresponding titles to house-lots, lands, and waters, granted to the new pobladors, or which may hereafter be granted to other residents, shall be made out by the governor, or commissary whom he may appoint for this purpose, records of which, and of the respective branding irons, must be kept in the general book of colonization, to be made and kept in the government archives, as a heading to which a copy of these instructions shall be placed.

18th. And whereas it is expedient for the good government and police of the pueblos, the administration of justice, the direction of public works, the distribution of water privileges, and the carrying into effect the orders given in these instructions, that they should be furnished with ordinary alcaldes and other municipal officers, in prorportion to the number of inhabitants, the gov-ernor shall appoint such for the first two years, and for the following ones, they shall appoint some one from amongst themselves to the municipal offices which may have been established, which elections are to be forwarded to the governor for his approbation, who if he sees fit, may continue said appoint-ment for the three following years.

APPENDIX No. 3.

In conformity with the opinion of the assessor of the *commandancia general*, I have determined in a decree of this date that, notwithstanding the provisions made in the 81st article of the ordinance of *intendentes*, the captains of presidios are authorized to grant and distribute house-lots and lands to the soldiers and citizens who may solicit them to fix their residences on.

And considering the extent of four common leagues measured from the centre of the presidio square, viz: two leagues in every direction, to be sufficient for the new pueblos to be formed under the protection of said presidios, I have likewise determined, in order to avoid doubts and disputes in future, that said captains restrict themselves henceforward to the quantity of house-lots and lands within the four leagues already mentioned, without exceeding in any manner said limits, leaving free and open the exclusive jurisdiction belonging to the *intendentes* of the royal hacienda, respecting the sale, composition, and distribution of the remainder of the land in the respective districts,

And that this order may be punctually observed and carried into effect, you will circulate it to the captains and commandants of the presidios of your province, informing me of having done so.

God preserve you many years.
CHIHUAHUA, *March* 22, 1791.

PEDRO DE NERVA.

Senor Don JOSEPH ANTONIO ROMEN.

APPENDIX No. 4.

Decree of the 18th August, 1824, respecting colonization.

The sovereign general constituent Congress of the United Mexican States has been pleased to decree—

1st. The Mexican nation promises to those foreigners who may come to establish themselves in its territory, security in their persons and property, provided they subject themselves to the laws of the country.

2d. The objects of this law are those national lands which are neither private property nor belong to any corporation or pueblo, and can therefore be colonized.

3d. To this end the Congress of the States will form, as soon as possible, the laws and regulations of colonization of their respective demarcation, with entire conformity to the constitutive act, the general constitution, and the rules established in this law.

4th. Those territories comprised within twenty leagues of the boundaries of any foreign nation, or within ten leagues of the seacoast, cannot be colonized without the previous approval of the supreme general executive power.

5th. If, for the defence or security of the nation, the federal government should find it expedient to make use of any portion of these lands for the purpose of constructing warehouses, arsenals, or other public edifices, it may do so, with the approbation of the general Congress, or during its recess with that of the government council.

6th. Before the expiration of four years after the publication of this law, no tax or duty (direcho) shall be imposed on the entry of the persons of foreigners, who come to establish themselves for the first time in the nation.

7th. Previous to the year 1840, the general Congress cannot prohibit the entry of foreigners to colonize, except compelled to do so, with respect to the individuals of some nation, by powerful reasons.

8th. The government, without prejudicing the object of this law, will take the precautionary measures which it may consider necessary for the security of the federation, with respect to the foreigners who may come to colonize. In the distribution of lands, Mexican citizens are to be attended to in preference; and no distinction shall be made amongst these, except such only as is due to private merit and services rendered to the country, or inequality of circumstances, residence in the place to which the lands distributed belong.

10th. Military persons who are entitled to lands by the promise made on the 27th of March, 1821, shall be attended to in the States, on producing the diploms granted to them to that effect by the supreme executive power.

11. thIf by the decrees of capitulation, according to the probabilities of life, the supreme executive should see fit to alienate any portion of land in favor of any military or civil officers of the federation, it may so dispose of the vacant lands of the territories.

12th. No one person shall be allowed to obtain the ownership of more than one league square, of five thousand varas, (5,000 v.) of irrigable land (de regadio,) four superficial ones of land dependent on the seasons (de temporal,) and six superficial ones for the purpose of rearing cattle (de abreradiso.)

13th. The new colonists cannot transfer their possessions in mortmain, (manos muertas.)

14th. This law guaranties the contracts which the grantees (empressrios) may make with the families which they may bring out at th pense; provided they be not contrary to the laws.

15th. No one who, by virtue of this law, shall acquire the ownership of lands, shall retain them if he shall reside out of the territory of the republic.

16th. The government, in conformity with the principles established in this law, will proceed to the colonization of the territories of the republic.

APPENDIX No. 5.

General rules and regulations for the colonization of territories of the republic.—Mexico, November 21, 1828.

It being stipulated in the 11th article of the general law of colonization of the 17th of August, 1824, that the government, in conformity with the principles established in said law, shall proceed to the colonization of the territories of the republic; and it being very desirable, in order to give to said article the most punctual and exact fulfilment, to dictate some general rules for facilitating its execution in such cases as may occur, his excellency has seen fit to determine on the following articles:

1st. The governors (gefes politicos) of the territories are authorized (in compliance with the law of the general Congress of the 18th of August, 1824, and under the conditions hereafter specified) to grant vacant lands in their respective territories to such contractors (empressarios,) families, or private persons, whether Mexicans or foreigners, who may ask for them, for the purpose of cultivating and inhabiting them.

2d. Every person soliciting lands, whether he be an *empressario*, head of a family, or private person, shall address to the governor of the respective territory a petition, expressing his name, country, profession, the number, description, religion, and other circumstances of the families or persons with whom he wishes to colonize, describing as distinctly as possible, by means of a map, the land asked for.

· 3d. The governor shall proceed immediately to obtain the necessary information whether the petition embraces the requisite conditions required by said law of the 18th of August, both as regards the land and the candidate, in order that the petitioner may at once be attended to; or if it be preferred, the respective municipal authority may be consulted, whether there be any objection to making the grant or not.

4th. This being done, the governor will accede or not to such petition, in exact conformity to the laws on the subject, and especially to the before-mentioned one of the 18th of August, 1824.

5th. The grants made to families or private persons shall not be held to be definitely valid without the previous consent of the territorial deputation, to which end the respective documents (espediontes) shall be forwarded to it.

6th. When the governor shall not obtain the approbation of the territorial deputation, he shall report to the supreme government, forwarding the necessary documents for its decision.

7th. The grants made to *empressarios* for them to colonize with many families shall not be held to be definitely valid until the approval of the supreme government be obtained; to which the necessary documents must be forwarded, along with the report of the territorial deputation. •

8th. The definitive grant asked for being made, a document signed by the governor shall be given, to serve as a title to the party interested, wherein it must be stated that said grant is made in exact conformity with the provisions of the laws in virtue whereof possession shall be given.

9th. The necessary record shall be kept in a book destined for the purpose, of all the petitions presented, and grants made, with the maps of the lands granted, and the circumstantial report shall be forwarded quarterly to the supreme government.

10th. No *capitulization* shall be admitted for a new town, except the *capitulizator* bind himself to present, as colonists, twelve families at least.

11th. The governor shall designate to the new colonists a proportionate time within which he shall be bound to cultivate or occupy the land on the terms and with the number of persons or families which he may have *capitulized* for, it being understood that if he does not comply, the grant of the land shall remain void; nevertheless, the governor may revalidate it in proportion to the part which the party may have fulfilled.

12th. Every new colonist, after having cultivated or occupied the land agreeable to his *capitulization*, will take care to prove the same before the municipal authority, in order that, the necessary record being made, he may consolidate and secure his right of ownership, so that he may dispose freely thereof.

13th. The reunion of many families into one town shall follow, in its formation, interior government and policy, the rules established by the existing laws for the other towns of the republic, special care being taken that the new ones are built with all possible regularity.

14th. The *minimum* of irrigable land to be given to one person for colonization shall be 200 varas square, the *minimum* of land called *de temporal* shall be 800 varas square, and the *minimum* for breeding cattle (*de obsevadeso*) shall be 1,200 varas square.

15th. The land given for a house-lot shall be 100 varas.

16th. The spaces which may remain between the colonized lands may be distributed among the adjoining proprietors who shall have cultivated theirs with the most application, and have not received the whole extent of land allowed by the law, or to the children of said proprietors, who may ask for them to combine the possessions of their families; but on this subject particular attention must be paid to the morality and industry of the parties.

17th. In those territories where there are missions, the lands occupied by them cannot be colonized at present, nor until it be determined whether they are to be considered as the property of the establishments of the neophytes, catechumens, and Mexican colonists.

APPENDIX No. 13.

Mexican law of the 17th August, 1833.

ARTICLE 1. Government will proceed to secularize the missions of Upper and Lower California.

ART. 2. In each of said missions a parish shall be established under the charge of a parish priest of the secular clergy, with a salary of from $2,000 to $2,500 per annum, at the discretion of the government.

ART. 3. These parish curates shall exact no enrolment for marriages, baptisms, burials, or any other religious functions. With respect to fees of pomp, they may receive such as shall be expressly stipulated in the tariff to be formed for this object, with as little delay as possible, by the reverend bishop of the diocess, and approved by the supreme government.

ART. 4. The churches which have hitherto served the different missions, with the sacred vessels, ornaments, and different appurtenances now belonging to them, shall be assigned to these new parishes, and also such buildings annexed to the said churches as the government may deem necessary for the most decent use of said parish.

ART. 5. The government will order a burial-ground to be erected outside of each parish.

ART. 6. There are $500 per annum assigned to each parish as a donation for religious worship and servants.

ART. 7. Of the buildings belonging to each mission, the most appropriate shall be designated for the habitation of the curate, with the addition of a ground lot which shall not exceed 200 varas square; and the remaining edifices shall be specially adjudicated for a court-house, preparatory schools, public establishments, and workshops.

ART. 8. In order to provide quickly and efficaciously for the spiritual necessities of both Californias, a vicar-generalship shall be established in the capital of Upper California, the jurisdiction of which shall extend to both territories; and the reverend diocesan shall confer upon its incumbent the necessary faculties, with the greatest amplitude possible.

ART. 9. For the donation of this vicar-generalship $3,000 per annum shall be assigned ; but the vicar shall be at all the expense of his office, and not exact under any title or pretext any fee whatever, not even for paper.

ART. 10. If by any motive the vicar-generalship should be filled by the parish curate of the capital of any other parish in those districts, said curate shall receive $1,500 yearly, in addition to the donation of his curacy.

ART. 11. No custom obliging the inhabitants of California to make oblations however pious they may be, although they may be called necessary ones, can be introduced ; and neither time, nor the consent of the citizens themselves, can give them any force or virtue.

ART. 12. The government will efficaciously take care that the reverend diocesan himself concur in carrying into effect the object of this law.

ART. 13. When these new curates are named, the supreme government will gratuitously furnish a passage by sea for them and their families ; and besides that, may give to each one from $400 to $800 for their journey by land, according to the distance, and the family they take with them.

ART. 14. Government will pay the passage of the missionary priests who return to Mexico ; and in order that they may comfortably reach their convents by land, it may give to each one from $200 to $300, and, at its discretion, what may be considered necessary for those to leave the republic who have not sworn to the independence.

ART. 15. The supreme government will provide for the expenses comprehended in this law out of the product of the estates, capitals, and revenues at present recognised as the pious fund of the missions of California.

APPENDIX No. 14.

Provisional regulations for the secularization of the missions of Upper California promulgated by Governor Jose Figueron on the 9th of August 1834.

ARTICLE 1. The governor, agreeable to the spirit of the law of the 17th August, 1833, and to the instructions which he has received from the supreme government, will, with the co-operation of the prelates of the missionary priests, partially convert into pueblos the missions of this territory, beginning in the next month of August, and commencing at first with ten missions and afterwards with the remainder.

ART. 2. The missionary priests will be exonerated from the administration of temporalities, and will only exercise the functions of their ministry in matters appertaining to the spiritual administration, until the formal division of parishes be made, and the supreme government and diocesan provide curates.

ART. 3. The territorial government will reassume the administration of temporalities in the directive part, according to the following bases :

ART. 4. The supreme government will, by the quickest route, be requested to approve of these provisional regulations.

Distribution of property and lands.

ART. 5. To every individual head of a family, and to all those above twenty-one years of age, although they have no family, a lot of land, whether irrigable or otherwise, if not exceeding 400 varas square, nor less than one hundred, shall be given out of the common lands of the missions ; and in community a sufficient quantity of land shall be allotted them for watering their cattle. Common lands shall be assigned to each pueblo, and, when convenient, municipal lands also.

ART. 6. One half of the self-moving property (cattle) shall be distributed among the said individuals, in a proportionable and equitable manner, at the discretion of the governor, taking as a basis the last accounts of all kinds of cattle presented by the missionaries.

ART. 7. One half or less of the chattels, instruments, and seeds on hand, and indispensable for the cultivation of ground, shall be divided proportionably among them.

ART. 8. The remainder of all the lands, landed property, cattle, and all other property on hand, will remain under the care and responsibility of the mayordomos, or other officers whom the governor may name, at the disposal of the supreme federal government.

ART. 9. From the common mass of this property the subsistence of the missionary padres, the pay of the mayordomos, and other servants, the expenses of religious worship, schools, and other objects of policy and ornament, shall be provided.

ART. 10. The governor, having under his charge the direction of temporal affairs, will determine and regulate, according to circumstances, all the expenses necessary to be laid out, as well for the execution of this plan as for the conservation and augmentation of this property.

ART. 11. The missionary minister will select the locality in the mission which may best suit him, for his own habitation and that of his servants and attendants ; and he shall be furnished with the necessary furniture and implements.

ART. 12. The library, sacred dresses, ornaments, and furniture of the church, shall be put in charge of the missionary padre, under the responsibility of the person who acts as subscriber, and whom the priest himself shall elect, and a reasonable salary be given for his trouble.

ART. 13. General inventories shall be made of all property on hand in each mission, with due separation and explanation of the different branches; of the books, debit, and credit, and all kinds of papers; of the amount owing by and to the missions; which document and account shall be forwarded to the supreme government.

Political government of the pueblos.

ART. 14. The political government of the pueblos shall be organized in perfect conformity with the existing laws; the governor will give the necessary instructions to have ayuntamientos established and elections made.

ART. 15. The economical government of the pueblos shall be under the charge of the ayuntamientos; but as far as regards the administration of justice in contentious affairs, they will be subject to the primary judges of the nearest towns constitutionally established.

ART. 16. The emancipated Indians will be obliged to assist at the indispensable common labor which, in the opinion of the governor, may be judged necessary for the cultivation of the vineyards, orchards, and cornfields, which, for the present, remain undisposed of until the resolution of the supreme government.

ART. 17. Said emancipated Indians will render to the missionary priest the necessary personal service for the attention of his person.

Restrictions.

ART. 18. They cannot sell, burden, or alienate, under any pretext, the lands which may be given them; neither can they sell their cattle. Whatever contracts may be made against these orders shall be of no value: the government will reclaim the property as belonging to the nation, and the purchasers shall lose their money.

ART. 19. The lands whose owners shall die without heirs, shall revert to the possession of the nation.

General orders.

ART. 20. The governor will name such commissioners as he may see fit to carry this plan and its incidents into effect.

ART. 21. The governor is authorized to resolve any doubt or matter which may arise relative to the execution of these regulations.

ART. 22. Until these regulations be put in force, the reverend missionary padres are prohibited from slaughtering cattle in large quantities, except the common and ordinary number accustomed to be killed for the subsistence of the neophytes, without allowing any waste.

ART. 23. The debts of the mission shall be paid in preference, out of the common mass of the property, at the time and in the manner that the governor shall determine.

And in order that these regulations be exactly complied with, the following order shall be observed:

As soon as the commissioners receive the order and their appointment they will present themselves in the respective missions and commence the execution of the plan, conforming themselves in all respects to the tenor thereof and to these orders. They will manifest their respective credentials to the priest in charge of the mission and act in concert with him, behaving towards him with the harmony, politeness, and respect which are his due.

Second. The priests will immediately deliver, and the commissioners receive, the cash books, accounts, and other documents relative to property and debts owing by and to the missions. They will afterwards proceed to make out the general inventories (agreeable to article 13 of these regulations) of all property on hand, including the buildings, church, workshops, and other premises, with distinction of what belongs to each department; that is, the utensils, instruments, or ornaments which belong to each. After enumerating all that belongs to the establishment, they will continue with the things belonging to the country; that is, landed property, such as vineyards, orchards, with the number of trees if possible, mills, fences, &c.; after this the cattle and all thereunto belonging. But, as it will be difficult to count said cattle, on account of the number, and want of horses, they shall be examined by two intelligent persons of probity, who will calculate as near as they can the number of each kind; and this shall be put in the inventory. As soon as anything is put into the inventory, it shall be taken out of the charge of the priest and placed at the disposal of the commissiner or mayordomo; but no innovation shall be made in the order of labour and servants until experience may render it necessary, excepting in such common matters as are commonly varied whenever it may be necessary.

Third. The commissioner, in conjunction with the mayordomo, will see that all superfluous expenses cease, and that a well regulated economy be established in everything which merits reform.

Fourth. Before making an inventory of the outside or country property, the commissioners will endeavour to explain to the Indians, with suavity and patience, that the missions are going to be converted into pueblos; that they will only remain subordinate to the priest in matters in relation to the spiritual administration; that the lands and property will be divided out among them, so that each one may work, maintain, and govern himself without dependence on any one; that the houses in which they live will become their own property; and that, in order to this, they must submit to what is commanded in these regulations and orders, which must be explained to them in the best possible manner. They will likewise have immediately divided out to them the lots for cultivation, agreeable to the fifth article of these regulations. The commissioner, padre, and mayordomo, will select the locality where this is to be, choosing the best and nearest to the mission; and they will give to each the quantity of land which they can cultivate, according to their aptness and family, without exceeding the maximum stipulated. They

will likewise see that each person marks his land in the manner most convenient to him.

Fifth. The debts (of the mission) shall be paid out of the common mass
of the property on hand; but neither the commissioner nor the mayordomos
shall do this without an express order from the government, which must be
informed in preference, respecting the matter, in order that it may resolve,
and in view thereof determine, the number of cattle which is to be divided
out amongst the neophytes, in order that it may take effect as soon as possible, according to what is stipulated in article sixth.

Sixth. The implements and tools necessary for cultivating the soil shall be
divided out in the quantity mentioned in article 7, either in community or
individually, as may appear best to the commissioner and the priest. The
grain shall remain undivided, and be served out to the Indians in the usual
rations.

Seventh. What is called the nunnery shall immediately be abolished, and
the girls therein shall be delivered over to their parents, recommending to
them the care which they ought to take of them, and explaining to them
their obligations as parents. The same shall be done with respect to the
boys.

Eighth. The commissioner, after having acquired the necessary information and acquaintance, will, as soon as may be proper, report to this government one or more individuals whom he may consider apt and honest for
mayordomos, according to article 8th, whether they be the same who are
actually employed in the missions or others. He will likewise suggest the
amount of salary which he thinks they ought to receive, according to the
labour of each mission.

Ninth. The rancherias situated at a distance from the missions, and containing more than twenty-five families, may, if they choose, form a separate
pueblo, and the distribution of lands and property shall there take place in
the manner pointed out for the rest. The rancherias which do not contain
twenty-five families, although they remain where they now reside, will form
a district or ward, and belong to the nearest pueblo.

Tenth. The commissioner will make known the number of souls in each
pueblo, in order to designate the number of municipal officers, and to order
the elections to be made, which shall be carried on, as far as possible, in the
manner prescribed by the law of 12th June, 1830.

Eleventh. The commissioners will take all such executive measures as the
state of affairs may demand, and inform the government; and in doubtful
or grave affairs they will consult it.

Twelfth. In all other respects the commissioners, the padres, the mayordomos, and Indians, will act in conformity with these regulations.

APPENDIX No. 15.

In the extraordinary session of the most excellent California deputation held in Monterey on the 3d of November, 1834, the following regulations were made respecting the missions which had been secularized agreeable to the supreme order of the 17th August, 1833, and the provisional regulations of Governor Figueron of the 9th August, 1834:

ARTICLE 1. In accordance with the 2d article of the law of the 17th August, 1833, the amount of $1,500 per annum is assigned to the priests who exercise the functions of parish priest in the curacies of the first class, and $1,000 to those of the second class.

ART. 2. As curacies of the first class shall be reputed San Diego, San Dieguito, San Luis Rey, Las Flores, and ranches annexed; San Gabriel and Los Angeles; Santa Barbara the mission and presidio annexed; San Carlos, united to Monterey; Santa Clara, joined to San Jose de Guadalupe, and San Jose, San Francisco Solano, San Rafael, and the colony. And the following shall be reputed of the second class: San Juan Capistrano, San Fernando, San Buenaventura, San Frues and la Purissima, San Luis Obispo, San Miguel, San Antonio and La Solidad, San Juan Bautista, Santa Cruz, San Francisco de Asis, and the presidio.

ART. 3. Agreeable to the 8th and 9th articles of said law, the reverend father commissary prefect, Father Francisco Garcia Diego, shall establish his residence in the capital, and the governor (gefe politico) shall request the reverend diocesan to confer upon said prelate the faculties appertaining to a foraneous vicar. He shall enjoy the salary of $3,000 assigned to him by said law.

ART. 4. The foraneous vicar and the curates shall be judged, in all other respects, by said law of the 17th August, 1833.

ART. 5. Until the government can furnish permanent parish priests, the respective prelates of the missionaries (religions) shall do so provisionally, with the approbation of the governor.

ART. 6. with respect to article 6th of said law, the $500 per annum shall be paid for public worship and for servants in each parish.

ART. 7. From the common stock of the property of the extinguished mission, the salaries of the foraneous vicar, the curates, and for religious worship, shall be paid either in cash (should there be any) or in produce or other articles at current prices. The governor will give the necessary orders to have this carried into effect.

ART. 8. The 17th article of the provisional regulations of secularization, which imposed upon Indians the duty of giving personal service to the priests, is annulled.

ART. 9. With respect to the 7th article of said law, the governor will order localities to be appointed for the habitation of curates, for the court-house, schools, public establishments, and workshops.

ART. 10. The other matters to which the observations of the reverend padre, Fr. Narciso Daran, extend, as they are of easy resolution, will be settled by the governor, who is authorized to do so by the provisional regulations.

ART. 11. This law, together with the opinion of the committee appointed to examine the above rations of Padre Daran on the provisional regulations, shall be communicated to the prelates for them to make it known to their subordinates.

ART. 2, (addition to.) The curacies which embrace two or more inhabited places will recognise the first one mentioned as the principal, and there the parish priest will reside, and in San Diego and Santa Barbara the missions will be the places of residence.

APPENDIX No. 16.

Mexican decree of the 7th November, 1835.

The President *ad interim* of the Mexican republic to the inhabitants thereof. Know ye that the general Congress has decreed the following :

"Until the curates mentioned in the 2d article of the law of August, 1833, shall take possession, the government will suspend the execution of the other articles of said law, and maintain things in the state they were in before said law was enacted."

APPENDIX No. 17.

Governor Alvarado's regulations respecting missions, January 17, 1839.

The fact of there not having been published in due season a set of regulations, to which the management of the administrators of the missions ought to have been subject from the moment that the so-called secularization was attempted, having caused evils of great transcendency to this Upper California, as these officers, authorized to dispose without limit of the property under their charge, do not know how to act in regard to their dependence upon the political government and that of the most excellent department junta, not being at present in session to consult with respecting the necessary steps to be taken under such circumstances, since the regulations of said secularization neither could nor can take effect on account of the positive evils attending the fulfilment thereof, as experience itself has demonstrated, has induced this government, in consideration of the pitiful state in which said establishments at present are, to dictate these provisional regulations, which shall be observed by said administrators, who will subject themselves to the following articles:

ARTICLE 1. All persons who have acted as administrators of missions will, as soon as possible, present to the government the accounts corresponding to their administration for due inspection, excepting those persons who may have already done so.

ART. 2. The present administrators who, at the delivery of their predecessors, may have received said documents as belonging to the archives, will return them to the parties interested, who, in virtue of the foregoing article, will themselves forward them to government, they being solely responsible.

ART. 3. Said officers will likewise remit those belonging to their adminis. tration up to the end of December of last year, however long they may have been in office.

ART. 4. Said officers will remit, as soon as possible, an exact account of the debts owing by and to the missions which at different times have been contracted.

ART. 5. Under no title or pretext whatever shall they contract debts, whatever may be the object of their inversion, nor make sales of any kind either to foreign merchants or to private persons of the country, without the previous knowledge of government, for whatever may be done to the contrary shall be null and without effect.

ART. 6. The amounts owed by the establishments to merchants and private persons cannot be paid without an express order from government, to which must likewise be sent an account of all such property of each mission as it has been customary to make such payments with.

ART. 7. Without previous permission from said government, no kind of slaughtering of cattle shall take place, except what is necessary for the maintenance of the Indians, and the ordinary consumption of the house ; and even with respect to this, the persons in charge will take care that, as far as possible, no female animals be killed.

ART. 8. The traffic of mules and horses for woolen manufactures, which has hitherto been carried on in the establishments, is hereby absolutely pro. hibited ; and in lieu thereof, the persons in charge will see that the looms are got into operation, so that the wants of Indians may thus be supplied.

ART. 9. At the end of each month, they will send to government a statement of the ingress and egress of all kinds of produce that may have been warehoused or distributed, it being understood that the Indians at all times are to be provided for in the customary manner with such productions ; to which end the administrators are empowered to furnish them with those which are manufactured in the establishment.

ART. 10. The administrators will in this year proceed to construct a building, on account of the establishment, to serve them for habitation, and they may choose the locality which they may deem most convenient, in order that they may vacate the premises which they now occupy.

ART. 11. They shall not permit any individual of those called *de razon* (white people) to settle themselves in the establishments while the Indians remain in community.

ART. 12. They will at an early period present a census of all the inhabitants, distinguishing their classes and ages, in order to form general statistics; and they will likewise mention those who are emancipated and established on the lands of said establishments.

ART. 13. The establishments of San Carlos, San Juan Bautista, and Sonoma are not comprehended in the orders of this regulation. The government will regulate them in a different manner; but the administrators, who at different times may have had the management of their property, will be subject to the orders contained in articles 1 and 2.

ART. 14. They will likewise remit an account of all persons employed under them, designating their monthly pay, according to the orders which may have been given, including that of the reverend padres, with the object of regulating them according to the means of each establishment; and these salaries shall not be paid now nor hereafter with self-moving property.

ART. 15. The administrators will, under the strictest responsibility, fulfil these orders, with the understanding that, in the term of one month, they shall send the information required of them.

ART. 16. Government will continue making regulations respecting everything tending to establish the police to be observed in the establishments, and the manner to be observed in making out the accounts.

ART. 17. For the examination of these accounts, and everything thereto relating, the government will appoint a person with the character of inspector, with a competent salary, to be paid out of the funds of said establishments; and this person will establish his office where the government shall appoint, and have regulations given therefor in due time.

Instructions to be observed by Mr. W. E. Hartwell in the inspection of the establishments of the missions of Upper California.

ARTICLE 1. It being a matter of the greatest importance that the missions be regulated as intended when I published my provisional regulations of the 17th of January last, you will methodize to order which you consider best adapted to obtain the monthly information required, and have the annual accounts of the missions kept ; and you will instruct the administrators how they shall organize them.

Art. 2. You will, with prudence an foresight, take an exact account of the self-moving property, and all other property in hand, calculating as near as possible the number of cattle, if it cannot be exactly got at.

Art. 3. In order to examine and count said cattle, you will take along with you a person of probity and information, who will attend to this business ; and you will offer him the compensation which you may deem just for his services while the inspection may last.

Art. 4. On presenting yourself at each of the establishments you will inform the administrator of the object of your arrival, referring to him or manifesting to him the respective orders, so that there may be no legal pretext for not punctually observing them.

Art. 5. If any of the administrators of the missions should make known to you any palpable wants which in your opinion ought to be immediately remedied, you will take the proper steps to do so, although it may be necessary to dispose of some of the produce on hand in the stores.

Art. 6. Should any of the reverend padres, or other persons employed, make any complaints, to you relating to the management of the administrators, you will with due prudence make the decision which you think most just, and use your utmost endeavors to keep up harmony among all classes.

Art. 7. You will exhort the administrators to use all possible economy in the use of provisions, weekly and annual slaughtering of cattle, and crops of of eatables, in order by all these means to further the progress of establish ments.

Art. 8. You are authorized to regulate the weekly and annual slaughtering which it has been customary to make in the missions, taking into consideration the number of calves marked, (annually,) so that the stock of cattle may not diminish.

Art. 9. You will likewise recommend the administrators to be affable in their treatment of Indians, and that the punishment they inflict be moderate and proportioned to their state of uncivilization ; and that they (the admin istrators) see that they frequent divine service, agreeably to the education which they have received.

Art. 10. If any of the administrators should disobey the orders of this government and not fulfil them duly, in spite of the good treatment you give them, you will inform the government by a courier, that it may determine what is to be done ; and in case that circumstances should require it, you are authorized to suspend such officer for the time that you may consider necessary, and put the mayordomos in charge in the mean time, in order that the labors of your commission be paralyzed ; and you will likewise inform the government, in order that it may determine what may be convenient.

ART. 11. The government expects, from your zeal, that you will be dil-
igent in your commission, collect all kinds of information, and make the
necessary observations for the formation of the police regulations which were
promised in those of the 17th already cited.

APPENDIX No. 18.

Regulations of Governor Alvarado respecting the missions of California,
obligations of the mayordomos, inspectors, &c., dated March 1, 1840.

Experience having proved in an undoubted manner that the missions of
Upper California, for want of regulations organizing the management of the
persons in charge of them, have in a short time suffered reverses and losses of
great moment, the many abuses which were found to exist in the administration of the property of said missions obliged this government to issue the
regulation of 17th January last year; but as it has been found that those
have not been sufficient to root out the evils which are experienced, particularly on account of the high salaries with which the establishments are bur-
dened, and which they cannot support, and being desirous to establish economy and a regular administration until the supreme government determine
what it may deem proper, I publish the present regulations, which are to be
strictly observed:

ARTICLE 1. The situations of administrators in the missions of Upper
California are abolished, and in their stead mayordomos are established.

ART. 2. These mayordomos will receive the following salaries: Those of
San Diego and San Juan Capistrano, $180; those of Santa Barbara, San
Luis Obispo, San Francisco de Asis, and San Rafael, $240; those of San
Buenaventura, la Purissima, San Miguel, and San Antonio, $300; those
of San Fernando and Santa Frues, $400; those of San Luis Rey and
San Gabriel, $420: the one of Santa Clara, $480; and the one of San
José $600.

ART. 3. The former administrators may occupy said situations, provided
that they be proposed in the manner pointed out by these regulations.

ART. 4. The situation of inspector and the office established agreeable to
the 17th article of the regulations of the 17th of January last year, shall
continue, with a salary of $3,000 per annum, and his powers will be here-
after designated.

Obligations of the mayordomos.

ART. 5. To take care of everything relative to the advancement of the
property under their charge, acting in concert with the reverend padres in
the difficult cases which may occur.

ART. 6. To compel the Indians to assist in the labors of the community, chastising them moderately for the faults they may commit.

ART. 7. To see that said Indians observe the best morality in their manners, and oblige them to frequent the church at the days and hours that have been customary, in which matter the reverend padres will intervene in the manner and form determined in the instructions given by the inspector to the administrators.

ART. 8. To remit to the inspector's office a monthly account of the produce they may collect into the storehouses, and an annual one of the crops of grain, liquors, &c., and of the branding of all kinds of cattle.

ART. 9. Said account must be authorized by the reverend padres.

ART. 10. To take care that the reverend padres do not want for their necessary aliment, and furnish them with everything necessary for their personal subsistence, as likewise to vaqueros and servants, which they may request for there domestic service.

ART. 11. To provide the ecclesiastical prelates all the assistance which they may stand in need of when they make their accustomed visits to the missions through which they pass ; and they are obliged under the strictest responsibility to receive them in the manner due to their dignity.

ART. 12. In the missions where the said prelates have fixed residence, they will have the right to call upon the mayordomos at any hour when they may require them, and said mayordomos are required to present themselves to them every day at a certain hour, to know what they may require in their ministerial functions.

ART. 13. To furnish the priests of their respective missions all necessary assistance for religious worship ; but in order to invest any considerable amount in this object, they will solicit the permission to do so from government through the medium of the inspector.

ART. 14. To take care that in the distribution of goods received from the respective office to the Indians, the due proportion be observed amongst the different classes and description of persons, to which end the reverend padres shall be called to be present, and they will approve of the corresponding list of distribution.

ART. 15. To observe all the orders which they receive from the inspector's office emanating from the government, and to pay religiously all drafts addressed to them by said conduct and authorized by said government.

ART. 16. They will every three months send to the respective office a list of the goods and necessaries they may stand in greatest need of, as well for covering the nakedness of the Indians and carrying on the labor of the establishment, as to provide for the necessities of the priests and religious worship, so that comparing these requisitions with the stock on hand, the best possible remedy may be applied. They will take care to furnish the necessary means of transport and provisions to the military or private persons who may be travelling on the public service, and they will provide said necessaries as well for the before mentioned persons, as for the commandants of stations who may ask for assistance for the troops ; and send in a monthly account to the inspector, that he may recover the amount from the commissariat.

ART. 18. They will likewise render assistance to all other private individuals who may pass through the establishments, charging them for food and horses an amount proportioned to their means.

ART. 19. They will take care that the servants under them observe the best conduct and morality, as well as others who pass through or remain in the establishments ; and in urgent cases they are authorized to take such steps as they may consider best adapted to preserve good order.

ART. 20. They may without any charge make use of the provisions produced by the establishments for their own subsistence and that of their families.

ART. 21. They may employ as many servants as they consider necessary for carrying on the work of the community, but their situations must be filled entirely by natives of the establishments themselves.

ART. 22. Said mayordomos are merely allowed to request the appointment of a clerk to carry on their correspondence with the inspector's office.

ART. 23. After the mayordomos have for one year given proofs of their activity, honesty, and good conduct in the fulfilment of their obligations, they shall be entitled (in times of little occupation) to have the government allow the Indians to render them some personal services in their private labors ; but the consent of the Indians themselves must be previously obtained.

ART. 24. The mayordomos cannot make any purchase of goods from merchants, nor make any sale of the produce or manufactures of the establishments, without previous authority from government. (Second.) Dispose of the Indians in any case for the service of private persons without a positive superior order. (Third.) Make any slaughtering of cattle, except what shall be ordered by the inspectors, to take place weekly, extraordinarily, or annually.

Obligations of the Inspectors.

ART. 25. To make all kinds of mercantile contracts with foreign vessels and private persons of the country for the benefit of the missions.

ART. 26. To provide said establishments with the requisite goods and necessaries mentioned in the lists of the mayordomos, taking into consideration the stock of each establishment.

ART. 27. To draw the bills for the payment of the debts contracted by his office and those already due by the establishments.

ART. 28. He shall be the ordinary conductor of communication between the government and the subaltern officers of said missions, as well as between all other persons who may have to apply to government respecting any business relative to said establishments.

ART. 29. He will pay the salaries of the mayordomos and other servants, take care that they fulfil their obligations, and propose to government, in conjunction with the reverend padres, the individuals whom they may consider best qualified to take charge of the missions.

ART. 30. He will determine the number of cattle to be killed weekly, annually, or on extraordinary occasions.

ART. 31. He will form the interior regulations of his office, and propose to government the subalterns which he may judge necessary for the proper management thereof.

General Orders.

ART. 32. All merchants and private persons who have any claims on said missions, will in due time present to the inspector an account of the amounts due to them, with the respective vouchers, in order that the government may determine the best manner of settling them, as the circumstances of said mission may permit.

ART. 33. With respect to the missions of San Carlos, San Bautista, Santa Cruz, La Solidad, and San Francisco Solano, the general government will continue regulating them as circumstances may permit.

ART. 34. Officers and magistrates of all kinds are at liberty to manifest to government the abuses they may observe in those charged with fulfiling these regulations, so that a quick remedy may be applied.

ART. 35. The government, after previously hearing the opinions of the reverend padres, will arrange matters respecting the expenses of religious worship and the subsistence of said padres, either by fixing a stated amount for both objects, or in some other manner which may be more convenient towards attending to their wants.

ART. 36. All prior regulations and orders conflicting with the present are annulled ; and if any doubt occur respecting their observance, the government will be consulted through the established channel.

ART. 37. During the defect or temporary absence of the mayordomos, the reverend padres will in the mean time take charge of the establishments.

APPENDIX No. 19.

Extracts from General Mitcheltorena's proclamation of the 29th of March, 1843, ordering the majority of the missions to be again placed in charge of the priests, in consequence of an arrangement entered into between said governor and the different prelates of said missions.

ARTICLE 1. The government of the department will order the missions of San Diego, San Luis Rey, San Juan Capistrano, San Gabriel, San Fernando, San Buenaventura, Santa Barbara, Santa Cruz, la Purissima, San Antonio, Santa Clara, and San José, to be delivered up to the very reverend padres whom the respective prelate may appoint to each of them, and said missions shall in future continue to be administered by the very reverend padres, as tutors to the Indians, in the same manner as they held them formerly.

ART. 2. As policy makes irrevocable what has hitherto been done, the missions will not claim any lands already granted up to this date; but they will collect the cattle, property, and utensils, which may have been lent by the priests or administrators, settling the time and manner in a friendly way with debtors or holders.

ART. 3. They will likewise take care to gather together the dispersed Indians, excepting, *first*, those legally emancipated by the superior departmental government; *second*, those who, at the date of this decree, are in the service of private persons, it being understood that even both these classes, if they voluntarily wish it and prefer returning to their missions, shall be admitted and protected with the knowledge of their masters and of the reverend missionaries.

ART. 4. The departmental government, in whose possession the missions have been up to this date, in virtue of the very ample faculties with which it is invested, authorizes the reverend padres to provide out of the produce of the missions for the indispensable expenses of the conversion, aliment, clothing, and other temporal necessities of the Indians, and to take from the same funds the moderate part which they may require for their own sustenance, for the economical salary of the mayordomo, and for the maintenance of divine worship, on the condition that they oblige themselves on their honor and conscience to deliver to the public treasury (notice first being given to this government by the reverend padres, and an express order in writing, signed by the undersigned, governor, commandant general, and inspector) for assistance, aliment, clothing for the troops, and wants of the civil officers, the eighth part of the total annual produce of every description; and they will take care to present, at the end of the year, an exact and true account of the number of neophytes' cattle property, and all kinds of fruits, or its representative value, belonging to each mission.

ART. 5. The departmental government, which prides itself in being religious, and at the same time entirely Californian, and, as such, interested in the same manner as each and every one of the inhabitants of both Californias, in progress of the holy Catholic faith and prosperity of the country, offers all its power for the protection of the missions, and, as commandant general, the force of arms to escort, defend, and sustain them, as it will likewise do in respect to individual and particular property and guaranties, securing to the owners thereof the possession and preservation of the lands which they this day hold, and promises not to make any new grants without the information of said authorities of the reverend padres, notorious unoccupancy, want of cultivation, or necessity.

APPENDIX No. 20.

Decree of the Departmental Assembly of 28th May, 1845, respecting the renting of some of the missions, and converting others into pueblos, &c.

ARTICLE 1. The departmental government shall call together the Indians of the missions of San Rafael, Dolores, Solidad, San Miguel, and la Purissima, which are abandoned by them by means of a proclamation, which it will publish, allowing them the term of one month from the day of its publication in their respective missions, or in those nearest to them, for them to re-unite for the purpose of occupying and cultivating them; and they are informed that, if they fail to do so, said missions will be declared to be without owners, (mostrencas) and the assembly and departmental government will dispose of them as may best suit the general good of the department.

2. The Carmelos, San Juan Bautista, San Juan Capistrano, and San Francisco Solano, shall be considered as pueblos, which is the character they at present have; and the government, after separating a sufficient locality for the curate's house, for churches and appurtenances, and a court-house, will proceed to sell the remaning premises at public anction in order to pay their respective debts, and the overplus, should there be any, shall remain for the benefit and preservation of divine worship.

3. The remainder of the missions, as far as San Diego, inclusive, may be rented out at the option of the government, which will establish the manner and form of carrying this into execution, taking care in so doing that the establishments move prosperously onwards. These respective Indians will consequently remain in absolute liberty to occupy themselves as they may see fit, either in the employment of the renter himself, or in the cultivation of their own lands, which the government must necessarily designate for them, or in the employ of any other private person.

4. The principal edifice of the mission of Santa Barbara is excepted from the renting mentioned in the foregoing articles; and the government will arrange, in the most suitable manner, which part thereof shall be destined for the habitation and other conveniences of his grace the bishop and his suite, and which for the reverend missionary padres who at present inhabit said principal edifice. And likewise one-half of the total rent of the other property of the mission shall be invested for the benefit of the church, and

for the maintenance of its minister, and the other half for the benefit of its respective Indians.

5. The product of the rents, mentioned in article 3, shall be divided into three equal parts, and the government shall destine one of them for the maintenance of the reverend padre minister, and the conservation of divine worship, another for the Indians, and the last shall necessarily de dedicated by government towards education and public beneficence as soon as the legal debts of each mission be paid.

6. The third part mentioned in the fifth article as destined for the main-tenance of the priests, and help towards divine worship, shall be placed at the disposal of the reverend prelates, for them to form a general fund, to be distributed equitably in the before-mentioned objects.

7. The authorities or ecclesiastical ministers, should there be any, in the missions referred to in article 1, or those in the nearest missions, or persons who may merit the confidence of government, will be requested by said gov-ernment to see that the proclamation above mentioned be published, and to give information immediately whether the said neophytes have presented themselves or not within the period fixed, in order that, in view of such documents, the necessary measures may be taken.

8. Government will, in the strictest manner, exact the amount owing by various persons to all the missions in general, as already ordered by the most excellent assembly in its decree of the 24th of August, 1844, and dispose of the same for the object mentioned in the last part of the 5th article.

APPENDIX No. 21.

Governor Pico's regulations for the alienation and renting of the missions, dated October 28, 1845.

OF ALIENATION.

ARTICLE 1. There will be sold in this capital, to the highest bidder, the missions of San Rafael, Dolores, Soledad, San Miguel, and la Purissima, which are abandoned by their neophytes.

ART. 2. Of the existing premises of the pueblos of San Luis Obispo, Carmelo, San Juan Bautista, and San Juan Capistrano, and which formerly belonged to the missions, there shall be separated the churches and appur-tenances—one part for the curate's house, another for a court-house and a place for a school, and the remainder of said edifices shall be sold at public auction, where an account of them will be given.

ART. 3. In the same manner will be sold the property on hand belonging to the missions—such as grain, produce, or mercantile goods—giving the preference for the same amount to the renters, and deducting previously that part of said property destined for the food and clothing of the reverend padre minister and the neophytes until the harvest of next year.

ART. 4. The public sale of the missions of San Luis Obispo, Purissima, and San Juan Capistrano shall take place on the first four days of the month of December next, notices being previously posted up in the towns of the department inviting bidders, and three publications being made in the capital at intervals of eight days one from the other before the sale. In the same manner will be sold what belongs to San Rafael, Dolores, San Juan Bautista, Carmelo, and San Miguel, on the 23d and 24th of January next year.

ART. 5. From the date of the publication of these regulations, proposals will be admitted in this capital to be made to government, which will take them into consideration.

ART. 6. The total proceeds of these sales shall be paid into the departmental treasury, to pay therewith the debts of said missions; and should anything remain, it will be placed at the disposal of the respective prelate for the maintenance of religious worship, agreeable to article 2d of the decree of the departmental assembly.

OF RENTING.

ART. 7. The missions of San Fernando, San Buenaventura, Santa Barbara, and Santa Ines shall be rented out to the highest bidder for the term of nine years.

ART. 8. To this end, bidders shall be convoked in all the departments, by fixing advertisements in the towns, in order that by the 8th December next they may appear in this capital either personally or by their legal agents.

ART. 9. Three publications shall be made in this capital at intervals of eight days each before the day appointed for the renting, and proposals will be admitted on the terms expressed in article 5.

ART. 10. There shall be included in said renting all the lands, out-door property, implements of agriculture, vineyards, orchards, workshops, and whatever, according to the inventories made, belongs to the respective missions, with the mere exception of those small portions of land which have always been occupied by some of the Indians of the missions.

ART. 11. The buildings are likewise included, excepting the churches and their appurtenances, the part destined for the curate's house, the court-house, and place for a school. In the mission of Santa Barbara no part of the principal edifice shall be included which is destined for the habitation of his grace the bishop and suit, and the reverend padres who inhabit it; and there shall be merely placed at the disposal of the renter the cellars, moveables, and workshops, which are not applied to the service of said prelates.

ART. 12. As the proceeds of the rent are to be divided into three parts, to be distributed according to article 5 of said decree, the renter may himself deliver to the respective padre, prefect, or to the person whom he may appoint, the third part destined for the maintenance of the minister and the religious worship; and only in the mission of Santa Barbara, the half of said rent-money shall be paid for the same object, in conformity with the 4th article of the decree of the departmental assembly.

ART. 13. The government reserves to itself the right of taking care that the establishments prosper; in virtue of which it will prevent their destruction, ruin, or decline, should it be necessary during the period of renting.

ART. 14. The renting of the missions of San Diego, San Luis Rey, San Gabriel, San Antonio, Santa Clara, and San José shall take place when the difficulties shall be got over which at present exist with respect to the debts of those establishments, and then the government will inform the public, and all shall be done agreeably to these regulations.

ADVANTAGES AND OBLIGATIONS OF THE RENTEES.

ART. 15. The renters shall have the benefit of the usufruct of everything delivered to them on rent according to the regulations.

ART. 16. The obligations of the rentees are: 1st. To pay promptly and quarterly, when due, the amount of the rent. 2d. To deliver back, with improvements, at the expiration of the nine years, whatever they may receive on rent, with the exception of the stills, moveables, and implements of agriculture, which must be returned in a serviceable state. 3d. They shall return at the same time the number of cattle which they receive, and of the same description, and of such an age as not to embarrass the procreation of the following year. 4th. They shall give bonds to the satisfaction of government before they receive the establishments of the rentees—one of which is the payment of the damages which the government may be obliged to find against them, agreeable to article 13.

OF THE INDIANS.

ART. 17. The Indians are free from the neophytism, and may establish themselves in their missions or wherever they choose. They are not obliged to serve the rentees, but they may engage themselves to them on being paid for their labor, and they will be subject to the authorities and to the local police.

ART. 18. The Indians radicated in each mission shall appoint from amongst themselves, on the 1st of January in each year, four overseers, who will watch and take care of the preservation of public order, and be subject to the justice of the peace to be named by government in each mission, agreeable to the decree of 4th July last. If the overseers do not perform the duty well, they shall be replaced by others to be appointed by the justice of the peace, with previous permission from government, and will remain in office for the remainder of the year in which they were appointed.

ART. 19. The overseers shall appoint every month, from amongst the rest of the Indians, a sacristan, a cook, a tortilla maker, a vaquero, and two washer-women, for the service of the padre minister, and no one shall be hindered from remaining in this service as long as he choose. In the mission of Santa Barbara, the overseers will appoint an Indian, to the satisfaction of the priest, to take care daily of the reservoir and water conduits that lead to the principal edifice, and he shall receive a compensation of four dollars per month out of the part of the rent belonging to the Indians.

ART. 20. The Indians who possess portions of land, in which they have their gardens and homes, will apply to this government for the respective title, in order that the ownership thereof may be adjudicated to them, it being understood that they cannot alienate said lands, but they shall be hereditary amongst their relatives, according to the order established by the laws.

ART. 21. From the said Indian population three boys shall be chosen as pages for the priest, and to assist in the ceremonies of the church.

ART. 22. The musicians and singers who may establish themselves the missions, shall be exempted from the burdens mentioned in article 18, but they shall lend their services in the churches at the masses and the functions which may occur.

OF THE JUSTICES OF THE PEACE.

ART. 23. The justices of the peace shall put in execution the orders communicated to them by the nearest superior authority ; they will take care that veneration and respect be paid to matters appertaining to our religion and its ministers, and that the 18th and 20th articles, inclusive, of these regulations, be punctually fulfilled ; they will see that no one be hindered in the free use of his property ; they will quiet the little disturbances that may occur, and, if necessary, enforce and impose light and moderate correction ; and if the occurrences should be of such a nature as to belong to the cognizance of other authorities, they will remit to such authorities the criminals and antecedents.

APPENDIX No. 22.

Decree of the Departmental Assembly of the 3d of April, 1846, respecting missions.

ARTICLE 1. The government is authorized to carry into effect the object of the decree of 28th May last, published by this honorable assembly, respecting missions ; to which end, seeing the impracticability of renting, mentioned in article 3 of said decree, the departmental government will act in the manner which may appear most conducive to obviate the total ruin of the missions of San Gabriel, San Luis Rey, San Diego, and the remainder which are in similar circumstances.

ART. 2. As most of these establishments are owing large amounts, if the property on hand should not be sufficient to satisfy their acknowledged debts, attention shall bo had to what the laws determine respecting bankruptcies, and steps shall be taken accordingly.

ART. 3. Should government, by virtue of this authority, find that, in order to prevent the total ruin which threatens said missions, it will be necessary to sell them to private persons, this shall be done at public auction, the customary notice being previously given.

ART. 4. In case of sale, if, after the debts be paid, any surplus should remain, this shall be divided among the Indians of the premises sold, government taking care to make the most just distribution possible.

ART. 5. In any case, care must be taken to secure a sufficient amount for the maintenance of the padres and the expenses of public worship, the government being at liberty to separate a part of the whole establishments, whether in lands for cultivation, landed or other property, at its discretion, which will be sufficient to secure both objects, the respective priests being previously heard and attended to.

ART. 6. The premises set apart according to the foregoing article shall be delivered as a sale at a perpetual interest of four per cent. ; and the proceeds shall be applied precisely to the objects mentioned in said article 5.

ART. 7. What has been done agreeably to what was ordained in the decree of the honorable assembly of the 28th May, before cited, remains in full force ; and these presents shall in no manner alter the contracts made and measures taken by government, in accordance with said decree of May, 1845 ; nor shall they in future put any obstacle in the way of what may be done in accordance thereto.

ART. 8. The government will remove any obstacles not foreseen in this decree ; and within six months at furthest will notify this honorable assembly of the result of its fulfilment.

APPENDIX. No. 23.

Decree of the Departmental Assembly of the 31st October, 1846, annulling the sale of missions and other acts of Don Pio Pico.

The citizen Jose Maria Flores, captain of cavalry in the Mexican army, governor and commandant general *ad interim* of this department, to its inhabitants :

Know ye the honorable departmental assembly, in an extraordinary session of yesterday, has decreed the following :

The most excellent departmental assembly, taking into consideration the urgent necessity of providing resources for carrying on the war against the invading forces of the United States of North America, and finding that the only way of obtaining them in a sure and prompt manner is to solicit a loan, has, in this day's session, found it expedient to decree the following, viz. :

1. The sales of missions made by Don Pio Pico as governor, as well as all other acts done by him on the same subject beyond his authority, are entirely annulled.

2. His excellency the governor *ad interim* is authorised to solicit a loan of such amount as he may consider necessary for the object indicated, it being stipulated that, in accomplishing this act in the most equitable and just manner, he may mortgage one or more of the missions for the corresponding security.

3. These establishments shall continue with the character of being rented and in possession of the rentees who shall have fulfilled the conditions stipulated in the proclamation upon that subject.

4. The missions which exist under the circumstances of the preceding article shall suffer no alteration until the term of their lease shall expire, even should they be of those mortgaged ; and with respect to the others the government will take care that the regulations formerly given on the subject be duly complied with.

His excellency the governor *ad interim* will be made acquainted herewith for his goverment and further ends.

Hall of sessions of the honorable assembly of California, in the city of Los Angeles, October, 20, 1846.

FRANCIS FIGUERON.

President.

AUGUSTINE OBVERA,

Department Secretary.

I Therefore command it to be published, circulated, and posted up in the usual places, for the knowledge of the public.

Given in the city of Los Angeles, October 31, 1846.

JOSE MARIA FLORES.

NARCISS BOTELLO, *Secretary.*

———

APPENDIX No. 24.

Know all men by these presents, that I, Brigadier General S. W. Kearney, governor of California, by virtue of authority in me vested, considering that, inasmuch as there are various claimants to the missions of San Jose, Santa Clara, Santa Cruz, and San Juan, and the houses, gardens, vineyards, &c., around and near them, do hereby decree that, until the proper judicial tribunals to be established shall decide upon the same, the above named missions and property appertaining thereto shall remain under charge of the Catholic priests, as they were when the United States flag was first raised in this territory, it being understood that this decree is not to affect the rights of any claimant and that the priests are to be responsible for the preservation of said missions and property while under their charge. The alcaldes of the jurisdictions in which the above named missions are situated will, upon the application of the priests, take the proper measures to remove therefrom all persons trespassing or intruding upon them.

Given at Monterey, capital of California, this 22d day of March, 1847.

S. W. KEARNEY,
Brigadier General and Governor of California.

APPENDIX No. 25.

HEADQUARTERS 10TH MILITARY DEPARTMENT,
Monterey, California, January 3, 1848.

REVEREND SIR: I have the honor to acknowledge the receipt of your letter of the 29th December, and its accompanying documents, purporting to give you authority to sell mission lands, bearing date 25th May and 16th June, 1846, signed by Jose Castro, and addressed to yourself.

This document certainly could give you no authority to sell any part of the mission lands after the 7th July, 1846, the day on which the United States flag was hoisted in California; indeed, if it could legally have conferred such authority before, since that date the mission lands can only be disposed of by virtue of authority from the United States government. I am therefore obliged to declare, and do hereby declare, all sales of any part of the mission lands made by your reverence to be illegal, null and void, and that the purchasers of such lands hold no legal title to them whatever by virtue of any sale made by your reverence.

I am, very respectfully, your obedient servant,

R. B. MASON,
Colonel 1st Dragoons, Governor of California.

Rev. Padre JOSE MA. DEL. R. S. DEL. REAL.,
Minister of the mission of Santa Clara.

PROCLAMATION

Of Gen. Kearney to the People of California.

The President of the United States having instructed the undersigned to take charge of the civil government of California, he enters upon his duties with an ardent desire to promote, as far as he is able, the interests of the country and the welfare of its inhabitants.

The undersigned has instructions from the President to respect and protect the religious institutions of California, and to see that the religious rights of the people are in the amplest manner preserved to them, the constitution of the United States allowing every man to worship his Creator in such a manner as his own conscience may dictate him.

The undersigned is also instructed to protect the persons and property of the quiet and peaceable inhabitants of the country against all or any of their enemies, whether from abroad or at home ; and when he now assures the Californians that it will be his duty and his pleasure to comply with those instructions, he calls upon them all to exert themselves in preserving order and tranquillity, in promoting harmony and concord, and in maintaining the authority and efficacy of the laws.

It is the wish and design of the United States to provide for California, with the least possible delay, a free government similar to those in her other Territories ; and the people will soon be called upon to exercise their rights as freemen, in electing their own representatives to make such laws as may be deemed best for their interests and welfare. But until this can be done, the laws now in existence, and not in conflict with the constitution of the United States, will be continued until changed by competent authority ; and those persons who hold office will continue in the same for the present, provided they swear to support that constitution, and to faithfully perform their duty.

The undersigned hereby absolves all the inhabitants of California from any further allegiance to the republic of Mexico, and will consider them as citizens of the United States. Those who remain quiet and peaceable will be respected in their rights, and protected in them. Should any take up arms against or oppose the government of this Territory, or instigate others to do so, they will be considered as enemies, and treated accordingly.

When Mexico forced a war upon the United States, time did not permit the latter to invite the Californians as friends to join her standard, but compelled her to take possession of the country to prevent any European power from seizing upon it ; and in doing so, some excesses and unauthorized acts were no doubt committed by persons employed in the service of the United States, by which a few of the inhabitants have met with a loss of property. Such losses will be duly investigated, and those entitled to remuneration will receive it.

California has for many years suffered greatly from domestic troubles; civil wars have been the poisoned fountains which have sent forth trouble and pestilence over her beautiful land. Now, those fountains are dried up; the star-spangled banner floats over California; and as long as the sun continues to shine upon her, so long will it float there - over the natives of the land, as well as others who have found a home in her bosom; and under it, agriculture must improve and the arts and sciences flourish, as seed in a rich and fertile soil.

The Americans and Californians are now but one people; let us cherish one wish, one hope, and let that be for the peace and quiet of our country. Let us as a band of brothers unite and emulate each other in our exertions to benefit and improve this our beautiful, and which soon must be our happy and prosperous home.

Done at Monterey, capital of California, the first day of March, A. D. 1847, and in the 71st year of the independence of the United States.

S. W. KEARNEY,

Brigadier General U. S. A., and Governor of California.

PROCLAMATION

Of Col. Mason to the people of California.

The undersigned has the pleasure to announce the ratification of a treaty of peace and friendship between the United States of America and the Mexican republic, by which Upper California is ceded to the United States.

The boundary separating this country from Lower California " consists of a straight line drawn from the middle of the Rio Gila, where it unites with the Colorado, to a point on the coast of the Pacific ocean distant one marine league due south of the southernmost point of the port of San Diego."

By the conditions of this treaty, those residing within the limits of this territory thus ceded, who may wish to become citizens of the United States, are absolved from all further allegiance to the Mexican republic, and will at the proper time (to be judged of by the Congress of the United States) be incorporated into the Union, and admitted to the enjoyment of all rights and privileges granted by the constitution to American citizens. Those who wish to retain the character of Mexicans will be at liberty to do so, and also to retain their property in this territory, or dispose of it and remove the proceeds thereof wherever they please; but they must make their election within one year from the 30th day of May last, and those who remain after the expiration of that year without declaring their intentions to retain such character will be considered to have elected to become citizens of the United States. In the mean time they will be protected in the free enjoyment of their liberty and property, and secured in the free exercise of their religion. They, however, are reminded that, as war no longer exists, and as Upper California now belongs to the United States, they owe a strict obedience to the American authorities, and any attempt on their part to disturb the peace and tranquillity of the country will subject them to the severest penalties.

The undersigned has received instructions from Washington to take proper measures for the permanent occupation of the newly acquired territory. The Congress of the United States (to whom alone this power belongs) will soon confer upon the people of this country the constitutional rights of citizens of the United States; and, no doubt, in a few short months we shall have a regularly organized territorial government: indeed, there is every reason to believe that Congress has already passed the act, and that a civil government is now on its way to this country, to replace that which has been organized under the rights of conquest. Such territorial government will establish all local claims and regulations which, within the scope of its legitimate powers, it may deem necessary for the public welfare. In the mean time the present civil officers of the country will continue in the exercise of their functions as heretofore, and when vacancies exist or may occur, they will be filled by regular elections held by the people of the several towns and districts, due notice of such elections being previously given. The existing laws of the country will necessarily continue in force till others are made to supply their place. From this new order of things there will result to California a new destiny. Instead of revolutions and insurrections, there will be internal tranquillity; instead of a fickle and vacillating policy, there will be a firm and stable government, administering justice with impartiality, and punishing crime with the strong arm of power. The arts and sciences will flourish, and the labor of the agriculturist, guided by the lamp of learning, will stimulate the earth to the most bountiful production. Commerce, freed from the absurd restrictions formerly imposed, will be greatly extended; the choked up channels of trade will be opened, and the poisoned fountains of domestic faction forever dried up. Americans and Californians will now be one and the same people, subject to the same laws, and enjoying the same rights and privileges; they should therefore become a band of brothers, emulating each other in their exertions to develope the wealth and resources, and to secure the peace, happiness, and permanent prosperity of their common country.

Done at Monterey, California, this seventh day of August.

R. B. MASON,
Colonel 1st Dragoons, Governor of California.

Communication of H. W. Halleck, by order of Gov. Riley, June 2, 1849.

STATE DEPARTMENT OF THE TERRITORY OF CALIFORNIA,
Monterey, June 2, 1849.

Sir: I am directed by Governor Riley to reply as follows to so much of your communication of the 16th ultimo as relates to the powers and duties of the ayuntamiento or town council of the town of Santa Cruz.

The laws of California, as they existed on the 1st of June, 1848, which are not inconsistent with the provisions of the constitution or the laws of Congress applicable to this country, as a part of the territory of the United States, are still in force, and must continue in force, till changed by competent authority. The powers and duties of town councils in California (except so far as they may be modified by the constitution and laws of Congress) are the same as they were previous to the conquest of the country. As the laws touching this subject may not be of convenient reference, I subjoin a few of their provisions.

The number of members of each town is regulated by the approbation of the governor, but can in no case exceed six alcaldes, twelve regidores or councilmen, and two syndicos.

They are charged with the police and good order of the town, the construction of roads, the laying out, lighting, and paving of streets, the construction and repair of bridges, the removal of nuisances, the establishment of public burying-grounds, the building of jails, the support of town paupers, the granting of town licenses, the examination of weights and measures, and the management and disposition of all municipal property. The council appoints its own secretary, who, as well the members of the council, before entering upon their respective duties, must take the usual oath of office. Each member of the council is bound to assist the alcaldes in executing the laws, and is individually liable for any mal-administration of the municipal funds. A full account of the receipts and expenditures of the council must be kept, and at the end of each year submitted to the prefect of the district, who, after his examination, transmits them to the governor, for file in the government archives. In case of the death of any member of the town council, the vacancy may be supplied by a special election; but if such vacancies occur within three months of the close of the year, it will not be filled until the regular annual election. In case of the suspension of the members of the council, those of the preceding year may be reinstated with their full powers.

Very respectfully, your obedient servant,

H. W. HALLECK,
Brevet Captain, and Secretary of State.

J. G. MAJORS,
Alcalde, Santa Cruz, California.

PROCLAMATION

Of Gen. Riley to the people of the District of San Francisco, June 4, 1849.

Whereas proof has been laid before me that a body of men styling themselves "the legislative assembly of the district of San Francisco" have usurped powers which are vested only in the Congress of the United States, by making laws, creating and filling offices, imposing and collecting taxes, without the authority of law, and in violation of the constitution of the United States and of the late treaty with Mexico: Now, therefore all persons are warned not to countenance said illegal and unauthorised body either by paying taxes or by supporting or abetting their officers.

And whereas due proof has been received that a person assuming the title of sheriff, under the authority of one claiming to be a justice of the peace in the town of San Francisco, did, on the 31st of May last, with an armed party, violently enter the office of the 1st alcalde of the district of San Francisco, and there forcibly take and carry away the public records of said district from the legal custody and keeping of said 1st alcalde: Now, therefore, all good citizens are called upon to assist in restoring said records to their lawful keeping, and in sustaining the legally-constituted authorities of the land.

The office of justice of the peace in California, even where regularly constituted and legally filled, is subordinate to that of alcalde ; and for one holding such office to assume the control of, and authority over, a superior tribunal, argues an utter ignorance of the laws or a wilful desire to violate them, and to disturb the public tranquillity. It is believed, however, that such persons have been led into the commission of this rash act through the impulse of the moment, rather than any wilful and settled design to transgress the law ; and it is hoped that on due reflection they will be convinced of their error, unite with all good citizens in repairing the violence which they have done to the laws. It can hardly be possible that intelligent and thinking men should be so blinded by passion, and so unmindful of their own interests and the security of their property, after the salutary and disinterested advice and warnings which have been given them by the President of the United States, by the Secretaries of State and of War, and by men of high integrity and disinterested motives, as to countenance and support any illegally-constituted body in their open violation of the laws, and assumption of authority which in no possible event could ever belong to them.

The office of alcalde is one established by law, and all officers of the United States have been ordered by the President to recognise and support the legal authority of the person holding such office ; and whatever feelings of prejudice or personal dislike may exist against the individual holding such office, the office itself should be sacred. For any incompetency or mal-administration the law affords abundant means of remedy and punishment—means which the executive will always be found ready and willing to employ to the full extent of the powers in him vested.

Given at Monterey, California, this 4th day of June, in the year of our Lord 1849.

B. RILEY,

Brevet Brig. Gen. U. S. A., and Governor of California.

Official :

H. W. HALLECK,

Brevet Captain and Secretary of State.

PROCLAMATION

Of Gen. Riley, to the people of California, June 3, 1849.

Congress having failed at its recent session to provide a new government for this country to replace that which existed on the annexation of California to the United States, the undersigned would call attention to the means which he deems best calculated to avoid the embarrassments of our present position. The undersigned, in accordance with instructions from the Secretary of War, has assumed the administration of civil affairs in California, not as a military governor, but as the executive of the existing civil government. In the absence of a properly-appointed civil governor, the commanding officer of the department is, by the laws of California, *ex officio* civil governor of the country ; and the instructions from Washington were based on the provisions of these laws. This subject has been misrepresented, or at least misconceived, and currency given to the impression that the government of the country is still *military*. Such is not the fact. The military government ended with the war, and what remains is the *civil* government recognised in the existing laws of California. Although the command of the troops in this department and the administration of civil affairs in California are, by the existing laws of the country and the instructions of the President of the United States, temporarily lodged in the hands of the same individual, they are separate and distinct. No military officer other than the commanding general of the department exercises any civil authority by virtue of his military commission ; and the powers of the commanding general as *ex officio* governor are only such as are defined and recognised in the existing laws. The instructions of the Secretary of War make it the duty of all military officers to recognise the existing civil government, and to aid its officers with the military force under their control. Beyond this, any interference is not only uncalled for, but strictly forbidden. The laws of California not inconsistent with the laws, constitution, and treaties of the United States are still in force, and must continue in force till changed by competent authority. Whatsoever may be thought of the right of the people to temporarily replace the officers of the existing government by others appointed by a provisional territorial legislature, there can be no question that the existing laws of the country must continue in force till replaced by others made and enacted by competent power. That power, by the treaty of peace, as well as from the nature of the case, is vested in Congress. The situation of California in this respect is very different from that of Oregon. The latter was without laws, while the former has a system of laws, which, though somewhat defective and requiring many changes and amendments, must continue in force till repealed by competent legislative power. The situation of California is almost identical with that of Louisiana; and the decisions of the Supreme Court in recognising the validity of the laws which existed in that country previous to its annexation to the United States, where not inconsistent with the constitution and laws of the United States, or repealed by legitimate legislative enactments, furnish us a clear and safe guide in our present situation. It is important that citizens should understand this fact, so as not to endanger their property and involve themselves in useless and expensive litigation by giving countenance to persons claiming authority which is not given them by law, and by putting faith in laws which can never be recognised by legitimate courts.

As Congress has failed to organize a new territorial government, it becomes our imperative duty to take some active means to provide for the existing wants of the country. This, it is thought, may be best accomplished by putting in full vigor the administration of the laws as they now exist, and completing the organization of the civil government by the election and appointment of all officers recognised by law; while at the same time a convention, in which all parts of the Territory are represented, shall meet and frame a State constitution, or a territorial organization, to be submitted to the people for their ratification, and then proposed to Congress for its approval. Considerable time will necessarily elapse before any new government can be legitimately organized and put in operation; in the interim, the existing government, if its organization be completed, will be found sufficient for all our temporary wants.

A brief summary of the organization of the present government may not be uninteresting. It consists, first, of a governor, appointed by the supreme government: in default of such appointment, the office is temporarily vested in the commanding military officer of the department. The powers and duties of the governor are of a limited character, but fully defined and pointed out by the laws. Second, a secretary, whose duties and powers are also properly defined. Third, a territorial or departmental legislature, with limited powers to pass laws of a local character. Fourth, a superior court (tribunal superior) of the Territory, consisting of four judges and a fiscal. Fifth, a prefect and sub-prefects for each district, who are charged with the preservation of public order and the execution of the laws: their duties correspond, in a great measure, with those of district marshals and sheriffs. Sixth, a judge of first instance for each district: this office is, by a custom not inconsistent with the laws, vested in the first alcalde of the district. Seventh, alcaldes, who have concurrent jurisdiction among themselves in the same district, but are subordinate to the highest judicial tribunals. Eighth, local justices of the peace. Ninth, ayuntamientos, or town councils. The powers and functions of all these officers are fully defined in the laws of this country, and are almost identical with those of the corresponding officers in the Atlantic and western States.

In order to complete this organization with the least possible delay, the undersigned, in virtue of power in him vested, does hereby appoint the 1st of August next as the day for holding a special election for delegates to a general convention, and for filling the offices of judges of the superior court, prefects, and sub-prefects, and all vacancies in the offices of first alcalde, (or judge of first instance,) alcaldes, justices of the peace, and town councils. The judges of the superior court, and district prefects are, by law, executive appointments; but, being desirous that the wishes of the people should be fully consulted, the governor will appoint such persons as may receive the plurality of votes in their respective districts, provided they are competent and eligible to the office. Each district will therefore elect a prefect and two sub-prefects, and fill the vacancies in the offices of first alcalde, (or judge of first instance,) and of alcaldes. One judge of the superior court will be elected in the districts of San Diego, Los Angeles, and Santa Barbara ; one in the district of San Luis Obispo and Monterey ; one in the districts of San José and San Francisco ; and one in the districts of Sonoma, Sacramento, and San Joaquin. The salaries of the judges of the superior court, the prefects and judges of first instance, are regulated by the governor, but cannot exceed, for the first, $4,000 per annum ; for the second, $2,500 ; and for the third, $1,500. These salaries will be paid out of the civil fund which has been formed from the proceeds of the customs, provided no instructions to the contrary are received from Washington. The law requires that the judges of the superior court meet within three months after its organization, and form a tariff of fees for the different territorial courts and legal officers, including all alcaldes, justices of the peace. sheriffs, constables, &c. All local alcáldes, justices of the peace, and members of town councils elected at the special election, will continue in office till the 1st of January, 1850, when their places will be supplied by the persons who may be elected at the regular annual election, which takes place in November, at which time the election of members to the territorial assembly will also be held.

The general convention for forming a State constitution or a plan for territorial. government will consist of thirty-seven delegates, who will meet in Monterey on the first day of September next. These delegates will be chosen as follows:

The district of San Diego will elect two delegates ; of Los Angeles, four ; of Santa Barbara, two ; of San Luis Obispo, two ; of Monterey, five ; of San José, five ; of San Francisco, five ; of Sonoma, four ; of Sacramento, four ; of San Joaquin, four. Should any district think itself entitled to a greater number of delegates than above named, it may elect supernumeraries, who, on the organization of the convention, will be admitted or not, at the pleasure of that body.

The places for holding the election will be as follows ; San Diego, San Juan Capistrano, Los Angeles, San Fernando, San Buenaventura, Santa Barbara, Nepoma, San Luis Obispo, Monterey, San Juan Bautista, Santa Cruz, San José de Guadalupe, San Francisco, San Rafael, Bodega, Sonoma, Benicia. (The places for holding elections in the Sacramento and San Joaquin districts will be hereafter designated.) The local alcaldes and members of the ayuntamientos, or town councils will act as judges and inspectors of elections. In case there should be less than three such judges and inspectors present at each of the places designated on the day of election, the people will appoint some competent persons to fill the vacancies. The polls will be open from 10 a. m. to 4 p. m., or until sunset, if the judges deem it necessary.

Every free male citizen of the United States and of Upper California, 21 years of age, and actually resident in the district where the vote is offered, will be entitled to the right of suffrage. All citizens of Lower California who have been forced to come to this Territory on account of having rendered assistance to the American troops during the recent war with Mexico should also be allowed to vote in the districts where they actually reside.

Great care should be taken by the inspectors that votes are received only from *bona fide* citizens, actually resident in the country. These judges and inspectors, previous to entering upon the duties of their office, should take an oath faithfully and truly to perform these duties. The returns should state distinctly the number of votes received for each candidate, be signed by the inspectors, sealed and immediately transmitted to the secretary of state, for file in his office. The following are the limits of the several districts :

1st. The district of San Diego is bounded on the south by Lower California, on the west by the sea, on the north by the parallel of latitude including the mission of San Juan Capistrano, and on the east by the Colorado river.

2d. The district of Los Angeles is bounded on the south by the district of San Diego, on the west by the sea, on the north by the Santa Clara river, and a parallel of latitude running from the head waters of that river to the Colorado.

3d. The district of Santa Barbara, is bounded on the south by the district of Los Angeles, on the west by the sea, on the north by Santa Inez river and a parallel of latitude extending from the head waters of that river to the summit of the coast range of mountains.

4th. The district of San Luis Obispo is bounded on the south by the district of Santa Barbara, on the west by the sea, on the north by a parallel of latitude including San Miguel, and on the east by the coast range of mountains.

5th. The district of Monterey is bounded on the south by the district of San Luis, and on the north and east by a line running east from New Year's Point to the summit of the Santa Clara range of mountains, thence along the summit of that range to the Arroya de los Leagas and a parallel of latitude extending to the summit of the coast range, and along that range to the district of San Luis.

6th. The district of San José is bounded on the north by the straits of Karquinez, the bay of San Francisco, the arroya of San Francisquito, and a parallel of latitude to the summit of Santa Clara mountains, on the west and south by the Santa Clara mountains and the district of Monterey, and on the east by the coast range.

7th. The district of San Francisco is bounded on the west by the sea, on the south by the districts of San José and Monterey, and on the east and north by the the bay of San Francisco, including the islands of that bay.

8th. The district of Sonoma includes all the country bounded by the sea, the bays of San Francisco and Suisun, the Sacramento river, and Oregon.

9th. The district of Sacramento is bounded on the north and west by the Sacramento river, on the east by the Sierra Nevada, and on the south by the Cosumnes river.

10th. The district of San Joaquin includes all the country south of the Sacramento district, and lying between the coast range and the Sierra Nevada.

The method here indicated to attain what is desired by all, viz: a more perfect political organization, is deemed the most direct and safe that can be adopted, and one fully authorized by law. It is the course advised by the President, and the Secretaries of State and of War of the United States, and is calculated to avoid the innumerable evils which must necessarily result from any attempt at illegal local legislation. It is therefore hoped that it will meet the approbation of the people of California, and that all good citizens will unite in carrying it into execution.

Given at Monterey, Cailfornia, this third day of June, in the year of our Lord eighteen hundred and forty-nine.

B. RILEY,
Brevet Brigadier General U. S. A,.
and Governor of California.

Official :

H. W. HALLECK,
Brevet Captain, and Secretary of State.

TREATY

BETWEEN SPAIN AND MEXICO.

Treaty of Amity and Commerce between Spain and the Mexican Republic. Dated at Madrid, November 28, 1836. Ratified by the President of the Mexican Republic May 3, 1837, and by Spain November 16, 1837; and ordered to be published by a decree of the Mexican Congress of Feb. 28, 1838.

Decree of the Mexican Congress of February 28, 1838.

TREATY OF AMITY AND COMMERCE WITH HER MAJESTY, THE QUEEN OF SPAIN.

THE President of the Mexican Republic to all to whom these presents shall come, Know Ye:—That having concluded and established at Madrid on the twenty-eighth day of December, one thousand eight hundred and thirty-six, a treaty of peace and amity between this republic and her Catholic majesty the queen regent of Spain through the medium of the plenipotentiaries of both governments for that purpose duly and respectively authorized, the tenor of what is as follows:—

In the name of the most holy Trinity—The Mexican republic on the one part, and on the other her Catholic majesty Doña Isabel 2d—by the grace of God and by the Constitution of the Spanish monarchy, queen of Spain and during her minority, the queen dowager Doña Maria Christina de Borbon her august mother, regent of the kingdom; earnestly desiring to bring to an end the state of non-intercourse and misunderstanding which has existed between the two governments and between the citizens and subjects of the respective countries and to cause to be forever forgotten the past differences and dissensions, by which for so long a time the relations of friendship and good understanding have been most unhappily interrupted between the people of both countries, although by their mutual bond of union, their identity of origin and reciprocal interests called upon to regard each other as brothers: and to establish and permanently to secure said relations for their mutual benefit by means of a definite treaty of peace and sincere friendship—and to this end they have nominated and appointed as their plenipotentiaries as follows—His Excellency the President of the Mexican Republic, His Excellency Jose D. Miguel Santa Maria, minister plenipotentiary of the same at the Court of London and Envoy extraordinary near that of Her Catholic majesty. And Her Catholic majesty, and in her

62

royal name the queen regent has appointed Sr. D. Jose Maria Calatrava, her Secretary of State and President of the council of ministers: who, after having interchanged their credentials, found to be in due form, have agreed upon the following articles.

ART. 1. Her majesty the queen regent of Spain in the name of her august daughter Doña Isabel II. recognises the republic of Mexico as a free, sovereign, and independent nation, composed of those states and countries specified in her Constitutional law, that is to say, the territory comprehended in the viceroyalty heretofore called New Spain, that styled the Captain-gen-eralship of Yucatan, that in the Commandicies so called, of the internal provinces of the East and West and of Lower and Upper California, and the lands annexed and the Islands adjacent, in both Seas which are actually in possession of said republic. And Her majesty renounces as well for herself as for her heirs and successors all claims to the government, proprietorship and territorial right in the said states and countries.

ART. 2. There shall be total oblivion as to all that has passed, and a general and complete amnesty in relation to all Mexicans and Spaniards without any exception, who may have been expelled, absent, banished or concealed, or who may chance to have been made prisoners, or confined without the knowledge of their respective governments, whatsoever part they may have taken during the wars and disputations happily terminated by the present treaty, both during the whole period of their continuance and until the ratification of this treaty. And the stipulation for this amnesty; and the granting of the same arise from the high interposition of her Catholic Majesty in proof of the desire which animates her that, united upon principles of justice and kindness, the strictest friendship, peace and union now, henceforth and forever, may be preserved between her subjects and the citizens of the Republic of Mexico.

ART. 3. The Republic of Mexico and her Catholic Majesty agree that the respective citizens and subjects of both nations shall enjoy their rights freely, and promptly to demand and obtain justice and ample satisfaction of debts contracted between them in good faith; and in like manner that there shall not be interposed on the part of the public authorities any legal impediment to the maintenance of their rights arising from marriage, inheritance by will or *ab intestato*, succession, or by any other of the modes of acquiring property recognised by the laws of the country where reclamation is sought to be obtained.

ART. 4. The high contracting parties also agree to proceed with all possible despatch to arrange and conclude a treaty of commerce and navigation, founded upon principles of reciprocal advantage to the respective countries.

ART. 5. The citizens of the Mexican Republic and the subjects of Her Catholic Majesty shall be treated, in relation to the imposition of duties on the products of the earth, goods, and merchandise which they shall import or export from the territories of the high contracting parties, and under their respective flags, as those of the most favoured nation, except in those cases in which, in order to obtain reciprocal advantages, they may agree upon such mutual concessions as may result in the advantage of both countries.

ART. 6. Merchants and other citizens of the Republic of Mexico, or subjects of Her Catholic Majesty who may be established in trading or passing through the whole or any part of the one or the other country, shall enjoy the most perfect security in their persons and property, and shall be exempt from all compulsory service in the army or navy, or in the national militia, and from every charge, contribution or impost, not payable by the citizens and subjects of the country where they reside; and as well in respect to the distribution of contributions, imposts and other general charges, as the protection and privileges in the prosecution of their business; and also in all that relates to the administration of justice, they shall be treated in the same manner as the native citizens of the respective nations, subject always to the laws, regulations, and usages of the country in which they may reside.

ART. 7. In consideration that the republic of Mexico, by a law of the general Congress of the twenty-eighth of June, 1824, has freely and spontaneously recognized as her own debt and that of the Nation, the debt contracted and charged upon the national treasury by the Spanish government of the metropolis, and its authorities while the present Mexican nation was under their dominion and until their authority ceased in the year 1821; and that in addition to this there is no confiscation of the property of Spanish subjects:—the republic of Mexico and Her Catholic Majesty, for herself and her heirs and successors in conformity therewith shall, mutually desist from any reclamation or claim which may be agitated in relation to the points aforesaid and hereby declare that the two high contracting parties shall be freed and discharged henceforth and forever from all responsibility in this particular.

ART. 8. The present treaty of peace and friendship shall be ratified by the two governments and the ratifications exchanged at the Court of Madrid, at the expiration of nine months from this day or sooner if it be possible to acccomplish the same with the greatest diligence.

In testimony of which, we the undersigned plenipotentiaries have signed and sealed the same with our respective seals.

Executed in triplicate at Madrid on the 28th day of the month of November, in the year of our Lord one thousand eight hundred and thirty-six.

[L. S.]   (Signed) MIGUEL SANTA MARIA,
[L. S.]   (Signed) JOSE MARIA CALATRAVA.

Wherefore after having seen and examined said treaty with the previous approbation of the National Congress and in virtue of the authority conferred on me by the Constitutional laws, I have ratified, accepted and confirmed it, and by these presents do ratify, accept and confirm the same, promising faithfully to observe and to cause to be observed everything therein contained and not to permit its violation in any manner whatever.

In testimony of which I have signed the same with my hand, commanded it to be sealed by the great seal of the nation, and to be countersigned by the ministers of foreign affairs.

Dated at the National palace of Mexico, on the 3d of May, one thousand eight hundred and thirty-seven, and the fourteenth of the Independence—*Auastasio Bustamente—Louis G. Cueras.* And the aforesaid treaty having been in like manner approved and ratified by her majesty, the queen Regent of Spain, for herself, and in the name of her august daughter Doña Isabel II, at Madrid, on the 14th of November, one thousand eight hundred and thirty-seven, after having enlarged the term fixed for the exchange of ratifications. I command that the same be printed, published and circulated and be duly obeyed.

---·•◦·---

TREATY

BETWEEN

THE UNITED STATES AND MEXICO.

Treaty of peace, friendship, limits and settlement, between the United States of America and the Mexican republic. Dated at Guadalupe Hidalgo, February 2, 1848 ; ratified by the President of the United States, March 16, 1848 ; exchanged at Queretaro, May 30, 1848 ; proclaimed by the President of the United States, July 4, 1848.

In the name of Almighty God :—

The United States of America and the United Mexican States, animated by a sincere desire to put an end to the calamities of the war which unhappily exists between the two republics, and to establish upon a solid basis relations of peace and friendship, which shall confer reciprocal benefits upon the citizens of both, and assure the concord, harmony and mutual confidence wherein the two people should live, as good neighbors, have for that purpose appointed their respective plenipotentiaries, that is to say, the President of the United States has appointed Nicholas P. Trist, a citizen of the United States, and the President of the Mexican republic has appointed Don Luis

Gonzaga Cuevas, Don Bernardo Couto and Don Miguel Atristain, citizens of the said republic, who, after a reciprocal communication of their respective full powers, have, under the protection of Almighty God, the author of peace, arranged, agreed upon, and signed the following

Treaty of peace, friendship, limits and settlement, between the United States of America and the Mexican republic.

ARTICLE I.

There shall be firm and universal peace between the United States of America and the Mexican republic, and between their respective countries, territories, cities, towns and people, without exception of places or persons.

ARTICLE II.

Immediately upon the signature of this treaty, a convention shall be entered into between a commissioner or commissioners appointed by the general-in-chief of the forces of the United States, and such as may be appointed by the Mexican government, to the end that a provisional suspension of hostilities shall take place, and that, in the places occupied by the said forces, constitutional order may be re-established, as regards the political, administrative and judicial branches, so far as this shall be permitted by the circumstances of military occupation.

ARTICLE III.

Immediately upon the ratification of the present treaty by the government of the United States, orders shall be transmitted to the commanders of their land and naval forces, requiring the latter (provided this treaty shall then have been ratified by the government of the Mexican republic, and the ratifications exchanged) immediately to desist from blockading any Mexican ports; and requiring the former (under the same condition) to commence, at the earliest moment practicable, withdrawing all troops of the United States then in the interior of the Mexican republic, to the points that shall be selected by common agreement, at a distance from the seaports not exceeding thirty leagues; and such evacuation of the interior of the republic shall be completed with the least possible delay; the Mexican government hereby binding itself to afford every facility in its power for rendering the same convenient to the troops, on their march and in their new positions, and for promoting a good understanding between them and the inhabitants. In like manner, orders shall be despatched to the persons in charge of the custom houses at all ports occupied by the forces of the United States, requiring them (under the same condition) immediately to deliver possession of the same to the persons authorized by the Mexican government to receive it, together with all bonds and evidences of debts for duties on importations and on exportations, not yet fallen due. Moreover, a faithful and exact account shall be made out, showing the entire amount of all duties on imports and on exports collected at such custom houses, or elsewhere in Mexico, by authority of the United States, from and after the day of the ratification of this treaty by the government of the Mexican republic ; and also an account of the cost of collection ; and such entire amount, deducting only the cost of collection, shall be delivered to the Mexican government, at the city of Mexico, within three months after the exchange of the ratifications.

The evacuation of the capital of the Mexican republic by the troops of the United States, in virtue of the above stipulations, shall be completed in one month after the orders there stipulated for shall have been received by the commander of said troops, or sooner, if possible.

ARTICLE IV.

Immediately after the exchange of ratifications of the present treaty, all castles, forts, territories, places, and possessions, which have been taken or occupied by the forces of the United States during the present war, within the limits of the Mexican republic, as about to be established by the following article, shall be definitively restored to the said republic, together with all the artillery, arms, apparatus of war, munitions, and other public property, which were in the said castles and forts when captured, and which shall remain rhere at the time when this treaty shall be duly ratified by the government of the Mexican republic. To this end, immediately upon the signature of this treaty, orders shall be despatched to the American officers commanding such castles and forts, securing against the removal or destruction of any such artillery, arms, apparatus of war, munitions, or other public property. The city of Mexico, within the inner line of entrenchments surrounding the said city, is comprehended in the above stipulations, as regards the restoration of artillery, apparatus of war, &c.

The final evacuation of the territory of the Mexican republic, by the forces of the United States, shall be completed in three months from the said exchange of ratifications, or sooner, if possible ; the Mexican government hereby engaging, as in the foregoing article, to use all means in its power for facilitating such evacuation, and rendering it convenient to the troops, and for promoting a good understanding between them and the inhabitants.

If, however, the ratification of this treaty by both parties should not take place in time to allow the embarkation of the troops of the United States to be completed before the commencement of the sickly season, at the Mexican ports on the Gulf of Mexico, in such case a friendly arrangement shall be entered into between the General-in-Chief of the said troops and the Mexican Government, whereby healthy and otherwise suitable places, at a distance from the ports not exceeding thirty leagues, shall be designated for the residence of such troops as may not yet have embarked, until the return of the healthy season.   And the space of time here referred to as comprehending the sickly season, shall be understood to extend from the first day of May to the first day of November.

All prisoners of war taken on either side, on land or on sea, shall be restored as soon as practicable after the exchange of ratifications of this treaty.   It is also agreed, that if any Mexicans should now be held as captives by any savage tribe within the limits of the United States, as about to be established by the following article, the Government of the United States will exact the release of such captives, and cause them to be restored to their country.

ARTICLE V.

The boundary lines between the two republics shall commence in the Gulf of Mexico, three leagues from land, opposite the mouth of the Rio Grande, otherwise called Rio Bravo del Norte, or opposite the mouth of its deepest branch, if it should have more than one branch emptying directly into the sea ; from thence up the middle of that river, following the deepest channel, where it has more than one, to the point where it strikes the southern boundary of New Mexico ; thence westwardly, along the whole southern boundary of New Mexico (which runs north of the town called *Paso*) to its western termination ; thence northward, along the western line of New Mexico, until it intersects the first branch of the river Gila ; (or if it should not intersect any branch of that river, then to the point on the said line nearest to such branch, and thence in a direct line to the same ;) thence down the middle of the said branch and of the said river, until it empties into the Rio Colorado ; thence across the Rio Colorado, following the division line between Upper and Lower California, to the Pacific ocean.

The southern and western limits of New Mexico, mentioned in this article, are those laid down in the map, entitled " *Map of the United Mexican States, as organized and defined by various acts of the Congress of said republic, and constructed according to the best authorities.   Revised edition Published at New York, in 1847, by J. Disturnell.*"   Of which map a copy is added to this treaty, bearing the signatures and seals of the undersigned plenipotentiaries.   And, in order to preclude all difficulties in tracing upon the ground the limit separating Upper from Lower California, it is agreed that the said limit shall consist of a straight line drawn from the middle of the Rio Gila, where it unites with the Colorado, to a point on the coast of the Pacific ocean distant one marine league due south of the southermost point of the port of San Diego, according to the plan of said port made in the year 1782 by Don Juan Pantoja, second sailing master of the Spanish fleet, and published at Madrid in the year 1802, in the Atlas to the voyage of the schooners *Sutil* and *Mexicana*, of which plan a copy is here-unto added, signed and sealed by the respective plenipotentiaries.

In order to designate the boundary line with due precision, upon authoritative maps, and to establish upon the ground landmarks which shall show the limits of both republics, as described in the present article, the two Governments shall each appoint a commissioner and a surveyor, who, before the expiration of one year from the date of the exchange of ratifications of this treaty, shall meet at the port of San Diego, and proceed to run and mark the said boundary in its whole course to the mouth of the Rio Bravo del Norte. They shall keep journals and make out plans of their operations; and the result agreed upon by them shall be deemed a part of this treaty, and shall have the same force as if it were inserted therein. The two Governments will amicably agree regarding what may be necessary to these persons, and also as to their respective escorts, should such be necessary.

The boundary line established by this article shall be religiously respected by each of the two republics, and no change shall ever be made therein, except by the express and free consent of both nations, lawfully given by the general government of each, in conformity with its own constitution.

Article VI.

The vessels and citizens of the United States shall, in all time, have a free and uninterrupted passage by the gulf of California, and by the river Colorado below its confluence with the Gila, to and from their possessions situated north of the boundary line defined in the preceding article; it being understood that this passage is to be by navigating the gulf of California and the river Colorado, and not by land, without the express consent of the Mexican government.

If, by the examinations which may be made, it should be ascertained to be practicable and advantageous to construct a road, canal, or railway, which should in whole or in part run upon the river Gila, or upon its right or its left bank, within the space of one marine league from either margin of the river, the governments of both republics will form an agreement regarding its construction, in order that it may serve equally for the use and advantage of both countries.

Article VII.

The river Gila, and the part of the Rio Bravo del Norte lying below the southern boundary of New Mexico, being agreeably to the fifth article, divided in the middle between the two republics, the navigation of the Gila and of the Bravo below said boundary shall be free and common to the vessels and citizens of both countries; and neither shall, without the consent of the other, construct any work that may impede or interrupt, in whole or in part, the exercise of this right; not even for the purpose of favouring new methods of navigation. Nor shall any tax or contribution, under any denomination or title, be levied upon vessels, or persons navigating the same, or upon merchandise or effects transported thereon, except in the case of landing upon one of their shores. If, for the purpose of making the said rivers navigable, or for maintaining them in such state, it should be necessary or advantageous to establish any tax or contribution, this shall not be done without the consent of both governments.

The stipulations contained in the present article shall not impair the territorial rights of either republic within its established limits.

ARTICLE VIII.

Mexicans now established in territories previously belonging to Mexico, and which remain for the future within the limits of the United States, as defined by the present treaty, shall be free to continue where they now reside, or to remove at any time to the Mexican republic, retaining the property which they possess in the said territories, or disposing thereof, and removing the proceeds wherever they please, without their being subjected, on this account, to any contribution, tax, or charge whatever.

Those who shall prefer to remain in the said territories, may either retain the title and rights of Mexican citizens, or acquire those of citizens of the United States. But they shall be under the obligation to make their election within one year from the date of the exchange of ratifications of this treaty ; and those who shall remain in the said territories after the expiration of that year, without having declared their intention to retain the character of Mexicans, shall be considered to have elected to become citizens of the United States.

In the said territories, property of every kind, now belonging to Mexicans not established there, shall be inviolably respected. The present owners, the heirs of these, and all Mexicans who may hereafter acquire said property by contract, shall enjoy with respect to it guaranties equally ample as if the same belonged to citizens of the United States.

ARTICLE IX.

The Mexicans, who, in the territories aforesaid, shall not preserve the character of citizens of the Mexican republic, conformably with what is stipulated in the preceding article, shall be incorporated into the union of the United States and be admitted at the proper time (to be judged of by the Congress of the United States) to the enjoyment of all the rights of citizens of the United States, according to the principles of the Constitution ; and in the mean time shall be maintained and protected in the free enjoyment of their liberty and property, and secured in the free exercise of their religion without restriction.

ARTICLE X.

[Stricken out.]

ARTICLE XI.

Considering that a great part of the territories, which, by the present treaty, are to be comprehended for the future within the limits of the United States, is now occupied by savage tribes, who will hereafter be under the exclusive control of the government of the United States, and whose incursions within the territory of Mexico would be prejudicial in the extreme, it is solemnly agreed that all such incursions shall be forcibly restrained by the Government of the United States whensoever this may be necessary; and that when they cannot be prevented they shall be punished by the said Government, and satisfaction for the same shall be exacted—all in the same way, and with equal diligence and energy, as if the same incursions were meditated or committed within its own territory, against its own citizens.

It shall not be lawful, under any pretext whatever, for any inhabitant of the United States to purchase or acquire any Mexican, or any foreigner residing in Mexico, who may have been captured by Indians inhabiting the territory of either of the two republics, nor to purchase or acquire horses, mules, cattle, or property of any kind, stolen within Mexican territory by such Indians.

And in the event of any person or persons, captured within Mexican territory by Indians, being carried into the territory of the United States, the government of the latter engages and binds itself, in the most solemn manner, so soon as it shall know of such captives being within its territory, and shall be able so to do, through the faithful exercise of its influence and power, to rescue them and return them to their country, or deliver them to the agent or representative of the Mexican government. The Mexican authorities will, as far as practicable, give to the government of the United States notice of such captures; and its agent shall pay the expences incurred in the maintenance and transmission of the rescued captives; who, in the mean time, shall be treated with the utmost hospitality by the American authorities at the place where they may be. But if the government of the United States, before receiving such notice from Mexico, should obtain intelligence, through any other channel, of the existence of Mexican captives within its territory, it will proceed forthwith to effect their release and delivery to the Mexican agent as above stipulated.

For the purpose of giving to these stipulations the fullest possible efficacy, thereby affording the security and redress demanded by their true spirit and intent, the government of the United States will now and hereafter pass without unnecessary delay, and always vigilantly enforce, such laws as the nature of the subject may require. And finally, the sacredness of this obligation shall never be lost sight of by the said government when providing for the removal of the Indians from any portion of the said territories, or for its being settled by citizens of the United States; but, on the contrary, special care shall be taken not to place its Indian occupants under the necessity of seeking new homes, by committing those invasions which the United States have solemnly obliged themselves to restrain.

ARTICLE XII.

In consideration of the extension acquired by the boundaries of the United Sates, as defined in the fifth article of the present treaty, the government of the United States engages to pay to that of the Mexican republic the sum of fifteen millions of dollars.

Immediately after this treaty shall have been duly ratified by the government of the Mexican republic, the sum of three millions of dollars shall be paid to the said government by that of the United States, at the city of Mexico, in the gold or silver coin of Mexico. The remaining twelve millions of dollars shall be paid at the same place, and in the same coin, in annual instalments of three millions of dollars each, together with interest on the same at the rate of six per centum per annum. This interest shall begin to run upon the whole sum of twelve millions from the day of the ratification of the present treaty by the Mexican government, and the first of the instalments shall be paid at the expiration of one year from the same day. Together with each annual instalment, as it falls due, the whole interest accruing on such instalment from the beginning shall also be paid.

ARTICLE XIII.

The United States engage, moreover, to assume and pay to the claimants all the amounts now due them, and those hereafter to become due, by reason of the claims already liquidated and decided against the Mexican republic, under the conventions between the two republics severally concluded on the eleventh day of April, eighteen hundred and thirty-nine, and on the thirtieth day of January, eighteen hundred and forty-three; so that the Mexican republic shall be absolutely exempt, for the future, from all expense whatever on account of the said claims.

ARTICLE XIV.

The United States do furthermore discharge the Mexican republic from all claims of citizens of the United States, not heretofore decided against the Mexican government, which may have arisen previously to the date of the signature of this treaty; which discharge shall be final and perpetual, whether the said claims be rejected or be allowed by the board of commissioners provided for in the following article, and whatever shall be the total amount of those allowed.

ARTICLE XV.

The United States, exonerating Mexico from all demands on account of the claims of their citizens mentioned in the preceding article, and considering them entirely and forever cancelled, whatever their amount may be, undertake to make satisfaction for the same, to an amount not exceeding three and one quarter millions of dollars. To ascertain the validity and amount of those claims, a board of commissioners shall be established by the government of the United States, whose awards shall be final and conclusive: provided, that, in deciding upon the validity of each claim, the board shall be guided and governed by the principles and rules of decision prescribed by the first and fifth articles of the unratified convention, concluded at the city of Mexico on the twentieth day of November, one thousand eight hundred and forty-three; and in no case shall an award be made in favor of any claim not embraced by those principles and rules.

If, in the opinion of the said board of commissioners, or of the claimants, any books, records, or documents in the possession or power of the government of the Mexican republic, shall be deemed necessary to the just decision of any claim, the commissioners, or the claimants through them, shall within such period as Congress may designate, make an application in writing for the same, addressed to the Mexican minister for foreign affairs, to be transmitted by the Secretary of State of the United States; and the Mexican government engages, at the earliest possible moment after the receipt of such demand, to cause any of the books, records, or documents, so specified, which shall be in their possession or power, (or authenticated copies or extracts of the same,) to be transmitted to the said Secretary of State, who shall immediately deliver them over to the said board of commissioners: *Provided*, That no such application shall be made by, or at the instance of any claimant, until the facts, which it is expected to prove by such books, records, or documents, shall have been stated under oath or affirmation.

ARTICLE XVI.

Each of the contracting parties reserves to itself the entire right to fortify whatever point within its territory it may judge proper so to fortify, for its security.

ARTICLE. XVII.

The treaty of amity, commerce, and navigation, concluded at the city of Mexico on the fifth of April, A. D. 1831, between the United States of America and the United Mexican States, except the additional article, and except so far as the stipulations of the said treaty may be incompatible with any stipulation contained in the present treaty, is hereby revived for the period of eight years from the day of the exchange of ratifications of this treaty, with the same force and virtue as if incorporated therein; it being understood that each of the contracting parties reserves to itself the right, at any time after the said period of eight years shall have expired, to terminate the same by giving one year's notice of such intention to the other party.

Article XVIII.

All supplies whatever for troops of the United States in Mexico, arriving at ports in the occupation of such troops previous to the final evacuation thereof, although subsequently to the restoration of the custom-houses at such ports, shall be entirely exempt from duties and charges of any kind ; the government of the United States hereby engaging and pledging its faith to establish, and vigilantly to enforce, all possible guards for securing the revenue of Mexico, by preventing the importation, under cover of this stipulation, of any articles other than such, both in kind and in quantity, as shall really be wanted for the use and consumption of the forces of the United States during the time they may remain in Mexico. To this end, it shall be the duty of all officers and agents of the United States to denounce to the Mexican authorities at the respective ports any attempt at a fraudulent abuse of this stipulation which they may know of or may have reason to suspect, and to give to such authorities all the aid in their power with regard thereto ; and every such attempt, when duly proved and established by sentence of a competent tribunal shall be punished by the confiscation of the property so attempted to be fraudulently introduced.

Article. XIX.

With respect to all merchandise, effects, and property whatsoever, imported into ports of Mexico whilst in the occupation of the forces of the United States, whether by citizens of either republic, or by citizens or subjects of any neutral nation, the following rules shall be observed :

1. All such merchandise, effects, and property, if imported previously to the restoration of the custom-houses to the Mexican authorities, as stipulated for in the third article of this treaty, shall be exempt from confiscation, although importation of the same be prohibited by the Mexican tariff.

2. The same perfect exemption shall be enjoyed by all such merchandise, effects, and property, imported subsequently to the restoration of the custom-houses, and previously to the sixty days fixed in the following article for the coming into force of the Mexican tariff at such ports respectively ; the said merchandise, effects, and property being, however, at the time of their importation, subject to the payment of duties, as provided for in the said following article.

3. All merchandise, effects, and property described in the two rules foregoing shall, during their continuance at the place of importation, and upon their leaving such place for the interior, be exempt from all duty, tax or

impost of every kind, under whatsoever title or denomination. Nor shall they be there subjected to any charge whatsoever upon the sale thereof.

4. All merchandise, effects, and property, described in the first and second rules, which shall have been removed to any place in the interior whilst such place was in the occupation of the forces of the United States, shall, during their continuance therein, be exempt from all tax upon the sale or consumption thereof, and from every kind of impost or contribution, under whatsoever title or denomination.

5. But if any merchandise, effects, or property, described in the first and second rules, shall be removed to any place not occupied at the time by the forces of the United States, they shall, upon their introduction into such place, or upon their sale or consumption there, be subject to the same duties which, under the Mexican laws, they would be required to pay in such cases if they had been imported in time of peace, through the maratime custom-houses, and had there paid the duties conformably with the Mexican tariff.

6. The owners of all merchandise, effects, or property described in the first and second rules, and existing in any port of Mexico, shall have the right to reship the same, exempt from all tax, impost, or contribution whatever.

With respect to the metals, or other property, exported from any Mexican port whilst in the occupation of the forces of the United States, and previously to the restoration of the custom-house at such port, no person shall be required by the Mexican authorities, whether general or State, to pay any tax, duty or contribution upon any such exportation, or in any manner to account for the same to the said authorities.

ARTICLE XX.

Through consideration for the interests of commerce generally, it is agreed, that if less than sixty days should elapse between the date of the signature of this treaty and the restoration of the custom-houses, conformably with the stipulation in the third article, in such case all merchandise, effects and property whatsoever, arriving at the Mexican ports after the restoration of the said custom-houses, and previously to the expiration of sixty days after the day of the signature of this treaty, shall be admitted to entry ; and no other duties shall be levied thereon than the duties established by the tariff found in force at such custom-houses at the time of the restoration of the same. And to all such merchandise, effects and property, the rules established by the preceding article shall apply.

ARTICLE XXI.

If unhappily any disagreement should hereafter arise between the governments of the two republics, whether with respect to the interpretation of any stipulation in this treaty, or with respect to any other particular concerning the political or commercial relations of the two nations, the said government, in the name of those nations, do promise to each other that they will endeavour, in the most sincere and earnest manner, to settle the difference so arising, and to preserve the state of peace and friendship in which the two countries are now placing themselves ; using, for this end, mutual representations and pacific negotiations. And if, by these means, they should not be enabled to come to an agreement, a resort shall not, on this account, be had to reprisals, aggression or hostility of any kind, by one republic against the other, until the government of that which deems itself aggrieved shall have maturely considered, in the spirit of peace and good neighbourship, whether it would not be better that such difference should be settled by the arbitration of commissioners appointed on each side, or by that of a friendly nation. And should such course be proposed by either party, it shall be acceded to by the other, unless deemed by it altogether imcompatible with the nature of the difference, or the circumstances of the case.

Article XXII.

If (which is not to be expected, and which God forbid !) war should unhappily break out between the two republics, they do now, with a view to such calamity, solemnly pledge themselves to each other, and to the world, to observe the following rules : absolutely, where the nature of the subject permits, and as closely as possible in all cases where such absolute observance shall be impossible :

1. The merchants of either republic then residing in the other shall be allowed to remain twelve months, (for those dwelling in the interior,) and six months, (for those dwelling at the seaports,) to collect their debts and settle their affairs, during which period they shall enjoy the same protection, and be on the same footing, in all respects, as the citizens or subjects of the most friendly nations ; and the expiration thereof, or any time before, they shall have full liberty to depart, carrying off all their effects without molestation or hindrance—conforming therein to the same laws which the citizens or subjects of the most friendly nations are required to conform to. Upon the entrance of the armies of either nation into the territories of the other, women and children, ecclesiastics, scholars of every faculty, cultivators of the earth, merchants, artisans, manufacturers, and fishermen, unarmed and inhabiting unfortified towns, villages, or places, and in general all persons whose occupations are for the common subsistence and benefit of mankind, shall be allowed to continue their respective employments unmolested in their persons. Nor shall their houses or goods be burnt or otherwise destroyed, nor their cattle taken, nor their fields wasted, by the armed force into whose power, by the events of war, they may happen to fall ; but if the necessity arise to take anything from them for the use of such armed force, the same shall be paid for at an equitable price. All churches, hospitals, schools, colleges, libraries, and other establishments, for charitable and beneficent

purposes shall be respected, and all persons connected with the same pro-tected in the discharge of their duties, and the pursuit of their vocations.

2. In order that the fate of prisoners of war may be alleviated, all such practices as those of sending them into distant, inclement, or unwholesome districts, or crowding them into close and noxious places, shall be studiously avoided. They shall not be confined in dungeons, prison-ships, or prisons; nor be put in irons, or bound, or otherwise restrained in the use of their limbs. The officers shall enjoy liberty on their paroles within convenient districts, and have comfortable quarters; and the common soldiers shall be disposed in cantonments, open and extensive enough for air and exercise, and lodged in barracks as roomy and good as are provided by the party in whose power they are for its own troops. But if any officer shall break his parole by leaving the district so assigned him, or any other prisoner shall escape from the limits of his cantonment, after they shall have been desig-nated to him, such individual, officer, or other prisoner, shall forfeit so much of the benefit of this article as provides for his liberty on parole or in can-tonment. And if any officer so breaking his parole, or any common soldier so escaping from the limits assigned him, shall afterwards be found in arms, previously to his being regularly exchanged, the person so offending shall be dealt with according to the established laws of war. The officers shall be daily furnished by the party in whose power they are with as many rations, and of the same articles, as are allowed, either in kind or by commutation, to officers of equal rank in its own army; and all others shall be daily fur-nished with such ration as is allowed to a common soldier in its own service —the value of all which supplies shall, at the close of the war, or at periods to be agreed upon between the respective commanders, be paid by the other party, on a mutual adjustment of accounts for subsistence of prisoners; and such accounts shall not be mingled with or set off against any others, nor the balance due on them be withheld, as a compensation or reprisal for any cause whatever, real or pretended. Each party shall be allowed to keep a commissary of prisoners, appointed by itself, with every cantonment of pri-soners, in possession of the other; which commissary shall see the prisoners as often as he pleases; shall be allowed to receive, exempt from all duties or taxes, and to distribute, whatever comforts may be sent to them by their friends; and shall be free to transmit his reports in open letters to the party by whom he is employed.

And it is declared that neither the pretence that war dissolves all treaties, nor any other whatever, shall be considered as annulling or suspending the solemn covenant contained in this article. On the contrary, the state of war is precisely that for which it is provided; and during which, its stipu-lations are to be as sacredly observed as the most acknowledged obligations under the law of nature or nations.

ARTICLE XXIII.

This treaty shall be ratified by the President of the United States of America, by and with the advice and consent of the Senate thereof; and by the President of the Mexican republic, with the previous approbation of its general Congress; and the ratifications shall be exchanged in the city of Washington, or at the seat of government of Mexico, in four months from the date of the signature hereof, or sooner if practicable.

In faith whereof, we, the respective plenipotentiaries, have signed this treaty of peace, friendship, limits, and settlement; and have hereunto affixed our seals respectively. Done in quintuplicate, at the city of Guadalupe Hidalgo, on the second day of February, in the year of our Lord one thousand eight hundred and forty-eight.

[L. S.]	N. P. TRIST,
[L. S.]	LUIS G. CUEVAS,
[L. S.]	BERNARDO COUTO,
[L. S.]	MIGL. ATRISTAIN.

ARTICLES REFERRED TO IN THE FIFTEENTH ARTICLE OF THE FOREGOING TREATY.

Articles I. and V. of the unratified Convention between the United States and Mexico, of the 20th November, 1843.

IN EXECUTIVE SESSION, SENATE OF THE UNITED STATES,
June 21, 1848.

Resolved, That the injunction of secrecy be removed from the first and fifth articles of the unratified convention for the settlement of claims of the citizens and Government of the Mexican Republic against the Government of the United States, and of the citizens and Government of the United States against the Government of the Mexican Republic, concluded at the city of Mexico the 20th of November, 1843, as proposed to be ratified by the Senate of the United States, which unratified convention is referred to, and the first and fifth articles thereof made a part of the fifteenth article of the treaty of peace, friendship, limits, and settlement between the United States of America and the Mexican Republic, concluded at Guadalupe Hidalgo, on the 2d day of Febuary, 1848.

"ARTICLE I.

" All claims of citizens of the Mexican Republic against the Government of the United States, which shall be presented in the manner and time hereinafter expressed, and all claims of citizens of the United States against the

Government of the Mexican Republic, which, for whatever cause, were not submitted to, nor considered, nor finally decided by the commission, nor by the arbiter appointed by the convention of 1839, and which shall be presented in the manner and time hereinafter specified, shall be referred to four commissioners, who shall form a board, and shall be appointed in the following manner, that is to say: Two commissioners shall be appointed by the President of the Mexican Republic, and the other two by the President of the United States, with the approbation and consent of the Senate. The said commissioners, thus appointed, shall, in presence of each other take an oath to examine and decide impartially the claims submitted to them, and which may lawfully be considered, according to the proofs which shall be presented, the principles of right and justice, the law of nations, and the treaties between the two Republics."

"ARTICLE V.

" All claims of citizens of the United States against the Government of the Mexican Republic which were considered by the commissioners, and referred to the umpire appointed under the convention of the 11th April, 1839, and which were not decided by him, shall be referred to and decided by the umpire to be appointed, as provided by this convention, on the points submitted to the umpire under the late convention, and his decision shall be final and conclusive. It is also agreed, that if the respective commissioners shall deem it expedient, they may submit to the said arbiter new arguments upon the said claims."

AN ACT

Adopting the Common Law of England.

Passed April 13, 1850.

The people of the State of California, represented in Senate and Assembly, do enact as follows:

The Common Law of England, so far as it is not repugnant to or inconsistent with the Constitution of the United States, or the Constitution or laws of the State of California, shall be the rule of decision in all the Courts of this State.

AN ACT

For the better regulation of the Mines, and the government of Foreign Miners.

Passed April 13, 1850.

The People of the State of California, represented in Senate and Assembly, do enact as follows:

§ 1. No person who is not a native or natural born citizen of the United States, or who may not have become a citizen under the treaty of Guadalupe Hidalgo (all native California Indians excepted,) shall be permitted to mine in any part of this State, without having first obtained a license so to do according to the provisions of this Act.

§ 2. The Governor shall appoint a Collector of Licenses to foreign miners for each of the mining counties, and for the county of San Francisco, who before entering upon the duties of his office, shall take the oath required by the Constitution, and shall give his bond to the State with at least two good and sufficient sureties, conditioned for the faithful performance of his official duties, which bond shall be approved by the Governor, and filed in the office of the Secretary of State.

§ 3. Each Collector of Licenses to foreign miners shall be commissioned by the Governor.

§ 4. It shall be the duty of the Comptroller to cause to be printed or engraved a sufficient number of licenses, which shall be numbered consecutively, and shall be in form following, to wit:

"Number ——. (Date.) A. B., a citizen of ———, age —— years, complexion ———, is hereby licensed to work in the mines of California for the period of thirty days."

The Comptroller shall countersign each of such licenses, and shall transfer them to the Treasurer, keeping an account of the number so transferred.

§ 5. The Treasurer shall sign and deliver to each Collector of Licenses to foreign miners so many of the licenses mentioned in the preceding section as he shall deem proper, and shall take his receipt for the same and charge him therewith. Such collector and his sureties shall be liable upon his bond for the number so furnished him, either for their return or the amount for which they may be sold; and the moneys collected, as herein provided, shall be paid into the treasury as prescribed in this Act.

§ 6. Every person required by the first section of this Act to obtain a license to mine, shall apply to the Collector of Licenses to foreign miners, and take out a license to mine, for which he shall pay the sum of twenty dollars per month; and such foreigners may from time to time take out a new license, at the same rate per month, until the Governor shall issue his proclamation announcing the passage of a law by Congress, regulating the mines of precious metals in this State.

§ 7. If any such foreigner or foreigners shall refuse or neglect to take out such license by the second Monday of May next, it shall be the duty of the Collector of Licenses to foreign miners of the county in which such foreigner or foreigners shall be, to furnish his or their names to the Sheriff of the county, or to any Deputy Sheriff, whose duty it shall be to summon a posse of American citizens, and, if necessary, forcibly prevent him or them from continuing such mining operations.

§ 8. Should such foreigner or foreigners, after having been stopped by a Sheriff or Deputy Sheriff from mining in one place, seek a new location and continue such mining operations, it shall be deemed a misdemeanor, for which such offender or offenders shall be arrested as for a misdemeanor, and he or they shall be imprisoned for a term not exceeding three months, and fined not more than one thousand dollars.

§ 9. Any foreigner who may obtain a licence in conformity with the provisions of this Act, shall be allowed to work the mines anywhere in this State, under the same regulations as citizens of the United States.

§ 10. It shall be the duty of each Collector of Licenses to foreign miners to keep a full and complete register of the names and description of all foreigners taking out licenses, and a synopsis of all such licenses to be returned to the Treasurer.

§ 11. Each license, when sold, shall be endorsed by the Collector selling or issuing the same, and shall be in no case transferable; and the Collector may retain out of the money received for each license, the sum of three dollars, which shall be the full amount of his compensation.

§ 12. Each Collector of Licenses to foreign miners shall, once in every two months, and oftener if called upon by the Treasurer, proceed to the seat of government, settle with the Treasurer, pay over to the officer all moneys collected from foreigners not before paid over, and account with him for the unsold licenses remaining in his hands.

§ 13. If any Collector shall neglect or refuse to perform his duty as herein provided, it shall be the duty of the Comptroller, upon receiving notice thereof from the Treasurer, to give information thereof to the District Attorney in whose district said officer may have been appointed, who shall bring an action against such Collector and his sureties upon his bond, before any court of competent jurisdiction; and upon recovery had thereon, the said District Attorney shall receive for his services ten per cent. upon the amount collected, the balance to be paid by him into the Treasury in the manner provided by law for like payments.

§ 14. It shall be the duty of the Governor, so soon as he shall have been officially informed of the passage of a law by the United States Congress, assuming the control of the mines of the State, to issue his proclamation, requiring all Collectors of Licenses to foreign miners to stop the issuing of licenses.

§ 15. It shall be the duty of the Secretary of State, immediately after the passage of this Act, to have two thousand copies each, in English and Spanish, printed and sent to the mining districts for circulation among the miners, and also to have the same published for thirty days in the Pacific News at San Francisco, and in some newspaper at Sacramento City and at Stockton.

AN ACT

For the Admission of the State of California into the Union.

Passed at the First Session of the 31st Congress.

Whereas the people of California have presented a constitution and asked admission into the Union, which constitution was submitted to Congress by the President of the United States, by message dated February thirteenth, eighteen hundred and fifty, and which, on due examination, is found to be republican in its form of government:

Be it enacted by the Senate and House of Representatives of the United States of America in Congress assembled, That the State of California shall be one, and is hereby declared to be one, of the United States of America, and admitted into the Union on an equal footing with the original States in all respects whatever.

SEC. 2. *And be it further enacted*, That, until the representatives in Congress shall be appointed according to an actual enumeration of the inhabitants of the United States, the State of California shall be entitled to two representatives in Congress.

SEC. 3. *And be it further enacted*, That the said State of California is admitted into the Union upon the express condition that the people of said State, through their legislature or otherwise, shall never interfere with the primary disposal of the public lands within its limits, and shall pass no law and do no act whereby the title of the United States to, and right to dispose of, the same shall be impaired or questioned; and that they shall never lay any tax or assessment of any description whatsoever upon the public domain of the United States, and in no case shall non-resident proprietors, who are citizens of the United States, be taxed higher than residents; and that all the navigable waters within the said State shall be common highways, and forever free, as well to the inhabitants of said State as to the citizens of the United States, without any tax, impost, or duty therefor: *Provided*, That nothing herein contained shall be construed as recognizing or rejecting the propositions tendered by the people of California as articles of compact in the ordinance adopted by the convention which formed the constitution of that State.

APPROVED, September 9, 1850.

AN ACT

To ascertain and Settle the Private Land Claims in the State of California.

Passed at the 2d Session of the 31st Congress.

Be it enacted by the Senate and House of Representatives of the United States of America in Congress assembled, That for the purpose of ascertaining and settling private land claims in the State of California, a commission shall be, and is hereby, constituted, which shall consist of three commissioners, to be appointed by the President of the United States, by and with the advice and consent of the Senate, which commission shall continue for three years from the date of this act unless sooner discontinued by the President of the United States.

SEC. 2. *And be it further enacted,* That a secretary, skilled in the Spanish and English languages, shall be appointed by the said commissioners, whose duty it shall be to act as interpreter, and to keep a record of the proceedings of the board in a bound book, to be filed in the office of the Interior on the termination of the commission.

SEC. 3. *And be it further enacted,* That such clerks, not to exceed five in number, as may be neccessary, shall be appointed by the said commissioners.

SEC. 4. *And be it further enacted,* That it shall be lawful for the President of the United States to appoint an agent learned in the law, and skilled in the Spanish and English languages, whose special duty it shall be to superintend the interests of the United States in the premises, to continue him in such agency as long as the public interest may, in the judgment of the President, require his continuance, and to allow him such compensation as the president shall deem reasonable. It shall be the duty of the said agent to attend the meetings of the board, to collect testimony in behalf of the United States, and to attend on all occasions when the claimant, in any case before the board, shall take depositions; and no deposition taken by or in behalf of any such claimant shall be read in evidence in any case, whether before the commissioners, or before the District or Supreme Court of the United States, unless notice of the time and place of taking the same shall have been given in writing to said agent, or to the district attorney of the proper district, so long before the time of taking the deposition as to enable him to be present at the time and place of taking the same, and like notice shall be given of the time and place of taking any deposition on the part of the United States.

SEC. 5. *And be it further enacted,* That the said commissioners shall hold their sessions at such times and places as the President of the United States shall direct, of which they shall give due and public notice; and the marshal of the district in which the board is sitting shall appoint a deputy, whose duty it shall be to attend upon the said board, and who shall receive the same compensation as is allowed to the marshal for his attendance upon the District Court.

Sec. 6. *And be it further enacted*, That the said commissioners, when sitting as a board, and each commissioner at his chambers, shall be, and are, and is hereby, authorized to administer oaths, and to examine witnesses in any case pending before the commissioners, that all such testimony shall be taken in writing, and shall be recorded and preserved in bound books to be provided for that purpose.

Sec. 7. *And be it further enacted*, That the secretary of the board shall be, and he is hereby, authorized and required, on the application of the law agent or district attorney of the United States, or of any claimant or his counsel, to issue writs of subpœna commanding the attendance of a witness or witnesses before the said board or any commissioner.

Sec. 8. *And be it further enacted*, That each and every person claiming lands in California by virtue of any right or title derived from the Spanish or Mexican government, shall present the same to the said commissioners when sitting as a board, together with such documentary evidence and testimony of witnesses as the said claimant relies upon in support of such claims ; and it shall be the duty of the commissioners, when the case is ready for hearing, to proceed promptly to examine the same upon such evidence, and upon the evidence produced in behalf of the United States, and to decide upon the validity of the said claim, and within thirty days after such decision is rendered to certify the same, with the reasons on which it is founded, to the district attorney of the United States in and for the district in which such decision shall be rendered.

Sec. 9. *And be it further enacted*, That in all cases of the rejection or confirmation of any claim by the board of commissioners, it shall and may be lawful for the claimant or the district attorney, in behalf of the United States, to present a petition to the District Court of the district in which the land claimed is situated, praying the said court to review the decision of the said commissioners, and to decide on the validity of such claim ; and such petition, if presented by the claimant, shall set forth fully the nature of the claim and the names of the original and present claimants, and shall contain a deraignment of the claimant's title, together with a transcript of the report of the board of commissioners, and of the documentary evidence and testimony of the witnesses on which it was founded ; and such petition if presented by the district attorney in behalf of the United States, shall be accompanied by a transcript of the report of the board of commissioners, and of the papers and evidence on which it was founded, and shall fully and distinctly set forth the grounds on which the said claim is alleged to be invalid, a copy of which petition if the same shall be presented by a claimant, shall be served on the district attorney of the United States, and if presented in behalf of the United States, shall be served on the claimant or his attorney; and the party upon whom such service shall be made shall be bound to answer the same within a time to be prescribed by the judge of the District Court; and the answer of the claimant to such petition shall set forth fully the nature of the claim, and the names of the original and present claimants, and shall contain a deraignment of the claimant's title; and the answer of the district attorney in behalf of the United States shall fully and distinctly set forth the grounds on which the said claim is alleged to be invalid, copies of which answers shall be served upon the adverse party thirty days before the meeting of the court, and thereupon, at the first term of the court thereafter, the said case shall stand for trial, unless, on cause shown, the same shall be continued by the court.

SEC. 10. *And be it further enacted*, That the District Court shall proceed to render judgment upon the pleadings and evidence in the case, and upon such further evidence as may be taken by order of the said court, and shall, on application of the party against whom judgment is rendered, grant an appeal to the Supreme Court of the United States, on such security for costs in the District and Supreme Court, in case the judgment of the District Court shall be affirmed, as the said court shall prescribe; and if the court shall be satisfied that the party desiring to appeal is unable to give such security, the appeal may be allowed without security.

SEC. 11. *And be it further enacted*, That the commissioners herein provided for, and the District and Supreme Courts, in deciding on the validity of any claim brought before them under the provisions of this act, shall be governed by the treaty of Guadalupe Hidalgo, the law of nations, the laws, usages, and customs of the government from which the claim is derived, the principles of equity, and the decisions of the Supreme Court of the United States, so far as they are applicable.

SEC. 12. *And be it further enacted*, That to entitle either party to a review of the proceedings and decision of the commissioners herein-before provided for, notice of the intention of such party to file a petition to the District Court shall be entered on the journal or record of proceedings of the commissioners within sixty days after their decision on the claim has been made and notified to the parties, and such petition shall be filed in the District Court within six months after such decision has been rendered.

SEC. 13. *And be it further enacted*, That all lands, the claims to which have been finally rejected by the commissioners in manner herein provided, or which shall be finally decided to be invalid by the District or Supreme Court, and all lands the claims to which shall not have been presented to the said commissioners within two years after the date of this act, shall be deemed, held, and considered as part of the public domain of the United States; and for all claims finally confirmed by the said commissioners, or by the said District or Supreme Court, a patent shall issue to the claimant upon his presenting to the general land office an authentic certificate of such confirmation, and a plat or survey of the said land, duly certified and approved by the surveyor-general of California, whose duty it shall be to cause all private claims which shall be finally confirmed to be accurately surveyed, and to furnish plats of the same ; and in the location of the said claims, the said surveyor-general shall have the same power and authority as are conferred on the register of the land office and receiver of the public moneys of Louisiana, by the sixth section of the act " to create the office of surveyor of the public lands for the State of Louisiana," approved third March, one thousand eight hundred and thirty-one : *Provided, always*, That if the title of the claimant to such lands shall be contested by any other person, it shall and may be lawful for such person to present a petition to the district judge of the United States for the district in which the lands are situated, plainly and distinctly setting forth his title thereto, and praying the said judge to hear and determine the same, a copy of which petition shall be served upon the adverse party thirty days before the time appointed for hearing the same. *And provided, further*, That it shall and may be lawful for the district judge of the United States, upon the hearing of such petition, to grant an injunction to restrain the party at whose instance the claim to the said lands has been confirmed, from suing out a patent for the same, until the title thereto shall have been finally decided, a copy of which order shall be transmitted to the commissioner of the general land office, and thereupon no patent shall issue until such decision shall be made, or until sufficient time shall, in the opinion of the said judge, have been allowed for obtaining the same ; and thereafter the said injunction shall be dissolved.

SEC. 14. *And be it further enacted*, That the provisions of this act shall not extend to any town lot, farm lot, or pasture lot, held under a grant from any corporation or town to which lands may have been granted for the establishment of a town by the Spanish or Mexican government, or the lawful authorities thereof, nor to any city, or town, or village lot, which city, town, or village existed on the seventh day of July, eighteen hundred and forty-six ; but the claim for the same shall be presented by the corporate authorities of the said town, or where the land on which the said city, town, or village was originally granted to an individual, the claim shall be presented by or in the name of such individual, and the fact of the existence of the said city, town, or village on the said seventh July, eighteen hundred and forty-six, being duly proved, shall be prima facie evidence of a grant to such corporation, or the individual under whom the said lot-holders claim ; and where any city, town, or village shall be in existence at the time of passing this act, the claim for the land embraced within the limits of the same may be made by the corporate authority of the said city, town, or village.

SEC. 15. *And be it further enacted*, That the final decrees rendered by the said commissioners, or by the District or Supreme Court of the United States, or any patent to be issued under this act, shall be conclusive between

65

the United States and the said claimants only, and shall not affect the interests of third persons.

SEC. 16. *And be it further enacted,* That it shall be the duty of the commissioners herein provided for to ascertain and report to the Secretary of the Interior the tenure by which the mission lands are held, and those held by civilized Indians, and those who are engaged in agriculture or labor of any kind, and also those which are occupied and cultivated by Pueblos or Rancheros Indians.

SEC. 17. *And be it further enacted,* That each commissioner appointed under this act shall be allowed and paid at the rate of six thousand dollars per annum ; that the secretary of the commissioners shall be allowed and paid at the rate of four thousand dollars per annum ; and the clerks herein provided for shall be allowed and paid at the rate of one thousand five hundred dollars per annum ; the aforesaid salaries to commence from the day of the notification by the commissioners of the first meeting of the board.

SEC. 18. *And be it further enacted,* That the secretary of the board shall receive no fee except for furnishing certified copies of any paper or record, and for issuing writs of subpœna. For furnishing certified copies of any paper or record, he shall receive twenty cents for every hundred words, and for issuing writs of subpœna, fifty cents for each witness; which fees shall be equally divided between the said secretary and the assistant clerk.

APPROVED, March 3, 1851.

THE COMMON LAW

IN RELATION TO MINES AND MINERALS.

CHAPTER I.

ON ROYAL MINES.

ACCORDING to the law of England, the only mines which are termed royal, and which are the exclusive property of the crown, are mines of silver and gold. (*a*) And this property is so peculiarly a branch of the royal prerogative, that it has been said, that though the King grant lands in which mines are, and all mines in them, yet royal mines will not pass by so general a description. (*b*)

This prerogative is stated to have originated in the King's right of coinage, in order to supply him with materials. (*c*) It may be observed, however,

(*a* 2 Inst. 577.   (*b*) Plowd. 336.   (*c*) 1 Black. Comm. 294.

that the right of coinage in the earlier periods of European society was not always exclusively exercised by the crown, that the same reason might apply to other metals, as copper and tin, and that in those rude times, the prerogative was perhaps as likely to have its origin in the circumstance of those rare and beautiful metals having always been among the most cherished objects of ambition, and which were, therefore, appropriated to the use of the crown, like the diamonds of India, in order to sustain the splendour and dignity of its rank.(1)

Whatever reason may be assigned for this right of the crown, and of whatever value that right may be, it has been long decided, not only that all mines of gold and silver within the realm, though in the lands of subjects, belong exclusively to the crown by prerogative, but that this right is also accompanied with full liberty to dig and carry away the ores, and with all other such incidents thereto as are necessary to be used for getting them. (a)

This right of entry is disputed by Lord Hardwicke in a case where there was a grant from the crown, of lands with a reservation of all royal mines, but not of a right of entry. The Lord Chancellor said he was of opinion that there was by the terms of the grant no such power in the crown, and that by the royal prerogative of mines, the crown had even no such power; for it would be very prejudicial if the crown could enter into a subject's lands, or grant a license to work the mines; but that when they were once opened, it could restrain the owner of the soil from working them, and could either work them itself, or grant a license for others to work them. (b)

This doctrine was, however, declared by Sir W. Grant, M. R., (c) to be liable to considerable doubt, as being inconsistent with the resolutions of the judges in the case just cited from Plowden. It may, therefore, be assumed that the latter case which was solemnly decided by all the twelve judges, has never been overruled; and Lord Hardwicke's case was decided also upon other grounds—viz., upon there not being a sufficient probability of there being royal mines at all, to disturb the possession of a purchaser. (d)

(a) The Queen and Earl of Northumberland, Plowd., 310. 336.

(b) Lyddal v. Weston, 2 Atk. 20. (c) Seaman v. Vaudrey, 16 Ves. 393.

(d) See chap. xii.

(1) Much more singular reasons however, for the right of property are given in Plowden's reports; we are there told that this right was considered by the Solicitor General of that day to exist in respect of the excellency of the thing, that the common law appropriated every thing to the persons whom it best suits, as common and trival things to the common people, and because gold and silver were most excellent things, the law had appointed them, to the person who is most excellent, and that was the king. And, finally we are entertained by Plowden himself with an alchemical theory on the origin and transmutation of all metals, which was no doubt designed to throw light upon the subject, but which, it must be admitted, leaves the law of the case in the same condition, however much that of the metals may have been changed. Plowd. 338. 9.

It seems formerly to have been a matter of considerable dispute, as to what constituted a royal mine. By some it was considered to be a principle of common law, that, if *any* gold or silver was found in metals of a baser nature, that was sufficient to bring the mine within the definition of a royal mine ; while by others, a mine was not to be deemed royal, unless the quantity of gold or silver exceed in *value* that of the other metal with which it was mixed. The latter opinion was adopted by three of the judges, viz., Harper, Southcot, and Weston, in the case of the Queen and the Earl of Northumberland, (*a*) although they agree in thinking that as the defendant, in this case, had confessed the production of some royal ore, he was concluded by his not having proceeded to show the relative difference of value, and that the mine must therefore be presumed to be royal. But all the other nine judges were of opinion that the existence of *any* portion of silver or gold was sufficient to constitute a royal mine. Plowden himself contends, that if the royal metals should bear the expense of extraction the whole should belong to the Crown, and if otherwise, to the owners of the base metals. This decision occurred in the time of Queen Elizabeth, when the prerogative of the Crown was perhaps at its greatest height, and the opinion of the nine judges does not appear to have gained the acquiescence of more recent lawyers. In 1640, the opinion of fifteen leading counsel, amongst whom are the names of Glanvil, Herbert, Grimston, and Maynard, was taken upon the subject. These gentlemen were all of opinion, that, although the gold or silver contained in the base metal of a mine in the lands of a subject, be of less value than the base metal, yet if the gold or silver countervail the charge of refining it, or be of more worth than the base metal spent in refining it, this is a mine royal, and as well the base metal as the gold and silver in it belong to the prerogative of the Crown. (*b*) It may be inferred, from this opinion, that if the gold or silver did not repay the charges of separation, those metals were not considered as belonging to the Crown. But it would appear, that if the royal metals had been found in a pure state and unmixed with ores of any baser metal, or if the mixture had been merely mechanical and not chemical, and the precious metals could have been extracted without necessarily submitting the whole mass to the ordinary smelting process used in the reduction of the inferior metals, the mine would have been considered a royal mine without reference to the cost of either production or separation. Silver mines are frequently mentioned as existing in England, but it is very questionable whether gold or silver have ever been found in a pure state in England, though small pieces have sometimes been discovered in Scotland (*c*) and in Ireland. And the silver said to have been produced in England was most probably extracted from lead, as at present. (*d*)

(*a*) Plowd. 336.   (*b*) Heton's Account of Mines, p. 21.
(*c*) Camd. Britt. 915, 923.   Boyle on Ores, 182.   Martin's Scotland, 339.
(*d*) Pryce's Mineralogia Cornubiensis, 59.   Heton's Account of Mines, 2, 5.

In the time of Queen Elizabeth, a society was eatablished on the part of the Crown for the management of royal mines, most probable in consequence of the decision reported by Plowden. Several rules were framed for its guidance, particularly in 1670. The opinion of the fifteen counsel before mentioned, seems to have been generally adopted. (a) But considerable difference of opinion still prevailed in many instances with respect to the actual fact of the royal metals bearing the charges of refinement. The royal refiners and assayers became either less skilful or dishonest. At length, the great case of Sir Carbery Price occurred. (b) This case produced repeated trials at bar, and at-nisi prius, and occasioned very considerble excitement in almost all parts of the kingdom. Sir C. Price succeeded at last in effectually precluding the claims of the Crown, but the spirit of mining adventure threatened to become extinct from the vexatious and uncertain state of the law. The right of entry in search of royal mines was oppressive in the extreme, for no damages were paid, and any mine which might have been discovered at great expense, and after infinite labour, seemed liable to be claimed as a royal mine. Valuable mines were concealed, and there was universal distrust. Such a state of things called loudly for a legislative remedy. (c)

This remedy was at last afforded. An act was passed, declaring that no mine of tin, copper, iron or lead, should thereafter be taken to be a royal mine, although gold or silver might be extracted out of the same. (d)

This provision was considered insufficient, and another statute was soon afterwards passed, (e) entitled "An Act to prevent Disputes and Controversies concerning Royal Mines," in which is recited the first act, and that many doubts and questions had arisen upon the said statute whereby great suits and troubles had arisen to many owners and proprietors of such mines.

It was then enacted, that all owners or proprietors of any mines in England or Wales, wherein any ore was then, or thereafter should be discovered or wrought, and in which there was copper, tin, iron, or lead, should hold and enjoy the same mines and ore, and dig and work the same, notwithstanding that such mines or ore should be pretended or claimed to be royal mines, any law, usage, or custom, to the contrary notwithstanding.

The third section, however, gives the Crown, or any persons claiming royal mines under it, the right to purchase the ore of any such mines (other than tin ore in the counties of Devon and Cornwall) upon payment, within thirty days after the ore is raised and laid upon the banks of the said mines, and before its removal thence, *but after being washed and made merchantable,* of the following sums and at the following rates :—For ore in which is copper, £16 per ton ; for ore in which is tin, forty shillings per ton ; for

(a) See Sir John Pettus' Fodinæ Regales.
(b) See Sir Humphrey Mackworth's Mine Adventure Expedient, p. 13.
(c) Heton, 27.   (d) 1 Will. and Mary, c. 30.   (e) 5 Will. and Mary, c. 6.

ore in which is iron, forty shillings per ton ; for ore in which is lead, £9 per ton ; and in default of payment it is declared to be lawful for the owners or proprietors to sell the said ore for their own use.

It is provided by the fourth section that nothing in the act should alter or make void the charters granted to the tinners of Devon and Cornwall, or any of their liberties, privileges or franchises, or the laws, customs, or constitutions of the stannaries of Devon and Cornwall. (a)

It should be observed, in the first place, that the right of the Crown, to all mines of gold and silver, in which the ores of those metals are found, in connection with any other substances than copper, tin, iron, or lead, remains unaffected by these statutes, and that the presence of any of the four metals just mentioned would seem to be sufficient to protect the ore against the claims of the Crown.

The right of pre-emption, reserved to the Crown, and the persons claiming under it, is limited to copper, iron, and lead, and to tin found in any other places than in the counties of Devon and Cornwall.

It might be contended that this right should extend equally to those metals specified in the act which contain no silver or gold at all, as to those which do actually contain them. But this construction must be considered to be excluded by the preamble and purpose of the act. Ores unmixed with any portion of gold or silver were undoubtedly the property of the subject before, and as the statute was not intended to apply to those, the right of pre-emption cannot be held to extend to any ores but those which the Crown might have pretended to claim.

This act seems to have given the most universal satisfaction to all mining adventurers, and the society for the royal mines appears to have been effectually broken up by its salutary operation.

It is stated by Sir W. Blackstone, that the Crown pays no more for the royal metal than the value of the base metal in which it is supposed to be.(b) This might certainly be quite true at the time when the statute was passed. But the value of all the metals mentioned in the act has since often and materially varied. At present, the price of almost all iron ores is under the sum fixed for the pre-emption—£2 per ton. But it is quite possible for very rich and peculiar ores, like the red hæmatite, to reach a price considerably above the rate of pre-emption. The price of copper ore is also usually under the sum fixed by the act—£16 per ton ; but the value of some copper ores now found in this country is much above that sum. In general, the sum fixed for tin ore would be greatly inadequate. It follows, therefore, that if it could be proved that any of the ores just mentioned contained any portion of gold or silver, the Crown would have the right of pre-emption at a price which might still seriously affect the interests of the producer.

(a) See chap. x.   (b) 1 Black. Comm. 295.

Neither of the royal metals, however, are usually found in this country in union with any other metals but lead, though silver has been found in Huel Alfred, in Gwinear, Cornwall, in green corbonate of copper, and in Huel Ann, in Phillack, Cornwall, with arsenical pyrites. And it may be considered, that, on this account, no fear need be apprehended of the Crown being enabled to exercise its right.

There is a considerable quantity of silver extracted from lead ores : and the rate of pre-emption has been raised by a recent statute, (a) by which, after reciting that in consequence of the lapse of time and change of circumstances, the former rate had been inadequate to the increased expense of raising lead, it is enacted that the rate shall thenceforth be £25 per ton. Since the passing of this act, the price of unsmelted lead has never been beyond the sum of £15 per ton, and even during the late war when the value of lead, like that of other metals, was extraordinarily high, it never reached the sum of £23 per ton. About the year 1807, the price closely approached to that sum, but it is now considerably reduced. Lead adventurers have, therefore, at present, nothing to apprehend from the right of pre-emption. But the subject cannot be dismissed without the observation, that the rate of pre-emption over all the metals ought to have been permanently fixed by reference to the market price of the day.

CHAPTER II.

ON THE RIGHT TO WORK MINES.

A person may have an undisputed right of property in mines, and may yet have no power to avail himself of that right ; and again, a person may have a distinct right of possession in mines, as part of his tenement, without being entitled to exert any act of ownership over them.

Such, is the condition of the lord and tenant, in the absence of special custom, with respect to mines in copyhold and customary lands.(b) And there are other persons who, from the limited nature of their interests, or the peculiar quality of their estates, are subject to similar incapacities, and are not permitted to despoil the inheritance by working mines.

It is unnecessary to say that when mines form part of the whole unsevered inheritance, an owner in fee simple possesses, in all freehold lands, an unrestricted right to work the mines in his estate.

It is equally clear, that all owners in fee whose title to mines depends upon *custom*, against the presumption of law, will be entitled to the right to

(a) 55 Geo. III. c. 134.   (b) See chap. ii.

work them, as the lord against the tenant, or the copyholder or commoner against the lord. For the right has been gained or preserved by the custom founded upon such acts of ownership. The right to work does not, in this instance, depend upon the right of property. The latter right is established by the former.

It has also been seen (*a*) that the lord is presumptively entitled to work mines in the commons and wastes of the manor, and that the Crown is supposed to have the right to enter the lands of a subject to search for and work mines of gold and silver. (*b*)

It remains, however, to be seen, in what cases the owner of mines is entitled to work them without the concurrence of the owner of the surface, when the property in mines forms a distinct inheritance and possession.

It has been expressly decided, in a case of some importance, first, that the right to enter and work mines is necessarily incident to a grant of mines, without any express authority for that purpose ; and secondly, that this power cannot be restrained by a special power given in the *affirmative*, which may authorise more acts than would be implied by law, but which will in no wise exclude the full operation of law. (*c*)

In that case, Sir Thomas Danby, a former owner of the demesne lands of a manor, had enfeoffed the Earl of Sussex of several closes, except and reserving unto himself and his heirs all the coals in the lands and premises, *together with* free liberty for Sir Thomas and his heirs at all times thereafter *during the time that the said Sir Thomas and his heirs should continue the owners and proprietors of the demesne lands of Farnley*, to dig pits, or otherwise to sough and get coals in the said lands and premises, and to sell and carry away the same with carts and carriages, or otherwise to dispose of the same coals at his and their wills and pleasures, making reasonable satisfaction for damages.—Afterwards the manor and demesne lands of Farnley were sold by the Danby family to the defendant. An action of trespass was brought by the plaintiff who was then owner of the lands in question, against the defendant, for entering and working for coal. On demurrer, it was argued for the plaintiff, that the heirs of Sir Thomas Danby having ceased to be owners and proprietors of the demesne lands of Farnley, the defendant had no right to enter and dig pits. It was admitted, that if there had been a general exception of the coal to the feoffor and his heirs, the law would imply a right to get it co-extensive with the reservation ; but it was contended, that the express liberty to take the coal limited the duration of the privilege by mutual consent and contract. Bayley, J., in delivering the judgment of the court, took an elaborate view of the subject, and said, that an exception was distinguished from a reservation by its being part of the thing granted, and in existence at the time of the grant, that it was always taken most strongly

(*a*) Chap. ii.   (*b*) Chap. iii.
(*c*) Earl of Cardigan *v.* Armitage, 2 Barn. & Cress. 197.   3 D. & R. 414.

against the feoffor or grantor, and that when any thing is excepted, all things that depend upon it, and are necessary for obtaining it are excepted also.(a) The coals were part of the thing granted, and in esse at the time. The consequence, therefore, was, that the property in the coals was never out of Sir Thomas Danby the feoffor, and would have remained in him and his heirs as before, without words of inheritance in the exception, and a right, as incident, to get the coals, and do all things necessary for the obtaining of them, would have been excepted also. The express liberty was introduced by the words "together with," as if the intention were to increase what had preceded, not to diminish; and he took it to be a general rule, that words tending to enlarge should not, unless the intention was very plain, be taken to restrain.(b) It might be taken as clear, that an express liberty did not always control what would otherwise exist, especially if the express liberty went beyond what would be implied. To give it a controlling power, the intention that it should have that effect must be very plain. (c)—The special power had its necessary use, for it went beyond the incidental power which the law would imply. The incidental power would warrant nothing beyond what was strictly necessary for the convenient working of the coals; it would allow no use of the surface; no deposit upon it to a greater extent or for a longer duration than should be necessary; no attendance upon the land of unnecessary persons. The express power gave great latitude in these respects. It had therefore its necessary use, though it worked nothing in restraint of the incidental right which Sir T. D. and his heirs would otherwise have had.

It would appear, therefore, that though a grant or exception may be controlled by express words of restriction or limitation, yet, if not so controlled, the grantor will have all the powers which are by law considered to be incident to such a grant for the full and necessary enjoyment of it. Any special power, as in the above case, will be limited in its duration and consequences, by the particular expressions which confer it.

The nature and extent of these implied powers, and of others arising from express stipulation, will be noticed in a subsequent part of the treatise. (d)

It is scarcely necessary to observe that the above remarks can have no application to mines in copyhold lands, which are not absolutely vested in the grantor. The lord may grant the property in mines, but he cannot grant what he may not himself possess—the right of entry to work them. It may sometimes happen, however, that the lord may have made a grant in fee of the minerals in copyhold lands not subject to any special custom, to third persons, and then enfranchises the lands, without excepting the minerals.—It might be contended that the mines, as in other freehold lands, formed a distinct inheritance, and that the grantees had then a right to the possession of their property. But it is presumed, the grantees would not be in the situa-

(a) Shepp. Touch. 78, 100.   (b) Winter v. Loveden, Lord Raym. 267.
(c) Stukeley v. Butler, Hobart, 168, and see 8 Ass. 10, and Dy. 19. (d) See chap. iv.

tion of parties claiming the full benefit of an unrestricted grant, inasmuch as at the time of their grant no right of entry could possibly be passed from the grantor, and no reservation had been made in the deed of enfranchisement, which might enure for the benefit of the grantor. The consequence would appear to be, that the mines would be severed from the demesnes of the manor, and would form a separate inheritance as freeholds generally, but that they would remain as inaccessible to the proprietor as before the act of enfranchisement. But if the grant of the minerals were made for a limited period, the owner of lands would, in such cases, of course be entitled to them after the expiration of that period. (a)

When the mines are excepted in the deed of enfranchisement, full powers to enter and work should be given ; for otherwise it might be doubted whether the lord or his grantee would be in any better condition with respect to the mines than before. The exception merely operates upon what he is already possessed of. Illa pars quam retinet semper cum eo est et semper fuit. (b) But it can confer nothing more, except what may be presumed to have been intended by the nature of the contract. The exception cannot itself form a reservation. The exception is always part of the thing granted, and in existence at the time of the grant. A reservation, on the other hand, is always of a thing not in existence, but newly created, and arising out of the subject of grant. (c) The mines may be excepted, but the right to work them should, in such cases, be also reserved. The owner of the land grants nothing to which a legal presumption can attach. But the reservation of a right to work will operate, by way of contract, as the grant of a new incorporeal hereditament in favour of the lord.

We are now to discuss the rights of those possessed of more limited interests, and we may first consider the privileges of proprietors, when the mines form an unsevered portion of the general inheritance.

Most of the different estates which may subsist in a fee simple can only be created by some of the common assurances recognized by law. It is not unusual to insert, in instruments of this description, distinct powers or reservations with respect to the working of mines. These powers, however, will be reserved for future consideration, and we shall at present confine our attention to the interests of those claiming either by act of law, or under instruments which contain no special clauses or directions with respect to mines.

It may, in the first place, be generally premised, that it is an act of waste to work mines or quarries. (d)

(a) Townley v. Gibson, 2 T. R. 701.

(b) Co. Litt. 47 a, Brooke's Abr. title Reservation, pl. 46.

(c) Shepp. Touch. 80. Fancy v. Scott, 2 Man. and Ry. 335. Doe. dem. Douglas v. Lock, 1 Ad. and Ell. 744.

(d) Co. Lit. 53' b, 54 b. Moyle v. Moyle, Ow. 66. Nowell v. Donning, 2 Rol. Abr. 816. Manwood's case, Moore, 101. Astry v. Ballard, 2 Mod. 193.

A tenant in tail has, like a tenant in fee simple, an estate of inheritance in the lands limited to him, but his estate must descend in the particular line marked out for its devolution. Notwithstanding this limited mode of descent, an estate in tail has certain incidents annexed to it which cannot be restrained by any condition, and amongst others, is the power of the tenant to commit waste. A tenant in tail, therefore, may fell timber, pull down houses, and open and work mines. But the waste or the act of severance from the inheritance must be committed in his own lifetime, for the heir will be entitled to the remainder as part of the fee. (a)

The Court of Chancery will never restrain a tenant in tail from committing waste. (b)

A tenant in tail after possibility of issue extinct, has only an estate for life in the lands. This estate has, however, been derived from an estate in fee tail; on this account, he possesses more than the ordinary powers of the tenant for life, and having once had the power of committing waste, he is still dispunishable for waste, because he continues in the seisin by virtue of the livery upon the estate tail. (c)

But although a tenant in tail after possibility of issue extinct has the power to commit waste, by the common law, yet he cannot commit wanton or malicious waste, in which he will be restrained by the Court of Chancery in analogy to the rule to be presently noticed with respect to a tenant for life without impeachment of waste. (d)

The privileges of a tenant in tail after possibility of issue extinct are personal, and arise from the privity of estate. His grantee, therefore, will be a mere tenant for life. (e)

A tenant for life, without being authorised, cannot commit waste. But he will be entitled to take the minerals upon his lands for the purposes of husbandry and repairs. One of the incidents to his estate is his right to estovers. (f) This word has been generally defined to mean an allowance of necessary wood; but there seems reason to contend that the original wood, estoffe, whence comes the English word stuff, might comprise all that was necessary for the cultivation and repairs of the estate generally. The statute of Westminster, 2. c. 25, gives an assize of novel disseisin de estoveriis bosci, which would seem to show that the word was not used in necessary connection with wood. At any rate, there can be no doubt that a tenant for life may, in all cases, dig for gravel, lime, clay, earth, stone, or similar minerals for the repair of buildings and the manuring of the land. (g) It

(a) 11 Rep. 50 a. Plowd. 259. Hard. R. 96.
(b) Forrester's Rep. 16. Glenorchy v. Bosville, Cas. Temp. Talb. 16.
(c) Co. Litt. 27 b. 2 Inst. 302. 1 Roll. Rep. 184.
(d) Abraham v. Bubb, 2 Freeman, 53. Anon. 2 Freem. 278. Lewis Bowles' case, 11 Rep. 83 a. Cook v. Winford, Abr. Eq. 221. Williams v. Williams, 12 East, 209.
(e) Co. Litt. 28 a. Aprice's case, 3 Leon. 241.   (f) Co. Litt. 41. b.
(g) Co. Litt. 53 b, 54. b. Moyle v. Moyle, Owen, 67. Roll. Abr. 816.

is said, that if a lessee of land with mines of coals, iron, and stones digs of the coals, iron and stones, so much as is necessary for him to use, without selling, it is no waste. (*a*)

A distinction has been taken between mines open and unopened. Lord Coke says, " a man hath land in which there is a mine of coals, or of the like, and maketh a lease of the land (without mentioning any mines) for life or for years, the lessee for such mines as were *open* at the time of the lease made, may dig and take the profits thereof. But he cannot dig for any *new* mine that was not open at the time of the lease made, for that should be adjudged waste, and if there be open mines, and the owner make a lease of the land, with the mines therein, this shall extend to the open mines only, and not to any hidden mine ; but if there be no open mine, and the lease is made of the land together with all mines therein, there the lessee may dig for mines and enjoy the benefit thereof, otherwise those words should be void." (*b*) It might certainly seem to be the true construction of an instrument granting lands with all mines therein, and the mines were unopened, that the tenant for life or for years should be unimpeachable for waste, and be at liberty to work the mines by express stipulation ; ut res magis valent quam pereat ; but this doctrine, notwithstanding Saunders' case where it was first resolved, was denied both by Lord Macclesfield and Lord King in a similar case, in which it was urged, that the mines being expressly granted by the settlement with the lands, it was as strong a case as if the mines themselves were limited to the tenant for life. But it was decided, that a tenant for life subject to waste shall no more open a mine than cut down the timber trees which were equally granted by the deed, and that the meaning of inserting mines, trees, and water, was, that all should pass, but as the timber and mines were part of the inheritance, no one should have power over them but such as had an estate of inheritance limited to him. (*c*)

The same reasoning might apply to mines that were opened which are equally part of the inheritance, but the presumption in favour of this construction of the deed is certainly stronger ; for the absence of more express stipulation would seem to show that the land was granted with all its current profits.(*d*) And, in the other case, there was, properly speaking, no mine at all, but only veins or strata. Indeed there can be no doubt that, though a tenant for life subject to waste cannot in any case open mines, he may, in the absence of stipulation to the contrary, for modus et conventio vincunt legem, proceed to work the mines that are opened.

It may be observed, however, that if a lease for life, or for years, were

(*a*) 2 Roll. Abr. 816.

(*b*) Co. Litt. 54 b. Saunders' case, 5 Co. 12. Lord Darcy *v*. Ashwith, Hob. 296. Hutt. 19.

(*c*) Whitfield *v*. Bewit, 2 Peere W. 240.

(*d*) Rutland *v*. Greene, 1 Sid. 152. 1 Lev. 107.

made in terms corresponding with the settlement in the case of Whitfield *v.* Bewit, and without embracing any ulterior objects, the reasoning contained in the decision of that case would scarcely apply. The intention of the parties would then appear more strongly in favour of the lessee's right to open mines, if there were no mines already opened.

It has been decided that a tenant for life, subject to waste, may open new workings to pursue old veins which were open when he came into possession of the estate. An injunction was moved for, but Lord King observed, that the question had been determined in the great cause of Hellier versus Twyford, in which he was of counsel, and which was tried at the assizes in Devonshire before Mr. Justice Powell, where it was proved by witnesses to be the course of the country, and a practice well known in those parts among the miners, that any person having a right to dig in mines may pursue the mine, and open new shafts or pits to follow the same vein ; and that otherwise the working in the same mines would be impracticable, because the miners would be choked for want of air, if new holes were not continually opened to let the air into them, that the same vein of coal frequently ran a great way, and the same mine of coals was very knowable, and easy to be discerned.(*a*)

In the same case, it was decided that, to enable a tenant for life to work mines, it is not necessary that they should have been open at the time of the settlement. It is sufficient if the mines are lawfully opened by any precedent tenant in tail, though subsequent to the settlement.

The actual distinction between an old mine and a new mine has never been plainly determined ; at least no case is reported. Such questions might be found too difficult of solution. From the case just cited, it would seem that the pursuit of the same vein or stratum would be permitted to a person claiming to work old mines, and there does not appear to be any objection to such a test. It might be doubtful, however, how far a mine which had been discontinued could be considered to be still an old mine. Much would, in all such cases, depend upon the particular facts.(*b*)

When a lessee for life, or years, is unable to work mines, and is subject in other respects to waste, it has been held that he cannot cut timber trees for use in carrying on the works, though without timber he could not avail himself of his right. The case was described as being similar to the case of a new house built after the demise, for the reparation of which the lessee cannot take timber on the land. (*c*)

Such is the law with respect to the rights of a tenant for life subject to waste, and we are now to consider the rights of a tenant for life, who is made expressly dispunishable for waste, or who is without impeachment of waste.

(*a*) Clavering *v.* Clavering, 2 Peere W. 388. Sel. Ch. Ca. 79.

(*b*) But see Stoughton *v.* Leigh, 1 Taunt. 410.   (*c*) Lord Darcy *v.* Ashwith, Putt. 19.

It has frequently been decided, that these words only extend to permissive waste, and not to the destruction of the estate itself, and that they will not authorise any malicious or extravagant acts of ownership, as in cutting down ornamental trees, or in wantonly pulling down houses. (*a*)   It had been decided in an old case at law, that the words, without impeachment of waste, gave the tenant the absolute property in the thing wasted, and courts of equity were for some time prevented by this case from interfering, as it would have been to declare that a man should not be allowed to make use of the property which the law allowed him. (*b*)   But it has also been held at law, that a tenant for life, under these circumstances, was only exempt from an action of waste, the penalty of the statute of Gloucester, the recovery of treble value, and the place wasted. (*c*)

It seems, however, never to have been disputed either at law or in equity, that a tenant for life, without impeachment of waste, may open and dig mines at his own pleasure. (*d*)

The right will, of course, be accompanied with all the necessary incidents; but if it could be shown that the tenant was exercising his privilege in a wanton or malicious manner, a court of equity, it is presumed, would interfere to control him, in analogy to the principle adopted in cases of the destruction of timber and houses.

A long lease had been granted by a former Bishop of London, without impeachment of waste, and the lessee had articled with some brickmakers, that they might dig and carry away the soil of 20 acres, 6 feet deep, provided they did not dig above two acres in the year, and levelled those acres before they dug up others.   A bill of injunction was brought by the then bishop, which alleged that this was carrying away the soil, part of the inheritance, and would in consequence turn the pasture field into a pit or pond; that the defendant, in digging all the soil for the bricks, was actually destroying the field.   It was argued for the defendant that frequent experience showed that the digging of brick did not destroy the field, there being many fields about the town where bricks had been dug, and those fields used again for pasture; but that admitting it was waste, yet there being a power to commit waste, the lessee might do it, as well as open a new mine, and carry away the mineral without filling it up again.   Lord Macclesfield said that the case was within the reason of Lord Barnard's case, (*e*) where as he

(*a*) Packington *v*. Packington, 3 Atk. 215.   Abraham *v*. Bubb, 2 Freem. Rep. 53.   Vane *v*. Lord Barnard, 2 Vern. 738, 1 Salk. 161.   Bishop of London *v*. Web, 1 P. Wms. 527.   Aston *v*. Aston, 1 Ves. 264.   Piers *v*. Piers, 1 Ves. 521.   Rolt *v*. Lord Somerville, 2 Ab. Eq. 759.   Strathmore *v*. Bowes, 2 Bro. Rep. 88.

(*b*) Lewis Bowles' case, 11 Co. 79.   See 1 Ves. 265.   See Pyne *v*. Don, 1 Term Rep. 55.

(*c*) 11 Rep. 82, Co. Litt. 220. 2 Inst. 146. 6 Rep. 63. Dyer, 184.   Wood's Inst. 574.

(*d*) Plowd. 135. Hard. 96.   Tracy *v*. Tracy, 11 Vern. 23.   Bray *v*. Tracy, 1 W. Jones, 51. Aston *v*. Aston, 1 Ves. 264.

(*e*) Vane *v*. Lord Barnard, 2 Vern, 738, 1 Salk. 161.

was not permitted to destroy the castle to the prejudice of the remainder man, so neither should the lessee destroy the field against the bishop who had the reversion in fee, to the ruin of the inheritance of the church. The defendant was permitted to carry away the brick he had dug, but restrained from digging further. (*a*)

Every mining operation is *pro-tanto* a destruction of the property and particularly if the surface is interfered with, as happens in almost all cases. Such powers, therefore, must be fairly exercised. In the above case, the lessee was carrying away not the minerals only, but the soil itself.

A jointress, tenant for life, is in the same situation with respect to mines as an ordinary tenant for life, and may be subject to or without impeachment of waste. (*b*)

In a case where there was a covenant that a jointure should be of a certain yearly value, and it fell short, and the estate was not without impeachment of waste, the court refused to prohibit the jointress from committing waste so far as to make up the defect of the jointure. (*c*) But though a court of equity may refuse to lend its assistance in preventing waste in a case when there was such a strong claim for the privilege, yet an action at law might be brought against her, and it does not follow from the above decision, that the court would interfere in her favour to restrain the action.

An estate by the curtesy, and an estate in dower, are also estates for life, and the tenants are punishable for waste; (*d*) for they cannot, in their origin, be freed from the liability by the consent of parties, their estates being created by act of law. (*e*) But like other tenants for life, they may work open mines. (*f*)

The right of curtesy, extends over the whole lands, and the right to customary dower or freebench is often equally extensive. The right to dower, however, at common law, attaches only to one-third of the lands. Hence arises a difference in the term and nature of the enjoyment of lands held in dower. An interest which extends over the whole land will, of course, be accompanied with an immediate right of exclusive possession, because it does not interfere with the rights of others, but in other cases, the dower, the right to which only attaches on the death of the husband, must be assigned. Dower ought to be assigned within forty days from that event; and it is not till assignment that the widow acquires an actual estate in the land. It will be afterwards shown how that assignment should be made with reference to mines, and what is the effect of it.

There is little difference between the rights of a tenant for life, and a tenant for years. Both hold their estates equally of the grantor, the estate

(*a*) Bishop of London *v.* Web, 1 Peere W. 527.

(*b*) Basset *v.* Basset, Finch. 190. Aston *v.* Aston, 1 Ves. 264.

(*c*) Carew *v.* Carew, Abr. Eq. 221.   (*d*) 2 Inst. 294. Stat. of Glou. 6 Ed. I. c. 5.

(*e*) See supra in this chapter.   (*f*) Stoughton *v.* Leigh, 1 Taunt. 411.

of a tenant for life not being within the provisions of the statute of quia emptores against subinfeudation. Both tenants are entitled to reasonable estovers, and to take minerals, for the purposes of husbandry, and necessary repairs. (a) They are now equally punishable for waste. (b) A tenant for years may work mines already opened. (c) A clause of impeachment of waste, when inserted in a grant or demise for years, will have the same effect as when contained in a grant for life, and the lessee will be equally restrainable by a court of equity from committing wanton waste. (d)

The mines in lands held for terms of years, are generally reserved to the owner of the inheritance.

A tenant at will has no power to commit any kind of waste, and an act of waste will determine his estate. (e) He is not bound to repair houses like a tenant for years, (f) and therefore has no right to estovers.

A tenant at sufferance has no rightful estate at all, and there is no privity of estate between him and the owner of the land. His continuance of possession, therefore, alone is an act of trespass, much more, when accompanied with acts of ownership. (g)

Tenants by statute and elegit have too uncertain an interest to enable them to do more than take the ordinary profits of the estate.

A mortgagee has, in law, an absolute estate in the lands mortgaged; and is consequently entitled to take immediate possession after default in payment, and to receive the rents and profits of the estate. And a court of equity will never interfere to prevent the mortgagee from exerting these rights. (h)

With respect to mines, the mortgagee in possession, it seems, will be clearly entitled to work old mines, in satisfaction of his demands, though it has been decided that he is not bound at the utmost to advance more money in a mining speculation than a prudent owner would do. For, as Lord Eldon justly said, if he were owner, he might speculate for himself as much as he pleased; the advantages, whatever they might be, would be his, and if it turned out unfortunate, he would bear the loss. But can a mortgagee be required to do that? Can he be required to risk his own fortune in speculation, and to incur hazard in an adventure which is ultimately to redound to the benefit of the mortgagor? (i)

There can, however, be no doubt that a mortgagee in possession will be accountable for wilful default; and if the nature of the property be such as

(a) Co. Litt. 41 b.
(b) Mitchell v. Dors, 6 Ves. 147. See also Hanson v. Gardner, 7 Ves. 308.
(c) Co. Litt. 54 b.
(d) Abraham v. Bubb, 2 Freem. 63. Bishop of London v. Web, 1 P. Wms. 527.
(e) Co. Litt. 57. a.
(f) Litt. S. 71. Lady Shrewsbury's case, 3 Rep. 13 b. 1 Show. 288.
(g) Co. Litt. 57 b. 270 b.   (h) Williams v. Medlicott, 6 Price, 496. See 2 Mer. 259.
(i) Rowe v. Wood, 1 Jac. and Walk. 555.

fairly to demand the expenditure and risk of a prudent owner, he will be answerable for the neglect, for he is bound to make the most reasonable use of the estate, and to satisfy his own claims with due diligence, and the nature of the estate should have been contemplated at the time of mortgage, or of taking possession.

On the other hand, it may be concluded, that if a mortgagee in possession exceed the expenditure and risk demanded from a prudent owner, he will be equally accountable for the consequences. He will not be allowed the expences of an unnecessary or extravagant enterprise, or, it is presumed, of pursuing an enterprise in a useless or chimerical manner, but in both instances must speculate at his own hazard. (a)

But although a mortgagee in possession may be, in some cases, bound to prosecute the working of old mines and quarries, it is submitted that, in the absence of stipulation, he may be prevented from opening new mines. At law, his estate is absolute, and he is therefore subject to no action of waste or trespass; but it has been long decided in equity where the mortgagor is, until foreclosure or sale, considered to be the actual owner of the land, that a mortgagee shall not be permitted to waste the estate. (b)

If the security of a mortgagee prove defective, it has been held that he may cut down timber, and apply the produce to the satisfaction of the interest, and then of the principal, and a court of equity will not restrain him from so doing. (c) A similar principle, it may be inferred, will apply to the mines, viz. that a mortgagee will be permitted to open mines if there is a deficiency in his mortgage security, and then he must speculate at his own risk.

In a case just cited, (d) the mortgagee had opened a slate quarry. It was decided that he did it at his own hazard; but an injunction was not applied for, and therefore the question of right did not arise.

When mines form a distinct inheritance or possession, and are the subjects of limitation and conveyance, the right to work them would seem to be necessarily incident to the right of possession. The ordinary doctrines with respect to waste appear quite inapplicable to such cases. The mines are then the express subjects of conveyance, and this circumstance would supply the absence of express stipulation. Any person, therefore, in possession under such circumstances, would appear to have an unlimited right to work mines, both opened and unopened, at his own pleasure, if not otherwise prevented. The privilege to commit waste may of course be conferred by any expressions which may sufficiently show the intention of the parties.

(a) Hughes v. Williams, 12 Ves. 493.　　(b) Hanson v. Derby, 2 Vern. 392.
(c) Witherington v. Bankes, Sel. Ca. Ch. 31.　　(d) Hughes v. Williams, Supra.

CHAPTER III.

ON THE TRANSFER OF MINES.

SECTION I.

ON THE STATUTE OF FRAUDS.

THERE can be no doubt that mines and minerals, whether forming a distinct possession or inheritance or not, are within the provisions of this statute. In either case, they form part of the land itself.

In a case in Ireland, the Chief Justice of the Court of King's Bench observed, that the mining company were engaged in a partnership in interests in lands, tenements, and hereditaments. The nature of mining implied at least a right to open the ground, and keep it open, and such right to the land for a limited time and purpose as induced the court, in Crosby *v.* Wadswords, (*a*) to hold a contract for the sale of a growing crop to be within the statute. But the evidence given upon the trial, by the secretary of the company put that part of the case out of doubt. He stated, that the company had many mines at work in different parts of Ireland; that they had purchased some and rented others; and that they had erected steam engines, and smelting houses, and built workmen's houses. Now, the shares of this company were transferable, and what did a purchaser of one of them acquire, and what would he be entitled to on the dissolution of the company? Why, a share of those houses and interests in land which the company had acquired. (*b*)

The following statement of the construction of four sections of the Statute of Frauds as applicable to mines and minerals, seems to be all that is necessary on a branch of the law so familiar.

1. The first section then, requires the creation of any lease, estate, or interest in mines to be in writing, and to be signed by the parties creating it, or their agents thereunto lawfully authorised by writing.

It must particularly be observed, that the authority of an agent to create any lease or interest must be in *writing* from the principal. The authority may, of course, be either general or special, under a general power of

---

(*a*) Infra.   (*b*) Boyce *v.* Green, Batty, 608.

attorney, or for a special purpose. In practice, however, a general deputation of authority is not usually resorted to. It would confer too great authority upon agents to invest them with the power of creating any interest whatever in the mines which may lawfully pass from the grantor, and upon any terms they may think proper. Special powers are, of course not liable to the same objection, and are adopted in cases when, as in other transactions, the signature of the grantor cannot be conveniently obtained at the proper time and place.

2. The exception contained in the second section cannot be said to have any practical reference to mines ; for though the duration of interest might be made to correspond with the requisitions of the exception, it can never happen that lessees would agree to give two-third parts of the full improved value of the thing demised. The profits of mines in general are too valuable ever to admit of any reservation to that amount. The usual render with respect to all minerals is of very much less amount ; and after great expenditure of capital, time, and labour, a rent of two-thirds of the profit of a mine in its most prosperous condition would form a most disproportionate deduction from the returns of an adventure which, in almost all cases, is uncertain in its results. Even in the demise of quarries and open workings, the labour of getting and disposing of the stone or mineral must always be too great to justify so large an amount of rent.

3. It has been already observed, that the operation of the third section extends to all cases within the meaning of both the first and second. All leases and other interests, therefore, in mines and minerals, whether originally created by writing, or subsisting by parol under the second section, must be assigned and surrendered in writing, by the party himself, or by an agent lawfully authorised by him in writing, as in the first section.

But the assignment or surrender need not be by deed. A note or any writing to that effect so signed by the party or his agent will be sufficient, (a) but it must be stamped.

4. The fourth section, so far as relates to our present purpose, is confined to any contract or sale of lands, or any interest in or concerning them. For it is quite clear that the words in the remaining part of the section " or upon any agreement not to be performed within a year," does not extend to an agreement concerning lands. (b) And it is equally clear that this section contemplates in its operation not only the origin of a contract, but also all transfers of subsisting interests. (c)

But this section differs materially from the preceding ones in not requiring the authority of an agent to be in writing. It follows, therefore, that though no agent can pass a legal interest under the first and third sections, unless

(a) Farmer v. Rogers, 2 Wils. 26.

(b) Hollis v. Edwards, 1 Vern. 159. Bracebridge v. Heald, 1 Barn. & Ald. 722.

(c) Anon. 1 Ventr. 361. Poultney v. Holmes, 1 Str. 405.

their authority, however lawful, be evidenced by writing, yet, under the fourth section, they may, if otherwise lawfully authorised, bind their principal by creating or transferring in writing an equitable interest *in fieri* without being authorised by writing. The extent and nature of this authority will be noticed presently.

———

A license to work mines is very distinguishable from a lease of mines. The former is an incorporeal hereditament, a mere right, which, in some instances may be revocable, in others, not exclusive of the similar rights of others, and, in all cases, only confers a right of property in the minerals when they have been severed from the freehold, and taken into the possession of the party. A lease, on the other hand, is a distinct conveyance of an actual interest in the thing demised, the right to which attaches even before the substance is extracted or taken. The difference in the creation and properties of a license and a lease will be discussed in the next chapter.

A license or liberty to work mines is very usual in mining countries. When an adventure is entered upon, a regular lease is not always obtained, till the prospects of the enterprise promise such results as may require a more particular arrangement; and the mine is, in these cases, often worked under a license. It becomes, therefore, very important to ascertain whether such a license be within the Statute of Frauds.

It is submitted, that licenses of this description are directly within the meaning of the statute, and that this opinion rests upon reasons very different from those applicable to some of the cases which have been decided upon the subject of licenses generally.

It has, certainly, been held that a mere license is, in some instances, not within the first, and by implication, the fourth sections of the statute.

A parol agreement was entered into for liberty to stack coals on part of a close for seven years, and, during this term, the person to whom it was granted should have the sole use of that part of the close upon which he was to have the liberty of stacking coals. Lee, C. J., and Dennison, J., were of opinion, that the agreement was good, and relied upon the authority of Webb and Paternoster, (*a*) where it was held, that a grant of a license to stack hay upon land, did not amount to a lease of the land. They maintained that the agreement in the present case was only for an easement, and not for an interest in the land—that it did not amount to a lease, and consequently it was not within the Statute of Frauds. Forster, J., said, that the agreement did not amount to a lease, but he inclined to think that the words in the statute, any " uncertain interest in land," extended to the

———

(*a*) Palm. 71.

agreement upon which the other judges observed, that these words related only to interests uncertain as to the time of their duration. It was ultimately decided that the agreement was good for the seven years. (*a*)

Now, with respect to the case of Webb and Paternoster relied upon in the above case, it is sufficient to observe that the decision there was come to upon another point, and that that case arose before the Statute of Frauds. It was even there held that the interest under the license was such as bound the land in the possession of a subsequent lessee. The statute does not apply exclusively to leases and estates in land. It applies to all *interests*. A right to enter alone is an interest, much more a right to use and occupy to the exclusion of others. The decision, therefore, in Wood *v*. Lake, was directly against both the spirit and language of the statute.

That decision, however, has been followed in several cases, but the point seems to have been very carelessly discussed. It has been successively held that a parol license to put a sky-light over an area, a parol agreement for leave to inhabit a house, a parol license to build a house on the waste of a manor, and a parol beneficial license to be exercised upon land, are all valid as not conferring interests in lands. (*b*)

In the above cases, there was simply a right either to control *pro tanto* the right of ownership in the lands of another, or to use and occupy the land for a definite purpose, and without any liberty for converting or appropriating the land for other purposes. But a license to work mines is of a very different description. It confers not only a right to enter and occupy, but to commit waste, and carry away part of the land itself—viz., the minerals. This right may, as we shall afterwards see, be in some instances revocable at the will of the party, but even then it will, of course, exist in full force till revocation. It seems, therefore, impossible to contend that this right is not an interest within the Statute of Frauds. To assert that, it would be necessary to maintain that the minerals are not part of the land.

An interest in land may exist where there is no actual estate in the land. And it has, in other cases, been determined that such an interest is within the meaning of the statute.

Thus, it has been decided that sales of growing poles, of standing underwood, of a crop of mowing grass, are all within the statute. (*c*) It is true the cases upon this subject are very conflicting, and that the leaning in the later decisions is certainly in favour of bringing the *produce* of the land not within the first and fourth sections, but the seventeenth section, which en-

(*a*) Wood *v*. Lake, Say. 3.

(*b*) Winter *v*. Brockwell, 8 East, 308. Rex *v*. Inhabs. of Standen, 2 Mau. and Sel. 461. Rex *v*. Inhabs. of Hornden, 4 Mau. and Sel. 562. Tayler *v*. Waters, 2 Marsh. 551. 7 Taunt. 374. But see Cocker *v*. Cowper, 1 Cro. Mees. and Rosc. 418. Fentiman *v*. Smith, 4 East. 107. Hewlins *v*. Shippam, 3 Barn. and C. 233.

(*c*) Teall *v*. Anty, 4 Moo. 542. Scorell *v*. Boxall, 1 You. and Jerv. 396. Crosby *v*. Wadsworth, 6 East, 602. See Carrington *v*. Roots, 2 Mees. and Wels. 248.

acts, that no contract for the sale of goods, wares, and merchandise, for the price of ten pounds or upwards, shall be allowed to be good, except the buyer shall accept part of the goods so sold, and actually receive the same, or give something in earnest to bind the bargain, or in part of payment, or that some note or memorandum of the bargain be made and signed by the parties, to be charged by such contract or their agents thereunto lawfully authorised. (*a*) But notwithstanding this inclination, it is not to be supposed that the courts will ever repudiate the distinction of Lord Ellenborough in the case of Crosby *v.* Wadsworth, where he said, with respect to a growing crop of grass, that, in the outset, he felt himself warranted in laying wholly out of the case, the provision contained in the seventeenth section, as not applicable to the subject matter of that agreement, which could not be considered in any proper sense of the words as a sale of goods, wares, or merchandise, the crop being at the time of the bargain (and with reference to which he agreed with Mr. Justice Heath in Waddington *v.* Bristow, (*b*) that the subject matter must be taken) an *unsevered* portion of the freehold, and not moveable goods or personal chattels. (*c*)

In a late case, (*d*) where a farm was agreed to be let by parol, and the tenant was to take the growing crops and pay for them, and also for the work, labour, and materials, in preparing the land for tillage, it was decided that this case was within the fourth section of the statute. It was held by the court, that at the time when the contract was made, the crops were growing upon the land, the tenant was to have had the land as well as the crops, and the work, labour, and materials were so incorporated with the land as to be *inseparable* from it. He would not have the benefit of the work, labour, and materials, unless he had the land, and they were of opinion that the right to the crops, and the benefit of the work, labour, and materials were *both* of them an interest in the land.

It must, therefore, be concluded, that a license to work mines is within the first, third, and fourth sections of the Statute of Frauds; that it must be in writing, either from the grantor or an agent lawfully authorised by writing under the first section; that it must be transferred, or surrendered in writing either by the assignor, surrenderor, or some agent also lawfully authorised by writing, under the third section; and that under the fourth section a bare agreement only for a license, if in writing, may be entered into either by the intended grantor or his agent lawfully authorised, and the authority of the agent need not be in writing. But a license cannot be within the exception of the second section, which applies only to leases.

(*a*) See Waddington *v.* Bristow, 2 Bos. and Pull. 452. Evans *v.* Roberts, 5 Barn. and Cress. 829. Parker *v.* Staniland, 11 East, 362. Warwick *v.* Bruce, 2 Mau. and Sel. 205. Smith *v.* Surman, 9 Barn. and Cress. 561. Sainsbury *v.* Matthews, 4 Mees. and Wels. 343. Dunne *v.* Ferguson. 1 Hayes, 541.

(*b*) Supra.   (*c*) See also Boyce *v.* Green, Batty, 608, supra.

(*d*) Lord Falmouth *v.* Thomas, 1 Crompt. and Mees. 89.

It was decided in the above case of Carrington *v*. Roots, (*a*) that an agreement under the fourth section, though altogether void, may have some operation in communicating a license, so far as to excuse what would otherwise be a trespass, but such a license could confer no interest, and would be always countermandable at the will of the party.

It is a general rule, that a bare personal right or a bare power cannot be assigned. We have seen, however, that a license to work mines confers a distinct interest in the land, which may, therefore, be assigned in the same manner as a power coupled with an interest, or a power to cut down trees. But the right or liberty must, of course, be exercised by the assignor in the manner pointed out by the original grantor. (*b*) A license often expressly extends to the assigns of a grantee.

The general construction and duration of a license will be considered in the next chapter.

An agreement was entered into by the committee of a lunatic, under the following circumstances. The lunatic was tenant for life, without impeachment of waste, with remainder to his first and other sons in tail, with other remainders over. The lunatic was unmarried. Coal was found upon the estate, but not in sufficient quantity to justify the sinking of a shaft; but the coal might be worked by means of a shaft in the adjoining land. Part of the estate of the lunatic was mortgaged, and the mortgagee was in possession. The income of the lunatic was considerably reduced, and there were other debts which could not be satisfied. The committee, therefore, agreed with the owner of the adjoining land to work the coal. The master, who was attended by the next of kin, reported this to be for the benefit of the lunatic. Lord Eldon, on confirming the report, said, the circumstances were singular. The next of kin had an interest that the coal should be worked. The heir at law had no interest, there being various remainders over. He thought it might be done by the committee; it was like cutting timber. (*c*)

Section II.

Transfer by Deed.

Having thus discussed the provisions of the first four sections of the Statute of Frauds with respect to the alienation of mining property, we may now proceed to enquire into the mode of alienation sanctioned and required by the common law, independent of that Statute.

(*a*) 2 Mees. and Wels. 257. See also 3 Barn. and C. 232.

(*b*) Warren *v*. Arthur, 2 Mod. 317.

(*c*) *Ex parte* Tabbert, 6 Ves. 428. As to leases and agreements on the part of lunatics and infants, See 1 Will. IV. c. 65.

All contracts and conveyances effected by deed or specialty, must be both signed and sealed. Signature is now required in all cases by the statute, and sealing is required by the common law. But, of course, when sealing is not required by the common law for giving validity to any instrument, signature alone will be sufficient.

Thus, leases were originally granted for a very small term of years, and though afterwards granted for longer periods, they continued to be created, before the statute, by parol, for any number of years. It follows, therefore that since the statute, leases for years may both be created and assigned by simple signature without sealing. But they will not, in this state, acquire the full operation of an indenture or deed, and the covenants which usually accompany them, are specialties which require the proper formalities to be observed. Leases and assignments therefore, are usually made in the same manner as deeds in general.

When the mines form part of the general inheritance, they will, of course, be transferred along with the lands without being expressly mentioned in the conveyance; but when they form a distinct possession or inheritance, a title to them must be established without reference to the general title to the lands in which they are situate.

In the latter situation, the mines will still, of course, retain the qualities of real estate, and will be transferred by conveyances applicable to the particular disposition of them intended to be made.

They are capable of livery, and of being made the subjects of ejectment. (a) " By the name of *minera*," says Coke, " or *fodina plumbi*, &c., the land itself shall pass in a grant, if livery be made, and also be recovered in an assise." (b)

It has been stated that if a grant of mines be made without livery, the grantor will only take a power to dig and work them. (c) But although the grantor would, in such a case, take no legal estate or right at all, except the liberty to work, yet his title might be perfected by a court of equity on the ground of contract.

It has been stated, indeed, that a common recovery could not have been suffered of a quarry, or a mine, because they are not in demesne, but in profit only. (d) But since the later cases upon the subject of mines, it may be clearly laid down that there is no distinction. Mines and minerals are parts of the very lands or demesnes themselves.

A distinction has been attempted to be taken between the transfer of opened and of unopened mines. Unopened mines have been thought so far to resemble an estate in remainder as to be incapable of livery of seisin, and to be only passed by grant. This opinion has been founded on the

(a) Comyn v. Kynoto, Cro. Jac. 150. Barnes v. Mawson, 1 Mau. and S. 77.
(b) Co. Litt. 6 a.   (c) Shepp. Touch. 96.   (d) Pigot, 96, 18 Vin. Abr. 218.

decision that unopened mines are not liable to dower. (*a*)   It will be afterwards shewn (*b*) that that doctrine rests upon very different grounds from those founded on the notion that unopened mines bear any resemblance to an estate in remainder.   All mines, whether opened or unopened, are parts of the freehold and inheritance, and they are equally, in all cases, in the possession of the tenant. (*c*)   It has been expressly held that mines do not lie in grant. (*d*)   As real hereditaments, they pass by livery of seisin.   Unopened mines are not incapable of livery.   The mines are not the subjects of transfer, but the minerals which are acquired by mining.   These minerals, or the mineral veins, are almost always so far accessible from the surface as to be capable, either by ordinary or mechanical means, of livery, without the actual operation of mining.   It is submitted, therefore, that there is no distinction in this respect, between opened and unopened mines; but it would certainly appear, that the modern form, by lease and release, is more applicable in both cases, than a conveyance depending upon livery of seisin.

It may here be observed, that a license for a grantor and his heirs to exercise a right over the lands of another person will confer a freehold interest; and will, therefore, require to be created by deed, without reference to its being an interest in land under the Statute of Frauds. (*e*)

It is scarcely necessary to add, that all leases and licenses for lives, or any other freehold interest, will require similar formalities.   A license being an incorporeal hereditament, should be created by grant ; but a license for years may be created, like a lease for years, by simple signature under the first section of the Statute of Frauds, although it is a usual practice to confer it in the form of a demise, accompanied with the ordinary covenants and stipulations.

The subject of leases and licenses will be resumed in the next chapter.

Mines are very frequently excepted in a conveyance.   When the exception contained in a deed of feoffment is in favour of the grantor, there can be no necessity for livery, because the grantor will never have been out of possession of the thing expected. (*f*)   But when the exception is in favour of third persons, or strangers to the legal estate, this livery cannot be dispensed with.

A conveyance in fee was made by a mortgagor and a mortgagee, in fee of certain lands to a purchaser ; and the purchaser, by the same deed, covenanted and granted to the mortgagor and his heirs, that it should be lawful for them to enter and work coal or other mines, with a proviso that deduction for damages done should be made from a yearly rent. which was also

(*a*) Burton's Comp. 386.   (*b*) Sec sec. 4 in this chapter.
(*c*) Lewis *v.* Branthwaite, 2 Barn. and Ad. 437.
(*d*) Chetham *v.* Williamson, 4 East, 476.
(*e*) Hewlins *v.* Shippam, 3 Barn. and C. 221.
(*f*) Co. Litt. 47 a, Doe dem. Douglas *v.* Lock, 1 Ad. and Ell. 743.
68

granted to the mortgagor. The mines were worked under the authority of persons claiming under a title derived from the purchaser; and an action of trover was brought against them by one claiming under a title derived from the mortgagee. The question was, whether the mortgagor had an exclusive right to the coal under the lands conveyed, or only a concurrent right with the purchaser, from whom the defendant claimed—and it was contended for the plaintiff, that the covenant and grant amounted to a reservation and exception of the coal in the grant to the purchaser; the legal estate and inheritance of which remained in the mortgagor, and those claiming under him. It was held by Lawrence J., that the covenant could not operate as an exception or reservation in favour of the mortgagor who had no legal estate in him at the time, but only the equity of redemption. He was in law no more than a stranger to the estate, and could not except or reserve that which he had not before. The covenant, therefore, could only operate as a grant; but a grant would not pass the land itself without livery. (*a*)

It must also be observed, that there must be an express exception or reservation of the mines, or a clear intention that they are not to pass under the conveyance, even when the grantor is in possession of the legal estate—for otherwise they may be granted over, and a mere license to work for, and carry away the minerals, may thus be only reserved.

This was the case of Lord Mountjoy, who was seised of two parts of a manor, and who conveyed them to purchasers, with a proviso and covenant, that it should be lawful for the grantor and his heirs to dig in the heath ground of the premises, sufficient ores for the making of alum or copperas, without interruption of the purchasers or their heirs. This was no exception of the minerals. (*b*)

SECTION III.

BY WILL.

There is nothing to engage particular attention in the transfer of mines and minerals by will, but there are some consequences arising from the duties of executors and trustees, which it will be proper to consider in this place.

Mines, under almost any circumstances, are of variable and uncertain value. They are described by Lord Hardwicke, as being in the nature of a trade. (*c*) Mines, therefore, constitute part of the perishable property of a testator, which is subject to particular regulations.

(*a*) Chetham *v*. Williamson, 4 East, 469. See Earl of Cardigan *v*. Armitage, 2 Barn. and C. 197.

(*b*) Lord Mountjoy's case, Godb. 17. 4. Leon. 147. 1 And. 307. Moore, 174.

(*c*) 1 Bro. C. C. 289. 3 Atk. 14.

These regulations, however, can only apply to personal property, or to real hereditaments.which are directed to be sold and converted into personal estate ; and which are in equity immediately upon the death of a testator invested with all the qualities of personalty. When mines, therefore,—whether worked or unworked, and whether forming a distinct inheritance or not, are devised as the freehold or copyhold hereditaments of the testator without any directions for conversion, or if they descend in this state to the heir, they will follow the course of alienation pointed out by the testator, or by the will of the law, without being subject to the rules applicable to personal property of a perishable description ; for, in such cases, mines will be placed beyond the general control of trustees and personal representatives. They must be enjoyed in the manner in which they devolve or descend.

If, again, the mines form part of the personal property of the testator, either in connection with the lands in which they are situate, or as a separate possession in the lands of others, and are devised as a specific bequest, either immediately to the parties entrusted, or through the intervention of trustees for them, the subject of devise must also be taken and enjoyed in the mode appointed by the testator. It will make no difference if the objects of the testator's bounty are directed to take absolutely or in succession for limited interests, with remainders over. As the testator has not thought proper to direct a sale, the law presumes that he intended his property to be enjoyed in the actual condition in which it is left by him. The ordinary principles of law which will be presently mentioned, and which arise from the propriety of avoiding risk in winding up the affairs of a testator, or of making adequate provision for persons successively interested in the subject of devise are, therefore, deprived of their operation. (a)

It remains only to consider, therefore, the consequences resulting from a devise of mines, when they form, or are directed to form, personal property, and are not the subjects of a specific devise, or of any special directions.

The law imposes upon an executor and administrator, the duty, and affords him the power, of collecting the assets, and distributing the effects of a testator ; generally speaking, they have the complete control over the personal property of the deceased. (b) It is their duty to perform their trust in a manner most advantageous to the estate. When mines, therefore, have been vested in an executor without any special directions with respect to them, or pass to the administrator by operation of law, these personal representatives will have full power to dispose of them, without reference to the fact of their being classed amongst property of a perishable and uncertain nature. It has been held, indeed, that direct acts of abuse, misapplication of assets, fraudulent or neglectful mismanagement of the estate, will charge them with the consequences of a *devastavit*, and will render them personally liable. (c)

(a) Gibson v. Bott, 7 Ves. 96. Howe v. Lord Dartmouth, 7 Ves. 147.
(b) Whale v. Booth, 4 T. R. 625. Nugent v. Gifford, 1 Atk. 463.
(c) See Wentworth. Off. Exors. 302. and Bac. Abr. Ex. (L) 1.

But courts of equity have always been extremely liberal in defining the duties of an executor or administrator, and cautious in rendering them liable upon slight grounds. (*a*)   There does not appear to be any reason for concluding that a personal representative is obliged, under such circumstances, to dispose of the mining property of the deceased, although he would certainly be liable for consequences induced by carrying on, or concurring in carrying on, mining stipulations in an unreasonable .or neglectful course of mismanagement.   It has been seen that mining is a kind of trade, though it would be impossible to establish any complete analogy to ordinary trading. Now the personal representatives of a deceased owner have, in general, no authority to carry on his business. (*b*)   And with respect to the public, they will become personally liable on failure of assets, to all debts contracted in connection with it since the death of the owner. (*c*)

It may be observed, however, that in cases of distinct contract by the deceased, the representatives will be bound to carry on a business. (*d*)   This sometimes happens in cases of partnership.

Such would appear to be the situation of an executor, when the mines are destined to devolve immediately for the benefit of persons taking permanent interests in the funds.   But if, on the other hand, they are to form a property, or part of a fund, limited first to tenants for life, and then to persons in remainder, it may be clearly deduced from the cases on this subject, not only that a tenant for life may call upon the executor or administrator to convert the property into the 3 per cent. consols—but that they will be personally liable for the consequences if they do not so convert it.   For it might otherwise happen, that the persons in remainder could derive no benefit from the devise, by the entire exhaustion of the profits and property during the enjoyment of the tenant for life.

This principle of the courts of equity is of such universal application, that it is contained in every decree under such circumstances, with respect to any wearing out funds, or any fund in which the tenant for life might ·have an advantage over those in remainder.   It applies to all the public funds, except those invariably selected by the courts for the investment of mines, viz., the per cent. consols. (*e*)

In a late case of importance, a testator gave the residue of his personal estate to trustees, with directions for them to convert and invest the proceeds in government or real securities, of which they were to stand possessed, upon trust for a tenant for life, with remainder over.   The trustees permitted a share which the testator had in an Indian loan, bearing interest

(*a*) See Powell *v*. Evans, 5 Ves. 843.   Raphael *v*. Boehm, 13 Ves. 410.   Tebbs *v*. Carpenter, 1 Madd. 298.   Garrett *v*. Noble, 6 Sim. 504.

(*b*) Barker *v*. Barker, 1 T. R. 295.   *Ex parte* Garland, 10 Ves. 119.

(*c*) Wightman *v*. Townroe, 1 M. and S. 412.

(*d*) Marshall *v*. Broadhurst, 1 Crompt. and J. 405. 1 Tyrw. 350.

(*e*) Howe *v*. Earl Dartmouth, 7 Ves. 150, and the cases cited in p. 141. .

at £10 per cent., to remain for several years unconverted, and paid, during that time, the whole of the interest to the tenant for life. The loan was afterwards paid off, and the money was invested in the 3 per cents., at a time the funds were so low, that the amount of stock purchased was considerably greater than if the conversion had taken place at the end of a year from the testator's death. It was held by Lord Gifford, that the tenant for life was not entitled to the actual interest which the money yielded on the Indian security, but only to the dividends of so much 3 per cent. stock as would have been purchased with it at the end of a year from the testator's death; that the trustees ought to be charged with the whole of the stock actually purchased, and all the sums actually received, and that they ought to be allowed in their discharge as paymemts to the tenant for life, not the sums actually paid to her, but only a sum equal to what she would have received for dividends, if the money had been transferred from the Indian security, and invested in the 3 per cents. at the end of a year from the testator's death. Lord Lyndhurst, on appeal, confirmed this judgment. (a)

The same principle will equally apply, when there is no express direction in the testator's will for the conversion of his personal estate; for it has been held, that what the court would decree, it will expect from an executor. (b)

In the case of Cranch v. Cranch, (c) an enquiry was directed under similar circumstances, whether it was for the benefit of the person entitled to the clear residue of the personal estate to have certain leasehold premises sold; and if it would be for their benefit, it was ordered that they should be sold, and that the money should be laid out in the 3 per cents., the dividends to be paid to the tenant for life, with liberty to apply after her death; and the practice of the court is stated by Lord Eldon to be, not to permit a real security to be called in without an enquiry whether it would be for the benefit of every person. (d)

But in the case of working mines, there can be no reason for supposing that it would be necessary to apply to the Court for an enquiry to be made, or that the Court would not order the conversion to be made at once, for the above principle of law applies with greater force to mines than perhaps any other description of property. In such cases the interest is infinitely variable and more perishable than those kinds of property which the Court has considered subject to conversion. A tenant for life might not only re-receive an annual sum far beyond the interest of the produce which would have resulted from a sale, but he might actually anticipate the whole fund reserved for those in remainder.

(a) Dimes v. Scott, 4 Russ. 195. See also Fearns v. Young, 9 Ves. 549

(b) Howe v. Earl Dartmouth, 7 Ves. 150.

(c) Cited in the report of the last case, p. 143.

(d) Howe v. Lord Dartmouth, supra.

The proper time for conversion is stated by Lord Eldon in the case last cited. If, he observed, the principle was, that the court, when its observation was thrown upon it, will order the conversion, it ought to be considered to all practicable purposes as converted, when it could be first converted; for no party ought to suffer by the circumstance, that what ought to have been done, and what the court would have directed to be done immediately on the testator's death, was not done.

But this duty is not so imperative as to require an immediate sale. Even when property is directed by the testator himself to be sold, as soon as conveniently after his decease, or with all convenient speed, and the property is not sold, the value of the property will not be taken at the time of his death.. In one case, Lord Eldon himself observed, that if a fund is to be converted with all convenient speed, those words never required it to be sold the very next day. The Court was obliged to take a general rule, as it was impossible to make the enquiry in every particular case. The rule was the end of a year after the death. (a)

If, therefore, the property be not sold within the year, the value will be taken at the end of the year from the death of the testator, and the trustees will be responsible for a depreciation after that period. But whether the property be actually sold or not, within that time, the person entitled for life will acquire a right to an interest from the time of the testator's death; (b) but the interest will be calculated upon the actual produce of a sale within the year; or if not sold, upon what would have been produced, if a sale had taken place at the end of a year from the testator's death. (c)

It is sometimes stipulated in copartnership deeds for carrying on mines for a term of years, that the parties and their personal representatives shall not be allowed to alien their shares without leave from the company. The question then arises when any of these shares are limited in the manner just mentioned, to a tenant for life, with remainder over, in what manner the tenant for life is to be precluded from the possibility of exhausting the fund. It does not appear that there is any ground of distinction from ordinary cases, except indeed, that the value of the property cannot be tested by an actual sale. Recourse must therefore be had, to valuation by competent persons. It is certainly very difficult to estimate the proper value of mining property. The adventure may be crowned with success, or its prospects may be blasted by the experience of a day. This difficulty would be seriously increased if a valuation were required to be made with reference to some remote period. Every thing, however, has its supposed value, though that value may differ most materially from its real worth. The law acts upon general rules—there is, in this instance, the same necessity for the exercise of the rule; and if re-

(a) Gibson v. Bott, 7 Ves. 89. See also Sitwell v. Bernard, 6 Ves. 520.
(b) Angerstein v. Martin, 1 Turn. and Russ. 232. Hewitt v. Morris, Ibid. 241.
(c) Dimes v. Scott, 4 Russ. 209.

course cannot be had to the best of all tests of value, viz., an actual sale, yet this does not preclude an approximation to the value by other means. In cases where no sale is effected for a considerable period, the interest payable to the tenant for life, as we have seen, must be calculated with reference to the same mode. In the case of Gibson v. Bott, (a) the Court directed that, as it was for the interest of all parties, that the leasehold property should not be sold, a value should be set upon them ; and the persons entitled for life should have the interest at 4 per cent. upon that value. In like manner, when an actual sale cannot be resorted to, as in the case we are discussing, a valuation must be made by competent persons, and interest allowed upon the amount. This valuation may be made at any time within a year from the death of the testator, but in the case of property liable to considerable fluctuation, to prevent disputes, it might be advisable to postpone the valuation till the end of the year. (b) It will be seen afterwards, that in cases of partnership, mines held for freehold interests in certain cases, on the death of an owner, will be classed amongst the personal property of the firm, and be transmissible accordingly. (c)

Section IV.

BY OPERATION OF LAW.

It is scarcely necessary to say that mines, like other kinds of real property, are subject to the usual laws of descent, devolution, and transfer, by act of law, according to the freehold or chattel interest acquired in them. We shall, therefore, only have occasion, in this section, to notice any peculiarities which may attend some cases of transfer by act of law.

Mines held in fee which are opened, are liable to dower. Dower should be assigned within forty days after the death of the husband, and an actual estate in dower does not arise till assignment by the sheriff or the tenant.

It has been held, however, that a widow is not entitled to dower in respect of mines which have not been opened. (d) The reasons for this decision are not recorded, but they may be presumed to consist in the uncertain nature of the property, and the impracticability of effecting an assignment.

There is no difference in the liability of mines forming a separate inheritance. (e)

In the case just cited, the Court was of opinion that the widow was dowable of all mines of the deceased husband, as well those in his own landed estates, as those in the lands of other persons, which had been wrought or opened before his death, and wherein he had an estate of inheritance,

---

(a) 7 Ves. 89.
(c) See Chap. viii.
(e) 1 Taunt. 410.

(b) See Dimes v. Scott, supra.
(d) Stoughton v. Leigh, 1 Taunt. 410.

and that her right to dower had no dependance upon the subsequent con-tinuance or discontinuance of working them, either by the husband, or those claiming under him.

It was also held that this right of dower could not be affected by leases made by the husband during coverture; but if any of the existing leases for years were made by the husband before marriage, then the endowment must be of the reversions and the rents reserved; in which case the widow would be bound, so long as the demises continued, to take her share of the renders, whether pecuniary or otherwise, according to the terms of reser-vation.

Dower may be assigned by parol, notwithstanding the Statute of Frauds, for her estate is not created but only ascertained by assignment; and when she has entered, after assignment, the freehold rests in her without livery of seisin, (a) whether the assignment has been accomplished by agreement, or by the course of law.

Dower may be assigned by mutual agreement between the owner of the freehold and the widow, and her acceptance of the provision by indenture will preclude her from asserting any further claim. (b)　But if her dower be refused to her, she may proceed either by writ of dower, at common law, or in equity by a bill for an assignment. In the former case, if her right is established, the sheriff is then directed to make the assignment; and, in the latter case, a commission usually issues for the same purpose, or the master may be directed to assign it. (c)　But the mode of proceeding, though varying in form, are substantially the same, with respect to the prin-ciple of assignment.

It is not necessary that the widow should have a third or other proportion of each part of the husband's estates. Thus, it has been held, that if the husband be possessed of several different mines, it is not necessary that the sheriff should divide each of them; but he may assign such a number of them as may amount to one-third in value of the whole. (d)

But when there is but one mine, or if it is not desirable to assign some in discharge of the whole, it it obvious that the ordinary mode of assignment by metes and bounds is impracticable, and some other means must be resort-ed to for determining the estate of the dowress. The following distinctions have been recognized :—

If the mines are within the lands of the husband, the sheriff must estimate the annual value; but he need not assign to her any of the mines themselves, or any part of them; the widow's part may consist wholly of lands set out by metes and bounds, in which are some of the mines.—But he may, if he chooses, include any of the mines or minerals in the assignment; and if the

(a) Co. Litt. 32. b, n. 1. 34 a. 35 a.　Rowe ♦. Power, 2 N. R, 134.
(b) Dyer, 91 b., pl. 12.　　　　　　　(c) Goodenough v. Goodenough, 2 Dick. 795.
(d) Stoughton v. Leigh, 1 Taunt. 411.　See 9 Vin. Ab. 257 ?60.

lands in which they are form no part of the lands assigned for dower, the mines should be specifically described; if, however, the mines assigned be included in the lands set out in dower, it is not necessary to particularise them, as they are parts of the lands assigned. But the sheriff may not adopt any of these methods; he may divide the enjoyment and perception of the profits of the mines between the parties—viz., by directing the separate alternate enjoyment of the whole for short periods, proportioned to the share each party had in the subject, or by giving to the widow an adequate part of the profits. (*a*)

If, again, the mines subject to dower are in the lands of other persons, the sheriff need not divide each of the mines; but he may assign such a number of them as may amount to one-third in value of the whole, or he may proportion the enjoyment of them in such a manner as to give each person a proper share of the whole. (*b*)

It would be to enter too minutely into the subject to discuss the remedies for excessive or defective assignments. (*c*) It may be observed, however, that when the assignment is made by the heir of full age and under no disability, and not by the sheriff, the heir will be bound by the assignment, although it exceeded the widow's part of the estate; for it is the act of a person *sui juris*, and uncontrolled in the distribution of his estate. (*d*) But a Court of equity, it is presumed, would relieve the heir against the consequences not only of fraud, but of evident mistake.

In the case of Stoughton *v.* Leigh, just cited, it appeared that the heir being of full age, let his ancestor's widow into possession of, and assigned to her for dower of a certain estate certain closes of land, in which there was an open coal mine wrought at times during the marriage, but which had been discontinued long before the husband's death.—The value of the closes was amply sufficient to answer any demand of dower, without regard to the value of any of the coal. The question was, whether the heir had any and what relief in respect to the excess of his own assignment. And it was held, that since the assignment was the act of the heir himself, he being of full age at the time, he had no remedy at law against the dowress for avoiding the consequences of that act, and that the dowress was at full liberty to work the mine, notwithstanding the excess of assignment.

But if the heir making an excessive assignment was only an heir in tail, it may be doubted whether those in remainder would be bound by his acts.

An infant heir may assign dower, for the widow's claim is urgent, and necessary for her immediate support. (*e*)—However, in consequence of his disability, the law protects him against the consequences of an excessive assignment, and he may, even before he arrives at full age, be supplied with the

---

(*a*) Stoughton *v.* Leigh, supra.   (*b*) Ibid.
(*c*) See Roper on Husband and Wife, chap. ix. sec. 3.
(*d*) Gilb. Dower, 300.   (*e*) 1 Roll. Abr. 137, 681. Gore *v.* Perdue, Cro. Eliz. 309.

writ of admeasurement, which is addressed to the sheriff, and which directs him to make the admeasurement finally. (*a*)

It has been doubted, whether, if an open mine of coals or lead were in the share assigned by the infant heir, so as to render the widow's third of greater value than the remaining two-thirds, a writ of admeasurement would lie.(*b*) It is difficult to conceive, in the case of an open mine not taken into the estimation, any ground of distinction from an ordinary case of excessive assignment ; and it is presumed, that there can be no doubt in such a case. But if the value of the mine had been taken into account, and its prospects, though since improved, were then such as to make no material distinction in the actual apportionment, it might of course be contended, that there was reason why the writ should be issued. It is presumed the value must be taken at the time of the assignment, and the heir would not be entitled to the writ if the value had increased since the assignment, for the writ is given to correct errors and unfair dealings ; and the assignment might be perfectly fair at the time it was made. All such questions may be brought by either party before the judges of the Court of Common Pleas, who will direct the writ, and proceed to make the proper admeasurement. (*c*)

It would appear, therefore, that if the value was fairly ascertained at the time of the assignment, the dowress will be entitled to all the increased value which may afterwards have resulted from the improved condition of the mine.

But if the value was not fairly ascertained at the time of the assignment, there must then be a proper re-valuation of the property at that period, and a fair distribution made accordingly. In the case of mines, this would be sufficiently difficult to determine. It might be a matter of great doubt, and subject to much conflicting evidence, to ascertain the value of a mine at any remote period of its history ; for the value of a mine not only depends upon the actual profits, but upon the difficulties which have been overcome, or which may be anticipated, and the general prospects of the adventure. It is sufficiently difficult to estimate the value of a mine at any period.

It is stated by Fitzherbert, that if the lands assigned by the infant heir exceed one-third of the whole, and they become more valuable than the remainder, by improvements made by the widow, a writ of admeasurement will not lie on account of such improvements, as that would be unjust, since she may have been induced to make them under a presumption that the assignment was proper (*d*) It has been suggested, that there seems no objection to the admeasurement of the lands assigned, and to the heir taking the overplus, upon allowing for the value of the improvements of the excess of lands assigned. Thus, if the assignment were of four acres when the number

---

(*a*) Fitz. N. B. 149 B.   Gilb. Dower, 385.   But see Co. Litt. 39, 2 Inst. 367.

(*b*) Fitz. N. B. 149 C.   (*c*) Fitz. N. B. 148, G. H.   Gilb. Dower, 385.

(*d*) Fitz. N. B. 149 C.

should have been three, the heir might take back the fourth upon the admeasurement, and make compensation to the widow for the value of its improvements. (a) But it does not appear clear that the sheriff of the Court of Common Pleas has the power under the writ, of awarding compensation, in such cases, to the widow. If this be the case, relief must be sought for in a Court of Equity, which would probably either put the parties to elect between the acceptance of certain terms, or a new assignment on the basis of the improvements. (b)

To what extent such a principle might be held to apply to mines, it would be impossible to say. If the dowress had been successful in converting her expenditure into a source of profit, there seems no reason why such a rule should not be made available in her favour. But in other instances, it is conceived, the uncertain nature of mining speculations would preclude her from demanding any amount of compensation.

It has been decided that when dower has been sued for at law, and a partial or improper return has been made by the sheriff, the heir or tenant may be relieved in equity. Thus, a suit was brought for relief against a fraudulent assignment of the sheriff, who had given to the widow a full third part in which there was a coal mine of considerable annual value, but in respect of which no consideration was had in the assignment. The Court proposed terms for the consideration and acceptance of the widow, and directed, if they were not accepted, that a new assignment of dower should be made. (c)

A widow will also be entitled to dower, when there is a licence or liberty in fee to work mines. Although this liberty only forms an incorporeal hereditament, yet it savours of the reality sufficiently to become liable to dower. (d)

Mines, of course, may also descend in coparcenery.

The case of Lord Mountjoy, (e) is the only one which seems to refer to this subject. In that case, there was only a liberty to work mines, and it appears to have been held that such a right descending in coparcenery, was incapable of division, and that the coparceners should continue to work the mines with one stock, participating equally in the expenditure and the profits.

It has been observed, that from the report of the case by Lord Anderson, it appears that this was a mere dictum, either of some of the judges, or of the other reporters. For this point of indivisibility is not noticed in Anderson, who gives the opinion of the judges as it was certified in writing to the

(a) Roper on Husb. and Wife, vol. i. p. 409.   (b) Hoby v. Hoby, 1 Vern. 218.
(c) Hoby v. Hoby, 1 Vern. 218. 2 Ch. Ca. 160. See also Sneyd v. Sneyd, 1 Atk. 442.
(d) Co. Litt. 32 a, and b. Cro. Jac. 621. Fitz. N. B. 148 c.
(e) Godb. 17. 1 And. 307, and Mo. 174.

privy council ; nor is it one of the questions stated by Anderson to have been referred to the judges. (a)

This dictum, however, meets with the approbation of Sir Edward Coke, and does not seem to be any reason for disputing it. After citing the case, Coke proceeds to say, that then it might be demanded what should become of these inheritances ?—The answer is, that it appeared that regularly the eldest should have the indivisible inheritance, and the rest should have a contribution, that is, an allowance of the value in some other of the inheritance. But what if the common ancestor left no other inheritance to give any thing in allowance, what contribution or recompense should the younger coparceners have ?—It is answered, that one coparcener shall have the subject matter for a time, and the other for a like time—as the one for one year, and the other for another, or more, or lesser time, *whereby no prejudice could grow to the owner of the soil.* (b)

The mere right to work mines, is, as we have seen, an incorporeal hereditament existing in the land of other persons ; and it is indivisible, because a division of the right would create new rights, and would prejudice the owner of the soil. All the coparceners cannot exercise the full right. This is the true reason why the enjoyment of coparceners must be distributed with respect to time, or limited to acts proceeding from a union of interests. Such is the law with respect to estovers, appendant to a freehold, a right of piscary uncertain, and common sans number, in all which and similar cases, a partition would enlarge the original grant beyond the intention of the grantor. (c)

But the case is very different when a distinct right of property in mines descends in coparcenery. And though this subject has never called for judicial discussion, there can be no doubt that, in analogy to what has been decided with respect to dower in mines, coparceners would be also held to be entitled to a partition. Their rights, in this case, have no such interference with the property of others. They are seised not of bare right, but of an estate in fee, divisible in its nature.

It is presumed, therefore, that mines whether forming a distinct inheritance or not, may be divided amongst any number of coheiresses under a commission issuing from the Court of Chancery. The writ of partition is now abolished. If there are other hereditaments or many mines, each coparcener may be entitled to a distinct and separate estate either in any of the mines or in other hereditaments, or in both, according to the circumstances of the case. If the property consist only of mines, and these are incapable of convenient and separate partition, the proper proceedings might easily be suggested by reference to the mode of partition in a case of a similar nature, or of assignment of dower. It is unnecessary to add, that

(a) See Co. Litt. 165 a. n. 1.   (b) Co. Litt. 165 a.
(c) Co. Litt. 32 a. Godb. 21. Perk. sec. 341.

coparceners may also, when competent, agree to any special enjoyment or partition in the usual way. (*a*)

Similar observations will apply to joint tenants, and tenants in common.

Mines, when held for chattel interest, will vest in administrators, in case of intestacy, and whether held for freehold or chattel interests, will also vest in the assignees of the estates of bankrupts and insolvents. They will also be subject to the ordinary processes of executions on judgment.

Under the third section of the Statute of Frauds, existing interests in land may still be assigned and surrendered by act and operation of law.

Thus, if during a lease from year to year, the landlord, with the assent of the tenant, who quits the premises, accept and treat a third person as his tenant, this will amount to a valid surrender of the former tenant's interest by operation of law. (*b*)   And the acceptance of a new lease for a term, to commence during the existence of a former demise, amounts to a surrender of the first term. (*c*)

SECTION V.

TRANSFER OF SHARES.

IN cases of partnership in mines, it usually happens, that the interest in the property is legally vested in one or more partners, in trust for themselves and the rest of the company. It may be useful, therefore, to consider in what manner a transfer of shares held under such circumstances should be effected.

When the property is thus vested, the existence of the trust may be shown by any written evidence or admission of the parties which may suffice to establish the fact, and a bill in equity may be filed for the discovery of the trust.—But when the adventure is of any consequence, there should either be a conveyance of the property to the other partners in the shares to which they are entitled, or the trust should be declared by the trustees in a regular deed, in which should be expressed the respective interests of all parties interested in the property at the time of the execution. It will be seen in a subsequent part of this treatise, that it is of great importance that the objects of a mining company should be fully developed in a deed of copartnership, by which the partners may prevent many of the legal and troublesome consequences arising from such connections. (*d*)   It is very usual to effect both purposes by the instrument. (*e*)   It may occasionally be

(*a*) See Bac. Ab. Coparc. C.

(*b*) Thomas *v.* Cook, 2 B. and Ald. 119.   Phipps *v.* Sculthorpe 1 B. and Ald. 50.

(*c*) Hamerton *v.* Stead, 3 Barn. and C, 478.   5 D. and R. 206.   And see Woodfall on Landlord and Tenant, by Harr. c. vii. s. 3.

(*d*) See chap viii.   (*e*) See Appendix.

sufficiently proper to include the stipulations of partnership in the deed of grant itself.

If the mines are held for a freehold interest, the cestuis que trust will, of course, be entitled to an equitable freehold ; and if only for terms of years, they will be entitled only to an equitable chattel interest. If, again, the property is held under a mere agreement, all the parties interested will stand merely in a similar condition, and will be equally entitled to equitable interests only, either of a freehold or personal nature. In all these cases, the shares of the cestuis que trust would be effectually bound by any written memorandum or agreement for transfer, which would, in equity, affect the legal estate, and control its disposition. In some cases, as where the adventure is of trifling importance, or when the period of enjoyment is very limited, it may be sufficiently prudent to dispense with any further means of security. But it will generally be most advisable to transfer the shares by an indenture of equitable grant or assignment, by which the conveying parties may be clearly estopped from asserting subsequent claims, and may enter into proper covenants with the persons acquiring the shares.

Notice of transfer should be immediately given to the trustees. This is often effected by the entry of the names of new partners upon the books of the concern, and recognition by their copartners. But if the trustees are not partners, express notice should be given.

If the person transferring the shares be one in whose name the property is held, and he disposes of his whole interest, it will, of course, be proper that he should also divest himself of all legal and equitable title to the general property as well as the particular shares. This object may be attained in the manner already pointed out in the preceding sections. If there be only an agreement for the mining property, no further conveyance than that of the shares can, of course, be obtained.

These observations will apply equally to licenses either for freehold or chattel interests.

It is almost unnecessary to say, that the shares will follow the course of devolution and descent, and be subject to the usual incidents of real property, according to the nature of the tenure. Equity follows the law. If they are freehold of inheritance, they will descend to the heir in cases of intestacy, except in cases where, as we shall afterwards see, they are still to be considered in the nature of personal estate, and even then the heir will hold an equitable interest for those beneficially entitled. If the shares are leasehold for years, they will devolve upon the executor or administrator who will hold them upon the trusts of the will, or as part of the general personal estate of the deceased.

Transfers of shares in mines are often effected in a most careless and irregular manner, and so as frequently to lead to vexatious litigation. It should be strongly impressed upon the minds of all adventurers that their shares in mines can only be effectually transferred in compliance with the Statute of Frauds, the provisions of which have been already discussed.

In some cases, however, Courts of Equity have supplied the wants of a strict observance with the requisitions of that Statute; but this doctrine has been carried, in some cases, to an exorbitant extent, and Lord Redesdale might justly make the observation that it was absolutely necessary for the Courts to make a stand, and not carry the decisions further. (a)

It is decided, however, that if a purchaser take rightful possession of the property, (b) or if he expend money in improving the condition of the property *according to the agreement*, (c) the contract will be considered as in part executed, and the Statute will be deprived of its operation. But the payment of a small part of the purchase money only will not have that effect.(d) And it appears to be the better opinion of the profession that even the payment of a considerable proportion will be equally inoperative. (e)

CHAPTER IV.

ON LEASES AND LICENSES.

I. *Description of a mining lease.*
II. *Construction of leases.*
III. *License to work mines.*

SECTION I.

DESCRIPTION OF A MINING LEASE.

THE greatest portion of mineral districts are worked under leases or licenses, and questions of importance are frequently arising with respect to the validity and construction of these instruments. This subject has, therefore, been reserved for distinct consideration.

(a) 2 Scho. and Lef. 5.

(b) Butcher v. Stapely, 1 Vern. 363. Pyke v. Williams, 2 Vern. 465. Lacon v. Mertins, 3 Atk. 1. Wills v. Stradling, 3 Ves. 378. Bowers v. Cator, 4 Ves. 91. Gregory v. Mighell, 18 Ves. 328. Kine v. Balfe, 2 Ball. and B. 343. Morphett v. Jones, 1 Swanst. 172.

(c) Foxcraft v. Lister, 2 Vern. 456. Floyd v. Buckland, 2 Freem. 268. Mortimer v. Orchard, 2 Ves. jun. 243. Toole v. Medlicott, 1 Ball. and B. 393.

(d) Seagood v. Meale, Prec. Ch 560. Lord Fingal v. Ross, 2 Eq. Ca. Abr. 46. pl. 12. Main v. Melbourn, 4 Ves. 720.

(e) Butcher v. Butcher, 9 Ves. 382. Clinan v. Cooke, 1 Scho. and Lef. 22. And see 1 Ca. and Or. 136 1 Sug. V. and P. 208.

In pursuing this investigation, we may proceed, in the first place, to give a general description of a mining lease, to define its construction, and some of its legal incidents ; to point out the distinction in the creation of an actual demise and a mere license to work mines ; and to describe the nature and properties of a license. The right to grant interests of this description, and the manner in which, in some cases, that right must be exercised, will be discussed in the next chapter.

A lease should, after a proper description of the parties, proceed to demise under an adequate description, the subject of contract. No cases are reported on the subject of insufficient description of mines, though many disputes have arisen, as might naturally be supposed. When all the mines or quarries of any particular metal or mineral within a certain district, form the subject of demise, as is usual in the coal fields and limestone beds of the kingdom, no dispute can well arise, except with respect to the actual boundary of the surface, or that below corresponding with the surface. In such cases, all the specified products found within the line of demarcation will belong to the lessee. But metals are usually deposited in veins or lodes ; and not like coal, which is always found in a state of stratification, corresponding more or less with the crust of the earth. Now, in such cases, it is not the invariable, though not an uncommon practice, to demise all the minerals within certain bounds which are ascertained on the surface ; but it is perhaps more usual to demise only particular veins, or known, or supposed deposits of metalliferous substances. These veins are demised for a certain length, and with a proportionate and adequate breadth. When there is only one adventure in operation within the same field, little difficulty is experienced ; for if a new vein is discovered in the course of workings, the right to which it is desirable to acquire, this desire may usually be gratified without infringing upon the rights of other adventurers. But the lessor may, in some cases, be induced to withhold any further extension of grant, though it must be acknowledged, that in general, the conduct of extensive owners towards mining adventures is marked by great liberality and fairness of dealing. It also often happens that many of the veins, which may have been traced from a greater or less distance, are actually in lease at the same time, in the same parcel of ground. Thus, veins in the possession of different lessees, may actually intersect each other ; or if not intersecting each other, the veins may, at any rate, come within the boundary prescribed for the proper breadth in each demise, or they may run into a district comprised in a deed of general grant. In such cases, there can be no doubt that the *first* grant must be sustained in all its vigour. Qui prior est in tempore, potior in jure. The second lessee cannot claim what has been already granted to the first. But the difficulty is frequently only half solved by the application of this plain rule of law. It may, in many cases, be exceedingly difficult to ascertain the *identity* of a vein, and a vein may be improperly or imperfectly described in the grant.

These difficulties may also be increased by the nature or disturbance of the stratification of the earth. It would be impossible, in a treatise of this description, to give any accurate idea of the difficulties which might be occasioned by imperfect description; and it would be equally impossible to enter into any particular enumeration of the geological phenomena which might render the clearest description of no avail in ascertaining the rights of the parties. To instances of the first kind, there are no limits but those prescribed to the imperfections of language. And Nature, in her subterraneous operations at least, is not more to be depended upon than human efforts are, for regularity of proceeding. Thus, the course of two different veins may be interrupted by the intersection of a strong cross vein, which may produce almost unavoidable confusion to the respective rights of different adventurers.

But it is not only in the exploration of metalliferous veins that the mining adventurer is exposed to unpleasant encounters of this description. The same result may take place even in the working of minerals found in a stratified state, and which are justly considered to be easier of search, though not always easier of attainment. For instance, a well ascertained stratum of coal may be the subject of accurate description and demise. There would appear to be little difficulty in such a case. But the whole stratification may be affected in a manner similar to the case just mentioned by an intersecting *dyke*, or vein of extraneous matter. Different strata of coal may have the same horizontal position on both sides of the disturbing dyke; but they may be totally changed in their relative situation to each other on each side. Thus, an upper stratum of coal may be thrown down so far as to correspond with the third or fourth stratum downwards on the other side; and these different but adjacent strata may be of the same thickness and quality, and may, in their general character, possess points of almost entire resemblance and identity. Such mistakes are often inevitable during what is called the process of boring or experimenting for coal; and even when the coal is actually in the course of working, it is possible that the error may still continue for a considerable time. The consequences resulting from such causes may be very serious. Veins and strata may be unconsciously worked by those who may, under circumstances of great hardship, be unexpectedly called upon to give up the produce of their successful labours to others who have established a superior claim. Again, the minerals may be fraudulently and violently extracted by persons who are conscious of their want of title, but who may disguise or pervert the facts, and take shelter under the colour of a legal claim. Disputes may arise, the law be appealed to, and an expenditure, which may require almost the wealth of a prosperous mine to satiate, may be incurred; and it may happen, after all, that when the rights of the parties have been adjusted by the judgment of the

70

law, the offenders may have found means to evade the consequences by a timely description or expenditure of property. The utmost that can be done in the preparation of a demise for avoiding any of these consequences, is to render the description as clear and intelligible as possible. No human language can control the operations of Nature. The rest must be left to be decided by the test of actual experience.

The direction, situation, nature, and quality of the vein or stratum, must be fairly proved by experiment, and in case of doubt, it will be for a jury to determine in whose favour the evidence preponderates.

After describing the subject matter, the instrument usually demises the full liberty to work the mines, and often in demises of metalliferous veins, to smelt the ores, and to erect washing and smelting apparatus, and to effect several other purposes particularly enumerated. Now it has been seen, before that the right to work mines is necessarily incident to the grant without any express authority for that purpose, and that this power cannot be restrained by a special power given in the *affirmative*, which may authorise more acts than would be implied by law, but which will in no wise exclude the full operation of the law. (*a*) A grant or lease of mines, therefore, will be attended with all the rights and incidents which may be necessary for the full enjoyment of the thing granted, unless any of those rights and incidents are restrained by express stipulation ; for modus et conventio semper vincunt legem. It is often a matter of great importance to ascertain what rights are necessarily incident to grants of this nature, and consequently how far any other rights should be expressly provided for, if the application of law is not sufficient to effectuate the intention of the parties. The only incidents which will be implied by law, will be those which may be necessary for giving the grantor the full benefit of his contract, and for enabling him to produce and carry away the mineral in a merchantable condition. He may enter, dig shafts, and pits, drive levels, make water gates, and aqueducts for draining the mines ; he may erect all such engines, machinery, and buildings which may be absolutely required for obtaining the minerals, or for protecting them when they are in his possession ; and he may, in short, make use of all such means as are usually and necessarily employed for the effectual and proper working of similar mines. Such rights must be incident to mining leases of every description. If the mineral, as coal or limestone for instance, be procured from the earth in such a state as to be immediately vendible without any additional process, no other incidents will be presumed, for no other are absolutely required ; but if the mineral, like the ores of the different metals, be found in a crude and imperfect state, or mixed up with the soil or other ingredients of the earth, an additional right will be presumed for the benefit of the grantee or lessee, viz., to erect washing mills and other apparatus for cleaning and washing the mineral from impurities mixed with it, and for

(*a*) Earl of Cardigan *v.* Armitage, 4 Barn. and C. 197. See chap. ii.

enabling him to produce the mineral in a state fit for smelting, or for immediate use, when, for the first time, it becomes, properly speaking, an article of commerce. The mineral may thus be effectually secured from the freehold, separated from extraneous substances, and procured in a pure and marketable condition. The objects of a simple grant will, therefore, have been fully attained, and the mineral may be taken from off the lands. Such incidents, therefore, as these, need not be specified in a lease, though it is always preferable to leave no room for dispute. But all other rights which are not implied by law, such as the right to erect houses for workmen, furnaces and buildings for smelting and refining ores, for making use of any of the other materials on the lands not included in the grant, must be expressly mentioned ; for, however important they may have been in the contemplation of the parties, they are not strictly necessary for the full operation of the grant or lease. In short, all rights which are not obviously implied by law, and which are intended to be conferred, should be clearly expressed on the face of the instrument.

It may be often very important to make special stipulations with respect to rights of way. A rights of way is incident to every grant, in cases where the grantor has the power to confer it. But it frequently happens that some required deviations from the proper course, some proposed alteration in the general condition of the property, or some particular mode or plan of shipment or delivery, demand a more particular arrangement. It may also here be observed that in leases of the surface, the grantor should, in all mining countries, make such reservation with respect to rights of way as may seem to be probably required for mining operations. If the minerals in the lands are reserved to the grantor, the tenant of the surface will then never have been in the possession of them. The exception will be construed as a grant, and a right of way will, of course, be presumed by law. But this right will not extend to minerals produced in the lands of others. Way leaves, in many mining districts, are of very great annual value ; and when they are likely to be required, they should always be properly reserved in all farming leases. It will be the duty of every prudent lessee, before he is far embarked in a mining speculation, to secure to himself all the necessary rights of way which may be required to be obtained from other persons as well as from the grantor of the mines. Few circumstances can be more harrassing to the enterprising lessee, than to find that after years of patience and expenditure, and when his efforts have been finally crowned with success, he will still be required to make an unconscionable bargain for a right of way, without which his acquisition will be comparatively worthless, and which by foresight and attention, might have been effectually provided for. Such cases, it is to be feared, are not uncommon. It will be often proper for the lessor to reserve rights of way through the mines demised for the purpose of working other mines. These are, in the coal districts of the

North of England, technically called outstrokes. Thus one pit may be used for bringing up the coal lying in distinct lands.

If any parts are to be *excepted* to the grantor, they should be set out and particularly described before the insertion of the habendum. Thus, if lands are demised at the same time with the mines, it is usual to except the trees and underwood; but by far the most important exceptions consist of distinct parts of the minerals which are intended to be reserved to the grantor. When minerals, *different* from those demised, are excepted out of the demise, there can be little difficulty as to the subject matter of the exception, though many difficulties might occur in the mode of working under both the demise and the exception. But when the minerals excepted, are of the same name and nature as those demised, it will be necessary to make the description both of what is demised, and what is intended to be excepted, sufficiently clear and express. Enough has already been said upon the necessity of accurate description in mining leases.

It has been stated, that an exception is to be construed as a grant, and therefore the same rights necessary for a full enjoyment of the subject of exception will be implied by law. But it had been also stated, that a grant is always to be taken most strongly against the grantor. There is, therefore, an additional reason why the language of exceptions should be full and clear, and why any other rights intended to be reserved should be expressly defined. Thus, in general, it is presumed, the mining operations under the exception must be carried on so as not to interfere with the working of the parts demised; for, otherwise, it would be in the power of the grantor to derogate from the force of his grant. This can only be allowed by express terms.—For *expressum facit cessare tacitum;* and a grantor may thus modify his grant in any manner suited to his purposes. In short, it will be the duty of the grantor or lessor who reserves to himself any thing out of his grant or lease, to observe that he does not in any way deprive himself of taking the full advantage of the thing reserved; and it may, in some cases, be advisable for him to secure even a superior advantage, if he has reason to contemplate any collision of interests.

It is not unusual to include in the exception, liberty to the lessor and his agents to visit the works. This right is more generally, perhaps, preserved by covenant—a mode equally effective, and, in many respects, preferable.

After the exception comes the *Habendum*, which should accurately state, if the lease be for years, the number of years intended for its duration, and the period of its commencement; if for lives, the number, names, and description of the cestuis que vie. In the latter case, it must be remembered that the lease cannot begin at a day to come; for a freehold interest is created by it, and a freehold cannot be made to commence in futuro. (*a*) It

---

(*a*) Plough *v.* Leeds (Duke), Cowp. 710, 725. Freeman d. Vernon *v.* West, 2 Wils. 165.

may be observed, that a lease may be granted for different periods of years, as, for instance, for seven, fourteen, or twenty-one years, and that in the absence of any other agreement on the face of the deed as to duration, the lessee only will have the option at which of the periods the lease shall determine. (a) The Habendum should also express when there are more lessees than one, whether it is intended they should take as tenants in common, or as joint tenants. When the lessees are numerous, it may be advisable to adopt the latter mode; in other cases, the former mode may be used, except in the grant of freehold interests of inheritance, where it is desirable to obviate as far as possible the descent of any portion of the legal estate upon infant heirs. In either case, however, the equitable rights of the parties really interested will remain the same; for the lessees will be only trustees on behalf of all persons having or acquiring shares in the property.

We next come to the *Reddendum* or reservation of rent, which forms, in general, the consideration for the granting of the lease.

It is said, that a reservation of rent must be of some other thing issuing or coming out of the thing granted, and not a part of the thing itself, for that would be an *exception* out of the grant, and not a rent reserved. (b) It would appear, therefore, that when, as is very usual in leases of metallic veins, the reservation consists of some proportion of the mineral in its natural state, there will not be strictly a rent, but an exception. The consideration, in such cases, will simply consist in the extraction and delivery of the part excepted to the lessor. There can be no distress for such a species of rent. No render, however, will, of course, be due till the mineral is severed from the land; and when that is effected the lessor may recover the proper proportion by an action either of trover, or in respect of the covenant of the lessees. A bill in equity for an account may also be maintained.

But if the reservation is of a proportion of the mineral in its smelted or manufactured state, it will constitute a legal rent subject to the usual incidents. (c)

Rents are generally payable in money in demises of quarries or open workings, and are often payable for mines. In mines of coal the render is also usually in money, and, in many instances, made to vary with the market price of the article. In the extensive coal districts belonging to the Dean and Chapter of Durham, the demise is made subject to an annual certain rent, and also to what is called a tentale rent. A Ten is a local measure equal in weight to about forty eight tons and a half. The lessee pays rent at the rate of twenty shillings for every ton of coals which is worked by him, till he has worked such a number of tons in the year as to make the payments in respect of them amount to the full certain rent mentioned in the

---

(a) Dann v. Spurrier, 3 Bos. and Pul. 399, 442. Price v. Dyer, 17 Ves. 356. Doe d. Webb v. Dixon, 9 East, 16.

(b) Co. Litt. 47 a. 142 a.   (c) Co. Litt. 142 a.

demise ; and after that period, he still continues to pay the rent of twenty shillings for every ton which he may afterwards raise in the same year. Thus the annual certain rent is payable to the lessor at all events, whether the mine be worked to the extent which would make up the rent at the rate mentioned, or not, and in fact, whether the mine is worked at all or not. But the lessee has also the right to make up the number of tons when the quantity raised has not kept pace with the rent, during any subsequent period of his tenancy, without any further payment. This is also a usual mode of render in other collieries of the North of England which are demised for from forty-two to sixty years. In other parts of England, a similar system prevails with respect to coal mines. Sometimes a rent of a certain sum for every ton is payable ; but in case the rent thus payable shall not amount to a certain sum in every year or part of a year, then the deficiency is to be made up by a further payment, unless the mine shall be incapable of producing to the extent which would be required for yielding the landlord's rent. The lessee is still left at liberty, during any subsequent period of his lease, to work a quantity of coal equal to the deficiency for the time being, without further payment. In other districts, a distinct proportionate part, as one-seventh, of the money realized by the sale of the coal which is raised from time to time is reserved, with such an additional sum, if required, as may always yield to the lessor a certain fixed rent, unless the mines are incapable of producing a specified number of tons in the week. This proportion, however, varies indefinitely, according to the nature of the operations, the supposed risk, the amount of expenditure, and the general circumstances of the case. Special provisions are often inserted for imposing a rent of so much per sack upon the coke which is made, and also upon so much of the slack or small coal which is raised and not consumed on the premises, and also upon the bricks or tiles which may be made from the clay which may be demised with the coal.

The rents made payable in respect of metalliferous mines are almost invariably proportioned to the quantity of ore actually raised, and without any stipulated certain rent in money. This rent is called the duty ore, or the lot ore, or the lord's dues. It is a common practice to stipulate that the rent shall be paid in money according to the market price of the day, or by delivery of the metals in a manufactured state. Thus, in demises of lead mines the reservation may consist of a certain quantity of smelted lead and of the silver actually extracted from the ore. In all such cases, an adequate allowance is made in the amount of reservation for the expense saved to the lessor in selling or smelting his proportion of the produce. But it is a frequent practice to stipulate for the lord's proportion of mineral to be rendered when it has been washed and cleansed by the lessee, and before it has undergone any process of manufacture, by which its quality is changed. The proportion to be rendered to the lessor differs not only with respect to the nature of the metals and substances which are discovered, but also to the circumstances under which they are produced. It would be impossible, therefore, to lay down any general rule.

It also sometimes happens, that fines or premiums are payable on the removal or grant of a lease of mines, either instead of, or, as is more usual, in addition to the annual rents.

It may be observed, that when there is a demise generally of all metals and minerals, the reservation should correspond with the different substances demised. The render is generally adapted to what is known or supposed to be discoverable in the land, but it may easily happen that, under a general demise of the minerals, other substances besides those which may be mentioned in the clause of reservation, may be met with, and these might be worked without any profit accruing to the lessor. If, on the other hand, there was a general proportion specified for all minerals found within the limits, it might still happen that many kinds of substances would be worked with injury either to the lessor or lessees. Thus, a render of the average amount of lead duty for copper would subject the lessee to much harder terms than are usual in such cases, and the contrary would prove equally disadvantageous for the lessor. As a general rule, it may be observed, that there should be either no general demise of minerals, without providing for the proper amount of rent in each case, which, with respect to all but the leading and most valuable minerals, may be done in general terms, or the amount of rent should be such as sufficiently to protect the lessor, whatever may be the result of the discoveries. Lessees, in general, know with tolerable exactness, what description of substances they may expect to meet with in the course of their enterprize, and will generally take care that these substances are included in the grant, and that the rent reserved is not beyond the usual amount. If other minerals than those anticipated by the lessor are found, although they will by the general description be in the possession of the lessee, yet if the duty payable should prove to be above the usual amount, the lessor will still have it in his power to control the proceedings of his lessees, or to receive an ample remuneration.

It is proper when duty ore or metal is reserved for rent, that the lease should sufficiently express the time and manner of delivery to the lessor. This may be expressed either in the reddendum or in the covenants afterwards entered into, or in both, but it should always be contained amongst the covenants; and the reddendum may refer to the covenant for the mode of delivery.

When lands are demised with the mines, it is usual to reserve a surface rent without reference to the mines.

We are now come to the consideration of the *Covenants*, by which the grants may be restrained, modified, or regulated; for it is a general rule, that he who has the *jus disponendi* may attach any conditions to his grant which are not unreasonable, repugnant, or illegal.

As the law regards only the intention of the parties as expressed by their deed, no particular form of words has been held necessary to constitute a valid covenant. (*a*) A recital of that intention even in the preceding part of the deed has been held sufficient. Thus, in the lease of a coal mine, it was recited that before the sealing of the indenture, it had been agreed that the plaintiff should have the part dug. It was decided by Lord Chief Justice Hale, that this amounted to a covenant. (*b*)

A covenant, like a grant, in cases of doubt, is always taken most strongly against the person making it. (*c*)

Many covenants will be implied by law, as for the payment of rent, and for the quiet enjoyment of the lessee.

The usual covenants common to all well drawn mining leases, on the part of the lessor, are the following :—That he will prosecute the adventure by opening pits or shafts, driving levels, and making effectual trials, and will use his best exertions for the discovery and attainment of the minerals, and work the mines in a proper and workmanlike manner—in coal mines, that he will raise certain quantity of tons per week, and pay the stipulated rents and taxes—in metallic mines, that he will employ at least a certain number of experienced workmen before the discovery of the veins, and at least a certain additional number afterwards, that he will remove the washed ore to a storehouse to be weighed in the presence of the parties, or their agents, and deliver the duty ore or metal to the lessor or his agents, at specified places and periods—that he will allow the lessor and his agents to inspect the works, and in case the mines are not worked in a proper manner, give such satisfaction and damages to the lessor as shall be decided by arbitration ; that he will provide proper books and accounts of the quantity produced, to be at all times open to the inspection of the lessor and his agents, who may take copies and extracts from them—that he will give up the possession of the mines in good condition at the end of the term, and for the payment of damages occasioned by the mining operations and works.

The usual covenants on the part of the lessor are for title, and for quiet enjoyment.

The remaining intentions of the parties are usually effected by provisoes or conditions. These differ from covenants in this respect, that they are binding on both parties, and a covenant only binds the covenantor. It may

(*a*) Holder *v* Taylor, 1 Rol. Abr. 518. 1. 19. 41. Bush *v.* Coles, Carth. 232. See Russell *v.* Galwell, Cro. Eliz. 637.

(*b*) Severn *v.* Clark, 2 Leon. 122. See Hollis *v.* Carr, 2 Mod. 87. Duke of Northumberland *v.* Errington, 5 T. R. 526. Saltoun *v.* Houston, 1 Bing. 433. Sampson *v.* Easterby, 9 Barn. and C. 505. 6 Bing. 644. 4 Moore. and P. 601. 1 Crompt. and J. 105.

(*c*) Bac. Abr. Cov. F.

often, however, be preferable to have also mutual covenants. When there is no penalty affixed to the non-performance of it, as a clause of re-entry, it will amount to a covenant. (a) A proviso, indeed, in many instances, will operate as a covenant. The usual provisoes are, that the lessor is to have the option of purchasing the tools, materials, and machinery, at a fair valuation, or otherwise the lessee is to be entitled to remove them—for re-entry or non-payment of the rent, or on the non-performance of the covenant and stipulation on the part of the lessee—and for referring all disputes to arbitration.

Such may be considered to be the usual contents of a mining lease; but there are few occasions which do not demand more particular explanations and agreements.

For instance, in leases of coal mines, it is frequently expressed that during any suspension of the works by any inevitable accident, the rents shall cease to be payable, and that in case of a partial suspension the rents shall be apportioned—that the lessee shall work the mines in a specified manner, and level the ground, and fill up all useless pits—that the rent shall be payable in a certain manner, by bills or other means, and that when the coal is exhausted, the term shall cease.

Again in general leases of mines, it is frequently expressed, that the mines may be shown, within a certain period from the termination of the term, to persons who may be desirous to become the tenants, and take demises of them—that the lessee shall not take any person into his service who may gain a settlement in the parish—that the lessor, if required, will grant a new lease to the same party—that the lessee shall erect certain buildings for particular or general purposes, and certain steam engines of defined power and application, and other works and machinery—that the mine shall be worked in a certain prescribed manner; and the levels, way gates, and passages be secured from injury by arching or other particular means. In short, all other purposes which may seem to be demanded on the occasion, must be stipulated for by the express covenants or agreements of the parties.

SECTION II.

CONSTRUCTION OF LEASES.

It will be proper, under this head, to mention the decisions which have taken place with respect to the working of mines under leases.

The terms of a demise which contained a condition or covenant to work mines as far as they ought to be worked, have been held to be satisfied by the lessees having made sufficient trials to show that there are no mines at all which ought to be worked.

(a) Doe dem, Wilson v. Phillips, 2 Bing. 13. 9 Moo. 46. See Simpson v. Titterell, Cro. Eliz. 242. See supra, page 143, and Doe d. Antrobus v. Jepson, 3 Barn. and Ad. 402.

Thus, several mines of coal in Lancashire were demised, subject to a covenant that the lessees would forthwith proceed to sink for coal, as far as could and ought to be accomplished by persons acquainted with the nature of collieries, and as in such cases was usual and customary, and immediately erect such fire engines as should be necessary for the above purpose before the 24th of June, 1806, or in default, to pay to the lessor such a sum as should be fixed by arbitration. Disputes arose soon afterwards, which were accordingly referred to arbitrators, who awarded that the lessees had not performed their covenants in the lease, inasmuch as they had not proceeded to sink for the coal in the manner mentioned in the lease, and had not erected the fire engines at the time appointed, and that in consequence of such non-performance, the lessees should pay to the lessor £150 for rent for the year ending in June, 1807; that the lessees should work the mines, and erect the engines before the 24th June, 1807, and, in default, that they should pay to the lessor the yearly rent of £200 as a compensation for the lord's rent reserved by the lease; and that as soon as the pits were sunk, and the engines erected, the rent should cease, and the lessees should pay the rent reserved by the lease, and when it should exceed £200 they might retain the excess until they had reimbursed themselves what had been paid for compensation before the colliery was begun to be worked. The lessees paid the £150, and before June, 1807, they proceeded to sink for coal. They afterwards desisted, and an action was brought by the lessor, to which the lessees pleaded that they would have continued to work the mines, and would have erected the engines, but that there were no mines of coal in the lands which ought to be worked by any person acquainted with the nature of collieries, or which it was, in such cases, usual, to work, or which would have defrayed the expense of working, and that they had ascertained the truth of these statements by sufficient experiments and trials. It was contended for the lessor, that it was no answer against the award of the umpire as to the breach of the covenant, for the lessees to say that there were no coals, or none worth the expense of getting. But it was held by Lord Ellenborough, C. J., that though it might be no answer to the damages awarded for the breach of the covenant for the time past, in not trying to get the coal, yet it was an answer to any further breach that they had tried as far as they could and ought to do in the judgment of persons of competent skill in such works, and as far as was usual and customary in such cases, and that no coal could be gotten. It was found upon competent trial to be impossible to get any coal fit to be worked, and no person could be bound to do impossibilities. It was suggested, however, by Bayley, J., that it would be better for the plaintiff, if the case would bear it, to take issue upon the sufficiency of the experiments made by the defendants; and leave was given to amend for that purpose, otherwise judgment would be given for the defendants. (a)

(a) Hanson v. Boothman, 13 East. 22.

In a similar case it was also held, at nisi prius, that when a tenant is bound to work a coal mine, as long as it was *fairly workable*, he is not compellable to work the mine at a dead loss. It was proved that there were coals in the mine, but of such a description as would not yield any profit by working them. (*a*)

Questions of this nature are of course, properly for the consideration of a jury ; but if there be any fraudulent delay on the part of a lessee, the Court of Chancery will interfere and order him to pay the rent which would have. accrued, if the mine had been properly worked.

A rent of £600 was reserved in a lease of coal mines, the first quarter's payment of which was to be made at the next feast after the lessee should have worked one thousand stacks of coal. There was a covenant by the lessor that he would dig the thousand stacks of coal without delay, and in a reasonable time, and that he would dig the pits in a workmanlike manner, and level the pits with the gin pit, viz., the pit where the engine is to carry away the water. There was a mutual covenant that the lessee might, on giving six months notice, determine the lease, on payment of all rents due and performance of the covenants. The lessor entered, and afterwards gave six months notice, by which he insisted that the lease was determined at Christmas, 1723. The lessor filed a bill in chancery, alleging that the defendant, after having entered, had worked before the first quarter day the thousand stacks of coal, except a small quantity, and had employed his workmen in other works, telling some of them that he was not such a fool as to pay a quarter's rent for a few days' work, and insisted that the first quarter's rent ought to have been paid at Lady Day, 1721. The Bill prayed a specific performance of the covenants, and that the lease might continue for twenty-one years, because the power to determine by notice was conditional, viz., on paying the rent and performing the covenants, which he had not done, for the pits were not levelled with the gin pit, and were overflowed with water, and rendered of no service to the lessor. It was contended for the lessee, first, that the Bill ought to be dismissed, because the plaintiff, if injured, might have his remedy at law, and secondly, that it was a question for the consideration of a jury whether the lessee had performed his covenants. Lord Chancellor King agreed with the counsel on the second point, for if the defendant had not performed his covenants, he could not then determine the lease, and if that was still subsisting, which was a fact for a jury to try, an action laid for the rent. But as to the first point, though the plaintiff might indeed have remedy by an action of covenant, upon the collateral covenant to dig the coal without delay, yet there was fraud in preventing the digging before the quarter day, in order that the rent might not commence so soon, and this fraud required the interposition of the Court. It was, therefore, decreed that the defendant should pay the first quarter's rent due at Lady day, 1721, and account and pay the rent to Christmas, 1723, till which time the defendant allowed the

(*a*) Jones *v.* Shears, 7 Carr. and P. 346. Per Coleridge, J.

lease to be subsisting, but that the Bill should be dismissed as to the second point, whether the lease was determined or not.   The costs were divided according to the issue of the suit. (*a*)

It will be afterwards seen, on what other occasions the Court of Chancery has interfered with respect to the enjoyment of mining property. (*b*)

The following decision may here be mentioned :—In a lease of mines and smelting mills in a waste there was the recital of an agreement that the lessees should take down a smelting mill, and erect a mill of larger dimensions, with several other buildings upon another peice of ground in the same waste, which were thenceforth to become the property of the lessor and the two other proprietors of the mines of the waste.   There was a covenant on the part of the lessees to keep and deliver up at the end of the term in good repair the new mill to be erected.   The lessor was not entitled to the general property in the waste, but he had power to erect buildings and smelting mills.   It was held, that, though the covenant did not expressly extend to the erection of the new mill, there was an implied covenant to fulfil the terms of the agreement.   It was also decided, that the covenant ran with the land, that is, the mines demised, so as to be available to the assignee of the reversion.   The covenant was considered to tend to the support and maintenance of the subject of demise. (*c*)

In another case, the owners of several distinct iron works joined with other persons in forming a railway, and severally engaged that they and their assigns would take all the lime-stone used in their works from a certain quarry, and carry it, and the ironstone from their mines to their furnaces along the railway, on payment of a certain tonnage.   The partnership deed of the railway recited that the strangers joined in the scheme in consideration of those benefits.—The owners of one of the iron works sold them to a purchaser with notice of the covenant.   It was held that he was not bound by the covenant, on the ground that the covenant was entered into by mere strangers, that there was a want of privity, and that parties could not be allowed to invent new modes for the enjoyment of property to be transmitted to remote persons, and impressed with peculiar conditions.   It was creating a new species of tenure. (*d*)   The latter reasons for this decision have not been aquiesced in, and they seem to be quite open to dispute.   The case must rest upon the want of privity. (*e*)

SECTION III.

LICENSES TO WORK MINES.

It has been before remarked, that there is a great distinction between a

(*a*) Greene *v.* Sparrow. Reg. Lib. A. 1725. fol. 120. 124 cited 3 Swanst. 408.

(*b*) See chap. viii., ix., and xii.

(*c*) Sampson *v.* Easterby, 9 Barn. and C. 505.   1 Cromp. and Jer. 105.

(*d*) Keppell *v.* Bailey, 2 Myl. and Keen. 517.   (*e*) 2 Sug. V. and P. 502.

lease of mines and a license to work mines. The former is a distinct conveyance of an actual interest or estate in lands, while the latter is only a mere right or incorporeal hereditament to be exercised in the lands of others.

We may now proceed to notice the difference in the creation of those interests, and to describe the general properties of a license which will be found to have much resemblance, in many respects, to an actual lease.

In order to ascertain whether an instrument must be construed as a lease or a license, it is only necessary to determine whether the grantee has acquired by it any estate in the land, in respect of which he might bring an action of ejectment. If the land is still to be considered in the possession of the grantor, the instrument will only amount to a license, and though the grantee of the license will certainly be entitled to search and dig for mines according to the terms of this grant, and appropriate the produce to his own use, on payment of the stipulated rent or proportion, yet he will acquire no property in the minerals till they are severed from the land, and have thus become liable to the recovery in an action of trover. It must be remembered, that in order to constitute an actual lease of mines it is not necessary for the grantor to acquire any right or interest in the surface ; for minerals have been shown to be capable of forming a distinct inheritance in the lands of which they are part, and, consequently, an actual estate may be both created in and restricted to any specified kinds of minerals. But a license is created only where the grantor has acquired no right of property to *any part* of the soil or minerals, till they are separated from the general inheritance.

If a man, says Lord Coke, grant to another to dig turves in his land, and to carry them at his will and pleasure, the land shall not pass, because but part of the profit is given, for trees, mines, &c., shall not pass. (*a*)

It has certainly been determined, that the intention of the parties may constitute an actual demise, whether the words be in the form of a licence, or a covenant, or an agreement. But it must sufficiently appear from the construction of the granting part, that it is clearly the intention of the parties, that the one should divest himself of the possession, and that the other should come into it for a determined time. (*b*) And it must be sufficiently apparent, that there is nothing in the grant of a liberty to work mines at all inconsistent with the possession being still reserved to the grantor.

This distinction has been clearly recognized by several decisions.

In a case before cited, there was a covenant for a person and his heirs and assigns at all times thereafter to enter and search and dig for coal and other minerals, and carry them away to their own use. It was decided, that

(*a*) Co. Litt. 4 b.   (*b*) See Bacon's Ab. Leases, K.

the words only amounted to a license or liberty to dig and work the mines. (*a*)

In another case, an owner of the land granted full and free liberty to work for tin, copper, and other minerals in the Crinnis Mines, in the county of Cornwall, for twenty-one years ; and there was a similar lease relating to another mine called Campdown. It was held by Lord Eldon, that this was nothing like a demise of mines, though he did not mean to say that similar principles would not apply to it. These leases, as they are called, were not demises of the mines, but simple grants of licenses and liberties to work, and there was no estate whatever in the grantees. (*b*)

The same case afterwards came before the consideration of the Court of King's Bench. The indenture was described as giving also full liberty to the grantees to erect *within the limits of the set thereby granted*, sheds, engines, and buildings, and to turn all water and water courses to their use, and to cut any channels over the lands for conveying the water ; and there was an exception to the grantor of full liberty to make use of any of the adits or levels, and of sinking any shafts for the purpose of working mines in other lands, and of conveying any water course over the *premises granted*. It was contended, that the language of these grants and exceptions, and the clause of re entry which enabled the grantor and his heirs to repossess and enjoy the lands in case of breach of any of the covenants, showed, that an interest in the soil was intended to pass. But it was held by the Court that the deed operated as a license only. Lord Tenterden, in delivering the judgment of the Court, observed, that the doubt had arisen from the inaccuracy of some of its expressions, which seemed to import that the grantor supposed himself to have done that by the granting a part of the deed, which, it was insisted, the words of the granting part did not warrant. But the instrument, though inaccurate, was a regular formal deed, containing all the formal and orderly parts of a deed of conveyance enumerated by Lord Coke, except the clause of warranty. (*c*) One of the proper offices of the premises or granting part of a deed, as stated by Lord Coke, " was to comprehend the certainty of the tenements" to be conveyed. This indenture, in its granting part, did not purport to demise the land, or the metals or minerals in it, but a liberty to dig for metals and minerals, and to dispose of *those only that should be found there within the term*, the grantor parting with no estate or interest in the rest. If so, the grantor had no estate or property in the land itself, or any particular portion of it, or in any part of the ore, metals or minerals, which are not obtained. He acquired no more than a mere right to a personal chattel, when obtained in pursuance of incorporeal privileges granted for the purpose of obtaining it. It had been contended

(*a*) Chetham *v.* Williamson, 4 East. 469. 1 Smith, 278.
(*b*) Norway *v.* Rowe, 19 Ves. 158.
                                                                    (*c*) Co. Litt. 6 a.

that there were words in the deed which showed an intent to demise, particularly in the clause of re entry. A proviso of that description was in itself not less applicable to a license to dig and work for mines, than to a demise of metals and minerals, because, under such a license, works may be effected, and a corporal possession had, which it might be competent for the grantor to resume. The expressions in the deed might probably be attributed to want of care and caution in its preparation ; but, supposing it otherwise, still they could have no further effect, than to show that the grantor who used them *supposed* that the soil or minerals, and not a mere liberty or privilege, passed by his deed ; and if the words used in the granting part of the deed were of doubtful import, and would bear the construction contended for, they might, with the aid of others showing the intent, be sufficient to pass the land or soil, and support an action of ejectment. But the words of the granting part were plain and not of doubtful import ; and as the proper office of that part of the deed is to denote what the premises are that are granted, and is the place where the intent of the grantor, and what he has actually done in that respect, is more particularly to be looked for, recourse must be had to it to see whether he has actually granted what it is urged his expressions denote that he supposed he had granted, for the question properly was not what he supposed he had done, *but what he really had done by his grant.* (a)

It will appear, therefore, from the preceding case, that, notwithstanding the rules of law that a grant is to be taken most strongly against the grantor, and that the intention of the parties is, if possible, to be supported, the deficiency of the granting part of a deed in the description of the thing granted, will not be assisted by the intention of the parties expressed in the other parts of the deed, unless that description may easily admit of an interpretation corresponding with the other portions of the deed. No expression of intention, it must be presumed, however strong, if it is not found in the proper place, will suffice so far to control the operation of this rule, as to vest any other premises in the grantee than those mentioned and described in the granting part. A more liberal rule of construction prevails with respect to wills. But a deed is a formal instrument, and is interpreted according to the strict rules of construction. But it will be obvious, that there may be recitals or expressions even in a deed, though they might not be discoverable in the deed mentioned in the above case, which might be construed by a Court of Equity as an agreement to perform what that particular act had failed to accomplish. In like manner, it is conceived, from the more indulgent construction which prevails in the interpretation of wills and agreements, expressions of still less force contained in such instruments might be held sufficient to effectuate the supposed intention of the parties. But it may well be doubted, whether the expressions made use of in the above deed

(a) Doe dem. Hanley v. Wood, 2 Barn, and Ald. 724.

would be sufficient to denote any further intention than that established by the decision.

A license to work mines is often framed, as in the above case, in the same manner as a regular demise, with formal provisoes and covenants entered into by both parties. The observations which have already been made with respect to the forms of leases, will, therefore, be generally applicable to licenses of this description.

But it remains to consider some incidents which are peculiar to licenses.

A license to work mines is not revocable or countermandable at the will of the grantor, because it confers an interest in lands (*a*) and because it is supported by a consideration, when a rent is paid to the owner of the land. (*b*) But it may be revocable by agreement.

Upon the subject of licenses, there arises a very important question with respect to mines—viz., whether those instruments are exclusive of the rights of others?

It may be stated, as a general rule, that a license to work mines is not exclusive of the similar rights of the grantor, or of those who may claim under him by virtue of a similar authority.

This was decided in a very early case. Lord Mountjoy, being séised in fee of the manor of Canford, sold it in fee with the reservation, and with a covenant on the part of the purchaser, that Lord Mountjoy, his heirs, and assigns might dig for ore in the lands, (which were great wastes) parcel of the manor, and dig turf also for the making of alum. It was held that, notwithstanding this grant, the purchaser, his heirs, and assigns might dig also, like the case of common sans nombre. (*c*)

In the case of Chetham *v.* Williamson, (*d*) a similar reservation of coals was made in a purchase deed, and the license was held not to confer an exclusive right to the coals. Lord Ellenborough observed, that no case could be named where one who had only a liberty of digging for coals in another's soil had an exclusive right to the coals, so as to enable him to maintain trover against the owner of the estate for coals raised by him ; and after citing the case of Lord Mountjoy, said that those who compared it to a grant of common sans nombre, used that as the strongest instance to show that it could not be an exclusive right.

It appears, therefore, that an exclusive right to minerals will not necessarily be conferred by the grant of a license to work them. But it must not be concluded from these decisions that the license to work may not be in such a form, as effectually to vest in the grantee a sole and undisturbable right to the minerals. It may be generally laid down, that if it appear to be the in-

(*a*) Doe d. Hanley *v.* Wood, 2 Barn. and Ald. 738.

(*b*) See Winter *v.* Brockwell, 8 East. 308. Taylor *v.* Waters, 7 Taunt. 374. Liggins *v.* Ingo, 5 Moo. and P. 712,

(*c*) Co. Litt. 165 a. Godb. 18. 1 And. 307. 4 Leon. 147.   (*d*) 4 East. 469.

tention of a deed of grant or license, that the grantee should be solely and exclusively entitled to work for minerals, the grantor will be afterwards precluded from abridging or derogating from his grant by any attempt to exercise a right, similar only indeed, but incompatible with his former disposition. This intention should properly appear in the granting part; for the use of the granting part as has been observed, (a) is to give an accurate description of the thing granted. It is an essential part of the thing granted, that it is freed from the interruptions and claims of others. If the description should fail in this respect, but the intention may still be gathered from other parts, or the general scope of the instrument, it would seem that, at law, the right to work would not be exclusive, but that the deed would create an equitable contract for an exclusive right, which would be binding upon the grantor, and those claiming under him. If this right could be considered to be included in a covenant entered into by the grantor, or if any particular recitals or expression should suffice to constitute a legal covenant, such a contract would even at law, be held to run with the land, and bind the assignees of any of its profits.

It would be useless, in the absence of decision, to consider by what particular expressions an exclusive right may be granted. It was contended, in one case, that the grant of " full and free liberty" to work was sufficient for that purpose, on the ground that if two persons had full liberty to work the mines, there would be a great interference with the rights of each other. (b) But it was not necessary to investigate that point in the case; and it may be safely asserted that such expressions would not be sufficient to confer an exclusive right; for they amount to no more than what would be implied by law. There must be some expression adequate to give the grantee a sole and exclusive privilege, incapable of being disturbed or interferred with. Questions of this nature seldom occur in practice; for almost all mines of any prospective value, not in the hands of the proprietors themselves, are worked under leases, when these can be obtained. If, however, the minerals of a district were worked under two different licences, and by different adventurers, it is quite clear that such questions might become not only of paramount consequence, but of very difficult solution. In different mining adventures carried on in search of distinct kinds of minerals, there might arise abundant causes of dispute with respect to interference. When the same kind of material is the joint object of attainment, the rights of the parties might become still more embarassing. It is submitted, that in cases of actual interference in the course of mining operations, the claimants, under the first grant, would be entitled to a general preference. *Qui prior est in tempore, potior in jure.* But it is difficult to assert any general principle upon a subject which might, from its nature, become so exceedingly com-

---

(a) See supra.   (b) Doe dem. Hanley v. Wood, 2 Barn. and Ald. 724.

plicated in actual practice. The mode of working, the nature of the inter-ference, the relative situation and priority of any particular operations, the designs of the parties, would all become important ingredients in the settle-ment of such questions ; and it would appear, from analogous cases on min-ing subjects, that an expenditure of capital, labour, and time might in them-selves create an equitable right to a sole enjoyment of the particular mines. (a)

From the above observations, it will be sufficiently obvious how important it is that mining adventurers should be furnished with either an exclusive license, or a regular lease. The latter is, in many respects, the preferable instrument.

It has been seen before, that leases, even for chattel interests, are now, under the proviso for making them void on breach of the covenants or con-ditions, only voidable at the election of the lessor—and that the same con-struction is applicable to licenses for years. (b) But a license, whether for a freehold or a chattel interest, may, upon forfeiture, be determined by simple notice.

In the above case of Roberts v. Davey, the license was for twenty-one years, and it was observed by Mr. Justice Littledale, that if it had been a freehold lease of land, it would have been necessary for the lessor to avoid it by entry, or if that were impossible, by claim. But that instrument was a mere license to dig, and did not pass the land—an actual entry, therefore, was unnecessary to avoid it—but by analogy to what was required to be done in order to determine a freehold lease, it seemed to follow that, to put an end to the license, the grantor should have given notice of his intention so to do. The giving of such notice in the case of such an instrument was equivalent to an entry or claim by the grantor of a freehold estate to which a condition is annexed. (c)

It was held in a case before cited, (d) that a proviso for re-entry was in itself not less applicable to a license to dig than to a demise of minerals, be-cause under such a license, works might be effected, and a corporal posses-sion had, which it might be competent for the grantor to resume. But this was not meant to convey the impression of the Court that entry was as ne-cessary for avoiding a license as a freehold lease. A license to work mines, whether it be for a freehold or a chattel interest, is still an incorporeal here-ditament, unattended with any present estate in the land out of which it issues. As such, it is, strictly speaking, incapable of actual entry. The works may be entered upon, but these do not constitute the subject of grant. It follows, therefore, that any such license may be determined by acts which

(a) See Norway v. Rowe, 19 Ves. 156-159.

(b) See last Section, and Doe d. Hanley v. Wood, 2 Barn. and Ald. 724. Roberts v. Da vey, 4 Barn. and Ad. 672.

(c) 4 Barn. and Ad. 672.　　　(d) Doe d. Hanley v. Wood, 2 Barn. and Ald. 740.

are applicable to the nature of the property, viz., by notice of the intention of the grantor to take advantage of the forfeiture committed by his grantee —and this notice, it is presumed, may be either express, or implied from acts of entry, or of notorious ownership. There is no distinction in this respect, between licenses for freehold interests and for years..

It is a general rule of law, that no rent can issue out of any incorporeal hereditament, because such inheritances are incapable of being distrained upon. (*a*) But the Crown is excepted from this rule, because by its prerogative all the lands of the lessee are liable to distress for rent (*b*) Rent, therefore, cannot, *eo nomine*, be reserved upon a license to work mines. Indeed, it may be doubted, whether in the case of an actual demise of mines without land, any rent liable to remedy by distress, can issue ; for the works would not be demised, and there would be nothing on the subject of demise to distrain. But the reservation of rent will, in either case, be good by way of contract, for the non-performance of which the lessor will be entitled to an action of covenant or debt—for the lessor might otherwise be left without a remedy. (*c*)

In other respects, the incidents and construction of licenses seem to correspond with what has already been said upon the subject of mining leases.

From the preceding observation and cases, it will appear very important, when any mining adventure is in contemplation, to ascertain whether the subject of speculation is entirely freed from previous grants and reservations. In cases of freehold leases, this subject should receive particular attention, although it has been seen that a sufficient entry may be completed by persons acting under the authority of the grantor. Allusion has already been made to this necessity for caution in treating of the relation of grantor and grantee. But prudence is equally required, and in all cases of grant, whether for freehold or personal interests, in adjusting the rights of different companies of adventurers. It very frequently happens, in mining districts, that a mine is worked under a license or a lease, containing the usual clauses of forfeiture and re-entry ; and from the want of success the enterprize is virtually abandoned by the company. It is not uncommon for another lease or license to be granted to other persons, or even to the same persons, in trust for another company of speculators, a great part of whom may have been members of the old compamy. At any rate, the mining agent and the leading directors of the first company may continue in the same capacity and situation with respect to the new company. There may be little change in any respect, except in the ordinary event of taking a new

---

(*a*) Co. Litt. 47 a, 142 a, 144.   (*b*) Ib. 47 a.   5 Co. Rep. 4, 56.
(*c*) Dalston *v.* Reeve, Ld. Raymond, 77.

interest in the mine, and in the substitution of a few dormant proprietors. All acts of ownership may thus be referred to either company, if the interest under the former grant is not effectually extinguished.

It very frequently occurs, particularly in operations for obtaining the metallic ores, that a second or a subsequent adventure, is attended with great, and perhaps unexpected success. Questions of prior claim may slumber when the result is doubtful, but when the prospects of a mine begin to be realized, these questions may cause, not only as in Hanley v. Wood, great embarassment, but great danger of a successful interference. A long course of litigation may ensue, and the mine may either cease to be worked, or the profits may flow into the hands of those who may be eventually be declared to possess no title to them. It is no less the duty of the lessor as of the miner to ascertain, that any grant under which mining operations are conducted, is not liable, from negligence and inattention, to be in any manner prejudicially effected by claims of prior origin, which should have been legally destroyed by properly carrying out the conditions which control them. To the lessor, indeed it might be of no consequence whatever, if the terms of the subsequent grant were equally favourable to his interests as those of the first. But every lessor is morally, if not legally, bound to furnish voluntarily, in such cases a valid title to the property he professes to dispose of; and especially in those particular matters which the lessee may not have the means of investigating for himself. On the other hand, it will readily be admitted, that no circumstance can be more vexatious to a mining adventurer, than after a long course of expense, doubt, and anxiety, to be harrassed by prior claims, when at length the enterprise has been favoured with the fulfilment of his hopes.

In such cases, however, a Court of Equity will often refuse to lend its assistance in favour of persons urging former claims.

In one case of this description, a motion for a receiver on the part of the first lessees was refused. Lord Eldon, on that occasion observed, that in disturbing possession with reference to such a subject as mines, the Court would be taking an extremely strong step; especially if great expenditure had been applied without the interposition of other claimants, until it was excited by the profitable result of that expenditure, in which they would take no share. (a)

In a case decided by Lord Rosslyn, (b) the plaintiff and defendant had been partners in a coal mine, under a lease, with a right of renewal. The renewal was obtained, and the mine worked, by the defendant alone, and the Bill was dissmissed, on the ground the plaintiff having waited till the concern appeared by the property embarked in it by the defendant to be profitable, keeping aloof while it was hazardous, had lost the equity he had by the renewal of his partner.

(a) Norway v. Rowe, 19 Ves. 156.   (b) Senhouse v. Christian, cited 19 Ves. 157. 159.

Lord Eldon, in commenting upon this case, said it involved a doctrine with regard to mining concerns, upon which at least the Court would not refuse to act without great consideration—speculations of that nature were very hazardous. He had known a copper mine produce £20,000 a-year, and the next week worth nothing, and that was as true of coal mines. There were persons who would stand by, see the expenditure incurred—if it turned out profitable, would set up their claim—if otherwise, would have nothing to do with it—and it deserved great consideration, whether the Court would interpose, even by Decree, much less on motion. (a)

These observations seem to apply to all mining adventurers.

It must be observed, that in both those cases, the plaintiffs had not the legal estate; and it may be concluded, that under such circumstances, a Court of Equity would refuse to interfere at all. It does not, however, appear to be settled, whether, after great expenditure incurred, without interruption or remonstrance, the Court would refuse to interfere against the owners of the legal estate who had not participated in the expenditure. It cannot, under any circumstances be considered to be a very equitable proceeding to encourage or acquiesce in an expenditure accompanied with great risk and delay, and afterwards to claim the whole benefit of the outlay. It would be a species of fraud. Every case will depend upon its own peculiar circumstances, but great injustice might result in many such cases, if a Court of Equity refused to interfere for the purpose of declaring such owners Trustees, as to the whole estate vested in them, for those adventurers who have carried on the mining operations.

A similar doctrine has even been maintained at law. An estate was sold at a remote period with a reservation of coal mines—they were reserved, because no one would give any thing for them. The application of machinery at length rendered them available, and the owner of the surface worked the coals after an enormous expense—and then the other party came forward. Upon the trial of the issue which seems to have been directed by the Court of Chancery, it was strongly laid down to the jury by Mr. Justice Buller, that as the proprietor had stood by during the whole of the expenditure, a grant should be inferred (b)

Lord Eldon, however, though admitting the great knowledge of Mr. J. Buller, with respect to mining concerns, established that the direction was wrong. (c) The circumstances of this case are not fully detailed. But the direction of the learned Judge was probably considered bad on the general ground of there being an insufficiency of time to warrant the presumption of a grant against the absolute owner of the inheritance. But the case is very different when a person is originally a trustee for himself and others claiming interests in the property. The legal estate vested in him

(a) 19 Ves. 159.   (b) Adair v. Shaftoe, cited 19 Ves. 156.   (c) Ibid.

may not be presumed to have passed from him. To affect this, would require a possession of the *cestuis que trust* for twenty years, without any formal recognition of the title of the trustee. And if such a possession has even subsisted for that period, it will be insufficient, if. the acts of ownership can be properly referred to the acquisition of an equitable estate only, or did not necessarily demand an investigation of the title. (*a*) It could only be contended that the conduct of the trustee has induced a sacrifice of his beneficial interest in the particular share to which he was originally and absolutely entitled. But, it is conceived, it would require. a strong case to call for the interference of a Court of Equity against an owner of the legal estate. *Vigilantibus non dormientibus leges subserviunt.* The other persons interested would make the expenditure with the .full knowledge of the circumstances. It was their duty, therefore, to have effected a different arrangement before entering upon such a course of expenditure.

CHAPTER V.

ON PARTNERSHIPS IN MINES.

WHATEVER may be the nature of mining, and whether the occupation may be so pursued as to be excluded from the.operation of the bankrupt laws or not, it may be carried on as a trade, in a manner which will subject the adventurer to all the consequences of a particular partnership.

The question of the existence of a partnership, however, may often depend upon very nice considerations, and is described in one case by Lord Eldon, as a very difficult question; (*b*) for the adventurers may only be the joint tenants, or tenants in common, of an estate in land, the profits of which they combine to enjoy and realize, by consenting to appoint a general system of management. In this situation, they will be considered, with respect both to themselves and third persons, as the ordinary owners of land, working their respective shares of the mines, responsible only for their own acts, subject to no laws of partnership whatever, and possessing distinct rights in the property.

It becomes, therefore, important to discuss a question which in cases of alleged partnership, must always be preliminary to further proceedings.

It may be laid down, as a general rule, that when the trade is carried on in such a manner as to bring the adventurers within the operation of the bankrupt laws, a partnership must, in such cases, always necessarily subsist,

---

(*a*) Doe d. Grosvenor *v.* Swymmer, 1 Lord Ken. 385. See also Doe d. Milner *v.* Brightwen. 10 East, 583.   (*b*) Crawshay *v.* Maule, *infra.*

for they will be commercial traders without reference to the production of minerals at all.

The quantity of interest which the owners for the time being may have in the lands will not influence the question of liability to the bankrupt laws.—For the same reasons it will not affect the question of partnership. Whether any or all of the owners have acquired an absolute or limited interest of any description, they may agree to enjoy the possession of the common object in a particular manner.

Neither does there appear to be any reason for supposing that, though one owner was possessed solely of the legal estate, and others had only equitable interests, arising too in different proportions, and evidenced by different means, any presumption of partnership would necessarily arise from that circumstance; for lands are frequently enjoyed in this manner by tenants in common, and there is nothing inconsistent with their rights of ownership.

If, however, it could be distinctly shown that the land was not intended to be held in common, but to remain the absolute property of any one or more of the parties, evidenced, for instance, by the payment of rent, a case of commercial partnership, it is conceived, might fairly be presumed with respect to all concerned.

The relation of partnership, as will be afterwards shown, may be constituted either by express stipulation, or by implication deduced from the acts of the parties.

When the mining operations are carried on by several landowners under a co-partnership deed or agreement, or even a verbal agreement, from which it may be clearly established that the parties intended to enter into a trading adventure, and to become co-partners in the ordinary and commercial sense of the word, a partnership will, of course, be constituted, not only as between themselves, but as to all other persons. But with respect to the presumption arising from persons holding themselves out to the world as partners, it is sufficiently obvious that something more is required in such cases than what would be necessary to establish a partnership under ordinary circumstances. For all the characteristic features of a general partnership *may* be equally applicable to persons who work the mines under their lands as parts of the profits of those lands. Such persons, in the absence of other circumstances, cannot fairly be presumed to have intended to render themselves liable to all the consequences of a commercial partnership. The question in such cases, will, therefore, naturally arise—viz., what additional circumstances will be requisite, in the absence of express agreement, to raise the presumption of partnership.

The first case which occurred on this subject was that of Crawshay *v.* Maule. (*a*) In that case certain lands had been held in tenancy in com-

(*a*) 1 Swanst 523.

mon, from which considerable quantities of iron and coal had been extracted, and upon which every extensive iron works had been erected. A Bill was filed by one of the co-tenants against the others for a dissolution of partnership. As the facts bearing upon this particular point were not sufficiently set out in the Bill, an affidavit in explanation of the nature of the business was ordered, in which it was stated, that the iron works at Cyfarthfa had been conducted as a trading concern—that the produce of the mines consisted of ironstone, coal, and limestone—and that at the works, large quantities of iron had been, and were manufactured, sometimes from the materials obtained from the leasehold land in question, and sometimes from pig iron and finers' metal purchased in London, Plymouth, and Bristol ; that from the first establishment of the works, the proprietors had been in the habit of making very considerable purchases of iron ore from Lancashire, pig iron, and finers' metal, and of old wrought iron, naval and ordnance stores, for the purpose of manufacture at the works into various sorts of iron, and re-selling them in that manufactured state ; that these purchases had been made by the successive firms with a view to profit, by manufacturing the articles purchased into bar and other iron for re-sale, and *not merely for mixing the same with the iron produced from the works for improving the latter, or bringing it to a better market.* Lord Eldon observed, that it was dfficult to establish that this was an interest in land, distinct from a partnership in trade—a mere interest in land, in which a partition could take place ; for when persons, having purchased such an interest, manufacture and bring to market the produce of the land (1) as one common fund, to be sold for their common benefit, it might be contended that they have entered into an agreement, which gives to that interest the nature, and subjects it to the doctrines of a partnership in trade.

It may be observed, that all these acts are equally applicable to strict owners of land who are not partners in a trade, and this idea must have suggested itself to the mind of Lord Eldon. For on a subsequent day he remarked, that a very difficult question might arise, whether, if the parties being originally tenants in common of a mine, agreed to become jointly interested in the manufacture of its produce for the purpose of sale, they continued mere tenants in common of the mine—still more, if not only carrying the produce of their own mine to market, they became purchasers of other property of a like nature, to be manufactured with their own. On a still subsequent day, Lord Eldon in delivering final judgment, said that after repeated consideration, he entertained no doubt that it was a trading concern, and that a partnership had subsisted.

If the contents of the affidavit alluded to in the above case were correct,

---

(1) It should be observed that the affidavit above referred to, by which it appears that they brought to market the manufactured produce of other lands, was not then before the Court.

there could be no doubt that the concern was a trade, which subjected the parties to the operation of the bankrupt laws, and therefore to the consequences of partnership. The purchase of other materials for the sake of manufacturing and selling them, as distinct articles of commerce, was quite sufficient to divest them of the exclusive character of owners of land.

It may be observed, that, in the above case, the parties were also interested in the lands in the same proportions, as in the trade itself. It may perhaps be presumed, that when the proportions differ, the intention of the parties to become partners will be more readily, though not necessarily implied.

The point was shortly afterwards adverted to in another case before the same Chancellor. But it did not form part of the ground of decision in that case, as it was decided that a manager of the mine might be appointed by the Court, even if the parties were not actual partners, but only tenants in common of land. (a)

In another case, six persons had taken a lease for years of mines, and also another lease of the surface lands, under which the mines were situated, and had worked the mines as a joint concern, divided into equal shares. One of them was appointed manager, and had become much indebted to it. He afterwards became bankrupt, and it appeared he had mortgaged his shares. A Bill was filed for the sale of the property; and that it might be declared, that the shares of the bankrupt should be applied, in the first place, in repaying to the partnership the debt which he had incurred in the management of the concern. The true question, therefore, was whether the parties stood in the relation of partners to each other. The above case of Crawshay v. Maule, was very properly distinguished, in the argument, from the present case, in which no other articles appear to have been purchased; and it was contended, that if the rules which are applicable to common trading partnerships, were to be extended to part owners of mines, it would be difficult to foresee what consequences might follow, affecting interests of the greatest magnitude, and placing many individuals of the highest rank and fortune in situations which they never contemplated—and that the parties must be considered as tenants in common of the mines and lands. But Sir John Leach, M. R. observed, it was true, a mining concern differs in some particulars from a common partnership—but it had been repeatedly held to be in the nature of a trading concern. He said that in Crawshay v. Maule, Lord Eldon had expressed a doubt, whether, if persons previously entitled as tenants in common to mines, were to form a mining concern, the general principles of partnership would apply, and he (the Master of the Rolls) was not aware that the particular point had ever been decided; but the distinction there was, that the interest in the mines was expressly acquired for the purpose of a partnership, and the general principle was therefore to be applied. (b)

(a) Jefferys v. Smith, 1 Jac. and W. 298.
(b) Fereday v. Wightwick, 1 Russ. and M. 45.

This decision seems to rest upon substantial reasons. The question is then one depending upon intention. And it may be concluded, that when persons acquire interests in lands apparently for the sole purpose of working the mines in them, they must be considered as entering into a commercial partnership. There does not appear to be any ground for distinction in such cases, if the parties have even acquired a permanent and absolute interest in the property. But it does not follow that, in every such case, such an inference can be drawn from the acts of the parties. An estate may be purchased or acquired for a definite period by a tenant in common, who may proceed forthwith to work the mines. But the mines may not have formed the only or even the primary inducements for effecting the purchase or acquisition. Much will always depend upon the particular facts. But it is submitted, as a general rule, that, in all such cases, there must not only be an express intention to work the mines, but this object must have been either *solely* contemplated by the parties, or of such paramount consequence as to effectually overbalance any other advantages anticipated from the estate. For the mines may form very important considerations in the arrangements of capitalists, and yet their existence need not preclude the motives which may proceed from the supposed general advantages of the investment.

This principle, however, will regulate, by far, the greater proportion of mining cases, not specially provided for, in this country, where it is usual for adventurers, only to obtain limited interests in the mines themselves, without acquiring any rights to the general inheritance. It may, therefore, be safely asserted, that, in all such cases, where the obvious intention of the parties to acquire interests in the land for the sole purpose of carrying on mining speculations can be deduced from the nature of those interests, and the manner of their acquisition, the parties will be considered, from these circumstances alone, to have entered into a particular partnership, and to be liable to all its consequences.

On the other hand, if it can be shown, that lands have been long in the possession of the different parties, or of those through whom they claim, or that they have been acquired without any intention to work the mines as an exclusive object, and if, after the mining operations have commenced, the parties have carefully avoided the assumption of the outward *indicia* of partnership, they must, it is conceived, be considered merely as the proprietors of land exercising the common acts of ownership in a manner adapted to the nature of their respective interests in it.

If an interest in opened mines is enjoyed by persons as a distinct inheritance or possession, it would appear, that it will only be under peculiar circumstances, that the parties can be considered to be exempt from the obligations of partnership. The intention, in general, will be too strongly expressed. It is quite possible, however, for persons to have been originally entitled to distinct shares in such a property, without ever having received profits as a partner, or having personally interfered in the management of the concern. It may also frequently happen that mines in this condition may devolve, by conveyance or operation of law, upon persons who have thus contracted no engagement of partnership. (*a*) A person may still continue to be entitled to the legal interest in his share, or to the legal or equitable reversion in it, and may cease, for a time, from becoming liable as a partner. Such experiments, however, are often dangerous, if it is desirable not to incur the liability.

In all cases, where it is intended that a trading partnership should be established, it is desirable that the parties should, by express agreement in writing, declare their intentions, and thus resolve all doubts upon the subject. This precaution seems not only to be reasonably required by the public, who may thus deal with them upon the faith, and with all the advantages, of a partnership; but it may often be indispensable for properly securing the interests of the parties themselves, by enabling them to prosecute the works in an efficient manner.

The consequences of the above distinction are these:—If the works are carried on by persons as mere owners of land, concurring in a general system of management for their common benefit, the shares of each person will only be liable for his individual engagements, and to the payment of debts contracted by himself or his authorized agent, without interfering with the shares of the other tenants in common. It is true, that, in cases of disagreement and mismanagement, a Court of Equity will appoint a general manager for the benefit of the whole. (*b*) But this remedy will very inadequately provide for the exigencies of such a case. In no other respect, will the parties be liable to the consequences of a partnership in trade. The shares cannot be sold for the liquidation of accounts as between the parties themselves; there cannot be enforced, as upon a dissolution, a general sale of the whole property; there will be no restraint upon the introduction of new partners, and there will, in short, be none of those general incidents of a commercial partnership, the exercise of which may prove of so much importance to the effectual and regular working of a mine.

(*a*) See Jefferys *v.* Smith, 3 Russ. 158.
(*b*) Jefferys *v.* Smith, 1 Jac. and W. 301.

CHAPTER VI.

ON THE REMEDIES RELATING TO MINES AND MINERALS.

I. Legal remedies.
II. Equitable remedies.

SECTION I.

LEGAL REMEDIES.

THE subject of remedies connected with mining property has been already incidentally discussed in various parts of the treatise. Much, therefore, which might otherwise have have been found under the present title, has been anticipated.—It will be proper, however, to lay before the reader a general view of the subject, which may include the discussion of those remedies which have not yet been particularly mentioned.

It has been seen that a property may be acquired in mines, which will be quite independent of the property in the lands in which they are situate. In this condition, the minerals, of whatever character they may be, will, of course, still form parts of the land itself, and will constitute land in strictly legal acceptation. As such, mines become liable to the adminstration of all the usual remedies relating to the law of real property, except in those cases which, in consequence of the peculiarity of this species of property, may necessarily demand some modification of those remedies. It may be proper to remind the reader that the word mine is not here used in its strict sense, but as descriptive of the strata, or minerals themselves.

An action of trespass may be maintained in respect of any improper interference with the enjoyment of mines, in all those cases in which that remedy is generally applicable. The same kind of action is usually resorted to for trying the validity of a trial. (*a*)

But an action of ejectment will also be maintainable for recovering possession of a mine. It might certainly be contended, when the mines form a distinct inheritance, that the action of ejectment is possessory ; that the object of contention must, at least, be such as to be capable of actual possession from the delivery of the sheriff; that all the excavated parts would be of an incorporeal nature, or, at any rate, would become part of the general freehold, through which a mere right of way would be permissible ; and that all the portions, which are severed, instantly lose the character of land, and become mere personal chattels. Such an action would certainly not seem to cor-

---

(*a*) Bourne *v.* Taylor, 10 East, 189.   Roberts v. Davey, 4 B. and Ad. 665.

respond, in such case, with its exact definition. But in this, as in some other instances, the action of ejectment has been carried beyond its original limits. And it has been expressly decided, that such an action for the recovery of mines may be supported. (*a*)

It would seem, however, to be doubtful whether such an action could be brought to recover the possession of unopened mines, the title to which is distinct from that to the surface (*b*) This subject has been already partially discussed in considering the operation of a feoffment with livery of seisin. In a case of unopened mines, it was observed by Lord Hardwicke, that the question was not, whether actual entry was necessary, and he denied that without entry an action of ejectment could not be brought; for the common rule, obliging the defendant to confess lease, entry, and ouster, was, in law, sufficient to support that. (*c*)

It has been seen, that an ejectment cannot be brought by the lord of a manor for the mines situate in the lands of his copyhold tenant, in the absence of special custom; for though the former is entitled to the right of property, the latter is entitled to the right of possession.(*d*)

It has been decided, that such an action will not properly lie in respect of a license only to work mines. In the case of a license, an action of this kind was brought for the recovery of mines. It was held by the Court of King's Bench, that a proviso for re-entry was not less applicable to a license to work mines, than to an actual demise of the minerals, because under such license works might be effected, and a corporal possession had, which it might be competent for the grantor to reserve, but that such an instrument did not confer a right sufficient to support the action of ejectment. (*e*)

But the grant of a license will support an action of trespass. (*f*)

When the minerals are severed from their native bed, and become the subject of manipulation, they are mere personal chattels, like the trees which are severed from the freehold, and an action of trover will, therefore, be maintainable for their recovery in that condition. This form of action has been often adopted to try the right to mines. (*g*)

But an action of trover cannot be maintained for the recovery of a certificate or voucher of a person being entitled to certain shares in a mining association, if the plaintiff can show no *legal* title to the document. (*h*)

(*a*) Comyn *v.* Kyneto, Cro. Jac. 150. De mineris carbonum in the county of Durham, Carth. 277. Wyld's case. Lawson *v.* Williams, cited Cro. Jac. 150. Cullen *v.* Rich, Bull. N. P. 102. Harebottle *v.* Placock, Cro. Jac. 21.

(*b*) Lewis *v.* Branthwaite, 2 Barn. and Ad. 437.

(*c*) Sayer *v.* Pierce, 1 Ves. sen. 234.

(*d*) Sayer *v.* Pierce, 1 Ves. sen. 232. See chap. iii. sec. ii.

(*e*) Doe d. Hanley *v.* Wood, 2 Barn. and Ald. 739, 740.

(*f*) Bishop of Winchester *v.* Knight, 1 P. W. 407. Harker *v.* Birkbeck, 1 W. Black. 482. 3 Burr. 1556. Roberts *v.* Davey, 4 Barn. and Ad. 665.

(*g*) Player *v.* Roberts, W. Jones, 243. Cullen (Lord) *v.* Rich, Bull. N. P. 102. 2 Str. 1142. Rowe *v.* Brenton, 8 Barn and C. 737. Rowe *v.* Grenfell, R. and M. 396.

(*h*) Dawson *v.* Rishworth, 1 Barn. and Ad. 574.

An action for use and occupation was held to be maintainable, in respect of a shaft or down, which had been let by a written agreement not under seal, if the defendant could be considered as having taken possession of the shaft; and he was also held liable, under those circumstances, to all the rent payable to the lessor till the determination of his tenancy, and whether he has continued to work the mine or not. But it was also said, that if he had merely caused holes to be dug, and had them filled up immediately, with a view to ascertain only what kind of a bargain he was about to make or had made, such acts would not amount to a taking of possession. (a)

Mines may also be taken possession of under the writ of elegit. A tenant in elegit, it has been seen, cannot open mines in lands of which he has taken possession. This restriction, it is presumed, would not apply to mines forming a separate inheritance; for such an exercise of power would not constitute waste. The point, however, is of little practical importance, as it can rarely, if ever, happen, notwithstanding the recent extension of the remedy, that such a temporary tenant would feel justified in proceeding to open mines.

At common law, an action of waste was maintainable to recover the place wasted, as well as damages for the injury done to the inheritance. This form of action, however, was attended with many difficulties and peculiarities, and gradually fell into disuse. It is now expressly abolished. (b) The modern remedies for punishing the commission of waste are an action on the case in the nature of waste, an action of covenant, and an action of assumpsit. The two latter actions are almost confined to cases between landlord and tenant. The action of assumpsit is resorted to when the tenancy is by agreement, not under seal, or in cases of an *implied* covenant. The action of covenant arises upon express and legal covenants. But an action on the case is most generally applicable, in cases of waste, and is maintainable by the reversioner or remainder man for life or years, against a stranger or tenant, even if the latter be a tenant at will or by sufferance. (c) It may be brought against a tenant after the expiration of his term. (d)

If a lease contain an express covenant against waste, the lessor may still bring an action on the case against the tenant. (e)

An action of trespass is also maintainable in cases of waste. (f)

In all these cases, damages may be recovered for the amount of injury sustained.

The remedies with respect to waste committed by ecclesiastical persons have already been discussed. (g)

(a) Jones v. Reynolds, 7 Carr. and P. 335. Per Coleridge, J.

(b) 3 and 4 Will. IV, c. 27, s. 36.

(c) 2 Wms. Saund. 252, n. 7. West v. Treude, Cro. Car. 187. Sir W. Jones, 224.

(d) Kinlyside v. Thornton, Bl. Rep. 1111. (e) Ibid. (f) West v. Treude, supra.

(g) See Chap. iv. See also Herring v. Dean and Chapter of St. Paul, 3 Swanst. 510. Per Sir Thomas Plumer. Bishop of Winchester v. Wolgar, cited ibid, 493.

A lessee covenanted to pay a certain proportion of the value of nine hundred Cwt. of the coals to be raised, unless prevented by unavoidable accident from working the pit. It was held, that if the accident were only of such a nature that the working of the pit was not physically impossible, but might have been effected, the defendant was liable, though the expense would be greater than the value of the coals to be raised. (a)

SECTION II.

EQUITABLE REMEDIES.

I. Courts of Equity have long ago adopted the practice of giving relief, in certain cases, by injunction to restrain persons from working mines. This remedy was always obtainable in cases of waste. It was extended to trespasses in mining cases, for the purpose of preventing irreparable mischief. (b) And it has even been carried so far as to restrain the taking of valuable stones, or nodules of clay, used for making cement under a patent, and which were found between high and low water mark, and below low water mark in the sea. (c)

In cases of a pressing nature, an injunction may be obtained on motion only, and before the answer of the defendant is put in. A contrary decision of Lord Hardwicke has been overruled. (d) The bill must, in such cases, be actually filed, and be supported by proper affidavits of title, and showing an actual or threatened interference.

But a distinction has always been observed with respect to the hasty disturbance of mines in active operation,—Mining operations may, in general, be prevented without much permanent injury even to the rightful owner, when no expenditure has been incurred, and when no extensive preparations have been made. But the nature of mining requires that the works should be kept in a constant state of repair and activity, and an injunction for causing such operations to be at once suspended, might produce an injury which might be of the most fatal consequences, both with respect to the costs of recommencing the suspended operations, and with respect to rival ownerships, by which the most favourable opportunity for disposing of the produce might be lost. As a general rule, therefore, the Court will not interfere by injunction, on motion, and before the cause is fully heard, in cases where there

(a) Morris v. Smith, 3 Doug. 279.

(b) Gibson v. Smith, Barn. Ch. Rep. 497, Player v. Roberts, W. Jones, 243, Anon. Amb. 209. Grey v. Duke of Northumberland, 13 Ves. 236. 17 Ves. 281. Mitchell v. Dors, 6 Ves. 147. Whitfield v. Bewit, 2 Pee. W. 240. Flamang's case, cited 7 Ves. 308. Norway v. Rowe, 19 Ves. 144. Field v. Beaumont, 1 Swans. 208. 3 Madd. 102.

(c) Earl Cowper v. Baker, 17 Ves. 128.   (d) Lowther v. Stamper, 3 Atk. 496.

has been either great expenditure or great delay. (*a*)   Delay alone, without much expenditure, will of itself sufficiently justify the Court in withholding the summary application of a remedy which is required to be sought for at once, and in the acquisition of which unusual facilities are afforded by the Court.   The only ground for so strong a measure is that a denial of it might be attended with irreparable mischief.—If persons are not prompt in proclaiming this mischief, the circumstance may be considered either to refute the extent of the injury, or their title to redress.

In one case, it was observed by Lord Eldon, that the grantees had actually worked the mines from 1808 till 1816, when the action of trespass was commenced—and that action was not brought to trial till 1817.   It had been very correctly stated, that if the defendants had filed a bill to stay the the working of the mines, the Court must have refused an injunction to parties who had permitted these operations to proceed from 1808 till 1816, without interruption.   To stop the working of a coal mine was a serious injury ; and the expenditure incurred in the course of eight years would raise an equitable ground to prevent the hasty interference of the Court. The defendants would have been directed first to bring an action, and to return when the result of the trial had enabled the Court better to deal with the application. (*b*)

In another case, the time of delay amounted to two years—and the injunction was refused. (*c*)

When a special injunction is granted, it is for the purpose of immediately protecting the rights of those interested in the property.   But whether issued in the first instance or not, it will be incumbent on the plaintiff, upon the hearing of the cause, to shew just grounds for the relief being granted or continued.   The Court may then proceed to the final decision of the question, or, as in cases of disputed title, may direct the plaintiff to establish his right in a court of law.

If there be any unnecessary delay in the plaintiff in such a case, in trying an action at law, this delay will, in itself, form just grounds for dissolving an injunction.   Thus, in the case of Grey *v.* the Duke of Northumberland, it was observed by Lord Eldon, after noticing that the action at law had miscarried by means of an error in pleading, in making the defendant a tenant in fee, instead of a tenant for life, that the merits of the question had not been tried from the fault of the plaintiff, which presented a strong case for dissolving the injunction ; unless some means of procuring a speedy trial could be insured, he should dissolve it. (*d*)

(*a*) Anon. Amb. 209, Grey *v.* Duke of Northumberland, 13 Ves. 236, 17 Ves. 282.   Birmingham Canal Comp. *v.* Lloyd, 18 Ves. 515.   Field *v.* Beaumont, 1 Swans. 208.   3 Madd. 102, nom. Beaumont *v.* Field, 1 Barn. and Ald. 247.

(*b*) Field *v.* Beaumont, 1 Swans. 204.

(*c*) Birmingham Canal Comp. *v.* Lloyd, 18 Ves. 515.   (*d*) 17 Ves. 281.

It must always require a strong case on the part of the plaintiff to demand the interference of the Court by injunction in cases of trespass by the working of mines. The remedy cannot be administered on every occasion of injury. There must exist an urgent necessity for so strong a proceeding, otherwise the parties will be left to their remedies at law.

A motion was made before Lord Hardwicke, to restrain a lessee from working a coal pit irregularly and detrimentally to the lessor. The Chancellor refused the injunction, and observed that the Court grants injunction to stay the working of a colliery with great reluctance, from the great inconvenience it occasions, and that it never will do it, but where there is a breach of an express covenant, or an uncontroverted mischief. (a)

In another case, it was observed by Lord Eldon, that the act of stopping a colliery *about to be wrought* might possibly, with reference to rival ownerships, be the means of making it absolutely unproductive twelve months afterwards, when it was to be wrought. The injunction was refused after the delay of two years. (b)

In another case, the same Judge observed, that inconceivable mischief might ensue from upholding the injunction too long, as the value of the opportunity of working a coal mine, if lost, might never be recovered, especially if it was contiguous to other mines belonging to the same person; and the interposition of the Court must be with a considerable pressure, that on the part of the plaintiff there should be no delay in going to trial. (c)

It has been doubted, whether after a verdict at law in an action of trespass, in favour of the plaintiff in equity, the Court will afterwards grant an injunction against future trespasses, when the plaintiff refused to produce at the trial documents which are necessary for a fair decision. (d)

II. It has been seen, that mining is considered as a species of trade. A Bill in Equity, therefore, may be brought for an account of the profits. (e) There are many instances in which the Court has decreed an account in cases of working mines, which it could not have decreed in cases of felling timber. (f)

An owner of a coal mine made a lease of it to a trustee, in trust for five other persons, in equal shares. The lessee entered and worked the mine,

(a) Clavering v. Clavering, 2 Pee. W. 388.
(b) Birmingham Canal Co. v. Lloyd, 18 Ves. 515.
(c) Grey v. Duke of Northumberland, 17 Ves. 231.   (d) Field v. Beaumont, 1 Swans. 210.
(e) Bishop of Winchester v. Knight, 1 Pee. W. 406. Whitfield v. Bewit, 2 P. W. 240. Story v. Lord Windsor, 2 Atk. 630. 1 Ch. Ca. 34. Clavering v. Westley, 3 P. W. 402. Pulteney v. Warren, 6 Ves. 89. Norway v. Rowe, 19 Ves. 144. Rowe v. Wood, 2 Jac. and W. 559.
(f) Jesus College v. Bloome, 3 Atk. 262. Amb. 54.

which some time afterwards became unprofitable, and was abandoned. The lessee was insolvent; and the lessor brought a bill against him and the five partners for the rent, and insisted that as the *cestui que trusts* were to have the profits while the lease continued to be a beneficial one, it was reasonable they should also bear the loss occasioned by it. The Master of the Rolls was of opinion, that, as an action at law lay against the lessee only, the landlord was debarred of any remedy against any other person; and that as the landlord gave credit entirely to the lessee, and made choice of him as the person liable for the rent, the bill ought to be dismissed, as against the partners. But this decision was reversed by Lord Talbot, on appeal; and it was decreed that an account should be taken of the amount of rent and sums due to the lessor, which was to be paid to him by the lessee; and in case of his default, that an account should be taken for the purpose of shewing whether the lessee had sufficient monies of the partners remaining in his hands to answer their shares of what should be found due to the plaintiff, and if the lessee had not sufficient, that the other defendants should pay the amount to the plaintiff, according to their respective shares. (*a*)

When mines are in the possession of assignees, or one of many persons entitled to share in the profits, all the reasonable expenses incurred in the management of the concern will be allowed in taking the account. (*b*)

A Bill for an account may be brought by the owners or lessees of mines against their agents; and if there are mutual accounts, the Court will restrain all proceedings at law and direct the whole accounts to be taken in equity.—In one case, the agent had received a regular salary previous to his dismissal. He afterwards brought an action for his wages against his former employers. The latter filed a bill to stay proceedings, and for an account, alleging the receipt of various sums by the agent, which had not been accounted for. The defendant admitted the existence of mutual accounts. But it was contended for him that the whole question depended upon the amount of compensation to be given to him for his services, and was a question for a jury. It was held, however, by the Court of Exchequer, that if it should become necessary to try the question before a jury, the Court could direct an issue. If the action proceeded it would have ended in a reference. The master was as good a judge of the matters in issue as a jury could be. (*c*)

But a bill for an account will not be supported unless the plaintiff does some act to show his possession.

A lease was made of a coal field, but no possession was taken of it by the lessee. The defendant, who was the owner or lessee of adjoining mines, was charged by the plaintiff with taking coals from the land included in his

(*a*) Clavering *v.* Westley, Clavering *v.* Reed, 3 Pee. W. 402. Reg. Lib. A. 1735. fol. 526.
(*b*) Scott *v.* Nesbitt, 14 Ves. 445. per Lord Eldon.
(*c*) Crease *v.* Penprase, 1 Jurist, 840. Ex. Eq.

lease. There were also disputes arising from a confusion of boundaries. Lord Hardwicke said, it was difficult to go through with an action at law in case of an account of the profits of coal mines; and therefore the Court would go no farther than in other cases. But the bill was the same as a bill for an account of rents and profits of an estate, which cannot be maintained merely on a legal title, unless there is infancy or something in the way so that no recovery could be obtained without it. An ejectment would have determined the right; and if the bill had been merely on account of the profits, it must have been dismissed; but being to ascertain the boundaries, the plaintiff might, if he recovered, want that relief; and then if leave were given to bring an ejectment abstracted from the direction of the Court, he must bring a new bill; and if it were dismissed entirely, he would be deprived of an injunction if wanted. The bill was then directed to be retained for a year with liberty for the plaintiff to bring an action of ejectment. (a)

The mine, in the above case, formed a possession distinct from that of the surface. If it had not been distinct, the objection could not have been raised unless it was also applied to the general inheritance.

A bill for an account may be brought by the mortgagor of mines against a mortgagee in respect of the proceeds arising during the period of his possession. In such cases, the mortgagee must account, not only for what he has actually received, but for what he might have received, but through his gross mismanagement or wilful neglect. (b) But as we have already seen, he will not be liable to account for any supposed benefits which might have resulted from any speculations in improvement, or from a more extensive scale of expenditure than is required from a prudent owner. (c)

The remedy of account between partners has been already considered. (d) A partner will not be bound to account in so particular a manner as a mortgagee, (e) for the acts of the former are identified with those of his copartners, who must, in due time, take measures for controlling his imprudent operations, and must, as in other respects, endure the consequences incident to the contract of partnership.

When the relations of a mortgagee and a partner are united in the same person, it has been doubted by Lord Eldon, whether an account should be directed with respect to the former or the latter character. But the mortgagee-partner was eventually declared to retain the possession of the mine in his character of mortgagee only. It is presumed, if a person takes possession as mortgagee, he must also account as a mortgagee. If he acquire the advantages resulting from the assumption of a higher character, it is only reasonable that he should bear the inconveniences. In the above

(a) Sayer v. Pierce, 1 Ves. sen. 232.

(b) Anon. 1 Vern. 45. 1 Eq. Ca. Ab. 327. Hughes v. Williams, 12 Ves. 493.

(c) See chap. ii.   (d) Chap. v. s. v.

(e) Rowe v. Wood, 2 Jac. and Walk. 556.

case the mortgagor was declared to have a clear right to insist that regular accounts should be kept of all receipts, payments, and transactions relating to the mine, and to have constant access for the purpose of inspecting the accounts. (*a*)

———

III. Contracts relating to mines may be enforced, as in other cases of real property, by bills for specific performance.

If a purchaser take possession of mines and manage the property under a contract stipulating that a good title should be made by a specified future day, and it appear to be the intention of the parties that the purchaser should immediately take possession, there will be no waiver of objections on the part of the purchaser. (*b*)

When specific performance is refused to be decreed to a vendor for want of a good title, and the purchaser is charged with gross mismanagement, the Court will not, upon a record so framed, and under a prayer for general relief, direct accounts or inquiries as to the defendant's possession or management, with a view to ascertain whether any compensation should be made by him to the plaintiff. Upon appeal from the Vice Chancellor, who dismissed the bill with costs, it was observed by Lord Lyndhurst, that it was true the bill contained charges of mismanagement of the property by the purchaser; but these charges were introduced, not with a view to demand compensation for any loss alleged to have been sustained, but in order to establish the fact of acceptance of the title by the defendant, and of waiver of all objections to it, and to make out the plaintiff's right to specific performance. Under such circumstances, it would be unjust to allow the plaintiff to abandon the case made by his bill, and to come at the hearing for a new remedy, upon a record framed with an aspect altogether different.

The appeal was then dismissed, but without prejudice to any suit which the plaintiff might think fit to institute, for the purpose of recovering compensation. (*c*)

In the above case there was only the purchase of shares, although the purchaser was in the possession of the whole mine. It was observed by the Court, there were other persons interested in the property when the alleged mismanagement took place. Under a decree between the vendor and purchaser of shares only, all the liabilities, which might be involved in giving the vendor the compensation he asked, could not be arranged. (*d*)

In a contract to purchase all the coal under an estate the purchase money was to be paid by instalments. A bill for specific performance was filed by the vendor, and a motion was made on his part to order the purchaser to pay into Court the amount of the first instalment which was then due. No con-

(*a*) Ibid. p. 559.   (*b*) Stevens *v.* Guppy, 3 Russ. 171.
(*c*) Ibid. 184.   (*d*) Jefferys *v.* Smith, 3 Russ. 158.

veyance had been made, but the contract was admitted, and the title was not disputed. The Court made the order for payment of the money in a month, as the defendant was in possession and working the mines. (*a*)

A purchaser under a decree, taking possession, will be ordered to pay the purchase money into Court, unless he entered with the express consent of the Court. (*b*)

Although the purchaser is not bound to acquaint a vendor with any latent advantage in the estate, yet any concealment for the purpose of obtaining an estate at a grossly inadequate price may be deemed fraudulent. (*c*)

Specific performance of a contract for the sale of lands in which there is a reservation of mines will be decreed, if there be a great improbability of the purchaser being disturbed.

In a case of this kind, it was objected that there was a reservation in a former grant from the crown, of tin, lead, and all royal mines. It was reported by the master, that there was a probability of the existence of such mines, and that the vendor could not make a good title. But it was held, at the hearing, by Lord Hardwicke, that the objection could not be sustained. It was the business of the Court, he observed, to carry such agreements into execution, and it must govern itself by a moral certainty; for it was impossible, in the nature of things, that there should be a mathematical certainty of a good title. There was no pretence that there had been any search for royal mines for one hundred and eleven years, and, upon examination, the probability was great there were no such mines. After denying the power of the crown, where there is only a bare reservation without a right of entry, to work for mines, (*d*) he said, it would be of mischievous consequence to allow such an objection to a title, especially as all grants from the crown have, for the most part, such a general reservation; but the fact in the present case was, that there had never been an exertion of this right in a single instance since the grant, and in all probability there never would. (*e*)

In like manner, specific performance of a contract for the sale of mines will be decreed, if there is no probability of the purchaser being disturbed by actions of trespass in the course of his operations. A purchaser, on one occasion, of some valuable mines, refused to perform his contract because the mines were situate under a common, and consequently he might be subject to actions for sinking shafts to work the mines. But Lord Eldon, having shewn the improbability of any obstruction from the commoners, said, that in case such an action were brought, he should think a farthing damages quite enough, and decreed a specific performance. (*f*)

(*a*) Buck *v.* Lodge, 18 Ves. 450.   (*b*) See 1 Sug. Vend. and P. 359, 10th ed.

(*c*) Deane *v.* Rastron, 1 Anst. 64. See, Turner *v.* Harvey, Jac. 169. Brenley *v.* Collins, You. 317.

(*d*) See chap. i.   (*e*) Lyddal *v.* Weston, 2 Atk. 19.

(*f*) Anon. Chan. 7 Sept. 1803. cited in Sugden's Vend. and P. vol. 2, p. 184.

It has been observed, that this case must have turned upon the improbability of the purchaser being disturbed, and that otherwise it has gone to the utmost verge of the law ; for although only trifling damages could be recovered, yet that would be no ground for a non-suit, and the estate might, therefore, subject the purchaser to litigation, whenever malice or caprice might induce any of the commoners to commence actions against him. (a)

If, however, there be a distinct reservation of the mines, it was held by Sir William Grant that the purchaser would be entitled to compensation, even if the reservation is of an old date, and the right under it has never been asserted by any actual attempts to work the mines.   In the case alluded to, the reservation was contained in a deed dated in 1704, and comprised all the springs, veins, and mines of salt in certain parts of the property, with full liberty, *without paying any thing*, to sink pits, and do all things necessary for carrying the minerals away.   This reservation was objected to by a purchaser, as a ground for compensation, and the Master of the Rolls decreed him compensation.   After noticing the fact of the ownership of the mines of salt, and that no inference of release or abandonment could be drawn from their non-user, Sir William Grant observed, that the case of Lyddal v. Weston, (b) instead of being an authority for the defendant, appeared to afford an argument by implication against him.   The grounds of that judgment were that, upon examination, the probability was great that there were no mines ; and that the Crown having merely reserved the mines without a right of entry, could not grant a license to enter and work them. That position was liable to considerable doubt; (c) but Lord Hardwicke thought it necessary to assume it, before he could determine against the validity of the purchaser's objection.   In the present case, it was not alleged, that there was no probability of mines upon the estate ; it was rather admitted, that there were, and there was a reservation of a right of entry, upon the want of which Lord Hardwicke had laid stress.   The defendant, he added, chose to consider this, not as an objection to the title, but as a ground for compensation, and he was entitled to it. (d)

It may evidently be gathered from the judgment of Sir William Grant, in the above case, that if the purchaser had altogether resisted the performance of his contract, he would have been allowed to do so.   It has been clearly shown that, in general, a right of entry is, in the absence of stipulation to the contrary, incident to the right of mines. (e)   The doctrine adopted by Lord Hardwicke upon this subject, and which was repudiated by Sir Wm. Grant, with respect to royal mines only, cannot be supported with respect to any mines.   One of the main reasons for his decision, therefore, in Lyddal v. Weston, is defective, and that decision must rest, and rest safely, upon the

---

(a) Ibid.   (b) Supra.   (c) See chap. i.
(d) Seaman v. Vandrey, 16 Ves. 390.   (e) See chap. ii.

evidence of the improbability of there being mines to create any disturbance to the purchaser. Such an improbability, however, should not rest upon slendor and inadequate evidence. If there is a legal reservation of mines, and mines are supposed, or even suspected to exist, it would be hard to force a title upon a purchaser, which might expose him to the complete waste of his estate. There was, in the case of Seaman v. Vaudrey, a stipulation in the deed of reservation, that the right to work the mines was exercisable without incurring any liability for damages. No compensation short of the amount of purchase money, might satisfy such a case as this. In such instances, extraordinary caution is required, and still stronger evidence of the non-existence of mines should be adduced, in order to compel the performance of a contract. It is quite enough, in all cases, where there is no probability of there being any mines, that the purchaser should be subject to the caprice or ignorance of individuals, who, in spite of appearances or the dictates of experience, may choose to embark upon a wild adventure in search of minerals which are not to be found. The fact of improbability, therefore, should be based upon such competent and substantial evidence as may justify the Court in exposing a purchaser to such a risk.

IV. On the other hand, if a vendor make false representations to a purchaser with respect to the advantages of an investment, it will amount to fraud, and the purchaser may be relieved in equity by a decree for setting aside the contract, or even the conveyance. (a)

In the great case of Small v. Attwood, (b) the vendor was charged with making or authorizing false statements, upon a treaty for the purchase of extensive iron mines and iron works, with respect to the cost of manufactured pig iron. The contract was silent upon the subject. A difference of 16s. per ton was stated to exist between the explanations of the defendant, and the actual cost. This would have produced a difference of £14,000 a year in the account of the concern. Similar mis-statements were charged with respect to the conversion of the metal into refined iron, blooms, and rods. Lord Lyndhurst, C. B., decided, that a case of mis-statement with the knowledge of the party, in other words, that a case of fraud had been proved against the defendant, and that the contract should be rescinded. But it was ultimately decided in the House of Lords, that such a case was not sufficiently proved.

In the above case, there was a disturbance of the stratification in an important part of the coal mines, amounting either to an actual fault, or producing similar consequences. The defect was discovered some months previous to the conclusion of the negotiation. The defendant did not sanction this concealment, but he was aware of the defect, and evaded the questions put with respect to the mine being a perfect mine. But the learned Judge

---

(a) Edwards v. M'Leay, Coop. 308.   (b) 1 Younge, 407.

held, that the purchasers, in taking possession, must have known immediately the circumstances connected with the fault, and that it was too late, after the expiration of six months, to file a bill for setting aside the contract. (*a*)

It is no objection to a bill for setting aside a contract that the purchasers have been in possession, and have made great alterations in the property. It is enough that they act fairly in the management of the property, and take the natural exercise of the rights of supposed owners. (*b*)

V. The purchaser of an estate sold under a decree in Chancery is entitled, as a general rule, to be let into possession from the quarter day preceding his purchase, on paying the purchase money before the succeeding quarter day. (*c*)   But this rule has been held to be inapplicable to the case of a colliery, in which the accounts of the concern were settled monthly, and in which there was no such thing as a quarter day; for the profits of such property may produce more in one quarter than in the preceding ten years.   A colliery is a trade, and not merely a property in land.   The purchaser was, therefore, declared to be entitled to the profits from the commencement of the month in which he purchased, paying his purchase-money in the course of that month. (*d*)   A person is not considered to be an absolute purchaser until the confirmation of the master's report. (*e*)

In the above case of Wren *v*. Kirton, a colliery had been put up to sale under a decree, and £23,000 was offered by a *bona fide* bidder.   The sale was defeated by setting up a fictitious bidder.   The property was again put up three times.   On the two first occasions £12,000 and £6,000 only were offered.   On the last occasion it was sold to a trustee for the agent and manager of the colliery for £15,000.   The motion to confirm this sale was opposed.—Lord Eldon observed, it was a very difficult and important case.   If it had been an original sale, and the agent had purchased in the name of another person, very slight circumstances would have induced him, even at some risk, to have set that aside—as it was the duty of the agent, if he meant to bid, to furnish all the knowledge he had to those who were to sell.   A regular proceeding in the master's office, which produced a bidding of £23,000 by a responsible person, was met by a very improper transaction in setting up a man of straw to defeat the sale, which occasioned the loss.   In general, the Court will at some risk put the property up again, if the sale has not been properly conducted. (*f*)   The difficulty was the danger of further loss by the re-sale.   He added, he would not hesitate to open the sale, if the least advance upon £15,000 was offered; but without such an offer, there was nothing leading him to suppose; it would ever again reach the sum originally bid.   An order was accordingly made, but with considerable reluc-

---

(*a*) Ibid. 503.   (*b*) Ibid. 506.   (*c*) Marfill *v*. Rudge, 2 You. and C. 566,
(*d*) Wren *v*. Kirton, 8 Ves. 502.   Williams *v*. Attenborough, Turn. and Russ. 70,
(*e*) Twigg *v*. Fifield, 13 Ves. 517.   Garrick *v*. Earl Camden, 2 Cox, 231.
(*f*) See Watson *v*. Birch, 2 Ves. Jun. 53.

tance, to confirm the report, unless before the first seal an application should be made to open the biddings, with security to answer the difference between the produce of the re-sale, and the sum of £15,000. (a)

The practice of opening biddings in sales under decrees in Chancery has often been justly reprobated. On one occasion, Lord Eldon said, during a period of nearly half a century which he had passed in the Court, he had heard one and all of its judges lament the introduction of the practice. (b) It is now, however firmly established by numerous cases, and almost daily experience.

But the rules with respect to opening biddings do not apply to the sales of mines. In the case of a colliery, an order for opening the biddings was made by the Vice Chancellor, but it was discharged by Lord Eldon, who observed, that land kept generally the same value; but collieries were liable not only to fluctuations in value, but to destruction; they were like land in a country liable to earthquakes. A gain, upon a re-sale of the property the purchaser might be tired of his bargain before he has completed his purchase; and although the Court might compel the final bidder to pay the money, the process was such, that in a great many cases, it was more for the interests of the vendors to abandon the bargain, than to put in force the process of the Court. Not even a *bona fide* bidder can, in any case be said to have any right to open the biddings.—The question was, whether regard being had to the nature of the property, the circumstances of the case, and the general interest of the suitors of the Court, not to the interests of purchasers, so much advantage was held out as to induce the Court to open the biddings. (c)

In the above case, the purchase could not be confirmed for a considerable time, and it became necessary to take into consideration who should have the intermediate management. It was finally agreed that the purchaser should work the colliery under the superintendance of the trustees. It was observed by the Court, it would have been folly in the purchaser if he had not insisted on having in some measure the management; for if, between the day of bidding and the confirmation of the purchase, the value of the mine had fallen from accidental causes injurious to the working, from some rival coal mine, or a destructive inundation, still, if the title had been completed at the time his report was confirmed, he would have been compelled to take the property without entering into the question, whether the management had been advantageous or disadvantageous. It was added that if the management had been advantageous, to discharge a purchaser under such circumstances, upon giving him his costs merely, without making some allowance for the expences incurred in the management, would be treating

(a) 8 Ves. 502.　　　　　　　　　　　　　(b) Turn. and Russ. 73.
(c) Williams *v.* Attenborough, Turn. and Russ. 70.

him in a way very detrimental to the general interests of all those who have collieries to dispose of, through the intervention of this Court. (*a*)

VI. In a case of alum works, there was a covenant by the lessee, to leave stock of a certain amount upon the premises. There was a fair ground of suspicion, that he did not mean to perform this covenant. Lord Eldon decided, that, though there might be compensation in damages, there was a reference to that sort of enjoyment for which the landlord had stipulated after the expiration of the term, and he decreed, by way of *quia timet*, the performance of the covenant. This decision was afterwards confirmed in the House of Lords. (*b*)

A Court of Equity will also, in certain cases, appoint a receiver or manager. (*c*)

It has been decided, that the Irish Statute, 11 and 12 George II. c. 10, does not authorize the appointment of a receiver over mines in the possession of the respondent; and that the Court will not order, upon a mortgage petition, the letting of any property which was not producing rent at the time when the receiver was appointed. (*d*)

A Bill in Equity may be brought for determining questions of disputed bonndaries in mining fields. (*e*)

(*a*) Ibid.   (*b*) Ward *v.* Duke of Buckingham, cited 10 Ves. 161.

(*c*) Jefferys *v.* Smith, 1 Jac. and W. 298.   Norway *v.* Rowe, 19 Ves. 144. Rowe *v.* Wood, 2 Jac. and W. 556.

(*d*) Frere *v.* The Hibernian Mining Comp. 2 Hog. 30.

(*e*) Sayer *v.* Pierce, 1 Ves. Sen. 232.

DECREES

OF THE

SUPREME GOVERNMENT OF MEXICO,

From the Year 1821 to 1848.

Extracted from the Printed Volumes, Published by Authority, to and including the Year 1838, and from the Official Publication of the Laws in the Newspapers of the City of Mexico, from 1839 to 1847, inclusive.

DECREE.

22d November, 1821,

Reduction of the duties on Silver.

THE Sovereign Provincial Governing Committee of the Mexican Empire having taken into consideration the deplorable and decaying condition of the mining business and the urgent necessity there is for extending to this important branch, whatever remedies lie within its power, that may contribute to its greater prosperity, have deemed it proper to decree and do decree :

1. That the duties of one per centum, tythe, and the seigniory tax of one real be abolished.

2. That the duty of of 8 maravedises on each marc of silver which is now collected on the refining of bullion, which may be subjected to such operation, be likewise abolished.

3. That the duty of 26 maravadises imposed upon every marc of mixed bullion which is now recovered by reason of the loss or waste of silver in the smelting rooms be also abolished.

4. That the duty of four eighths on the coined price of silver and of a half an eighth on the coined price of gold which is now collected, under the name of *bocado* in the Mint, be likewise abolished.

5. All the duties which were imposed on bullion of gold or silver and on coin, during the period of the revolution are equally abolished.

6. As an only contribution, there shall be recovered a duty of 3 per cent. on the true value of silver, and the same upon gold, this tax being collected in the same manner as was formerly the tax of one per cent. and the tythe.

7. In the Mint established at the capitol there shall only be collected two reals on each marc of silver, and the same on each marc of gold, as the

entire cost of coining the metals ; and at the other Mints of the kingdom, inasmuch as they are but newly established, a calculation of the expense shall be made which shall be the rule for the first year, at which time this calculation being corrected by an examination of the accounts of expenditures, this corrected calculation shall govern for the following second year.

8. There shall not be levied for costs of smelting more than two reals on the marc of mixed bullion, in place of the five and a half reals heretofore exacted and all the bullion brought to the smelting rooms shall be smelted for the introducers of it, if according to its quality said bullion will pay the expense of the operation. The owners of mixed silver are at liberty to perform this operation by themselves whenever it may be most convenient for them.

9. On assays for strangers, there shall only be collected the real costs of the operations of assaying and those of fusion, in the coined pieces which require it. Suppressing the duty of bocado.

10. The payment of the only contribution as designated in Art. 6. on bullion of gold and silver having been made at the National Treasury and the stamps to show the payment placed upon the pieces of these metals, the owners are at liberty to sell them or employ them in any uses they may desire, without any official designation of value whatever.

11. Six grains weight of deficient shall only be allowed in the Mint in place of the 18 now allowed.

12. In future the scientific offices of the Mint and Smelting Rooms shall be given to persons who possess the necessary knowledge of Natural Philosophy, Chemistry and Mineralogy to discharge the duties of them.

13. Quicksilver (in caldo) liquid shall be entirely exempt from tax, whether it proceeds from Europe or Asia, or be drawn from the mines of the Empire.

14. The powder which the miners require in working the mines, the government shall deliver to them at prime cost.

DECREE.

13th February, 1822.

Prescribing the grain of deficiency in weight, which are allowed in Silver coin.

The sovereign, Provisional, Governing Committee, which from the first moments of its installation took under consideration the deplorable and decaying condition of the mining business, and the urgent necessity of affording to this branch of industry whatever means were in its power, in order to contribute to its greater prosperity, on which depends that of the Empire, having deliberately considered the exposition made to it by the Regency in consequence of the resolution taken on the 22d of November last, and of the opinion which the commission on mining rendered on this important question, in the exercise of its powers, and in conformity with the provision of Article 11th, Chapter xith, regulating it, has determined to decree, and does decree :

" There shall only be allowed eight and a half grains of deficient weight in silver coin, in place of the eighteen which have heretofore been allowed."

DECREE.

29th October, 1823.

Exemption from the duty of ten per cent. on specie funds remitted to the mining Villages.

The Sovereign Congress of Mexico have decreed as follows :

Specie funds destined for the mining villages, with a custom house permit, shall be free from the payment of the two per cent. duty ; the proper officers taking care to require a corresponding return from it in conformity to the disposition made of the same.

DECREE.

13th February, 1824.

Concerning the importation of Quicksilver.

The Sovereign Constituent Congress have thought proper to decree :

That quicksilver arriving at our ports shall, without regard to its origin, or the place of shipment, be admitted, in whatever quantities the same has arrived or shall arrive under a friendly or neutral flag ; provided that this shall not effect the decision of any causes now pending for the forfeiture of the article.

DECREE.

24th July, 1824.

Permission to Don Juan Bautista Binnón, to work Quicksilver mines.

The Sovereign Mexican Congress of the United Mexican States having taken with consideration the application of D. Juan Bantista Binnon, relative to granting him the privilege of working quicksilver mines, have thought proper to decree :

1. The exclusive privilege is hereby granted to the said Binnon for the period of five years, to work the quicksilver mines in the territory of the republic, he conforming in all respects to the mining ordinances.

2. This privilege, in accordance with the request of the person interested,

shall commence two years from the date of this decree, which shall be held without prejudice to those who in the meantime shall acquire mines of the same article, and those who now hold those previously acquired.

3. In like manner permission is given to him to erect at his own expense three factories for the working the minerals of quicksilver in those places where he may have discovered the mines.

4. If at the expiration of the term named in the second article the said Binnón shall not have commenced work with the utensils which he proposes, at that date all the privileges named in this law shall terminate.

5. The expenditure for labor in the quicksilver mines which said Binnón shall work, it shall be his duty to maintain at a weekly average of not less than two hundred dollars.

6. The quicksilver which said Binnón shall extract from said mines shall not be sold by him at more than forty dollars per quintal.

7. Whenever the establishments of the contractor shall produce all the quicksilver necessary for the consumption of the mining operations of the republic, and shall prove the same to the satisfaction of the government, the introduction of foreign quicksilver shall be prohibited.

8. If in addition to what may be necessary for the consumption of the said mining operations, and a reserved stock of one quarter more, which it is the duty of said Binnón to keep, he shall have accumulated any surplus, he shall be at liberty to export the same from the republic, free of duty.

9. The privilege of cutting the wood which may be necessary in the establishment, for the reduction of the quicksilver, is hereby granted, he complying with all the regulations which govern that subject.

10. The nation, at the expiration of the term of the grant, receives a transfer which the said Binnón hereby makes of the business, and the several factories connected with the same.

DECREE.

May 20th, 1826.

The suppressing of the Tribunal of the Miners.

1. The tribunal general of the miners according to the constitution, shall cease to exist in so far as relates to the administration of justice with which it was charged.

2. Its functions shall also cease so far as relates to the executive, economical and administrative attributes which characterised its institution and laws.

3. The late tribunal shall immediately proceed to liquidate within such period as the government shall designate, not exceeding two months, the accounts of the funds which have been placed in their possession.

4. The general meeting of the miners shall select an individual who, with

an accountant named by the government and an attorney of the creditors of the mining funds, appointed in such time and manner as the government shall designate, who shall receive and audit the accounts, having first taken in charge the archives, &c. pertaining to the tribunal.

5. The individual members of the tribunal shall receive their salaries during the period mentioned in the third article.

6. The accounts audited as is provided in Article 4, shall be transmitted to the government who with such report as they may think proper, shall send them to the General Congress for their approval.

7. The avails of what is called the *real de mineria*, and other available credits of the late tribunal shall be applied to the payment of their officers, the maintenance of the College, the payment of taxes and the redemption of loans; and the *real de mineria* shall cease where the debts chargeable upon the mining funds shall have been extinguished.

8. Such portions of those funds as have been received by the State shall be reimbursed to the establishment within such time as the government shall designate.

9. The nation recognises its obligation for the amounts which have been taken from the funds of the tribunal to meet the urgent wants of the state.

10. The collection of the means belonging to this fund shall be made by respective commissaries, who under their own responsibility shall remit the avails to the mint at Mexico, in the nature of a special deposit, and in the meantime said establishment will, in relation to the same, govern itself accordingly.

11. The distribution of the funds in conformity with this law, shall be made through warrants drawn by the person named by the general meeting of miners, subject to the careful supervision of the Secretary of the Treasury.

12. Such person shall be regarded as the general attorney of the body of miners, and in that capacity shall make such representations to the government as he may judge proper, as to the most effectual execution of this law.

13. Extracts from the accounts taken at the tribunal, shall be printed and published each month successively of the receipts and expenditures of the establishment.

14. The persons in the permanent employment of the late tribunal shall continue in the class of *cesantes*, payable out of the funds of the establishment.

15. The government shall require of the *cesantes* to engage in the labors of the establishment if they think it necessary.

16. The college of miners shall continue henceforth, in the same manner as heretofore and with the endowment which has been assigned to it which shall be drawn from the mining fund.

17. The College shall be under the direction of the person who, under

the provision of this law, is appointed by the general meeting of miners, who shall exercise in relation to it those functions heretofore enjoyed by the tribunal, subject to the President of the United Mexican States.

18. The government shall obtain the opinion of Congress as to the salary which the director should have, and with their approbation will form a new plan for the regulation of the college according to the intention of its endowment, leaving to the general Congress to pass on the subject whatever they may determine to be proper.

Lorenzo de Zavala, President of the Senate ; Bernardo Gonzales Perez de Angulo, President of the House of Deputies ; Demetrio del Castillo, Secretary of the Senate ; Antonio Fernandez Monjardin, Deputy Secretary.

DECREE.

September 15, 1829.

Persons who have the Collection of what belongs to the Mineral Fund.

The President of the United States of Mexico to the inhabitants of the Republic.—Know Ye :

That great inconveniences having appeared in the establishment of the miners which have arisen in the collection of the foundation funds made by the general commissaries of the States, to whom, in the meantime and until the said establishment was organized the same was committed, in conformity with the law and regulation of the 20th May, 1826 : and consequently, desiring that in future the collection of the duties shall be made by persons in the employment of and named by the gentlemen who compose said establishment, with whom they can have a more ready intercourse and can thus have more conveniently at hand the funds for the purpose of securing their appropriation to the important objects for which they were designed. In the exercise of the extraordinary powers conferred on me, I have thought proper to command :

1st. That the authority of the commissaries general in the collection of the mining fund, be discontinued.

2d. That this duty shall successively be performed by persons respectively, whom said establishment shall appoint, at least at one of the points where the mining duty is to be collected, said persons being responsible to the same, and having previously given suitable security.

3d. That the same establishments assign to the collectors a compensation in proportion to the sum collected, observing always the greatest economy in the disposition of the funds.

4th. That the commissaries general present to the establishment the general accounts of the amount produced by the mining duty during the time in which they have been charged with its collection, with a statement of the amount remitted to the mint and of the balance resulting in favour of the miners.

5th. That the foregoing articles be substituted for the 10th, and 11th articles of the 20th May, 1826.

Mexico, 15th September, A. D., 1829.

LORENZO DE ZAVALA.

LAW.

May 12th, 1838.

A reward to persons who during the period named shall import in national or neutral vessels quicksilver not French property.

1. During the blockade and six months thereafter, persons who shall import quicksilver in neutral or national vessels, shall receive a premium of five dollars for each quintal introduced by the ports or frontiers of the republic, which shall be credited at the respective custom houses, in account of duties there collected.

2. If the quicksilver which is introduced into the ports of the republic be French property, it shall not be included in the provisions of the previous article, and the same shall besides be subjected to the penalty of forfeiture.

DECREE.

" Diario del Gobierno."—(*Vol.* 22, *No.* 2426, *p.* 173.)

Mexico, February, 18th, 1842.

Department of justice and public instruction. His Excellency the provisional president has been pleased to issue the following decree :

Antonio Lopez de Santa Anna, general of division *benemérito* of the country, and provisional president of the republic of Mexico, to the inhabitants thereof. Know ye : That the piety fund of California being a matter of general interest, and all the objects to which it is destined being truly national, and should therefore be under the immediate care and management of the supreme government, as it has formerly been, I have thought proper to decree :

Art. 1. The 6th article of the decree of the 19th September 1836, whereby the government is deprived of the management of the piety fund of the Californias, and the same placed at the disposition of the reverend bishop of that new diocese, is hereby repealed.

Art. 2. Consequently the management and disposition of the property shall return to and be under the care of the supreme national government, in the manner and on the terms fitted to give effect to the object proposed by the donation—the civilization and conversion of the barbarians.

76

Wherefore I command that the same be printed, published, and carried into effect.

Palace of the national government, Mexico, February 8, 1842.

ANTONIO LOPEZ DE SANTA ANNA,

CRISPINIANO, *of Castile,*

Minister of Justice and Public Instruction.

And I communicate it to you for your information and consequent action.

God and Liberty.——Mexico, February 8, 1842.   Castello.

DECREE.

" Diario del Gobierno." (Vol. XXIV. No. 2687, *p.* 361.

Mexico, October 31st, 1842.

Department of Justice and Public Instruction.

His Excellency the provisional president of the Mexican Republic, has been pleased to issue the following decree :

" Antonio Lopez de Santa Anna, general of division, benemérito of the country and provisional president of the Mexican Republic, to the inhabitants thereof.   Know ye : That having had in consideration that the decree of the 8th of February of the present year, which provided that the safe keeping and administration of the (piadoso) piety fund of the Californias should be restored to and continue in charge of the supreme government, as was the case formerly, directed that the benefits and national objects proposed by the founders should be enjoyed with all exactitude, without the slightest loss to the property destined to this purpose ; and considering also, that this can only be accomplished by converting the same property into capital and putting it out to rent under due security, so as thus to avoid the expenses of administration and any others that may arise ; exercising the powers conceded to me by the seventh of the bases accorded in Tacubaya, and sanctioned by the nation, I have thought proper to decree as follows :

1. The country and town estates, the active credits and other property belonging to the piety fund of the Californias, are incorporated into the national treasury.

2. The Department of the Treasury will proceed to sell the estates and other property belonging to the piety fund of California, as the capital which they represent at six per cent for their annual product, and the public treasury will borrow at the rate of the same 6 per 100 the total proceeds arising from these transfers.

3. The revenue from tobacco remains hypothecated especially for the payment of the revenue, corresponding to the capital of the aforesaid fund of California, and the administration of this branch will deliver the sums neces-

sary to carry into effect the objects to which the same fund is destined, without any deduction for expenses of administration or any others.

Wherefore, I order the same to be printed, published, circulated and carried into full effect.

National Palace of the Government, Mexico, 24th October, 1842.

ANTONIO LOPEZ DE SANTA ANNA.
PEDRO VELEZ,
Minister of Justice and Public Instruction.

And I communicate the same to you for your information and consequent action.

God and Liberty. Mexico, October 24, 1842.

VELEZ.

" *Diario Del Gobierno.*"—(*Vol. XXIV. No.* 2730, *page* 537-8.)

November 13th, 1842.

Government of the Department of Mexico.

EDICT.

Citizen Luis Gonzaga Vieyra, Brevet Brigadier General and Governor of the Department of Mexico.

By the department of war and navy, under date of the 2d. instant, the following decree has been communicated to me.

His Excellency the substitute President has been pleased to issue the following decree.

" Nicholas Bravo, general of division, benemérito of the country and substitute president of the Mexican Republic, to the inhabitants thereof, Know ye : That having in consideration the necessity, as well as at the same time the inportance of encouraging the interesting branch of mining and remembering that although many regulations are in existence having relation to this public benefit, they have either fallen into disuse or have been entirely forgotten, without dilating upon the very great importance, principally to the Republic, of preserving one of the most necessary elements of its prosperity and greatness, I have thought proper to grant in the exercise of powers conceded by the seventh of the bases adopted in Jacubaya, and attested by the representatives of the Department, the following Regulations :

Regulation for the board of encouragement and management of the Mining
Corporation.

TITLE I.

Of the board of encouragement and improvement of the mining corporation, its formation, renewal and attributes.

ART. 1st. There shall be established a Board which shall direct the en-

couragement of mining.   It shall be composed of an attorney of the miners,
another of the creditors of the fund instituted, and of a person commissioned by the Supreme Government.   Their mode of election and powers
will be detailed in the following articles.

ART. 2. The presidency of this board shall be held by turns by the
three persons who compose it, alternating every year.   The first year, the
person commissioned by the Supreme Government shall be the president.

ART. 3. As soon as the present decree is published, the Supreme Government and the creditors of the funds of the establishment, shall proceed
to appoint their respective Commissioners, and the miners residing in this
Capital shall also on their part, appoint a commissioner ad interim.

ART. 4. The Governor of the department of Mexico shall call together
and preside over the creditors and miners in separate meetings, in order
that each class may appoint their respective commissioner conforming in vot-
ing to the existing laws and those in force in the present establishment.

ART. 5. When the board is formed, it shall require from the individuals who may withdraw the delivery by formal and exact inventory of whatsoever may appertain to the establishment, as also the surrender of the accounts for the whole time which has elapsed since the last were presented,
and it will take care the same be laid before the tribunal of revision of accounts within the space of three months.   It will hold its session in the
buildings of the same establishment, and there also shall its office be located.

ART. 6. Three months after the publication of the present decree, the
special attornies who may have been appointed in the mining districts by the
meetings of minors, shall meet in this capital, under the presidency of the
governor of the department, in order to elect the person who is to represent
them in the board of encouragement, which election being completed, and
the proprietary commissioner being put in possession, the one appointed
ad interim shall retire.   Three substitutes shall also be elected, who as well
as the commissioner must be miners or suppliers of mines, (aviadores) who
shall be substitutes for the proprietors in the order of their appointment, and
shall also act as advisers in cases in which the board may desire to hear
their opinion.   If from any places the special attornies of the meetings cannot
come, on account of their being very remote, or their inability to bear the
expense of travelling and staying in Mexico, it will be sufficient that the
meetings at the localities of mines send authority and instructions to a person
in whom they have confidence, and who resides in this capital.

ART. 7. On the 31st of December 1844 this Board of Miners shall be renewed, in order to make a similar election, in the same manner as the creditors shall do, in regard to their attornies, and both shall have power to re-
elect the persons whose terms may expire, the renewal taking place successively every three years.

ART. 8. Each of the members of this board shall enjoy an annual salary of $3000, which shall be paid out of the fund which this law establishes, and a half salary shall be paid to the substitutes when they enter upon duty through any legal impediment to the proprietor, and whenever the duty exceeds fifteen days.

ART. 9. The Board shall propose the reforms it may deem proper in the secretary's and other offices of the establishment. In the regulation of which mention will be made in the next article, the salary of all the persons whom it shall consider necessary for the office to employ shall be fixed, and in the appointment, under equal circumstances, preference shall be given to those retiring, who may receive a salary from the treasury.

ART. 10. The attributes of this Board shall be those which include an economical and faithful management of the funds mentioned in the present decree, in conformity with the regulations which it shall draw up and submit to the supreme government for its approval. In this regulation shall be decided :

1st. The manner in which quicksilver shall be obtained, distributed and sold, to the workers of metals, determining the cases and mode in which the working of quicksilver mines in the Republic is to be encouraged by rewards, or in any other way promoted.

2d. Everything relating to the redemption of the debt of the subscribed fund, according to what may be decreed in the item relating thereto.

3d. The government and direction of the Board itself : and finally, it shall be an attribute and object of its most particular solicitude, to promote the encouragement of the branch, by its funds and by its school.

ART. 11. The Board, after hearing the director and professors of the school, shall submit to the Supreme Government for its approval the reforms it may think necessary in the ordinances of the said establishment.

ART. 12. The Board, in conjunction with the advisers, shall submit to the Supreme Government a ternary list for the appointment of director of the school, the individuals named in the ternary list to have the qualifications detailed in Art. 13. of title 1. of the ordinances of mining ; it being understood that the Supreme Government shall be empowered to return the ternary list in order that a new one may be made, should it think proper so to do, and the President of the Board having in the votings the casting vote.

ART. 13. In the charge of the board of encouragement shall be all the property which may produce the funds mentioned in this law ; that arising from the quicksilver which may be distributed, and the stock of quicksilver itself. The responsibility for everything comprised in the management, preservation and safe keeping, shall be jointly in the members of the Board. That of the management and distribution shall be confided to an auditor treasurer, whom the Supreme Government shall appoint on the submission of a ternary list by the board, at a salary which shall be fixed in the regulations, and shall be paid out of the funds of the establishment, he giving the bonds which shall be designated in the same regulation; it being the duty of the said auditor treasurer to draw up and present the accounts for each year, and to be accountable for the quicksilver which the establishment may have on hand. For the custody and security of the property there shall be a chest with four keys, each of the commissioners holding one, and the auditor treasurer the other. The regulations which the board shall draw up for the management of the property shall be founded upon these bases.

ART. 14. The Board shall not have power to invest the funds which may come into its coffers in any other objects than those prescribed by the present law, or those for which it may obtain the previous authority of the government. In the ordinary repairs of the building, or other extraordinary expenses, it shall only have power to expend, without such permission, not exceeding $250 per annum.

ART. 15. The Board shall transmit to the Supreme Government monthly statements of its cash account, and each year it shall transmit another of its general receipts and expenditures. The first are to be published every four months by the board, and the second annually at the proper period by the same board.

ART. 16. The Board shall have power to settle with the parties interested the business left pending by the late tribunal of mines, and which the establishment may at present hold; these transactions are to be submitted for the approval of the Supreme Government.

ART. 17. The privilege is granted to the same board that the mines of the establishment may put in operation in Tasco, may not be denounced during two years, and for that purpose the articles relative to the ordinance of mining are suspended in this case.

TITLE II.

Of the Quicksilver fund.

ART. 18. A fund shall be created destined to the acquisition of quicksilver which the board shall manage, distributing it exclusively among the workers of metals at cost and expences. The said fund shall be formed with two thirds of the amount of the import duties, imposed upon linens and textures of foreign cotton, according to the decree of this date.

ART. 19. The Board may transfer the quicksilver with the corresponding guaranty, and on the terms established, by the regulation, being authorized, in order to render effectual the collecting of the duty, to have recourse either by themselves or by their agents, to the judges " de hacienda," in order that they may enforce upon the contractors a fulfilment of their obligations, and coerce payment from those who refuse to make it.

ART. 20. Every four months the board shall publish a statement of the issues of quicksilver, expressing the quantities sent to each mine, and the names of the beneficiaries who shall receive it; and in case of complaint of partiality or injustice in the distribution, the supreme government shall decide; the said statement shall also comprehend a report of the quantities purchased by the board, and the cost thereof.

ART. 21. When the board may have succeeded in collecting a fund equivalent to twenty four thousand quintals of quicksilver, the portion assigned out of the proceeds of the increase of duties upon foreign linens and textures of cotton shall cease to be applied to this object, conformably with the appropriate decree of this date.

TITLE III.

Of the foundation fund and redemption.

ART. 22. The proceeds of the so called Real de Mineria, the active credits of the old tribunal, and those of the establishment which by this law is reformed, continue to be liable to the charges and obligations designated in the decree of May 20, 1826 in Art. 7, and shall continue to be scrupulously complied with.

ART. 23. Every four months there shall be made by the Board a partial redemption of debts from the amounts which have been realised, taking care as far as possible to concede the preference to which they are justly entitled, who as creditors to said fund, offer the most favorable terms.

TITLE IV.

Of the administration of justice in the affairs of mining. Of the primary courts.

ART. 24. The Governors of the departments, in concert with the Departmental Juntas, and having the previous approval of the Supreme Government, shall establish in each the number of tribunals of the first instance, which are necessary within their limits.

ART. 25. Each tribunal shall be composed of three territorial deputies, elected in the same manner as is prescribed in the ancient ordinance of mining; and of these three individuals, the first shall be the president of the court and the other two the associates.

ART. 26. Each of these three tribunals shall exercise in their territory the governing and economical powers committed to them by the ancient ordinance of the branch, and in judicial matters they shall also conform to the same ordinance, as respects simplicity and brevity in their proceedings.

ART. 27. In suits in which the tribunal may have occasion to consult with a counsellor, it shall be with the Judge of the first instance of the respective district.

ART. 28. Each tribunal of the first instance shall choose a secretary, and the clerks it may deem necessary for the despatch of the business of its secretaryship and of the court, specifying the salaries they are to receive, which it will report to the respective governors of the departments, in order that with their assent the determination to which the Supreme Government may consent, may be heard.

ART. 29. From the definite decisions pronounced by these courts, in which the amount in dispute does not exceed five hundred dollars, there shall be no room for appeal when the sentence of the court of the second instance is in conformity with that of the first, and the amount in litigation does not exceed two thousand dollars.

ART. 30. Besides the three persons who are to compose the court of the first instance, three others shall be appointed who shall act as consulters in all the governing matters in which the same tribunal may desire to hear their opinion, and they shall supply the place of the judges, in case of inability or resignation of the same.

Of the second and third instances and extraordinary appeals.

ART. 31. The second and third instances which may occur in the business of mining, and the extraordinary appeals which may arise, shall be proven and decided in the superior courts of justice of each respective department, and in the courts designated by the laws, or which shall be hereafter designated.

Wherefore I order, that the same be printed, published, circulated, and carried into full effect.

Palace of the National Government, Mexico, 2d December, 1842.

JOSE MARIA TORNEL,
NICOLAS BRAVO,
Minister of War and Navy.

And I communicate the same to your Excellency, for your information and consequent action.

God and liberty.——*Mexico, December* 2d, 1842.

TORNEL.

To His Excellency, the Governor of this department:

And in order that it may come to the notice of every one, I order that it be published by Edict in this Capital, and in all the other cities, towns and places comprehended in this department, exposing it in the usual places, and circulating it among whom it may concern.

LUIS G. VIEYRA.

MIGUEL ZERES,
Secretary.

" Diario del Gobierno."—(*Vol. XXVI. No.* 2899, *page* 117.)

Mexico, 31st May, 1843.

Department of Foreign Affairs and Government.

" Antonio Lopez de Santa Anna, General of division, benemérito of the country, and president of the Mexican Republic to the inhabitants thereof: Know ye : That it being consistent with my purposes to encourage whatsoever may contribute to the national advancement and wealth, and considering as one of the means most tending thereto, that of granting premiums and incentives to the important branch of the mines of quicksilver, so necessary for the working of the precious metals, the first branch of the industry of the Republic, without which the others can make no progress, having heard the report of the Committee on advancement of mining, in the exercise of the powers conceded to me by the seventh of the bases accorded in Tacubaya, and sanctioned by the nation, I have thought proper to decree as follows.

ART. 1. The royal orders of the 13th January 1783, 12th November 1791, 6th December 1796 and 8th August 1814, as to exemption from excise duties granted to the articles for the use of mines, are to be punctually observed in regard to the mines of quicksilver of the Republic.

ART. 2. No general or municipal impost shall be laid upon the quicksilver which may be derived from the possessions of the Republic.

ART. 3. Quicksilver shall be sold throughout the nation without permits, passes, or other custom house papers.

ART. 4. A premium of $25,000 is granted to each of the four first proprietors who shall extract in one year from the mines of the Republic, 2000 quintals of liquid quicksilver.

ART. 5. There shall be paid during three years for each quintal of quicksilver which shall have the above origin, the sum of $5.

ART. 6. The laborers in the mines of quicksilver, shall be exempted from all military duty, and from personal taxes.

ART. 7. The committee on advancement and administration of mining, will draw up the proper regulation for the distribution of the aforesaid premiums, paying them at maturity out of the fund designated by the 2nd article of the decree of 2nd December, 1842, and the 4th article of the decree of 17th February of this year : Therefore, I order the same to be printed, published, circulated and carried into full effect.—Palace of the National Government, Tacubaya, 24th May, 1843.

ANTONIO LOPEZ DE SANTA ANNA.

JOSE MARIA DE BOCANEGRA,
Minister of Foreign affairs and Government.

77

FOREIGNERS.

DECREE.

October 7th, 1823.

Office of the Principal Secretary of State, Mexico.

The Supreme Executive Power has directed to me the following decree :—

The Sovereign Mexican Congress has resolved and decreed,

1st. That for the present, there shall be a suspension of the Law 12, Title 10, Book 5 ; and of the Law 5, Title 18, Book 6, of the Collection of Castile ; and also of the Law 1, Title 10, Book 8 ; and of the Laws comprehended in Title 27, Book 9, of the Collection of the Indies, together with the Article 1, Title 7, of the Ordinances of the Mines; which Laws enact that foreigners, in order to acquire and work Mines, on their own account, should be naturalized, or tolerated with the express permission of the Government.

2dly. This suspension only enables foreigners to contract with the owners of such mines, as are in want of capital, for supplying them with capital, in all the modes which are usual in such contracts, upon the terms that shall be most convenient to both parties, so that they may even acquire in property, shares in the concerns to which they supply capital ; (*hasta poder adquirir en propriedad acciones en las negociaciones que habiliten ;*) such foreigners remaining liable, in all respects, to our Ordinances, concerning the working of the Mines, and the reduction of the ores, and to all the taxes and duties, subject to which the nation grants to its citizens the right of enjoying such property.

3dly. By consequence they are prohibited from registering new Mines, from denouncing those which have been deserted, and from acquiring a share in any Mine, except those to which they supply capital, under any colour or pretence whatsoever.

4thly. No alteration whatever shall take place for the present, in respect of the excise duties, and the law relating to quicksilver, which article is excepted from all duty ; all others used in the Mines, remaining subject to the usual excise duties.

The Supreme Executive power are desirous that the above article should be generally understood and carried into effect, and order that it be printed, published, and circulated.

Mexico, 7th October, 1823.

FRANCISCO MANUEL SANCHEZ DE TAGLE,
Presidente,
JOSE ARCADIO DE VILLALOA,
Diputado Secretario,
MANUEL TEXADA,
Diputado Secretario, &c.

Addressed to DON LUCAS ALAMAN.   ALAMAN.

" *Diario del Gobierno.*"—(*Vol. XXII. No.* 2457, *page* 297·8.)

Mexico, March 16th, 1842.

Government of the Department of Mexico.

EDICT.

Citizen Luis Gonzaga Vieyra, brevet brigadier general, and governor of this department.

By the department of foreign affairs and government the following has with this date been communicated to me.

MOST EXCELLENT SIR :—His Excellency the Provisional President of the republic has been pleased to transmit to me the following decree :

Antonio Lopez De Santa Anna, general of division, benemérito of the country, and provisional president of the Mexican Republic, to all the inhabitants thereof. Know Ye :—That after a mature and the most cautious examination into the benefits which will result to the republic from permitting foreigners to acquire property; having heard the opinion of the council of representatives, which with the greatest exactitude examined this subject ; the reports of several juntas of the departments, many well informed persons, and the pro and contra supported in print : having seen the various projects for a law which to this effect have been offered ; being also convinced that a frank policy and a well understood interest demand that there should no longer be delayed a concession which may tend to the advancement of the republic, by the increase of population, the extension and division of property, which consequently makes the national wealth the greater ; having also in consideration that by these means the safety of the nation may be more and more secured, since foreign proprietors will be so many more defenders of the national rights, at the same time that they are interested in the common property : considering also the impulse which will be given to agriculture, industry and commerce, which are the sources of public wealth ; and finally, that the opinion generally expressed is in favor of the said concession, I have thought proper, exercising the powers conceded to me by the seventh of the bases accorded in Tacubaya, and attested by the representatives of the departments, to decree as follows :

ART. 1. Foreigners not citizens, residing in the republic may acquire and hold town and country property, by purchase, adjudication, denouncement or any other title established by the laws.

ART. 2. They may also acquire ownership in mines of gold, silver, copper, quicksilver, iron and coal, of which they may be the discoverers, in conformity with the ordinance of the branch.

ART. 3. Each individual foreigner cannot acquire more than two country estates in the same department, without a license from the Supreme Government, and only under the boundaries which they now have, each independent of the other.

ART. 4. In the acquisition of town property in the cities, towns and villages, as also in the lands contiguous thereto, in which they may wish to construct new estates, they shall enjoy the right to so much under similar circumstances and conditions.

ART. 5. Foreigners who in virtue of this law may acquire property, remain absolutely liable in regard to it, to the existing laws, or those which may prevail in the republic, as to transfer, use, preservation and payment of imposts, without the power of alleging any right appertaining to being foreigners, in regard to those points.

ART. 6. Consequently, all the questions of this nature, which may arise, shall be decided in the ordinary and usual manner of the national laws, with the exclusion of all other intervention whatsoever.

ART. 7. Foreigners who may acquire country property, city property, or property in mines, and foreigners who may labor in them as servants, laborers or journeymen, are not obliged to take part in the service of arms, unless in the way of police; but they are to pay the imposts which have for their object to keep up the militia.

ART. 8. If the foreign proprietor absent himself for more than two years with his family from the republic, without obtaining permission from the government, or if the property pass by inheritance or by any other title into the possession of persons non-resident in the republic, he shall be obliged to sell it within two years, counted from the day when his absence took place, or the change of ownership. If this be not done, the sale shall be officially proceeded with, with all the legal formalities, and of the proceeds the tenth part shall go to the informer; the nine tenths remaining shall be safely deposited at the disposal of the owner. This shall always be done when it is proven that the owner of the estate resides out of the republic, and he who is the nominal proprietor is only so in place of the absentee.

ART. 9. These arrangements do not include the departments on the frontier and bordering upon other nations, in regard to which special laws of colonization will be enacted, without the power to foreigners to ever acquire property in them, without the express license of the Supreme Government of the Republic.

ART. 10. In the departments which are not on the frontier, and which may have coasts, only at five leagues distance from the coasts can foreigners acquire country property.

ART. 11. In order that foreigners who may have acquired property in the republic may be citizens thereof, it is sufficient that they prove before the political authority of the place of their residence that they are proprietors, that they have resided two years in the republic, and that they have conducted themselves well. The expediente drawn up in this manner will be sent to the proper department, by which the certificate of citizenship will be issued.

ART. 12. Foreigners cannot acquire royal or public lands in all the departments of the republic, without contracting for them with the government which possesses this right as representing the domain of the Mexican nation.

Wherefore I order that it be printed, published, circulated and carried into full effect.

Palace of the national government, Mexico, 11th March, 1842.

ANTONIO LOPEZ DE SANTA ANNA.

JOSE MARIA DE BOCANEGRA,
Minister of Foreign Affairs and Government.

And I communicate it to your excellency for your information and consequent action.

God and Liberty.——Mexico 14th March, 1842.

BOCANEGRA.

And in order that it may come to the knowledge of every one, I order that it be published by edict in this capital and the other cities, towns and places within the limits of this department, exposed in the usual places, and circulated among those who are concerned in taking care to see it observed.

Given in Mexico on the 14th March, 1842.

LUIS G. VIEYRA.

MIGUEL ZEREZ, *Secretary.*

———

" *Diario del Gobierno.*"—(*T. XXIII. No. 2579. page 285.*)

Mexico, July 15th, 1842.

Department of Foreign Relations and Government.

MOST EXCELLENT SIR:

His Excellency the provisional president has been pleased to issue the following decree:

" Antonio Lopez de Santa Anna, general of division benemérito of the country, and provisional president of the Mexican Republic, to all the inhabitants thereof,

Know ye: That the decree of the 11th March of this year, which so empowers foreigners to acquire landed property in the republic, in the manner set forth in the same decree, having been made public, some doubts have arisen as to the true meaning of the 2nd Article, and appeals have been brought to the supreme government arising from the different meaning which has been given to said article. In view of all which, and, bearing in mind the respective provisions and ordinances, I have thought proper, in the exercise of the powers conceded to me by the seventh of the bases accorded in Tacubaya, and attested by the representatives of the nation, to declare as follows :

"Natives or foreigners who shall fully prove that they have been the restorers of old mines fallen into disuse or abandoned, shall be considered as discoverers and consequently empowered by the 2nd Article of the decree of 11th March of the present year, to acquire property in mines.

Wherefore, I order the same to be printed published, circulated and carried into full effect."

National Palace, Mexico 12th July, 1842.

ANTONIO LOPEZ DE SANTA ANNA.

JOSE MARIA BOCANEGRA,
   Minister of Foreign Relations and Government.

And I communicate it to your Excellency, for your information and consequent action.

God and Liberty.——Mexico July 12, 1842.

BOCANEGRA.

———

"*El Siglo diez y nueve.*"—(*No.* 331, 1st. *Year, 4th Quarter.*)

Mexico, September 7th, 1842.

Department of Foreign Relations and Government.

MOST EXCELLENT SIR :—His Excellency, the provisional President, has been pleased to issue the following decree :

"Antonio Lopez de Santa Anna, general of division, benemérito of the country and provisional president of the Mexican Republic, to all the inhabitants thereof, Know Ye: That in the exercise of the powers conceded to me by the seventh of the bases accorded in Tacubaya and attested by the representatives of the Departments, I have thought proper to declare as follows :

"The Law of the 11th March of this year which empowered foreigners to acquire landed property, did not annul that of the 7th of October, 1823.

"Wherefore I order that it be printed, published, circulated and carried into full effect."

National Palace, Mexico, 31st August, 1842.

ANTONIO LOPEZ DE SANTA ANNA.

JOSE MARIA DE BOCANEGRA,
   Minister of Foreign Relations and Government.

And I transcribe it for your Excellency, for your information and consequent action.

God and Liberty.——Mexico, 31st August 1842.

BOCANEGRA.

" *Diario del Gobierno.*"—(*Vol.* 27, *No.* 3021, *p.* 121.)

Mexico, September 30th, 1843.

Department of Justice and Public Instruction.

His Excellency the provisional President of the Republic has been pleased to transmit to me the following decree.

" Antonio Lopez de Santa Anna, General of division, benemérito of the county, and provisional president of the Mexican Republic, to the inhabitants thereof, Know Ye : That desiring to render effective the benefit which the government purposed to confer upon the mining interests in the authority which it granted to the board of encouragement of the branch, by decree of the 5th of July last, to enable it to establish and encourage the working of quicksilver mines, I have thought proper to decree as follows :

ART. 1. The Board of encouragement of mining shall appoint at least one commission in each department of the Republic, to explore and examine all the quicksilver mines that may be in said department.

ART. 2. The examination which these Commissions are to make, shall be scientific, and they shall also be charged to report upon the following points. *First :* If in the respective department there are or have been mines of quicksilver which may at present be worked, or which have heretofore been worked. *Second :* What is their present condition. *Third :* Which of them are most susceptible of being worked. *Fourth :* What works are necessary to put them in operation, and the expense required to put them in order. *Fifth :* The alloy contained in the yield which may be produced. *Sixth :* The cost of its extraction and working.

ART. 3. The Board of encouragement in view of all the above reports will decide upon the places which should be established in preference, and the sum with which the establishment is to be put in operation.

ART. 4. The aforesaid examinations must be concluded within six months, counted from this date ; and within seven months, also counted from this date the supplies for the working of the mines shall be decreed, some facilities being prior to that time conceded to the mines which evidently deserve them.

ART. 5. Out of the funds which may be designated for the supply of the quicksilver mines, and out of those which this decree may designate, the facilities mentioned in the foregoing articles shall be conceded.

ART. 6. In order to furnish the supplies mentioned in this decree, the board shall make use of one of two modes. First : To furnish the necessary funds in the character of a loan at the annual interest of 6 per 100. Second : To constitute itself the [*aviador*] mines supplier, keeping an account of the losses and gains as in the ordinary advances.

ART. 7. When it advances money on interest, it shall be secured precisely as follows : that the money is to be returned within the fixed period agreed upon : that the capital and interest are to be secured on bond to the satisfaction of the board : that it is to be invested necessarily and exclusively in the business in question, to which end a supervisor shall be appointed by the board and paid by the owner of the mine, and that these loans shall only be made in favor of establishments which the same board shall have qualified as being worthy of being put in operation, according to the examinations provided for in this decree.

ART. 8. If the supplies be furnished the board constituting itself the [*aviador*,] the mine supplier, the following will be observed. *First :* That the supplies be furnished to a mine worth working, according to the result of the examinations ordered in this decree. *Second :* That the sum which is to be advanced, be regulated according to the opinions which the commission who may have examined the mine, may arrive at. *Third :* That the half at least, of the profits be stipulated in favor of the supplier. *Fourth :* That the exclusive direction shall be in charge of the supplier, with the right on the part of the owner of the mine to appoint a supervisor. *Fifth :* That every four months, there shall be a settlement and distribution of profits, if any there be. *Sixth :* That the board shall, under its responsibility, have the certifying of the accounts ; and *Seventh,* That the profits which arise, be applied first to the redemption of the capital supplied, and until this be entirely covered, no distribution of profits among the participants shall take place.

ART. 9. The board shall draw up a regulation for supplies according to the bases of the two foregoing articles, submitting the same to the government for its approval.

ART. 10. The funds which are destined for the supplies decreed, are, *First :* One per cent. of the duties laid upon hard coin, conveyed from one department to another. *Second :* The $150,000 which have been decided to appertain to the mining interest, out of the fund created by the decree of the 2nd December last.

ART. 11. The one per cent. fund shall be collected by the Board of mining, for which purpose it shall have power to appoint and designate the commissioners who are to receive it.

ART. 12. The sum of $150,000 shall be paid by the maritime custom houses of Vera Cruz and Tampico, the first furnishing $80,000 per annum, and the second $50,000, payable in eight monthly instalments, which they shall remit in bills of exchange in favor of the board of encouragement.

ART. 13. The latter shall apply out of the said funds destined for working the mines of quicksilver, $15,000 designated in the decree of 18th August of this year, for the foundation and annual expenses of the school of mining.

Wherefore, I order that the same be printed, published, circulated and carried into full effect.

Palace of the National Government. Tacubaya, 25th September, 1845.

ANTONIO LOPEZ DE SANTA ANNA.

MANUEL BARAUDO.

Minister of Justice and Public Instruction.

And I communicate it to you for your information and consequent action. God and Liberty.——Mexico, September 25th, 1845.

BARAUDO.

LAWS, DECREES, &c.

IN RELATION TO

COLONIZATION.

From the Printed Volumes, Published by Authority, and the Official Publications in the Newspapers of the City of Mexico.*

National Colonization Law

Of 4th January, 1823.

ART. 1. The government of the Mexican nation will protect the liberty, property, and civil rights, of all foreigners, who profess the Roman Catholic apostolic religion, the established religion of the empire.

ART. 2. To facilitate their establishment, the executive will distribute lands to them, under the conditions and terms, herein expressed.

ART. 3. The empresarios, by whom is understood those who introduce at least two hundred families, shall previously contract with the executive, and inform it what branch of industry they propose to follow, the property or resources they intend to introduce for that purpose ; and any other particulars they may deem necessary, in order that with this necessary information, the executive may designate the province to which they must direct themselves ; the lands which they can occupy with the right of property, and the other circumstances which may be considered necessary.

ART. 4. Families who emigrate, not included in a contract, shall immediately present themselves to the Ayuntamiento of the place where they wish to settle, in order that this body in conformity with the instructions of the executive, may designate the lands corresponding to them, agreeably to the industry which they may establish.

* For the law of the Mexican Congress of the 18th August, 1824, on the subject of Colonization and general regulations of 21st March, 1828, see pages 451, 453.

ART. 5. The measurement of land shall be the following :—establishing the *vara* at three geometrical feet, a straight line of five thousand *varas* shall be a league ; a square, each of whose sides shall be one league, shall be called a Sitio ; and this shall be the unity of counting one, two, or more Sitios ; five Sitios shall compose one Hacienda.

ART. 6. In the distribution made by government, of lands to the colonists for the formation of villages, towns, cities and provinces, a distinction shall be made between grazing lands, destined for the raising of stock, and lands suitable for farming or planting, on account of the facility of irrigation.

ART. 7. One labor shall be composed of one million square *varas*, that is to say, one thousand varas on each side, which measurement shall be the unity for counting one, two, or more labors. These labors can be divided into halves and quarters, but not less.

ART. 8. To the colonists whose occupation is farming, there cannot be given less than one labor, and those whose occupation is stock raising, there cannot be given less than one Sitio.

ART. 9. The government, of itself, or by means of the authorities authorized for that purpose, can augment said portions of land as may be deemed proper, agreeably to the conditions and circumstances of the colonists.

ART. 10. Establishments made under the former government which are now pending, shall be regulated by this law in all matters that may occur ; but those that are finished shall remain in that state.

ART. 11. As one of the principal objects of laws in free governments, ought to be to approximate, so far as is possible, to an equal distribution of property, the government, taking into consideration the provisions of this law, will adopt measures for dividing out the lands, which may have accumulated in large portions, in the hands of individuals or corporations, and which are not cultivated, indemnifying the proprietors for the just price of such lands to be fixed by appraisers.

ART. 12. The union of many families at one place, shall be called a village, town or city, agreeably to the number of its inhabitants, its extension, locality, and other circumstances which may characterize it, in conformity with the law on that subject. The same regulations for its internal improvement and police, shall be observed as in the others of the same class in the empire.

ART. 13. Care shall be taken in the formation of said new towns, that, so far as the situation of the ground will permit, the streets shall be laid off straight, running north and south, east and west.

ART. 14. Provinces shall be formed whose superfices shall be six thousand square leagues.

ART. 15. As soon as a sufficient number of families may be united to form one or more towns, their local government shall be regulated, and the constitutional Ayuntamientos and other legal establishments formed, in conformity with the laws.

ART. 16. The government shall take care, in accord with the respective, ecclesiastical authority, that these new towns are provided with a sufficient number of spiritual pastors, and in like manner, it will propose to Congress a plan for their decent support.

ART. 17. In the distribution of lands for settlement among the different provinces, the government shall take care, that the colonists shall be located in those which it may consider the most important to settle. As a general rule, the colonists who arrive first shall have the preference in the selection of land.

ART. 18. Natives of the country shall have a preference in the distribution of land ; and particularly the military of the army, of the three guarantees, in conformity with the decree of the 27th of March, 1821 ; and also those who served in the first epoch of the insurrection.

ART. 19. To each Empresario, who introduces and establishes families in any of the provinces designated for colonization, there shall be granted at the rate of three haciendas and two labors, for each two hundred families so introduced by him, but he will lose the right of property over said lands, should he not have populated and cultivated them, in twelve years from the date of the concession. The premium cannot exceed nine haciendas and six labors, whatever may be the number of families he introduces.

ART. 20. At the end of twenty years the proprietors of the lands, acquired in virtue of the foregoing article, must alienate two thirds part of said lands, either by sale, donation, or in any other manner he pleases. The law authorizes him to hold in full property and dominion one third part.

ART. 21. The two foregoing articles are to be understood, as governing the contracts made within six months, as after that time, counting from the day of the promulgation of this law, the executive can diminish the premium as it may deem proper, giving an account thereof to congress, with such information as may be deemed necessary.

ART. 22. The date of the concession for lands, constitutes an inviolable law, for the right of property and legal ownership; should any one, through error or by subsequent concession, occupy land belonging to another, he shall have no right to it, further than a preference in case of sale, at the current price.

ART. 23. If, after two years from the date of the concession, the colonist should not have cultivated his land, the right of property shall be considered as renounced ; in which case, the respective Ayuntamiento can grant it to another.

ART. 24. During the first six years from the date of the concession, the colonists shall not pay tithes, duties on their produce, nor any contribution under whatever name it may be called.

ART. 25. The next six years from the same date, they shall pay half tithes, and the half of the contributions, whether direct or indirect, that are paid by the other citizens of the empire. After this time, they shall in all things relating to taxes and contributions, be placed on the same footing with the other citizens.

ART. 26. All the instruments of husbandry, machinery, and other utensils, that are introduced by the colonists for their use, at the time of their coming to the empire, shall be free, as also the merchandise introduced by each family, to the amount of two thousand dollars.

ART. 27. All foreigners who come to establish themselves in the empire, shall be considered as naturalized, should they exercise any useful profession or industry, by which, at the end of three years, they have a capital to support themselves with decency, and are married. Those who with the foregoing qualifications marry Mexicans, will acquire particular merit for the obtaining letters of citizenship.

ART. 28. Congress will grant letters of citizenship to those who solicit them in conformity with the constitution of the empire.

ART. 29. Every person shall be free to leave the empire, and can alienate the lands over which he may have acquired the right of property, agreeably to the tenor of this law, and he can likewise take away from the country all his property, by paying the duties established by law.

ART. 30. After the publication of this law, there can be no sale or purchase of slaves which may be introduced into the empire. The children of slaves born in the empire, shall be free at fourteen years of age.

ART. 31. All foreigners who may have established themselves in any of the provinces of the empire, under a permission of the former government, will remain on the lands which they may have occupied, being governed by the tenor of this law, in the distribution of said lands.

ART. 32. The executive, as it may deem necessary, will sell or lease the lands, which on account of their local situation, may be the most important, being governed with respect to all others, by the provisions of this law.

This law shall be presented to his Imperial Majesty, for his sanction, publication, and fulfilment.—Mexico, 3rd Janury, 1823. 3rd of the independence of the empire.—Juan Francisco, Bishop of Durango, President.—Antonio de Mier, Member and Secretary.—Juan Batista de Arispe, Member and Secretary.

Therefore, we order all tribunals, judges, chiefs, governors, and all other authorities, as well civil, as military, and ecclesiastical, of whatever class or dignity they may be, to comply with this decree, and cause it to be complied with, in all its parts; and you will cause it to be printed, published, and circulated.—Given in Mexico, 4th January, 1823.—Signed by the Emperor.—To Don Jose Manuel de Herrera, Minister of Interior and Exterior Relations.

DECREE.

The Vice President of the Mexican United States, to the inhabitants of the Republic :

KNOW YE, that the General Congress has decreed as follows :

ART. 1. The entry of those descriptions of cotton goods, prohibited by the law of 22d May last, shall be permitted in the ports of the republic generally, until the 1st January 1831, and in those ports situated on the south sea, until the last of June, 1831.

ART. 2. The duties arising from the importation of such goods, shall be appropriated to maintaining the indivisibility of the Mexican territory, to the formation of a fund of reserve, to be used in case of a Spanish invasion, and to the encouragement of national industry.

ART. 3. The government shall appoint one or more commissioners, whose duty it shall be, to visit the colonies of the frontier states ; to contract with the legislatures of said states, for the purchase by the nation of lands suitable for the establishment of new colonies of Mexicans and foreigners ; to enter into such arrangements as they may deem proper, for the security of the republic, with the colonies already established ; to watch over the exact compliance of the contracts on the entrance of new colonists ; and to investigate how far the contracts already made have been complied with.

ART. 4. The executive is empowered to take possession of such lands as may be suitable for fortifications and arsenals, and for the new colonies, indemnifying the state in which such lands are situated, by a deduction from the debt due by such state to the federation.

ART. 5. The Government may cause such number of the convicts destined for Vera Cruz and other places, as it may deem proper, to be conducted to the colonies it may establish, paying at the same time the expense of removal, of such families as may desire to accompany them.

ART. 6. The said convicts shall be employed in the construction of the fortifications, public buildings, and roads which the respective commissioner may judge necessary ; and every convict who, at the expiration of his term of service, shall desire to become a colonist, shall receive a grant of land, and shall be furnished with implements of husbandry and a subsistence during one year.

ART. 7. Mexican families who may voluntarily desire to become colonists, shall be conveyed free of expense, subsisted during the first year, and receive a grant of land and the necessary implements of husbandry.

ART. 8. The individuals spoken of in the anterior articles, shall conform to the laws of colonization of the federation, and the state in which they are settled.

ART. 9. The entrance of foreigners by the frontier of the north, under any pretence whatsoever, is prohibited, unless furnished with a passport, signed by an agent of the republic in the country from which the individual may come.

ART. 10. No change will be made with respect to the colonies already established, nor with respect to the slaves which they now contain ; but the general government, and that of each particular state, shall exact, under the strictest responsibilities, the observance of the colonization laws, and the prevention of the further introduction of slaves.

ART. 11. In exercise of the right reserved to the general congress, by the 7th article of the law of 18th August, 1824, the citizens of foreign countries lying adjacent to the Mexican territory, are prohibited from settling as colonists in the states or territories of the republic adjoining such countries. Those contracts of colonization, the terms of which are opposed to the present article, and which are not yet complied with, shall consequently be suspended.

ART. 12. For and during the term of four years, the coasting trade shall be free to foreign vessels for transportation of produce of the colonies to the ports of Matamoras, Tampico, and Vera Cruz.

ART. 13. For and during the term of two years, the introduction of frame houses, and of every kind of foreign provisions, shall be admitted into the ports of Galveston and Matagorda, free of duty.

ART. 14. The Government is authorized to expend in the construction of fortifications and public buildings on the frontier, in the transportation of convicts and Mexican families to the new colonies, in the subsistence of such during one year, in implements of husbandry, transportation of troops, and premiums to agriculturists who may distinguish themselves amongst the colonists, and for the general purposes contemplated by the foregoing articles, the sum of five hundred thousand dollars.

ART. 15. For the purpose of raising promptly one half of the said sum, the government is authorized to negotiate a loan, payable from the duties received on coarse cotton goods, at the rate of three per cent. per month, to to be paid at the term fixed by the *Arancel*.

ART. 16. The twentieth part of the above-mentioned duties, shall be employed to encourage cotton manufactories, by purchasing machines and looms, by furnishing small sums to aid in their establishment, and by such other means as the government may deem most advisable ; apportioning the aid among the states where this branch of industry exists. This appropriation shall be placed at the disposition of the Minister of Relations, to be applied to the above stated interesting objects.

ART. 17. Out of the produce of said duties, shall also be reserved three hundred thousand dollars for the formation of a fund, to be deposited in the treasury, under the most strict responsibility of the government, that it shall not be touched except in case of a Spanish invasion.

ART. 18. The Government shall form a system for the regulation of the new colonies, and shall, within one year, lay before congress an account of the colonies established under this law, and a statement of the increase of the new settlement on the frontiers.—Jose Dòminguez, Pres't of the Ch. of Dep., Miguel Duque de Estrada, Pres't of the Senate, Juan Vicente Campos, dep. sect., Rafael Delgado, sect. of the Senate.

Wherefore, I command the present to be printed, published and circulated and fulfilled.

Palace of the Federal Government, Mexico, April 6th, 1830.

ANASTACIO BUSTAMENTE.

To D. Lucas Alaman.

DECREE.

November 25th, 1833.

Art. 1. The eleventh article of the law of the sixth of April 1830 is repealed, in all its parts.[*]

Art. 2. The government is authorised to expend the sums necessary in the colonization of the territories of the confederation, and other vacant places which it has the right to colonize.

Art. 3. The Government is also authorised with respect to lands subject to colonization, to adopt such measures as they [may consider conducive to the security, advancement and stability of the colonies which shall be established.

Art. 4. The repeal spoken of in the first article of this decree shall not take effect until the expiration of six months after its publication.

Art. 5. In the authority conceded by the second article is comprehended that of raising fortresses at those points on the frontiers where the executive may think them useful and expedient.

CIRCULAR

Of the Secretary of Relations.

February 4th, 1834.

In relation to the Colonization of the the lands of Coahuila and Texas.

The Vice President of the Mexican United States, in the exercise of the supreme executive power, availing himself of the authority conferred upon

---

[*] For the act of 6th April 1830, see page 621. The 11th article above repealed is as follows:

" 11. In the exercise of the authority reserved to the general congress in the 7th article of the law of the 18th August 1824, the colonization of foreigners of adjacent countries is prohibited in the state and territories which adjoin such foreign nations. Consequently, contracts which are opposed to this law shall be suspended.

him by the law of the 6th April 1830, and impressed with the necessity of re-lieving a multitude of persons whose condition has been and now is most un-fortunate by reason of political errors, the paralization of trade, the destruc-tion of fortunes, and all those evils which attend a state in a condition of con-stant revolution as has been the state of this republic for many years, it has resulted in the opening of the coffers of the public in order to repair as far as possible, a state of things so deplorable. The territories situated adjoin-ing the dividing line of our republic all crossed by navigable rivers, situated immediately on the Atlantic Ocean, open to commerce, unexhausted by culti-vation and fruitful in the extreme, and inviting the robust arms of the Mexi-can to all kinds of employment which can no where else be so well rewarded and the same facilities afforded, as within their limits.

No other measures are necessary to effect the colonization of those beauti-ful and fruitful territories, but the incipient advances for the enterprise, and the Supreme government have the disposition and power to make them. The public funds should not be wasted, but neither should the necessary means be niggardly applied, nor as those affected be withheld, anticipating on proper occasions the means of bringing into action the industry of the nation, until their accumulated means shall place the colonists in a position not only of supplying for themselves the bare necessaries of life, but to form for themselves a capital by which to extend their operations and to reproduce continually the product of agricultural industry, the true source of wealth, and that upon which alone new communities can rely.

The republic finds itself infested by families, which in one mode or another, from this or that cause, have lost their fortune and their peace : all such the Supreme government invites to better their condition in the peaceful pursuits of agriculture : this will restore their estates, improve their fortunes, make them to forget their errors and wanderings, and convert into useful citizens a multitude of persons, whom the pressure of circumstances have widely separa-ted from the existing communities and the imperious necessity of living, which could not be satisfied by lawful means, has ranked with the class of criminals.

The vice president is sincerely desirous of attaining this happy result, but he cannot omit adopting the precautions to secure it by avoiding the result that the transport of the colonists shall possess no other character than that of a costly journey. If they are to abandon their land shortly after their arri-val, and if they are to do nothing to render it productive by their labor, and confine themselves to consuming the appropriations made for the sacred pur-pose of supplying their want of capital, the object is entirely frustrated, and the republic instead of recovering its erring citizens, only lose their funds, and increase their wants by an enterprise, which instead of securing, exposes to greater risks the integrity of its territory. At no period has it been so important to provide for the security of the frontiers, and to give employment to the innumerable hands which by the most sad fatality are found unemployed. To objects so beneficent and salutary has the attention of the goverment been directed, and he believes that the following provisions are not unlikely to secure them.

1. Every person who is free and not under local engagements in other parts of the republic shall be admitted to colonize the lands which are or may be at the disposition of the supreme government in the state of Coahuila and Texas.

2. This invitation is most particularly given to the officers and soldiers who have been thrown out of employment from having taken part in the present revolution, to those who are under obligation for debts due to the government, to those expelled from the States and to those who already remain with arms in their hands.

3. To each family which shall engage to colonize in said State there shall be given a tenth part of a *sitio de ganado mayor*.

4. To every person more than fifteen years of age the expense of cattle or carts necessary for transportation, shall be borne by the government, and they shall become the property of such persons at the moment of arriving at the sitio where they intend colonizing.

5. Each of the persons aforesaid past the age of fifteen years, shall be assisted from the day of his departure from the place of his residence to the end of a year, by receiving four reals daily, and to those less than fifteen years of age, two reals.

6. No person shall separate from the colony before the expiration of two years without the permission of the government, and those who do so shall lose the land which had been given to them, and continue bound to pay whatever may have been received from the government.

7. To each of the families comprising the colonies shall be given a yoke of cattle and a cow, or their value, two ploughs and such carpentering and farming tools as the government shall consider necessary.

8. From the land which is appropriated for a village there shall be given to each family a building lot on which to erect a house as his own dwelling.

9. The transportation shall be conducted under the direction of the person or persons which the government shall select.

10. The colonies shall be subject to such political regulations as the government shall direct and when they shall have distributel their house lots, they shall establish a municipal government.

[Published by decree, on the 6th. instant.]

In the declaration circulated by the Secretary of the Treasury of the 11th of April, of this year, and published by decree of the 13th, the 10th article is published in the following terms :

" The Colonies shall be subject to such political ruler or rulers as the government shall designate and when they shall have distributed their house lots they shall establish a municipal government in conformity with the laws of the same State."

LAW.

April 24, 1835.

In relation to the decree of the Legislature of Coahuila and Texas, and the unoccupied lands of those states.

1. The decree of the Legislature of Coahuila and Texas, of the 14th of March of the present year, is contrary, in its first and second articles, to the law of the 18th of August 1824; consequently, the alienations of property made in pursuance of said decree, are void and of no effect.

2. In the exercise of the power which is reserved to the general congress in the 7th article of said law of the 18th of August 1824, the states on the frontiers and on the coast are prohibited from alienating their vacant lands for colonization, until the regulations proper to be observed therein shall be established.

3. If any one of those states desire to alienate any portion of their vacant lands, they cannot do so without the previous approbation of the general government, said government in every case shall be preferred, if they see fit to take it, and shall give to the state the corresponding indemnification.

4. The general government may, in accordance with the 3d and 4th articles of the law of the 6th of April 1830, purchase to that amount of the state of Coahuila and Texas the four hundred sitios which it says it is under the necessity of selling.

[Circulated by the secretary of relations on said 25th of April, and published by edict on the 2d of May following.]

The decree cited in Article 1 of the foregoing law is as follows:

Supreme Government of the free states of Coahuila and Texas. The provisional governor of the state of Coahuila and Texas, in the exercise of supreme executive power, to all the inhabitants thereof. Know ye :—

That the Congress of said state have decreed as follows:

The Constitutional Congress of the free, sovereign and independent state of Coahuila and Texas, have thought proper to decree:

1. The government may dispose to the extent of four hundred sitios of land, of the vacant lands of the state, in order to meet the urgent wants of the public, which are actually existing.

2. The colonization of said lands shall be regulated on the bases and conditions which may be considered expedient, without being subject to the provisions of the law of the 26th March of the last year.

3. The government will direct the measures necessary for the collection of the amounts due the state, whatever their source and origin.

The provisional constitutional governor will cause the same to be complied with, and to be printed, published and circulated.

JOSE ANTONIO TEJERINA,
President.

AUDRES DE LA VIESCA, *y Montes,*
Deputy Secretary.

DIEGO,
Grand Deputy Secretary.

Monclava, March 14, 1835.

LAW.

Mexico, 4th April, 1837.

Providing for rendering effective the colonization of the lands which are, or should be the property of the Republic. All directions heretofore issued in relation to colonization, so far as they are contrary to this law, are repealed. See decree of the Supreme government of the 12th of the present month.

The government with the consent of the Council, will proceed to give effect to the colonization of the lands which are, or should be the property of the Republic by means of sale, *enfiteusis,* or mortgage, applying the amount (which for the best lands should not be less than ten reals per acre) to the redemption of the national debt, contracted, or to be contracted, reserving always a sufficient amount in order to fulfil the promise to the troops who aided in achieving the independence, and for the rewards and grants decreed by Congress in favor of the native tribes or nations, and of those aiding in the restoration of Texas; not being hindered by the laws heretofore passed in relation to colonization, the provisions of which, so far as they are contrary to this law, are repealed,—the prohibition of the 11th Article of the law of the 6th April, 1830 being renewed.

DECREE.

Mexico, 12th April, 1837.

Decree of the Supreme Government in virtue of the authority conferred by the Law of the 4th instant.

Creation of a national consolidated stock at an interest of 5 per cent. per annum, for the express purpose of converting the entire foreign debt and redeeming the same on the terms expressed.

1. A consolidated national stock with interest at five per cent. per annum, is hereby created for the sole and determinate object of converting the entire foreign debt if the existing creditors consent, and for the redemption of the same in the manner expressed in the following articles. For this purpose

Messrs. F. de Lizardy and Company are appointed as agents for the Republic in said transaction, and are authorized in the name of the Mexican nation to issue accordingly the bonds of said consolidated national stock in pounds sterling, payable in London on the 1st October, 1866 with coupons for interest in the margin payable every six months and running to the aforesaid date. These bonds shall also be *viscéd* by the minister plenipotentiary of the Republic at London or by the person acting in his stead.

2. The holders of the bonds of the foreign debt in circulation, the proceeds of the two loans negotiated in London at 5 and 6 per cent. interest, may convert the same together with the interest coupons over due, into bonds of the new consolidated stock on the following conditions. *First:* That the bonds of five per cent. interest shall be received in exchange, cent. per cent. *Secondly:* That those of six per cent. interest shall be at the rate of a hundred twelve and a half for a hundred. *Third:* That the over due coupons of interest of both loans shall be exchanged cent. per cent. *Fourth:* That they shall receive in payment of the sums which they desire to convert, one half of the amount in bonds of the consolidated stock at five per cent. interest, and the other half in public land scrip in the departments of Texas, Chihuahua, New Mexico, Sonora and the Californias, at the rate of four acres per pound sterling; and this scrip shall also bear interest at five per cent. to the day on which the owners are placed in possession of the lands, increasing thereby proportionally the amount of property acquired, and security shall be given by those interested that they will be present to take possession within the period designated in article 5th.

3. The interest on the bonds of the national consolidated stock, shall be payable in London, at intervals of six months, on the first days of April and October of each year, commencing on the first of October of the present year, one thousand eight hundred and thirty-seven. In the meantime and until arrangements are made for remitting periodically the funds destined to this object, the holders of the interest coupons which become due shall have the right to present them to the agents of the republic in London, on the day of their maturity, and to require of them in exchange for such coupons, a certificate of their value, *viseéd* in like manner by the minister of the republic at said court; and these shall be received on presentation as ready money in payment of a sixth part of the duties collected at the maritime custom houses of Vera Cruz and Santa Anna de Tamaulipas. The agents of the republic in London shall not, consequently be at liberty to refuse to give such certificates when thereto requested by the holders of the unpaid coupons. In such case the value of each pound sterling shall be computed at the rate of five dollars, and the amount of each certificate shall be increased six per cent. in full compensation for difference of exchange and all expenses, including in such six per cent. one per cent., which the persons interested shall pay on receiving the certificates, to the agents, one fourth part

of which they shall relinquish in favor of the minister plenipotentiary of the Republic.

4. The public land scrip shall, in like manner be issued in the name of the Mexican nation by the agents aforesaid, and shall be *viseéd* by the diplomatic agent accredited at London, the tenor of which shall be as follows : " To all to whom these presents shall come,—Know Ye : That the Mexican nation acknowledges that (*the name*,) or his representative, is the proprietor of (*the number*) of acres of land in the department of (*the place*) of which he shall be placed in immediate and full possession by competent authority, with the aid of the public surveyor and on the delivery of this scrip. Dated at London (*the day of the year.*)" No scrip shall be issued for less than four hundred acres nor for more than ten thousand. Those interested shall pay to the agents on receiving their scrip at the rate of twelve reals for every hundred acres, and of these, three reals shall belong to the minister his *visa.*

5. The property of the land scrip may pass from person to person by endorsement, but after taking possession of the land of which the scrip gives the right, and receiving a new title, the same cannot be transferred to another person except in virtue of a public instrument of sale.

6. It is necessary that the scrip should be presented when the same is to be redeemed by the delivery of lands at the office of the secretary of the several departmental governments, in order that he may make a list of them as presented (obtaining a book for that purpose) with the view of giving to those interested a preference in the selection of land according to the order of presentation. For the same purpose, shall be delivered to them a certificate, in which shall appear the number and place entered in the scrip, in order that it may be presented to the local authorities, and this with the aid of the surveyor of the department, will give to them possession of the land which they select, taking care, without fail, to observe the 11th article of the law of the 6th April 1830, which declares :—" in the exercise of the authority reserved to the general Congress in the 7th article of the law of the 18th August, 1824, the colonization of foreigners of adjacent countries is prohibited in those states and territories which adjoin such foreign nations ; consequently, contracts which are opposed to this law shall be suspended."

7. For the greater security of the payment of the principal and interest of the consolidated stock, the Mexican government, in the name of the nation, specially pledges one hundred millions of acres of public land in the departments of the Californias, Chihuahua, New Mexico, Sonora and Texas, as a special guarantee of said stock until the total extinction of said debts ; but if any sale shall be made of said lands so pledged, it shall be at least at the rate of four acres to the pound, and the proceeds shall be paid by the purchaser to the government agents in London, from whom alone can he receive the corresponding scrip, and they shall use the product of the sale in

the redemption of the bonds of the new consolidated stock, which also may be received in payment for said lands at the price said bonds bear in market.

8. The proper period for the making the application for the change of securities treated of in article 2nd of this decree, will be from the day on which the appropriate notice is published in London by the agents of the republic till the corresponding day of the following year ; when this period shall have passed no further opportunity shall be afforded for such change.

9. During said period and until the thirty-first day of December 1839, the holders of the bonds of the consolidated stock shall have the right either on receiving them from the agents or at any other time, for the purpose of extinguishing the same to take in exchange public land scrip for the amount with ten per cent. premium added to the same, at the rate as aforesaid, of four acres to the pound sterling ; but if this be not done before the first of January 1840, although the same right will be at all times recognized of extinguishing these bonds by receiving scrip in like manner with ten per cent. premium, there shall not be granted to them more than three acres to the pound sterling.

10. Finally, those foreigners who in virtue of the scrip which they hold, come to the Republic and establish themselves in their new estates, shall acquire from that moment, the title of colonists, and they and their families shall enjoy all the rights and advantages which are or may be granted by law to other naturalized foreigners and on the same conditions : but it shall not be allowed that there be held by a single person or the owner, more than a league square of five thousand *varas* of *regadio*, four of *superficie temporal*, and six leagues of *superficie de abrevadero ;* and the usufruct of the mines which are found in said lands, shall be subject to the provisions of the general mining ordinances. (Circulated on the same day by the department of the Treasury, and published by edict on the 17th May following.)

" Diario Del Gobierno."—*(Vol. II. No.* 113.)

Mexico, November 27th, 1846.

Department of Interior and Foreign Relations.

His excellency the general charged with the Supreme executive power, has been pleased to send me the following decree.

" Jose Mariano de Salas, general, charged with the executive power of the Mexican United States, to the inhabitants of the Republic, Know ye:

That being authorized by the plan proclaimed in the citadel on the 4th of August last, to dictate all the measures which the security of the Republic may demand, and considering that one of the most necessary and urgent is that of promoting foreign immigration in order to people our immense lands which are at this time, the object of foreign cupidity ; that for this purpose it is indispensible to establish the board of colonization heretofore decreed, so that it may labor with zeal and industry in the rapid increase of the population, upon which great benefits will depend : that the economy of the treasury is now more than ever necessary, and requires that the aforesaid board be established in the office of industry, which junction does not in any other veiw present any inconvenience. I have thought proper to decree as follows :

1st. In conformity with the provision in the 16th Art. of the regulations issued for the execution of the law of 1st June 1839 the board of colonization is established under the immediate consent of the department of relations.

2nd. This board shall be composed, as provided in the foregoing regulations, of three persons, appointed by the Supreme government.

3rd. In order to save expense, the board of colonization shall be established in the office of industry, and shall exercise the functions and attributes thereof. In regard to colonization it shall promote the same effectually by all means possible, consulting the government with respect to those involving expenses which its funds may not meet, and endeavouring to combine the rapid increase of population with the revenue coming to the treasury from the sales it shall make of the public lands. It shall also exercise the faculties given to it by the aforesaid regulation of the 1st. June 1839, and those which shall be specified in the one it shall draw up and present for the approval of the government.

4th. The board of colonization and industry shall have the funds assigned to the board of this name in the decree of 2nd. October 1843, the 5 per 100 from the sales of lands belonging to the confederation, and the proceeds of the prohibited goods confiscated, which shall be sold, but which cannot be passed through the country by permits, but consumed in the precise place of sale ; or the 20 per 100 of the duties which these goods shall give rise to on their importation, should it be hereafter permitted.

Wherefore, I order the same to be printed, published, circulated, and carried into full effect. Palace of the general government.

JOSE MARIANO DE SALAS.

To Don Jose Maria Lafragna."

And I enclose it to you for your information.

God and liberty.——Mexico, November 27, 1846.

LAFRAGNA.

" *Diario del Gobierno.*" (*Vol. II. No.* 124.)

Mexico, December 8th 1846

His Excellency the general charged with the supreme executive power, has been pleased to transmit to me the following decree :—

" José Mariano de Salas, general of brigade, charged with supreme executive power of the Mexican United States, to the inhabitants of the republic. Know Ye :—

That, being constantly desirous of rendering available the benefits which the system of colonization ought to produce in the republic, and considering that the decree issued on the 27th of last month, which established the direction of the branch, will not produce all the effects which ought to be anticipated, if its powers are not at once detailed : keeping in view the project in which these are proposed, presented by the same direction which has been so diligently and efficaciously engaged in drawing up the same, from the moment of entering upon its duties, in compliance with the provisions in Art. 3 of the aforesaid decree of the 27th of last month, and whilst the congress, taking into consideration the initiative which the government has consented to make, is digesting the principal bases on which will depend the advancement of colonization ; I have thought proper to decree the following

REGULATIONS :

1. In order that the direction of colonization may not suspend its labors from accidental impediments to its members, three substitutes shall be appointed, who shall be called upon in the order of their appointment, whenever any disability, or absence of any of the members shall occur.

2. In case of the absence or disability of the president, who shall always be the first named, the second shall discharge his duties, and in case of his absence or disability, the third shall do so.

3. In order to have concord in the direction, the concurrence of a majority of the members, and the joint vote of two, shall be sufficient.

4. The proprietary members and substitutes of the direction shall remain four years in the exercise of their functions.

5. The president shall have in his charge the correspondence and the whole management of the office.

6. The appointment of clerks in the office appertains to the board, with the approbation of the government : the provisions of the 11th Art. of the decree organizing the direction of Industry, of the 2nd December 1842, governing in regard to the perpetuity of these employments.

7. The direction of colonization shall use particular diligence in having plats drawn of the lands of the republic which may be colonized, and in collecting the data which are filed in the archives, in order to know whatever may be of importance for the better direction of the business relating to colonization ; procuring information and reports of the kind of land, of their waters, mountains, mineral and salt regions, and also of the climate and production of the said lands.

8. The same direction shall appoint competent persons who shall without any delay make surveys of the public lands which either now or hereafter

may belong to the confederation, it being understood by such public lands, those lands which are not the property of individuals, societies or corporations; and if hereafter it be thought convenient, it may appoint a surveyor general, by commission, to reside in that capital, who may revise the plats and surveys. In these duties and others, it may employ, by commission, the retiring and withdrawing clerks, and those who are in actual service.

9 These surveyors shall take an oath before the direction, or the authority whom it may entrust therewith, to faithfully execute the surveys. Those employed in carrying the chains in the said surveys, shall take an oath before the surveyors. The direction shall have power to remove these to save expense, from failure to perform their duties, and to appoint others in their stead, when vacant from illness, death or resignation.

10. The surveyors shall work and proceed in their surveys, in entire conformity with the orders they may receive from the direction.

11. The surveys shall be made by *sitios*, which shall be squares of six miles of $1666\frac{2}{3}$ Mexican varas per side, or $18,948\frac{6}{100}$ acres. The lines to form the squares shall be drawn due north and south, one to each mile. Upon these lines shall be drawn others from east to west, at the same distance of one mile from each other, forming perfect squares by right angles; so that each square shall be one mile square.

12. This division must not fail to be made in the surveys, save when physical and legal obstacles prevent it—that is to say when natural obstructions, or the ownership of lands in contact do not permit; but then the surveyors shall always endeavor, so far as possible, to make the surveys in squares.

13. The surveyors shall assist in person in drawing the first and last lines from north to south, and from west to east, and all those lines which on account of the surface of the land, are necessarily irregular.

14. The lines must be drawn with a straight iron rope or chain, and exactly copied or drawn in the plat which must be made. By notes on the same plat, the streams of water which may be in the land will be indicated, their courses to be drawn in the places through which they pass, and their capacity estimated. Mention shall also be made of the lakes, pools, mountains, mineral regions, salt regions and others, the climate of the locality, and the apparent character of the soil, and everything else which may give an idea of the improvements of which they may be susceptible.

15. The squares into which a *sitio* is divided, will be numbered on the plat, beginning with No. 1.

16. Each square of one mile square, will make a *lot* of 526 $33\frac{1}{2}$ acres. The *lot* No. 16 shall always remain unsold, for the public uses to which the government may think proper to appropriate it.

17. The surveyors being responsible for the correctness of the surveys, will take the greatest care to execute them well, and in the variations of the compass, will state and note the true meridian.

18. The surveyors shall have the salary which they shall agree for with the direction.

19. The same direction may advance to the surveyors under bond, the amounts which in its discretion they may require, and at the end of each year it shall settle them and pay what they may have earned, or they shall return what they may not have earned of the previous advances, if they should not continue.

20. With this intent, and in order that the drawn plats may be on file in the office of the direction, the surveyors shall transmit them thereto, retaining copies.

21. The confederation reserves to itself the mines discovered and to be discovered in the public lands, which were not known at the time the lands may have been alienated.

22. It will also reserve the sixth part of the lands which may be surveyed, at the disposal of the war department, for military rewards, and the portion necessary in the judgment of the direction, to make a capital for the salaries of the persons employed who may desire to retire from the service ; this capital being made by giving them in value a quantity of land which invested at five per cent. will produce the amount of the annual salary they receive.

23. The price of each acre of land for the present, and so long as the direction of colonization does not propose any modification, and the government does not decree in conformity therewith, shall be at least four reals, except in Lower and Upper California, where it shall not exceed 2 reals per acre. The price of the public lands shall be hereafter increased by the government, on the proposition of the same direction, where their situation, the improvements which may be given them, and other circumstances, render them peculiarly valuable.

24. The surveyors, when they survey lands lying alongside of private property, or surrounded thereby, shall summons the parties interested in said property to concur therein, and exhibit their titles. In case of any dispute, the survey shall be made, considering as public land what the surveyor may judge to be such, and the business shall be referred to the respective district court, for its judicial decision. Connivance or corruption between the proprietors and the surveyors shall be reputed as a fraud on the public treasury, and the latter shall be tried as such defrauders, for the sole fact of not reporting to the direction of colonization, without delay, the public lands which they may discover occupied without a right thereto, at the time of making the surveys. Those who report those lands which may be possessed without right by individuals, companies, or corporations, shall be rewarded with 25 per 100 of their value, on the sale of the land by the direction, in the funds in which the price of the sale may be paid, or in the land itself, if

it can be conveniently divided, in the opinion of the said direction, with the obligation of cultivating and settling it.

25. All surveyed land shall remain with the landmarks used by the surveyors, or marked by permanent bounds, of which mention shall be made in the plats.

26. The plats of the surveyed lands shall be open for inspection in the office of the direction of colonization, and in those of its agents in the states and territories where sales of the lands are to take place.

27. These sales shall take place in the office of the direction of colonization, and by the agents and commissioners thereof in the states and territories; they shall be conformable with the regulations of this decree, and with those which may be received from the said direction of the branch.

28. The said sales shall be made at public auction, to the highest bidder, under the following rules:—

1. As soon as the direction receives the plat of a portion of land, it shall publish in the newspapers the announcement of its sale three months beforehand, specifying the place where it will take place; and if it is to be effected by its agents, the latter will also advertise the same at least one month beforehand.

2. On the specified day, the land will be put up at auction at the price and on the conditions established by this decree. That situation will be held as the best in which the introduction of the greatest number of families may be secured in a given period. The shortest period for this introduction will be considered the best: and in default of bidding upon this basis, the best bid offered with proposals for ready money, and those with cash will be accepted.

3. Payment will be made with 20 per 100 in money, which will be payable in four instalments, one at once, and the three others in the twelve months ensuing, one instalment every four months. The remainder shall be paid within two years counted from the day of sale or auction, in money or in credits against the treasury, of the internal or external debt, which may be in the course of payment, and which may cause revenue.

29. As a general rule in all contracts of sale, the purchaser shall bind himself to settle the land he purchases, with at least two families, of five individuals each, per square mile, within the space of two years counted from the date of the sale or purchase.

30. To the person with whom the bidding shall close, which being once accomplished, cannot be re-opened, shall be issued the corresponding evidence of title, by the direction of the branch.

31. Each bill of sale shall be signed by the board, and shall be recorded in the general treasury of the confederation.

32. Neither for the auction nor for the issue of the title of ownership shall any fees be incurred. The purchasers shall pay no more than the

cost of the stamped paper upon which the title is written out, which shall in all cases be of the third seal, and two dollars to the office in which the auction may take place.

33. When on the day specified for the auction of a portion of land no bidders appear, the sale shall be suspended until a purchaser shall present himself, to whom the sale shall be made.

34. The direction of colonization shall announce every month in the newspapers of this capital, the sale of the lands which have remained over unsold, from there not having been any bidder on the day specified for the auction.

35. The same direction shall have power to make contracts with individuals or companies for the formation of new colonies upon the following bases.

1. That none of the colonists who may be introduced therein, shall be a subject or native of, or come from a nation whose territory lies contiguous to the lands which are to be granted, nor of a power with which the Republic may be at war, save in the cases in which the government may make exceptions for special reasons and motives.

2. That in the colonies at no time shall slavery be permitted.

3. That the plats of the surveys of the lands made by a competent person in its confidence, shall be produced to the direction, which person in case of default herein, shall be liable to the penalties laid down in Art. 23, within a period specified thereby, which shall not exceed two years, and that if the survey should have been already made, the cost thereof shall be paid.

4. That the price of the public lands shall be realized in annuities, or secured by credits in course of payment which may cause revenue, on paying twenty per cent. in money. The said price shall be fixed by the government on the proposition of the direction, according to the localities, and shall not be less than the half of that fixed in Art. 23.

5. That the number of families agreed upon with the direction, shall be introduced within a determined period.

6. That the grants of lands and the payments made, shall be forfeited in default of any of the foregoing conditions.

36. These contracts for new settlements, shall be made at public auction, the right being granted for the same price to those who may have made the first proposals, unless from the nature of these, and the circumstances of the case, this requisite in the opinion of the direction cannot be proceeded with.

37. The direction shall also have power with the approbation of the government, to contract for the establishment of banks for the colonization of large territories, and for the opening and constructing of highways for the colonies, with the pledge of the value of the public lands. In this case the government shall fix the price of the lands, and this shall be paid with the bills which the bank may issue. Its creation shall be fixed upon the bases contained in the decree of 25th October, 1842, the government signifying,

in each case the effective capital with which it is to be provided, the amount of bills it may issue, the time of their duration, and that of the redemption of the bills.

38. The lands which may be granted for new settlements, shall be, first: the public lands belonging to the confederation; second: those which the owners may cede for the purpose by agreements with the direction of the branch; third: those of ownership acquired by grants from the government, or by any other title, which remain uncultivated and depopulated, and which the direction may qualify as being open to colonization. With regard to these lands, the same direction shall require from their owners to cultivate and settle them, specifying to them a limited period, which shall not exceed five years: and if within that time they be not cultivated or settled at the rate of ten persons per square mile, it shall propose to them to put them up for sale to be colonized. If they do not consent thereto, the direction shall apply to the government, laying before it the case and the reasons for which it is of opinion that the sale should take place, and if the government consider them well founded, it shall decree the occupation of the lands in the manner prescribed in the third paragraph of the 112th Art. of the federal constitution.

39. The [empresarios] contractors for colonization, shall distribute the lands among the colonists conformably with the contracts they may have made with them, saving the obligation of the recognition of the annuity upon the part upon which the price is not paid in ready money, which annuity the colonists will pay in proportion to the lands they may occupy.

40. The Judges and authorities of the Republic shall enforce the fulfilment of said contracts on petition from the party interested.

41. The new foreign settlers shall be considered as citizens of the Republic, from their arrival in the colony, conformably with the decree of the 10th of September last.

42. The [empresarios] contractors for new settlements shall have, according to the decree of 3d of October, 1843, a direct intervention in everything relating to the management of the colony and its primary organization, in regard to the administrative and judicial branches, the laws of the Republic will be observed, with the exceptions and privileges in favor of new settlements.

43. All the public acts and documents of the colonies, shall be written in the Spanish language.

44. In conformity with the decrees of 25th October, 1842, and 5th November of the present year, the new settlements shall enjoy the following exemptions.

1. Exemption from active military service for twenty years, except in case of foreign aggression.

2. Exemption from all tax except municipal, for the same term of twenty years.

3. Exemption from all duty for ten years after the colonies may be established, upon all articles of subsistence, clothing, furniture and other articles useful in the construction and furnishing of houses, which may be imported into the colonies. These effects shall be conveyed to the colonies with proper precautions, in order to prevent their being carried to other places, and they cannot be shipped from the colonies in the way of commerce, without falling under the penalty of confiscation.

4. That if free importation, without payment of duties, of implements of art and agriculture, of books and printed matter, for twenty years, and for the same period no exaction will be imposed upon the country or town estates.

5. That of tonnage duty upon the vessels which may convey at least ten families of new settlers, or which may come fully laden with articles destined for the colonies.

45. Military colonies shall also be established, composed of Mexicans and of foreigners, or of both, on the coasts and frontiers where the government may indicate, especially for preventing the inroads of the savages: and in them shall be granted to the colonists, gratis, the lands which the direction of colonization may, with the approval of the government, designate for that purpose.

46. The following classes shall appertain to the military colonies :

1. Retired and invalid soldiers of the Republic, who may apply therefor.

2. Those who may be permitted by legal grant, and those who may desire to invest their savings in lands and settlements in order to cultivate them.

3. Mexican and foreign peasantry to whom the direction of colonization may grant the same.

4. Those who in future may be forcibly transported thither through the provisions of the laws. For the individuals of the military colonies, the expense of their conveyance thither will be borne, and they will be furnished with a place of residence, implements and tools for labor, or for the trades they may follow, and the means upon which to subsist during the first year.

47. The Military colonies shall have the same privileges as the other colonies, and shall be governed like those which are not military ; but all the individuals who can bear arms, shall be organized into companies and corps, it being the duty of the government to provide them with arms, ammunition, and every thing requisite for the service.

The government, upon a report from the direction of colonization, shall draw up the regulations for the instruction of, and service which these militia are to perform, the pay they are to receive when in active service, and whatever else may concern these settlements in carrying out this object without withdrawing them from their domestic occupations.

48. A military colony, composed wholly of foreigners, cannot be estab-

lished unless contiguous to another composed of Mexicans or of other foreigners of various countries.

49. The direction of colonization will make application for parishes to be erected in the military colonies, and shall establish in each of them a primary school and a medical practitioner.

50. The same direction shall take the necessary steps for the founding of missions in the colonies nearest to the savage tribes, and shall propose to the government the means of sustaining and increasing them, and of encouraging those already existing.

51. The direction of colonization shall appoint agents, commissioners, or auxillary boards in the states and territories, whose labors in the business of colonization shall be executed under the instruction of the same direction.

52. It shall also have power to appoint agents in foreign countries who may promote colonization, and enter into communication with the ministers consuls of the Republic, for the trust it may think proper to confide to them.

53. With the data which it shall collect together, the direction of colonization shall submit to the government the means of marking the boundaries of the lands on the frontiers of the Republic, and whatever may concern the internal navigation of the rivers. Colonization of the frontiers shall not take place without the express approbation of the government, at less than twenty leagues from the boundaries of the Republic, nor less than ten from the coasts, conformably with Article 4 of the law of 13th August, 1844.

54. The office of the direction shall keep clear and methodical registers of all the public lands, of the titles of transfers which it may issue in consequence of sales at auction or by contracts, and of the documents of grants of lands where the issues of the title remains pending upon the surveys. It shall also keep the judicial record of the revenue which may arise from the amount of the price of the lands, and shall draw up a table showing the report of the measures which, up to this time, have been used by the surveyors, with the measures of the acre and of the mile.

55. The direction shall submit to the government every thing which may have relation to the better administration and government of the new settlements; it shall report against the abuses which may be committed therein; and in order that they may be effective, shall report the guarantees and exemptions conceded to the colonists.

56. The direction, as far as concerns the branches of the agricultural and manufacturing industry of the colonies, the district and the territory of the confederation, and as far as may be within the province of the general government in the states, shall exercise the following powers:

1st. It shall be the organ of communication between the assemblages of manufacturing or agricultural industry of the colonies, and of the district and territories of the confederation and the supreme government, and through its

channel all petitions or memorials which may be made to the government relative to matters appertaining to agriculture and the arts, shall be conveyed
to it, the direction expressing its opinion upon the same.

2d. It shall enter into correspondence with the juntas (societies) of agriculture or industry of the states, in relation to its designs.

3d. It shall make to the government such reports as may be desired, in
relation to matters of the same industry.

4th. It shall have in its charge the formation of industrial statistics.

5th. It shall promote the advancement of agriculture and the arts, by all
proper means, and especially by premiums for industrial inventions, and improvements in cultivation, in vegetables, and breeding of animals, and by
the establishment of schools of arts and agriculture, and the publication of
instructive works.

6th. It shall take cognizance of all the records of applications for patents
for the invention, perfection, or introduction of new processes in industry,
and in its archives shall be deposited the models and specifications presented
by those who obtain patents, and it shall publish both, when the inventions
become public property.

7th. It shall take care that public exhibitions at stated periods shall be
made in the capital of the republic, of the national agricultural and manufacturing products.

8th. It shall put into operation, as early as possible, the establishment of
the schools of arts and of agriculture, which are placed under the inspection
and care of the direction of industry, taking charge immediately of the
funds destined for said establishments.

57. In the treasury of the direction shall be kept a set of books, with the
formalities which shall be decreed, on the recommendation of the board, and
the following rules shall henceforth be observed :—

1st. No payment shall be made which shall not be decreed by law, without an order from the president, and without the assent of the board, and the
further approval of the government, in the cases where the law expressly demands the same.

2d. Every month there shall be a settlement of accounts, and a general
settlement at the close of the fiscal year.

3d. The treasury account shall be settled on the 30th of June of each
year, and shall be presented before the month of November, together with a
statement which shall comprehend the condition of the branch in charge of
the direction, in which shall be exhibited the present state of colonization,
and that of industry, their progress, or the causes of their backwardness, if
such be the case, with an indication of what ought to be done to remedy the
same, in order that the government, taking the whole into consideration,
may on its part dictate such measures as may be within its functions, and

may call the attention of Congress at its next following session to what may be requisite from the legislative power.

Wherefore, I order that the same be printed, published and circulated and carried into full effect.

Palace of the Federal Government of Mexico.

JOSE MARIANO DE SALAS.

To Don Jose Maria Lafragna."

And I communicate it to you for its fulfillment.

God and Liberty.——Mexico, December 4th, 1846.

LAFRAGNA.

Colonization Law

Of the State of Coahuila, and Texas.

The Governor provisionally appointed by the Sovereign Congress of this State—to all who shall see these presents ; Know—That the said Congress have decreed:

Decree, No. 16. The Constituent Congress of the free, Independent, and sovereign state of Coahuila and Texas, desiring by every possible means to augment the population of its territory ; promote the cultivation of its fertile lauds ; the raising and multiplication of stock, and the progress of the arts, and commerce ; and being governed by the Constitutional act, the Federal constitution, and the basis established by the National decree of the general congress, No. 72, have thought proper to decree the following law of colonization :

ART. 1. All foreigners, who in virtue of the general law, of the 18th August, 1824, which guarantees the security of their persons and property, in the territory of the Mexican nation, wish to remove to any of the settlements of the State of Coahuila and Texas, are at liberty to do so ; and the said state invites and calls them.

ART. 2. Those who do so, instead of being incommoded, shall be admitted by the local authorities of said settlements, who shall freely permit them to pursue any branch of industry, that they may think proper, provided they respect the general laws of·the nation, and those of the state.

ART. 3. Any foreigner, already in the limits of the state of Coahuila and Texas, who wishes to settle himself in it, shall make a declaration to that effect, before the Ayuntamiento of the place, which he selects as his residence, the Ayuntamiento in such case, shall administer to him the oath, which he must take to obey the federal and state constitutions, and observe the religion which the former prescribes; the name of the person, and his family if he has any, shall then be registered in a book kept for that purpose, with a statement of where he was born, and whence from, his age, whether married, occupation, and that he has taken the oath perscribed, and considering him from that time and not before, as domiciliated.

ART. 4. From the day in which any foreigner has been enrolled, as an inhabitant, in conformity with the foregoing article, he is at liberty to designate any vacant land, and the respective political authority will grant it to him in the same manner, as to a native of the country, in conformity with the existing laws of the nation, under the condition that the proceedings shall be passed to the government for its approbation.

ART. 5. Foreigners of any nation, or a native of any of the Mexican States, can project the formation of new towns on any lands entirely vacant, or even on those of an individual, in the case mentioned in the 35th article; but the new settlers who present themselves for admission, must prove their christianity, morality and good habits, by a certificate from the authorities where they formerly resided.

ART. 6. Foreigners who emigrate at the time in which the general sovereign congress may have prohibited their entrance, for the purpose of colonizing, as they have the power to do, after the year 1840, or previous to that time, as respects those of any particular nation, shall not then be admitted; and those who apply in proper time, shall always subject themselves to such precautionary measures of national security, which the supreme government, without prejudicing the object of this law, may think proper to adopt relative to them.

ART. 7. The government shall take care that within the 20 leagues bordering on the limits of the United States of the north, and ten leagues in a straight line from the coast of the Gulf of Mexico, within the limits of this state, there shall be no other settlements, except such as merit the approbation of the supreme government of the Union, for which object, all petitions on the subject, whether made by Mexicans or foreigners, shall be passed to the superior government, accompanied by a corresponding report.

ART. 8. The projects for new settlements in which one or more persons offer to bring at their expense, one hundred or more families, shall be presented to the government, and if found conformable with this law, they will, be admitted; and the government will immediately designate to the contractors, the land where they are to establish themselves, and the term of six years, within which they must present the number of families they contracted for, under the penalty of losing the rights and privileges offered in their favor, in proportion to the number of families which they fail to introduce, and the contract totally annulled if they do not bring, at least, one hundred families.

ART. 9. Contracts made by the contractors or undertakers, *Empresarios* with the families brought at their expense, are guaranteed by this law, so far, as they are conformable with its provisions.

ART. 10. In the distribution of lands, a preference shall be given to the military entitled to them, by the diplomas issued by the supreme executive power, and to Mexican citizens who are not military, among whom there shall be no other distinction than that founded on their individual merit, or services performed for the country, or in equal circumstances, a residence in the place where the land may be situated; the quantity of land which may be granted is designated in the following articles.

ART. 11. A square of land, which on each side has one league or five thousand varas, or what is the same thing, a superficie of twenty-five million varas, shall be called a sitio, and this shall be the unity for counting one, two, or more sitios; and also the unity for counting one, two, or more labors, shall be one million square varas or one thousand on each side, which shall compose a labor. The vara for this measurement shall be three geometrical feet.

ART. 12. Taking the above unity as a basis, and observing the distinction which must be made, between grazing land, or that which is proper for raising of stock, and farming land, without the facility of irrigation; this law grants to the contractor or contractors, for the establishment of a new settlement, for each hundred families, which he may introduce and establish in the State, five sitios of grazing land, and five labors at least, the one half of which shall be without the facility of irrigation; but they can only receive this premium for eight hundred families, although a greater number should be introduced, and no fraction whatever less than one hundred shall entitle them to any premium, not even proportionally.

ART. 13. Should any contractor or contractors in virtue of the number of families which he may have introduced, acquire in conformity with the last article, more than eleven square leagues of land, it shall nevertheless be granted, but subject to the condition of alienating the excess, within twelve years, and if it is not done, the respective political authority shall do it, by selling it at public sale, delivering the proceeds to the owners, after deducting the costs of sale.

ART. 14. To each family comprehended in a contract, whose sole occupation is cultivation of land, one labor shall be given, should he also, be a stock raiser, grazing land shall be added to complete a sitio, and should his only occupation be raising of stock, he shall only receive a superficie of grazing land, equal to twenty-four million square bars.

ART. 15. Unmarried men shall receive the same quantity when they enter the matrimonial state, and foreigners who marry native Mexicans, shall receive one fourth more; those who are entirely single, or who do not form a part of some family, whether foreigners or natives, shall content themselves with the fourth part of the above mentioned quantity which is all that can be given them until they marry.

ART. 16. Families or unmarried men, who, entirely of their own accord, have emigrated, and may wish to unite themselves to any new towns, can at all times do so, and the same quantity of land shall be assigned them, which is mentioned in the two last articles, but if they do so within the first six years from the establishment of the settlement, one labor more shall be given to families; and single men, in place of the quarter designated in the 15th article, shall have the third part.

ART. 17. It appertains to the government to augment the quantity indicated in the 14th, 15th, and 16th articles, in proportion to the family industry, and activity of the colonists, agreeably to the information given on these subjects by the Ayuntamientos and Commissioners; the said government always observing the provisions of the 12th article, of the decree of the general congress on the subject.

ART. 18. The families who emigrate in conformity with the 16th article, shall immediately present themselves to the political authority of the place which they may have chosen for their residence, who finding in them the requisites, prescribed by this law for new settlers, shall admit them, and put them in possession of the corresponding lands, and shall immediately give an account thereof to the government; who of themselves, or by means of a person commissioned to that effect, will issue them a title.

ART. 19. The Indians of all nations, bordering on the state, as well as wandering tribes that may be within its limits, shall be received in the markets, without paying any duties whatever for commerce, in the products of the country; and if attracted by the moderation and confidence, with which they shall be treated, any of them, after having first declared themselves in favor of our religion and institutions, wish to establish themselves in any settlements that are forming, they shall be admitted, and the same quantity of land given them, as to the settlers spoken of in the 14th and 15th articles, always preferring native Indians to strangers.

ART. 20. In order that there may be no vacancies between tracts, of which great care shall be taken in the distribution of lands; it shall be laid off in squares, or other forms although irregular, if the local situation requires it; and in said distribution, as well as the assignation of lands for new towns, previous notice shall be given to the adjoining proprietors, if any, in order to prevent dissentions and law suits.

ART. 21. If by error in the concession, any land shall be granted, belonging to another, on proof being made of that fact, an equal quantity shall be granted elsewhere, to the person who may have thus obtained it through error, and he shall be indemnified by the owner of such land, for any improvements he may have made; the just value of which improvements, shall be ascertained by appraisers.

ART. 22. The new settlers, as an acknowledgement, shall pay to the state, for each sitio of pasture land, thirty dollars; two dollars and a half, for each labor without the facility of irrigation, and three dollars and a half, for each one that can be irrigated, and so on proportionally, according to the quantity and quality of the land distributed; but the said payments need not be made until six years after the settlement, and by thirds; the first within four years, the second within five years, and the last within six years under the penalty of losing the land, for a failure in any of said payments; are excepted from this payment, the contractors, and military, spoken of in the 10th article; the former, with respect to lands given them, as a premium, and the latter, for those which they obtained, in conformity with their diplomas.

ART. 23. The Ayuntamientos of each municipality (*Comarca*,) shall collect the above mentioned funds, gratis, by means of a committee, appointed either within or without their body; and shall remit them as they are collected, to the treasurer of their funds, who will give the corresponding receipt, and without any 'other compensation than two and a half per cent. all that shall be allowed him, he shall hold them at the disposition of the government, rendering an account every month of the ingress and egress, and of any remissness or fraud, which he may observe in their collection; for the correct management of all which, the person employed, and the committee, and the individuals of the Ayuntamientos who appoint them, shall be individually responsible, and that this responsibility may be at all times effectual, the said appointments shall be made *viva voce*, and information shall be given thereof immediately to the government.

ART. 24. The government will sell to Mexicans *and to them only*, such lands as they may wish to purchase, taking care that there shall not be accumulated in the same hands more than eleven sitios; and under the condition, that the purchaser must cultivate what he acquires by this title, within six years from its acquisition, under the penalty of losing them; the price of each sitio, subject to the foregoing condition, shall be one hundred dollars, if it be pasture land; one hundred and fifty dollars, if it be farming land without the facility of irrigation; and two hundred and fifty dollars if it can be irrigated.

ART. 25. Until six years after the publication of this law, the legislature of this state, cannot alter it as regards the acknowledgement, and price to be paid for land, or as regards the quantity and quality, to be distributed to the new settlers, or sold to Mexicans.

ART. 26. The new settlers, who within six years from the date of the possession, have not cultivated or occupied the lands granted to them, according to its quality, shall be considered to have renounced them, and the respective political authority, shall immediately proceed to take possession of them, and recall the titles.

ART. 27. *The contractors and* military, heretofore spoken of, and those who by purchase have acquired lands, can alienate them at any time, but the successor is obliged to cultivate them in the same time, that the original proprietor was bound to do ; the other settlers can alienate theirs when they have totally cultivated them, and not before.

ART. 28. By testamentary will made in conformity with the existing laws, or those which may govern in future, any new colonist, from the day of his settlement, may dispose of his land, although he may not have cultivated it, and if he dies intestate, his property shall be inherited by the person or persons entitled by the laws to it ; the heirs being subject to the same obligation and condition imposed on the original grantee.

ART. 29. Lands acquired by virtue of this law, shall not by any title whatever, pass into mortmain.

ART. 30. The new settler, who, wishing to establish himself in a foreign country, resolves to leave the territory of the state, can do so freely, with all his property ; but after leaving the state, he shall not any longer hold the land, and·if he had not previously sold it, or the sale should not be in conformity with the 27th article, it shall become entirely vacant.

ART. 31. Foreigners who in conformity with this law, have obtained land, and established themselves in any new settlement, shall be considered from that moment, naturalized in the country ; and by marrying a Mexican, they acquire a particular merit to obtain letters of citizenship of the state, subject however to the provisions which may be made relative to both particulars, in the constitution of the state.

ART. 32. During the first ten years, counting from the day on which the new settlements may have been established, they shall be free from all contributions, of whatever denomination, with the exception of those which, in case of invasion by an enemy, or to prevent it, are generally imposed, and all the produce of agriculture or industry of the new settlers, shall be free from excise duty *Alcabala*, or other duties, throughout every part of the state, with the exception of the duties referred to in the next article ; after the termination of that time, the new settlements shall be on the same footing as to taxes, with the old ones, and the colonists shall also in this particular, be on the same footing with the other inhabitants of the state.

ART. 33. From the day of their settlement, the new colonists shall be at liberty to follow any branch of industry, and can also work mines of every description, communicating with the supreme government of the confederation, relative to the general revenue appertaining to it, and subjecting themselves in all other particulars, to the ordinances or taxes, established or which may be established on this branch.

ART. 34. Towns shall be founded on the sites deemed most suitable, by the government, or the person commissioned for this effect, and for each one, there shall be designated *four square* leagues, whose area may be in a regular or irregular form, agreeably to the situation.

ART. 35. If any of the said sites should be the property of an individual, and the establishment of new towns on them should notoriously be of general utility, they can notwithstanding, be appropriated to this object, previously indemnifying the owner for its just value, to be determined by appraisers.

ART. 36. Building lots in the new towns shall be given gratis, to the contractors of them, and also to artists of every class, as many as are necessary for the establishment of their trade; and to the other settlers they shall be sold at public auction, after having been previously valued—under the obligation to pay the purchase money by instalments of one third each; the first in six months, the second in twelve months, and the third in eighteen months; but all owners of lots, including contractors and artists, shall annually pay one dollar for each lot, which, together with the produce of the sales, shall be collected by the Ayuntamientos, and applied to the building of churches in said towns.

ART. 37. So far as is practicable, the towns shall be composed of natives and foreigners, and in their delineations, great care shall be taken to lay off the streets straight, giving them a direction from north to south, and from east to west, when the site will permit it.

ART. 38. For the better location of the said new towns, their regular formation and exact partition of their lands and lots, the government on account of having admitted any project, and agreeing with the contractor or contractors, who may have presented it, shall commission a person of intelligence and confidence, giving him such particular instructions as may be deemed necessary and expedient; and authorising him under his own responsibility, to appoint one or more surveyors, to lay off he town scientifically, and do whatever else may be required.

ART. 39. The Governor in conformity with the last fee bill *Arancel*, of notary public's of the ancient audience of Mexico, shall designate the fees of the commissioner, who in conjunction with the colonists, shall fix the surveyor's fees; but both shall be paid by the colonists, and in the manner which all parties among themselves may agree upon.

ART. 40. As soon as at least forty families are united in one place, they shall proceed to the formal establishment of the new towns, and all of them shall take an oath, to support the general and state constitution: which oath will be administered by the commissioner, they shall then, in his presence proceed for the first time, to the election of their municipal authority.

ART. 41. A new town, whose inhabitants shall not be less than two hundred, shall elect an Ayuntamiento, provided there is not another one established within eight leagues, in which case, it shall be added to it. The number of individuals which are to compose the Ayuntamiento, shall be regulated by the existing laws.

ART. 42. Foreigners are eligible, subject to the provisions which the con-stitution of the state may prescribe, to elect the members of their municipal authorities, and to be elected to the same.

ART. 43. The municipal expenses, and all others which may be necessary, or of common utility to the new towns, shall be proposed to the Governor, by the Ayuntamientos through the political chief, accompanied with a plan of the taxes *arbitrios,* which in their opinion may be just and best calculated to raise them, and should the proposed plan be approved of by the Governor, he shall order it to be executed, subject however to the resolution of the legisla-ture, to whom it shall be immediately passed with his report and that of the political chief, who will say whatever occurs to him on the subject.

ART. 44. For the opening and improving of roads, and other public works in Texas, the government will transmit to the chief of that depart-ment, the individuals, who in other parts of the state, may have been sen-tenced to public works as vagrants, or for other crimes, these same persons may be employed by individuals for competent wages, and as soon as the time of their condemnation is expired, they can unite themselves as colo-nists, to any new settlement, and obtain the corresponding lands, if their reformation shall have made them worthy of such favor in the opinion of the chief of the department, without whose certificate, they shall not be ad-mitted.

ART. 45. The government in accord with the respective ordinary ecclesi-astics, will take care to provide the new settlements with the competent number of pastors, and in accord with the same authority, shall propose to the legislature for its approbation, the salary which the said pastors are to receive, which shall be paid by the new settlers.

ART. 46. The new settlers as regards the introduction of slaves, shall subject themselves to the existing laws, and those which may hereafter be established on the subject.

ART. 47. The petitions now pending relative to the subject of this law, shall be despatched in conformity with it, and for this purpose, they shall be passed to the Governor, and the families who may be established within the limits, of the state, without having any land assigned them, shall subject themselves to this law, and to the orders of the supreme government of the Union, with respect to those who are within twenty leagues of the limits of the United States of America, and ten leagues in a straight line of the coast of the Gulf of Mexico.

ART. 48. This law shall be published in all the villages of the state, and that it may arrive at the notice of all others, throughout the Mexican con-federation, it shall be communicated to their respective legislatures, by the secretary of this state; and the Governor will take particular care, to send a certified copy of it, in compliance with the 161st article of the federal con-stitution, to have the two houses of congress, and the supreme executive power of the nation, with a request to the latter, to give it a general circulation through foreign states, by means of our ambassadors.

The Governor pro tem. of the state will cause it to be published and circulated.—Saltillo, 24th March, 1825.—Signed.

RAFAEL RAMOS Y. VADEZ, President,

JUAN VICENTE CAMPOS, Member & Sec'y.

JOSE JOAQIN ARCE ROSALES, Mem. & Sec'y.

Therefore I command all authorities, as well civil as military and ecclesiastical, to obey, and cause to be obeyed, the present decree in all its parts.

RAFAEL GONZALES, Governor.

INSTRUCTIONS

To the Commissioners appointed by the Legislature of the State.
EXECUTIVE DEPARTMENT   }
of the State of Coahuila and Texas. }

Instructions by which the Commissioner shall be governed, in the partition of lands to the new colonists, who may establish themselves in the State, in conformity with the colonization law of the 24th of March, 1825.

ART. 1. It shall be the duty of the commissioner, keeping in view the contract which an empresario may have entered into with the government, and also the certificates or recommendations which foreign emigrants must produce from the local authorities of the place where they removed from, accrediting their christianity, morality, and steady habits, in conformity with the 5th article of said law; without which requisite they shall not be admitted to the colony.

ART. 2. In order to prevent being imposed on by false recommendations, the commissioner shall not consider any as sufficient, without a previous opinion in writing as to their legitimacy, from the empresario, for which purpose they shall be passed to him by the commissioner.

ART. 3. The commissioner shall administer to each of the new colonists, the oath in form, to observe the federal constitution of the United Mexican States, the constitution of the State, the general laws of the nation, and those of the State which they have adopted for their country.

ART. 4. He shall issue, in the name of the state, the titles for land, in conformity with the law, and put the new colonists in possession of their lands, with all legal formalities, and the previous citation of adjoining proprietors, should there be any.

ART. 5. He shall not give possession to colonists who may have established, or who may wish to establish themselves within twenty leagues of the

United States of the north, or within ten leagues of the coast, unless it should appear that the supreme government of the nation had approved thereof.

ART. 6. He shall take care that no vacant lands be left between posses-sions, and in order that the lines of each one may be clearly designated, he shall compel the colonists, within the term of one year, to mark their lines, and to establish fixed and permanent corners.

ART. 7. He shall appoint under his own responsibility the surveyor, who must survey the land scientifically, requiring him previously to take an oath truly and faithfully to discharge the duties of his office.

ART. 8. He shall form a manuscript book of paper of the 3d stamp, in which shall be written the titles of the lands distributed to the colonists, specifying the names, the boundaries, and other requisites, and legal circum-stances; and a certified copy of each title shall be taken from said book on paper of the 2d stamp, which shall be delivered to the interested person as his title.

ART. 9. Each settler shall pay the value of the stamp paper used in issu-ing his title both for the original and copy.

ART. 10. This book shall be preserved in the archives of the new colony, and an exact form of it shall be transmitted to the government, specifying the number of colonists with their names, and the quantity of land granted to each one, distinguishing that which is farming land with or without the facilities of irrigation, and that which is granted as grazing land.

ART. 11. He shall select the site which may be the most suitable for the establishment of the town or towns, which are to be founded agreeably to the number of families composing the colony, and keeping in view the provi-sions of the law of colonizations on this subject.

ART. 12. After selecting the site destined for the new town, he shall take care that the base lines run north and south, east and west, and he will de-signate a public square, one hundred and twenty varas on each side, exclu-sive of the streets, which shall be called the *principal or constitutional square*, and this shall be the central point from which the streets shall run, for the formation of squares and blocks in conformity with the model hereto annexed.

ART. 13. The block situated on the east side of the principal square, shall be destined for the church, curate's house, and other ecclesiastical buildings. The block on the west side of said square shall be designated for public buildings of the municipality. In some other suitable situation a block shall be designated for a market square, another for a Jail, and house of correction, another for a school, and other edifices for public instruction, and another beyond the limits of the town for a burial ground.

ART. 14. He shall, on his responsibility, cause the streets to be laid off straight, and that they are twenty varas wide, to promote the health of the town.

Art. 15. Mechanics, who at the time of founding a new town, present themselves to settle in it, shall have the right of receiving one lot apiece, without any other cost than the necessary stamp paper for issuing the title, and the light tax of one dollar annually, for the construction of the church.

Art. 16. The lots spoken of in the preceding article, shall be distributed by lot, with the exception of the empresario, who shall be entitled to any two lots he may select.

Art. 17. The other lots shall be valued by appraisers according to their situation, and sold to the other colonists at their appraised value. In case there should be a number of applicants for the same lot, owing to its situation or other circumstances which may excite competition, it shall be decided by lot as prescribed in the preceding article, the product of said lots shall be appropriated to the building of a church in said town.

Art. 18. He shall, in union with the empresario, promote the settlement of each town by the inhabitants belonging to its jurisdiction, who take lots in it, and cause them to construct houses on said lots within a limited time, under the penalty of forfeiting them.

Art. 19. He shall form a manuscript book of each new town, in which shall be written the titles of the lots which are given as a donation, or sold, specifying the boundaries and other necessary circumstances, a certified copy of each one of which on the corresponding stamp shall be delivered to the interested person as his title.

Art. 20. He shall form a topographical plan of each town that may be founded, and transmit it to the government, keeping a copy of it in the said register book of the colony.

Art. 21. He shall see that at the crossing of each of the rivers on the public roads where a town is founded, a ferry is established at the cost of the inhabitants of said town, a moderate rate of ferriage shall be established to pay the salary of the ferryman and the cost of the necessary boats, and the balance shall be applied to the public funds of the towns.

Art. 22. In places where there are no towns, and where ferries are necessary, the colonists who may be settled there, shall be charged with the establishment of the ferry, collecting a moderate ferriage until such ferries are rented out for the use of the state. Any colonist who wishes to establish a ferry on the terms above indicated, shall form an exact and certified account of the costs which he may be at for the building of boats, and also an account of the produce of the ferry, in order that when said ferry is rented out for the use of the state, he shall have a right to receive the amount of said expenses which had not already been covered by the produce of the ferry, which for the present he will collect.

Art. 23. He shall preside at the popular elections mentioned in the 40th article of the colonization law, for the appointment of the Ayuntamiento, and shall put the elected in possession of their offices.

ART. 24. He shall take special care that the portions of land granted to the colonists by article 14, 15, and 16, shall be measured by the surveyors with accuracy, and not permit any one to include more land than is designated by law, under the penalty of being personally responsible.

ART. 25. Should any colonist solicit, in conformity with the 17th article of the law, an augmentation of land beyond that designated in the preceding articles on account of the size of his family, industry, or capital, he shall present his petition in writing to the commissioner, stating all the reasons on which he founds his petition, who shall transmit it to the Governor of the State, together with his opinion; for which opinion he shall be responsible in the most rigid manner, in order that the Governor may decide on the subject.

ART. 26. All the public instruments, titles, or other documents, issued by the commissioner, shall be written in Spanish, the memorials, decrees, and reports of the colonists or empressarios on any subject whatever, shall be written in the same language, whether they are to be transmitted to government, or preserved in the archives of the colony.

ART. 27. All public instruments or titles of possession, and the copies signed by the Commissioner, shall be attested by two assistant witnesses.

ART. 28. The Commissioner shall be personally responsible for all acts or measures performed by him, contrary to the colonization law or these instructions.

A Copy.—Saltillo, September 4th, 1827.

> TIJERINA, } Secretaries of
> ARCINIEGA, } the Legislature.

A Copy, JUAN ATONIO PADILLA, Secretary of State.

GLOSSARY.

GIVING THE SIGNIFICATION OF SOME OBSCURE TERMS, USED IN THE MIN-
ING ORDINANCES OF NEW SPAIN.

A

Abras (clefts or fissures). Are fissures in the hills, demonstrating the force of some subterraneous expansion, which has torn them asunder. They are indications of veins, as is the spar generally found about their entrance.

Achicar (to diminish). A mining term, referring to the lowering of the water in any work or level. The workmen employed for this purpose are called *Achicadores*.

Achichinques. Workmen employed to collect the water from the lower springs in the mines, in buckets of ox hide, and to empty it into the cisterns, or into the sump of the pit.

Ademes. Coverings or linings of timber, by means of which the pits, pillars of support, and works generally, are secured and strengthened. The workman employed in this business is called an *Ademador*.

Afinacion (refining). Is the separating from the plates or ingots of silver, the dross always combined with them after smelting.

Alcribis or *Tovera* (twer or tuyere). A kind of funnel, into which the nozzle of the bellows of smelting furnaces is fitted, to conduct the blast.

Aparejo (tackel). A machine for raising the timber linings of the pits, when they give way or become loose ; also for raising certain large beams called *llaves*, on which the whims rest.

Aperos (implements). All the requisites for keeping in working order the pits and draw wells, for erecting sheds, and for other matters relating to the underground works of the mines. The person who has all such articles under his care, and who distributes them when called for, is called the *Aperado*.

A pique (downwards). To work *à pique* is to work by sinking perpendicularly downwards, in the perpendicular veins.

Apuradores (gleaners.) Men or women who seek for particles of metal in the refuse of the amalgamation works.

Atacador (rammer.) A smooth cylindrical tool, more slender than a borer (*barrcna*,) for ramming in the cartridge with which the rock is blasted.

No part of it should consist of steel, lest it should strike fire too soon.

Atajador (interceptor.) A boy who brings the mules or horses for the grinding mills and draining, when relieved.

Atecas. Workmen who bale the water from the lower levels of the mine into the skins, in order to be raised by the pit.

Atierres. (rubbish.) Ground which interferes with the work, and which should be removed to the rubbish heaps.

Azogueria (from *azogue*, quicksilver.) Used to express the reduction of gold and silver by quicksilver, and the establishments where it is effected.

B

Bancos (banks.) Strong rock, which throws up and contracts the vein, or alters its direction.

Barra (crow.) An iron tool tipped with steel. Also one of the twelve or twenty-four shares into which mines are divided.

Barrena (borer.) A cylindrical iron tool, of the diameter of a two real piece ; the lower end shaped like a chisel, or with four edges placed crosswise ; the head and point tipped with steel, and two thirds or three fourths (of a *vara*) in length ; it is used for boring the rock, preparatory to blasting.

Barreno (hole bored.) Is the hole bored in the rock for the insertion of the cartridge. *Barreno* is also used to express a communication between two mines, which are said to *barrenarse* when they communicate underground.

Barretero. A working miner who uses a crow bar (*barra,*) wedge (*cuña,*) or pick (*pico.*)

Boca (mouth.) Is the first opening made on the vein.

Boca mejora (mouth, improved.) Pit or mouth made to communicate with the fixed stake or principal pit, in order to facilitate the underground working of the mines.

Bochorno (glow.) Excessive heat, which extinguishes the lights within the mines, arising from a want of ventilation, and from working without driving cross-cuts to promote a due circulation of the air. It is increased by the effluvia thrown off from the bodies of the workmen during their labour, and extinguishes the lights. When this is the case, some of the workmen ought immediately to leave the spot, upon which the flame usually revives.

Bonanza (fair weather.) Is generally applied to a work when in rich ore.

Borrasca (foul weather.) Vide *emborrascarse.*

Botas (buckets.) Are made of the entire hide of an ox, for drawing off the water by the pit.

Buscones (searchers.) Persons who search for ore in abandoned mines, either with the view to carry it off, or to give information of the discovery, for the sake of a reward.

C

Calentadura (from *calentar*, to heat.) The first ingot reduced in a smelting furnace.

Camino (road or way.) Besides its usual sense, is applied in some places to the bags or sacks of ore.

Cañones (levels.) Narrow underground passages or galleries, by means of which the mine is worked.

Capellina (hood.) A vessel consisting of two pieces, employed in separating the quicksilver from the silver.

Cata (taste or trial.) A mine of small depth.

Caballo (horse.) A mass of firm and hard rock met with in working a mine, or sinking a pit.

Cebar (to feed.) A mode of reducing rich ore in a refining furnace. Also said, when the furnace will not contain all the ingots, in which case fresh ingots are supplied, as the metal goes off.

Cendrada. The bottom of the smelting or refining furnace, which is made of fine earth, or of the ashes of plants.

Cendradilla or *galeme.* A small test or refining furnace for rich ores.

Charqueo interior. To clear off the water from the cisterns or pools by channels, so as to guide it into the pit.

Chiflon. To work *à chiflon* is to extend the works, at the same time, both in length and depth.

Cielo (sky.) Working *de cielo* is when the workmen, either on foot or on his knees, works at the vault or roof of the work.

Cohetazo (blast.) A mode of breaking the rock, by wrapping up gunpowder in paper tied together with palm leaf, or any other flexible vegetable, and secured with sifted white earth. A small reed is left projecting out, for the purpose of applying the match, to ignite it.

Colores (colours.) Colours with which the surface of the earth is tinged, shewing a vermillion or yellow appearance in the sun; which is an indication of ore.

Comerse los pilares (to consume the pillars.) To break down, pare away or weaken the supports or pillars of the mine.

Consumido. See *Lis.*

Contramina. A work of communication between two or more mines, by means of which they may be cleared, and the rubbish and ore got out. The adits also, made to communicate with the pits, are called *contraminas.* An adit is driven from the side of the hill. A pit is sunk from the surface.

Cortar pilar. (to cut a pillar). To finish a pillar by making a cross cut, and forming a landing place, also called *tapextle.* See *tapextle.*

Cortar sogas (to cut away the ropes.) To abandon a mine.

Crestones (crests.) Ridges consisting of crude ore, the effect of fire; spar or rocks on the surface, which have burst out from the pressure of the vein, in the form of a cock's comb, so as to be visible at a league's distance. They are, as it were, the crust of the vein.

Criadero. A kind of *cul de sac* or vault, in which the ore lies loose. It is also called a *bohedal.*

Crucera (cross-cut.) *Dar crucero,* is to work horizontally along or across the vein, to give air to the works, or to avoid some insuperably hard mass of rock; or to drive in search of the vein, in which case the work is also called a level (*cañon*). A *crecero* crosses the principal work, which is carried on by winzes in the inclined veins, or by ends in the horizontal veins.

Cuña (wedge). An iron tool, usually of two pounds weight for soft ground, and one pound or under, for hard ground. The edge is of steel, and it is struck with the pick.

D

Denuncio (denouncement). Properly, *denunciacion;* the giving information that a mine has been insufficiently worked more than four months, in order that it may be adjudged to the denouncer, with the due solemnities of proclamation and summons.

Demasias. Unappropriated grounds.

Derrumbe or *derrumbamiento* (a falling down). The falling in of a mine, from the roofs and works giving way through weakness. Also called *hundido* (a sinking in).

Desagues (unwatering, draining). The drawing off water from the lower works of the mine by the pits, or by means of adits.

Descargue (discharge). The last and largest ingot reduced in a smelting furnace, To *descargar* the furnace is to demolish it.

Desmonte (that which has been cut away). All the barren rock removed from the sides and roof of the vein, which, when the rubbish, rock and barren ground are removed, is left clear.

Despensa (pantry). A safe room for storing up the rich ores; the shed (*galera*) serving for the common ores.

Despueble (dispeopling). Abandoning the mine; neglecting to employ four laborers about some external or internal work, agreeably to the ordinance.

E

Echadero (resting place). Platform on the hill, for loading the mules, for spreading out, cleaning and weighing the ore.

Echado (inclination). Lateral inclination of the vein.

Emborrascarse la mina (from *borrasca*). Is applied, when instead of ore, spar is found, or when the vein loses itself.

Ensayes (assays). Trial of a small quantity of ore by fire or quicksilver, in order to ascertain its standard, and whether it will answer to work it. It is also said when the assayer determines the standard of gold or silver, marking each piece.

Escaleras (ladders). Round pieces of 8, 10 or more yards in length, with notches, which serve for stairs, in ascending the pits. The landing places between, enable the workmen to ascend and descend without interfering with each other.

Escorial (slag heap). Vide *grassero*.

Espejuelo (glassy substance). A kind of spar less consistent than the common spar, with an oily lustre, like talc or gypsum.

Estaca fixa (fixed stake). The principal pit by which the mine is registered, and which is not to be altered when the miner measures out or alters his boundaries. The boundary stakes set out between the mine and that of a neighbor, are also called *fixed stakes*.

F

Faenas (fatigues). Dead works which are not carried on in ore, but in barren ground, and which tend to bring the mine into a working state; such as driving an air hole, adit, level or work of drainage. To work *a faena* is to pay less wages to the barman, sharing the ore equally with him. (Vide *tequio*).

Fierros (iron). Dross removed from the ingots after letting off the lead into the float; or from the ore first smelted.

Fronton (wall). Is a work which the laborers carry on standing, proceeding onwards, or straight forward.

Fuelles (bellows). Applied both to those used for the forges (above ground or beneath), where the bars and picks are sharpened, and to those used in the smelting furnaces, for smelting and refining the ore and metal.

G

Galeme. See *cendradilla.*

Galera. See *dispensa.*

Gallos (cocks). Rich ore, with threads and grains of gold and silver.

Golpeador (striker). The person who strikes the head of the borer with the pick, to bore the rock for the insertion of the cartridge.

Grassas (grease). Scum or scoriæ removed from the metal, when it runs out of the smelting furnace into the float. From this scum the *plomillos* are detached.

Grassero or *escorial* (slag heap.) Where the scoriæ are thrown out.

Guarda-raya (limit or boundary mark). A mark or boundary of stone and mortar, or stone and mud, erected at the spot where a communication has occurred between two mines; the boundary being first ascertained.

Guardas (guards.) Rock at the sides of the vein, and roof of the work.

Guia (guide). An indication, guiding or conducting to the rich part of a vein, or to the discovery of a new vein. Also applied to the ingredients added to the *montons* of ore, when mixed for reduction, to ascertain their state.

Guija (spar or gravel). Is a hard flint of a dusky color; or a more crystalline substance of not very firm texture, which breaks to pieces with a slight blow. It varies in color, and affords the best indication of ore when black.

Guija Iron spike on which the mortar (of the stamping mill?) rests.

H

Hueco (hollow). Vide *demasias*.

Hundido (sinking in). See *derrumbe*.

I

Incorporadero (mixing place). A place, court, yard or shed, where the quicksilver and other ingredients are mixed with the ore, in the process of reduction by amalgamation.

J

Jaboncillos (diminutive of *jabon*, soap). Whitish, unctious ore, which is an indication and forerunner of treasure.

Jalsontles. Portions of ore not properly ground, and which have to be reground. Also the slime or dust from the washing vats in the amalgamation works, which is afterwards made into *montons* (for reduction?)

L

Labor (working). Generally, all mining labor is so called. It is either performed in an *end*, which is when the workman drives straight forward; in a back or rise, which is when he works upwards; or it may be downwards.

Lamas (slime). The earthy matter taken from the vats in the amalgamation works, and which is again made into *montons* (for reduction?).

Lamero. A place in the amalgamation establishments for the slime and ore after grinding.

Lampazo (mop). An instrument formed of green boughs, fixed to the end of a long pole, which is used to moderate the heat of the smelting furnaces, when excessive.

Lavadero (washing place.) A large wooden vat, in the middle of which is a contrivance for stirring, in the form of a chocolate mill. The montons of ore are washed in this vat, and this earthy matter being separated, is carried off through a channel, with the water; the silver remaining at the bottom.

Llaves (keys). Supports of oak, with notches and circular joints, which extend to the four corners of the pit, and support the lining or timber covering. Also the two timbers which support the shed for draining.

Lazadores (persons who use a *lazo* or noose). Persons employed to collect hands for working the mines, in case of a scarcity of workmen; so called from their remarkable dexterity in throwing a *lazo*.

Leñador (woodman) Workman employed in carrying or supplying wood for the smelting furnaces.

Limadura (filings.). A film with which the metal becomes coated in the small assays made for the purpose of ascertaining the state of the *monton*, and what additions of quicksilver or other ingredients it may require.

Lis. The silver is said to form *lis*, when the quicksilver is resolved into almost imperceptible particles, which occasions the loss and consumption in washing and stirring the *montons* of ore, in the course of the reduction by amalgamation.

Lumbreras (sky-lights). Communication between two works, for the sake of ventilation, and to make the lights burn.

M

Malacate (whim). A machine moved by mules or horses. It consists of a wheel, a cage or drum, and an axle (*exe*). It is used for winding, the ropes, so as to raise and let down the bags of ore or skins of water by the pit.

Mantas (blankets). Sacks made of the thread of the aloe, and filled with ore or rubbish.

Mantos (cloaks). Veins of ore spreading horizontally through the mountain, but of no depth.

Marca (mark). The royal arms, stamped on a piece of assayed silver, as a token of its having paid the duties to the crown.

Mecha (match). A twist of cotton and grease, made by the workman called *cohetero* or *golpeador*, usually from his drawers or shirt, and used for firing the cartridge.

Medidas de mina (dimensions or boundaries of a mine). As to silver mines, they form a parallelogram of 160 varas in length and 80 in width, in the discoverer's, and 120 and 60 in an ordinary mine. As to gold mines, the discoverer's is 100 varas in length, and 50 in width; and an ordinary mine, 80 in length, and 40 in width. The internal dimensions should correspond with the external ones.

Metal de ayuda (assistant ore). What the words denote, that is to say, ore used to assist the smelting of other ore, and to temper it.

Metal de cebo. Very rich ore, which is smelted in refining tests.

Metal pepena. Rich picked gold or silver ore; the common ore is called *ordinario*.

Mina (mine). The *descubridora* is the first mine discovered on the vein, or on a new vein in the same hill; all others are called *ordinary mines*.

Mogrollo. The same as *metal de cebo*, being very rich. It is not smelted in a furnace, being safer in the hollow of a test.

Molonque. A piece of ore, of uniform richness, containing more silver than extraneous matter, or at any rate, equal parts.

N

Natas or *escorias* (scum or scoriæ). Dross thrown off in the smelting furnace; in which case the furnace is said to *texear* well.

P

Panino. A person is said to know the *panino*, when he possesses experience and skill in judging from the appearance of the ground, the colour or shade of the ore, and other signs, whether there be metal.

Parcionero (partner). Part-owners of mines.

Partido (share). The division of the ore amongst partners in their respective shares. Also, the division made by the barmen, of the ore they raise—over and above the *tequio*, or quantity they have to contribute at stated hours. Also a payment made by the miners to the owner of an adit, or general work of draining, for getting out the rubbish and ore, and for the draining.

Pepe (short for Joseph). Boy who lights each barman at his work, and assists him in it at certain hours.

Pepena. See *metal pepena*.

Pico (pick). A kind of iron hammer, tipped with steel at both ends, of 8, 10 or 12 pounds in weight, and longer or shorter, according to the fancy of each barman.

Piedras de mano (stone carried by hand). Ore of good quality, which the miners usually set apart for various pious purposes, which is called, giving a *piedra de mano*.

Pilar (pillar). Part of the substance of the hill, left between the excavations made cross-wise upon the vein; in other words, a support for the roof or back of the work, being the intermediate ground left between the winzes, cross-cuts and levels. It ought to be lined with timber, and should not be worked into or weakened.

Pileta (cistern). In which the waters within the mine are collected, to prevent them from pouring down and inundating the lower works. In a smelting furnace, the breast-pan or vessel into which the melted metal flows down from the bottom stone.

Pina (pine apple,) or *Pella* (mass.) The amalgam of silver and quicksilver, before the latter is driven off.

Pinta (spot or mark.) An indication of this or that ore, by which its degree of richness is estimated, according to the colour, grain, weight or lightness. Amongst the good indications are the *gallos*, or threads of gold and silver in the ore ; the ores called *polvorilla*, *jaboncillos*, *ayemado*, *apericado*, *cardenillo*, *arenillas* ; copper and lead. And amongst the bad ones, are mundic and antimony. But it is always necessary to prove the ore by an assay, as these indications are sometimes fallacious.

Plan. (floor.) To work *de plan*, is to work either perpendicularly downwards, or *a chiflon*, that is to say, extending both forward and downwards.

Planes. The floor or deepest part of the mine.

Planchera. A place or float made of white earth, connected with the smelting furnace, and in which the ingots are formed.

Plomillos. Particles charged with lead, which the scum or scoria of the metal carries off with it. See *Natas*.

Pueble (peopling.) The actual working of a mine by labourers, for its improvement, as regulated by the ordinance, whether in ore or dead work.

Puertas (gates.) Very firm rock concealing the vein. When this is got through by blasting, the vein is generally discovered again, in a richer state than previously.

Q

Quemazon. (effect of heat.) Light metallic dross, vesicular and scorched, which is one of the indications of a vein.

Quita-pepena. He who attends to the entrance of the mine and the getting out the ore, to guard against theft.

R

Rebolturon or *Reboltura* (from *revolver*, to mix.) A mixture of ground ore with assistant ore, litharge, impregnated cupels, *plomillos* and slag, preparatory to smelting.

Rebotalleros. Persons who search for ore amongst the heaps of refuse or rubbish, which generally contain a little ore. It would be much better if these persons would work, being generally idle.

Recogedores. See *Lazadores*.

Registro (registry.) A description of the mine and its situation, and an exhibition of the ore before the justice ; which, after the depth of three *estados* has been sunk, possession judicially given, and the boundaries defined, serves as an evidence of title. Upon every change of ownership, and upon the making of a new pit or *contramina*, there should be a new registry.

Repasar (to stir.) To stir the *montons* of ore, in which *magistral* and quicksilver are mixed, from time to time, in the process of reduction.

Reposadero (from *reposar*, to rest. A black, soft and vesicular (*hoyoso*) stone, placed at the bottom of the smelting furnace.

Rescatadores (purchasers.) Persons who purchase ore from the mine-owners, or who buy the *partido* or share of ore alloted to the workmen.

Riscos. A substance partly crystalline (though not transparent) and partly granular, like a cauliflower ; the colour being yellow or white.

S

Saca (sack ; also, a substance raised or extracted.) Is a sack of ore ; and it is also said that the mine gives a good *saca*, when the vein being soft, or of great width, plenty of ore is raised.

Socabon (adit.) One or more narrow subterraneous passages driven from the skirt of a hill, and communicating with the pit ; its use being to drain the mine, and for getting out ore, barren ground and rubbish. It ought therefore, to be driven from a point situated lower than the bottom of the workings of the mine.

T

Tanates. Baskets made of hide, or of the thread of the aloe (called *Mecate*,) in which the ore and rubbish is carried out by the workmen called *Tanateros*.

Tanda. (turn.) Is a cessation of working on certain days.

Tapextle. A small wooden platform for working upwards, in the back of the work. Likewise the timber lining with which the roof is propped up, to prevent its giving way, and resembling the centering of an arch, or a palisading. Most commonly a landing place, made where there is no pillar of support, both to make the ladders more secure, and to give the labourers an opportunity of taking breath.

Temescuitate. The earthy part of the ground ore.

Tentadura (from *tentar*, to try.) An assay of the mixture of quicksilver and ore, made in a cup, for the purpose of ascertaining what addition the *monton* may require to bring it to the proper point. It is performed by washing a small portion of the ore, by which means the earthy parts being removed, the sediment, which contains the quicksilver and silver, is examined.

Tepetate. All the ground in the mine which is destitute of ore.

Tequio (duty). A certain portion of ore, which the barman, according to the hardness or softness of the ground, has to deliver to his employer in working hours. The remainder of what the barman raises is divided between him and his employer, and is called *partido*.

Terrero (rubbish heap). The place where the earth, barren ground and rubbish is thrown out.

Texear bien el horno. Is said when the furnace throws off fine and brittle dross or scoriæ.

Tiro (pit). A perpendicular shaft of three *varas*, more or less, in diameter, either square, octagonal or hexagonal. Its use is to raise the ore in bags and the water in buckets, by means of whims. A perpendicular pit, is one which descends vertically. An inclined pit, has an underlay, and the bags and skins are therefore dragged along the side in removing them.

Trompa (trumpet) of the smelting furnace. Applied when the blast from the bellows makes no noise, and does not disperse the cinders. It is said to *entromparse*, because the ore collects into the form of a trumpet, at the orifice of the twer, through which the blast enters.

V

Vapor (vapor). Rather worse than *bochorno ;* for besides putting out the lights, it is noxious. It proceeds from something in the nature of the ground, combined with the want of ventilation in the cavities of the mine.

Vena (vein.) Is applied to the branches or small veins, of three, two, or one finger in breadth, or not wider than the back of a knife.

Veta (lode or vein). A vein of metallic ore intersecting the ground. It is called a *manto* (bed), when it spreads horizontally through the hill ; *clavadar* (perpendicular), when it proceeds perpendicularly downwards ; *echada* (underlying or inclined), when it extends sideways in length and depth ; *obliqua* (oblique), when it crosses the hill ; *serpenteada* (tortuous), when it winds ; *socia* (combined) when it unites with another ; *rama* (branch), when it branches off from the primary lode.

Vuelta (turn). The silver in the refining furnaces is said to *dar vuelta* (turn over), when, after all the dross is driven off, the ingot remains of a red color.

X

Xacal. A hut, either covered with straw, or roofed with shingles or squares of deal, in which the tools are kept, and likewise the ore, until removed to the amalgamation or smelting works. The places where the ore is kept are also called *galeras* or *despansas.* A *xacal*, that is to say, a hut or covering, is also erected over the pits, to keep off the rain and to shelter the workmen.

Table of Land Measures adopted in the Republic of Mexico.

Names of the Measures.	Figures of the Measures.	Length of the figures expressed in varas.	Breadth in varas.	Areas, in square varas.	Areas in caballerias.
Sitio de ganado mayor	Square	5,000	5,000	25,000,000	41.023
Criadero de ganado mayor	Square	2,500	2,500	6,250,000	10.255
Sitio de ganado menor	Square	3,333⅓	3,333⅓	11,111,111⅑	18.232
Criadero de ganado menor	Square	1,666⅔	1,666⅔	2,777,777⁷⁄₉	4.558
Caballeria de tierra	Rightangled parallelogram	1,104	552	609,408	1
Media caballeria	Square	552	552	304,704	½
Cuarto caballeria ò suerte de tierra	Rightangled parallelogram	552	276	152,352	¼
Fanega de sembradura de maiz	Rightangled parallelogram	376	184	56,784	1⁄12
Salar para casa	Square	50	50	2,500	0.004
Fundo legal para pueblos	Square	1,200	1,200	1,440,000	2.036

The Mexican vara is the unit of all the measures of length, the pattern and size of which is taken from the Castillian vara of the mark of Burgos, and is the legal vara used in the Mexican republic. Fifty Mexican varas make a measure which is called cordel, which instrument is used in measuring lands.

The legal league contains 100 cordels or 5,000 varas, which is found by multiplying by 100 the 50 varas contained in a cordel. The league is divided into two halves and four quarters—this being the only division made of it. Half a league contains 2,500 varas, and a quarter of a league 1,250 varas.

Anciently, the Mexican league was divided into three miles, the mile into a thousand paces of Solomon, and one of these paces in to five thirds of a Mexican vara; consequently the league had 3,000 paces of Solomon. This division is recognized in legal affairs, but has been a very long time in disuse—the same as the pace of Solomon, which in those days was called vara, and was used for measuring lands. The mark was equivalent to two varas and seven-eighths—that is, eight marks contained twenty-three varas, and was used for measuring lands.